# 500
# BEST
## BRITISH AND
## FOREIGN

✦✦✦✦✦✦✦✦✦✦✦✦✦✦✦✦✦✦✦✦✦✦✦✦✦✦✦✦✦✦✦✦✦✦✦✦✦✦✦✦✦✦✦

# FILMS

✦✦✦✦✦✦✦✦✦✦✦✦✦✦✦✦✦✦✦✦✦✦✦✦✦✦✦✦✦✦✦✦✦✦✦✦✦✦✦✦✦✦✦

## TO BUY, RENT OR
## VIDEOTAPE

# 500
# BEST
## BRITISH AND FOREIGN

****************************************************************
# FILMS
****************************************************************

## TO BUY, RENT OR VIDEOTAPE

Selected by The National Board of Review of Motion
Pictures and the editors of Films in Review

EDITED BY JERRY VERMILYE

Quill

William Morrow • New York

Copyright © 1988 by The National Board of Review of Motion
Pictures.
Preface copyright © 1988 by Robert Giroux.

6-88        BT                     2200

Library of Congress Cataloging-in-Publication Data

500 best British and foreign films to buy,
    rent, or videotape.

    1. Moving-pictures—Reviews—Dictionaries.
2. Moving-pictures—Film catalogs.  3. Video
recordings—Reviews—Dictionaries.  4. Video
recordings—Film catalogs.  I. Vermilye, Jerry.
II. National Board of Review of Motion Pictures
(U.S.)  III. Films in review.  IV. Title: Five hundred
best British and foreign films to buy, rent,
or videotape.
PN1993.45.A15  1988    016.79143'75    87-28260
ISBN 0-688-07798-6
ISBN 0-688-06897-9 (pbk.)

Printed in the United States of America

First Quill Edition

1 2 3 4 5 6 7 8 9 10

BOOK DESIGN BY BARBARA MARKS

# Preface

By Robert Giroux

\* \* \* \* \* \* \* \* \* \* \* \* \* \* \* \* \* \* \* \* \* \* \* \* \* \* \* \* \* \* \* \* \* \* \* \* \* \* \* \* \* \* \* \* \* \* \* \* \* \* \* \* \* \* \*

The movies, as well as being the 20th century's newest and greatest art form, have been an *international medium* from the start. Long before Hollywood became the film capital, and we Americans were making the earliest movies at Edison's studio in New Jersey, in Biograph's converted brownstone house on Fourteenth Street and on lots at Fort Lee and elsewhere, the Lumière Brothers of Paris had their cameramen traveling around Europe—even into tsarist Russia for the coronation of Nicholas II in 1894—turning their hand-cranked cameras in the open air. In France, there were also the fantastic films of the professional magician Georges Méliès, who used every resource of cinematography for his startling effects and whose hundreds of one-reelers between 1896 and 1912, including *Journey to the Moon* (1902), are among the wonders of film history. At the same time early filmmakers were pioneering in Germany, Italy, Scandinavia, and England. One of Adolph Zukor's earliest (1912) business coups was to import Sarah Bernhardt's *Queen Elizabeth* from France; the first superlength spectacle, the four-hour *Cabiria,* a story of ancient Rome whose scenarist was the poet d'Annunzio, came from Italy as early as 1913; the success of this foreign film encouraged D. W. Griffith to proceed with his long planned *The Birth of a Nation* in 1914; the German expressionist film, *The Cabinet of Dr. Caligari* (1919), revolutionized the aesthetics of filmmaking—and so on. This rich history provides a vast treasury from which to pick the best foreign films for this book. Space limitations have forced The National Board of Review and the editors of *Films in Review* to eliminate silents and documentaries from consideration in these pages.

What is The National Board of Review? It is the oldest continuous body in America involved in assaying movies, domestic and foreign. It is older than the American Academy and the annual Oscars, which date from 1927. The National Board was founded in 1909 in New York, because of a threat of censorship by Mayor George McClellan, who was under pressure to close the city's movie theaters and nickelodeons on complaints that "movies tend to degrade or injure the morals of the community." When Mayor McClellan actually revoked exhibitors' licenses on Christmas eve, 1908, the threatened movie industry turned to the People's Institute at Cooper Union for help. This progressive civic body was

5

almost alone in its public stand that movies had positive qualities that contributed to the cultural life of the city and provided one of the few inexpensive forms of entertainment for all the people. The institute assigned one of its young members, John Collier—who later had a distinguished career as commissioner for Indian affairs in the Department of the Interior and as the author of books about American Indians—to find a solution to the impasse. Collier, at age 25, became a founder and the first executive secretary of what was originally known as The National Board of Censorship of Motion Pictures. It served as the lifesaver of the movies at a moment of crisis. Since the board always insisted on *voluntary* censorship, as against political or capricious censorship, it adopted the slogan "Selection, not Censorship." The industry's pledge to exhibit only films that received the Board's approval was an effective means of freeing movies from the caprices of politically controlled state and local boards of censors. The name was changed to The National Board of *Review* in 1916, when W. D. McGuire, Jr., succeeded John Collier as the executive secretary.

The legend "Passed by The National Board of Review" can still be seen occasionally on reruns of old silent films. It was dropped in the 1930s, soon after the advent of sound, when Wilton A. Barrett was serving as the NBR's executive secretary. Barrett—who had collaborated as a researcher with Terry Ramsaye on *A Million and One Nights* (1926), the first authoritative history of American films—turned the NBR into a superior and reliable source of critical writing about films by the best writers of the day. He picked James Shelley Hamilton to edit the NBR monthly bulletin, with its cream-colored paper and excellent photos. A fine selection of early film criticism from Hamilton's era is preserved in *From Quasimodo to Scarlett O'Hara: A National Board of Review Anthology, 1920–1940,* a book edited by Stanley Hochman and published by Ungar in 1982.

Dr. A. A. Brill, who had studied with Sigmund Freud and was his first translator in English, became The National Board's first president and continued for many decades until 1941. He was succeeded by Quincy Howe, who also served over thirty years (1942–75). Member of a famous Boston family, Howe was also well known as an author, editor, and radio news correspondent. I served as the Board's third president from 1976 to 1982, succeeded by Lewis Turner who piloted NBR during the crisis years of 1983 and 1984. Hartley Ramsay assumed the presidency in 1985.

Henry Hart, a longtime member, persuaded Quincy Howe to launch *Films in Review* in 1950. His long tenure as editor of the magazine and as custodian and preserver of NBR traditions lasted from 1950 to 1973. Hart's previous career in publishing had started at Scribner's; he became editor-in-chief at Putnam's, consulting editor at Macmillan, contributing editor at *Time,* associate editor at *Fortune,* and he was the author of several books. Hart was succeeded in 1973 by Charles Phillips Reilly, under whose editorship *Films in Review* achieved a worldwide reputation with subscribers in sixty countries. Ronald Bowers became editor in 1979 and Brendan Ward in 1981. Robin Little took over the editorship of *Films in Review* in 1983. Mrs. Little, whose background was also in book publishing, is also in charge of the advance screenings of new films for NBR's reviewing committee, held every week throughout the year. Readers interested in the Board's activities can write to P.O. Box 589, New York, NY 10021.

The national pastime of choosing the ten best movies of the year was started by NBR as early as 1919. We soon had many imitators, and we have been announcing our lists annually ever since. In 1979 the NBR inaugurated the annual David Wark Griffith Awards for the best English-language and foreign-language films, the best performances, and the best director. The winners so far of our Career Achievement Awards include James Cagney, John Huston, Jack Lemmon, Myrna Loy, Patricia Neal, Gregory Peck, Gloria Swanson, and Orson Welles. There have been special tributes to the Kaufman Astoria Studios under George S. Kaufman for his contribution to the film industry, and in television the NBR has honored Alistair Cooke, Mobil Corporation, Exxon, and *The New York Times* critic John J. O'Connor.

In 1985, The National Board of Review and the editors of *Films in Review* joined forces to produce *The 500 Best American Films to Buy, Rent or Videotape,* an eminently successful venture that the *American Library Association Bulletin* called "a good basic reference volume."

Here is the Board's follow-up book, this time listing the best of British and foreign-language films. You, the reader, may acquire, temporarily or permanently, all the films chosen in this book. It's great fun to view foreign movies, as The National Board of Review and its members have known for over 75 years.

# Foreword

With the lowering of consumer appliance costs, the age of the VCR that has burgeoned with the Eighties has brought thousands of home-video owners an excellent reason to become "couch potatoes," staying home to enjoy favorite films as many times as desired in personal comfort, free from long waiting lines at cinemas and unruly audiences. Instead of being trapped by the available television or pay-cable programming menu of the day, one can instead turn to one's own home-video library of motion-picture choice, be it eclectic, cultist, concentrated on a favorite performer or, perhaps, the works of a revered director.

As was discussed in The National Board's 1985 companion volume, *500 Best American Films to Buy, Rent or Videotape,* most of our important movies of the past 58 years—in short, the sound era—are now obtainable on prerecorded videocassette (as well as videodiscs) that can be acquired at prices ranging from a lofty $89.95 (for recent releases) down to below $10.00 (for public-domain titles) at neighborhood videotape outlets, video clubs, bookstores, and even drugstores. In some areas, there are chains like Video Shack that are entirely devoted to videotapes, while audio outlets such as Tower Records are opening up annexes specifically for video. West Coast sources like Music Plus and the Wherehouse are prime targets for the movie-cassette shopper. And there are the ever-growing, much-advertised video clubs, of which the current biggest seems to be the CBS Video Club, with its sizable monthly catalog of recent films, popular classics, and even popular foreign-language movies. More recently, the RCA Video Club and Time-Life Home Video have joined the bandwagon.

But rather than purchase prerecorded tapes, most movie buffs prefer to rent them, at nominal rates, from a host of video-rental stores that are mushrooming into view everywhere across the country. And then there are the public libraries, many of which are making the borrowing of videocassettes—on a standard library card—as easy as checking out the latest novel.

Taping right off the TV set is yet another popular method of adding to a collector's home library. In that way, one can have a copy of an otherwise unavailable movie for the bargain price of a blank tape. Is this legal? Yes! The U.S. Supreme Court allows that it is—provided that the taping is for one's own home use and not for subsequent sale.

Quite naturally, the majority of films available on prerecorded video-cassette are of American origin, with British pictures coming in a close second. But while this book was being contemplated, an informal survey revealed that, as of the close of 1985 alone, there were already well over 500 foreign-made movies available on video in the United States, ranging from established classics like *Grand Illusion, La Strada,* and *Wild Straw-berries*—which are frequently available in their original languages with English subtitles—to the English-dubbed likes of such frankly "exploitation" films as martial-arts adventures, "spaghetti" Westerns, and soft-core "adult" material like the *Emmanuelle* series.

Depending on the enterprise of various distributors, some of the more popular foreign films are being issued in *both* dubbed and subtitled versions—admittedly a costly gamble—while other distributors consider they're playing it safer to stick to English-dubbed product, no matter how sloppily executed (for example, Columbia's inexcusably inept job on the Vittorio De Sica classic *The Garden of the Finzi-Continis*—which is better taped off PBS stations in its still-available Italian-language original!). Some companies have issued their foreign films only in the original language with English subtitles, which may or may not be easily readable on the home screen. Apart from the out-and-out exploitation movie, English-dubbing of foreign product has usually been limited to those imports whose initial big-city, subtitled engagements have proven successful enough to warrant going to the expense of dubbing them for more widespread "general" release—as with *La Dolce Vita, Diabolique,* and *Elvira Madigan.*

As British and foreign-language films continue to become increasingly more available to the home viewer, the choice of titles is considerable. Which ones merit a place on your shelf? Their selection, of course, must be personal. To facilitate the choice, The National Board of Review of Motion Pictures has, through a committee of seasoned film writers, reviewers, and historians, compiled in these pages 500 of the best British and foreign-language movies that it would recommend for any motion picture collection on tape. Committee members who helped select the titles for this book are, for the most part, regular contributors to *Films in Review,* The National Board's distinguished monthly journal.

In consideration of spatial limitations and lack of mass-market appeal, the decision was made to bypass documentaries and silent films. But apart from the committee's selection of established classics that are likely to provide the foundation of any foreign movie collection, there are many titles on the board's A to Z list (from *A Nous La Liberté* to *Zulu*) that reflect a wide spectrum of film genres and countries of origin, although the majority of selections necessarily must represent the more prolific filmmakers of France, Italy, and the United Kingdom.

Acquiring prerecorded videocassettes and videodiscs usually assures motion pictures of high-quality image, as these were made from clear master prints. But the buyer should be wary of any extraordinary over-the-counter bargains—a possible signpost of counterfeit tapes. Taping off television, of course, has its pros and cons. Public broadcasting stations and commercial-free pay-cable systems are naturally your best bet. Otherwise, one is faced with the intrusion of commercial messages and those ever-present "edited for television" disclaimers that can herald anything from cutting that will simply "shoehorn" a lengthy movie into an unreasonable time slot to those censorship snips that eliminate what a station's (or a network's) "standards and practices" deem too sexy, too violent, or simply too likely to offend. Such cuts may range from the excision of mere seconds to an outright desecration of the movie. In rare instances, as with Britain's multipart 1945 thriller *Dead of Night,* its TV showing may introduce a longer and more complete version than was originally seen, even in its U.S. theatrical run!

The *500 Best British and Foreign Films* that have been selected by The National Board of Review are arranged here alphabetically, according to the titles—in most cases, either the original or translated one—by which they are best known in the United States (alternate titles are in parentheses), followed by the original year of release (as well as the American release date, if different), the country of origin, the director's name, and those of its leading players. Also designated is whether the film is in color or B/W (black and white). Other information includes:

*Running Time.* With transcontinental editing, this is necessarily problematical, although the editors have made every effort to be as accurate as possible. Especially with foreign films, running times may vary considerably from their original foreign showings to their U.S. release. And, finally, time lengths printed on videocassette packaging is frequently in error and cannot be trusted!

*Availability.* The name of the distributor of the videocassette is supplied if the film is known to be available. But in most cases, the buyer is advised to purchase the tape through a retail outlet, as distributors do not generally deal directly with the public. Where no availability is stated and the words *TV only* appear, then that film, as of this book's publication, is not known to be on prerecorded tape. Consequently, the viewer would be advised to monitor local TV program guides for a showing that could be privately taped. *Public domain* means that a movie's original copyright has run out and that it may be distributed by any videocassette company enterprising enough to secure a print of the film (no matter how poor in quality) and issue it on one of the many—usually very inexpensive—public-domain labels. In those cases, let the buyer beware! In some cases, however, public-domain titles have also been issued by reliable, responsible companies like Embassy Home Entertainment, in which cases we have listed those organizations. Otherwise, we have simply indicated "Public Domain."

*Synopsis/production details.* A succinct description of the film offers plot, background information, and data on major awards that could influence the indecisive buyer/taper.

*Dubbing/subtitling.* More often than not, foreign-language films are made available in their original tongue, with the inclusion of subtitles. Where such subtitling is known to be particularly good—or poor—we have so indicated. Other movies are available only in English-dubbed versions, and appropriate commentary has been included where possible. Embassy frequently issues tapes of foreign-language films in both dubbed

11

*and* subtitled versions, so buyers should be cognizant of that fact when purchasing Embassy tapes. Display boxes are marked accordingly.

Comments and suggestions with regard to the committee's chosen movies will be gratefully accepted and may be addressed to the publisher of this book or to The National Board of Review of Motion Pictures, P.O. Box 589, New York, NY 10021.

# Contributors

★★★★★★★★★★★★★★★★★★★★★★★★★★★★★★★★★★★★★★★★★★★★★★★★★★★★★★★

Pat Anderson is a movie critic for *Films in Review* and contributes articles to the magazine as well. She is also a member of The National Board of Review's Screening Group.

Howard Brown, whose plays have been produced off-off Broadway by the 7th Sign and Quaigh theatres, is also a writer-editor for Standard & Poor's.

Michael Buckley is Consulting Editor for *Films in Review* and writes regularly for the magazine. His articles have also appeared in the New York *Daily News* and the Home Box Office magazines.

Kenneth M. Chanko is a regular contributor to *Films in Review*. His movie reviews and feature stories appear in *The Sunday Daily News Magazine, USA Weekend, Details, Daily News Record, Eastside Express* and are syndicated through Universal Press.

Ross Claiborne is the Vice President of The National Board. He has had a long career in publishing, holding top executive positions, and has sponsored many books having to do with films and film personalities.

John Cocchi has worked for *Box Office* magazine, reviewed for *The Film Journal*, directed The Cooperative Film Society for twenty years, and has collaborated on over a hundred movie books, including all of those of James Robert Parish.

Frank Farel is a filmmaker and writer who has just produced the motion picture *Spookies*. He lectures and writes on movie production and history.

C. M. Fiorillo is a movie critic for *Films in Review* and works as an editor for a woman's magazine. Her articles have appeared in leading film publications.

Roy Frumkes is a contributor and movie critic for *Films in Review*. He is a producer, director, and screenwriter. His films include the award-winning *Burt's Bikers*, as well as *Document of the Dead* and *Street Trash*. He teaches filmmaking and screenwriting at the School of Visual Arts.

Keith Gardner who has a master's degree in film from Columbia University, writes for Manhattan Cable Television, and was associate producer in *The Midnight Muse* on MCTV. He contributes articles and motion picture reviews to *Films in Review*.

William H. Gibbons, III, is a staff reporter for Fairchild Publications. He contributes movie articles to *How . . .* magazine and is a motion picture critic for *Films in Review*.

Eva Kissen reviews movies for *Films in Review*, her specialty being foreign-language motion pictures. She contributes articles and interviews to the magazine as well.

Kevin Lewis is a contributor and critic for *Films in Review*, a Special Projects Coordinator for the Shubert Archives, and guest curator of the Museum of the Performing Arts at Lincoln Center. He worked for many years with Herman Weinberg subtitling foreign-language films.

Robin Little is Editor-in-Chief of *Films in Review*. Before assuming that title, she was a book publishing executive often involved with books dealing with motion pictures and motion picture personalities.

Marcia Magill is Consulting Editor for *Films in Review* as well as a frequent contributor. A former book publishing executive, she was responsible for many books dealing with motion pictures.

Anthony Osnato, Artistic Director for off-off Broadway's 7th Sign Theatre, will have his adaptation of Ibsen's *The Lady from the Sea* produced shortly.

Charles Phillips Reilly, former Editor-in-Chief of *Films in Review*, continues to contribute to the magazine. He is a Director of The National Board and former Man Power Director of the State of New Jersey.

Cesar J. Rotondi, author of *Grand Obese* and *Obsessions*, worked as a film consultant in Europe. He is a motion picture critic for *Films in Review* as well as a contributor of feature articles.

Charles Sawyer, former advertising executive and movie critic for *Our Town*, now is a contributor to *Films in Review*.

Thomas P. Sciacca is a film historian, researcher, and writer whose work appears regularly in *Films in Review*.

Michael Scheinfeld, who was one of the contributors to Leonard Maltin's *TV Movies*, is producer of *Master Reels*, Manhattan Cable TV's weekly film series.

Gregory Solman, a New York-based freelance writer, is an editor of *Millimeter Magazine* and a broadcast critic for WFNX-FM, Boston. He also contributes reviews to *Films in Review*.

Louise Tanner is a Director of The National Board, a contributor and critic for *Films in Review*, and the author of five books. She is the widow of Patrick Dennis, author of *Auntie Mame*.

Bill Thompson programmed the weekly Japanese series at the Beekman Cinema in New York City for five years. He is a contributor to *Films in*

*Review, Cineaste, OCS News,* and Magill's *Survey of International Cinema.*

Jerry Vermilye has contributed to *Films in Review, Screen Facts, Film Fan Monthly,* and *Andy Warhol's InterView.* He is the author of ten books on movies, including *The Films of the Thirties, The Great British Films,* and *The Films of the Twenties.* He is currently Movie/Opera Listings Editor for *TV Guide.* An experienced actor and stage manager, Vermilye acts off-off Broadway in his spare time.

Armond White is a regular contributor to *Films in Review.* He is also a writer and critic for *Film Comment,* the *Village Voice,* the *Daily News,* the *City Sun,* and Soho's *Paper.*

Jack Wolf is a freelance writer and critic whose articles appear in a number of publications, including *Films in Review,* the HBO guides, *Cinemax,* and *Festival.*

# Contents

*(All foreign-language films are alphabetically arranged beginning with the first words of their titles)*

17

20

23

# A Nous la Liberté

★★★★★★★★★★★★★★★★★★★★★★★★★★★★★★★★★★★★★★★★★★★★★★★★★★★★★★★

**Nationality**: French                    **Year**: 1931 (U.S. release: 1932)
**Cast**: Raymond Cordy, Henri Marchand, Germaine Aussey, Rolla France, Paul Olivier
**Director**: René Clair                    **Running Time**: 87 minutes
**B/W or Color**: B/W                    **Availability**: Public Domain

This ambitious comedy was the most complex movie ever conceived by René Clair. It was the direct inspiration for Chaplin's *Modern Times* made five years later, and has been said to raise more social questions than it was prepared to answer. But compared with most films, *A Nous la Liberté* is brilliant and a joy to behold.

Two former down-and-outs meet years later. One has become the head of a corporation, while the other works in his friend's factory. The film uses this premise to set up various satirical set pieces involving dehumanizing machinery, greed, social hypocrisy, and, oddly, the corrupt nature of France (the Stavisky currency scandal broke three years later). The movie's most famous episode is a speech about justice, patriotism, and country, counterpointing a money chase by industrialists and aristocrats. It is a chilling prophecy of the capitulation of France in 1940.

Georges Auric's music contributes to the greatness of the film, as do the marvelous, fluid camerawork by Georges Perinal and the abstract, stylized sets of Lazare Meerson, who creates an Art Deco fantasy. It would be fair to say that Clair, who always wrote his own scenarios (in fact, he considered himself first and foremost a writer who directed his scripts), is an auteur.

Whether or not the film answers its central question about *"moi d'abord"* (me first) is not crucial to its appreciation. Clair falls back on the old canard that life is for enjoyment, so why worry about a buck (or a franc). Chaplin used the same argument in his tramp films, but we know that Clair and Chaplin both enjoyed honors and wealth. See *A Nous la Liberté* for its balletic movements, its symphonic blend of music and dialogue, and its brilliant design.

At the very first Venice Film Festival, in 1932, *A Nous la Liberté* was named Most Amusing Film. The National Board voted it the year's Best Foreign Film.

# The Abominable Dr. Phibes
## (Dr. Phibes Rises Again)

\* \* \* \* \* \* \* \* \* \* \* \* \* \* \* \* \* \* \* \* \* \* \* \* \* \* \* \* \* \* \* \* \* \* \* \* \* \* \* \* \* \* \* \* \* \* \* \* \* \*

*Nationality*: British

*Year*: 1971/1972 (U.S. release: 1973)

*Cast*: Vincent Price, Joseph Cotten, Hugh Griffith, Terry-Thomas/Vincent Price, Robert Quarry, Valli Kemp, Peter Cushing.

*Director*: Robert Fuest

*Running Time*: 94 minutes/89 minutes

*B/W or Color*: Color

*Availability*: VESTRON VIDEO (Both)

The *Abominable Dr. Phibes* was an Art Deco avenger, punishing those responsible for the death of his beloved wife, with the help of a mysterious siren named Vulnavia. One by one his enemies met gruesome, creative deaths with Victorian objets d'art used as murder weapons, while the once-good doctor (Vincent Price), masked to hide the skeletal remains of his face, poeticized away their collective deaths.

There was a second *Phibes,* an unpolished gem that may remain director Robert Fuest's crowning achievement. *Dr. Phibes Rises Again* has the stamp of a wittily unbridled perverse mind. Price is back, pitted against Robert Quarry in a deadly quest for the secret of immortality. Two bumbling British cops are on their trail. Black humor abounds, with several new and devilish deathtraps, as well as such art department trappings as a Rolls-Royce coffin. The ending is about as cathartic a capper as you'll ever find . . . but I leave it to you to experience, unspoiled by critical review.

Director Fuest seemed to have been possessed of a mischievous cinematic mind. Though his antic *Phibes* series promised much, the lamentable bomb of his first American film, *The Devil's Rain,* sent his career slipping into the uninspired, as if his arcane sensibilities were squashed by the Hollywood powers he encountered.

At one point, plans were announced to make a third *Phibes* picture—dealing with Hitler and featuring Ruby Keeler dancing. Just how this would have fit into the scenario is delicious to imagine, but it never came to pass. More recently, George Romero (*Night of the Living Dead*) was toying with resurrecting Phibes, but Price has yet to sign on.

# Accident

\* \* \* \* \* \* \* \* \* \* \* \* \* \* \* \* \* \* \* \* \* \* \* \* \* \* \* \* \* \* \* \* \* \* \* \* \* \* \* \* \* \* \* \* \* \* \* \* \* \* \* \* \* \* \* \*

Nationality: British                    Year: 1967
Cast: Dirk Bogarde, Stanley Baker, Jacqueline Sassard, Michael York, Vivien Merchant, Delphine Seyrig
Director: Joseph Losey            Running Time: 105 minutes
B/W or Color: Color                 Availability: THORN/EMI-HBO
                                                   VIDEO

A deceptively simple film, *Accident* examines the ambiguities of relationships and the games that people play—both physically and emotionally. The critic for the London *Times* considered the film director Joseph Losey's "clinching masterpiece."

The picture begins and ends with a car crash that occurs outside the home of an Oxford philosophy don (Dirk Bogarde). As he assists the survivor, a young Austrian student (Jacqueline Sassard), a flashback reveals that he is secretly (and rather mildly) in love with her. Complicating matters are his pregnant wife (Vivien Merchant) and the don's old flame (Delphine Seyrig). Also in love with Sassard are Bogarde's best friend, another married don (Stanley Baker), and a student (Michael York). Sassard has announced that she will wed York, and they had been on their way to meet Bogarde when the accident occurred.

Based on a novel by Nicholas Mosley, the screenplay was written by Harold Pinter (who makes a brief appearance as a television producer). Several of the events are open to audience interpretation. Pinter and Losey had earlier collaborated on *The Servant* and would later do so again with *The Go-Between*. Bogarde, who won the British Film Academy's Best Actor award for *The Servant,* here flawlessly depicts the inner conflicts of a man who realizes that his once-promising career has faded and that he is getting older. Although he is surrounded by things that should make him happy, he is not. Another exceptional performance is given by Vivien Merchant (at the time, the offscreen wife of Harold Pinter). Mention should also be made of Gerry Fisher's expressionistic cinematography and the carefully detailed art direction of Carmen Dillon.

*Accident* shared the Special Jury Prize at the 1967 Cannes Film Festival with Yugoslavia's *I Even Met Happy Gypsies* and was named one of the ten best pictures of the year by The National Board of Review.

# Aguirre, The Wrath of God
### (Aguirre, Der Zorn Gottes)

★ ★ ★ ★ ★ ★ ★ ★ ★ ★ ★ ★ ★ ★ ★ ★ ★ ★ ★ ★ ★ ★ ★ ★ ★ ★ ★ ★ ★ ★ ★ ★ ★ ★ ★ ★ ★ ★ ★ ★ ★ ★ ★ ★ ★ ★ ★ ★ ★ ★

*Nationality*: West German      *Year*: 1973 (U.S. release: 1977)
*Cast*: Klaus Kinski, Ruy Guerra, Helena Rojo, Cecilia Rivera, Del Negro
*Director*: Werner Herzog      *Running Time*: 90 minutes
*B/W or Color*: Color      *Availability*: CONTINENTAL VIDEO

Tauntingly called a "director of dwarfs" by Klaus Kinski, his star in *Aguirre, The Wrath of God,* Werner Herzog has also presented phantoms, images of woodchucks and auctioneers, volcanoes about to erupt, ecstasies, outsiders, iconoclasts, and other enigmatic fanatics as a routine part of his cinema. The true Herzogian hero is a romantic, half-mad, half-visionary, completely out of whack with a normal environment. Likewise, Herzog's special compositions are strange, defying those found in conventional cinema, yet ethereal and alluringly beautiful.

*Aguirre, The Wrath of God* begins with the morning mist of the Andes gleaming through a steamy jungle. Slow, airy music by Popol Vuh breathes with the Peruvian Amazons. Meanwhile, Spanish conquistadores, invaders in this magical jungle, hack their way through the dense vegetation. The Spanish soldiers are part of Gonzalo Pizarro's search for El Dorado, the legendary city of gold, in 1560. Realizing that the South American jungle is much larger than originally imagined, he sends forth a small party headed by the loyal Ursúa. When Ursúa later realizes that he, too, must eventually turn back, Aguirre, his second-in-command, leads a revolt and usurps power.

Aguirre's men continue their journeys through the jungle and down the river in their raft. But as they claim the lands surrounding them for their emperor, a nobleman who is Aguirre's puppet, they journey into their own hallucinations and madness. Supplies dwindle, crew members die or are lost, but nature perseveres. By the end, Aguirre is drifting into a turbulent whirlpool, his raft overrun by monkeys and littered with corpses, but he obsessively reasserts his power by declaring, "I am the wrath of God."

Herzog has achieved a cult status for feverish, hypnotic, visionary works highlighted by *Aguirre, The Wrath of God.* In interviews, he has declared that his films are always concerned with the same subject. Perhaps they are, perhaps this antirational output climaxed with *Aguirre* and *The Mystery of Kaspar Hauser.* But it still continues with further layers of madness and newer, more different images.

*(The videocassette is subtitled.)*

# Alexander Nevsky

★★★★★★★★★★★★★★★★★★★★★★★★★★★★★★★★★★★★★★★★★★★★★★★★★★★★★★★

Nationality: Russian                    Year: 1938

Cast: Nikolai Cherkassov, N. P. Oklophkov, A. L. Abrikossov

Director: Sergei Eisenstein and      Running Time: 117 minutes
D. I. Vassiliev

B/W or Color: B/W                    Availability: CORINTH VIDEO

W hen the Teutonic knights invade the Russia of 1241, Alexander
Nevsky, the fisherman prince, and the "proletariat" (read serfs
and muzhiks) turn back the German horde. Director Eisenstein knew what
he was doing in the Russia of 1938. Substitute Stalin for Nevsky and the
Nazis for the Teutonic knights, and add Stalin's distrust of Eisenstein's
*Bezhin Meadow* (being filmed in 1937) as having too much of a religious
message (it would never be completed), and you'll understand why *Alexander Nevsky* saved Eisenstein's career, and perhaps his life. Soon after
the release of the movie, he was elevated to head of Mosfilm and began
what turned out to be his final picture, *Ivan the Terrible*.

As an epic, *Nevsky* ranks with *The Battleship Potemkin* and *Ten Days
That Shook the World,* and in the character of Nevsky, Eisenstein has
created a starring role, rare in his other works. The Teutonic knights, on
the other hand, are mainly caricatures of evil, slyly glancing and dressed
like early versions of Darth Vader. One caustic critic observed that the
film benefited from Eisenstein's "discriminating taste and his supreme
mastery of crowd scenes, and the absence of Errol Flynn."

The Battle on the Ice in *Nevsky* is a splendid tour de force, with the
two opposing armies charging across the frozen lake, accompanied by
Sergei Prokofiev's marvelous score, which has already taken its place among
the 20th century's best.

Eisenstein has been called by some the D. W. Griffith of Russian cinema, and film historian Leslie Halliwell says Eisenstein "virtually invented montage." There are those who might argue with both opinions,
but all will agree that *Alexander Nevsky* is a landmark in moviemaking.

(*Corinth Video offers an excellent print in Russian with English subtitles.*)

# Alphaville

### (Alphaville, une Etrange Aventure de Lemmy Caution)

★★★★★★★★★★★★★★★★★★★★★★★★★★★★★★★★★★★★★★★★★★★★★★★★★★★

Nationality: French-Italian      Year: 1965
Cast: Eddie Constantine, Anna Karina, Akim Tamiroff, Howard Vernon, Lazslo Szabo
Director: Jean-Luc Godard        Running Time: 100 minutes
B/W or Color: B/W                Availability: Public Domain

Godard takes on science fiction and makes the most influential sci-fi movie of the modern era (next to *2001*). Starting from the French B-movie serials about Lemmy Caution (played by Eddie Constantine, the expatriate American actor), Godard imagined the future in terms of film noir paranoia. This is a bleak but poetic vision of the world's soulessness, once machines and technology have taken over and fascism has made people forget art and emotion. Caution's heroic efforts seem to come out of a time warp. He's Godard's emissary, standing in for the principles of the caring, educated humanism of our day. Godard combines an Aldous Huxley-type presentiment to the then-new sociological perceptions of Marshall McLuhan. His future is so close to contemporary theory that it seems merely a visionary, abstract version of the present. In fact the entire film was designed and shot without any special effects: Godard simply selected the most modern, futuristic-looking aspects of Paris and photographed them in a newer, documentary style.

When Caution attempts to escape the totalitarian zone of the future world and save Natacha von Braun (Anna Karina), a robot with feelings, Godard achieved a striking combination of Arthurian legend and Murnau's *Nosferatu*. The mythology has been reprised in the plots of Ridley Scott's *Blade Runner* and Robert Altman's *The Long Goodbye*. This is the only sci-fi film to contain a poignant romanticism. But the plot is not nostalgic. Godard's yearning, even when placed into the future, is for the best potential of the human race—not for the world as it was, but for the most responsive and individualistic world people can make. The movie is superbly photographed by Raoul Coutard, whose wizardry turns Paris into Alphaville. Godard himself is the voice of the computer god.

# Amarcord

\* \* \* \* \* \* \* \* \* \* \* \* \* \* \* \* \* \* \* \* \* \* \* \* \* \* \* \* \* \* \* \* \* \* \* \* \* \* \* \* \* \* \* \* \* \* \* \* \* \*

Nationality: Italian                Year: 1974
Cast: Bruno Zanin, Magali Noel, Pupella Maggio, Armando Brancia
Director: Federico Fellini          Running Time: 127 minutes
B/W or Color: Color                 Availability: WARNER HOME
                                    VIDEO

In May 1974, when Vincent Canby reported on *Amarcord* from the Cannes Film Festival, he wrote, "*Amarcord* looks as if Fellini were spending his time extravagantly doodling while awaiting an idea for his next real movie." Four months later he wrote in his review, "*Amarcord* may possibly be Federico Fellini's most marvellous film." The consensus is with Canby's latter opinion. The movie went on to win the Oscar for Best Foreign Film that year.

*Amarcord* is a film of memory and of growing up, with the events of Fellini's early life washed over with the golden brush of sentiment. The town's characters, and especially its eccentrics, are introduced with compassion and understanding. The stiff schoolteacher, the lusty tobacconist, the local flirt, and the quirky relatives all hold the stage for a set piece and then allow the camera to move on to a new sequence. The cruelty and pomposity of the Fascists are shown, but even here there is no hard-edged bitterness to their portraits. It's rather as if they existed and were a nuisance, but in the end weren't terribly important.

What we're offered is a poetic *Our Town* with images of unexpected beauty and startling poetic values. The townfolk assemble to watch the steamship *Rex* pass through the harbor, and the appearance of the liner is more awesome than the arrival of an alien craft in the space movies of later years.

There is humor in the sexual awakening of the town adolescents; a good deal less so in the awkward portrait of the local nymphomaniac. Bruno Zanin, who plays the young Fellini, had never appeared in films before but gives a distinguished and noteworthy performance. Fellini wraps it all up with one of his most splendid symbolic images—the arrival of a peacock on a snowy morning. The bird's breathtaking preening becomes Fellini's affirmation of the immortality of the human spirit.

# The American Friend
## (Der Amerikanische Freund)

* * * * * * * * * * * * * * * * * * * * * * * * * * * * * * * * * * * * * * * * * * * * * * * * * * * * * *

*Nationality*: West German          *Year*: 1977
*Cast*: Bruno Ganz, Dennis Hopper, Lisa Kreuzer, Gerard Blain, Nicholas Ray
*Director*: Wim Wenders          *Running Time*: 127 minutes
*B/W or Color*: Color          *Availability*: PACIFIC ARTS VIDEO

W im Wenders, one of the best-known directors of the "New German Cinema," has gained a cult following by making films that generally feature restless heroes, distanced from society. Born just after the close of World War II, Wenders grew up in West Germany obsessed with Hollywood films, and his cinema reflects his heritage of Goethe and Heidegger fused with Hawks, Fuller, Nicholas Ray, and Ford. His work illustrates the consciousness and confusion of many of his directionless generation.

Wenders' first features, including *The Goalie's Anxiety at the Penalty Kick* and the trilogy *Alice in the Cities, The Wrong Move,* and *Kings of the Road,* were all made in or near Germany. *The American Friend,* made in 1977 immediately following his trilogy, captures often interchangeable images of deterioration and loneliness in Hamburg, Paris, and New York. His source material is the thriller *Ripley's Game,* by the acclaimed Patricia Highsmith, who also wrote the novels upon which Hitchcock's *Strangers on a Train* and Clement's *Purple Noon* are based. Wenders quickly fashions the two main characters into his own universe, while making references to Hitchcock—with Highsmith (a proposal of murder made by strangers on a train) and without (menacing birds at a window).

An American (Dennis Hopper) involved in an art scam meets a Hamburg framemaker (Bruno Ganz), who believes he has a terminal blood disease, and suggests him as a possible hired killer. In order to provide financial security for his wife and son, the man murders two rival Mafia leaders—one in a train station, and the other on a train.

Several directors, American (Nicholas Ray, Samuel Fuller) and foreign, play parts in the movie.

Among The National Board's best films of 1977, *The American Friend* was the first new German film shot in the United States to depict Hollywood's America as viewed by Germans.

# And God Created Woman

### (Et Dieu Créa la Femme/And Woman Was Created)

★★★★★★★★★★★★★★★★★★★★★★★★★★★★★★★★★★★★★★★★★★★★★★★★★★★★

**Nationality**: French       **Year**: 1957

**Cast**: Brigitte Bardot, Curt Jurgens, Jean-Louis Trintignant, Christian Marquand

**Director**: Roger Vadim      **Running Time**: 92 minutes (95 minutes in France)

**B/W or Color**: Color      **Availability**: VESTRON VIDEO

The American ads were typical Hollywood exploitation: "*And God Created Woman* . . . but the devil invented Brigitte Bardot!" It wasn't the first time U.S. filmgoers had witnessed the sex-kittenish charms of Bardot—she had already appeared in such foreign imports as *Doctor at Sea* and *The Light Across the Street*—but nothing had quite prepared America for the blatant sensuality of *And God Created Woman*. Directed by the star's then-husband Roger Vadim, this wasn't sleazy trash, but, rather, a handsomely produced romantic melodrama about an amoral young woman and the men whose lives she upsets—or destroys—in the vicinity of colorful St. Tropez.

*Variety*'s review from Paris at the outset of 1957 was surprisingly brief and dismissive, predicting, ". . . this is just average for any U.S. possibilities." Little did the industry's "Bible" anticipate the incredible overseas popularity this picture would enjoy, unleashing a floodgate of older, tamer Bardot efforts. By the end of 1957, she was an international sex symbol, and throughout the late Fifties and early Sixties, B.B. was a household synonym for eroticism. A trained dancer (her abandoned mambo sequence in a seaside nightclub is among *And God Created Woman*'s more arousing highlights), the 22-year-old Gallic beauty with the tawny blonde hair and the drop-dead body had been well-schooled by Vadim. For him, she exhibited a magnetic screen presence that was perhaps never better displayed than in this cunningly Bardot-tailored vehicle, whose more explicit nudity was excised prior to its American release. But the film wasn't designed to win awards; it only made money.

While making *And God Created Woman*, Bardot left Vadim for co-star Jean-Louis Trintignant, although Vadim went on to direct her in several subsequent movies, in hopes of recapturing that original screen magic. And, 30 years later, Vadim was busy working on a remake of the film, this time showcasing yet another beautiful blonde, Rebecca De Mornay.

*(The videocassette is dubbed in English.)*

# Andrei Rublev

\* \* \* \* \* \* \* \* \* \* \* \* \* \* \* \* \* \* \* \* \* \* \* \* \* \* \* \* \* \* \* \* \* \* \* \* \* \* \* \* \* \* \* \* \* \* \* \* \* \* \* \* \* \*

Nationality: Russian                     Year: 1967 (U.S. release: 1973)
Cast: Anatoli Solonitzine, Ivan Lapikov, Nikolai Grinko
Director: Andrei Tarkovsky          Running Time: 146 minutes (181
                                                         minutes in the USSR)
B/W or Color: B/W and Color      Availability: TV only

More stark in its apocalyptic severity than even the cerebral *Stalker* (1979) and *Solaris* (1972)—in which Andrei Tarkovsky's inner self was reflected in Stanislav Lem's science fiction—*Andrei Rublev* stands with *The Mirror* (1975) as his testament. The director died at 54 in 1986, having made only eight feature-length films, each of which was celebrated by some faction of free (or repressed) society.

*Andrei Rublev* concerns the solitary, poor, nasty, brutish, and short life of a 15th-century Russian monk and icon painter (Anatoli Solonitzine). The story was co-authored by Tarkovsky and Andrei Michalkov-Konchalovsky, now a Russian director of considerable reputation (*Siberiade, Runaway Train*), and is spare but richly rewarding. Tarkovsky pictures a world pitched on the perilous edge of conflicting, confusing systems of belief that inchoately characterize the civilization he experienced. When one man is destroyed by having boiling oil forced down his throat, it attests not to the dissimilarity of medieval evil, but to a certain continuity in how creative methods of killing—casting death as if a sculpture—mime artistic production throughout the ages. Does the artist, Rublev, stand outside that system, or is his passivity in its face complicit with it? A long portion of the narrative is devoted to a simple, yet completely compelling tale of how a young artisan must be brought from a distant village to supervise the creation of a huge cathedral bell. So desperate for such knowledge is the town that they accept the second-generation artisan's word; however, he has lied about his experience, frantically trying to enter into the new, graced segment of society allowed to heal, not hack. Tarkovsky's mystic vision is carried off to perfection by Vadim Youssov's stunning photography.

# Angry Harvest
## (Bittere Ernte)

★★★★★★★★★★★★★★★★★★★★★★★★★★★★★★★★★★★★★★★★★★★★★★★★★★★★★

Nationality: West German          Year: 1985 (U.S. release: 1986)
Cast: Armin Müller-Stahl, Elisabeth Trissenaar, Käthe Jaenicke
Director: Agnieszka Holland        Running Time: 102 minutes
B/W or Color: Color               Availability: TV only

Perhaps the best compliment to this film came from a critic present at the 1985 New York Film Festival. On the same day as the Gloria hurricane scare, he told director Agnieszka Holland, "Your film was worth coming out in a hurricane to see!" And it truly is an electrifying storm of a film.

Set in Silesia during World War II, *Angry Harvest* concerns a farmer (Armin Müller-Stahl) who shelters an escaping Holocaust victim (Elisabeth Trissenaar). An ignorant man who had just been allowed to care for the estate of an aristocrat, he uses that power against the beautiful Jewess, who longs to join her husband. He falls in love with her, and she is powerless to resist because he is hiding her in his cellar, à la *The Collector*. They have an affair and set up housekeeping as a husband and wife. But he isn't content with this and seeks to convert her to Catholicism so they can be married in reality. Tragedy results, and the wretched man tries to help others as repentance.

An unusual, original allegory of war—a war within a war—it is human and haunting in its emotions. One hesitates to write that it could be directed only by a woman, but it is a brilliant depiction of the battle of feelings that can create havoc. The differences in a man-woman relationship have seldom been better realized than here, and the performances of not only the leading actors but also those of Käthe Jaenicke, Isa Haller, and Anita Höfer—as, respectively, Anna, Magda, and Pauline—are superb.

Nominated as West Germany's Academy Award nominee in the Best Foreign-Language Film category for 1985, *Angry Harvest* lost out to *The Official Story*.

# The Angry Silence

★★★★★★★★★★★★★★★★★★★★★★★★★★★★★★★★★★★★★★★★★★★★★★★★★★★★★★

*Nationality*: British        *Year*: 1960
*Cast*: Richard Attenborough, Michael Craig, Pier Angeli, Bernard Lee
*Director*: Guy Green        *Running Time*: 95 minutes
*B/W or Color*: B/W        *Availability*: TV only

O ne of The National Board's best films of 1960, *The Angry Silence* concerns courage—one man's stand against a labor union. "If people can't be different," he claims, ". . . there's no point to any of it. . . ."

Based on fact, the film was the first co-production for actors Richard Attenborough, who also starred, and Bryan Forbes, who wrote the screenplay (and appears unbilled as a reporter who interviews Attenborough's wife, played by Pier Angeli). The film reflected the new honesty and realism introduced to British cinema by the previous year's *Look Back in Anger* and *Room at the Top*.

Machine operator Attenborough is ostracized by his fellow workers when his conscience forces him to stay on the job during a wildcat strike. He even gets the silent treatment from his treacherous best friend, Michael Craig, who rents a room in the Attenborough home. When another strike is called and he again stays at work, Attenborough is beaten by two young thugs and loses an eye. A remorseful Craig finds those responsible and is able to bring the factory workers to their senses.

Attenborough turns in an extremely fine performance. Having made his first screen appearance in *In Which We Serve* (1942), his directorial debut was 1962's *Oh! What a Lovely War*. In 1982, *Gandhi* brought him several awards—including The National Board's plaque and the Oscar—as Best Director.

As Attenborough's pregnant wife, Pier Angeli perhaps does her finest acting. The Italian-born beauty, who enjoyed brief Hollywood stardom in the early Fifties, committed suicide (age 39) in 1971.

Along with *The Mark* (1961), this film is considered to be the best directorial work of Guy Green, who won an Oscar for his cinematography of *Great Expectations* (1947).

The story (by Michael Craig and Richard Gregson) and screenplay received an Academy Award nomination.

# Anne of the Thousand Days

★★★★★★★★★★★★★★★★★★★★★★★★★★★★★★★★★★★★★★★★★★★★★★★★★★★★★★

**Nationality**: British                   **Year**: 1969
**Cast**: Richard Burton, Geneviève Bujold, Irene Papas, Anthony Quayle
**Director**: Charles Jarrott          **Running Time**: 145 minutes
**B/W or Color**: Color                  **Availability**: MCA HOME VIDEO

D ue to the success of *Becket* (1964), its producer, Hal Wallis, de-
        cided to cast one of that film's stars, Richard Burton, in another
historical drama. He chose Maxwell Anderson's 1948 Broadway play
*Anne of the Thousand Days*, which had starred Rex Harrison (who won
the Tony Award as Best Actor).

Wallis switched from Paramount (where he had worked for 30 years)
to Universal, because the former studio refused to meet Burton's salary
demands. As King Henry VIII, the actor received a sixth Oscar nomination but lost to John Wayne (*True Grit*).

*Anne of the Thousand Days* is the story of Henry and his second wife,
Anne Boleyn, and extends from his infatuation in 1527 to her execution
in 1536. The king's unsuccessful attempts to have the Catholic Church
sanction a divorce from his first wife, Katharine of Aragon, in order to
marry Anne, caused a rift with Rome and the establishment of the Protestant Church. Henry married his Anne, but even the birth of their
daughter, Elizabeth, did nothing to revive his rapidly diminishing passion. She had been queen for only 1,000 days when Henry had Anne
beheaded and soon after married Jane Seymour.

Anne is played by Geneviève Bujold, a French-Canadian actress who
made her screen debut in Jean Renoir's *French Can-Can* (1956). Prior to
this, she was best known for her role in *King of Hearts* (1967). As Henry's queen, she received an Oscar nomination but lost to Maggie Smith
for *The Prime of Miss Jean Brodie*. In his *New York Times* review, Vincent Canby found Bujold "a constantly delightful surprise" and Burton
"in excellent form and voice—funny, loutish and sometimes wise." There
are fine performances by Irene Papas as Henry's first wife (of six), John
Colicos as Cromwell, and Anthony Quayle, who received an Oscar nomination as Best Supporting Actor, as Wolsey. Of its ten Academy Award
nominations, the film won only for its costume design.

Between *Becket* and *Anne*, the only memorable film (of 11) made by
Burton was *Who's Afraid of Virginia Woolf?* With the exception of *Equus*
(his seventh and last nomination), his work deteriorated seriously following *Anne of the Thousand Days*.

# Another Country

★★★★★★★★★★★★★★★★★★★★★★★★★★★★★★★★★★★★★★★★★★★★★★★★★★★★★★

**Nationality**: British        **Year**: 1984

**Cast**: Rupert Everett, Colin Firth, Michael Jenn, Robert Addie, Anna Massey, Betsy Brantley

**Director**: Marek Kanievska       **Running Time**: 90 minutes

**B/W or Color**: Color       **Availability**: EMBASSY HOME ENTERTAINMENT

In the Fifties, Great Britain was rocked by a spy scandal involving three men who leaked British intelligence secrets to the Soviet Union: Guy Burgess, Donald MacLean, and Kim Philby. All were products of England's "public school" system, where the sons of upper-class families learn political power and the snobberies of Britain's old-guard society. It's hardly the expected breeding ground for three such notorious traitors.

Julian Mitchell's adaptation of his successful West End stage play centers on just such an institution. It's the Thirties, and Guy Bennett (read Guy Burgess) is a charming and clever student in his penultimate year of study. He envisions a brilliant future for himself in the diplomatic service. His best friend, already a committed Marxist, is Tommy Judd (an amalgam of Donald MacLean and two lesser-known English communists), who appears unconcerned at his colleague's obviously homosexual interest in a younger student named Harcourt. Another student commits suicide after being caught in a gay act, and the school is subsequently rife with tension and hypocrisy. In refusing to adhere to the unspoken rules of the British class system, Bennett finds his covert love affair exposed, and he undergoes a ritual punishment by the school prefects. Ultimately, he comes to respect—and embrace—Judd's theories on the injustice of privilege.

Marek Kanievska's direction takes a straightforward approach to this story, while the cinematography of Peter Biziou evokes the postcard-pretty nostalgia of a *Brideshead Revisited*. Re-creating his extraordinary stage performance, Rupert Everett makes a striking film debut as Bennett, with his matinee-idol looks and kinetic energy, and he's well supported by Colin Firth's Judd and Cary Elwes as the object of Bennett's all-too-obvious affections.

# Any Number Can Win

## (Melodie en Sous-Sol/The Big Grab)

\* \* \* \* \* \* \* \* \* \* \* \* \* \* \* \* \* \* \* \* \* \* \* \* \* \* \* \* \* \* \* \* \* \* \* \* \* \* \* \* \* \* \* \* \* \* \* \* \* \* \* \* \* \*

*Nationality*: French        *Year*: 1963
*Cast*: Jean Gabin, Alain Delon, Viviane Romance
*Director*: Henri Verneuil      *Running Time*: 118 minutes
*B/W or Color*: B/W          *Availability*: KARTES VIDEO
                                          COMMUNICATIONS

This slick, stylish crime caper boasts a strong cast and a neat plot twist that raises it a notch above other such comedy-suspense films.

Directed by Henri Verneuil, a Turkish-born filmmaker best known for the successful Fernandel comedies of the Fifties (*The Sheep Has Five Legs, The Cow and I, Forbidden Fruit*), this picture concerns the attempt by an aging French exconvict named Charles (Jean Gabin) and his young accomplice Francis (Alain Delon) to carry out an elaborate plan to rob the gambling casino at Cannes.

On the night of the robbery, Francis lowers himself down an elevator shaft (the only access to the basement vault where the casino proceeds are kept) and, disguised by a black mask, confronts the head cashier with a gun and obtains the keys to the exit door. He unlocks it to admit Charles, who gathers the francs into two valises.

As they plan to make their getaway from Cannes the following morning, Francis overhears the head cashier telling police he could recognize the bags the robbers used to store the money. Francis, who's holding the suitcases, becomes desperate and drops them into the swimming pool. The valises open, and the money floats to the surface as the two thieves watch helplessly.

The charismatic performances of Gabin and Delon are first rate, and Verneuil's use of locations is excellent. The film slowly builds in suspense to the final half hour, when tensions run high.

The National Board of Review named *Any Number Can Win* one of the best foreign films of the year.

(*The tape is of very good quality, with reduction of the print at top and bottom to retain the wide-screen image. Kartes employs the movie's original French name,* Melodie en Sous-Sol, *without mentioning its more familiar U.S. release title of* Any Number Can Win.)

# Ashes and Diamonds
## (Popiol i Diament)

**★★★★★★★★★★★★★★★★★★★★★★★★★★★★★★★★★★★★★★★★★★★★★★★★★★★★★**

*Nationality*: Polish            *Year*: 1958 (U.S. release: 1961)

*Cast*: Zbigniew Cybulski, Eva Krzyzewska, Adam Pawlikowski, Waclaw Zastrzezynski, Bogumil Kobiela

*Director*: Andrzej Wajda       *Running Time*: 105 minutes

*B/W or Color*: B/W           *Availability*: EMBASSY HOME ENTERTAINMENT

This is the final part of Andrzej Wajda's trilogy on the Polish Resistance, preceded by *A Generation* (1954) and *Kanal* (1957). But it was *Ashes and Diamonds* that established Wajda's reputation in the West— as well as that of his charismatic star, Zbigniew Cybulski, whose sobriquet, "the Polish James Dean," later achieved a tragic irony when, like Dean, he died prematurely in a violent accident.

*Ashes and Diamonds* is among the most successful films ever made in Poland, and a reviewing proves that its popularity owes a lot to Cybulski's magnetic blend of humor, kinetic vitality, and acting skills, which enabled him to submerge his pleasant-faced personality in the role of a youth who is something of a World War II Hamlet.

The movie begins on May 7, 1945, the last day of the war in Europe. Maciek (Cybulski, sporting his signature tinted sunglasses) is one of two Resistance fighters with one final assignment—to assassinate the town's newly arrived Communist Party secretary. By mistake, two innocent men are needlessly killed instead, and Maciek agonizes over the prospect of pursuing his deadly mission. And, while others celebrate victory around him, the young man allows himself to be distracted by a beautiful barmaid named Krystyna (Eva Krzyzewska), with whom he spends the night. Early the next morning, Maciek carries out the murder plan, but his suspicious behavior gets the youth shot as he runs from a military patrol, and he dies crumpled on a field of rubbish.

Largely because of Cybulski's performance, *Ashes and Diamonds* remains a haunting experience. But its visual style, which owes so much to Jerzy Wojcik's craftily lit photography, suggests the care with which Wajda planned his mise-en-scene.

*(Embassy offers this film in excellent-quality prints, both dubbed and subtitled, although the latter version's titles are frequently out of focus.)*

# The Assault
## (De Aanslag)

**********************************************************

Nationality: Dutch                    Year: 1986 (U.S. release: 1987)
Cast: Derek de Lint, Monique van de Ven, John Kraaykamp
Director: Fons Rademakers          Running Time: 149 minutes
B/W or Color: Color                    Availability: TV only

This Dutch-made motion picture won the Academy Award for Best Foreign Film of 1986 and the Golden Globe Award from Hollywood's Foreign Press Association.

The Assault takes us back to the final days of World War II, just before the collapse of the Third Reich. The scene is rural Haarlem in occupied Holland. A Nazi collaborator is assassinated by the underground as he rides home on a bicycle. The Steenwijks watch terror-stricken as the traitor falls dead in front of a neighbor's house and are petrified as those neighbors drag the body away and dump it on their doorstep. There is no time to explain as the Nazis roar up. They are summarily executed in retaliation, and their home is burned to the ground. Only the youngest boy, Anton, survives the assault. The film tells the story of his life for the next 25 years, and his single-minded search to wreak vengeance on the neighbors who did not come forth to save his family.

Rademakers pulls no punches with his graphic description of the Nazi reign of terror in the Netherlands. The German soldiers seen on screen are not the usual faces of tired Hollywood extras and bit players, but rather the faces of fanatics. The Assault is a multilayered drama shown to us in bits and pieces through the eyes of a man obsessed with the past. The mosaic spreads over a long period of time, with the pieces falling into place at the end, to give us the tragic details of the crime and the betrayal.

The Assault was adapted from the Dutch best-seller, written by Harry Mulisch, whose mother was of Jewish descent and died in a German concentration camp; his father, in contrast, was imprisoned after the war for collaborating with the Nazis.

# Autumn Sonata

## (Herbstsonate/Höstsonat)

★ ★ ★ ★ ★ ★ ★ ★ ★ ★ ★ ★ ★ ★ ★ ★ ★ ★ ★ ★ ★ ★ ★ ★ ★ ★ ★ ★ ★ ★ ★ ★ ★ ★ ★ ★ ★ ★ ★ ★ ★ ★ ★ ★ ★ ★ ★ ★

*Nationality*: Swedish/British/West German    *Year*: 1978

*Cast*: Ingrid Bergman, Liv Ullmann, Lena Nyman, Halvar Björk, Gunnar Björnstrand, Erland Josephson

*Director*: Ingmar Bergman    *Running Time*: 97 minutes

*B/W or Color*: Color    *Availability*: CBS/FOX HOME VIDEO

Ingrid Bergman and Liv Ullmann act out the Master's (Ingmar Bergman) belief that "of all the relationships I know, that of mother and daughter is . . . the most mysterious, complicated and charged with emotion."

Charlotte (Ingrid Bergman) comes to visit her dowdy daughter, Eva (Liv Ullmann), in a remote Norwegian parsonage. Cosmopolite Charlotte immediately establishes her superiority over her provincial daughter and son-in-law (Halvar Björk) by remarking in a surprised and injured tone, "You eat dinner at four o'clock!" Undercurrents abound: Charlotte has just lost her lover Leonardo; Eva still grieves over the death of her son; sister Helena (Lena Nyman), dying of a mysterious disease, appalls Charlotte with her unintelligible cries. In the dark watches of the night, mother and daughter have at each other. Was childhood worse during Charlotte's endless tours, Eva asks bitterly, or when she was at home, giving a perfect performance as wife and mother? Charlotte dissects Eva's playing of a Chopin piece, justifying her cruelty. "For forty-five terrible years I've battled these preludes." Faces grow ugly in tearful closeup, revealing raw wounds underneath.

The unresolved generational battle may have echoes of real life. Does Bergman's superb performance (she won both the 1978 National Board of Review and New York Film Critics awards for Best Actress) project some guilt over her own career, and her relationship with her daughter, Pia? Was Leonardo based on Rossellini? Ullmann's own daughter Linn plays Eva as a child. To this film's variation on a universal theme is added the piquancy of a *roman à clef*. *Autumn Sonata* was also the winner of two other National Board of Review Awards: Best Picture; and, to Ingmar Bergman, Best Director.

*(CBS FOX offers the film in its English-dubbed version.)*

# The Baker's Wife
## (La Femme du Boulanger)

★ ★ ★ ★ ★ ★ ★ ★ ★ ★ ★ ★ ★ ★ ★ ★ ★ ★ ★ ★ ★ ★ ★ ★ ★ ★ ★ ★ ★ ★ ★ ★ ★ ★ ★ ★ ★ ★ ★ ★ ★ ★ ★ ★ ★ ★ ★

**Nationality**: French           **Year**: 1938 (U.S. release: 1940)
**Cast**: Raimu, Ginette Leclerc, Charles Moulin, Charpin, Robert Vattier
**Director**: Marcel Pagnol         **Running Time**: 124 minutes
**B/W or Color**: B/W             **Availability**: Public Domain

The Baker's Wife is a delicious, yeasty combination of those Gallic imperatives: food, sex, and emotions. Shot in Provence and filled with quintessentially French "types," it is as indigenous as the daily crusty loaf.

A middle-aged baker of considerable circumference and generally comic proportions is uniquely played by Raimu. He sets up shop with his pretty young wife, who is soon taken with a handsome young shepherd. The wife disappears, and the mortified baker refuses to supply bread to the village until she returns. The village is in turmoil.

Raimu, a serious comedian in the Chaplin tradition, mirrors a thousand emotions in his agony as he turns first to the church and finally to Pernod for comfort. He eventually grasps the extent of his wife's betrayal and the shepherd's deceit when he says, wryly, "I invited the fellow into my house for a cookie, and he took all I had." Later, after the village has rallied in the defense of its daily bread, his wife returns. Now his genuine breadth is revealed in his cautious but concerned conversation with the house cat, who has also deserted its mate for a similar fling. Within earshot of his wife, in his gentle way, the plump baker questions the feline, "Will you leave in the future? If so, it would be less cruel to go immediately than to wait a while." The heart-shaped loaf of bread he has baked for his errant wife is not as corny within its context as it would seem.

In short, a gem of a film filled with universal human quirks and genuine human feeling. Marcel Pagnol, a director in the grand tradition, was the first filmmaker to be immortalized in the Academie Francaise. His companions there are in good company.

The National Board voted The Baker's Wife 1940's Best Foreign Film, as did the New York Film Critics.

# Ballad of a Soldier
## (Ballada o Soldate)

★ ★ ★ ★ ★ ★ ★ ★ ★ ★ ★ ★ ★ ★ ★ ★ ★ ★ ★ ★ ★ ★ ★ ★ ★ ★ ★ ★ ★ ★ ★ ★ ★ ★ ★ ★ ★ ★ ★ ★ ★ ★ ★ ★ ★ ★ ★ ★ ★ ★ ★ ★ ★ ★

*Nationality*: Russian          *Year*: 1960

*Cast*: Vladimir Ivashov, Shanna Prokhorenko, Antonina Maximova, Evgenie Urbanski

*Director*: Grigori Chukhrai          *Running Time*: 89 minutes

*B/W or Color*: B/W          *Availability*: Public Domain

This ballad carefully traces the six-day leave of a 19-year-old Russian soldier who chooses a pass to go home instead of a medal for his heroic bravery on the battlefield.

En route, he encourages and helps a frightened amputee soldier to reach his home and attempts to deliver a precious gift of soap to the apparently unfaithful wife of another comrade. He also meets the inevitable shy and frightened girl for an unforgettable brief encounter. But in a typical wartime "snafu," the soldier arrives home too late for his specific purpose—to mend his widowed mother's roof. In fact, he barely sees her at all. Her lonely figure standing on the empty road, after his momentary visit, is dignified and telling. This poetic film has much of the humane feeling and characteristic lyricism of the great 19th-century Russian novels.

The photography is both forceful and luminous with strong, and frequently tender, closeups. Grigori Chukhrai's direction, vital and yet not overdone, is in the style of the great Russian master Eisenstein. Mikhail Ziv has provided a moving music score.

The actors are well cast and convincing in their essential innocence and freshness. Each one is archetypical—from the brightly energetic young soldier to the innocent but generous young woman, to the mother who must fight her own lonely war at home. Films like this provide more insight into the contemporary Russian mood than all the formal meetings between highly placed foreign ministers.

*Ballad of a Soldier* won a special prize at 1960's Cannes Film Festival and was an Oscar nominee for Original Story and Screenplay. In 1961, it tied with *The Hustler* for the British Film Academy's Best Film award.

# Barry Lyndon

\*\*\*\*\*\*\*\*\*\*\*\*\*\*\*\*\*\*\*\*\*\*\*\*\*\*\*\*\*\*\*\*\*\*\*\*\*\*\*\*\*\*\*\*\*\*\*\*\*\*\*\*\*\*\*\*\*

*Nationality*: British                 *Year*: 1975
*Cast*: Ryan O'Neal, Marisa Berenson, Patrick Magee, Hardy Kruger
*Director*: Stanley Kubrick        *Running Time*: 184 minutes
*B/W or Color*: Color              *Availability*: WARNER HOME
                                                VIDEO

After his success with sadomasochism in *A Clockwork Orange* (1971), director Stanley Kubrick confidently switched in 1975 to the romantic yet violent world of William Thackeray's first novel, *The Luck of Barry Lyndon*, originally published serially in 1841.

William K. Everson, reviewing the picture in the February 1976 issue of *Films in Review*, called "*Barry Lyndon* . . . a work of consummate craftsmanship, and one with a notably civilized stance, ingredients increasingly rare in movies today," adding, "Critics who carp at the changes Kubrick wrought in Thackeray's novel and in its hero fail to note that while in the book Barry Lyndon talked too much and in the film hardly at all, both approaches are able to say the same thing about him and about the futility and pointlessness of his odyssey." Everson ended his review by advising us not to let "anyone keep you from seeing *Barry Lyndon*." And, indeed, to this day, the film is one that should be seen by all—it is one of the most gorgeous ever made, unrivaled in scene after scene for its extraordinary beauty and sumptuousness. It is a Lucullan feast for the eyes. Although Kubrick freely confessed that he did not fully understand Thackeray's scathing satire, he felt he had included in the film qualities that had "eluded" Thackeray. Nevertheless, the movie's deficiencies in some areas can in no way detract from its singular beauty.

*Barry Lyndon* was chosen by The National Board of Review as the best film of 1975 and picked up Oscars at the 1976 Academy Awards ceremony for Best Costumes; Best Musical Adaptation (Leonard Rosenman, the winner, expressed his gratitude to Mozart, Handel, and Vivaldi); Best Cinematography; and Best Art Direction. The beauty of the film, especially the lighting of candlelit scenes, is unforgettable and brilliantly conveys all the decadence of the *haute monde* of the 18th century.

The cast, Ryan O'Neal particularly, is often less interesting than the costumes and decor, and Marisa Berenson is as beautiful—and as moving—as a gorgeously dressed mannequin. It is one's eyes that are dazzled.

# The Battle of Algiers
## (La Battaglia di Algeri)

\* \* \* \* \* \* \* \* \* \* \* \* \* \* \* \* \* \* \* \* \* \* \* \* \* \* \* \* \* \* \* \* \* \* \* \* \* \* \* \* \* \* \* \* \* \* \* \* \* \* \* \*

Nationality: Italian-Algerian    Year: 1966 (U.S. release: 1967)
Cast: Yacef Saadi, Jean Martin, Brahim Haggiag, Tommaso Neri, Samia Kerbash
Director: Gillo Pontecorvo    Running Time: 120 minutes
B/W or Color: B/W    Availability: Public Domain

The Battle of Algiers is excruciatingly pertinent in view of the increase in similar anguished confrontations today. The faces of colonialism and revolution are pitted against each other more wrenchingly than in anything before or since.

Not one foot of newsreel was used in the reenactment of the battle. Nonetheless, Pontecorvo demanded and achieved documentary realism in his reconstructed scenes of historical events. Sponsored by the victorious Algerians and produced by the rebel leader Yacef Saadi, The Battle of Algiers is potentially propagandistic. The French didn't allow it to be screened in France until 1971 and boycotted its screening at the Venice Film Festival as well as the award ceremony. At the St. Severin Film Festival in 1981 the theater showing it was fire bombed by fascists.

In 1954 a message from the National Liberation Forces incites the Arab population to break from colonialism. Over the next three years there are terrorist attacks from both sides. An innocent Arab worker is accused of killing a policeman, and in retaliation a French official has a bomb planted near the Arab's residence. The NLF seeks vengeance. Three women from the Casbah penetrate the French section and plant bombs in a milk bar, a cafeteria, and an Air France terminal. Sound familiar? Colonel Matthieu and his parachutists then systematically eliminate the guerrilla movement. The Battle of Algiers, 1954–57, is a victory for the French, but in 1960 the independence movement rises phoenix-like out of the Casbah, and independence is finally won in 1962.

Some of the most effective statements are from the French officers themselves, who show admiration for the valor of the Algerians. A highly explosive film that prudent distributors might be reluctant to show today, but a must for the thoughtful.

# The Beachcomber
## (Vessel of Wrath)

\* \* \* \* \* \* \* \* \* \* \* \* \* \* \* \* \* \* \* \* \* \* \* \* \* \* \* \* \* \* \* \* \* \* \* \* \* \* \* \* \* \* \* \* \* \* \* \* \* \* \*

**Nationality**: British            **Year**: 1938
**Cast**: Charles Laughton, Elsa Lanchester, Robert Newton
**Director**: Erich Pommer            **Running Time**: 92 minutes
**B/W or Color**: B/W            **Availability**: Public Domain

Based on W. Somerset Maugham's short story *Vessel of Wrath,* this film was retitled *The Beachcomber* in the United States. A top-notch cast helps make it memorable—particularly Charles Laughton as Ginger Ted, the tippling beachcomber of the title. Real-life wife Elsa Lanchester (*Bride of Frankenstein*) makes a rare appearance with her husband as Miss Jones, a prim and proper missionary who disapproves of Ted's drunken and promiscuous ways. Ginger Ted is also the bane of the *Controleur* of the small island (Robert Newton), and a friend of sorts, as well, since he is the only white man the official can talk to. Miss Jones's complaints escalate when Ted helps a native girl play hooky from one of the missionary's classes. Ted and the girl prefer lessons in love, and Ted is finally arrested by the authorities and sentenced to hard labor. Ultimately, Miss Jones discovers that beneath his sodden exterior Ted is an English gentleman who went to pieces when his father, a country vicar, refused to allow him to marry the barmaid at the local pub, the Fox and Rabbit. Encounters between Ted and Miss Jones culminate in his saving her life, and the two marry. She reforms him while he melts her frigidity, and at the finale the two are running a local pub called the Fox and Rabbit.

Laughton and Lanchester are absolutely marvelous together and were listed among the year's best performers by the National Board, which also chose *The Beachcomber* as one of its best films for 1938.

Initially, the puritans in the Breen Office trimmed the delightful British comedy for its (God forbid) sexual connotations, but the complete film is available on videocassette.

Robert Newton, better known to fans as the character Long John Silver, is a young, clean-cut, and sober character herein. In 1954, he assayed the Laughton role in an undistinguished color remake of *The Beachcomber.*

# Beauties of the Night
## (Les Belles de Nuit)

★★★★★★★★★★★★★★★★★★★★★★★★★★★★★★★★★★★★★★★★★★★★★★★★★★★★★

**Nationality**: French          **Year**: 1952

**Cast**: Gérard Philipe, Gina Lollobrigida, Martine Carol, Magali Vendeuil, Paolo Stoppa

**Director**: René Clair        **Running Time**: 84 minutes (originally 90 minutes in France)

**B/W or Color**: B/W        **Availability**: TV only

Although the great French director René Clair often made films of social comment, this comedy-fantasy was done solely in the spirit of fun, with little regard for the morals haunting Hollywood at the time. Clair's only message, if you can call it that, was that it's fine to indulge in fantasies, especially when the ladies of your dreams are as dazzling as these.

Gérard Philipe is a poor Parisian composer whose efforts to create a successful opera are thwarted by the din in the streets beneath its garret windows. A Gallic Walter Mitty, the shy young man takes solace in daydreaming. He fancies himself back at the turn of the century, as an acclaimed composer with the world at his feet. Retreating farther back in time, he's a soldier in Louis Philippe's army in Algiers, with Gina Lollobrigida begging for the merest favor. Her disrobing in a bathing sequence was considered too racy for American audiences, however, and was cut from the film.

From Algiers, our amorous hero retreats to the days of Louis XVI, and thence to the reign of Louis XIII, with the Three Musketeers making a command appearance. It's back to the future, finally, in this imaginative romp, performed with great style and photographed ravishingly.

Gérard Philipe brings an intensity to his portrayal of the dreamy musician who conjures up this amiable frenzy—an intensity that was the hallmark of this actor who died at 37 of a heart attack in 1959. Eight years later, co-star Martine Carol also succumbed to a heart attack, at 45.

Along with *Les Grandes Manoeuvres*, *Beauties of the Night* ranks high among Clair's latter-day memorable films. The National Board named it Best Foreign Film of the year.

# Beauty and the Beast
## (La Belle et la Bête)

★★★★★★★★★★★★★★★★★★★★★★★★★★★★★★★★★★★★★★★★★★★★★★★★★★★★★★

Nationality: French          Year: 1946 (U.S. release: 1947)

Cast: Jean Marais, Josette Day, Marcel André, Mila Parely, Michel Auclair

Director: Jean Cocteau        Running Time: 92 minutes

B/W or Color: B/W            Availability: EMBASSY HOME VIDEO

E nough has been written about this film, even at the time it was made, to fill days of intense reading. Jean Cocteau, the writer-director-scenographer, was no modest individual either in artistic range or personality. Said W. H. Auden, "To enclose the collected works of Cocteau, one would need not a bookshelf, but a warehouse."

Versed in every field from poetry to opera to film, Cocteau was chosen by the French government to help rejuvenate the crippled film industry in the wake of World War II. Money and equipment and qualified crew members and even film stock were at an appalling low. His film, whatever it would be, was one of several expected to bring state-of-the-art motion pictures back to France. Perhaps this was why the classic fairy tale was chosen—to give him access to the largest possible audience.

Cocteau's diary of the production, available in soft cover, indicates that he felt up to the task spiritually, but that all elements, both human and mechanical, were conspiring against him. He was plagued by illness and constantly in pain—so much so that his health threatened to terminate the production—but he pressed on. "The work of art hates us and contrives by any foul means to get rid of us." Film stock came out of the lab scratched, continuity was often mismatched, and he was constantly told to rush shooting, which, since he was rediscovering cinema, was a poor decision on the part of the producers.

Jean Marais, a dashingly handsome actor, was given three roles to play in the film—including that of the Beast. Marais and Cocteau were close friends, and giving him the key role was the director's gift to the actor. As Beauty, Josette Day glides down haunted corridors, shrinks from the Beast's advances, but grows to love him. Extraordinarily photographed by Henri Alekan, and scored by Georges Auric, it possesses a mystical feeling that is truly timeless.

(Embassy's videocassette is subtitled.)

# Becket

★ ★ ★ ★ ★ ★ ★ ★ ★ ★ ★ ★ ★ ★ ★ ★ ★ ★ ★ ★ ★ ★ ★ ★ ★ ★ ★ ★ ★ ★ ★ ★ ★ ★ ★ ★ ★ ★ ★ ★ ★ ★ ★ ★ ★ ★ ★ ★ ★ ★ ★ ★

*Nationality*: British        *Year*: 1964
*Cast*: Richard Burton, Peter O'Toole, John Gielgud, Donald Wolfit
*Director*: Peter Glenville      *Running Time*: 148 minutes
*B/W or Color*: Color       *Availability*: MPI VIDEO

**B**ecket led The National Board's ten best list for 1964. After receiving 11 Academy Award nominations—including Best Picture, Best Director, Best Actor (for both Burton and O'Toole), Supporting Actor (John Gielgud), and Cinematography—the film won only for its screenplay by Edward Anhalt. The source was Jean Anouilh's stage play, which starred Laurence Olivier as Thomas Becket (the Archbishop of Canterbury) and Anthony Quinn as King Henry II. In the picture, Burton is Becket and O'Toole, Henry.

Told in flashback, as an inconsolable Henry does penance for his responsibility for the murder of Becket, the film details the agonizing drama of the conflict between two men, once fine friends. The time is 800 years ago, and the issue is who is to be the more powerful—the King and his crown or the Archbishop and his church? Deadly enemies now, Henry orders the murder of his former drinking and wenching companion, and death comes for the Archbishop on the high-altar of Canterbury Cathedral.

This stunning historical drama reestablished Burton's appeal at the box office, following the scandal of his affair with Elizabeth Taylor. O'Toole would later play Henry II again in *The Lion in Winter* and would once more be nominated for the Oscar. The two actors share the unfortunate distinction of having the most nominations (seven) without having won an Oscar.

Sian Phillips, at that time Mrs. O'Toole, appears as Gwendolyn—Becket's mistress before he became Archbishop—who commits suicide rather than join the king in his bedchamber, as he demands.

# Belle de Jour

**\*\*\*\*\*\*\*\*\*\*\*\*\*\*\*\*\*\*\*\*\*\*\*\*\*\*\*\*\*\*\*\*\*\*\*\*\*\*\*\*\*\*\*\*\*\*\*\*\*\***

*Nationality*: French-Italian          *Year*: 1967
*Cast*: Catherine Deneuve, Jean Sorel, Michel Piccoli, Geneviève Page, Pierre Clementi
*Director*: Luis Buñuel          *Running Time*: 100 minutes
*B/W or Color*: Color          *Availability*: TV only

Buñuel's first color film is an enigmatic "comedy," rather a departure from his darker, more brooding work, but it operates on the same soaring level of fantasy as his other films. There is the usual formula, Buñuel's melange of religious and bourgeois decay, but where we have become accustomed to an undertone of morbid eroticism, in *Belle de Jour* it becomes a central theme. Catherine Deneuve plays the beautiful but bored wife of a French medical student (Sorel). She is dutiful and loving, but when she hears about a kinky brothel from a middle-aged roué (Piccoli) she is intrigued. Given the address, she introduces herself to the madam (delightfully played by Geneviève Page) and sets about occupying every afternoon until 5:00 P.M. as one of the girls. Her encounters are mostly amusing, and we're treated to a series of vignettes featuring the whimsies of the oddball clientele, rather in the manner of Jean Genet's *The Balcony*. She caters to the whims of a sadistic candy manufacturer, a Japanese businessman who wants to pay by credit card (no longer a farfetched notion), and a young gangster (Clementi) who has been outfitted with an alarming set of steel teeth. Clementi plays his role to the hilt, and gives us a wonderful spoof of movie gangsters, principally Belmondo. A complication ensues when he falls in love with her and insists on more than an afternoon tryst.

In less capable hands, the movie could have bogged down into a series of successively less amusing investigations into derailed sex, but Buñuel is always one step ahead of us and keeps it fresh. The movie ends ambiguously so that we are not allowed to be certain we haven't witnessed more than a series of the heroine's unconventional daydreams. Deneuve gives what is possibly the best, and certainly the most animated, performance of her career.

# The Belles of St. Trinian's

\* \* \* \* \* \* \* \* \* \* \* \* \* \* \* \* \* \* \* \* \* \* \* \* \* \* \* \* \* \* \* \* \* \* \* \* \* \* \* \* \* \* \* \* \* \* \* \* \* \* \* \* \* \* \*

*Nationality*: British                    *Year*: 1954

*Cast*: Alastair Sim, Joyce Grenfell, George Cole, Beryl Reid, Hermione Baddeley

*Director*: Frank Launder         *Running Time*: 91 minutes

*B/W or Color*: B/W                   *Availability*: THORN/EMI-HBO VIDEO

Ronald Searle's macabre cartoons depicting the anarchic goings-on at St. Trinian's, that never-never school for uniformed little female monsters, inspired this often hilarious farce, whose commercial success was sufficient unto spawning three sequels: *Blue Murder at St. Trinian's* (1957), *The Pure Hell of St. Trinian's* (1960), and *The Great St. Trinian's Train Robbery* (1966). But, for many, the first St. Trinian's movie is the best.

Occasionally, Searle's sick-joke cartoons are woven into the plot devised by Frank Launder, Sidney Gilliatt, and Val Valentine, but more often (and more successfully) the scriptwriters merely use Searle's characters as a springboard for their own fertile ideas, while remaining faithful to the ambience of that Gothic institution of dubious learning.

A plot summary would give little indication of the madness and mayhem that loom large in those academic corridors, where keeping a racehorse in the dormitory is no more unusual than cheating at sports or making gin in chemistry. Indeed, what goes on in the classrooms is outrageously amusing, with a faculty so disreputable that it would look more at home in a women's prison.

*The Belles of St. Trinian's* is a marvelously mindless entertainment, played to the hilt by a cast of both seasoned character performers and suitably awful little sub-ingenues. Leading the whole charade in splendidly ridiculous fashion is the inimitable Alastair Sim, quite literally beside himself as both Fritton, the master bookmaker, and *Miss* Fritton, that genteel gargoyle of a giddy headmistress who's nevertheless permissably cognizant of the monstrous capabilities of her adolescent charges.

Cartoons don't often translate well into another medium, but in the mirthful hands of Launder and Gilliatt, the unique world of St. Trinian's here enjoys a splendidly Searleistic new shadow-life of its own.

(*The tape is of very good quality.*)

# Bellissima

\* \* \* \* \* \* \* \* \* \* \* \* \* \* \* \* \* \* \* \* \* \* \* \* \* \* \* \* \* \* \* \* \* \* \* \* \* \* \* \* \* \* \* \* \* \* \* \* \* \* \* \* \* \*

Nationality: Italian           Year: 1951
Cast: Anna Magnani, Walter Chiari, Tina Apicella, Gaston Renzelli, Alessandro Blasetti
Director: Luchino Visconti       Running Time: 100 minutes
B/W or Color: B/W           Availability: TV only

Considering all the big names involved in this "small" film, it's a miracle that it has retained the simplicity that gives it "heart." This can be attributed to its star—arguably one of the world's greatest screen actresses—Anna Magnani. Directed by Luchino Visconti and co-written by Cesare Zavattini, Francesco Rosi, Visconti, and others, *Bellissima* also credits Franco Zeffirelli among its contributors. These names are the building blocks of modern Italian cinema, yet *Bellissima* remains rarely seen in this country. In some ways it is even more "Italian" than Visconti's *Rocco and His Brothers*.

A seriocomic look at stage mothers and Cinecittà (the Roman Hollywood), *Bellissima* is stylistically the least Visconti-like of his films. Spare in style, verbose, and surprisingly feminist, *Bellissima* is a confounding item in the master's *oeuvre*.

Magnani plays the star-struck mom. She is one of the thousands who herd their moppets into Cinecittà to audition for a film directed by Alessandro Blasetti (played by himself). The cruelty that the dream factory exhibits in its treatment of the mothers and their children and the way all of Rome gets involved in these machinations are Visconti and company's not-too-subtle self-criticism. That Magnani's awakening at the film's end—her return to "maturity"—comes at the expense of the film world is of considerable interest as far as Visconti is concerned, let alone plot and theme.

Once again, *Bellissima* is Magnani. Four years following this picture she would receive an Academy Award for *The Rose Tattoo*, which Tennessee Williams would write for her, but here she is her woman of the people. Magnani is both riveting and combustible; she is at her most moving and fascinating. As the actress sits with her film-husband appreciating the scenery of Hawks's *Red River*, she says, "Montgomery Clift, *simpatico*—eh?" Anna Magnani, *simpatica . . . sì!*

# Betrayal

★★★★★★★★★★★★★★★★★★★★★★★★★★★★★★★★★★★★★★★★★★★★★★★★★★★★

*Nationality*: British       *Year*: 1983

*Cast*: Jeremy Irons, Ben Kingsley, Patricia Hodge

*Director*: David Jones       *Running Time*: 95 minutes

*B/W or Color*: Color       *Availability*: CBS/FOX HOME VIDEO

The celebrated British playwright Harold Pinter (*The Caretaker, The Birthday Party*) is no novice to screenplay writing, having adapted not only his own work but the work of others, i.e., *The Servant, The French Lieutenant's Woman*. Nothing attempted previously, however, is perhaps as successfully realized as his screenplay for *Betrayal*, his own absorbing and stylish London play, which was performed in New York in 1980 with Raul Julia, Blythe Danner, and Roy Scheider.

In the film version the *ménage à trois* stars Jeremy Irons as Jerry, a literary agent who has conducted a long affair with Emma (Patricia Hodge), the wife of a publisher, Jerry's best friend, Robert (Ben Kingsley). Pinter has retained the play's chronological order, which moves backward in time over nine years. The film announces each time change with a title, and it opens with Emma and Jerry meeting in a London pub two years after the end of their seven-year affair. Their conversation, though outwardly banal, is, in the Pinter manner, far from being all small talk. Beneath the surface are revealed the fascinating foibles of unsentimental characters caught up in a liaison they are hard pressed to understand. Much of Pinter's skill lies in the unpredictability and sense of irony inherent in this seemingly ordinary love triangle, his talent for producing quiet suspense (who is actually betraying whom?), and, surprisingly, even a sense of the comic (Pinter admits to being a fan of Noel Coward's).

The play has been opened up for the film in various locations, and the performances are superb. The versatile Ben Kingsley, fresh from the triumph of *Gandhi*, gives another sensitive portrayal as the cuckolded husband. Irons's character is intelligent, even interestingly tiresome, and, though many critics preferred Danner's "incandescent" performance as the stage wife, British actress Patricia Hodge manages to hold her own in a role that is strongly overshadowed by the men in her life.

The National Board of Review gave the film the Best Picture of the Year Award.

# The Bicycle Thief
### (Ladri di Biciclette/Bicycle Thieves)

* * * * * * * * * * * * * * * * * * * * * * * * * * * * * * * * * * * * * * * * * * * * * * * * *

**Nationality**: Italian       **Year**: 1948 (U.S. release: 1949)

**Cast**: Lamberto Maggiorani, Lianella Carell, Enzo Staiola, Elena Altieri, Vittorio Antonucci

**Director**: Vittorio De Sica       **Running Time**: 90 minutes

**B/W or Color**: B/W       **Availability**: CORINTH VIDEO

"My idea is to de-romanticize the cinema," said Vittorio De Sica, the brilliant director of *The Bicycle Thief*. His goal was more than achieved in this remarkable neorealist film, shot in documentary fashion, with its almost totally amateur cast taken from the poverty-ridden streets of postwar Rome.

This is the director's film from start to finish, in its combination of apparent effortlessness and profound social and emotional power. The story is simple. It concerns the survival of a young couple and their family in a period of incalculable misery and unemployment. The husband finally gets work posting bills up and down the streets of Rome. His wife sells the sheets from their bed so that he can buy a bicycle from the local pawn shop in order to perform his job. In one terrible moment, we watch the bicycle being stolen. In his desperate and futile hunt for the lost bike, we observe the degradation of a decent man attempting to support his family in a society in which unemployment is the rule. We see him slap his child undeservedly in his frustration. We watch him turn into a bumbling, inadequate thief in his despair. Caught and beaten, he is profoundly humiliated in front of his young son in yet another unforgettable scene.

In this film, the average Roman struggles to survive in an indifferent and uncaring world. Although the picture is thoroughly realistic, it never punches us between the eyes with its message. De Sica's sensitive hand knows just how far to go.

The National Board voted *The Bicycle Thief* 1949's Best Picture and named De Sica Best Director. The New York Film Critics named it the year's Best Foreign Film, and Hollywood awarded it a Special Oscar as Outstanding Foreign Film.

*(Corinth offers a subtitled videocassette.)*

# The Big Deal on Madonna Street
## (I Soliti Ignoti/Persons Unknown)

★★★★★★★★★★★★★★★★★★★★★★★★★★★★★★★★★★★★★★★★★★★★★★★★★★★★

*Nationality*: Italian          *Year*: 1958 (U.S. release: 1960)

*Cast*: Vittorio Gassman, Marcello Mastroianni, Toto, Renato Salvatori

*Director*: Mario Monicelli      *Running Time*: 91 minutes (105 minutes in Italy)

*B/W or Color*: B/W           *Availability*: Public Domain

Oscar-nominated as Best Foreign Film of 1958, under the title *The Usual Unidentified Thieves*, *The Big Deal on Madonna Street* is an hilarious story of unbelievably incompetent crooks who plan a robbery. It's a clever spoof of Jules Dassin's superb 1955 crime caper *Rififi*. Many critics claimed that the sight gags did credit to the best of the silent-screen comedy talents, and director Mario Monicelli's frenetic pace is maintained throughout.

Arrested for trying to steal a car—with a horn that gets stuck—Cosimo (Memmo Carotenuto) is willing to pay someone to serve his sentence. Peppe (Vittorio Gassman), an unsuccessful boxer, agrees; however, the scheme backfires, and both men end up in jail. Once released, the daring duo decide to follow through on a robbery that Cosimo has devised, and they gather their gang.

The motley crew consists of Tiberio (Marcello Mastroianni), an inept photographer; Mario (Renato Salvatori), who formerly stole baby carriages and now sells popcorn in a seedy movie house; Ferribotte (Tiberio Murgia), a hot-tempered type who's extremely jealous of his beautiful sister Carmelita (Claudia Cardinale); and Campannelle (Carlo Pisacane), a constantly hungry ex-jockey. They are instructed (in a highlight of the movie) by safecracker Dante (Toto).

Nothing goes according to plan: the *vacant* apartment next door to the robbery site turns out to be occupied by spinster sisters; attempts to gain entry through a coal chute lead to the discovery that the building has been converted to oil; drilling into a wall bursts a water pipe . . . and so on. Though *The Big Deal* doesn't materialize, the undaunted desperadoes retain their hope for a brighter future.

Not shown in the American prints was a sequence wherein Cosimo is accidentally killed after bungling a holdup.

A sequel, *Big Deal on Madonna Street . . . 20 Years Later,* was made 27 years later, and an unsuccessful American version, 1984's *Crackers,* was directed by Louis Malle.

# Bitter Rice
## (Riso Amaro)

★★★★★★★★★★★★★★★★★★★★★★★★★★★★★★★★★★★★★★★★★★★★★★★★★★★★

**Nationality**: Italian                **Year**: 1949 (U.S. release: 1950)
**Cast**: Silvana Mangano, Vittorio Gassman, Doris Dowling, Raf Vallone
**Director**: Giuseppe De Santis        **Running Time**: 109 minutes
**B/W or Color**: B/W                   **Availability**: TV only

I n 1950, with its provocative poster-art poses of busty, sullen-faced Silvana Mangano standing in a rice field, her nubile figure clad in tight sweater, short shorts, and thigh-length hose, *Bitter Rice* promised forbidden pleasures to the American foreign-film patron as it advertised "An earthy drama of human passions!" Older readers of this volume will recall this period as an era of severe Hollywood censorship restrictions, when the only respite was to be gleaned from foreign movies. In short, *Bitter Rice* was then pretty hot stuff!

In this steamy tale of tensions and passions amid the rice fields of the Po Valley, neorealism clashes head on with sexy exploitation melodrama. *Bitter Rice* may have aired pretentions of social realism and responsibility of championing the plight of exploited female rice workers, but that wasn't what made the movie a hit. Instead, we have an impressionable young woman (Mangano), fascinated by the hollow glamour of movie magazines and gangsters, who becomes involved with a slick crook (Vittorio Gassman, playing somewhat beyond the hilt), who plans to steal the rice crop. American actress Doris Dowling makes a good impression as Mangano's rice-gathering fellow worker, a reformed moll, and rugged Raf Vallone, as a police sergeant, rounds out the starring quartet. But it's 19-year-old Mangano's picture, and her impassioned final scenes are as unforgettable as the best operatic exercise in *verismo* melodrama.

*Bitter Rice* remains director Giuseppe De Santis's most significant contribution to the evolution of the Italian film in America. And, for Silvana Mangano, it was the erotic stepping-stone to an international career that was curtailed only by her desire to first fulfill her responsibilities as Mrs. Dino De Laurentiis.

# Bizet's Carmen

★★★★★★★★★★★★★★★★★★★★★★★★★★★★★★★★★★★★★★★★★★★★★★★★★★★★★★

*Nationality*: French-Italian      *Year*: 1984

*Cast*: Julia Migenes-Johnson, Plácido Domingo, Faith Esham, Ruggero Raimondi

*Director*: Francesco Rosi      *Running Time*: 152 minutes

*B/W or Color*: Color      *Availability*: RCA/COLUMBIA PIC-TURES HOME VIDEO

Prosper Mérimée's familiar tale of the seductive gypsy Carmen, for whose love men ruined their lives, has probably been filmed more times than any other in classic literature. This Franco-Italian co-production, directed in Spain by Francesco Rosi *(Eboli)*, has been hailed by critics and moviegoers as the ideal transference of opera to film and dismissed by a cranky minority as too little opera and too much movie.

*Bizet's Carmen* utilizes the Opéra Comique version—with spoken dialogue. Indeed, such natural sounds as crickets, birds, and horses' hooves occasionally replace the music altogether on the soundtrack, as though to allow a rest for the opera's offscreen conductor, Lorin Maazel, and the Orchestre National de France.

This is a flavorful and rewarding *Carmen,* and Rosi's expansive use of the dusty Andalusian locations (in and around the city of La Ronda) lend pastel-muted verisimilitude to a *Carmen* more given to passionate, earthy realism than the pseudo-Spanish glamour of so many past adaptations. The leading players enact their roles as well as they sing them, from Julia Migenes-Johnson's brazenly sexy gypsy temptress to Faith Esham's Micaela, the country girl so often portrayed as merely a sweet-voiced cipher. Plácido Domingo is justly celebrated for his Don José, and Ruggero Raimondi embodies the perfect toreador. Bizet purists may miss some minor music that has been dropped, but those are the necessary compromises that make this an effective opera-film and not just another filmed opera.

The National Board of Review listed *Carmen* among the five best foreign films of the year.

# Black Narcissus

★ ★ ★ ★ ★ ★ ★ ★ ★ ★ ★ ★ ★ ★ ★ ★ ★ ★ ★ ★ ★ ★ ★ ★ ★ ★ ★ ★ ★ ★ ★ ★ ★ ★ ★ ★ ★ ★ ★ ★ ★ ★ ★ ★ ★ ★ ★ ★ ★ ★ ★ ★ ★

*Nationality*: British                         *Year*: 1947

*Cast*: Deborah Kerr, Sabu, David Farrar, Flora Robson, Jean Simmons, Kathleen Byron

*Director*: Michael Powell and         *Running Time*: 100 minutes
Emeric Pressburger

*B/W or Color*: Color                    *Availability*: VIDAMERICA


The distinguished producer-director-writer team of Michael Powell and Emeric Pressburger, who called their company Archer Films, had impressed critics and audiences alike with the variety of their productions, released at the rate of one per year. Following the varied successes of 1945's *I Know Where I'm Going* and *A Matter of Life and Death/Stairway to Heaven* in 1946, they turned the following year to Rumer Godden's novel *Black Narcissus*, about Anglican nuns trying to operate a school-cum-hospital in a remote stretch of the Himalayas, using an edifice that had once been a potentate's harem. Of course, they must cope with the inevitable clash of cultures, but there is also the potentially profane influence of Mr. Dean, a sensual, cynical British agent, played by a muscular, pipe-puffing David Farrar. His presence is particularly disturbing to the neurotic and unstable Sister Ruth (Kathleen Byron), who's driven to shed her habit for a red dress in an effort to win Dean's interest. In so doing, she comes into conflict with the serene and gentle Sister Clodagh (Deborah Kerr), leader of the order, who must also cope with a nubile native girl (Jean Simmons) who's courted by a bejeweled young general (Sabu) whose signature scent is the disturbing Black Narcissus perfume. In this colorful and relaxed atmosphere, Sister Philippa (Flora Robson), a senior nun, finds her waning faith conflicting with her native wisdom. The occasionally melodramatic story line hinges on whether or not the well-intentioned sisters will be able to win their battle against an environment uncongenial with their mission.

Surprisingly, the entire film was shot in England. Deborah Kerr won the New York Film Critics Best Actress award for her double duty in this picture and *I See a Dark Stranger/The Adventuress*.

(*VidAmerica's cassette contains footage cut from the film's initial U.S. release, showing Kerr recalling her preconvent life.*)

61

# Black Orpheus
## (Orfeu Negro)

★★★★★★★★★★★★★★★★★★★★★★★★★★★★★★★★★★★★★★★★★★★★★★★★★★★★★★

*Nationality*: French-Italian-Brazilian     *Year*: 1959

*Cast*: Breno Mello, Marpessa Dawn, Lourdes De Oliveira, Lea Garcia

*Director*: Marcel Camus     *Running Time*: 100 minutes

*B/W or Color*: Color     *Availability*: CBS/FOX HOME VIDEO

Winner of the 1959 Academy Award for Best Foreign Film and the Grand Prize as Best Film at the Cannes Festival, *Black Orpheus* is a multinational co-production, made in Brazil and based on a Greek legend. The cast was mostly nonprofessional, and the film was the second feature (and eventually the only success) for director Marcel Camus.

Jean Bourgoin's cinematography was praised; *Films in Review* noted that it was "excellent, and some of his shots of Rio de Janeiro and its environs are sheer beauty." The New York *Herald Tribune* critic termed it "the most sensuous use of color I have ever seen on film . . . it is not so much dressed in color as created out of color." Also notable is the infectious music by Antonio Carlos Jobim and Luis Bonfa.

The Orpheus legend has the celebrated musician's love, Eurydice, die soon after they are married. He goes to the Underworld to ask the gods for her return. They grant his request, with a warning: he is to go first and lead Eurydice out of Hades, without looking back. Just before the journey's end, a love-sick and frightened Orpheus turns to make certain Eurydice is following him. She disappears, never to be seen by him again.

The film is based on the play *Orfeu da Conceicao*, by Vinicius De Moraes. Director Camus has guitarist (rather than lyre-player) Orpheus (Breno Mello) fall in love with Eurydice (American dancer Marpessa Dawn), who is visiting her cousin in Rio de Janeiro. Eurydice is being pursued by a former lover (Adhemar da Silva) who, on Carnival Day, dresses in the costume of Death. Eurydice flees wildly through the city, as both Death and Orpheus follow. Hiding in a darkened power plant, she is accidentally electrocuted by Orpheus.

Later, as he carries her body, his jealous former fiancée (Lourdes De Oliveira) follows. Still holding Eurydice in his arms, Orpheus falls from a cliff to his death.

Comparing this work with Cocteau's 1949 *Orpheus*, Hollis Alpert wrote in *Saturday Review*, "*Black Orpheus* is a far more brilliant movie . . . Through it all sound the pulsing drums . . . the insistent rhythms of carnival . . . all quite irresistible."

*(The videocassette is subtitled.)*

# Black Sunday
## (La Maschera del Demonio/The Mask of the Demon)

★ ★ ★ ★ ★ ★ ★ ★ ★ ★ ★ ★ ★ ★ ★ ★ ★ ★ ★ ★ ★ ★ ★ ★ ★ ★ ★ ★ ★ ★ ★ ★ ★ ★ ★ ★ ★ ★ ★ ★ ★ ★ ★ ★ ★ ★ ★ ★ ★ ★

**Nationality**: Italian          **Year**: 1960

**Cast**: Barbara Steele, John Richardson, Ivo Garrani, Andrea Checci, Arturo Dominici

**Director**: Mario Bava          **Running Time**: 83 minutes

**B/W *or* Color**: B/W          **Availability**: TV only

The colorful, if often aesthetically questionable, history of the Italian horror movie may have been simultaneously inaugurated and attained its zenith in this savage, brooding tale of 19th-century vampirism, set in Moldavia. Taking inspiration from the highly profitable horror period pieces being made by Hammer Films in Britain, *Black Sunday* manages to surpass them on many aesthetic levels. Based on Gogol's novel *The Vij*, *Black Sunday* rivals Murnai's *Nosferatu*, for not since that 1922 silent chiller has the vampire of legend been depicted as such a truly loathsome and unnatural abomination.

In the early 1800s, two traveling physicians inadvertently restore to life a centuries-dead female vampire-witch and her devoted servant-lover. The revived pair proceed to wreak vengeance on the family that condemned them to death, while the two courageous doctors attempt to return these demons to hell.

Former cinematographer Mario Bava's directorial feature-film debut is easily his handsomest, most carefully wrought production. Few supernatural thrillers have succeeded so well in terms of purely charnel imagery and atmosphere. Castle and forest locations, exquisitely lit and photographed, provide an oppressively foreboding environment.

Italian filmmakers have never been as squeamish about the graphically unpleasant as their British and American counterparts. *Black Sunday*'s surreal Gothic trappings are generously layered with startling moments of explicit gore and sadism (almost unprecedented at the time in a mainstream horror film), and edited prints have long-circulated in varying lengths. In more recent years, Italian horror cinema, unfortunately, has more or less eschewed atmosphere and suspense (not to mention plot, character, and even the rudiments of basic film technique!) in favor of radical violence and buckets of entrails.

# Blithe Spirit

★★★★★★★★★★★★★★★★★★★★★★★★★★★★★★★★★★★★★★★★★★★★★★★★★★★★★★★★

*Nationality*: British        *Year*: 1945

*Cast*: Rex Harrison, Constance Cummings, Kay Hammond, Margaret Rutherford

*Director*: David Lean       *Running Time*: 96 minutes

*B/W or Color*: Color       *Availability*: TV only

Noel Coward termed his satire on spiritualism "an improbable farce," and of all four Coward-David Lean movie collaborations *Blithe Spirit* is certainly the most delightfully entertaining, if the least important in content. Owing much of its witty inspiration to the whimsical ghosts of the *Topper* movies, *Blithe Spirit* centers on Elvira, the late first-wife accidentally conjured up in a private séance. Responsible for this unwanted visitation is the eccentric medium named Madame Arcati, a dinner guest of the remarried writer Charles Condomine, who is researching spiritualism for a novel. Because only the astonished Charles can see or hear the capricious Elvira, his second wife, Ruth, believes that either madness or drink must be the cause of his irrational behavior. Arcati vainly tries to send the ghost back whence she came, but Elvira won't leave without Charles, and she tampers with his car so that an auto accident will enable him to join her in the afterlife. Instead, Ruth is killed, leaving the again-widowed writer with *two* ghosts about the house. When Charles attempts to escape his apparitions, the tampered car causes *his* death, as well. The film ends with a ghostly *ménage à trois* adorning the garden wall.

In the wildly outrageous role of Madame Arcati, which Coward had tailored to her eccentric talents, Margaret Rutherford re-created her stage characterization—one no other actress has yet surpassed (not even the inimitable Beatrice Lillie's interpretation in the 1960s stage musical *High Spirits*). The urbane Rex Harrison's subsequent U.S. popularity—and career—owed much to *Blithe Spirit*. And the total effect of chartreuse-colored Kay Hammond, with blood-red lips and fingernails, is biliously right.

As slightly more than a well-photographed play—albeit a superbly written and flawlessly acted one—*Blithe Spirit* remains, in its David Lean film version, a permanently frozen daiquiri of a delightful stage fantasy.

# Blow-Up

★ ★ ★ ★ ★ ★ ★ ★ ★ ★ ★ ★ ★ ★ ★ ★ ★ ★ ★ ★ ★ ★ ★ ★ ★ ★ ★ ★ ★ ★ ★ ★ ★ ★ ★ ★ ★ ★ ★ ★ ★ ★ ★ ★ ★ ★ ★ ★ ★ ★ ★

*Nationality*: British-Italian        *Year*: 1966
*Cast*: David Hemmings, Vanessa Redgrave, Sarah Miles, Jane Birkin, John Castle
*Director*: Michelangelo Antonioni    *Running Time*: 111 minutes
*B/W or Color*: Color                 *Availability*: MGM/UA HOME VIDEO

"I've just seen Antonioni's *Blow-Up*. These Italian directors are a century ahead of me in terms of technique. What have I been doing all this time?" These extraordinary words were spoken in 1966 by none other than the Master himself, Alfred Hitchcock. In a sense, *Blow-Up* did signal the beginning of a new, modern era in filmmaking when it was first released. The nudity and glamorous models, the rich textures and color schemes, the abstract reflective sets, elaborate compositions and jump-cuts, and Herbie Hancock's jazz score all set to a "swinging" London milieu combined to create Antonioni's first (and only) commercial hit, as well as a genuinely fascinating work of art.

The story of fashion photographer David Hemmings discovering he may have inadvertently taken shots of a murder is merely a pretext for an open-end meditation on illusion and reality, art vs. life, and a myriad of other existential concerns. Unlike many "hip" Sixties films that were popular when they first came out, *Blow-Up* doesn't seem dated today. The mod world of mimes, marijuana, war protesters, and London nightclubs may seem quaint, but the film still retains its gripping hold on the viewer once Hemmings goes through the long, detailed process of blowing up individual sections of photos in an effort to determine if there is a hidden killer. As the sound of wind blows through trees, each picture is edited into a brilliantly designed sequence that seems to break down film into its most basic and powerful elements.

Antonioni's elliptical style is perfectly suited to his allegory of a man who is rich in material goods but is compelled by inner emptiness to search for some meaning in his life, even if it is searching for a possibly imaginary murderer. That we never learn if there even was a crime is beside the point. By 1966, audiences (mostly young) were ready to accept puzzles without solutions. In this and many other respects, *Blow-Up* remains the quintessential Sixties time capsule.

# The Blue Angel
## (Der Blaue Engel)

**************************************************

Nationality: German                    Year: 1930

Cast: Emil Jannings, Marlene Dietrich, Kurt Gerron, Hans Albers

Director: Josef von Sternberg        Running Time: 106 minutes

B/W or Color: B/W                    Availability: Public Domain

This truly legendary film owes its longevity chiefly to the equally legendary Marlene Dietrich. The lady became an international star with this movie, after appearing in 17 previous German pictures dating back to 1923—which she later tried to cover up by promoting the legend that Josef von Sternberg took her out of drama school for *The Blue Angel*.

This was quite likely the most important film of Sternberg's then-waning career, and it came about at the behest of the great German character actor Emil Jannings, whose performance in Sternberg's American-made *The Last Command* had brought Jannings Hollywood's first Best Actor Academy Award. The actor, who had returned to work in Germany, knew that his first talkie would be a career milestone, and he insisted Sternberg be imported to direct him in this adaptation of Heinrich Mann's *Professor Unrat*.

It was the story of a stuffy, middle-aged professor who becomes infatuated with a cheap nightclub singer, whom he foolishly allows to ruin his life and career. Finally, humiliated and abandoned, he returns to die in his old classroom.

*The Blue Angel* was simultaneously shot in both German and English, which Jannings had to learn phonetically. In America, Paramount released the English-language *Blue Angel*. This was a shorter, less flavorful version of the German original, with enough subtle changes to make it, in historian William K. Everson's opinion, "a totally different movie from the German version most classic-movie buffs know."

*The Blue Angel* remains a powerful film, and it's interesting to note how light-voiced Dietrich was when she introduced her signature song, "Falling in Love Again."

(*The film is available in at least two acceptable video prints: in German, with occasional subtitles, from Kartes—and in English, from Silver Mine Video.*)

# The Blue Lamp

**Nationality**: British       **Year**: 1950 (U.S. release: 1951)
**Cast**: Jack Warner, Jimmy Hanley, Dirk Bogarde, Robert Flemyng, Bernard Lee
**Director**: Basil Dearden       **Running Time**: 84 minutes
**B/W or Color**: B/W       **Availability**: Public Domain

M any British films have suffered a mid-Atlantic name change, but *The Blue Lamp* proves that one can succeed despite a title that tells little. In this semidocumentary melodrama about an urban crime and its detection, set against the everyday workings of London's Metropolitan Police Force, that lamp is the one that shines above British police stations.

Producers Michael Balcon and Michael Relph, director Basil Dearden, and screenwriter T.E.B. Clarke had the full cooperation of Scotland Yard, and this tribute reflects the dedication of all who contribute to Britain's prevention and detection of crime, from the lab scientist to the bobby on the beat.

*The Blue Lamp* deals with the tracking down of Tom Riley (Dirk Bogarde), a neurotic, small-time crook who fatally shoots veteran policeman Dixon (Jack Warner) during a cinema holdup. Since Warner is among the film's leading players, and since Clarke's script has carefully established Dixon as a well-liked member of the force, audience emotions are carefully manipulated to root for the men in uniform. Nor does Clarke glamorize Riley, his hysterical moll (Peggy Evans), or his punk sidekick (Patric Doonan). Nevertheless, through artful direction and writing, a heavy use of realistic London locations (well photographed by Gordon Dines), and some ingenious editing by Peter Tanner, Ealing Studios emerged with a winner. Among 1950's biggest money-makers in England, it also copped their Academy Award for the year's Best British Film.

*The Blue Lamp* also made a star of Dirk Bogarde. But it is Basil Dearden's wholly convincing mise-en-scene that one recalls most about the movie, from the authenticity of London's meaner streets and the station at Paddington Green, to the cleverly staged multicar chase through the city and the final, inspired entrapment of the killer during a greyhound race at the crowded White City Stadium.

# Bob Le Flambeur

★ ★ ★ ★ ★ ★ ★ ★ ★ ★ ★ ★ ★ ★ ★ ★ ★ ★ ★ ★ ★ ★ ★ ★ ★ ★ ★ ★ ★ ★ ★ ★ ★ ★ ★ ★ ★ ★ ★ ★ ★ ★ ★ ★ ★ ★ ★ ★ ★ ★ ★ ★ ★

*Nationality*: French        *Year*: 1956 (U.S. release: 1982)
*Cast*: Roger Duchesne, Isabelle Corey, Daniel Cauchy, Guy Decomble
*Director*: Jean-Pierre Melville       *Running Time*: 102 minutes
*B/W or Color*: B/W        *Availability*: RCA/COLUMBIA PIC-
TURES HOME VIDEO

"**B**ob Le Flambeur is not a pure policier, but a comedy of manners, a love letter to a Paris that never existed—and it en-
shrines a nostalgia for the past." That is how Jean-Pierre Melville described
what is arguably his finest film, but it could also serve as a philosophy
for almost all his pictures. They are dark, ironic tales of men and women
caught in the city between midnight and dawn, when the underworld
comes out to play. They're about loyalty and betrayal, trust and love
between crooks and their pursuers. Melville was so enamored of American culture and films that he changed his given last name (Grumbach) to
that of the great author of *Moby Dick*, Herman Melville.

*Bob Le Flambeur* is an extremely entertaining tale of an inveterate
gambler (Roger Duchesne) who decides to engage in one last fling—a
robbery at the Deauville casino. Complicating matters are the young petty
thief who idolizes Bob and the beautiful, ambitious young girl (Isabelle
Corey) who gets mixed up with the wrong crowd. Corey, who was only
16 at the time, predates Bardot in her role as a remarkably seductive and
sensuous sex-kitten, using men to get what she wants.

Henri Decae's peerless monochrome cinematography paints the blacks
ultra-dark and the whites ultra-bright. The whole design of the film is
similar, with walls and floors made up of black-and-white checkerboard
squares.

Melville believes intensely in the dignity and conviction of the crime
drama. One could compare *Bob* to another heist film, Jules Dassin's *Rififi*. But Melville's treatment is more poetic, deeper, and richer than Dassin's. We care for the characters more than in *Rififi*, and the robbery itself
is played out as a stylized imaginary sequence that Bob describes to his
cohorts. In fact, *Bob* more closely resembles John Huston's *The Asphalt
Jungle*, one of Melville's all-time favorite movies.

*(The videocassette is subtitled.)*

# Born Free

★ ★ ★ ★ ★ ★ ★ ★ ★ ★ ★ ★ ★ ★ ★ ★ ★ ★ ★ ★ ★ ★ ★ ★ ★ ★ ★ ★ ★ ★ ★ ★ ★ ★ ★ ★ ★ ★ ★ ★ ★ ★ ★ ★ ★ ★ ★ ★ ★ ★ ★

*Nationality*: British        *Year*: 1966
*Cast*: Virginia McKenna, Bill Travers, Geoffrey Keen, Peter Lukoye
*Director*: James Hill        *Running Time*: 96 minutes
*B/W or Color*: Color        *Availability*: RCA/COLUMBIA PIC-
TURES HOME VIDEO

A superb family film, *Born Free* placed second (following *A Man for All Seasons*) on The National Board of Review's ten best list for 1966.

Based on the popular book by Joy Adamson, it's the story of the extraordinary trust and bond that develops between Adamson (Virginia McKenna), her husband, George (Bill Travers)—a senior game warden in Kenya—and a lion cub named Elsa (actually portrayed by a dozen different lions).

When George brings home three orphaned cubs, his wife takes a fancy to the smallest and names her Elsa, after a school chum. The two biggest cubs are eventually sent to a zoo, but the Adamsons keep Elsa as a pet. They're ordered to get rid of her, however, when Elsa accidentally starts an elephant stampede that wrecks a nearby village. Joy Adamson requests time to teach Elsa how to survive in the wild. Given two months, she succeeds in schooling Elsa just before the time limit is up.

A year later, the Adamsons return from a trip to England and are reunited with Elsa, who now has three cubs of her own. The special bond between the lioness and the humans she loves and trusts remains.

The popular title song won Academy Awards for lyricist Don Black and composer John Barry, who also won the Oscar for Best Score. Two literary sequels followed, *Living Free* and *Forever Free*; a 1970 documentary, *The Lions Are Free* (about Bill Travers and wife Virginia McKenna's return to Kenya); an overwrought sentimental 1971 film, *Living Free*, starring Susan Hampshire and Nigel Davenport; and a 1975 television series.

The end of the lioness' saga is dark. The real Elsa died in 1968. One of the lionesses that had portrayed her in the film had to be shot by George Adamson, after it had killed one of his assistants. Joy Adamson perished under very mysterious circumstances in January 1980. To this day, the details are oddly conflicting or alarmingly absent. It appears certain, however, that the initial verdict that Ms. Adamson had been mauled to death by a marauding lion was incorrect.

# Bread and Chocolate
## (Pane e Cioccolata)

**************************************************

*Nationality*: Italian               *Year*: 1974 (U.S. release: 1978)
*Cast*: Nino Manfredi, Anna Karina, Johnny Dorelli, Paolo Turco
*Director*: Franco Brusati          *Running Time*: 111 minutes
*B/W or Color*: Color               *Availability*: TV only

Migrant workers are a common sight in Europe, comparable to Latin Americans who come to the United States to work the land. They arrive from the poorest parts of the Continent to the more affluent countries and often labor as kitchen help, graduating to waiters. As in America, the work permit is of paramount importance. Nino (Nino Manfredi), from the south of Italy, is an apprentice waiter in a grand, luxurious Swiss hotel, and he's determined to make good and defeat his Turkish rival for the only upcoming permanent waiter's job.

Alas, as Vincent Canby said in his *New York Times* review, "The hotel guests are people who travel through life first-class. Nino is forever steerage." He's eager and willing to work long and hard, but something always goes awry with Nino. Trying to emulate the Turk peeling an orange so deftly it becomes a perfect sphere, Nino is all thumbs so that *his* orange ends up misshapen; sitting on the lawn of the hotel with a staid string quartet playing nearby, he chomps loudly on his sandwich and everybody, including the quartet, turns to glare at him. Exonerated for the murder of a young girl whose body he finds, on his release from the police station Nino relieves himself in public (all right where he comes from) and is promptly rearrested; this act is grounds for his dismissal from the restaurant.

Poor Nino, after a couple of more abortive jobs, he must either return home in disgrace or work illegally, despite the temporary help of his Greek refugee girlfriend (Anna Karina), who spurns him by deciding the best way out of her dilemma is to marry her Swiss policeman suitor.

Seesawing between hilarity and genuine pathos, *Bread and Chocolate* becomes something close to a masterpiece because of Nino Manfredi's inspired and antic performance in the leading role.

A prizewinner at 1974's Berlin Film Festival, *Bread and Chocolate* was named Best Foreign Film by the New York Film Critics—and one of 1978's five best by The National Board.

# Breaker Morant

∗∗∗∗∗∗∗∗∗∗∗∗∗∗∗∗∗∗∗∗∗∗∗∗∗∗∗∗∗∗∗∗∗∗∗∗∗∗∗∗∗∗∗∗∗∗∗∗∗∗∗∗∗∗∗∗

**Nationality**: Australian          **Year**: 1979 (U.S. release: 1980)
**Cast**: Edward Woodward, Bryan Brown, Lewis Fitz-Gerald, Jack Thompson
**Director**: Bruce Beresford          **Running Time**: 107 minutes
**B/W or Color**: Color          **Availability**: RCA/Columbia Pictures Home Video

B ased on a true incident during the Boer War in South Africa in 1901, *Breaker Morant* is the story of three Australians court-martialed for breaking the military law that forbade killing prisoners. Under normal circumstances, this local bloodshed might have escaped the glare of publicity, but Australia, newly a Commonwealth, was eager to show the British Empire her respect for the law.

It is obvious that director Bruce Beresford (who co-wrote the screenplay, which was nominated for an Academy Award and was on The National Board of Review's ten best list) considers the courts-martial a shocking miscarriage of justice. Breaker Morant (Edward Woodward), a folk hero whose nickname derived from his talent as a horse breaker, was only seeking reprisal for the death of a comrade when he allowed his men to kill Boer prisoners. The Boers were using guerrilla tactics. Why not the Aussies?

The story, beautifully photographed in South Australia, unfolds in skillfully handled flashbacks, culminating in the trial. As fascinating as the mounting suspense, however, are the characters of the three defendants and their lawyer. Lieutenant Morant's inner fears are hidden behind a heavy veil of sarcasm. The gregarious Lieutenant Handcock (Bryan Brown) is given to verbal outbursts in court. ("Anytime, mate," he threatens one witness.) The third lieutenant, Witten (Lewis Fitz-Gerald), reveals his overwhelming terror by remaining silent. Jack Thompson, as Major Thomas, the lawyer for the defense, far removed from his simple country practice, must battle resourcefully for the lives of his three clients.

Beresford's script may cast a slightly more sympathetic light on the turbulent event than is warranted by the historical facts, but he has produced a superior film, genuinely moving in its depiction of officers forced to become military scapegoats, but whose humanity transcends both their "crime" and their ultimate fate.

# Breaking the Sound Barrier
## (The Sound Barrier)

★★★★★★★★★★★★★★★★★★★★★★★★★★★★★★★★★★★★★★★★★★★★★★★★★★★★★★

**Nationality**: British          **Year**: 1952

**Cast**: Ralph Richardson, Ann Todd, Nigel Patrick, John Justin, Dinah Sheridan, Denholm Elliott

**Director**: David Lean          **Running Time**: 118 minutes

**B/W or Color**: B/W          **Availability**: TV only

Director David Lean has had a long and illustrious career spanning many decades, and on the way garnered Oscars for *The Bridge on the River Kwai* and *Lawrence of Arabia* and, in 1985, the D. W. Griffith Award for *A Passage to India*. When Lean made this movie, few people outside the aeronautics field had even thought about traveling faster than sound, so the film not only dramatized the wealth of events leading to supersonic flight but also interpreted it for the general public in deceptively simple terms.

The plot concerns Ralph Richardson as an autocratic aircraft manufacturer whose son (Denholm Elliott) crashes on his maiden solo flight; Richardson's daughter (Ann Todd), quarreling violently with her father, blames him for her brother's death. At the outbreak of war, Todd joins the WAAF and marries a fighter pilot (Nigel Patrick), who is drawn into Richardson's orbit. When the war ends, he accepts a job as test pilot with his father-in-law, and the young couple moves into Richardson's house. Todd is uncomfortable living in such close proximity to her father and is fearful about his determination to launch a supersonic plane using her husband as a guinea pig. She's sure that Patrick will be sacrificed as was her brother.

Well directed and impeccably acted though this picture is, its real stars are the planes. Jet engines were revolutionary in 1952, and those wonderful sequences showing the diving pilots' attempts to break the sound barrier are as thrilling—36 years later—as are those in *Top Gun*.

Hollywood's Motion Picture Academy awarded *Breaking the Sound Barrier* an Oscar for Best Sound Recording. The National Board of Review gave the film a triple salute, including Best Foreign Film and Best Director, and named Ralph Richardson 1952's Best Actor.

# Breathless
## (A Bout de Souffle)

★★★★★★★★★★★★★★★★★★★★★★★★★★★★★★★★★★★★★★★★★★★★★★★★★★★★★★

**Nationality**: French          **Year**: 1960 (U.S. release: 1961)
**Cast**: Jean-Paul Belmondo, Jean Seberg, Daniel Boulanger, Liliane David, Jean-Pierre Melville
**Director**: Jean-Luc Godard      **Running Time**: 89 minutes
**B/W or Color**: B/W          **Availability**: V.P. VIDEO

A pioneering film of the New Wave in France, *Breathless* revolutionized filmmaking around the world. The audacious Jean-Luc Godard popularized jump cuts and hand-held camera techniques, among other dazzling effects, and created a new film language. He was financed by François Truffaut, his *Cahiers du Cinema* colleague.

On the surface, *Breathless* chronicles the love affair of a Parisian hood and an American girl in Paris. She is full of pretentious notions about life and art, beautifully illustrated in a scene she has with Jean-Pierre Melville, but is fascinated with the anarchist life-style of the crook. Mercurial, she soon is bored and made even more restless by her inability to understand the Frenchman. She blithely betrays him to the police, and he is killed in the ensuing shootout.

Jean-Paul Belmondo became an international star with this film, as well as the natural heir to the Bogart mystique. As late as the mid-Seventies, he was still playing this character in movies. But he was never better than in this first, low-budget opus. Unsentimental (unlike Bogart), Belmondo brought a unique sensuality to the gangster, and though the character has the viewer's sympathy, he doesn't consciously elicit it. He is a true outsider in society.

*Breathless* revived Jean Seberg's career, after the well-publicized Otto Preminger star flopped in *Saint Joan*. She magnificently updated a character created in fiction by Henry James in *Daisy Miller*—the independent, cool, but spoiled American girl in a foreign setting. We first see Patricia in T-shirt and slacks, with a close-cropped hair style, hawking the *Herald-Tribune* in Paris. That hair style is still in fashion today among the punk set. Arrogance characterizes Patricia, and her actions clearly are not from moral choice, but from boredom and viciousness.

*Breathless* still delights audiences today because of its carefree, nonjudgmental attitude toward the outsiders in society. The 1983 remake with Richard Gere and Valerie Kaprisky was arch, hard to relate to, and very badly acted. Small wonder it flopped.

# The Bride Wore Black
## (La Mariée Etait en Noir)

* * * * * * * * * * * * * * * * * * * * * * * * * * * * * * * * * * * * * * * * * * * * * * * * * * * * * *

Nationality: French-Italian     Year: 1968
Cast: Jeanne Moreau, Jean-Claude Brialy, Michel Bouquet, Charles Denner
Director: François Truffaut     Running Time: 107 minutes
B/W or Color: Color     Availability: TV only

On a terrace overlooking the Côte d'Azur, a young Frenchman (Claude Rich) stands beside a mysterious-looking woman (Jeanne Moreau) dressed in white. She pushes him over the railing to his death. The same woman later poisons the wine of a bank clerk (Michel Bouquet), and then seals an aspiring politician (Michel Lonsdale) inside a cabinet, leaving him to suffocate. Before each victim dies, the woman reveals her identity.

Why is Julie Kohler (Moreau) committing these murders? This is the theme of The Bride Wore Black, which the National Board selected as one of the best films of 1968. Directed and co-authored (with Jean-Louis Richard, Moreau's first husband) by François Truffaut, it pays homage to Alfred Hitchcock. The screenplay is based on a novel by William Irish (a pseudonym for Cornell Woolrich, who wrote the short story from which Hitchcock's Rear Window derives).

"François Truffaut is such a rare talent," stated The New York Times review, "that one knows instantly . . . this is what movies are about, this is how they can be done, this is why so few people do them beautifully."

Moreau's character, it turns out, is seeking revenge on the five men accidentally responsible for the death of her husband—on their wedding day. He was shot on the steps of the church, and the fatal bullet came from a building across the street, where five men were playing with a rifle.

Number four on Julie's list, a dishonest car dealer (Daniel Boulanger), is arrested and thereby saved from her vengeance. For Julie's fifth victim (Charles Denner), she poses as Diana the Huntress, using a bow and arrow to kill the artist.

Allowing herself to be caught, Julie is sent to the same prison as the car dealer. While helping to serve meals to prisoners, she steals a carving knife. Will she be able to complete her list?

Critic Judith Crist wrote: "It's a beautiful film. The cast is uniformly excellent, the plotting absorbing and the final scene masterly—and what more can one want?"

# The Bridge on the River Kwai

★ ★ ★ ★ ★ ★ ★ ★ ★ ★ ★ ★ ★ ★ ★ ★ ★ ★ ★ ★ ★ ★ ★ ★ ★ ★ ★ ★ ★ ★ ★ ★ ★ ★ ★ ★ ★ ★ ★ ★ ★ ★ ★ ★ ★ ★ ★ ★ ★ ★ ★

Nationality: British  Year: 1957
Cast: William Holden, Alec Guinness, Jack Hawkins, Sessue Hayakawa
Director: David Lean  Running Time: 161 minutes
B/W or Color: Color  Availability: RCA/COLUMBIA PIC-
TURES HOME VIDEO

A David Lean classic, *The Bridge on the River Kwai* led The National Board of Review's ten best list for 1957.

Based on a Pierre Boulle novel, which depicted the futility and insanity of war, the story is set in 1943 at a Japanese POW camp in Thailand. Ordered to participate in the construction of a bridge—part of Japan's "death railroad"—Colonel Nicholson (Alec Guinness) cites the Geneva Convention rules, insisting that his officers perform no manual labor. The commandant, Colonel Saito (Sessue Hayakawa), places him in solitary confinement but, in acknowledgment of Nicholson's resolute courage, releases him. Oblivious to the fact that he's aiding the enemy, the British colonel orders his troops to work overtime, and the bridge is finished ahead of schedule—proving, in the colonel's mind, the invincibility and superiority of the British soldier.

Meanwhile, Shears (William Holden), an American soldier posing as an officer, escapes from the camp and agrees to lead back a commando raid to destroy the bridge. The confrontation results in the deaths of both Nicholson and Shears. (In the novel, the bridge is not destroyed, making the point that no one wins in war.)

The National Board also chose David Lean, Alec Guinness, and Sessue Hayakawa, respectively, as Best Director, Actor, and Supporting Actor. The New York Film Critics cited the film, Lean, and Guinness. Of its eight Academy Award nominations, seven were won: Best Picture, Director, Actor (Guinness), Screenplay (Pierre Boulle, though it is believed that most of it was written by the then-blacklisted Carl Foreman), Cinematography, Editing, and Score.

Cary Grant was offered the role of Shears, and the original choice for the part of Nicholson was Noel Coward, with whom David Lean had made *Brief Encounter* (1946). Filming took place in Ceylon, where a quarter of a million dollars was spent to build the bridge.

# Brief Encounter

★★★★★★★★★★★★★★★★★★★★★★★★★★★★★★★★★★★★★★★★★★★★★★★★★★★★★★★★★

Nationality: British                          Year: 1945 (U.S. release: 1946)

Cast: Celia Johnson, Trevor Howard, Cyril Raymond, Stanley Holloway, Joyce Carey

Director: David Lean                          Running Time: 86 minutes

B/W or Color: B/W                            Availability: CBS VIDEO LIBRARY

O f Noel Coward's nine short plays produced collectively in 1936 as *To-Night at 8:30,* six have reached the screen to date, but only one—*Still Life* (retitled *Brief Encounter*)—has been fully realized. If its moral values seem outmoded in the permissive Eighties, this movie still merits its classic status for the brilliant craftsmanship of its acting and direction.

Laura and Alec meet by chance at a small-town railroad station, where he helps her remove a cinder from her eye. He's a doctor; she's a housewife. Both are middle-class, middle-aged, and happily married to others. But they establish an immediate rapport. She comes there from a neighboring village each Thursday to shop and see a film; he journeys from the opposite direction for morning duties at a local hospital. At first, they continue to meet there innocently on successive Thursdays, then compulsively and surreptitiously, sharing a pot of tea, a cinema visit, and even a tryst in a friend's apartment. But when they realize that their clandestine affair can lead nowhere, they part.

Casting the attractive but ordinary-looking Celia Johnson and Trevor Howard in these pivotal roles was a stroke of genius. Neither one makes a false move, playing in that typically English style of understated naturalism that renders their doomed affair all the more poignant. The film is beautifully lit and photographed by Robert Krasker, and underscored by Eileen Joyce's excellent soundtrack rendition of Rachmaninoff's appropriately romantic—if now overly familiar—Second Piano Concerto.

Unbelievably, this movie was none too successful in 1945, despite the London critics' calling it one of the best ever to come from a British studio. America was especially impressed with Celia Johnson; Hollywood nominated her for an Oscar, and the New York Film Critics gave her 1946's Best Actress award. The National Board of Review listed *Brief Encounter* among that year's ten best films.

*(CBS Video Club offers a print of excellent, sharp quality.)*

# A Brief Vacation
## (Una Breve Vacanza)

\* \* \* \* \* \* \* \* \* \* \* \* \* \* \* \* \* \* \* \* \* \* \* \* \* \* \* \* \* \* \* \* \* \* \* \* \* \* \* \* \* \* \* \* \* \* \* \* \* \* \* \* \* \*

*Nationality*: Italian-Spanish      *Year*: 1973
*Cast*: Florinda Bolkan, Renato Salvatori, Daniel Quenaud, Jose Maria Prada, Teresa Gimpera
*Director*: Vittorio De Sica      *Running Time*: 106 minutes
*B/W or Color*: Color      *Availability*: TV only

While not in the classic vein of his greatest films, this is the last really excellent motion picture to be made by Vittorio De Sica. The master of Italian neorealism fashioned a touching tale from Cesare Zavattini's screenplay, with shadings of his own, of course. And he obtained a fine performance from his star, Florinda Bolkan.

Casting her in a role obviously ideal for Sophia Loren, De Sica helped transform Bolkan's glamorous personality into that of an accomplished actress, as he'd done with Loren before her. Of Spanish and Indian parentage, the Brazilian beauty put aside her cool and sophisticated image for that of a hardworking and ill-appreciated wife and mother. This is her warmest and most sensitive portrayal.

A Calabrese, Bolkan lives near Milan with husband Renato Salvatori, their three sons, and her in-laws. Recovering from an accident, Salvatori is insensitive to the hardworking Bolkan and is more annoyed than concerned when she is sent to a clinic in northern Italy to recuperate from tuberculosis. There, amidst the beautiful snow-capped mountains of Sondalo, she befriends and emotionally attends to the other female patients and is loved by young machinist Daniel Quenaud and fellow Calabrese doctor Jose Maria Prada. Although her joy is brief, Bolkan comes to the realization that she has a worth far beyond her depressing and demeaning existence at home.

De Sica, who died in 1974, a few months prior to the film's American release, often accepted acting roles in secondary movies in order to invest the money he earned in the sort of stories he wanted to make. Had he lived, he could have turned Florinda Bolkan into a major name, a la Loren. Her career as a serious actress went into a decline after De Sica's death, and like the heroine of *A Brief Vacation,* she returned to her old life—and more glamorous roles.

# Brimstone and Treacle

★★★★★★★★★★★★★★★★★★★★★★★★★★★★★★★★★★★★★★★★★★★★★★★★★★★★★

*Nationality*: British            *Year*: 1982

*Cast*: Sting, Denholm Elliott, Joan Plowright, Suzanna Hamilton, Mary MacLeod

*Director*: Richard Loncraine      *Running Time*: 85 minutes

*B/W or Color*: Color             *Availability*: MGM/UA HOME VIDEO

**B**rimstone and Treacle, a Grand Prize winner at the 1982 Montreal Film Festival, is a stylish psychological thriller engagingly directed by Richard Loncraine, from a script by Dennis Potter, and starring sensual British rock singer Sting.

Martin Taylor (Sting) forces himself upon Thomas Bates (Denholm Elliott), a cynical publisher of hymns and evangelical prayers, insisting they know each other. When the frustrated Bates mentions his paralyzed daughter Patty (Suzanna Hamilton), the mysterious Taylor immediately passes himself off as Patty's old friend. Bates manages to elude his daughter's suspiciously fraudulent acquaintance, but not before Taylor lifts his wallet. When Taylor returns the wallet, he becomes a malevolent force in the Bates household, destroying the precariously balanced equilibrium, dredging up new hope, old guilt, and vile secrets. Taylor quickly ingratiates himself with Mrs. Bates (Joan Plowright), eventually appeases Mr. Bates's suspicions, and brings the fractured couple together. Their newfound serenity, however, is abruptly shattered when Bates discovers Taylor raping Patty. Taylor escapes by crashing through a window. Patty immediately blames her father for the attack. And back on the streets, Taylor is confronted by a stranger who unceremoniously traps him in insidious recognition.

*Brimstone and Treacle* is a clever film that works hard to capture underlying tensions with low camera angles, dream sequences, plays on shadow and light, and mood music. It's an almost surreal film of contrasts, of religious frenzy, and sexual hostility. This is a striking yet subtle film.

# The Brothers

\* \* \* \* \* \* \* \* \* \* \* \* \* \* \* \* \* \* \* \* \* \* \* \* \* \* \* \* \* \* \* \* \* \* \* \* \* \* \* \* \* \* \* \* \* \* \* \* \* \* \* \*

*Nationality*: British        *Year*: 1947 (U.S. release: 1948)
*Cast*: Patricia Roc, Finlay Currie, Maxwell Reed, Duncan Macrae, Will Fyffe
*Director*: David Macdonald      *Running Time*: 98 minutes
*B/W or Color*: B/W           *Availability*: TV only

In 1947, a banner year for British melodrama, *The Brothers* offered moviegoers unusual diversion with its blend of grim, ethnic naturalism and lyric romanticism. It was based on L.A.G. Strong's novel set on the Hebridean island of Skye in 1900, and its central character was Mary Lawson, an outsider whose attractive presence among the islanders (with one family of whom she comes to live and work as a servant) ignites old feuds and arouses varying aspects of jealousy, lust, and family destruction.

Patricia Roc realized her best performance in this role, when she replaced Ann Todd, the original Mary. Todd had not enjoyed the experience of playing opposite mean, moody Maxwell Reed in *Daybreak*, and balked at repeating the ordeal.

A plot synopsis of *The Brothers* would scarcely sound credible, but that's more than made up for by the fine acting of such strong Scots types as Finlay Currie, Duncan Macrae, and, in his last role, scene-stealer Will Fyffe.

*The Brothers* was director David Macdonald's best film, and it obviously owes a debt to his Scottish heritage, reflected in a near-documentary approach to ancient Celtic manners and mores. In one powerful sequence, an informer is tendered clan vengeance by being floated on the water with a herring tied to his head, to be pecked to death by the birds. This scene is so grim that it's frequently cut for TV.

Stephen Dade's cameras eloquently capture the terrible beauty of that rugged and remote stretch of Britain, enforcing the strength of *The Brothers'* visual imagery. Since British prints occasionally surface on American TV, it's possible that viewers may see this film with its original tragic resolution; in 1947; its U.S. distributor demanded of J. Arthur Rank—and got—an adulterated version with a *happy* ending!

# The Browning Version

★ ★ ★ ★ ★ ★ ★ ★ ★ ★ ★ ★ ★ ★ ★ ★ ★ ★ ★ ★ ★ ★ ★ ★ ★ ★ ★ ★ ★ ★ ★ ★ ★ ★ ★ ★ ★ ★ ★ ★ ★ ★ ★ ★ ★ ★ ★ ★ ★ ★ ★ ★ ★ ★

**Nationality**: British                    **Year**: 1951
**Cast**: Michael Redgrave, Jean Kent, Nigel Patrick, Wilfrid Hyde-White, Ronald Howard, Brian Smith
**Director**: Anthony Asquith          **Running Time**: 90 minutes
**B/W or Color**: B/W                    **Availability**: TV only

The Browning Version, an obvious forerunner of *Who's Afraid of Virginia Woolf?*, is a more cynical and less sentimental *Goodbye, Mr. Chips*. Andrew Crocker-Harris, the tragic central figure of Terence Rattigan's long, one-act 1948 play, offers a great acting challenge. But this defeated, middle-aged classics professor, prematurely facing the twilight of both a failed teaching career and a disastrous marriage, is by no means actor-proof, for the pitfalls are tricky.

Always a cerebral, intelligent actor of the Stanislavsky school, 42-year-old Michael Redgrave makes brilliant use of the camera to establish the subtlest of Crocker-Harris's emotions. His precise and restricted mannerisms are uncannily accurate for this self-contained, frustrated martinet, and his pinched, nasal voice with its sarcastic undertones is cunningly resourceful. This is arguably *the* performance of Redgrave's uneven film career, winning him the Best Actor prize at Cannes.

In poor health, Crocker-Harris is forced to give up his position as instructor of classic languages at an English boys' school. This is an annoying inconvenience to his callous wife, Millie (shrewishly portrayed by Jean Kent), who has been maintaining an affair with the popular science teacher (Nigel Patrick). Crocker-Harris has never been popular with *his* students, but a pupil named Taplow (Brian Smith) makes him a gift of Robert Browning's translation of the *Agamemnon*, and the instructor is moved to tears. In an uncharacteristic speech, departing from his prepared text, he delivers a straightforward apologia for his failure as a teacher.

Terence Rattigan's sensitive screenplay opens up and fleshes out his excellent play, and Anthony Asquith's unobtrusive, understanding direction moved Rattigan to praise his "superb instinct and impeccable taste."

The National Board named *The Browning Version* among 1951's ten best films.

# Caesar and Cleopatra

★ ★ ★ ★ ★ ★ ★ ★ ★ ★ ★ ★ ★ ★ ★ ★ ★ ★ ★ ★ ★ ★ ★ ★ ★ ★ ★ ★ ★ ★ ★ ★ ★ ★ ★ ★ ★ ★ ★ ★ ★ ★ ★ ★ ★ ★ ★ ★ ★ ★ ★

*Nationality*: British          *Year*: 1945 (U.S. release: 1946)

*Cast*: Vivien Leigh, Claude Rains, Stewart Granger, Flora Robson, Francis L. Sullivan, Basil Sydney, Cecil Parker

*Director*: Gabriel Pascal          *Running Time*: 138 minutes

*B/W or Color*: Color          *Availability*: VIDAMERICA

I n the Forties—and for a long time thereafter—*Caesar and Cleopatra* was notorious for its then-outrageous production costs, which set J. Arthur Rank back by some £1,300,000 (at 1944 exchange rates, $5,200,000). Its Transylvania-born director, Gabriel Pascal, virtually made a career out of directing the filmed plays of George Bernard Shaw, but this one nearly did him in, with his reckless extravagance and slow, time-consuming production methods. That it was ultimately a box-office failure doesn't lessen the historical importance of this opulent and beautifully acted film. It remains an extraordinary achievement for the British movie industry, especially considering that it was produced during 1944 and 1945, when wartime Britain was going through one of the most critical periods in her history.

Vivien Leigh makes an enchanting Cleopatra, starting out as a timid young monarch under the thumb of her overbearing servant Ftatateeta (Flora Robson in blackface) and developing before our eyes into a sparkling creature of many facets. Her growth, of course, is achieved under the benevolent tutelage of Caesar, as impersonated by Claude Rains in a witty and masterful performance. A huge cast surrounds them with the sort of acting we have come to expect from British performers, with their comprehensive background in the stage classics. Those with sharp eyes might notice such future stars among the bit players as Jean Simmons as a harpist, Michael Rennie as a centurion, and Kay Kendall, then only an extra.

In the United States, the film's success was limited. It seemed American moviegoers were disappointed at not finding the DeMille-type spectacle suggested by the picture's ads.

# Cal

\* \* \* \* \* \* \* \* \* \* \* \* \* \* \* \* \* \* \* \* \* \* \* \* \* \* \* \* \* \* \* \* \* \* \* \* \* \* \* \* \* \* \* \* \* \* \* \* \* \* \* \* \* \* \* \*

*Nationality*: Irish          *Year*: 1984
*Cast*: Helen Mirren, John Lynch, Donal McCann, John Kavanagh
*Director*: Pat O'Connor          *Running Time*: 102 minutes
*B/W or Color*: Color          *Availability*: WARNER HOME
VIDEO

Cal is the chilling portrait of a 19-year-old Catholic boy growing up in Northern Ireland. It is through his tormented eyes that the audience first enters a war-torn world, where peace and quiet, like the calm in the eye of a hurricane, loom ominously over the damp city streets. It is a world divided by politics and religion and shattered by bullets and bloodshed. This is not a film that allows its audience to sit back and relax.

Helen Mirren as Marcella and newcomer John Lynch as Cal give passionate performances as the lonely and isolated lovers. He lives with his father in a Protestant neighborhood amidst threats of violence that leave them afraid to speak above a whisper in their own home. She is the widow of a man shot down by the I.R.A., living on a secluded farm with her aloof in-laws. When they are together, their eyes fight to tell tales that they are otherwise unable to articulate.

Bernard MacLaverty has turned his novel into a powerful screenplay. And director Pat O'Connor tackles a hair-raising subject with a delicate hand. He has combined beautiful photography, dramatic lighting, and subtle sound effects to create not a moving image, but a living environment into which audience and characters are immediately drawn.

# Careful, He Might Hear You

\* \* \* \* \* \* \* \* \* \* \* \* \* \* \* \* \* \* \* \* \* \* \* \* \* \* \* \* \* \* \* \* \* \* \* \* \* \* \* \* \* \* \* \* \* \* \* \* \* \* \* \* \*

*Nationality*: Australian  *Year*: 1983 (U.S. release: 1984)
*Cast*: Wendy Hughes, Robyn Nevin, Nicholas Gledhill, John Hargreaves
*Director*: Carl Schultz  *Running Time*: 116 minutes
*B/W or Color*: Color  *Availability*: CBS/FOX HOME
VIDEO

Winner of eight of Australia's equivalent of the Oscars (including Best Picture, Director, Actress), this popular film centers on a bitter family struggle over the custody of a six-year-old boy. Young P.S. (so-named by his mother, who died after giving him birth: "the postscript to a ridiculous life") has lived contentedly with his working-class Aunt Lila, his mother's sister, and her husband, George. Suddenly, his world is turned upside down when the worldly and glamorous Vanessa, his mother's other sister, arrives from abroad and attempts to gain control of P.S.'s life.

Despite first appearances, the elegant Vanessa proves to be a neurotic, severely repressed spinster who still yearns for Logan, P.S.'s ne'er-do-well father, who disappeared years before. When P.S. finally summons the courage to rebel against all the adults trying to control his life, the results are both tragic and inevitable.

The production of the film is impeccable. Carl Schultz's direction and the photography by John Seale, often viewing adult behavior from a child's perspective, are excellent. Wendy Hughes (who won the Australian Film Institute's Best Actress Award) has the showy role of Vanessa, but the entire cast is superlative—with Nicholas Gledhill an adorable and thoroughly believable P.S.

This intense human drama is based upon the acclaimed 1963 novel by Sumner Locke Elliott. The Australian-born Elliott came to the United States just after World War II, and along with a handful of talented writers (Paddy Chayefsky, Rod Serling, Tad Mosel, et al.) provided TV with its so-called Golden Age of Drama, during the Fifties. He turned to fiction in the Sixties and has published nine well received novels, none more compelling than this autobiographical first one.

# Carnival in Flanders
## (La Kermesse Heroïque)

\*\*\*\*\*\*\*\*\*\*\*\*\*\*\*\*\*\*\*\*\*\*\*\*\*\*\*\*\*\*\*\*\*\*\*\*\*\*\*\*\*\*\*\*\*\*\*\*\*\*\*\*\*\*\*\*

*Nationality*: French               *Year*: 1935 (U.S. release: 1936)
*Cast*: Françoise Rosay, Jean Murat, Micheline Cheirel, Louis Jouvet
*Director*: Jacques Feyder          *Running Time*: 95 minutes
*B/W or Color*: B/W                 *Availability*: Public Domain

Flemish art comes to life in this magnificently detailed depiction of the Netherlands under Spanish rule in the 17th century. Perhaps this is Jacques Feyder's masterpiece, and it is certainly his wife Françoise Rosay's finest performance. Louis Jouvet as the sophisticated monk is a delight. A film that never dates, it has some pointed comments about not only nations coexisting but also about the relationship between men and women. The National Board of Review named *Carnival in Flanders* among the best foreign films of 1936.

The women save their Flemish town when their men hide from the Spanish conquerors. As the mayor's wife, Rosay leads the peaceful welcoming expedition. The Spanish soldiers don't know what to make of all this hospitality, and graciously accept it. In a few days, they leave the town intact, with friendships made.

*Carnival in Flanders* doesn't need acceptance of its viewpoint to succeed. It is the great humor, set design, acting, script (by Charles Spaak), and cinematography (by Harry Stradling) that make this a great artistic achievement. The combination brilliantly illustrates Feyder's theme that sex is more potent a communicator than patriotism. Feyder has created a sort of reverse *Lysistrata*.

Jouvet further underscores the theme in his droll portrayal of the monk. Knowing full well what is going on under the guise of hospitality, he conveys worlds of meaning and understanding with just the arch of an eyebrow. Jouvet's angular, wedge-shaped face was singularly suitable at conveying skepticism.

Rosay is best known in America for this film; she is one of the few Frenchwomen stars to be seen in good Hollywood movies, although Hollywood capitalized only on her majestic, imperious appearance and cast her in humorless parts. She was a woman of great, wry wit, and it is good to know this masterpiece is still widely seen.

# Casque d'Or
## (Golden Marie)

★★★★★★★★★★★★★★★★★★★★★★★★★★★★★★★★★★★★★★★★★★★★★★★★★★★★★★★

Nationality: French          Year: 1952
Cast: Simone Signoret, Serge Reggiani, Claude Dauphin
Director: Jacques Becker      Running Time: 94 minutes
B/W or Color: B/W         Availability: TV only

Almost the reverse coin from René Clément's *Gervaise* is this lovingly re-created portrait of the Parisian underworld in the 1890s. The *Cahiers du Cinema* critics loved this film, and Jacques Becker was one of the few veteran French directors to win their praise. Certainly, this is Becker's masterpiece, and it's one of the most authentic of all period movies. Yet the characters seem contemporary and fresh. Simone Signoret became a major international star because of this film.

Serge Reggiani plays Manda, a poor laborer who becomes involved with a gang in order to win the beautiful Marie, the golden-haired temptress of the title. He is forced to kill another gang member because of Marie and is betrayed by the leader, who also hopes to win her. Marie loves Manda, and their (fully clothed) love scenes are some of the most sensuous ever filmed. Reggiani and Signoret had a real chemistry between them. Claude Dauphin is wittily wicked as the two-faced Leca.

But Becker is responsible for the overall success of this richly designed film, and the influence of Jean Renoir is everywhere evident. Becker was Renoir's assistant in the Thirties, and the compassion Becker feels for his characters and their life-style echoes that of Renoir's. Becker doesn't halt his story for meaningless romanticism; instead, his poetic but gritty technique is completely incorporated into the film.

Reggiani was never better. His intensity is controlled here and sublimated into internal strength. Signoret displays a subtle sexiness that's more cerebral than outwardly obvious, wearing her sensuousness as casually as her carelessly arranged clothing. But she is her own woman, which makes her fascinating. The British Film Academy named her the year's Best Foreign Actress.

# Cat and Mouse
## (Le Chat et La Souris)

\*\*\*\*\*\*\*\*\*\*\*\*\*\*\*\*\*\*\*\*\*\*\*\*\*\*\*\*\*\*\*\*\*\*\*\*\*\*\*\*\*\*\*\*\*\*\*\*\*\*\*\*\*\*

Nationality: French          Year: 1975

Cast: Michèle Morgan, Serge Reggiani, Philippe Léotard, Jean-Pierre Aumont, Valerie Lagrange

Director: Claude Lelouch          Running Time: 107 minutes

B/W or Color: Color          Availability: RCA/COLUMBIA PICTURES HOME VIDEO

Wealthy Jean-Pierre Aumont is dead. Who killed him and why is the object of this comedy-mystery produced, directed, and written by Claude Lelouch. The real purpose of the film, however, is to introduce as many offbeat situations and characters as possible. Done in tongue-in-cheeky style, the Lelouch travesty was praised as being the best Hitchcock imitation (topping, some say, even the Master) in a decade. The title could easily refer to Lelouch and the viewer, as clue piles upon clue, making it easy to miss a plot twist that may be important (the reverse knob on your VCR will come in handy here).

Police Inspector Serge Reggiani's attempts to teach his police dog Samy to respond to his commands account for much humor; there are high-speed views of Paris and the French countryside, and even Reggiani's character's name in the film is a joke—Lechat ("the cat").

Jean-Pierre Aumont is pushed by wife Morgan from the top of a high-rise he's built. It's only in a dream, but she becomes a suspect when he is actually shot. Inspector Reggiani and assistant Philippe Léotard sort out the clues and find that Aumont had a mistress, Valerie Lagrange, who in turn has another lover, as does Michèle Morgan (oh, la, la!). The investigation drags on. Reggiani settles down on a farm with prostitute Anne Libert to write about the case, and Léotard weds his superior's daughter, Christine Laurent. Then the case comes to a singularly surprising conclusion.

A star since her late teens, the ever-glamorous Michèle Morgan was in her mid-fifties here; unfortunately, the film remains her last significant role. For that matter, Lelouch hasn't attained the impudence he displays here on any subsequent assignment.

(The videocassette is dubbed in English.)

# Chance Meeting
## (Blind Date)

★★★★★★★★★★★★★★★★★★★★★★★★★★★★★★★★★★★★★★★★★★★★★★★★★★★★★★

**Nationality**: British        **Year**: 1959 (U.S. release: 1960)

**Cast**: Hardy Kruger, Stanley Baker, Micheline Presle, John Van Eyssen, Robert Flemyng, Gordon Jackson

**Director**: Joseph Losey        **Running Time**: 96 minutes

**B/W or Color**: B/W        **Availability**: TV only

A taut suspense drama, director Joseph Losey's *Chance Meeting* is based on a Leigh Howard novel titled *Blind Date* (which it was originally called in Britain).

As the film opens, Jan Van Rooyen (Hardy Kruger), a penniless Dutch artist living in England, is accused of murdering his mistress. Protesting his innocence, Van Rooyen describes their affair to Inspector Morgan (Stanley Baker).

The audience sees (in flashback) his first meeting, at an art gallery, with Jacqueline Cousteau (Micheline Presle), an older, married Frenchwoman. A relationship of secret trysts develops. It was Jacqueline, the artist insists, who called him and said to wait for her at the address where he was arrested—and, in another room, Cousteau's body was discovered.

Inspector Morgan is aware that Jacqueline Cousteau was not married and that she was also the mistress of a renowned politician, whose name is to be kept out of the case. On a hunch, the inspector takes the artist to an airport where the politician's plane is due to land.

Out of the plane steps the politician's wife, the same woman known to the artist as Jacqueline Cousteau! However, the woman denies knowing Van Rooyen. Did she commit the murder? Will she change her story? Had she planned the first encounter, or was it a *Chance Meeting*?

Excellent performances are given by Kruger and Baker. As the socialite described by her lover as "carved in ice," Presle's performance, according to *The New York Times*, ". . . eloquently demonstrates that ice not only freezes but also burns." The critic complimented director Joseph Losey for having "taken a taut scenario and given a fresh and ironic treatment to a flashback mystery with a denouement comparable to the memorable *Laura*."

The film's American release stirred some controversy because its writers (Ben Barzman and Millard Lampell) and director Losey had been blacklisted during the McCarthy era.

# Chariots of Fire

★ ★ ★ ★ ★ ★ ★ ★ ★ ★ ★ ★ ★ ★ ★ ★ ★ ★ ★ ★ ★ ★ ★ ★ ★ ★ ★ ★ ★ ★ ★ ★ ★ ★ ★ ★ ★ ★ ★ ★ ★ ★ ★ ★ ★ ★ ★ ★ ★ ★ ★ ★ ★ ★

*Nationality*: British          *Year*: 1981
*Cast*: Ben Cross, Ian Charleson, Alice Krige, Ian Holm, Cheryl Campbell
*Director*: Hugh Hudson        *Running Time*: 123 minutes
*B/W or Color*: Color           *Availability*: WARNER HOME
                                          VIDEO

Not unlike its track-star heroes, *Chariots of Fire* crossed the finish line first to win the race for the Oscars. Four were bestowed: Best Picture; Best Original Screenplay (Colin Welland); Best Original Score (Vangelis); and Best Costume Design (Milena Canonero); plus two nominations: Hugh Hudson, Editing, and Supporting Actor Ian Holm. *Chariots of Fire* also won the Best Picture Award from The National Board of Review.

Based on the stunning track victories of two Cambridge University students in the 1924 Paris Olympics, the film, a true story, follows the maverick classmates who go up against British tradition. Harold Abrahams (Ben Cross), the "Cream of Cambridge," son of a Lithuanian Jew, runs to beat the Wasp Establishment, and Eric Liddell (Ian Charleson), "The Flying Scot," a Scottish preacher, runs because "when I run, I can feel His pleasure." However, Liddell will not run on the Sabbath, which exasperates the Cambridge dons, notably two crusty snobs impeccably played by John Gielgud and Lindsay Anderson. While Liddell juggles to make room for running in his life, his sister (Cheryl Campbell) fears it is taking over his religion. Abrahams discovers his obsession with running is complicating his romance with a lovely young actress (Alice Krige). It is Abrahams who hires the Italian-Turkish track coach, Sam Mussabini (Ian Holm). The wily coach craftily points out that Abrahams wins—not for king, country, or even God. "You win for us," he convinces his pupil.

The races, often in slow motion, are exquisitely filmed, conveying an intimate sense of the power of competition and sheer physical drive. The haunting score is taken from a popular British hymn based on a poem by William Blake.

Producer David Puttnam's primary goal was to show how sport can be "the meeting between idealism and expediency," but his film also reveals how the honorable pursuit of excellence can honor, celebrate, and reward both the competitor and the sport.

*Chariots of Fire* became the most successful British film in the United States up to that time.

# Children of Paradise
## (Les Enfants du Paradis)

\*\*\*\*\*\*\*\*\*\*\*\*\*\*\*\*\*\*\*\*\*\*\*\*\*\*\*\*\*\*\*\*\*\*\*\*\*\*\*\*\*\*\*\*\*\*\*\*\*\*

Nationality: French            Year: 1945 (U.S. release: 1947)
Cast: Arletty, Jean-Louis Barrault, Pierre Brasseur, Maria Casares, Louis Salou, Albert Remy
Director: Marcel Carné            Running Time: 195 minutes
B/W or Color: B/W            Availability: TV only

Often called the *Gone With the Wind* of France, the plot of *Children of Paradise* bears little resemblance to that Civil War romantic epic. But like *GWTW*, the French film is a romantic drama about unrequited love. Unlike the American film, the French classic is philosophic and poetic.

Arletty plays a fascinating *demimonde* who loves, and is loved by, a gifted mime (Jean-Louis Barrault). But circumstances prevent them from marrying. She is also loved by three other men, a flamboyant actor (Pierre Brasseur), a jealous nobleman, and a common criminal, nicely illustrating her universal appeal. Barrault is relentlessly pursued and finally caught by a possessive woman (Maria Casares). When the mime and the adventuress decide years later to run away together, his youngest son shames Arletty into rejecting Barrault. The famous last scene shows Barrault chasing Arletty's carriage through the teeming Parisian streets and being swallowed up in the crowd.

What makes the film extraordinary is not just its love story, but its recreation of 1840s Paris and the world of the theater. The magnificent canvas of characters, scenes from period plays, costumes, the glimpses of ordinary Parisians have never been more precisely realized. One forgets that this is a movie and feels part of that long-gone glittering world.

Arletty joins the pantheon of screen goddesses on the strength of this one film. She superbly realizes the Garboesque and Dietrichesque dimensions of her role, transcending even those two actresses by adding her own brand of Gallic sensibility.

Barrault made his reputation in America with this film, and after the war appeared on the New York stage with his wife, Madeleine Renaud. Until Marcel Marceau played in America in the 1960s, the classical art of pantomime was associated solely with Barrault.

*Children of Paradise* was initially shown in the United States some 50 minutes shorter than its original European version, which runs more than three hours.

# A Christmas Carol
## (Scrooge)

\*\*\*\*\*\*\*\*\*\*\*\*\*\*\*\*\*\*\*\*\*\*\*\*\*\*\*\*\*\*\*\*\*\*\*\*\*\*\*\*\*\*\*\*\*\*\*\*\*\*\*\*

*Nationality*: British      *Year*: 1951

*Cast*: Alastair Sim, Kathleen Harrison, Jack Warner, Michael Hordern, Mervyn Johns, Glyn Dearman

*Director*: Brian Desmond Hurst      *Running Time*: 86 minutes

*B/W or Color*: B/W      *Availability*: UNITED HOME VIDEO

Over the years, there have been many versions of the Charles Dickens classic *A Christmas Carol*: Hollywood filmed it several times, and in 1935 Seymour Hicks starred in a British adaptation called *Scrooge*. The 1938 MGM version, starring Reginald Owen as Scrooge, was well received, and Albert Finney headlined 1970's big-budget musical *Scrooge*. And even Mr. Magoo got into the act for a cartoon edition in the Sixties. More recently, George C. Scott and Henry Winkler portrayed the character in separate TV editions of the yuletide classic. But, somehow, none has surpassed Alastair Sim as Scrooge in the 1951 *A Christmas Carol*.

Director Brian Desmond Hurst worked an almost mystical, dreamlike quality into the film, perfectly capturing the Victorian atmosphere, so that his audience is drawn into the period and locale of 19th-century England. And Sim gives Ebenezer Scrooge a three-dimensional quality that no other actor has ever quite managed on the screen. At first, he appears a mean and rotten fellow, but flashbacks help make his behavior understandable in light of the setbacks of his unfortunate formative years.

The scenes with the Ghost of Christmas Yet to Come are quite chilling, and the graveyard scene is as scary as anything Hammer Films ever came up with. Sim's supporting cast is equally good, with Kathleen Harrison wonderfully amusing as his housekeeper. Mervyn Johns makes a fine Bob Cratchitt, and Glyn Dearman is endearing as Tiny Tim. In the minor role of an undertaker, Ernest Thesiger reminds us how good a character actor he always was.

This version of *A Christmas Carol* is one to treasure—and the one most requested of TV programmers.

# Chushingura
## (The Loyal 47 Ronin)

\* \* \* \* \* \* \* \* \* \* \* \* \* \* \* \* \* \* \* \* \* \* \* \* \* \* \* \* \* \* \* \* \* \* \* \* \* \* \* \* \* \* \* \* \* \* \* \* \* \*

*Nationality*: Japanese

*Year*: 1962 (U.S. release: 1963)

*Cast*: Koshiro Matsumoto, Yuzo Kayama, Chusha Ichikawa, Toshiro Mifune, Yoko Tsukasa

*Director*: Hiroshi Inagaki

*Running Time*: 204 minutes (released in Japan in two parts; in one part in the U.S., at 108 minutes)

*B/W or Color*: Color

*Availability*: TV only

C*hushingura* ranks among the most popular and frequently revived plays in Japan and has been filmed more than any other Japanese story. Based on an actual event, this enduring tale is well known to all Japanese.

In 1701, the young Lord Asano received an appointment to a ceremonial position serving the shogun. Special training was needed to perform these rituals, for which one generally "rewarded" one's instructor. However, Asano refused to pay the customary bribe to the pompous Lord Kira, who then taunted and deceived the younger lord. The frustrated Asano then drew his sword and slashed Kira while in the shogun's castle. In recompense for this blasphemous act, Asano's lands were seized, his retainers were dismissed to become masterless samurai (*ronin*), and he was ordered to commit ritual *seppuku* (suicide).

Twenty-one months later, a group of 47 warriors loyal to Asano, led by his chief retainer, decapitated Kira in revenge. This event stirred the imagination of a Japan which, after nearly a century of peace, had not seen such a dramatic demonstration of traditional samurai loyalty for some time. Following the trial, the noblemen were permitted to die by *seppuku*, a death befitting true samurai.

Of the more than 20 film versions of *Chushingura*, two endure as classics. Director Hiroshi Inagaki (*Rikisha Man*, the *Samurai* trilogy) remains close to the traditional story, and his 1962 *Chushingura* is a lavish, episodic offering with ornate sets and costumes in a slow but beautiful spectacle of color and action.

The most cinematically interesting, however, is *Genroku Chushingura* (1941–42), a two-part motion picture made by the great Kenji Mizoguchi (*Ugetsu, The Life of Oharu*), whose emphasis on strong characterizations, mood, and atmosphere over action have made this *Chushingura* a major recent discovery in the West.

# A Clockwork Orange

★ ★ ★ ★ ★ ★ ★ ★ ★ ★ ★ ★ ★ ★ ★ ★ ★ ★ ★ ★ ★ ★ ★ ★ ★ ★ ★ ★ ★ ★ ★ ★ ★ ★ ★ ★ ★ ★ ★ ★ ★ ★ ★ ★ ★ ★ ★ ★ ★ ★ ★ ★ ★ ★ ★

*Nationality*: British  *Year*: 1971

*Cast*: Malcolm McDowell, Patrick Magee, Adrienne Corri, Aubrey Morris, James Marcus

*Director*: Stanley Kubrick  *Running Time*: 137 minutes

*B/W or Color*: Color  *Availability*: WARNER HOME VIDEO

In 1970, Americans were reading *Blue Movie*, Terry Southern's narrative tale of a famous Hollywood director who decides to break the last taboo and make a pornographic mainstream film. The character of the director was loosely based on Stanley Kubrick, for whom Southern had co-authored the screenplay of *Dr. Strangelove*. During that time, sexuality was being cautiously liberated on the screen, and Kubrick had often discussed the possibility of an X-rated project with Southern.

In 1971, without Southern's participation, and with violence as much as sexuality deciding its rating, Kubrick delivered his X-rated film. With the substitution of different shots from those objected to, an R-rated version was released several months later. Today, America's conservative attitudes, as well as altered rules on the part of the MPAA concerning the release of X- and R-rated versions of the same film, would prevent Kubrick from making *A Clockwork Orange* for purely business reasons.

A graphic, highly stylized study of cause and effect in a violent London of the near future, *A Clockwork Orange* was adapted by Kubrick from the Anthony Burgess novel, which he'd bought for a pittance. Burgess's beautifully poetic slang of the future, using English, Russian, and hybrid words, was augmented by a hybrid score: classical pieces processed through the moog synthesizer of Walter Carlos, one of the pioneers of modern electronic music. By the time Kubrick worked with the composer again, eight years later on *The Shining*, Carlos had become a hybrid of sorts himself, now known as Wendy Carlos.

The most memorable scene in *Clockwork*, wherein Malcolm McDowell, as the youthful thug, rapes and murders a woman while singing and dancing to "Singin' in the Rain," was based on a similar, horrible incident in Burgess's own life. Apparently it was McDowell who suggested using the song, and Kubrick decided to go with the idea, revealing something of a democratic nature behind a film that otherwise was completely controlled by the director.

# The Clouded Yellow

★ ★ ★ ★ ★ ★ ★ ★ ★ ★ ★ ★ ★ ★ ★ ★ ★ ★ ★ ★ ★ ★ ★ ★ ★ ★ ★ ★ ★ ★ ★ ★ ★ ★ ★ ★ ★ ★ ★ ★ ★ ★ ★ ★ ★ ★ ★ ★ ★ ★

*Nationality*: British          *Year*: 1950 (U.S. release: 1951)
*Cast*: Jean Simmons, Trevor Howard, Sonia Dresdel, Barry Jones, Maxwell Reed, Kenneth More
*Director*: Ralph Thomas          *Running Time*: 95 minutes
*B/W or Color*: B/W          *Availability*: TV only

This film's unusual title refers to a species of butterfly belonging to wealthy Nicholas Fenton (Barry Jones), who hires ex-Secret Service agent David Somers (Trevor Howard) to catalog his large collection. Also present at Fenton's country estate: his beautiful but eccentric niece Sophie (Jean Simmons), his neurotic wife Jess (Sonia Dresdel), and Hick (Maxwell Reed), the hulking handyman whom Jess covets and Sophie repulses.

The movie's slow-paced opening exposition serves to build and establish the subtle conflicts of these diverse characters. But the pace accelerates when Hick is found dead and circumstantial evidence points to the innocent, muddled Sophie. Before the police can arrest her, David helps her escape, and they are pursued through Britain's lake district. An exciting climactic chase across the rooftops of Liverpool nearly results in Sophie's death—before the real killer is revealed.

This high class chase thriller certainly offers no innovations to the genre, but Ralph Thomas's direction of an expert cast manages to extract every ounce of suspense Janet Green's screenplay has to offer, and the film drew favorable comparisons with Hitchcock.

For 21-year-old Jean Simmons, *The Clouded Yellow* marked an end to the British-ingenue phase of her career, just prior to her departure for Hollywood—and an unfortunate Howard Hughes contract. But the role of this fey and over-protected child-woman, who matures under stress, presented a considerable challenge to the young actress, and much of the movie's sustained excitement owes a debt to her intense performance.

*The Clouded Yellow* offers some fascinating Freudian sidelights to the old-fashioned hunt-and-chase melodrama, and Geoffrey Unsworth's cameras atmospherically capture the natural highlights of London, Liverpool, Newcastle-upon-Tyne, and England's northern lakes and hills. In *The Clouded Yellow*, we have an indigenous British art form—the whodunit—at its intriguing best, entertainingly recounted.

# Colonel Redl
## (Oberst Redl)

\*\*\*\*\*\*\*\*\*\*\*\*\*\*\*\*\*\*\*\*\*\*\*\*\*\*\*\*\*\*\*\*\*\*\*\*\*\*\*\*\*\*\*\*\*\*\*\*\*\*\*\*\*\*

*Nationality*: Hungarian-West German-Austrian

*Year*: 1985

*Cast*: Klaus Maria Brandauer, Armin Mueller-Stahl, Gudrun Landgrebe, Jan Niklas, Hans-Christian Blech

*Director*: Istvan Szabo

*B/W or Color*: Color

*Running Time*: 149 minutes

*Availability*: PACIFIC ARTS

One of the finest films produced in the last decade, *Colonel Redl* is hardly a bittersweet elegy to the lost Austro-Hungarian Empire. Rather it dissects the politically bloated nature of that conglomerate of eastern European nations. Colonel Redl was a real person, and he did die because of his intrigues, but Istvan Szabo completely fictionalizes his character and story.

Klaus Maria Brandauer is superb as the opportunistic, but socially insecure, military officer. Although there is some rather unconvincing homosexuality grafted onto his character toward the end, his motivations are meticulously explored by the actor. One should dislike Redl, but one can't. Instead, genuine sorrow is felt for this man who is betrayed by everything and everyone around him. Brandauer skillfully interprets the psyche of the complex but ultimately naive man pictured in this film. Armin Mueller-Stahl almost matches him as Franz Ferdinand, the crown prince, who cunningly arranges Redl's downfall.

The cinematography of Lajos Koltai is outstanding and captures the color and drama of old Vienna. The sets by Jozsef Romvari and the costumes of Peter Pabst, full of rococo detail and claustrophobic in their overwhelming effect, perfectly sum up the decadent era preceding the defeat and fall of the Hapsburg Empire.

Perhaps the most fascinating aspect of this film is the fact that Szabo has altered history in the screenplay. An officer in the Austro-Hungarian army during World War I, the real-life Redl began selling military secrets to the Russians early in his career in order to support his homosexual lover. His costume parties, where all men dressed in ball gowns, were notorious. Heavily in debt, Redl, in his final act of treachery, sold the Russians the entire Austrian war plan for the Eastern Front, resulting in the slaughter of thousands of his fellow soldiers. Unmasked, he committed suicide. It is interesting to speculate why Szabo chose to alter Redl's biography so, and why he felt the true story was less interesting than the fictional one he created.

*(The videocassette is in subtitled German.)*

# Comfort and Joy

\* \* \* \* \* \* \* \* \* \* \* \* \* \* \* \* \* \* \* \* \* \* \* \* \* \* \* \* \* \* \* \* \* \* \* \* \* \* \* \* \* \* \* \* \* \* \* \* \* \* \* \* \* \*

*Nationality*: British                  *Year*: 1984
*Cast*: Bill Paterson, Eleanor David, C.P. Grogan, Alex Norton
*Director*: Bill Forsyth          *Running Time*: 106 minutes
*B/W or Color*: Color          *Availability*: MCA HOME VIDEO

Sweetness is a rare thing in adult movies, and Bill Forsyth has found it and plays it like a violin in *Comfort and Joy*. Set at Christmastime in Scotland, the film has an emotional amplitude that sustains Forsyth's flats, sharps, and grace notes. The story of a radio disc jockey (Bill Paterson) who loses his girlfriend during the holidays and then gets involved in the product competition of two rival ice-cream manufacturers offers a constant unfolding and revelation of the characters' idiosyncrasies and absurd actions.

The great modern influence in this film is Robert Altman. Bill Forsyth follows Altman's display of the commonplace as something wonderful and thrilling. The audio density of the radio station scenes in *Comfort and Joy* may be a direct tribute to Altman's full, vivid soundtracks.

Forsyth and his remarkable cameraman Chris Menges convey a sparkling, bracingly clean countryside so that even the disclosure of social inactivity is viewed kindly. By now, in his fourth film, Forsyth can give most everything he shows a distinctive emotional touch. Paterson's reveries about his relationship with Eleanor David are filmed in a soft light, yet they practically glisten and have a palpable eroticism. As Paterson's fantasies end, Forsyth brings the story back to reality with masterful subtlety. The modulation from ecstasy to melancholy seems as simple as turning the corner from one room to the next, but one can think of comparable scenes only in some of the greatest films of Altman, De Sica, or Chaplin.

# Confidentially Yours
## (Vivement Dimanche!)

★★★★★★★★★★★★★★★★★★★★★★★★★★★★★★★★★★★★★★★★★★★★★★★★★★★★★★★

Nationality: French          Year: 1983

Cast: Fanny Ardant, Jean-Louis Trintignant, Philippe Laudenbach, Caroline Sihol

Director: François Truffaut          Running Time: 111 minutes

B/W or Color: B/W          Availability: KEY VIDEO

A highly enjoyable film, *Confidentially Yours* was the last film directed by François Truffaut (1932–84). His screenplay was based on an American novel, *The Long Saturday Night*, by Charles Wilson. Titled *Finally Sunday* in England, it opened the 1983 London Film Festival.

Truffaut acknowledged Alfred Hitchcock's influence on his work, and the plot is typical Hitchcock—a man is charged with crimes about which he knows nothing. Homage is also paid to film noir, several of the scenes being reminiscent of the Forties' detective movie genre. Praise was paid to Nestor Almendros's cinematography. He had worked with Truffaut on *The Green Room*, which was also in black and white.

Fanny Ardant is excellent as Barbara Becker, a wise, sarcastic, and self-assured secretary who is secretly smitten with her real-estate broker boss Julien Vercel (Jean-Louis Trintignant) and sets out to clear him of murder charges.

Julien remains in hiding, the chief suspect in the killings of his wife (Caroline Sihol) and her lover. Even the loyal Barbara initially disbelieves him. The theme of a man on the run turning for assistance to a suspicious woman also echoed Hitchcock.

Ardant, who had played a very different type of heroine in Truffaut's *Woman Next Door* (*La Femme d'à Côté*), won kudos. Wrote *Newsweek* magazine critic David Ansen, "If you can imagine Irene Papas rolled into the young Katharine Hepburn playing a very sensual Nancy Drew, in French, you'll have a clue to the fun in store."

Trintignant became a star in *And God Created Woman*. His later films include *Les Liaisons Dangereuses*, *A Man and a Woman*, *Z*, *My Night at Maud's*.

Once described as "a man who was born to live his life in the cinema," former movie critic Truffaut's 25-year career as a director began with the autobiographical *The 400 Blows* in 1959.

(*Key Video offers a subtitled cassette.*)

# The Conformist
## (Il Conformista)

∗∗∗∗∗∗∗∗∗∗∗∗∗∗∗∗∗∗∗∗∗∗∗∗∗∗∗∗∗∗∗∗∗∗∗∗∗∗∗∗∗∗∗∗∗∗∗∗∗∗∗∗∗∗∗∗

**Nationality**: Italian-French-West German     **Year**: 1970

**Cast**: Jean-Louis Trintignant, Stefania Sandrelli, Dominique Sanda, Pierre Clementi, Gastone Moschin

**Director**: Bernardo Bertolucci     **Running Time**: 115 minutes

**B/W or Color**: Color     **Availability**: PARAMOUNT HOME VIDEO

Bertolucci's film is a vast improvement over the Alberto Moravia novel from which it is adapted. This was Bertolucci's first film after joining the Communist party, but it's far from a doctrinaire exploration of the link between sex and politics. The rise and fall of Fascism are convincingly tied to the appalling romantic life of Marcello (Jean-Louis Trintignant), the conformist of the tale. Some adroit flashbacks show us that, as a boy, Marcello was sexually exploited by the family chauffeur (Pierre Clementi), whom he shoots and believes he has killed. As an adult, he confesses the crime to a priest, who absolves the young Fascist. Marcello marries a lovely woman of his class (Stefania Sandrelli), whom he doesn't truly love, but this is yet another act of conformism. He doesn't hesitate to combine his honeymoon with a political job, the assassination of an anti-Fascist professor in Paris, who it turns out was Marcello's mentor in school, before he went bad. Marcello's father was insane, and the professor became a surrogate father, just as the Fascist party subsequently did. His object of desire becomes the professor's wife, Anna (Dominique Sanda), a luscious and intriguing woman who succeeds in conveying a hint of her own androgynous nature. She has an affair with Marcello, but it is really his wife who excites her, and the two women dance an unabashedly erotic tango that is memorable. The professor is duly assassinated, and the film's denouement occurs later, in 1943, when Marcello glimpses the chauffeur he believed he had killed. He recognizes his conformity was an obsession formed after their traumatic encounter and sees his life is a sham. The film re-creates the period depicted with great style. Mussolini architectural details dwarf the characters in a Fascist minister's office, while Paris is all seductive art nouveau tendrils. A period piece par excellence and a fascinating exploration of its theme, justifying its National Board Award as one of 1971's five best foreign-language films.

(*The videocassette is dubbed in English.*)

# Contempt
## (Le Mépris)

★★★★★★★★★★★★★★★★★★★★★★★★★★★★★★★★★★★★★★★★★★★★★★★★★★★★★★★

*Nationality*: French-Italian     *Year*: 1963 (U.S. release: 1964)

*Cast*: Brigitte Bardot, Jack Palance, Michel Piccoli, Fritz Lang, Georgia Moll

*Director*: Jean-Luc Godard     *Running Time*: 103 minutes

*B/W or Color*: Color     *Availability*: EMBASSY HOME ENTERTAINMENT

This was the iconoclastic Godard's only concession to mainstream filmmaking. Producers Carlo Ponti and Joseph E. Levine hired the New Wave master to do a film adaptation of the Alberto Moravia novel *Il Disprezzo* with a cast of guaranteed international box-office appeal: Bardot, Palance, and Piccoli. The story is about infidelity, actual or suspected, among the international filmmaking set. A screenwriter and his wife, Paul and Camile (Piccoli and Bardot), are at odds with each other due to the interference of the scenarists' crass producer Prokosch (Palance). The soap opera premise is as commercial as Godard's storytelling ever became. Instead he used the situation for a serene, modernist meditation on his favorite subjects: filmmaking and sexual love. The opening scene—Bardot nude, spread across the CinemaScope screen, asking Piccoli which of her physical features he likes best—confronts the audience with the issues of filmic representative and the erotic/emotional confusions of love. Godard also added a role for the legendary German director Fritz Lang, here playing a pontificating filmmaker who hires Piccoli to write an adaptation of Homer's *Odyssey*. Each character represents a level of inquiry that Godard intends the simple plot to support: sex, love, power, and creativity. Although the plot is about filmmakers, the filmmaking itself never happens: the astonishing Mediterranean locations are used as the settings for philosophical discussions. Because Godard is more poet than pedant, he counters the verbal emphasis of the film with nearly overwhelming sensual and visual beauty.

Hailed as the greatest color work by cinematographer Raoul Coutard, *Contempt* also stands as a ravishing nature study. The splendid sea, mountain, and skyscapes are matched by the play of sunlight Godard and Coutard discover for the interiors. The celebrated scene of Paul and Camille's marital disagreement is set in one room for nearly half an hour with few cuts—just the camera moving seductively, following the smooth, bright sunlight from the windows; their poignant dialogue, highlighted by Georges Delerue's evocative score, has been likened to opera.

*(Embassy offers the film in both dubbed and subtitled versions.)*

# Cousin, Cousine

\* \* \* \* \* \* \* \* \* \* \* \* \* \* \* \* \* \* \* \* \* \* \* \* \* \* \* \* \* \* \* \* \* \* \* \* \* \* \* \* \* \* \* \* \* \* \* \* \* \* \* \* \* \*

Nationality: French                    Year: 1975
Cast: Marie-Christine Barrault, Victor Lanoux, Marie-France Pisier, Guy
Marchand
Director: Jean-Charles Tacchella    Running Time: 95 minutes
B/W or Color: Color                      Availability: CBS/FOX HOME
                                                     VIDEO

One of France's greatest imports was—and is—this charming sex
comedy. It was the first Best Picture Award winner in the 33-
year history of the Prix Louis Delluc to be voted upon unanimously on
the first ballot, and it won the Cesar (French equivalent of the Academy
Award) for Best Supporting Actress for Marie-France Pisier as the wonderfully madcap neurotic wife. In this country, Cousin, Cousine seemed
a sure bet to win the Best Foreign Film Oscar, but it lost to the less
memorable Black and White in Color. The National Board named it one
of the year's five best foreign films.

When Ginette Garcin, 50, weds Pierre Plessis, 60, the celebrating goes
on all day. Continuing their own festivities are cousins by marriage Marie-
Christine Barrault, her daughter, and Victor Lanoux, his nephew. They
get together when *their* respective spouses, Guy Marchand and Marie-
France Pisier, have a brief fling. The new lovers decide not to consummate their affair, for the time being, so they do nothing to also hide their
relationship. Each family gathering seems to end in turmoil and to inten-
sify their relationship, which includes sharing a tub in which they paint
each other's body. Although Marchand and the wacky Pisier attempt to
win back their mates, they fight a losing battle. At Christmas, Lanoux
and Barrault leave to begin a new life together and, presumably, consummate their affair.

Writer-director Jean-Charles Tacchella, a film critic and scriptwriter,
made just two shorts and the feature Voyage en Grande Tartarie before
this, his triumph. It became one of the most popular French movies ever
to be released in America. Tacchella, whose inspiration was the screwball
American comedies of the Thirties, shows that he had learned his lesson
well. For your pleasure.

(The videocassette is in subtitled French.)

# The Cranes Are Flying
## (Letiat Jouravly)

**★★★★★★★★★★★★★★★★★★★★★★★★★★★★★★★★★★★★★★★★★★★★★★★★★★**

*Nationality*: Russian                    *Year*: 1958 (U.S. release: 1960)

*Cast*: Tatyana Samoilova, Alexei Batalov, Vasily Merkuryev, Alexander Shvorin

*Director*: Mikhail Kalatozov          *Running Time*: 94 minutes

*B/W or Color*: B/W                       *Availability*: TV only

An earlier cultural thaw in Russian-American relations permitted this sensitive, moving film to be released here. Directed with apparently relative freedom by Mikhail Kalatozov, the movie is essentially devoid of the usual propaganda.

This lyrical antiwar film recaptures some of the romance of 19th-century Russian literature with its two lovers, Veronica and Boris, separated by the German invasion in 1941. Each is a particularly attractive Russian type. Boris, for his essential decency and wholesomeness; and Veronica for her prototypical, handsome, young Soviet womanhood. However, played by Tatyana Samoilova, she bears still richer references. Lithe, slender, dark haired, vibrant in her sexuality, she embodies our vision of the eternal Russian young woman, the archetypal Natasha of *War and Peace*.

Too late to say good-bye to her lover, Veronica experiences further traumas of war. Her parents die in an air raid, and she is forced to move in with Boris's family. His cousin, a pianist, courts the lonely young woman and, in the midst of a bombing, seduces her. She marries him in spite of her feelings for Boris and is filled with guilt when she hears of his death at the front.

Although Russian films are generally puritanical and moralistic, *The Cranes Are Flying* is relatively open about the victimization of individuals by war. Veronica's "mistake" is delineated within the context of the era, and the possibility of peace suggests a new life for her.

The film is important because it presents the Russians both as they see themselves and as they want the world to see them. In addition, it is a motion picture of moving, poetic quality and visual excellence. There is some fascinating photography, especially the shots of large groups of people. *The Cranes Are Flying* genuinely merits its Best Film prize at the Cannes Festival and *The New York Times*'s naming it as one of the ten best foreign films of the year.

# Cria!

## (Cria Cuervos . . . )

\* \* \* \* \* \* \* \* \* \* \* \* \* \* \* \* \* \* \* \* \* \* \* \* \* \* \* \* \* \* \* \* \* \* \* \* \* \* \* \* \* \* \* \* \* \* \* \* \* \* \* \*

*Nationality*: Spanish          *Year*: 1976
*Cast*: Geraldine Chaplin, Ana Torrent, Conchita Perez, Mayte Sanchez, Monica Randall
*Director*: Carlos Saura          *Running Time*: 112 minutes
*B/W or Color*: Color          *Availability*: TV only

"If you raise ravens," states an old Spanish proverb quoted in *Cria!*, "you can expect them to peck out your eyes." The haunting *Cria!*—also called *Raise Ravens*, a literal translation of its original title—received a Special Jury Award at the Cannes Festival because of its "perceptive examination of a child's world as seen through the eyes of adults, contrasted with adults as seen through the eyes of a child."

Carlos Saura, *Cria!*'s director, is Spain's best-known filmmaker from the postwar generation. He is particularly known for his rich, multilayered portrayals of family life during the uncertain period immediately following the Spanish Civil War. His obsessions with personal memory blend reality with fantasy, while overlapping the present with the past, and sometimes with the future.

A very subtle work, *Cria!* is Saura's most acclaimed picture within this particular *oeuvre* (*Blood Wedding* and his other recent Spanish dance works have also received considerable attention). Geraldine Chaplin, Saura's frequent collaborator during the late Sixties and Seventies, sensitively depicts a woman (Ana) searching her childhood memories to piece together the forces that have plagued her adult life. She remembers that following the death of her overbearing father, her Aunt Paulina moved in to help care for her two sisters and herself. Although the aunt attempts to be friendly, little Ana prefers to retreat into her fantasy world, where she reverentially remembers her mother (also played by Chaplin), who had died many years before. When she sees the aunt passionately embracing a neighbor (the husband of *her* husband's mistress), Ana decides to poison the older woman by pouring baking powder, which she believes is poison, into the aunt's milk.

In piecing together the clues recalling Ana's past with transitions that are deliberately blurred, Saura occasionally plays with conflicting tricks of memory. He has compared this technique to someone reviewing fading photographs of incidents that occurred long ago and are not fully remembered. Saura's formative years, like Ana's, immediately followed the Spanish Civil War. In this delicate allegory made only a year before Franco's death, the forces troubling the adult Ana are those that have impeded the psychological and social growth of the Spanish people since their civil war.

# Cries and Whispers

## (Viskningar och Rop)

★ ★ ★ ★ ★ ★ ★ ★ ★ ★ ★ ★ ★ ★ ★ ★ ★ ★ ★ ★ ★ ★ ★ ★ ★ ★ ★ ★ ★ ★ ★ ★ ★ ★ ★ ★ ★ ★ ★ ★ ★ ★ ★ ★ ★ ★ ★ ★ ★ ★ ★ ★ ★ ★

Nationality: Swedish        Year: 1972

Cast: Liv Ullmann, Harriet Andersson, Ingrid Thulin, Kari Sylwan, Erland Josephson, George Ahlin

Director: Ingmar Bergman        Running Time: 106 minutes

B/W or Color: Color        Availability: WARNER HOME VIDEO

W ho knows what evil lurks in the bourgeois heart? Players in this domestic Ingmar Bergman psychodrama are the terminally ill Agnes (Harriet Andersson), her sisters Maria (Liv Ullmann) and Karin (Ingrid Thulin), who carry on a deathbed vigil, and Anna, the maid (Kari Sylwan). Meals are served in this household by minions in white aprons. Enameled clocks are immaculately dusted. Yet deadly emotions seethe beneath this tranquil facade. Karen and Maria are wrenched by the knowledge that they don't really love Agnes. A disillusioned lover and a loveless husband turn the ritual of dining into an orgy of hate. The family doctor (Erland Josephson) traces the source of every early wrinkle on Liv Ullmann's face, knowing that her slothful, calculating ways are his own. As Agnes dies, her sisters run in disgust from her illness. It is Anna who cradles Agnes's head against her breast. The melodrama of the primal scream is enhanced by the vivid red and gray interiors for which cinematographer Sven Nykvist won an Oscar.

Bells toll. Shafts of light pierce the forest. Sisters run in their long white dresses toward a swing where they played as children. The setting may be pre-World War I Sweden, but the motivations in this superb picture are universal, from the heights of passion to the depths of pettiness. They will strike a particularly responsive chord in every child, sibling, or faithful retainer who has sat anxiously awaiting the reading of a family will. A well-deserved Best Foreign Film Award was given by The National Board of Review, which also cited Bergman's screenplay and Nykvist's cinematography.

(Warner's videocassette is dubbed in English.)

# "Crocodile" Dundee

★★★★★★★★★★★★★★★★★★★★★★★★★★★★★★★★★★★★★★★★★★★★★★★★★★★★★★

Nationality: Australian  Year: 1986
Cast: Paul Hogan, Linda Kozlowski, John Meillon, Mark Blum
Director: Peter Faiman  Running Time: 98 minutes (102
minutes in Australia)
B/W or Color: Color  Availability: PARAMOUNT
HOME VIDEO

Australia's most successful box-office hit (to date), *"Crocodile" Dundee* also became a surprise financial and critical winner in the United States—where at least one studio passed on the distribution rights, mistakenly assuming that the picture would not do as well with audiences this side of the wallabies.

It's a fun movie, an audience pleaser that was partially written by its star, Australian TV personality Paul Hogan (who was recognizable to American audiences because of his commercials that invited viewers to journey Down Under). The screenplay received a 1986 Academy Award nomination.

The entertaining charmer is sort of an updating of *Tarzan's New York Adventure* (1942), with the hero transported from the African jungles to the Australian outback. Michael J. "Crocodile" Dundee (Paul Hogan) is a modern adventurer whose exploits are depicted in a New York newspaper article by a reporter (Linda Kozlowski). She brings 'im back alive to the wilds of Manhattan and also manages to fall in love with the likable bloke.

Comedy and action are neatly juggled, especially in the New York scenes. When Dundee is accosted by a knife-wielding mugger, the Australian crocodile-fighter is amused by the size of the weapon. "Ya call that a knife?" he scoffs, as he produces a machete-like blade that scares off the offender. Dundee has a far greater trouble distinguishing transvestites and develops an up-front manner of determining them. There are also encounters with prostitutes and various other urban types uncommon to the outback. Perhaps his biggest challenge, however, is facing a morning rush-hour crowd in a subway station, as he attempts to win his lady fair.

Directed by Peter Faiman, the popular hero is destined for additional adventures in a sequel, which, if successful, would lead to further exploits for *"Crocodile" Dundee.*

# The Cruel Sea

*********************************************************

Nationality: British                    Year: 1953

Cast: Jack Hawkins, Donald Sinden, Stanley Baker, Virginia McKenna

Director: Charles Frend           Running Time: 121 minutes

B/W or Color: B/W                  Availability: THORN/EMI-HBO
                                                       VIDEO

A documentary-style account of a British warship vs. Nazi subs during World War II, *The Cruel Sea* received an Oscar nomination for Eric Ambler's screenplay. Based on the best-selling novel by Nicholas Monsarrat, the film initiated a cycle of World War II films on the British screen during the early Fifties.

Depicting the heroism of ordinary men in wartime, the story centers on the crew of the corvette HMS *Compass Rose,* under the command of Captain Ericson (Jack Hawkins), an intrepid officer who must make able seamen out of bank clerks, journalists, lawyers, et al. The *Compass Rose,* part of the British convoys in the North Atlantic, must steer through a hidden gauntlet of Nazi submarines. The corvette is torpedoed, and the scenes of destruction and evacuation that follow are considered by many the best ever filmed. Director Charles Frend never again equalled the quality displayed here. Following a hazardous night in "the cruel sea," the survivors are rescued. As the picture ends, Ericson is seen taking command of another corvette.

Jack Hawkins, who possessed one of the more distinctive voices in British cinema, retired briefly when cancer claimed his vocal cords. He returned to play a silent role in *Great Catherine* (1967) and was dubbed in subsequent parts, prior to his death.

Hawkins's performance is first rate, as is Donald Sinden's as a former journalist who becomes an experienced leader and Denholm Elliott's as a former lawyer, another officer under Hawkins's command.

As its prologue claims, *The Cruel Sea* remains an exciting story of "an ocean, of two ships, and a handful of men."

# Curse of the Demon
## (Night of the Demon)

★ ★ ★ ★ ★ ★ ★ ★ ★ ★ ★ ★ ★ ★ ★ ★ ★ ★ ★ ★ ★ ★ ★ ★ ★ ★ ★ ★ ★ ★ ★ ★ ★ ★ ★ ★ ★ ★ ★ ★ ★ ★ ★ ★ ★ ★ ★ ★ ★ ★ ★

Nationality: British

Year: 1957 (U.S. release: 1958)

Cast: Dana Andrews, Niall MacGinnis, Peggy Cummins, Athene Seyler, Liam Redmond, Brian Wilde

Director: Jacques Tourneur

Running Time: 83 minutes

B/W or Color: B/W

Availability: RCA/COLUMBIA PICTURES HOME VIDEO

In 1942, Val Lewton (producer) and Jacques Tourneur (director) fashioned a poetic tale of shadow and suggestion called *Cat People*. RKO studio brass (the same who insisted on that miserable title) demanded that the title creature be visible. Tourneur and editor Mark Robson saw to it that the animal was only glimpsed, rather than seen.

Fifteen years later Tourneur, working abroad, tried to recapture the subtle horrors of his RKO period with M. R. James's story *Casting the Runes*, adapted for the screen by Hitchcock collaborator Charles Bennett. But his film version, *The Haunted*, became *Night of the Demon* at studio insistence, then *Curse of the Demon* when it reached America. And once again the brass insisted on a cameo appearance by the title monster. Tourneur capitulated to the tune of several frames of film, but after he left the project, the executive producer conjured up a slathering ancestor of the muppets and dumped it into two sequences. Following this, as much as 13 minutes were cut from the film to make it a tidy length for double billing, which didn't do wonders for its continuity. It is a testament to Tourneur's artistry that the film survived such butchering.

*Curse of the Demon* is an enduring B masterpiece, tightly written, sympathetically acted by Dana Andrews playing a zealously skeptical parapsychologist and by Niall MacGinnis as a politely insidious alchemist. The research Bennett poured into the film, about satanic tunes, runes, woodcuts, games, and spells—about seances and the obdurate mentality of the scientific community—creates a compelling sense of inner realism (he also gave us a very Hitchcockian villain with an equally familiar troublesome mother). The art direction and cinematography are remarkable for a low-budget film, and Clifton Parker's foreboding score is memorable.

# The Damned
## (La Caduta degli Dei/Götterdämmerung)

★★★★★★★★★★★★★★★★★★★★★★★★★★★★★★★★★★★★★★★★★★★★★★★★★★★★★★★

**Nationality**: Italian-West German    **Year**: 1969
**Cast**: Dirk Bogarde, Ingrid Thulin, Helmut Griem, Helmut Berger, Charlotte Rampling, Florinda Bolkan
**Director**: Luchino Visconti    **Running Time**: 155 minutes (164 minutes in Europe)
**B/W or Color**: Color    **Availability**: WARNER HOME VIDEO

Luchino Visconti claimed that William L. Shirer's *The Rise and Fall of the Third Reich* ". . . really became our Bible" during this film's production. When questioned why he had chosen Nazism over Fascism as his subject, he replied, ". . . Nazism seems to me to reveal more about a historic reversal of values." The description "operatic" often fits Visconti's films, and *The Damned* has its share of melodramatic excesses, though they're justifiably integral to this powerful and shocking work. Many have suggested that the fictitious German munitions family of this film is really the Krupps, but Visconti maintained that he drew his characters from *eight* such wealthy German clans.

*The Damned* conjures up thoughts of Shakespeare's *Macbeth* and Sartre's *The Condemned of Altona* with its large-scale story of greed, corruption, murder, and perversion, concurrent with the Nazi rise to power in 1933–34 Germany. And it provides a virtual six-ring circus of colorful villains and their victims as it dissects this specimen of familial decay that culminates in an ambitious woman's rape by her own son, whose love-hatred of her fired his own rise to power.

*The Damned* can only leave its audience with a wealth of nightmare images to ponder—or try to forget: among them, the all-male orgy of the notorious "Night of the Long Knives," the bizarre but uncanny drag impersonation of Marlene Dietrich, and the enforced post-rape wedding of the mother and her Nazi-uniformed lover, followed by her son's nuptial gift—cyanide tablets!

Superbly acted, especially by Ingrid Thulin and Helmut Berger as that deadly mother and son, Dirk Bogarde as her consort, and Helmut Griem as a Nazi charmer, *The Damned* was rated X in America. *The New York Times* listed it among 1969's ten best movies, and The National Board named it one of the year's five best foreign imports.

*(The videocassette is in English with some segments in German.)*

# Danton

**************************************************************

Nationality: French-Polish        Year: 1982
Cast: Gérard Depardieu, Wojciech Pszoniak, Patrice Chereau, Angela Winkler
Director: Andrzej Wajda        Running Time: 136 minutes
B/W or Color: Color        Availability: RCA/COLUMBIA HOME VIDEO

Filming in France, Polish director Andrzej Wajda used French, Polish, and German actors to make this story of the French Revolution (1789–95), based on a play (by Stanislawa Przybyszewska) that Wajda had directed on the Warsaw stage.

In November 1793, Georges Danton (Gérard Depardieu) leaves his brief, self-imposed exile in the country and returns to Paris, where he protests the murderous Reign of Terror, as executed by his nemesis (and former friend), "the incorruptible" Maximilien de Robespierre (Wojciech Pszoniak). Convinced that Danton's moderation is a betrayal of the Revolution, Robespierre has Danton and his followers arrested and engineers their trial. Not allowed to call witnesses, they are declared guilty in absentia and sent to the guillotine. The earthy, passionate Danton tells the stern and solemn Robespierre that he, too, will be sent to the guillotine—within three months. (Robespierre's July 1794 execution did follow three months after Danton's death.)

Though many noted parallels between the 18th-century events in France and problems that existed in present-day Poland, Wajda denied that any were intended, although he admitted that Danton represents the West and Robespierre the East.

The screenplay, by Jean-Claude Carriere, presents a series of mostly small, skillfully defined confrontations between the robust Danton and the steely Robespierre, and as the rivals, Gérard Depardieu and Wojciech Pszoniak are memorable. German actress Angela Winkler appears as Lucile Desmoulins, the wife of Dantonist journalist Camille Desmoulins, played by stage director Patrice Chereau. Another stage director, Roger Planchon, is noteworthy as the judge.

Wajda's use of artistic composition, cold coloring, and classic lighting brilliantly illustrates the time depicted and makes Danton as visually striking as it is dramatically absorbing.

(The videocassette is subtitled.)

# Dark Journey

★ ★ ★ ★ ★ ★ ★ ★ ★ ★ ★ ★ ★ ★ ★ ★ ★ ★ ★ ★ ★ ★ ★ ★ ★ ★ ★ ★ ★ ★ ★ ★ ★ ★ ★ ★ ★ ★ ★ ★ ★ ★ ★ ★ ★ ★ ★ ★ ★ ★ ★ ★ ★ ★

*Nationality*: British                    *Year*: 1937
*Cast*: Conrad Veidt, Vivien Leigh, Joan Gardner, Anthony Bushell, Ursula Jeans
*Director*: Victor Saville                 *Running Time*: 82 minutes
*B/W or Color*: B/W                        *Availability*: Public Domain

Alexander Korda was a Hungarian producer-director who came to England in the early Thirties and, on the strength of his film *The Private Life of Henry VIII* (1933), created a film empire and helped to gain prestige and respect for the British film industry. With his brothers Zoltan (a director) and Vincent (a designer), he made such films as *The Scarlet Pimpernel* (1934), *Rembrandt* (1936), *Things to Come* (1936), and *The Thief of Baghdad* (1940). Commercial and artistic success enabled Korda to form his own company, London Film Productions, and to buy Denham Studios in England, while in America he became a partner in United Artists. Alternating between producing and directing, he made big-budget "important" films back-to-back with more simple entertainments. One of the latter was *Dark Journey,* an unpretentious and wholly enjoyable World War I spy melodrama starring Vivien Leigh.

Korda was building Leigh up as a big leading lady in England, and this was her first really important starring role. She plays a dress-shop owner in Stockholm who is really a French spy. Meeting Conrad Veidt, the head of the German secret service, she pretends to give him helpful information and, somewhat surprisingly, they fall in love. This somewhat implausible plot is countered by the undeniable charm and chemistry of the two stars. Leigh is still the sweet, unspoiled English young lady, and Veidt is his usual slightly sinister but suave self.

Victor Saville's direction is smooth, imaginative, and well-crafted, emphasizing the romantic angle amidst a turbulent atmosphere. The photography of Georges Perinal and Harry Stradling is highly skillful, in keeping with Korda's always first-class production values. All in all, a thoroughly pleasing entry in the spy genre.

# Darling

★ ★ ★ ★ ★ ★ ★ ★ ★ ★ ★ ★ ★ ★ ★ ★ ★ ★ ★ ★ ★ ★ ★ ★ ★ ★ ★ ★ ★ ★ ★ ★ ★ ★ ★ ★ ★ ★ ★ ★ ★ ★ ★ ★ ★ ★ ★ ★ ★ ★ ★ ★ ★ ★

**Nationality**: British                      **Year**: 1965

**Cast**: Julie Christie, Dirk Bogarde, Laurence Harvey, Roland Curram

**Director**: John Schlesinger          **Running Time**: 122 minutes

**B/W or Color**: B/W                      **Availability**: EMBASSY HOME
ENTERTAINMENT

Darling is as much a movie product of the Sixties as is its amoral heroine, Diana Scott. Ten years earlier, the Code would have demanded that Diana pay for her sins, but here, in a dramatic reversal, it's the people she uses who pay for her sins, while she blithely seeks fresh diversion. In spite of the relaxed Code restrictions, the American print of *Darling* was cut by five minutes, reportedly a Paris orgy sequence. And, in Julie Christie, the film celebrated the arrival of a new superstar.

Diana Scott is the beautiful, pampered daughter of an upper-middle-class family, whom she defied with a brief but doomed teenage marriage. A model in London's TV and advertising circles, she meets video journalist Robert Gold (Dirk Bogarde). He leaves his wife and children to live with her—until ambition drives her into the arms of Miles Brand (Laurence Harvey), an executive who gets her a small role in a horror film. Pregnant by Robert, she returns to him, then decides on an abortion. Thinking she really wants security, Diana marries a wealthy, middle-aged Italian prince—and enters a new life of affluent tedium.

Christie's is an astonishing, true portrait of an amorous but amoral child-woman, equally adept at helplessness, guileless joy, or crafty bitchery. Laurence Harvey is perfect as the smooth jet-setter-on-the-make, but the most affecting performance is Bogarde's as the movie's only sympathetic character. As Diana's photographer pal Malcolm, Roland Curram contributes what in 1965 was considered a daringly frank portrait of a well-adjusted gay.

*Darling,* sparkling with devastating satirical thrusts, justifiably won screenwriter Frederic Raphael both an American Oscar and a British Academy Award. Julie Christie not only duplicated both of these honors but also copped the New York Film Critics Award and The National Board of Review's Best Actress citation. The Board also gave its Best Director award to Schlesinger and listed *Darling* among 1965's best films.

# Das Boot
## (The Boat)

\* \* \* \* \* \* \* \* \* \* \* \* \* \* \* \* \* \* \* \* \* \* \* \* \* \* \* \* \* \* \* \* \* \* \* \* \* \* \* \* \* \* \* \* \* \* \* \* \* \* \* \* \* \* \* \*

Nationality: West German          Year: 1981 (U.S. release: 1982)
Cast: Jürgen Prochnow, Herbert Grönemeyer, Klaus Wennemann
Director: Wolfgang Petersen     Running Time: 145 minutes
B/W or Color: Color                    Availability: RCA/COLUMBIA PIC-
                                                    TURES HOME VIDEO

D*as Boot* is a visually stunning and emotionally gripping tale of the tension-filled and danger-ridden lives of young sailors aboard German U-boats chasing British ships in the North Atlantic during World War II. An introductory title states that 75 percent of the seafarers did not safely return to Germany, thereby preparing the audience for the morbid drama that ensues. This film resembles the classic black-and-white war dramas in its depiction of the crew's struggle to survive and longing for loved ones left behind. *Das Boot* is a different kind of war film, however, in that emotional involvement with the characters is created by *not* depicting the sailors as stereotypical (Nazi) heroes and by *not* glorifying the honor of serving in the submarine. The captain and his officers display a distinct lack of enthusiasm for their commands. Director Wolfgang Petersen (*The Consequence*) compresses characters, mobile camerawork, and narrow spaces into a choreography of claustrophobia and tension. The image vibrates at moments when the submarine is hit, and the camera holds very still when the boat sinks, lingering on the tense faces of the protagonists, not knowing if they will live or die. The director enriches the scenes with visually beautiful images: mist, dripping water, and filters of blue, red, and orange light infuse the interiors with an ethereal quality. Such formal loveliness is interlaced with aesthetic shots of colorful sunrises and sunsets and white starry light dappling on moonlit water.

This film about survivors, however, contains an ironic twist. In its final moments, the audience's sympathy with the German sailors and fascination with the submarine are shattered by the horror of war and the sudden intrusion of death.

The National Board voted *Das Boot* one of 1982's five best foreign films.

*(RCA/COLUMBIA's videocassette is English-dubbed.)*

# Day for Night
## (La Nuit Américaine)

\*\*\*\*\*\*\*\*\*\*\*\*\*\*\*\*\*\*\*\*\*\*\*\*\*\*\*\*\*\*\*\*\*\*\*\*\*\*\*\*\*\*\*\*\*\*\*\*\*\*\*\*\*\*\*\*\*

*Nationality*: French        *Year*: 1973
*Cast*: François Truffaut, Jacqueline Bisset, Jean-Pierre Léaud, Valentina Cortese, Jean-Pierre Aumont
*Director*: François Truffaut        *Running Time*: 116 minutes
*B/W or Color*: Color        *Availability*: KEY VIDEO

Making a film has been likened to living a lifetime in a few months. Thrown into close quarters under near-deprivation conditions, false facades are quickly stripped away and true emotions spring up. It is a time of communal creativity, but it is not easy, and everything that can go wrong will. People like George Lucas have ceased directing for reasons akin to these, while others like Truffaut have embraced the experience, as he does in *Day for Night,* playing a director based not so much on himself as on a pastiche of several.

Films like this one, that talk about themselves, are part of a small genre called reflexive film and include such titles as *8½, The Projectionist,* and *The Day of the Locust.* Truffaut uses the genre in an almost docudramatic manner, definitively capturing the complex odyssey of feature filmmaking, with all its insanity, hilarity, pathos, and love. He has neither overdirected nor catered to stereotypes. It feels real, and though episodic, has drama enough, as does any film set.

Jean-Pierre Léaud's manic *Day for Night* performance is particularly interesting now, in light of his subsequent life. Collaborators on his later films have testified to his increasingly violent behavior and often absent manner, and neighbors in his building witnessed his standing naked in the courtyard, swinging a crucifix over his head and screaming, "Back, Satan!" One might, therefore, question the extent to which Truffaut allowed the real lives of his cast to reshape the structure of his film . . . especially the young star he had discovered in *The 400 Blows.*

*Day for Night* won a carload of awards, including an Oscar as 1973's Best Foreign Film. The New York Film Critics seconded that citation and went on to name Truffaut the year's Best Director and Valentina Cortese Best Supporting Actress. And, in Hollywood, when Best Supporting Actress Ingrid Bergman found herself the recipient of an Oscar for which Cortese was also nominated, she saluted her colleague's wonderful *Day for Night* performance, adding, "Please forgive me, Valentina. I didn't mean to."

*(The videocassette is dubbed in English.)*

# Day of Wrath
## (Vredens Dag)

**★★★★★★★★★★★★★★★★★★★★★★★★★★★★★★★★★★★★★★★★★★★★★★★★★**

*Nationality*: Danish          *Year*: 1943 (U.S. release: 1948)
*Cast*: Thorkild Roose, Lisbeth Movin, Sigrid Neiindam, Preben Lerdorff
Rye
*Director*: Carl Theodor Dreyer      *Running Time*: 105 minutes
*B/W or Color*: B/W          *Availability*: TV only

A story of witchcraft in 17th-century Denmark lends itself to exploitation, but Carl Theodor Dreyer isn't interested in manipulating
his audience. His other classic films (*The Passion of Joan of Arc, Vam-
pyr,* and *Ordet*) are all mystical and concerned with psychological torment, often revolving around religious matters. His characters cannot
resolve their spiritual drives, because they are caught in the center of
them.

*Day of Wrath* explores spiritual witch hunts in society. A woman loves
the son of her aged husband, a pastor. Her husband's mother, the boy's
grandmother, knows this and stirs up suspicion against—and hostility
toward—her daughter-in-law. When the husband dies, shortly after being
cursed by an old woman he had denounced as a witch, the mother-in-
law accuses the wife of also being a witch. The stepson draws away from
the distraught woman, who then accepts her fate.

Though set in the past, the film is a chilling forecast of America's "Red
scare" of the Fifties. It is more powerful and less obvious than Raymond
Rouleau's *The Crucible/The Witches of Salem,* and also less dated. Dreyer
poses the actors in painterly composition—and that is his point. His
characters are frozen, lonely, and full of frustration. When the woman is
deserted by her illicit lover, she allows herself to be swallowed up by the
hateful, suspicious, and emotionally dead community. The villagers have
no humanity, as evidenced in their burning of the eccentric but kindly
old woman. Her counterpart, the pastor's aged mother—a respected
member of the community—is the *true* witch.

Dreyer made *Day of Wrath* during World War II, and it reflects his
bleak outlook on the human condition during the Holocaust, for he has
made a timeless statement on "fear and trembling and the sickness unto
death."

The National Board named it one of 1948's ten best films.

# Daybreak
## (Le Jour Se Lève)

\*\*\*\*\*\*\*\*\*\*\*\*\*\*\*\*\*\*\*\*\*\*\*\*\*\*\*\*\*\*\*\*\*\*\*\*\*\*\*\*\*\*\*\*\*\*\*\*\*\*\*

**Nationality**: French      **Year**: 1939 (U.S. release: 1940)

**Cast**: Jean Gabin, Jacqueline Laurent, Jules Berry, Arletty

**Director**: Marcel Carné      **Running Time**: 87 minutes (95 minutes in France)

**B/W or Color**: B/W      **Availability**: Public Domain

A psychological study in despair, *Daybreak* was one of several films made by director Marcel Carné and writer Jacques Prévert. It stars three of France's major actors: Jean Gabin, long the most famous of all French leading men, Arletty, and Jules Berry; and features a fine performance by Jacqueline Laurent, who did not work again in films.

As the picture begins, an argument is heard, followed by the sound of a shot. Out of a fourth-floor flat emerges a man who falls dead on the landing. When the police arrive, another shot is fired—signaling the start of a siege.

Holding off police is François (Gabin), a sandblaster at a steel foundry. In flashback, it is learned that he had fallen in love with a flower seller named Françoise (Laurent), whom he had met on their name day, the feast of St. Francis. She, however, is fascinated by Valentin (Berry), a dog trainer whose partner Clara (Arletty) left him during a performance.

Circumstances lead to Clara's moving in with François, but the man's rivalry with Valentin is because of Françoise. Intending to kill François, Valentin goes to his apartment. An argument results in the trainer's death when François, in a rage, kills him with his own gun. Dawn brings no hope, and François uses the last bullet to kill himself.

A great deal of attention is paid to the movie's decor and to inanimate objects (a teddy bear named Bolop, a brooch, a pack of cigarettes, etc.), the significance of which is explained in flashbacks. Much of the dialogue spoken by François is uncharacteristically poetic, yet the superb performances and Carné's expert direction contribute to a haunting, lasting impression.

*Daybreak* was remade—less successfully—in an American version called *The Long Night* (1947), directed by Anatole Litvak and featuring Henry Fonda, Barbara Bel Geddes, Vincent Price, and Ann Dvorak.

# Dead of Night

* * * * * * * * * * * * * * * * * * * * * * * * * * * * * * * * * * * * * * * * * * * * * * * * * * *

**Nationality**: British        **Year**: 1945 (U.S. release: 1946)

**Cast**: Michael Redgrave, Googie Withers, Mervyn Johns, Roland Culver, Sally Ann Howes, Ralph Michael

**Directors**: Basil Dearden, Alberto        **Running Time**: 104 minutes
Cavalcanti, Robert Hamer, and
Charles Crichton

**B/W or Color**: B/W        **Availability**: THORN-EMI VIDEO

The most unusual British film production of 1945 was undoubtedly Ealing Studio's ingenious thriller *Dead of Night*, comprising five supernatural tales connected by a linking story. Based on the works of four different writers, the film also represents the efforts of four different directors: Basil Dearden ("The Hearse Driver" and the linking footage), Alberto Cavalcanti ("The Christmas Story" and "The Ventriloquist's Dummy"), Robert Hamer ("The Haunted Mirror"), and Charles Crichton ("The Golfing Story").

In *Dead of Night,* the five ghost stories are cleverly and logically cemented together like stones in a circular tower. Circular, because the film concludes where it begins, thereby suggesting an endlessly repeating nightmare for the architect (played by Mervyn Johns) whose dream the whole thing is (or is it really a dream, after all?) that connects the various tales together. Of this collection, the most memorable involve an antique mirror that begins to reflect a sinister old room in which it once hung— and where a murder took place—with Googie Withers and Ralph Michael in top form as the unsuspecting affianced giver and petrified recipient; and the bizarre episode in which Michael Redgrave brilliantly portrays an increasingly more disturbed ventriloquist, whose dummy begins to take on a life of its own.

When Universal imported this film in 1946, it was decided to shorten *Dead of Night* to 77 minutes by lopping off two episodes that were apparently considered dispensable, the Christmas and golfing stories. While admittedly tightening the continuity, the cut nevertheless opened gaps that failed to explain some of those present in the linking segments. Years later, this lamentable situation was rectified when original British prints surfaced on American TV—*complete*!

(*THORN-EMI offers cassettes of the full-length version.*)

# Death in Venice

★★★★★★★★★★★★★★★★★★★★★★★★★★★★★★★★★★★★★★★★★★★★★★★★★★★★★★

**Nationality**: Italian-French    **Year**: 1971
**Cast**: Dirk Bogarde, Silvana Mangano, Bjorn Andresen, Marisa Berenson, Mark Burns
**Director**: Luchino Visconti    **Running Time**: 130 minutes
**B/W or Color**: Color    **Availability**: WARNER HOME VIDEO

I t is hard to think of two artists further apart in technique, philosophy, and personality than Thomas Mann and Luchino Visconti. No wonder so many critics were dismayed that Visconti failed to capture the complexity of Mann's intellectual theses in *Death in Venice*. What we have instead is a spectacular operatic version of Mann's theme, dazzling to behold and heart-wrenching to follow. In place of Aschenbach's interior monologues we have a profound wedding of scene and action. Aschenbach is an inhibited moralist, a refugee from a cold, restrictive environment, who suddenly finds himself in a baroque city where the air is dappled with gold and every turn invites a new assault on the senses. If Aschenbach hadn't developed his morbid crush on teenaged Tadzio, he'd be just as likely to develop a fixation on one of the San Marco pigeons. It is the inevitability of his fate that Visconti pursues, and does so at least as successfully as Mann did. The first image of the character is revealing. Huddled in his coat and virtually bandaged in his muffler, he is dreamily transported toward a city of legendary seductive powers. Perhaps his mistake is not in foolishly falling in love with a forbidden object, but staying too long in a city infected with a secret pestilence. He is a man who is heedless of warnings, once his obsession grips him, and so seals his own doom.

Bogarde's performance is flawless. He has mastered his subject's precise walk and static, helpless gestures. His attempt to convert to something he is not, when he submits to his hairdresser's dyes and paints, is agonizing to watch.

Visconti's most notable achievements are in the details of his settings. Every color, entrance, and costume down to the last feather is expressive. As an adaptation of a novel, it is lacking. As moviemaking in the grand style, it has few peers.

(*The movie was filmed in English.*)

115

# Death on the Nile

**★★★★★★★★★★★★★★★★★★★★★★★★★★★★★★★★★★★★★★★★★★★★★★★★★★★★★★★**

*Nationality*: British                    *Year*: 1978

*Cast*: Peter Ustinov, Bette Davis, David Niven, Mia Farrow, Angela Lansbury, Maggie Smith

*Director*: John Guillermin          *Running Time*: 140 minutes

*B/W or Color*: Color                   *Availability*: HBO/CANNON
                                                         HOME VIDEO

Peter Ustinov first portrayed Agatha Christie's famous Belgian detective Hercule Poirot in *Death on the Nile*. He was to play him again in *Evil Under the Sun* (1982), and later on television. The canny, well-combed sleuth was first seen on screen in *Alibi* (1931), with Austin Trevor, who repeated the role in *Lord Edgware Dies* (1934). Tony Randall is the only American to play Poirot, appearing in that role in *The Alphabet Murders* (*The ABC Murders*, 1966), and Albert Finney received an Oscar nomination for his depiction of the courtly supersleuth in *Murder on the Orient Express* (1974).

This time the intrepid investigator is faced with a shipload of suspects, following the murder of Lois Chiles, playing a much disliked American heiress. The only party above suspicion is Poirot's friend, Colonel Rice (David Niven). Could the killer be jealous Mia Farrow, whose former fiancé (Simon MacCorkindale) was seduced by Chiles and was honeymooning with her? Might it possibly be Bette Davis, a wealthy woman who coveted pearls belonging to the deceased? George Kennedy, the bride's greedy uncle, was embezzling money from her; Maggie Smith's family was ruined by the dead woman's father; and tipsy romance novelist Angela Lansbury was being sued by Chiles for libel. And they're not the only possible culprits aboard.

The all-star cast shines. Ustinov does a fine job, while Bette Davis parodies Bette Davis. But the particular delight is Angela Lansbury; when she first meets Ustinov, she greets him as "Hercules Porridge." Lansbury was selected as The National Board of Review's Best Supporting Actress of 1978 for this role. (She would later play Agatha Christie's Miss Marple in 1980's *The Mirror Crack'd* and gain her widest popularity as television's Jessica Fletcher, an American cousin to Marple, on *Murder, She Wrote*.) Anthony Shaffer wrote the screenplay for *Death on the Nile*, and Anthony Powell won an Oscar for his costume design.

# Dersu Uzala
## (The Hunter)

★★★★★★★★★★★★★★★★★★★★★★★★★★★★★★★★★★★★★★★★★★★★★★★★★★★★★

**Nationality**: Russian-Japanese     **Year**: 1975 (U.S. release: 1978)

**Cast**: Maxim Munzuk, Yuri Solomin, S. Danilchenko

**Director**: Akira Kurosawa     **Running Time**: 137 minutes (141 minutes overseas)

**B/W** *or* **Color**: Color     **Availability**: EMBASSY HOME ENTERTAINMENT

D*ersu Uzala*, an Academy Award winner for Best Foreign Film, marks both advance and decline in the remarkable career of Akira Kurosawa. Prior to 1965, he had averaged a film a year for over two decades. But his 1970 *Dodes 'Ka-Den* had failed commercially, and his health was declining, along with his career. Then, in 1973, Kurosawa received an unprecedented offer from Mosfilm, the Soviet Union's largest studio, and *Dersu Uzala* was the result.

Based on a work by Russian explorer, ethnographer, and writer Vladimir Arseniev, the film centers on a daring hunter-pathfinder named Dersu Uzala, whom Arseniev met while exploring the Ussuri Territory, near the Russian-Manchurian border, shortly after the turn of the century. He is a warm-hearted, compassionate man, free from the corruption of civilization. Although diminutive in contrast to the tall, handsome Russian explorers, it is he who must teach them how to survive the wilderness. The film follows Arseniev during two mapping expeditions through the Ussuri Taiga. With failing eyesight, Dersu later attempts to live within "civilization" but cannot adjust to the restrictive city life.

Kurosawa is at his best in this allegory when he celebrates nature, its backwoods and deep rivers—and Dersu himself. The film's most haunting scene features Arseniev and his guides trapped on a frozen lake, struggling to cut grass for shelter as a blinding blizzard approaches. This remarkable episode features breathtaking cinematography and cinematic techniques as crisp and powerful as in any Kurosawa film. *Dersu Uzala*'s success enabled Kurosawa to turn his filmmaking career around.

*(The videocassette is shown with subtitles, but is listed at only 124 minutes.)*

# Devi
## (The Goddess)

* * * * * * * * * * * * * * * * * * * * * * * * * * * * * * * * * * * * * * * * * * *

*Nationality*: Indian          *Year*: 1961 (U.S. release: 1962)

*Cast*: Chhabi Biswas, Sharmila Tagore, Soumitra Chatterjee, Karuna Bannerjee

*Director*: Satyajit Ray          *Running Time*: 96 minutes

*B/W or Color*: B/W          *Availability*: Public domain

I f Indian culture is already "exotic," then Kali-worship is beyond the pale of a Westerner's understanding. The strength of Satyajit Ray's *Devi* is that it not only makes the motivation of the most extreme characters palpable but moving. That we get caught up in what is probably one of the most bizarre and frightening fantasies imaginable is Ray's art, and our response is prefigured in his world view. *Devi* is not only Indian film at its best but film technique at its most demonstrative.

An older, wealthy gentleman mistakes his new daughter-in-law for an incarnation of the goddess Kali. Intoxicated by the atmosphere of her father-in-law's home and wishing only to please, the daughter-in-law slowly begins to believe that she truly is Kali's incarnation. Her marriage is destroyed after she performs a "miracle," and so is she, after the second "miracle" fails.

This is the stuff of Buñuel nightmares, but Ray plays it straight. The air is languid and ripe, and the performances are just about perfect. Sharmila Tagore is transcendent as the daughter-in-law and could be the object of just about anyone's fantasies—Oedipal or not. Ray's art is seamlessly organic. The characters spiral forth from their culture. They can't help their actions.

Wherein Ray's "Apu Trilogy" had an almost seasonal approach to narrative, *Devi* is much more structured. As told from the young husband's viewpoint, the film is about helplessness in the face of beliefs. These beliefs may seem alien to the Westerner, but the ways in which they entangle the characters are universal. This is cultural examination and critique at its highest brow and, despite Ray's deceptively simple approach, most complex. *Devi* is cinema at its best.

# Devil in the Flesh
## (Le Diable au Corps)

\*\*\*\*\*\*\*\*\*\*\*\*\*\*\*\*\*\*\*\*\*\*\*\*\*\*\*\*\*\*\*\*\*\*\*\*\*\*\*\*\*\*\*\*\*\*\*\*\*\*\*\*\*

Nationality: French                    Year: 1947 (U.S. release: 1949)
Cast: Gérard Philipe, Micheline Presle
Director: Claude Autant-Lara        Running Time: 110 minutes
B/W or Color: B/W                      Availability: TV only

Some of the most beautiful love scenes ever put on film are among the best remembered moments from this famous French romantic drama, which catapulted young Gérard Philipe to international stardom. Extraordinarily frank, the film is based on the autobiographical novel by the legendary Raymond Radiguet, written when he was only 17 and three years before his tragic death. Set in World War I France, a time of almost hopeless confusion, this is the story of a young married woman whose husband is away at the front. She falls in love with a handsome, passionate, but irresponsible college youth and becomes pregnant by him, with unhappy results. Philipe himself was only 25 at the time of the film, and many great successes, including *Fanfan the Tulip* (1951), were to follow this elegant performance before his own untimely death at 37 in 1959. Philipe's brilliant performance is matched by Micheline Presle. The actress makes the total surrender of the older woman completely believable. Also 25 at the time and on screen since the age of 16, she was born Micheline Chassagne and first took the name of Micheline Michel. She later changed it to Presle. After Hollywood captured the sophisticated, coquettish star, it was changed to Prelle. Her American stint was brief, and she soon resumed her career in Europe. Director Claude Autant-Lara is best known for stylish romantic dramas, but he never again matched this film, which so movingly explores the raptures and torments of two sensitive people whose lives are turned upside down by events around them. A former assistant to René Clair, he first came to fame with *Fric-Frac* (1939). He later directed Philipe in *The Red and the Black*, co-starring Danielle Darrieux. *Devil in the Flesh* was named one of the year's best foreign films by The National Board. A new—and more explicit—version, from the Italian director Marco Bellocchio, was released in 1987.

# The Devils

***************************************************

Nationality: British          Year: 1971
Cast: Oliver Reed, Vanessa Redgrave, Dudley Sutton, Max Adrian, Gemma Jones
Director: Ken Russell          Running Time: 109 minutes
B/W or Color: Color          Availability: WARNER HOME VIDEO

Ken Russell was able to smother his sensationalism in enough creativity and originality to make it palatable in *Women in Love* and many of his BBC biographical features. But when he sublimated his artistic abilities to sensationalism, the critics and the public came gunning for him.

*The Devils* was X rated when it opened in 1971. Unlike *Midnight Cowboy, A Clockwork Orange,* and *The Killing of Sister George,* all of which were X rated then and would undoubtedly be rated downward today, *The Devils'* X is there to stay. This tale of demoniac possession is one of the most gratuitously violent, savage, and sexually explicit films ever made. Russell told this reviewer that the cut we see actually is less extensive than one he originally prepared, but while this version was being screened, the other segments were stolen and never recovered.

The story of Aldous Huxley's *The Devils of Loudun* has a very modern feel. Zeffirelli made *Romeo and Juliet* appealing to young audiences of today by using contemporary emotions they understood, whereas Russell chose recognizable "types"—the hippie exorcist, the amoral politician-priest, etc., and populated the film with them so we have the fun of seeing the Middle Ages as precursor to our own hypocritical times.

Set designer Derek Jarman's city of Loudun is the most arresting element in the film. It has the look of a medieval Disney World; its immaculate towering white brick walls decorate David Watkin's compositions in hundreds of aesthetic and dramatically pleasing ways, its awesome symmetry belying the decadence and horror hidden within. It ranks with the great set designs of all time.

Russell's stock company, including the unsympathetic Oliver Reed, all perform admirably. Vanessa Redgrave, new to Russell's clutches, gives a properly hysterical and grotesque performance. On her road to spiritual salvation from possession by the devil, she is made to go through physical tortures best not described here. One hopes it was somehow cleansing to her as an actress, as well.

# Diabolique
## (Les Diaboliques/The Fiends)

**★★★★★★★★★★★★★★★★★★★★★★★★★★★★★★★★★★★★★★★★★★★★★★★★★★★★★★**

*Nationality*: French                    *Year*: 1955
*Cast*: Simone Signoret, Vera Clouzot, Paul Meurisse, Charles Vanel
*Director*: Henri-Georges Clouzot    *Running Time*: 114 minutes
*B/W or Color*: B/W                    *Availability*: Public Domain

D irected by master craftsman Henri-Georges Clouzot, *Diabolique* is a brilliantly suspenseful murder mystery. Based on the 1952 novel *Celle Qui N'Etait Plus,* by Pierre Boileau and Thomas Narcejac (published in America as *The Woman Who Was No More*), *Diabolique* won a Prix Louis Delluc in 1954 and tied with De Sica's *Umberto D* for the New York Film Critics Award as Best Foreign Film in 1955. There were kudos also from The National Board.

The mystery unfolds at a boys' school run by Michel Delasalle (Paul Meurisse), a cruel headmaster and sadistic husband who flaunts his relationship with his schoolteacher-mistress Nicole (Simone Signoret) in front of his frail wife, Christina (Vera Clouzot). The two women plot to rid themselves of him. The headmaster is drugged and drowned in a bathtub; his body is tossed into the silt-filled school pool. As the film's tension builds, events conspire to further weaken Christina's already ailing heart. Michel's body disappears, and clues surface suggesting he's still alive. A visit to the morgue turns up Inspector Fuchet (Charles Vanel), who insists on helping the now-frantic Christina locate her missing husband. Cool no more, Nicole leaves Christina to fend for herself. When Christina sees Michel rise from his bathtub, eyes rolled back in their sockets, she's frightened into a heart attack. But to reveal more of the plot would be unfair.

Henri-Georges Clouzot, Jerome Geronimi, Frederic Grendel, and Renee Masson conspired to write the absorbing screenplay, and Clouzot directed his leads, including wife Vera, to haunting performances. Armand Thirard's murky photography enhances the menacing atmosphere. *Diabolique* is a genuine thriller—a shocking, satisfying chunk of *Grand Guignol* psychological suspense.

# Diamonds Are Forever

★★★★★★★★★★★★★★★★★★★★★★★★★★★★★★★★★★★★★★★★★★★★★★★★★★★★★★★★★

*Nationality*: British        *Year*: 1971

*Cast*: Sean Connery, Jill St. John, Charles Gray, Lana Wood, Jimmy Dean, Bruce Cabot

*Director*: Guy Hamilton        *Running Time*: 119 minutes

*B/W or Color*: Color        *Availability*: CBS/FOX VIDEO

In several aspects, this is a notable James Bond adventure. It's the eighth to use the services of Ian Fleming's ace superspy, the seventh to be produced by Albert R. (Cubby) Broccoli and Harry Saltzman, the sixth to star Sean Connery, and the first Bond to be shot on American locations. The $7 million extravaganza was also the first Connery-Bond in four years (George Lazenby in *On Her Majesty's Secret Service* intervened) and his last for a dozen more (with Roger Moore succeeding him). Among other distinctions, it's the last film of veteran American actor Bruce Cabot, who died five months after its release, and one of the few dramatic appearances of country-and-western singer Jimmy Dean. Guy Hamilton, who also did *Goldfinger,* directs in crackling style.

Agent 007 (Sean Connery) disposes of old enemy Blofeld (Charles Gray), then is assigned to break up a plot to corner the world diamond market. With beautiful Jill St. John acting as a contact, Bond learns that Blofeld is not dead (he had killed a double). The villain has been impersonating wealthy recluse Dean and using his missile laboratory. A laser has been developed with the diamonds and is to be used in demanding a world ransom before its destructive powers are unleashed. A more mature Bond survives death by cremation and must fight both homosexual henchmen and lesbian guards before smashing his adversary.

If Connery, who originated the role of James Bond on screen with *Doctor No,* were bidding good-bye to his character for the time being, he was not doing so quietly. The Richard Maibaum-Tom Mankiewicz screenplay contains enough action for any four ordinary films and offers a world's tour of glamorous locales: Nice, Amsterdam, London, Frankfurt, Las Vegas, Reno, Palm Springs, and Los Angeles. The tantalizing title song, by John Barry and Don Black, is rendered by Shirley Bassey.

# The Discreet Charm
# of the Bourgeoisie
## (Le Charme Discret de la Bourgeoisie)

★ ★ ★ ★ ★ ★ ★ ★ ★ ★ ★ ★ ★ ★ ★ ★ ★ ★ ★ ★ ★ ★ ★ ★ ★ ★ ★ ★ ★ ★ ★ ★ ★ ★ ★ ★ ★ ★ ★ ★ ★ ★ ★ ★ ★ ★ ★ ★ ★ ★

*Nationality*: French        *Year*: 1972

*Cast*: Fernando Rey, Delphine Seyrig, Stéphane Audran, Jean-Pierre Cassel, Paul Frankeur, Bulle Ogier

*Director*: Luis Buñuel      *Running Time*: 102 minutes

*B/W or Color*: Color      *Availability*: MEDIA HOME ENTERTAINMENT

"The picture is a joke," Luis Buñuel described his Oscar winning (Best Foreign Film) comedy-fantasy, which The National Board voted one of the year's best. And the critics went wild over this farce, which combines reality and fantasy to the point at which most observers give up trying to determine what is supposed to be real and just enjoy the bizarre goings-on. Minus most of the savagery—but none of the bite—of his other films, it concentrates on six upper-class people and their efforts to eat dinner. This simple synopsis masks a very complex story that ridicules Buñuel's favorite targets—members of the establishment—while also smiling at them benignly.

Fernando Rey, doubling as diplomat and dope smuggler, portrays the ambassador of the Latin American republic of Miranda. In France, he visits friends Jean-Pierre Cassel and Paul Frankeur, their respective wives, Stéphane Audran and Delphine Seyrig, and Seyrig's sister, Bulle Ogier. Their efforts to get together and enjoy dinner are interrupted by numerous happenings, often revolving around death. Linking the episodes are scenes of the six trudging along a country road.

Buñuel, co-scripting with Jean-Claude Carriere, originally intended the dream sequences to be real, but changed his mind when he saw their absurdity. Buñuel's rather simplistic philosophy—that this is not the best of all possible worlds—is hilariously restated. In 1962's *The Exterminating Angel*, he presents a group literally unable to leave a dinner; in this, yet another group cannot *get* to dinner. The earlier film may be the darker opposite of this charmer, which remains an appetizing feast on any level.

(*The videocassette is subtitled.*)

# Diva

★ ★ ★ ★ ★ ★ ★ ★ ★ ★ ★ ★ ★ ★ ★ ★ ★ ★ ★ ★ ★ ★ ★ ★ ★ ★ ★ ★ ★ ★ ★ ★ ★ ★ ★ ★ ★ ★ ★ ★ ★ ★ ★ ★ ★ ★ ★ ★ ★ ★ ★ ★ ★ ★

*Nationality*: French  *Year*: 1981

*Cast*: Wilhelmina Wiggins Fernandez, Frederic Andrei, Richard Bohringer, Thuy An Luu

*Director*: Jean-Jacques Beineix  *Running Time*: 123 minutes

*B/W or Color*: Color  *Availability*: MGM/UA HOME VIDEO

An imaginative film, *Diva* marked the debut of director Jean-Jacques Beineix, who also co-authored the screenplay with Jean Van Hamme. Critic Pauline Kael called it "a mixture of style and chic hanky-panky, but it's also genuinely sparkling." And David Denby (*New York* magazine) termed it "a put-on raised to the level of art."

While the plot involves thieves, murderers, and a crooked chief of police, its main theme concerns the obsession of a Parisian mail carrier, Jules (Frederic Andrei), with an American soprano, Cynthia Hawkins (Wilhelmina Wiggins Fernandez). Cynthia performs only live. She refuses to record her voice, feeling that in the transition the profound relationship she shares with her audience will be lost. In his blind devotion, Jules, however, has secretly taped the soprano and hidden the recording in his delivery bag. This move sends a recording company executive chasing after him with blackmail on his mind. And unknown to Jules, a prostitute, moments before her murder, placed in his bag a second recording, one that reveals the identity of the local drug and prostitute kingpin. So Jules is chased throughout the film by all manner of bad guys, managing to evade their clutches by hair-raising escapes aboard his trusty moped, and running into all manner of odd characters en route.

At one point, the hero evades his followers by riding his moped down the steps and onto a subway train. The *London Times* critic termed it "the single best chase sequence I have ever seen."

Hilton McConnico's art direction and Philippe Rousselot's cinematography garnered praise, and *Diva* won the French film award for Best First Film.

(Diva *is available on a subtitled videocassette.*)

# Divorce—Italian Style
## (Divorzio all'Italiana)

\* \* \* \* \* \* \* \* \* \* \* \* \* \* \* \* \* \* \* \* \* \* \* \* \* \* \* \* \* \* \* \* \* \* \* \* \* \* \* \* \* \* \* \* \* \* \* \* \* \*

Nationality: Italian                 Year: 1961 (U.S. release: 1962)
Cast: Marcello Mastroianni, Daniela Rocca, Stefania Sandrelli, Leopoldo Trieste
Director: Pietro Germi             Running Time: 104 minutes (108 minutes in Italy)
B/W or Color: B/W                 Availability: TV only

In this beautifully realized black comedy, Marcello Mastroianni is a man with a problem, namely a wife he wants to be free of and a gorgeous blond 16-year-old cousin he's in love with.

Italy did not have a divorce law at the time the film was made, and the plot centers about this regrettable legal obstacle.

Ferdinando (Mastroianni) lusts after his young, nubile cousin Angela (Stefania Sandrelli), and the only way to possess her is to see to it that his wife dies. Ferdinando concocts a scheme based on an obscure Italian law that provides a very light sentence for a man who commits murder to defend his honor.

Ferdinando unearths a former beau to seduce his now-plump wife Rosalia (Daniela Rocca). Carmelo (Leopoldo Trieste), a timid fellow, has to be bullied into making love to his former girlfriend, but once he has summoned up his courage, his passion knows no bounds. The lovers flee the village, and a stunned Ferdinando frantically searches for them. He finds the lovers, breaking in on them as they roll about in bed. Ferdinando receives an 18-month sentence for disposing of his despised mate, and is released into the arms of his young love Angela, not noticing on his honeymoon cruise that she is seductively eyeing a handsome young sailor.

Divorce—Italian Style, a black comedy belonging to the same school of humor as the British Kind Hearts and Coronets, was one of Mastroianni's first U.S. successes. Stefania Sandrelli isn't bad to look at either, and she plays her Lolita-like role to the hilt. The black-and-white photography perfectly offsets this wild comedy.

The film won an Oscar for its screenplay, while Mastroianni and director Germi were nominated for Best Actor and Director. The National Board cited the movie among 1962's best.

Marriage, Italian Style was the 1964 follow-up to this movie, with Sophia Loren teaming up with a rascally Mastroianni.

125

# The Divorce of Lady X

★★★★★★★★★★★★★★★★★★★★★★★★★★★★★★★★★★★★★★★★★★★★★★★★★★★★★

Nationality: British                     Year: 1937
Cast: Merle Oberon, Laurence Olivier, Binnie Barnes, Ralph Richardson
Director: Tim Whelan                Running Time: 92 minutes
B/W or Color: Color                   Availability: EMBASSY HOME
                                                      VIDEO

Alexander Korda's first picture in color, *The Divorce of Lady X* is a charming bedroom farce that explores an attitude toward women that would not be tolerated in a modern film.

Forced by a dense fog to take a room at the Royal Park Hotel, barrister Everard Logan (Laurence Olivier) has his privacy invaded by Leslie Steele (Merle Oberon), who had been attending a costume ball at the hotel. Thinking she is an errant married woman, he calls her Lady X. She tricks him into sleeping on the sitting room floor, while she claims his bed, his pajamas, and even the book he'd been reading. Naturally, their initial friction leads to a mutual attraction.

The following morning, Leslie leaves (still wearing Logan's pajamas). Later, at his office, Logan is visited by Lord Mere (Ralph Richardson), who wants to divorce his wife (Binnie Barnes) because she has spent the night in a man's room at the Royal Park Hotel. Logan assumes that his Lady X is really Lady Mere, and the mistaken identity leads to a humorous battle of the sexes that is eventually resolved during a weekend at Mere Hall.

Merle Oberon and Laurence Olivier play their roles with great style and enthusiasm. They would later co-star in *Wuthering Heights,* which Olivier wrote about in his autobiography: "I had done one film with Merle Oberon and liked her reasonably well; but now . . . I was blinded with misery at being parted from Vivien, who would have been the perfect Cathy [heroine of *Wuthering Heights*]."

Ralph Richardson is superb as Lord Mere, his best moment coming when the inebriated lord climbs into bed still wearing his suit and hat—and carrying his umbrella! Binnie Barnes, who played Oberon's role in the earlier version of the movie titled *Counsel's Opinion* (1932), handles herself with her usual stylish good humor.

# Doctor in the House

* * * * * * * * * * * * * * * * * * * * * * * * * * * * * * * * * * * * * * * * * * * * * * * * * * * * * *

*Nationality*: British          *Year*: 1954
*Cast*: Dirk Bogarde, Muriel Pavlow, Kenneth More, Donald Sinden, Kay Kendall, James Robertson Justice
*Director*: Ralph Thomas          *Running Time*: 92 minutes
*B/W or Color*: B/W          *Availability*: TV only

The first in the series of *Doctor* movies, all produced by Betty Box and directed by Ralph Thomas, *Doctor in the House* examined the misadventures of medical students during their five years of training at London's prestigious hospital St. Swithin's. It was based on a novel by Richard Gordon (the pseudonym of a real-life M.D.).

Dirk Bogarde became a box-office star as Simon Sparrow. The picture, said Bogarde, "was the most important thing that had happened (up to that time) in my career." He would play the role in three sequels: *Doctor at Sea* (1955), *Doctor at Large* (1957), and *Doctor in Distress* (1963). (The 1960 film *Doctor in Love* starred Michael Craig.)

Bogarde displays just the right comic touch—whether fainting at the first operation he observes or dropping a skeleton on a bus where the passengers are engrossed in newspaper accounts of a grisly murder.

As a student repeating the courses because he'll receive his income from an inheritance only as long as he's attending medical school, Kenneth More won the British Film Academy's Award as Best Actor.

James Robertson Justice is enjoyable as Sir Lancelot Spratt, the gruff chief surgeon who secretly helps Sparrow survive his mishaps. He reprised the role in *Doctor at Large* and *Doctor in Distress*. (Though he co-starred with Bogarde in *Doctor at Sea*, he played a ship's captain.)

Muriel Pavlow as Joy, the nurse who's Simon's love interest, and Donald Sinden as Benskin, the rugby enthusiast, repeated their roles in *Doctor at Large*.

Kay Kendall, whose career ended too soon (due to cancer), is seen briefly as a wealthy woman who dates Bogarde, convinced that he's already a doctor.

Barry Evans starred in the 1968 British TV series *Doctor in the House*.

# Dr. No

★★★★★★★★★★★★★★★★★★★★★★★★★★★★★★★★★★★★★★★★★★★★★★★★★★★★★★★

*Nationality*: British

*Year*: 1962 (U.S. release: 1963)

*Cast*: Sean Connery, Ursula Andress, Joseph Wiseman, Jack Lord

*Director*: Terence Young

*Running Time*: 111 minutes

*B/W or Color*: Color

*Availability*: CBS/FOX HOME VIDEO

Although Sean Connery is the actor most readily identified with author Ian Fleming's popular secret agent James Bond, he was not the first to portray 007. Barry Nelson played Bond live on CBS television in 1954. However, producers Broccoli and Saltzman, impressed with Scottish actor Connery in his film roles in *On the Fiddle* and *Darby O'Gill and the Little People,* signed him, at a salary of $30,000, over stiff competition from actors Patrick McGoohan, Richard Johnson, and Richard Burton (whom the author wanted).

Bond's first major film adversary is the wily Dr. No (Joseph Wiseman), a Fu Manchu-type character who, working for SPECTRE, the international crime ring, is sabotaging NASA space launches from his underwater fortress in Jamaica. Ian Fleming's choice to play Dr. No was his friend Noel Coward, whose cabled reply to the suggestion read: "No, no, no, no!" Ursula Andress is the sexy shell collector, Honey Wilder, and Jack Lord appears as Bond's CIA contact, Felix Leiter.

What were to become permanent James Bond trademarks are obvious throughout this first (and last) low-budget film: Maurice Binder's opening-logo view of 007 down a gun barrel; John Barry's striking theme music from his instrumental "Bea's Knees"; Ken Adam's imaginative and ingenious art direction; sophisticated gadgetry; tongue-in-cheek humor; beautiful and bedable women, both good and bad; and the characters of 007's boss, M (Bernard Lee), and M's secretary, Moneypenny (Lois Maxwell).

In 1971 Connery declared himself tired of portraying the world's most famous double agent, and George Lazenby took over in *On Her Majesty's Secret Service.* Roger Moore followed in seven Bond films. And most recently, Welsh actor Timothy Dalton won the role over *Remington Steele*'s Pierce Brosnan when the latter could not be released from his TV commitments.

Twenty-four years after *Dr. No,* the Bond films have earned in excess of $600 million.

# Doctor Strangelove or:
# How I Learned to Stop Worrying and
# Love the Bomb

\* \* \* \* \* \* \* \* \* \* \* \* \* \* \* \* \* \* \* \* \* \* \* \* \* \* \* \* \* \* \* \* \* \* \* \* \* \* \* \* \* \* \* \* \* \* \* \* \* \* \* \* \* \*

**Nationality**: British          **Year**: 1964

**Cast**: Peter Sellers, George C. Scott, Sterling Hayden, Slim Pickens, Keenan Wynn

**Director**: Stanley Kubrick          **Running Time**: 93 minutes

**B/W or Color**: B/W          **Availability**: RCA/COLUMBIA PICTURES HOME VIDEO

Few today could imagine that *Dr. Strangelove* was originally conceived as a straight dramatic nightmare akin to Sidney Lumet's *Fail-Safe* (released the same year). But script sessions were inspiring such lunacy that Kubrick decided satire was the more appropriate way to go with the project. Terry Southern was brought in to add his absurdist touches, and Peter George's draft was abandoned.

Producer James Harris felt ambivalent about the humorous treatment of the subject and eventually directed his own version of the story, *The Bedford Incident* (also released within the year), a taut little thriller with Richard Widmark and Sidney Poitier.

Before his success in motion pictures, Kubrick played professional chess in Washington Square Park. *Strangelove* is much like a chess game structurally, moving tensely between four confined sets toward an apocalyptic conclusion, and editor Anthony Harvey (who later directed *The Lion in Winter*) admits that Kubrick left him very few moves.

*Strangelove*'s bleak vision of our future (balanced later in the decade by Kubrick's upbeat alternative, *2001*) was everywhere touched with genius. Peter Sellers is brilliant in three roles. Originally set for a fourth—the bomber pilot—he injured himself near the end of filming and was quickly replaced by Slim Pickens, whom Kubrick had earlier cast in *One-Eyed Jacks* (a film whose directorship he had relinquished to star Marlon Brando). Pickens flew to London with nary an idea of what he was involved in and was stuffed into the cockpit without having read the screenplay. "Just play it straight," advised the director, "and they'll laugh their heads off." Aided by Southern, a fellow Texan, Pickens ad-libbed much of his dialogue, and we're still laughing 20 years later, though perhaps our guffaws grow more shrill as the threat of atomic annihilation draws ever nearer . . .

# Dr. Syn

★★★★★★★★★★★★★★★★★★★★★★★★★★★★★★★★★★★★★★★★★★★★★★★★★★★★★★★

Nationality: British          Year: 1937
Cast: George Arliss, Margaret Lockwood, John Loder, Roy Emerton
Director: Roy William Neill     Running Time: 80 minutes
B/W or Color: B/W              Availability: Public Domain

George Arliss, the third actor ever to win an Academy Award (*Disraeli*), preceded Paul Muni as Hollywood's foremost interpreter of the biofilm with such portrayals as *Alexander Hamilton* (1931), *Voltaire* (1933), and *Cardinal Richelieu* (1935). *Dr. Syn* (the actor's last film, shot when he was 68), isn't in the same league with those distinguished Arliss vehicles, but it *is* an entertaining movie that has faded into undeserved obscurity in the 50 years since its release.

*Dr. Syn* probably holds the most interest for those curious to see the final screen work of this once-esteemed actor, as well as those interested in Margaret Lockwood's work prior to Hitchcock's *The Lady Vanishes*. Unfortunately, the beautiful young actress, as Arliss's unacknowledged daughter, has as little to do here as does her romantic counterpart, John Loder. Director Roy William Neill (1886–1946) was a specialist in the B-melodrama and is now best remembered for his Forties Sherlock Holmes series with Basil Rathbone.

*Dr. Syn* derives from a Russell Thorndyke novel of pirates and smugglers in late-18th-century England, where Dr. Syn, the vicar of coastal Dymchurch, is in reality a supposedly dead buccaneer named Captain Clegg. But in his current, respectable calling, this elegant old gentleman secretly carries on as a maritime Robin Hood, leading a gang of smugglers whose activities are soon curtailed by suspicious revenue officers.

Neill's direction keeps the proceedings lively and diverting, and Arliss, ever the old scene-stealer, manages to make viewers believe in the unbelievable, for this is unlikely casting, to say the least.

Peter Cushing portrayed this character in 1962's *Captain Clegg* (U.S. title: *Night Creatures*), coincidentally the same year Walt Disney produced a TV film called *Dr. Syn Alias the Scarecrow* with Patrick McGoohan.

(*Kartes offers a videotape of mediocre quality.*)

# Doctor Zhivago

\*\*\*\*\*\*\*\*\*\*\*\*\*\*\*\*\*\*\*\*\*\*\*\*\*\*\*\*\*\*\*\*\*\*\*\*\*\*\*\*\*\*\*\*\*\*\*\*\*\*\*\*\*\*\*\*\*\*\*\*\*

*Nationality*: British          *Year*: 1965
*Cast*: Omar Sharif, Julie Christie, Geraldine Chaplin, Tom Courtenay, Rod Steiger, Alec Guinness, Ralph Richardson
*Director*: David Lean          *Running Time*: 197 minutes
*B/W or Color*: Color          *Availability*: MGM/UA HOME VIDEO

One of The National Board's ten best of 1965, *Doctor Zhivago* is also one of director David Lean's best films. Based on the epic novel by Boris Pasternak, the Oscar-winning screenplay by Robert Bolt details the life and times of physician and poet Yuri Zhivago (Omar Sharif) during the tumultuous years between 1905 and 1935.

Unlike the novel, the story is told in flashback by Yuri's brother, played by Alec Guinness, to a girl (Rita Tushingham) who might be the child of Zhivago and his mistress Lara (Julie Christie).

Young Yuri, an orphan raised by an aristocratic couple (Ralph Richardson and Siobhan McKenna), marries their daughter (Geraldine Chaplin). During the war, he meets Lara, a nurse with whom he falls in love. At war's end, an unhappy Yuri returns to his wife and family, now stripped of their wealth by the Bolsheviks. He meets Lara again, but their affair is interrupted when he's kidnapped by soldiers involved in the Revolution. He later escapes and returns openly to Lara, since his family has fled to Paris. Their idyll ends when Lara is forced to leave Russia because of the activities of her estranged husband, a revolutionary (Tom Courtenay). So perilous are the times that if she remains, Zhivago might also be killed. Lara is helped in her flight by Boris Komarovsky (Rod Steiger), who years before had forced her to become his mistress.

Later, an ill Zhivago, while riding on a bus, sees a passerby whom he thinks is his beloved Lara and dies in an attempt to reach her.

Julie Christie was chosen Best Actress by The National Board for this picture and for *Darling* (which won her an Oscar). Of its ten Academy Award nominations, there were five wins: Score, Costumes, Cinematography, Art Direction, and Screenplay. The only performance nominated was Courtenay's as Best Supporting Actor. The haunting score, "Lara's Theme" ("Somewhere My Love"), became as popular as this romantic and epic film.

# Doña Flor and Her Two Husbands
## (Doña Flor e Seus Dos Maridos)

★★★★★★★★★★★★★★★★★★★★★★★★★★★★★★★★★★★★★★★★★★★★★★★★★★★★★

*Nationality*: Brazilian      *Year*: 1977

*Cast*: Sonia Braga, José Wilker, Mauro Mendonca

*Director*: Bruno Barreto      *Running Time*: 106 minutes

*B/W or Color*: Color      *Availability*: WARNER HOME VIDEO

One of the few Brazilian-made films to capture a large American audience, it is remarkable on several levels. Based on the famed erotic novel by Jorge Amado, *Doña Flor* was the most successful film to play in Brazil up to its time. Made in the old section of Bahia, it kept the 1943 setting of the novel. Director-adapter Bruno Barreto managed to be both very funny and very sexy in his vision, and did all this at the tender age of 23. Before one wonders at what sort of a childhood he must have had, consider that Barreto started writing, directing, photographing, and editing—as well as winning awards—when he was 11. Father Luiz Carlos was one of the film's producers, and Sonia Braga earned worldwide attention with her starring role.

During the 1943 carnival in Bahia, devilish José Wilker drops dead from a lifetime of dissipation. Widow Sonia Braga is inconsolable; although Wilker constantly cheated, ignored, and even abused her, he was a fantastic lover. She remembers their passion vividly. Druggist Mauro Mendonca, respected and refined, courts her, and they wed in a short time. About ten years her senior, he proves to be a true gentleman and the complete opposite of Wilker. One night, Braga is shocked to find a naked Wilker in her bed, he having returned in spirit. Since he wants nothing except to resume their lovemaking, Braga attempts to exorcise him. Finally, she settles down with both men, Wilker being visible only to her.

A model and stage actress, Braga's roles have called more for lovemaking than dramatic abilities (*Kiss of the Spider Woman* being a notable exception). While a big hit as a film, *Doña Flor* obviously doesn't translate well: a Broadway musical version (*Saravà*) and the U.S. remake *Kiss Me Goodbye* (1982) with Sally Field, James Caan, and Jeff Bridges, were not successes.

*(The cassette is dubbed in English.)*

# Don't Look Now

**★★★★★★★★★★★★★★★★★★★★★★★★★★★★★★★★★★★★★★★★★★★★★★★★★★★★★★**

*Nationality*: British                    *Year*: 1973
*Cast*: Donald Sutherland, Julie Christie, Hilary Mason, Clelia Matania, Massimo Serato
*Director*: Nicolas Roeg            *Running Time*: 110 minutes
*B/W or Color*: Color                *Availability*: PARAMOUNT
                                                  HOME VIDEO

This is a remarkably unified film, which means you may find it an overwhelming experience. Stylized performances; dank, dark, and haunted sets; bizarre editing all counterpoint the rich technique, weaving an affecting vision rare in motion pictures.

But equally important as all its virtues of unity is the filmmaker: Nicolas Roeg, gadfly of celluloid, whose sins against "film normale" caught up with him long ago. The last decade has seen him working far too seldom.

Roeg and Donald Cammell co-directed *Performance,* a violent (X-rated), often inaccessible film co-starring Edward Fox and Mick Jagger in 1970. Prior to, and during this, he had been an accomplished cinematographer (*Far From the Madding Crowd, Fahrenheit 451*). When asked what exactly his contribution to *Performance* had been, he compared his relationship with Cammell to a marriage. "A fight begins. One starts yelling, but who really started it, and how long before? I knew who told whom to do what, but I don't know who was responsible."

There's an insight into his style. *Walkabout* followed, and David Bowie in *The Man Who Fell to Earth.* Since *Don't Look Now,* there have been *Insignificance, Eureka,* and *Bad Timing*—consciously nonmainstream films all.

*Don't Look Now,* aside from being about style and form, is an expanded version of a Daphne du Maurier (*Rebecca*) supernatural story about a grieving couple whose daughter may or may not have drowned in a wintry Venice you'll hardly recognize. Symbols, psychics, visual obtuseness, all meld and challenge the viewer. It's Roeg's best work and an invitation to marvel at his esoteric manipulation of the visual medium.

# Double Agents
## (La Nuit des Espions/Night Encounter)

★ ★ ★ ★ ★ ★ ★ ★ ★ ★ ★ ★ ★ ★ ★ ★ ★ ★ ★ ★ ★ ★ ★ ★ ★ ★ ★ ★ ★ ★ ★ ★ ★ ★ ★ ★ ★ ★ ★ ★ ★ ★ ★ ★ ★ ★ ★ ★ ★ ★ ★ ★ ★

Nationality: French                         Year: 1959
Cast: Robert Hossein, Marina Vlady
Director: Robert Hossein               Running Time: 85 minutes
B/W or Color: B/W                         Availability: VIDEO YESTERYEAR

The films directed by actor Robert Hossein have played in the United States mostly in "exploitation houses" under titles like *Riff Raff* and *Nude in a White Car*. And, for a time, they all seemed to team him with his then-wife, Marina Vlady.

Both were French-born and of Russian descent, and both brought a photogenic magnetism to the screen in their 1950s prime. Eleven years her senior (they wed when she was 17 and he 28), Hossein had rugged good looks bordering on the villainous; Vlady's film presence centered on a striking face with sensuous, feline eyes. And in those days (before Ferreri's *The Conjugal Bed* and Godard's *Two or Three Things I Know About Her*) she was a slim blonde, reminiscent of Veronica Lake. Together, they realized an unusual love affair with the camera.

Among the more interesting Hossein-Vlady vehicles was this 1959 melodrama, a claustrophobic yarn set almost entirely during the course of one night, within the confines of a cabin on the Normandy coast, where a 1941 rendezvous has been arranged between two Germans, a female agent and the officer to whom she's carrying secret documents. But the story opens with deliberate ambiguity, and the audience soon becomes a pawn in the cat-and-mouse game in which these characters may, or may not, be what they seem. Is she really an *English* spy? Or could *he* be a British spy masquerading as a German officer? During the night, this attractive pair progress beyond their wary opening encounter to an impassioned romance (perhaps somewhat less passionate in the 80-minute U.S. print), only to return to positions of distrust in its aftermath. In the interests of suspense, the movie's denouement won't be revealed here.

(*Video Yesteryear offers this movie in an excellent print, dubbed into suitably British-accented English.*)

# Dreamchild

★★★★★★★★★★★★★★★★★★★★★★★★★★★★★★★★★★★★★★★★★★★★★★★★★★★★★★★★★

*Nationality*: British        *Year*: 1985
*Cast*: Coral Browne, Ian Holm, Peter Gallagher, Amelia Shankley
*Director*: Gavin Millar        *Running Time*: 94 minutes
*B/W or Color*: Color        *Availability*: HBO/CANNON
                                            VIDEO

With a wistful, romantic air, and liberally intermixing fact and fantasy, Gavin Millar's film concerns the "real" Alice, Alice Liddell Hargreaves, an aging woman who as a child inspired Lewis Carroll—Dr. Charles Dodgson—to write *Alice's Adventures in Wonderland*.

In New York to speak at Columbia on the occasion of a Carroll centennial, Mrs. Hargreaves (Coral Browne) unwillingly dredges up memories of her special relationship with Dodgson (Ian Holm), and at first you may suspect Alice has suppressed shame over improprieties common to man-girl love. But Millar has a genteel sensibility: it's more likely guilt she feels for having acted cruelly indifferent in the face of a love she was too immature to appreciate. And having carried into adulthood the spoiled, willful side of her childhood, she's a curmudgeonly presence to a teenage traveling companion who is discovering her first love.

Millar reveals her past through the young Alice (Amelia Shankley), who seems always aware of a shared secret. In the end, she is comforted to discover Dodgson's to be as pure and gracious a love as ever she knew, and she clings to—even replays in her mind—the one moment she was sufficiently grateful. Both Alices give remarkable performances, but Browne's stands out: unafraid to show the disoriented, often dislikable side of aging, Browne does not rely on the tics and theatrical mannerisms that often replace *acting* in performers of her age. As the sweet, stuttering Dodgson, Holm, too, is a heartbreaker, delivering perhaps the most underappreciated work of his cinematic career, expressing the frustrated elan of unrequitable affection with a mere drop of his hand.

*Dreamchild* was named by The National Board as one of the ten best films of the year. Cinematographer Billy Williams finally proves worthy of his considerable reputation. The film looks great, even on cassette.

# The Dresser

*******************************************************

Nationality: British        Year: 1983

Cast: Albert Finney, Tom Courtenay, Edward Fox, Zena Walker, Eileen Atkins, Michael Gough

Director: Peter Yates        Running Time: 119 minutes

B/W or Color: Color        Availability: RCA/COLUMBIA PICTURES HOME VIDEO

One of The National Board's ten best for 1983, *The Dresser* is based on Ronald Harwood's play about the relationship between an aging actor, whose survival depends upon constant pampering, and his dresser, who lives vicariously through the star's performances.

In wartime England, "Sir" (Albert Finney) leads his less-than-fine Shakespearean repertory troupe through the hinterlands, playing as many as four towns a week. He's having problems with his memory, often forgetting where he is and what play he's about to perform. At one point, he starts to apply Othello's blackface on an evening when he's to appear as King Lear. He must constantly rely on Norman (Tom Courtenay), his prissy dresser, to bolster his ego and attend to his every need. Norman, in turn, thinks that Sir looks on him as a friend, only to learn to his despair and outrage that, to the actor, he's merely a servant.

Both Finney and Courtenay (who created his role on stage) received Oscar nominations as Best Actor but lost to Robert Duvall (*Tender Mercies*). Courtenay and Duvall tied for the Golden Globe as Best Actor. Among its other Academy Award nominations were Best Picture and Best Director (Peter Yates).

Ronald Harwood is said to have based his story on his career as a dresser for English actor Sir Donald Wolfit (1902–68), who for many years performed Shakespeare in the provinces and whose films include *Lawrence of Arabia* and *Becket*.

There are marvelous backstage scenes and wonderful actors' outbursts—such as Sir warning a fellow thespian: "If you don't keep downstage of me, I'll have you nailed to the orchestra pit!" Finney, under layers of makeup to age his features—and employing a vocal quality to match—does marvelously well—either as the forgetful old man or the bombastic star who can command a train to be held until his troupe is aboard; and Courtenay perfectly captures every nuance of his character.

*The Dresser* is a succulent slice of backstage life.

# Drums
## (The Drum)

\* \* \* \* \* \* \* \* \* \* \* \* \* \* \* \* \* \* \* \* \* \* \* \* \* \* \* \* \* \* \* \* \* \* \* \* \* \* \* \* \* \* \* \* \* \* \* \* \* \* \* \*

**Nationality**: British        **Year**: 1938

**Cast**: Sabu, Raymond Massey, Roger Livesey, Valerie Hobson

**Director**: Zoltan Korda      **Running Time**: 101 minutes

**B/W or Color**: Color        **Availability**: EMBASSY HOME
ENTERTAINMENT

Sabu became an international sensation in *Elephant Boy* (1937), which introduced him to the screen, and Alexander Korda quickly put the India-born teenager back in front of the camera. He was cast as Prince Azim in *Drums* (released in England as *The Drum*).

Since the earlier movie had been shot on location in India (sans script) and took almost a year and a half, Korda decided it would be wiser to film *Drums* closer to home, substituting the hills outside Harlech in Wales for the Indian terrain.

Zoltan Korda (co-director of *Elephant Boy*) was assigned to direct the picturesque, action-packed melodrama, and a superb cast was assembled to support Sabu. Raymond Massey plays the evil Prince Ghul, Roger Livesey is the stalwart Captain Carruthers, and Valerie Hobson appears as the officer's wife. Desmond Tester does a very nice job as the young British drummer boy who becomes Sabu's friend.

Set in the then-present-day India, *Drums* is a story of good vs. evil with Prince Ghul as usurper to the throne to which young Prince Azim is the rightful heir. Ghul plans to massacre Captain Carruthers and his regiment while they're visiting the palace, thus starting a war with the British. Luckily, the day is saved because Azim has learned the drum signals from his young drummer friend and is able to issue a warning and to summon help.

The production notes given to reviewers carefully stated that the actions of Prince Ghul did not reflect in any way "the Indian nationalistic viewpoint" but were "for his own selfish glory."

*The New York Times* critic invited viewers to "lean back and enjoy the crowding Oriental splendors and the devious Oriental politics . . . hiss Raymond Massey . . . be charmed by [Sabu]. . . ."

Many considered the color photography to be the best up to that date. *Drums* ensured Sabu's popularity and, according to the Korda studio, he began receiving over 100 fan letters a day.

# The Earrings of Madame de . . .
## (Madame de . . . )

★★★★★★★★★★★★★★★★★★★★★★★★★★★★★★★★★★★★★★★★★★★★★★★★★★★★★★

Nationality: French-Italian          Year: 1953 (U.S. release: 1954)
Cast: Charles Boyer, Danielle Darrieux, Vittorio De Sica, Lia di Lea
Director: Max Ophuls          Running Time: 102 minutes
B/W or Color: B/W          Availability: CORINTH VIDEO

The circuitous route of a pair of heart-shaped earrings is the basis for a bittersweet love story, acted with charm by an elegant cast and directed with great style by Max Ophuls.

In late-19th-century Paris, a General (Charles Boyer) presents the earrings to his wife (Danielle Darrieux), Madame de . . . (the remainder of the name is never revealed, skillfully concealed from view or, when spoken, covered by sundry noises).

Privately in need of funds. Madame de . . . sells the earrings, telling her husband that they have been lost. The worried jeweler (Jean Debucourt), fearful that he might be accused of possessing stolen property, informs the general of the transaction. Purchasing the earrings, the officer then gives them, as a parting gift, to his mistress (Lia di Lea). She, in turn, sells them to pay a gambling debt. The new owner, Baron Fabrizio Donati (Vittorio De Sica), eventually meets and falls in love with Madame de . . . and gives her the precious trinkets.

Wishing to wear them, Madame de . . . informs the general that she has found the lost items. The truth is eventually revealed, which ends the affair with an angered baron and causes the general to challenge the baron, an old friend, to a duel. On the field of honor, Madame de . . . suffers a fatal heart attack.

Nominated for an Academy Award for Best Costume Design, the film was the next-to-last for Max Ophuls, who later directed *Lola Montes* (1955) and died in 1957.

Boyer and Darrieux had memorably co-starred in *Mayerling* (1936). As the aristocratic beauty Madame de . . . , Darrieux gives one of her best-remembered performances. Boyer's handsome military man and De Sica's gallant lover complete the tragic triangle in this masterful tale of failed romance.

*(Corinth offers a cassette with English subtitles.)*

# Ecstasy

## (Extase)

★★★★★★★★★★★★★★★★★★★★★★★★★★★★★★★★★★★★★★★★★★★★★★★★★★★★

**Nationality**: Czech

**Year**: 1933 (U.S. release: 1940)

**Cast**: Hedy Kiesler (Hedy Lamarr), Aribert Mog, Jaromir Rogoz, Leopold Kramer

**Director**: Gustav Machaty

**Running Time**: Release prints range from 67 to 90 minutes.

**B/W or Color**: B/W

**Availability**: Public Domain

Because of its fairly frank sexual content, 1933's *Ecstasy* stirred up censorship storms, both in Europe and the United States, where it didn't reach the public until 1940. By then, its Austrian-born leading lady had undergone an M-G-M name-change from Hedy Kiesler to Hedy Lamarr. Shown discreetly nude in a rural swimming sequence that's followed by a bare-breasted run through the woods, 18-year-old Hedy became notorious long before she was ever seen on American screens. In this, her fifth European movie (and first leading role), she expressively runs the gamut from youthful naiveté to romantic frustration to sexual excitement and recrimination. Hedy's first husband, industrialist Fritz Mandl, found *Ecstasy* such a source of embarrassment that he made a costly but futile effort to buy up and destroy every existing print of the film.

*Ecstasy* presents Hedy as a young bride who finds her stodgy, middle-aged husband so inattentive that she soon institutes a divorce. She discovers fulfillment in the arms of a handsome young engineer she encounters in the countryside after that naked swim. But then her husband seeks her out, hoping for a reconciliation, and, upon uncovering his wife's relationship with the younger man, he commits suicide. The girl is so overcome with guilt that she leaves her lover asleep on a waiting-room bench as she either boards a train or steps in front of it (writer-director Gustav Machaty makes the ending deliberately ambiguous).

The film's lack of dialogue is covered by an intrusive musical score leaning heavily on oboes, violins, and Tchaikovsky's "None But the Lonely Heart." But *Ecstasy*'s best asset is its lyrical photography, which alternately celebrates the beauties of nature and its teenaged star.

(*Kartes offers a 67-minute, English-dubbed version in a clear print of mediocre quality.*)

# Educating Rita

\* \* \* \* \* \* \* \* \* \* \* \* \* \* \* \* \* \* \* \* \* \* \* \* \* \* \* \* \* \* \* \* \* \* \* \* \* \* \* \* \* \* \* \* \* \* \* \* \* \* \* \*

*Nationality*: British

*Year*: 1983

*Cast*: Michael Caine, Julie Walters, Malcolm Douglas, Maureen Lipman

*Director*: Lewis Gilbert

*Running Time*: 110 minutes

*B/W or Color*: Color

*Availability*: RCA/COLUMBIA PICTURES HOME VIDEO

A well-worn, time-honored Broadway and Hollywood formula that has usually worked successfully is one in which the hero-heroine, hungry for knowledge or to better his/herself, seeks out—or is sought out by—a special teacher who is able to impart that knowledge and polish. Along the way, both are enriched by the learning experience. Other films with this theme include *Pygmalion, The Corn is Green,* and *To Sir with Love.* In the witty and engaging *Educating Rita,* the familiar formula works beautifully.

Michael Caine, in one of his best roles (for which he won an Academy Award nomination), plays the cynical Dr. Frank Bryant, a boozing English professor who resents having to teach "while the pubs are open." His marriage has failed, and his current relationship with his live-in girl-friend, Julia (Jeananne Crowley), isn't going too well. Into the disillusioned professor's study bursts—literally—a lively 26-year-old hairdresser named Rita (her new name in honor of the author of her favorite trashy novel). The brash, down-to-earth Rita is married to a complacent electrician (Malcolm Douglas), who wants his wife to have a baby but not an education. Bemused by the wisecracking, street-smart housewife, Frank encourages Rita to become an intellectual free spirit. Their shared hours form the basis of a tender and unique friendship. As Rita prepares for her exams, both teacher and student learn a great deal about themselves.

It would have been easy for director Gilbert and screenwriter Willy Russell (who based the film on his successful London play, which had only two characters) to have kept the story within its narrow theatrical confines or to have included the obvious: a romantic relationship between the leading characters. Rita's romantic focus, however, remains on Shakespeare and Chekhov rather than on her erudite mentor. By opening up the play cinematically, they also manage to infuse it with even more charm, humor, and insight.

In her first screen appearance, Julie Walters's luminescent performance as Rita (re-creating her London Stage role) earned her an Academy Award nomination. More credit to Gilbert and Russell for considering no other actress for the role. The picture also won second place on The National Board of Review's ten best list.

# 8½
## (Otto e Mezzo)

★★★★★★★★★★★★★★★★★★★★★★★★★★★★★★★★★★★★★★★★★★★★★★★★★★

**Nationality**: Italian          **Year**: 1963

**Cast**: Marcello Mastroianni, Anouk Aimée, Claudia Cardinale, Sandra Milo, Guido Alberti

**Director**: Federico Fellini          **Running Time**: 135 minutes (148 minutes in Italy)

**B/W or Color**: B/W          **Availability**: VESTRON VIDEO

Fellini's lifelong search for meaning leads him finally to the mirror, where in this masterwork of self-reflective cinema, he faces his own inability to love. Yet, despite the parallel lines that run through the film, Fellini has said this motion picture contains the least about his life (and here, like many great artists, he's not to be trusted).

Though he's committed to finishing the project, famous filmmaker Guido Anselmi (Marcello Mastroianni) is stuck on a sci-fi movie "where everything happens"—about survivors of nuclear holocaust escaping earth—and the monstrous, empty set suggests both his creative sterility and existential crisis. "There is not even a film," Guido says. "There's nothing. Nothing at all." What's on Guido's mind? "Asa Nisi Masa"—anima, in Fellini's pig-Latin—says the mind reader Maurice (Jan Dallas). Guido escapes his professional anxiety by taking faddish cures and cheating on his pretty but doubtful wife, Luisa (Anouk Aimée), with Carla (Sandra Milo), a passing fancy of baroque tastelessness. But in the afterglow of adultery comes an awakening of a sense of family—which conjures up his dead parents and a bittersweet desire for their motivation, and yearning for his youth. Other spirits appear, most dramatically, his ideal woman, Claudia (Claudia Cardinale), and, with scrupulous honesty, also the fat fishmonger, La Saraghina (Edra Gale), to whom Guido owes his sexual debut. In the end, he does not understand the exact influence the people in his life have had—he chooses only to love them, regardless.

A rich, open (and profoundly funny) text by one of cinema's great trail blazers, Fellini shows not—in the words of one of the actors—"the deformed footprint of a cripple," but the sure step of a master.

(*Vestron's videocassette is English-dubbed.*)

# El Super

* * * * * * * * * * * * * * * * * * * * * * * * * * * * * * * * * * * * * * * * * * * * * * * * * * * *

*Nationality*: Cuban-American     *Year*: 1979
*Cast*: Raymundo Hidalgo-Gato, Zully Montero, Reynaldo Medina
*Director*: Leon Ichaso and Orlando *Running Time*: 90 minutes
Jimenez-Leal
*B/W or Color*: Color     *Availability*: TV only

E *l Super* is a remarkable example of the independent, New Cuban Cinema—in exile. Made on a shoestring budget, the film, directed by Leon Ichaso and Orlando Jimenez-Leal (who also did the fine cinematography), is smooth, moves well, and has excellent production values.

In Spanish, *El Super* is a slice-of-life film made in New York about a Cuban émigré who has become the superintendent of an Upper West Side tenement. It is based on an award-winning play by Ivan Acosta that was originally produced at New York's Cuban Cultural Center in 1977. Raymundo Hidalgo-Gato, from the stage production, gives a thoughtful, complex, and brilliantly comic performance as the unhappy, bedraggled, and frustrated *el super*, and is supported by a fine cast of Hispanic actors. Especially interesting is the movie's depiction of New York as a "city of foreigners," in which displaced, isolated minorities wait for word from home, hope for reunion with their families, and yet manage somehow to survive the brutal conditions of ghetto existence.

In *El Super*'s treatment of the Cuban exodus after the revolution and the continuing courage of Cubans in the face of adversity some ten years later, the film sparkles with warmth, wit, and extraordinary humanity.

In its review, *The Hollywood Reporter* said, "*El Super* deserves industry focus, not only because it's an able accomplishment done with energy and enthusiasm, but because its . . . filmmakers have so handsomely accomplished what few of their peers have managed in the past: how to rap home a basically serious human theme in a thoroughly watchable, entertaining manner." *El Super* offers a rare and unique glimpse of Hispanic family life in America.

142

# Elephant Boy

*★ ★ ★ ★ ★ ★ ★ ★ ★ ★ ★ ★ ★ ★ ★ ★ ★ ★ ★ ★ ★ ★ ★ ★ ★ ★ ★ ★ ★ ★ ★ ★ ★ ★ ★ ★ ★ ★ ★ ★ ★ ★ ★ ★ ★ ★ ★ ★ ★ ★*

*Nationality*: British          *Year*: 1937

*Cast*: Sabu, W. E. Holloway, Walter Hudd, Allan Jeayes

*Director*: Robert Flaherty and Zol-  *Running Time*: 80 minutes
tan Korda

*B/W or Color*: B/W          *Availability*: EMBASSY HOME
                              ENTERTAINMENT

One of The National Board's best films for 1937, *Elephant Boy* is based on Rudyard Kipling's *Toomai of the Elephants,* the story of a youngster descended from four generations of mahouts (the Indian riders and keepers of elephants).

The father of Toomai (Sabu) is killed, and the family elephant, Kala Nag, is given to another driver, despite the boy's protests. The new mahout—a mean man—attempts to beat the elephant—leading to some broken bones for the driver and near execution for the animal. One night, Toomai succeeds in stealing Kala Nag, and the pair happily escapes to the jungle. The accidental discovery of a herd of wild elephants the British have been tracking results in Toomai becoming a full-fledged mahout.

The story behind the making of *Elephant Boy* is almost as interesting as the film itself. In February 1935, Alexander Korda sent famed documentary director Robert Flaherty to India. By July 1936, Flaherty had shot over 55 hours of film—all of it background for a nonexistent story. (He often worked in this manner, shaping a finished product in the editing room.) Taking control, Korda assigned John Collier to construct a simple story that could utilize the footage and had his brother, Zoltan Korda, direct the screenplay in England. The finished product was half-Flaherty, half-Korda—and, ironically, received the award for best direction at the 1937 Venice Film Festival.

Sabu Dastagir was discovered by Flaherty in Mysore, India, where he was born in 1924. Following his screen debut in *Elephant Boy,* he made three other Korda films: *Drums, The Thief of Bagdad,* and *Jungle Book.* In 1944, he became a U.S. citizen and enlisted in the Air Force. Married and the father of two, he died of a heart attack, at 39, in 1963. His last film was *A Tiger Walks* (1964). *The New York Times* review of *Elephant Boy* noted that Sabu was "a sunny-faced, manly little youngster, whose naturalness . . . should bring blushes to the faces of the precocious wonder children of Hollywood."

# The Elephant Man

\* \* \* \* \* \* \* \* \* \* \* \* \* \* \* \* \* \* \* \* \* \* \* \* \* \* \* \* \* \* \* \* \* \* \* \* \* \* \* \* \* \* \* \* \* \* \* \* \* \* \* \* \*

**Nationality**: British  **Year**: 1980

**Cast**: Anthony Hopkins, John Hurt, Anne Bancroft, John Gielgud, Wendy Hiller, Freddie Jones

**Director**: David Lynch  **Running Time**: 123 minutes

**B/W or Color**: B/W  **Availability**: PARAMOUNT HOME VIDEO

Selected as one of The National Board's ten best for 1980, *The Elephant Man* remains a tribute to the dignity of the human spirit. Based on the true story of John Merrick, a grossly deformed man with a misshapen, enlarged head, this was *not* an adaption of Bernard Pomerance's 1979 Broadway play, in which the title character wears no makeup.

In turn-of-the-century England, a caring physician, Sir Frederick Treves (Anthony Hopkins), rescues Merrick (John Hurt) from a freak show and brings him to a hospital, where the chairman (John Gielgud) protests his presence but the head matron (Wendy Hiller) becomes protective of him.

Merrick becomes a celebrity and is befriended by actress Mrs. Kendal (Anne Bancroft), who dedicates the performance of a Christmas pantomime to him, as he sits in the royal box. After receiving a standing ovation from the audience, he dies later that night.

Hurt, in a skillfully crafted "head mask," is not seen on-camera until midway through the film. He is perhaps most touching when he tells the doctor's wife about his mother: "She had the face of an angel. I must have been a great disappointment to her. I tried so hard to be good . . ."

Eight Oscar nominations, including Best Picture, Actor (Hurt), Director (David Lynch), and Screenplay, resulted in no wins.

Cinematographer Freddie Francis (who has a following for having directed many of the Hammer Studios' horror films) received praise for his black-and-white photography.

David Lynch's previous film had been *Eraserhead*, the story of a mutant child, which attracted a cult audience. He has since directed *Dune* and *Blue Velvet*.

The play, which starred Kevin Conway, Philip Anglim, and Carole Shelley (who won a Tony Award as Best Actress), was later performed on television with the same actors and Penny Fuller as Mrs. Kendal.

# Elvira Madigan

★★★★★★★★★★★★★★★★★★★★★★★★★★★★★★★★★★★★★★★★★★★★★★★★★★★★★

**Nationality**: Swedish  **Year**: 1967

**Cast**: Pia Degermark, Thommy Berggren, Lennart Malmen, Nina Widerberg, Cleo Jensen

**Director**: Bo Widerberg  **Running Time**: 89 minutes

**B/W or Color**: Color  **Availability**: THORN/EMI-HBO VIDEO

They could not live without each other, the lovely tightrope walker (Pia Degermark) and the handsome soldier (Thommy Berggren). She quits her job with the circus. He leaves his wife and children and becomes a deserter from the Swedish army. Around the turn of the century, this was tantamount to social suicide. Their idyll, of vagabond wanderings, lovemaking, and country picnics, is beautifully photographed by Jorgen Persson—to the sublime accompaniment of Mozart's Twenty-first Piano Concerto.

Lady Luck, at first, smiles on them. Missing a button, the lieutenant fortuitously picks just the right one off a scarecrow. They are marvelously free from the realities of modern travel. As newspaper accounts of their disappearance reach the inn where they are staying, an employee lends them a horse to escape the police. Though both have quit their jobs, and a container of cream strains their budget, they walk out unopposed, apparently without paying the bill. While laundry is well beyond their means, Elvira catches fish and runs through fields, bustled, corsetted, and ever-immaculate in white. You or I would have picked a darker color. In this ideal world, sylvan couplings take place, causing not so much as a grass stain.

Based on a true story, the escape of this handsome pair requires a suspension of belief. It is, however, visually breathtaking and well worth the price of admission. A gorgeous tour de force: Elvira's tightrope dance on a clothesline, which might be a symbol of their precarious voyage. Love conquers all, for a while, at least. Then Elvira slips money to her lover so he won't lose face with an old army buddy, and their feet finally hit the ground on which most of us walk. Named the Best Foreign Film of the year by The National Board.

*(The cassette is in Swedish with English subtitles.)*

# The Emigrants
## (Utvandrarna)/The New Land (Nybyggarna)

★★★★★★★★★★★★★★★★★★★★★★★★★★★★★★★★★★★★★★★★★★★★★★★★★★★★★

**Nationality**: Swedish

**Year**: 1971 (U.S. release: 1972)/ 1972 (U.S. release: 1973)

**Cast**: Max von Sydow, Liv Ullmann, Eddie Axberg, Svenolof Bern, Aina Alfredsson

**Director**: Jan Troell

**Running Time**: 151 minutes (190 minutes in Sweden)/161 minutes (205 minutes in Sweden)

**B/W or Color**: Color/Color

**Availability**: TV only/TV only

This is a two-part saga of a band of hardworking Swedish peasant farmers who left their country during the 1850s for America. The unyielding Swedish soil and changeable weather produced poor crops in spite of untiring efforts, and the ancient caste system relegated the peasants to their traditional roles without hope for a better existence. Furthermore, only the oldest son was permitted to work his father's land. The others had to fend for themselves.

The first film properly deals with a small group who left home together for individual reasons. Yet they all shared the anticipation of fertile land and the freedom of the American experience.

The journey, however, was not an easy one. The ten-week Atlantic crossing in tight, filthy quarters, where they were assaulted by seasickness, lice, and scurvy, appeared to be almost "God's test" to those who managed to survive. The rest of the journey to Minnesota by steamer, train, and on foot was equally arduous, although it was eventually rewarded by the rich, green fields of the new country. Here, in a significant moment, the grateful leader finally carves his work on a tree in what is to be *his* land.

*The Emigrants* is classic in the power of its concept, in the implication of the meaning of America for so many European settlers. Cinematically, it moves slowly in appreciation of its great theme and absorbs us like a rich novel, as we keep pace with the settlers and accompany them on their trek.

Aesthetically, the film is magnificent. The camera reflects the mood of the film, from the drab browns of the old country to the bright green of the Minnesota farm land.

Director Jan Troell co-authored the screenplay, based on the four novels of Vilhelm Moberg. His cast, especially Max von Sydow and Liv Ullmann, was remarkably right. Liv Ullmann was chosen Best Actress of 1972 (for *The Emigrants*) by the New York Film Critics and Best Actress of 1973 (for *The New Land*) by The National Board of Review, which selected both pictures among its best of their years.

# The Entertainer

★ ★ ★ ★ ★ ★ ★ ★ ★ ★ ★ ★ ★ ★ ★ ★ ★ ★ ★ ★ ★ ★ ★ ★ ★ ★ ★ ★ ★ ★ ★ ★ ★ ★ ★ ★ ★ ★ ★ ★ ★ ★ ★ ★ ★ ★ ★ ★ ★ ★ ★ ★ ★ ★ ★ ★ ★ ★

*Nationality*: British                *Year*: 1960

*Cast*: Laurence Olivier, Brenda de Banzie, Joan Plowright, Roger Livesey, Alan Bates

*Director*: Tony Richardson        *Running Time*: 97 minutes

*B/W or Color*: B/W               *Availability*: TV only

Taking the role of Archie Rice, the seedy, over-the-hill song-and-dance man of John Osborne's 1957 play *The Entertainer*, marked a radical acting departure for Sir Laurence Olivier, Britain's most distinguished interpreter of Shakespeare, Ibsen, Sheridan and their ilk. In Osborne's words: "It was a remarkable thing to do. Quite remarkable at the time. The part of Archie Rice seemed to go against everything he stood for." And Olivier himself echoed those thoughts, admitting, "I was boring the public, I was boring myself. I was predictable as hell, and it was a wonderful, wonderful part."

*The Entertainer* was even better on screen, as directed to perfection by Tony Richardson in a 1960 film that added dimensions to Olivier's role and opened up a small-scale play to the location possibilities of a typically English seaside town. A fine cast features Brenda de Banzie as Archie's pathetic but irritating wife and Joan Plowright (the future Lady Olivier) as his daughter. Roger Livesey is moving as the elderly former-vaudevillian father Archie can only exploit, and, in promising movie debuts, Alan Bates and Albert Finney have their moments as Archie's sons. But it's Olivier's vehicle all the way, and it's a profound tribute to the actor's art that he can make so fascinating a character out of a man who's little more than an insufferable bore, an unrepentant heel, and a manipulative charlatan whose songs are as awful as his charm is transparent. And underscoring it all is John Addison's cheap, tinkly music that provides so fitting a background for a brilliant classical artist in his greatest contemporary role.

# Entertaining Mr. Sloane

★ ★ ★ ★ ★ ★ ★ ★ ★ ★ ★ ★ ★ ★ ★ ★ ★ ★ ★ ★ ★ ★ ★ ★ ★ ★ ★ ★ ★ ★ ★ ★ ★ ★ ★ ★ ★ ★ ★ ★ ★ ★ ★ ★ ★ ★ ★ ★ ★

Nationality: British                    Year: 1970
Cast: Beryl Reid, Harry Andrews, Peter McEnery, Alan Webb
Director: Douglas Hickox            Running Time: 94 minutes
B/W or Color: Color                    Availability: THORN/EMI-HBO
                                                      VIDEO

In the Sixties, playwright Joe Orton offended critics and audiences alike
with his wildly outrageous comedies *Loot, What the Butler Saw,* and
*Entertaining Mr. Sloane*—which won awards in London but failed on
Broadway.

Grotesque, off-the-wall humor is the essence of *Entertaining Mr. Sloane.*
The movie opens in a cemetery, where middle-aged Kath (Beryl Reid),
vulgarly attired in a see-through mini-dress, watches a funeral service
while crunching on a Popsicle. When she spies young, blond Sloane (Peter McEnery) sunbathing half-naked on a tombstone, she invites him to
her adjacent home, where he joins an odd menagerie. Aside from the
aggressive Kath, there's her upstanding, closet-gay brother Ed (Harry Andrews) and their crotchety old father Dadda (Alan Webb), who recognizes Sloane as a fugitive killer.

Kath seduces Sloane and becomes pregnant, Ed grows jealous, and Dadda
plans vengeance—while Sloane cannily plays them all off against one another. Tired of the old man's accusations, the amoral youth beats Dadda
to death. And although Kath and Ed feel no loss, they use the incident
to compromise Sloane, guaranteeing their secrecy in exchange for his eternal
fidelity. The film closes with a most unusual private ceremony—as Sloane
successively marries them both!

Faced with the bald outrageousness of this repellently baroque farce,
Douglas Hickox directs with commendable restraint. But it's the excellent cast that puts the icing on this cake. Reid makes Kath's rapacious,
matter-of-fact amorality at once amusing and even touching, and Andrews plays against type with taste and subtlety. In perhaps the film's
most challenging role, Peter McEnery may lack Sloane's underlying evil,
but he nevertheless approximates this conscienceless charmer skillfully.

*Entertaining Mr. Sloane* cannot help but shock, offend, and outrage
less sophisticated audiences. But for others, it remains a unique and hilarious delight.

# Entre Nous
## (Coup de Foudre)

\*\*\*\*\*\*\*\*\*\*\*\*\*\*\*\*\*\*\*\*\*\*\*\*\*\*\*\*\*\*\*\*\*\*\*\*\*\*\*\*\*\*\*\*\*\*\*\*\*\*

*Nationality*: French                    *Year*: 1983
*Cast*: Isabelle Huppert, Miou-Miou, Guy Marchand, Jean-Pierre Bacri
*Director*: Diane Kurys          *Running Time*: 111 minutes
*B/W or Color*: Color            *Availability*: MGM/UA HOME
                                 VIDEO

In *Peppermint Soda* (1977), writer-director Diane Kurys explored the childhood of herself and her sister. In *Entre Nous,* Kurys goes farther back to depict the hardships of her parents' lives during World War II and the years immediately following.

Lena (Isabelle Huppert), a Russian-Jewish refugee in France, marries Michel (Guy Marchand), a French Legionnaire, in order to avoid deportation to a concentration camp. She and her new husband cross the Alps on foot to wait out the Occupation in comparative safety.

Ten years later, they're parents of two daughters and living in Lyons, where Michel operates a garage. At a school fete, Lena meets an artist named Madeleine (Miou-Miou), who's married to a romantic and chronically out-of-work actor, Costa (Jean-Pierre Bacri), and has a son. The two women are immediately attracted to each other, and soon the two couples are constantly together.

Michel and Costa have little in common, but Lena and Madeleine become inseparable. Under Madeleine's influence, Lena is gradually transformed from a staid housewife and mother into a rather smart, stylish woman, who begins to express opinions and demands more freedom for herself. She and Madeleine take trips to Paris together and eventually open their own boutique, for which a reluctant and very jealous Michel puts up the money.

The performances are meticulous. In its coverage of the twenty-first New York Film Festival, *Films in Review* noted that "Isabelle Huppert runs off with the best acting."

*Entre Nous* was nominated for an Academy Award as Best Foreign Film.

This is no tale of lesbianism, but a feminist statement sensitively written and directed by Diane Kurys. It's her personal feelings beautifully expressed. This is how it was, she says, this is how my mother and her friend changed each other's lives.

(*The videocassette is subtitled.*)

# The Europeans

*************************************************************

Nationality: British                    Year: 1979
Cast: Lee Remick, Robin Ellis, Wesley Addy, Tim Choate, Lisa Eichhorn
Director: James Ivory                   Running Time: 90 minutes
B/W or Color: Color                     Availability: VESTRON VIDEO

The natural autumnal splendor of New England provides a colorfully contrasting setting for the puritanical austerity of its American characters in this charming Merchant-Ivory production of *The Europeans*, Henry James's 1878 romantic study in contrasting cultures. Like most of the carefully turned out films of this distinguished team, production values are truly excellent, with Larry Pizer's photography of the Massachusetts settings a prime asset, as are Judy Moorcraft's costumes and the art direction of Jeremiah Rusconi. But *The Europeans* isn't just a visual feast; producer Merchant and director Ivory had the skilled adaptation of their frequent collaborator Ruth Prawer Jhabvala, whose team efforts produced so charming a mood piece that The National Board named it one of the year's ten best films.

Set in the environs of 1850s Boston, the story centers on a wealthy but puritanical New England family whose lives are altered by the unexpected arrival of their more worldly—but less solvent—European cousins. Eugenia (Lee Remick) is married to a German prince, but that union is threatened with dissolution, and so quiet, wily desperation has sent her to the colonies, in search of a husband and a fortune. Her carefree brother Felix (Tim Woodward) is equally agreeable to finding a rich wife, and together they proceed to charm their way into the Wentworth household, despite the sternly disapproving family patriarch (Wesley Addy).

The pleasures of *The Europeans* are manifold, from the overall joy of witnessing innocent Americans best the Continental sophisticates to the small wonders of manners and mores so meticulously re-created. From dappled sunlight to rural birdsong, the sights and sounds of *The Europeans* are as absolutely breathtaking as they are mesmerizing.

# Evergreen

\* \* \* \* \* \* \* \* \* \* \* \* \* \* \* \* \* \* \* \* \* \* \* \* \* \* \* \* \* \* \* \* \* \* \* \* \* \* \* \* \* \* \* \* \* \* \* \* \* \* \* \* \* \*

Nationality: British  Year: 1934 (U.S. release: 1935)
Cast: Jessie Matthews, Sonnie Hale, Betty Balfour, Barry Mackay
Director: Victor Saville  Running Time: 90 minutes
B/W or Color: B/W  Availability: Public Domain

B illed as "The Dancing Divinity," graceful and long-limbed Jessie Matthews was one of England's most enchanting musical stars, enjoying her greatest motion picture fame in the Thirties, when she starred in *The Good Companions* and *Evergreen*. The latter was based on a Rodgers and Hart show, a stage hit for her in 1930. Actor-playwright Emlyn Williams helped adapt Benn W. Levy's *Ever Green*, a theater piece changed for its screen version, with new production numbers and four Harry Woods songs added. Only three songs remained from the original Rodgers and Hart score. Michael Balcon, the film's producer, attempted to sign the fast-rising American dancing star Fred Astaire as co-star, but a contract with RKO prevented Astaire from accepting. Surprisingly, Jessie Matthews filmed *Evergreen* on the edge of a nervous breakdown. In her autobiography, *Over My Shoulder,* she credits director Victor Saville with helping her survive the experience.

*Evergreen* affords Matthews a dual role, as both mother and daughter. In the Edwardian music halls of 1909, she's a headliner named Harriet Green, skillful enough to put over a coy production number like "Daddy Wouldn't Buy Me a Bow-Wow." London's favorite is then blackmailed into early retirement, and her daughter (who resembles her Mum) later becomes a star—by pretending to be an "ageless" Harriet Green attempting a comeback. The finale uncovers her masquerade, when she performs a strip-dance to the foot-tapping "Over My Shoulder," which Harry Woods wrote especially for Matthews. She's equally charming delivering the Rodgers and Hart song "Dancing on the Ceiling" and Wood's "When You've Got a Little Springtime in Your Heart."

*Evergreen* was a hit in 1934 Britain. Its U.S. success, the following year, brought Matthews a Hollywood offer from MGM, which she couldn't accept; like Fred Astaire, her home studio wouldn't release her, considering her too valuable a property at home.

151

# Fahrenheit 451

★★★★★★★★★★★★★★★★★★★★★★★★★★★★★★★★★★★★★★★★★★★★★★★★★★★★★

Nationality: British          Year: 1966
Cast: Julie Christie, Oskar Werner, Cyril Cusack, Anton Diffring
Director: François Truffaut          Running Time: 112 minutes
B/W or Color: Color          Availability: MCA HOME VIDEO

Director François Truffaut's only film in English, *Fahrenheit 451* (the title refers to the temperature at which paper burns) is set in a futuristic society where minds are controlled and all reading material is burned. An adaptation of Ray Bradbury's 1953 classic sci-fi novel, it depicts one man's struggle for individual freedom.

Oskar Werner, who had earlier starred in Truffaut's *Jules and Jim* (1961), plays Montag, a fireman who does not extinguish flames, but instead sets books afire and is an expert at ferreting out concealed works and destroying them. His captain (Cyril Cusack) informs him that if such superior work continues, he's in line for promotion.

In a dual role, Julie Christie (who had just won an Oscar for *Darling*) plays the women in Montag's life: his wife, Linda, who spends her days tranquilized in front of a wall-screen television, and Clarisse, who wants to know if Montag ever reads the books he burns. Her question prompts the fireman to steal a copy of *David Copperfield,* and he soon becomes a secret reader who hoards literature—much to his wife's alarm.

After Linda reports him, he turns the flames on the captain and becomes a fugitive. Clarisse takes him to a community of forest dwellers who commit books to memory, and Montag sets about memorizing a novel by Edgar Allan Poe.

Truffaut, who also co-authored the screenplay, was uncomfortable working in English. A Hitchcock devotee, he acknowledged the master's influence on *Fahrenheit 451,* and assigned Bernard Herrmann, who often worked with Hitchcock, to compose the film's score. (As an inside joke, one of the publications being burned in one scene is a copy of *Cahiers du Cinema,* the publication for which Truffaut had been a film critic.)

Future director Nicolas Roeg received considerable praise for his cinematography.

# The Fallen Idol

**★ ★ ★ ★ ★ ★ ★ ★ ★ ★ ★ ★ ★ ★ ★ ★ ★ ★ ★ ★ ★ ★ ★ ★ ★ ★ ★ ★ ★ ★ ★ ★ ★ ★ ★ ★ ★ ★ ★ ★ ★ ★ ★ ★ ★ ★ ★ ★ ★ ★ ★ ★ ★ ★**

*Nationality*: British　　　　　　　*Year*: 1948

*Cast*: Ralph Richardson, Michèle Morgan, Bobby Henrey, Sonia Dresdel, Jack Hawkins, Denis O'Dea

*Director*: Carol Reed　　　　　　*Running Time*: 94 minutes

B/W *or* COLOR: B/W　　　　　　*Availability*: Public Domain

The Fallen Idol was showered with awards: Best Picture of the Year (1948), British Film Academy; Carol Reed, Best Director, New York Film Critics; Best Screenplay for Graham Greene (from his short story), Venice Film Festival; and Best Actor for Ralph Richardson, The National Board of Review. But with all the acclaim for the many talents involved, it was Carol Reed's picture.

Although he had great success at the outbreak of World War II with *The Stars Look Down* (1939) and the internationally popular thriller *Night Train to Munich* (known in the United States as *Night Train*), in 1940, it was in the postwar years that Reed came resoundingly into his own with a glorious triple play: *Odd Man Out* (1947), *The Fallen Idol* (1948), and *The Third Man* (1949). Classics all.

The entire focus of *The Fallen Idol* is on the astonishing child actor Bobby Henrey, who was guided by Reed into one of the great performances by a young actor on screen. Playing the shy son of a foreign ambassador, left alone in the giant embassy with the butler (Richardson) and his shrewdish wife (Sonia Dresdel), young Henrey does not fully comprehend a number of things taking place around him. Among them is his idol's (Richardson) domestic unhappiness and the affair he is having with an embassy typist (Michèle Morgan). When Richardson's wife dies violently, it is the boy's belief that his friend is the killer and must be protected. His efforts to help have devastating results, culminating in a scene with the police that is harrowing in its suspense.

It is to Bobby Henrey and Carol Reed's eternal credit that there is never a hint of sentimentality or condescension in the film. This child's-eye-view of an adult world is an absolute stunner.

# The Family Way

* * * * * * * * * * * * * * * * * * * * * * * * * * * * * * * * * * * * * * * * * * * * * * * *

*Nationality*: British                    *Year*: 1966 (U.S. release: 1967)
*Cast*: Hayley Mills, Hywel Bennett, John Mills, Marjorie Rhodes, Avril Angers
*Director*: Roy Boulting          *Running Time*: 115 minutes
*B/W or Color*: Color             *Availability*: TV only

This charmingly candid comedy-drama about a young couple and their unconsummated marriage brought an end to the on-screen innocence of 20-year-old Hayley Mills. Audiences could now see the former child star smoking, drinking, and even displaying her naked backside. Offscreen, Hayley shocked her less worldly admirers by becoming romantically involved with her 53-year-old married director, Roy Boulting. While this scandal rocked Britain, *The Family Way* became a box-office hit.

But this is quite a wonderful motion picture, handling a genuinely adult theme with an earthy warmth that provokes both laughter and tears without resort to sentimentality. Bill Naughton craftily expanded his original stage play to meet screen requirements, with the aid of co-scenarists Jeffrey Dell and director Roy Boulting, who artfully guides a superlative cast around the possible pitfalls inherent in such "sensitive" subject matter.

In view of *The Family Way*'s plot, the taste and care with which it reached the screen—devoid of either leering farce or needless explicitness—is quite remarkable. But neither does it sugarcoat its pill; the issue of marital consummation is faced squarely, as well as the insensitive cruelty with which people often carelessly treat one another.

As the tense and troubled young newlyweds, Hayley Mills and Hywel Bennett are as near perfection as are the wonderful character actors who surround them—especially John Mills and Marjorie Rhodes, a little-known player cited as the year's Best Supporting Actress by The National Board of Review, which also listed *The Family Way* among the best English-language films released in the United States during 1967.

# Fanfan the Tulip
### (Fanfan La Tulipe)

\*\*\*\*\*\*\*\*\*\*\*\*\*\*\*\*\*\*\*\*\*\*\*\*\*\*\*\*\*\*\*\*\*\*\*\*\*\*\*\*\*\*\*\*\*\*\*\*\*\*\*\*\*

Nationality: French:         Year: 1952 (U.S. release: 1953)
Cast: Gérard Philipe, Gina Lollobrigida, Geneviève Page
Director: Christian-Jaque      Running Time: 96 minutes (104
                                minutes in France)
B/W or Color: B/W            Availability: TV only

Arousing, good-natured parody of swashbuckling Errol Flynn-style movies, this popular French film starred Gérard Philipe, France's leading young male actor of the 1950s. At the height of his career, Philipe played the country bumpkin who has had his way with many a farmer's daughter when he is recruited into Louis XV's 18th-century army. Young braggart Fanfan gets himself into and out of one scrape after another as he brandishes his sword in the classic style of Flynn and Douglas Fairbanks, Sr. The deliciously impudent movie spoofs the traditional military spirit and the stubbornness of old-time monarchs. Philipe is charming and dashing as the buffoon turned courtier and hero as the winds of fortune lead him. Gina Lollobrigida was well into her career as a glamorous international actress when she made *Fanfan the Tulip*. As Philipe's co-star, she showed a remarkable screen presence and acting ability, as well as her famous figure, in her role as the recruiting sergeant's daughter. She went on the next year to co-star again with Philipe in *Belles de Nuit*. Now in her sixties, she has had a successful second career as a photographer.

The handsome, exuberant, but ill-fated Philipe made film after film in fast succession after *Fanfan* until his death at the young age of 37 in 1959. Other films of his include *Devil in the Flesh* (1947), *The Red and the Black* (1954) with Danielle Darrieux, and *Les Liaisons Dangereuses* (1959) with Jeanne Moreau. French actress Geneviève Page plays *Fanfan*'s Madame Pompadour, who is impressed with the hero's one-man saber battle with a pack of bandits who hold her up in her coach. Director Christian-Jaque (Christian Maudet) was a former journalist as well as screenwriter. His career spans five decades, from 1938 to the 1980s. Among his films: *Bluebeard* (1951), *Nana* (1954), and *The Black Tulip* (1963).

# Fanny and Alexander

## (Fanny och Alexander)

★★★★★★★★★★★★★★★★★★★★★★★★★★★★★★★★★★★★★★★★★★★★★★★★★★★★

**Nationality**: Swedish-French-West German    **Year**: 1982 (U.S. release: 1983)

**Cast**: Pernilla Allwin, Bertil Guve, Borje Allstedt, Harriet Andersson, Erland Josephson, Gunn Wallgren, Jarl Kulle

**Director**: Ingmar Bergman    **Running Time**: 188 minutes

**B/W or Color**: Color    **Availability**: EMBASSY HOME ENTERTAINMENT

Alexander Eckdahl (Bertil Guve), through whose eyes and imaginings *Fanny and Alexander* is told, plays out scenes from Bergman's life, hiding beneath the furniture (as Bergman did at his grandmother's apartment in Upsala) and casting flickering images on the wall with a magic-lantern projector. Like Bergman, Alexander is haunted by the ghosts of his twin muses, art and religion.

Among the Eckdahls, who comprise this 1907 family chronicle, is the melodramatic matriarch Helena (exquisitely played by Gunn Wallgren), a retired stage-actress who must be convinced by her daughter-in-law that Strindberg's *Dream Play* mustn't be discarded because of vague mutterings of misogyny. Her son Carl prefers male-bonding to family gatherings and borrows money to make ends meet. Gustav (Jarl Kulle) is a jovial satyr who wants his family-sanctioned mistress Maj to run the coffee shop of his petit-bourgeois dreams. Another brother, Oscar (father of Fanny and Alexander), has a stroke on stage while rehearsing *Hamlet*.

After Oscar dies, his wife, Emilie (Ewa Froling), marries a stern Protestant clergyman (Jan Malmsjo) whose house is an owned-and-operated torture chamber, bringing her children under the bishop's iron crosier. Bergman even seems to hold the couple's physical beauty in disdain—they bring a pox on each other's houses. Meanwhile, Christmas-cavorting at Helena's suggests (refreshingly) that homelier people can and do enjoy their sexuality and (stalely) that a little infidelity among friends never hurt anybody, but beware of those churchgoers!

The interiors are divided between the rich, warm hues of Helena's and Isak's cluttered, backstage homes and the austere coldness of the bishop's cave, with nary a table under which to hide. Outside, Bergman becomes elegiac, directing his legendary cinematographer Sven Nykvist to shoot Brueghellian exteriors of unmodulated blacks and whites and to punctuate sentences with lyrically descending camera movements that seem to echo the paths of rain and snow from the heavens.

*Fanny and Alexander* won the Best Foreign Language Film Oscar and The National Board's Best Foreign Film Award.

(*The videocassette is in subtitled Swedish.*)

156

# Fantastic Planet
## (La Planète Sauvage)

\*\*\*\*\*\*\*\*\*\*\*\*\*\*\*\*\*\*\*\*\*\*\*\*\*\*\*\*\*\*\*\*\*\*\*\*\*\*\*\*\*\*\*\*\*\*\*\*\*\*\*\*

*Nationality*: French-Czech

*Director*: René Laloux

*B/W or Color*: Color

*Year*: 1973
*Running Time*: 72 minutes

*Availability*: EMBASSY HOME ENTERTAINMENT

Animation has always been an intriguing business, but because its target audience has primarily been children, it has been taken seriously only peripherally.

Al Kilgore took Bullwinkle and achieved the difficult end of aiming scripts simultaneously at adults and kids. Disney found his way into the Abrams's art books through the sheer artistry of his staff. His most ambitiously adult cartoon—*Fantasia*—certainly succeeded on many levels, but not without a certain queazy pretentiousness. Ralph Bakshi (*Fritz the Cat, American Pop*) aims at adolescent audiences and deals in autobiographical material: he's one of America's true auteurs.

But very few feature cartoons are conceived with adult audiences in mind. One was the grim, noble, and depressing *Plague Dogs,* which tragically saw no U.S. release to speak of but is available on video. Another is *Fantastic Planet,* shot in the animation studios of Jiri Trnka in Prague.

*Fantastic Planet* is based on the novel *Oms En Serie,* by Stefan Wul, and was a French-Czech co-production. The film's creators have given us a sensitive, contemplative story that is inherently moral and engagingly surreal. The animation is basic compared to American sophistication. For example, simple dissolves are used to create the sense of movement. But it is effective—which animation of the Saturday morning TV cartoons is not.

Roland Topor, the surrealist artist who co-authored Roman Polanski's autobiographical *The Tenant,* has lent the film his narrative and visual ideas: the innumerable abstract life forms that populate the alien terrain of the film are provocative, haunting, and disturbing, as are the two races of humanoid creatures pitted against one another by destiny. It is the achievement of all involved that we both care for and identify with the blue giants and the tiny, inarticulate Ohms whom they enslave.

# Far from the Madding Crowd

*********************************************************

*Nationality*: British                     *Year*: 1967
*Cast*: Julie Christie, Terence Stamp, Peter Finch, Alan Bates, Prunella Ransome
*Director*: John Schlesinger         *Running Time*: 169 minutes
*B/W or Color*: Color                    *Availability*: TV only

Two years after the sensational success of *Darling*, producer Joseph Janni and director John Schlesinger teamed again with their Oscar-winning star and screenwriter, Julie Christie and Frederic Raphael, for an expensive adaptation of *Far from the Madding Crowd*, Thomas Hardy's 1874 Victorian romance about the loves of a headstrong young woman farmer in the verdant southwest of 19th-century England. This was an unusual choice of source material for Schlesinger, whose previous films had included the very contemporary *Billy Liar* and *A Kind of Loving*. With sweeping English locations in Dorset and Wiltshire, Hardy's beloved "Wessex" country was lovingly re-created by the teamwork of production designer Richard MacDonald, cinematographer Nicolas Roeg, and the haunting, folk-flavored score of Richard Rodney Bennett. The result was pure "Masterpiece Theatre," with the stamp of David Lean.

A reappraisal of this beautiful motion picture continues to reward the viewer, as it pits the handsome protagonists against the joys and frustrations of love, lust, and fate. Equally interesting are those tortured, sub-plot lovers portrayed by dashing Terence Stamp and wistfully beautiful Prunella Ransome.

Like those of Jane Austen, Hardy's plot and characters seem almost quaint after a century of progress and social change. However, the nearly three hours of aural and visual beauty, and a cast of infinitely more glamour and charisma than is likely to be found in the present lackluster era, result in a ravishing and diverting film. The National Board named *Far from the Madding Crowd* 1967's Best English-Language Picture and voted Peter Finch the year's Best Actor.

# Fellini Satyricon

★★★★★★★★★★★★★★★★★★★★★★★★★★★★★★★★★★★★★★★★★★★★★★★★★★★★★★★

*Nationality*: Italian-French        *Year*: 1969 (U.S. release: 1970)
*Cast*: Martin Potter, Hiram Keller, Max Born, Capucine, Salvo Randone
*Director*: Federico Fellini        *Running Time*: 129 minutes
*B/W or Color*: Color        *Availability*: TV only

This is the first full-length Fellini film based on an outside source, but Fellini has put his personal stamp on every detail of the classic. What emerges is a fully realized projection of the director's most fevered dreams. In at least one sense, it is Fellini's most original film. He creates an entire world and peoples it with the familiar creatures of his fantasies, so that it becomes a surreal Italianate Oz.

The shred of plot revolves around young Encolpius (Potter), whose boy lover Giton (Born) has been stolen from him by his best friend Ascyltus (Keller). Encolpius goes after them, and the three of them wander through the Roman Empire, witnessing an astonishing progression of murders, orgies, feasts, abductions, bizarre couplings, and dastardly plots. Whether Encolpius recovers his boy or prefers his rival's charms is unimportant. The hero never reaches a point of psychological crisis that will alter his circumstances or outlook. All the figures move at the director's will, and any glimpse of understanding they attain is dispensed with his approving nod. Encolpius is conceived as a creature manipulated by fate, but fate is clearly Fellini. Encolpius does not move so much as he is moved through a world governed entirely by chance. There are no values and no ethics. We witness the unfolding of a catalog of perversities, most of them sexual. Albino hunchbacks, harpies, and other mythical monsters people this poetic hallucination just as credibly as do the central characters. John Simon called it "a sort of Roman s/m holiday." It would be futile to dwell too long on precisely what Fellini had in mind. The film uncovers truths that must have astonished him, as well as puzzles that confused him.

# Fellini's Roma

★ ★ ★ ★ ★ ★ ★ ★ ★ ★ ★ ★ ★ ★ ★ ★ ★ ★ ★ ★ ★ ★ ★ ★ ★ ★ ★ ★ ★ ★ ★ ★ ★ ★ ★ ★ ★ ★ ★ ★ ★ ★ ★ ★ ★ ★ ★ ★ ★ ★ ★

*Nationality*: Italian               *Year*: 1972
*Cast*: Peter Gonzales, Britta Barnes, Pia de Doses, Fiona Florence, Marne
Maitland
*Director*: Federico Fellini          *Running Time*: 128 minutes
*B/W or Color*: Color                 *Availability*: TV only

**R**oma is Fellini's last installment in his Roman trilogy, following *La Dolce Vita* and *Fellini Satyricon*. The film is an impressionistic autobiography, with a young man (Gonzales) coming to Rome to seek his fortune. The city he explores is overwhelmingly decadent, the spiritual as well as physical capital of a bankrupt Fascist system. Two bordellos, one for the rich and one for the poor, illustrate the social definitions of the period. Fellini proceeds to explore the life of the city, often with casual disregard for its impact on his protagonist. In the contemporary segments we watch the horrors of traffic on the *anulare,* the maze of motorways that encircles Rome. We see the perils of digging the new subway system in a city where archeological treasures abound, we watch the whores at their roadside encampments, join the working class families of Trastevere in outdoor dining, and finally view an ecclesiastical fashion show. Fellini's satire is at its sharpest, if not his wittiest, here, as priests and nuns parade on roller skates and an archbishop preens for a cardinal's approval in Daliesque vestments.

The city bears little resemblance to the real Rome, but is rather an imaginative celebration of its spirit. Fellini salutes the manner in which Romans eat, work, and copulate. Someone said the film is his vision of Rome as the last great expression of the Middle Ages. *Roma* was filmed mostly indoors on a sound stage, and it is typical of Fellini that when he does take the camera outside he treats the whole city as a sound stage. The performances are, as usual, competently orchestrated. The film stands as an amusing observation of the mores of a society, with little pretense of developing the theme beyond this.

# Fire over England

★★★★★★★★★★★★★★★★★★★★★★★★★★★★★★★★★★★★★★★★★★★★★★★★★★★★★

**Nationality**: British          **Year**: 1937

**Cast**: Flora Robson, Laurence Olivier, Leslie Banks, Vivien Leigh, Raymond Massey, Robert Newton, James Mason

**Director**: William K. Howard     **Running Time**: 88 minutes (92 minutes in Britain)

**B/W or Color**: B/W           **Availability**: Public Domain

Following the international success of *The Private Life of Henry VIII*, Alexander Korda produced this costume picture about Henry's dynamic monarch-daughter, Queen Elizabeth I, tailoring it for the talented young character actress Flora Robson.

As adapted by Clemence Dane from A.E.W. Mason's novel, *Fire over England* is an episodic, romanticized drama of Britain's 16th-century queen vs. Philip of Spain (Raymond Massey) and the Spanish Armada. In the interests of popular entertainment, historical events were liberally distorted, with athletic young Laurence Olivier as an impetuous naval lieutenant who arouses his queen's jealousy by romancing her lady-in-waiting (Vivien Leigh), when not engaged in spy missions to Spain. This fictional hero ultimately saves England from Spain in a swashbuckling Armada sequence (with a skillful use of ship models in the studio tank).

Although on the brink of full-fledged movie stardom, Olivier and Leigh—who herewith began their extramarital four-year love affair—are somewhat less interesting in their first screen teaming than the scene-stealing Raymond Massey and the rather benevolent Elizabeth of Flora Robson (looking like a made-up Carol Burnett!) in a characterization she would later reprise for *The Sea Hawk*. Olivier's acting borders on the overwrought, and Leigh had yet to develop the character and beauty that Hollywood would eventually glorify so brilliantly.

In small supporting parts, one notes effective performances by Robert Newton (who received billing) and James Mason (who did not). In the latter case, this was odd, since Mason—who had already appeared prominently in seven motion pictures—had a three-scene speaking role that set the stage for Olivier's subsequent impersonation of him. To quote Mason: "Mine was a vitally important role, but after one day's and one night's shooting, it was all over."

*(Kartes offers a videocassette of very mediocre quality.)*

# Fitzcarraldo

* * * * * * * * * * * * * * * * * * * * * * * * * * * * * * * * * * * * * * * * * * * * * * * * *

*Nationality*: West German          *Year*: 1982
*Cast*: Klaus Kinski, Claudia Cardinale, Jose Lewgoy, Miguel Angel Fuentes, Paul Hittscher
*Director*: Werner Herzog          *Running Time*: 157 minutes
*B/W or Color*: Color          *Availability*: WARNER HOME VIDEO

This is Werner Herzog's magnificent statement on the nature of obsession, and it is as eccentric as it is powerful. The film opens with Irishman Brian Sweeney Fitzgerald (Klaus Kinski)—called Fitzcarraldo by his fellow Europeans in Peru—arriving at the Manaus, Brazil, Opera House in 1906 to hear Enrico Caruso sing. Fitzcarraldo has traveled, along with a lovely lady named Molly (Claudia Cardinale), 1,200 miles down the Amazon from his home in Iquitos, Peru. More than moved by Caruso's performance, Fitzcarraldo becomes obsessed with the idea of building an opera house in Iquitos and of having Caruso sing there on opening night. He decides that the way to finance such an undertaking is to buy what would appear to be a worthless piece of land from the government in the Ucayali. Although the land has thousands of rubber trees, it is located in a region off the Ucayali River that cannot be reached by ship because of the perilous "Pongo das Mortes" rapids. But there is another river, the Pachitea, that at one point winds within a mile of the Ucayali, above the rapids. Fitzcarraldo is convinced that he'll be able to pull a 300-ton-plus riverboat over the mountain that separates the rivers, and sail on to claim his land.

The major portion of the film focuses on Fitzcarraldo's attempts to pull the ship over the mountain, with the help of the strangely cooperative but ominously enigmatic local Jivaro Indians. The grounded ship soon becomes the film's central image, an immovable object that simply must be moved. Pulling it even slightly represents a victory, a joyous triumph—practically an end unto itself. Fitzcarraldo's plight becomes ours as well, through Werner Herzog's brutally realistic but passionately poetic direction. As we witness Fitzcarraldo's mad struggle to move the ship, we are also witnessing Herzog's mad struggle as filmmaker in the Peruvian Amazon jungle. The ship is no plastic model; there are no back-lot-created sets. *Fitzcarraldo* is a truly rare piece of filmmaking.

(*The Warner videocassette is subtitled.*)

# Floating Weeds
## (Ukigusa)

\*\*\*\*\*\*\*\*\*\*\*\*\*\*\*\*\*\*\*\*\*\*\*\*\*\*\*\*\*\*\*\*\*\*\*\*\*\*\*\*\*\*\*\*\*\*\*\*\*\*\*\*

*Nationality*: Japanese        *Year*: 1959 (U.S. release: 1970)

*Cast*: Ganjiro Nakamura, Haruko Sugimura, Machiko Kyo, Ayako Wakao, Koji Mitsui

*Director*: Yasujiro Ozu        *Running Time*: 119 minutes

*B/W or Color*: Color        *Availability*: EMBASSY HOME VIDEO

E ven today, when the phrase "unique directoral style" has been greatly overused, it can be truly applied to Yasujiro Ozu. The most distinct stylistic element of this Japanese master, who made films from late in the silent era until his death in 1963, is the low-angle shot: his camera is, at most, two feet off the ground, the height of one seated on the traditional *tatami* mat. His camera is almost always stationary, his frames rigid but carefully and beautifully composed. Characters appearing in the same shot usually face the same direction, and even strike identical poses, very rarely moving. Ozu uses a large number of cuts, but no optical effects. Much more interested in character development than plot, he used a very slow and deliberate pacing to generate a special rhythm in his films. As a result of his austere techniques, Ozu is acclaimed for his simple but sensitive dramas of the family and everyday life.

*Floating Weeds*, made near the end of Ozu's career and his first color film, depicts a troupe of traveling actors hitting rock bottom in a remote island town. Less typical than most of his films, here his "family" is Komajiro, the aging troupe leader; his longtime mistress; a local woman he has not seen in years; and their illegitimate son, who believes Komajiro to be his uncle. The two women become rivals for Komajiro, and the jealous mistress even hires another actress to seduce the teenage boy. In the end, the troupe has disbanded, the actress falls in love with the son, and Komajiro and the mistress finally reconcile.

A remake of his silent *A Story of Floating Weeds*, this film features more melodrama and a stronger story line than most of Ozu's works. Over the 25 years between films Ozu mellowed, and the native woman, who was very bitter in the first version, is much more resigned here.

Many consider Yasujiro Ozu to be the most "Japanese" of all film directors. The Japanese themselves were afraid his work would be regarded as too "Japanese" to be appreciated in the West. Only near the end of his lifetime were they entered in international film festivals, where their true universality and beauty were discovered.

# For Your Eyes Only

★★★★★★★★★★★★★★★★★★★★★★★★★★★★★★★★★★★★★★★★★★★★★★★★★★★★★

Nationality: British:                    Year: 1981

Cast: Roger Moore, Carole Bouquet, Chaim Topol, Lynn-Holly Johnson, Julian Glover, Jill Bennett

Director: John Glen                    Running Time: 128 minutes

B/W or Color: Color                    Availability: CBS/FOX HOME VIDEO

For Your Eyes Only is the most controversial of the James Bond series, returning to the simpler story lines rather than the hi-tech heroics of more recent entries, but still retaining the trademark chase sequences and spectacular stunts. Director John Glen, making his debut (though he had previously done second-unit work on several Bond films), keeps the action at breakneck speed. He also directed its successors, *Octopussy* (1983) and *A View to a Kill* (1985).

Bond (Roger Moore) is assigned to recover a vital computer that could be used to turn British submarines against their own country and, as if the super agent didn't have enough to do, he must also deal with a sinister opium smuggler. Assisting him is the attractive Carole Bouquet, who has a mean way with a crossbow. Many consider this Moore's most accomplished outing as Agent 007, whom he first portrayed four features earlier in *Live and Let Die* (1973).

Ian Fleming introduced James Bond to readers in his 1950 novel *Casino Royale,* which was adapted for the television series *Climax* in the mid-fifties, with Bond played (for the first time ever) by Barry Nelson.

Sean Connery brought Bond to the big screen with *Dr. No* (1963) and continued to dispense debonair mayhem in *From Russia with Love* (1963), *Goldfinger* (1964), *Thunderball* (1965), *You Only Live Twice* (1967), and *Diamonds Are Forever* (1971). Claiming that he was through with the role forever, he went on to other pictures but returned as the secret agent in *Never Say Never Again* (a remake of *Thunderball*) in 1983.

In 1967, *Casino Royale* was brought to the screen with David Niven playing Sir James Bond; and, in 1969, *On Her Majesty's Secret Service* featured newcomer George Lazenby as 007.

Moore's other Bond adventures were *Man with the Golden Gun* (1974), *The Spy Who Loved Me* (1977), *Moonraker* (1979), *Octopussy* (1983), and *A View to a Kill* (1985).

To date, on screen, James Bond has reached sweet 16.

# Forbidden Games

## (Jeux Interdits/The Secret Game)

★★★★★★★★★★★★★★★★★★★★★★★★★★★★★★★★★★★★★★★★★★★★★★★★★★★★★

**Nationality**: French        **Year**: 1952
**Cast**: Brigitte Fossey, Georges Poujouly, Lucien Hubert, Suzanne Courtal
**Director**: René Clément      **Running Time**: 87 minutes
**B/W or Color**: B/W         **Availability**: NELSON ENTER-
TAINMENT

One of the most shattering, intense antiwar films ever made, *Forbidden Games* views the desolation through the eyes of children. With lyric purity, it contrasts the tragedy of war with the innocence of youth and children's honesty with the deceptive values of adults.

It is based on a novel by Françoise Boyer, who originally wrote it as a screenplay but was unable to get it filmed. She received an Academy Award nomination (in 1954) for Best Original Story.

In the summer of 1940, 5-year-old Paulette (Brigitte Fossey) is orphaned by a German air raid. She meets 11-year-old Michel (Georges Poujouly), the son of farmers who agree to temporarily care for the girl. Paulette and Michel bury her dog (killed in the air raid), which is the beginning of a secret cemetery and the start of their "forbidden games."

One of The National Board's best foreign films for 1952, *Forbidden Games* was also honored by the New York Film Critics, the Japanese Critics, and the Venice and Cannes Film Festivals. It received an honorary Oscar and (in 1953) was chosen as Best Film by the British Film Academy.

Brigitte Fossey next appeared on screen as a 10-year-old with Gene Kelly in *The Happy Road* (1957) and began her adult film career in 1967's *The Wanderer.*

*Forbidden Games* is a gripping experience from that heartrending moment, after the attack, when Paulette tries to rouse her dead mother, to the ending at the railway station, as she's about to be sent to an orphanage. Hearing someone call out "Michel," Paulette runs through the crowd— only to discover that it's not her friend, but an adult. She cries, "Mama," and then "Michel" repeatedly, as the camera moves away—leaving her ticketed and labeled in the crowd of displaced persons. It is a harrowing conclusion to director René Clément's masterpiece.

*(Nelson offers a subtitled French print.)*

# The Four Feathers

*****************************************************

*Nationality*: British       *Year*: 1939

*Cast*: John Clements, Ralph Richardson, June Duprez, C. Aubrey Smith

*Director*: Zoltan Korda      *Running Time*: 115 minutes (130 minutes in Britain)

*B/W or Color*: Color      *Availability*: EMBASSY HOME ENTERTAINMENT

A classic adventure film, *The Four Feathers* is the story of Harry Faversham (John Clements), the son of a military man who's expected to carry on in the family tradition.

Faversham resigns his commission when his regiment is ordered to the Sudan and is branded a coward by his fiancée, Ethne Burroughs (June Duprez), daughter of an officer (C. Aubrey Smith), and by his three friends: Durrance (Ralph Richardson); Burroughs, his fiancée's brother (Donald Gray); and Willoughby (Jack Allen). They send him their cards, each with a white feather (a symbol of cowardice) attached. Faversham himself attaches a feather to Ethne's card.

Questioning his conscience, Faversham sets out on his own for Egypt. With the help of a doctor, he disguises himself as a Singli (North African natives who bear a mark on their foreheads and are without tongues). He infiltrates a group of fanatics and is able to warn the British soldiers of an attack.

The regiment is under the command of Durrance, who keeps secret the fact that he's been blinded. After the battle, Durrance is left for dead but is found by Faversham, who leads him to safety—quietly slipping into his old friend's pocket the card bearing the white feather.

Faversham also manages to rescue Burroughs and Willoughby from prison—winning the day and Ethne's hand.

Filmed on location, *The Four Feathers* is based on A.E.W. Mason's 1901 novel, previously made into movies in 1915, 1921, and 1928. This version was the work of the Brothers Korda (Alexander produced, Zoltan directed, and Vincent was art director). Zoltan Korda also directed the 1955 remake, *Storm Over the Nile,* which used location footage from the 1939 production. A TV movie was made in 1977.

Action, spectacle, and romance make this epic of bravery and tradition an evergreen entertainment.

# The 400 Blows
## (Les Quatres Cent Coups)/Stolen Kisses
## (Baisers Volés)/Bed and Board (Domicile Conjugal)/
## Love on the Run (L'Amour en Fuite)

**************************************************

**Nationality**: French

**Year**: 1959/1968 (U.S.: 1969)/1970 (U.S.: 1971)/1979

**Cast**: Jean-Pierre Léaud, Claire Maurier, Albert Remy, Claude Jade, Delphine Seyrig, Michel Lonsdale, Hiroko Berghauer, Daniel Ceccaldi, Marie-France Pisier

**Director**: François Truffaut

**Running Time**: 98 minutes/90 minutes/97 minutes/93 minutes

**B/W or Color**: B/W; Color; Color; Color

**Availability**: KEY VIDEO; RCA/COLUMBIA PICTURES HOME VIDEO; TV only; WARNER HOME VIDEO

When *The 400 Blows* won in Cannes in 1959 (Best Director François Truffaut and the Catholic Film Office Award) the starting gun was sounded for the French New Wave. Along with Godard's *Breathless*, Chabrol's *Les Cousins*, Rivette's *Paris Belongs to Us*, and Resnais's *Hiroshima, Mon Amour*, the inmates had finally taken over the asylum, and cinema would never be the same again. As the enfant terrible of French film critics, François Truffaut was given the legendary "So you think you can do better, kid?" offer by his father-in-law, and delivered his autobiographical masterwork, *The 400 Blows*.

This is one of the best-made films on the subject of misunderstood youth. A large part of its fine reputation stems from the excellent performance of its star, Jean-Pierre Léaud. Although Léaud has worked well with other directors, he is primarily associated with Truffaut. In a history of famed symbiotic relationships between director and star, the Léaud/Truffaut act is probably the most celebrated. The four films in the so-called Antoine Doinel cycle become more Léaud and less Truffaut as they progress through *Stolen Kisses* (1968) and *Bed and Board* (1970) to *Love on the Run* (1979).

*The 400 Blows* is Truffaut's most autobiographical statement in a career of autobiographical statements. It is a film about the claustrophobia of youth and the few avenues open for a young boy to grow. Antoine's dreams lie only with Balzac and the movies. His sensibility is very Fifties. His combination of alienation and well-meaning empathy remind one of Salinger's Holden Caulfield and James Dean's rebels. Truffaut brilliantly shows Antoine's bewilderment and confusion while trying to deal with his near-whore mother, impotent father, and authoritarian teacher.

The camerawork, soundtrack, and editing are cut loose here, as Truffaut's style is at its freshest, "let's try this" mode. *The 400 Blows* tore open the film world and helped rewrite French film history. The New York Film Critics named it the year's Best Foreign Film.

167

# The 4th Man
## (De Vierde Man)

* * * * * * * * * * * * * * * * * * * * * * * * * * * * * * * * * * * * * * * * * * * * * * * * * * * *

*Nationality*: Dutch        *Year*: 1983 (U.S. release: 1984)
*Cast*: Jeroen Krabbé, Renée Soutendijk, Thom Hoffman, Dolf De Vries
*Director*: Paul Verhoeven        *Running Time*: 104 minutes
*B/W or Color*: Color        *Availability*: MEDIA HOME EN-
                                                   TERTAINMENT

**P**aul Verhoeven, idiosyncratic Dutch director, came splashing across the cinema scene in 1972 with *Turkish Delight*. It was, beyond a display of his stylish gifts, the film that introduced Rutger Hauer, and the second Dutch feature ever to be nominated for an Academy Award.

*Soldier of Orange*, again with Hauer and with Jeroen Krabbé, won the Los Angeles Critics Best Foreign Film Award of 1979. In 1980 came *Spetters*, a disturbing sexual tragedy set within the biker community, featuring, not surprisingly, Hauer and Krabbé.

In 1984 *The 4th Man* arrived, adapted from the novel by Gerard Reve, a highly controversial, openly homosexual writer. The film was originally conceived to be shot in a documentary fashion, but the final look was almost diametrically different—surrealistic, with super-saturated colors. It cost $1,800,000 and took eight weeks to shoot.

In it, Krabbé gives a sly, complex performance as Gerard Reve, a rude, disenchanted writer. On his way to deliver an out-of-town lecture, he is attracted to a young man at the railway station. Events (real or imagined?) spin around him, much as the spider in the title sequence dizzyingly spins its web. Symbols and dreams of creativity, homosexuality, woman as murderous sexual aggressor, Catholicism, and psychic premonition abound. The comic turns of Reve/Krabbé/Verhoeven's film noir keep us on our toes, as does our growing awareness that the protagonist is being set up for the Big Fall. Christine, a local widow, begins to woo him into a financially secure relationship—he has other motives, and so does she.

The voluptuous, tormented score by Loek Dikker strongly supports the characterizations and narrative. Verhoeven has spun us a sure-handed, ironic vision of modern decadence and redemption.

The National Board named *The 4th Man* one of the best foreign films of the year.

(*The videocassette is dubbed in English.*)

# The French Lieutenant's Woman

★★★★★★★★★★★★★★★★★★★★★★★★★★★★★★★★★★★★★★★★★★★★★★★★★★★★★★

*Nationality*: British            *Year*: 1981

*Cast*: Meryl Streep, Jeremy Irons, Leo McKern, Hilton McRae, Patience Collier, Lynsey Baxter

*Director*: Karel Reisz        *Running Time*: 127 minutes

*B/W or Color*: Color         *Availability*: CBS/FOX VIDEO

John Fowles's best-selling novel took more than ten years to reach the screen, having challenged and defeated such major-league directors as Fred Zinnemann and Mike Nichols. And up until this film, Fowles had had generally dismal luck with adaptations of his novels. William Wyler's *The Collector* (1965) was an uneasy blend of pretentious talk and little suspense. *The Magus* (1968), for which Fowles wrote the screenplay, was a disaster of almost epic proportions. *The French Lieutenant's Woman* was indeed a challenge—a high charged, very romantic Victorian novel in which the author's present day voice is constantly used to comment on issues as varied as Freud, Darwin, or the plight of the mid-19th-century prostitute. Unable to find a satisfactory solution to this problem of the commentator, screenwriter Harold Pinter devised the not entirely fresh notion of a film within a film, so that the freewheeling actors in the present form the counterpart to the conventional Victorians. It's a device that only partially succeeds, since the contemporary film folk are not nearly as interesting as their 19th-century counterparts. However, there is no denying the magnificence of this production. The exceedingly photogenic Dorset coast and the fishing village of Lyme Regis have been gorgeously photographed. The Art Direction, Costume Design, and Film Editing were nominated for Academy Awards (as were Pinter for Best Screenplay Adaptation and Meryl Streep for Best Actress). None won. The film may be a disappointment for a few lovers of the novel, but be assured there is much here to enjoy, particularly Meryl Streep's technically dazzling virtuosity and Jeremy Irons who, in this his major film debut, was likened to the young Olivier of *Wuthering Heights*.

# From Russia with Love

*******************************************************

Nationality: British          Year: 1963 (U.S. release: 1964)
Cast: Sean Connery, Daniela Bianchi, Pedro Armendariz, Lotte Lenya, Robert Shaw
Director: Terence Young          Running Time: 110 minutes
B/W or Color: Color          Availability: CBS/FOX VIDEO

Considered by many to be the best of the James Bond films, *From Russia with Love* is a superior spy chiller with fascinating characters and interesting gadgetry (a formula that was reversed in some of the later entries). The second of the Bond series, it brought back the dashing Agent 007 with the license to kill, played by Sean Connery, who gained stardom when he introduced that character to the screen in *Dr. No*. The story line adheres closely to the Ian Fleming book on which it's based (although the international crime syndicate, SPECTRE—Special Executive for Counterintelligence, Terrorism, Revenge and Extortion—was borrowed from others of Fleming's Bond adventures: *Thunderball* and *On Her Majesty's Secret Service*).

In the movie, SPECTRE lures Bond with the possibility of obtaining a Russian coding device, the Lektor. They plan to avenge the death of Dr. No (this is the only Bond movie with a direct reference to any of the others ), as well as embarrass the East and West. Viewers will get a kick out of Rosa Klebb (Lotte Lenya), a toadlike KGB colonel who conceals a poisonous dagger in the tip of her shoe. There's a beautiful Russian, Tatiana Romanova (Daniela Bianchi), who's used as bait and falls in love with her catch (guess who); and a ruthless killer, Red Grant (Robert Shaw), who temporarily poses as a British Agent (whom he murdered). He arouses 007's suspicions, however, by ordering red wine with fish.

After battling a helicopter and what appears to be the entire SPECTRE naval force, Bond encounters Grant (in one of the screen's most exciting fights) on board the Orient Express.

Bond keeps his gadgets (a lethal briefcase) intact and his tongue in cheek throughout the intrigue and action of *From Russia with Love*.

# Gallipoli

★★★★★★★★★★★★★★★★★★★★★★★★★★★★★★★★★★★★★★★★★★★★★★★★★★

Nationality: Australian                    Year: 1981
Cast: Mel Gibson, Mark Lee
Director: Peter Weir                        Running Time: 110 minutes
B/W or Color: Color                        Availability: PARAMOUNT
                                                         HOME VIDEO

Gallipoli was Australian film director Peter Weir's idea, and he commissioned David Williamson to write the screenplay from Weir's story in three parts. The first explores the friendship between two young runners, the naive Archy (Mark Lee) from Australia's rugged outback and Frank (Mel Gibson), a street-smart city boy from Perth, who join up to fight for king and country. Part two follows their basic training near Cairo, and part three the 1915 battle for Gallipoli, the military manuever by which the Allies hoped to control the Dardanelles, but which, through monumental blunders at the top, resulted in a crushing defeat, claiming the lives of thousands of Australians and New Zealanders.

Despite its title and denouement, however, Gallipoli is not a war movie. Its principal theme is the developing friendship between two young men, which just happens to culminate in their participation in a historical conflict. The predominant mood is one of delicacy and warmth; there are delightful touches of humor—notably a scene in which the Aussies attempt to cope with Mid-East hustlers—and director Weir's masterful use of naturalism contributes to the film's strong, overall sense of universality.

Mel Gibson, on his way to international stardom, reveals here, as the cynical Frank, the broad range of his acting talents, and newcomer Mark Lee, a former model with no previous acting experience, turns in an impressive performance as Gibson's boyish comrade.

After Paramount trumpeted its release with the publicity tag line "From the place you may never have heard of, the story you'll never forget," producer Robert Stigwood and his partner, newspaper mogul Rupert Murdoch, watched Gallipoli become Australia's most successful film till then, one of forty-nine originating from Down Under that year. The National Board of Review named it one of the best pictures of the year.

# Gandhi

\* \* \* \* \* \* \* \* \* \* \* \* \* \* \* \* \* \* \* \* \* \* \* \* \* \* \* \* \* \* \* \* \* \* \* \* \* \* \* \* \* \* \* \* \* \* \* \* \* \* \* \* \* \* \*

*Nationality*: British          *Year*: 1982

*Cast*: Ben Kingsley, Candice Bergen, Edward Fox, Rohini Hattangady, Roshan Seth, Saeed Jaffrey, Trevor Howard, John Mills, John Gielgud, Martin Sheen

*Director*: Richard Attenborough     *Running Time*: 188 minutes

*B/W or Color*: Color           *Availability*: RCA/COLUMBIA
                      HOME VIDEO

I t took twenty years for Sir Richard Attenborough to raise financing for a film biography of Mohandas K. Gandhi, the Mahatma (meaning "Great Soul"). The studios, said Attenborough, "felt a film about a little brown man in a sheet . . . wasn't exactly going to pack them in." His dream led to a memorable film that received numerous best picture honors, including that of The National Board of Review, the New York Film Critics, and the Academy Award.

Producer-director Attenborough accepted Oscars for Best Picture and Director. Of its nine other nominations, there were seven wins: Best Actor (Ben Kingsley), Screenplay, Cinematography, Art Direction, Editing, Sound, and (surprisingly) Costumes. The evocative music by Ravi Shankar and George Fenton failed to be selected, as did the superb makeup by Tom Smith.

The picture opens with the assassination of Gandhi in 1948 and an unforgettable aerial shot of the funeral procession, as thousands follow the cortege and line the streets. It then flashes back to Gandhi's arrival, as a young barrister, in South Africa in 1893. He learned the hard way— by being bodily thrown off the train—that Indians were not permitted to travel first class.

Gandhi remained in South Africa until 1915, making the world aware of that government's racial repressions. Having arrived with all the trappings of an upper-middle-class Westerner, he left for India wearing a dhoti and proudly traveling third-class. In India, Gandhi triumphed over and over, defeating the British Empire through his steely resolution of "passive resistance."

Born in England, Ben Kingsley (real name: Krishna Bhanji) was one of three finalists for the title role; he was chosen over Dustin Hoffman and John Hurt. The elderly Gandhi, claimed Kingsley, was imprinted on everybody's mind, but his re-creation of the younger man was a combination of "some books and an actor's imagination."

# The Garden of the Finzi-Continis
## (Il Giardino dei Finzi-Contini)

\* \* \* \* \* \* \* \* \* \* \* \* \* \* \* \* \* \* \* \* \* \* \* \* \* \* \* \* \* \* \* \* \* \* \* \* \* \* \* \* \* \* \* \* \* \* \* \* \* \* \* \*

**Nationality**: Italian-German

**Year**: 1970 (U.S. release: 1971)

**Cast**: Dominique Sanda, Lina Capolicchio, Helmut Berger, Fabio Testi, Romolo Valli

**Director**: Vittorio De Sica

**Running Time**: 95 minutes (103 minutes in Italy)

**B/W or Color**: Color

**Availability**: COLUMBIA PICTURES HOME ENTERTAINMENT

Vittorio De Sica (1894–1974) began working in films as an actor in 1918. When, in the Forties, age relegated him to lesser roles, he became active as a director, and as the first neorealist Italian filmmaker, made such prizewinning movies as *Shoeshine*, *The Bicycle Thief*, and *Umberto D*. Following a spate of glossy, empty star vehicles in the Sixties, De Sica enjoyed a major comeback with *The Garden of the Finzi-Continis*. As he told an interviewer, "I accepted this subject because I intimately feel the Jewish problem. I myself feel shame, because we are all guilty of the death of millions of Jews. I wasn't a fascist, but I belong to the country that collaborated with Hitler."

Set in the town of Ferrara (where it was filmed), the movie centers on the elegant estate of the Jewish Finzi-Contini family during the years 1938–43. In those spacious grounds, Micol (Dominique Sanda) and her brother Alberto (Helmut Berger) cling to their sheltered past, sharing their afternoons with the friends with whom they bicycle and play tennis. But it's a temporary joy that soon turns ominous as the reality of war and concentration camps intrudes. Against this fearsome backdrop De Sica portrays the romantic frustrations of these attractive young protagonists, for whom life on the edge of the precipice is fraught with psychological complexities they cannot begin to comprehend.

*The Garden of the Finzi-Continis* is a beautiful and ultimately heartbreaking film, well deserving of its many international awards, including the Berlin Film Festival's Golden Bear, Italy's David di Donatello Award, and a Hollywood Oscar for 1971's Best Foreign Film. The National Board named it one of the year's five best foreign films.

*(Unfortunately, Columbia's videocassette is an English-dubbed version that seldom matches the actors' lips.)*

# Gate of Hell
## (Jigokumon)

★★★★★★★★★★★★★★★★★★★★★★★★★★★★★★★★★★★★★★★★★★★★★★★★★★★★★★★★

*Nationality*: Japanese  **Year**: 1953 (U.S. release: 1954)
*Cast*: Kazuo Hasegawa, Machiko Kyo, Isao Yamagata
*Director*: Teinosuke Kinugasa  **Running Time**: 86 minutes (90 minutes in Japan)
B/W *or Color*: Color  *Availability*: EMBASSY HOME ENTERTAINMENT

In 1954, two years after the West witnessed a sensational Japanese movie "breakthrough" with the monochromatic *Rashomon*, that country's filmmakers now showed the world how artfully they could employ color with the feudal romantic drama *Gate of Hell*. After winning the Grand Prix at Cannes, this exquisite gem went on to garner Academy Awards for Costume Design and Best Foreign Film. The National Board of Review not only listed *Gate of Hell* among the year's best, but also cited its beautiful leading lady, Machiko Kyo, "For the modernization of traditional Japanese acting in *Gate of Hell* and *Ugetsu*."

Set in 12th-century feudal Japan, the film depicts a bloody rivalry among warrior clans. In the aftermath of a palace revolt, a desperate romantic triangle is played out among the impulsive, excitable samurai Moritoh (Kazuo Hasegawa), Kesa (Miss Kyo), the noblewoman he rescues, and her dignified courtier husband, Wataru (Isao Yamagata). Its outcome is more like Greek tragedy.

Although the richness of its original color may have faded slightly over the years, *Gate of Hell*—never the gaudiest of color films to begin with—still impresses with the delicacy of its palette, whose emphasis lies in the realm of pale blues and yellows, with dabs of red against the green pine trees. As are its settings, the film's cinematography is beautiful in its austerity, its deceptive simplicity masking layers of subtle Japanese custom and tradition.

Teinosuke Kinugasa, who directed *Gate of Hell*, was among the pioneers of Japanese motion pictures, playing a major part in their evolution during the silent era. He made his directing bow in 1922 and was much influenced in the late Twenties by the Russian filmmakers Eisenstein and Pudovkin, whom he met in 1928. An active director until 1966, when he was 70, Kinugasa remains little known in the West, where only *Gate of Hell* is likely to be met with recognition.

*(Embassy offers an excellent videotape, subtitled in English.)*

# General Della Rovere

*★ ★ ★ ★ ★ ★ ★ ★ ★ ★ ★ ★ ★ ★ ★ ★ ★ ★ ★ ★ ★ ★ ★ ★ ★ ★ ★ ★ ★ ★ ★ ★ ★ ★ ★ ★ ★ ★ ★ ★ ★ ★ ★ ★ ★ ★ ★ ★ ★ ★ ★ ★ ★ ★ ★*

**Nationality**: Italian                    **Year**: 1960

**Cast**: Vittorio De Sica, Hannes Messemer, Vittorio Caprioli, Giuseppe Rossetti, Sandra Milo

**Director**: Roberto Rossellini          **Running Time**: 160 minutes

**B/W or Color**: B/W                      **Availability**: TV only

After eleven years of not-so-private living (Ingrid Bergman and *Stromboli*), Roberto Rossellini made his best picture since *Open City* and *Paisan* (1945 and 1946, respectively). And he did this in 33 days.

*General Della Rovere* takes place during the German occupation of Italy in 1945, a period of profound defeat for Italy and demoralization for her people. In this picture as in his previous two, Rossellini selects the little man as his hero and describes the way he rises above his own mean and shifty nature.

This particular "little guy" is magnificently played by a very big one, Vittorio De Sica, who provides a brilliant performance in his characterization of a deceitful, shabby, petty criminal who hangs around Genoa taking money from Italians by promising to get their loved ones out of Nazi prisons. The German occupiers, aware of his particular talents and inclinations, hire him to infiltrate the political prison and obtain information about the partisans. They promise a financial reward and a pass to the good life across the border in Switzerland.

Bardone (Vittorio De Sica) is given the new identity of a heroic leader of the Resistance, General Della Rovere. Only the Nazis know the real general is dead.

Once inside the prison, Bardone's new role commands respect and admiration. Furthermore, his experiences with the essential decency of some of the prisoners change him from his old, seedy, fraudulent self into the man he is impersonating—a patriot, hero, and martyr.

In depicting Bardone's growth, Rossellini is clearly saying the individual has a choice even under the most dire circumstances. He is also suggesting the human potential is always possible.

*General Della Rovere* restored Rossellini to the pantheon of cinema masters. The National Board named it among the year's five best foreign films, and it was an Oscar nominee for Original Story and Screenplay.

# Genevieve

★ ★ ★ ★ ★ ★ ★ ★ ★ ★ ★ ★ ★ ★ ★ ★ ★ ★ ★ ★ ★ ★ ★ ★ ★ ★ ★ ★ ★ ★ ★ ★ ★ ★ ★ ★ ★ ★ ★ ★ ★ ★ ★ ★ ★ ★ ★ ★ ★ ★ ★ ★ ★

**Nationality**: British          **Year**: 1953 (U.S. release: 1954)

**Cast**: John Gregson, Dinah Sheridan, Kenneth More, Kay Kendall, Joyce Grenfell

**Director**: Henry Cornelius          **Running Time**: 86 minutes

**B/W or Color**: Color          **Availability**: EMBASSY HOME ENTERTAINMENT

The title-named heroine of this vintage comedy is an antique 1904 automobile, the proud possession of one Alan McKim (John Gregson). For his wife Wendy (Dinah Sheridan), she's an object of envious exasperation, since Genevieve has quite usurped Alan's attentions, preparatory to the annual London-to-Brighton old-car race. His automaniac pal Ambrose (Kenneth More) brings along a girlfriend named Rosalind (Kay Kendall), and Wendy accompanies her husband, although she deplores his vintage-auto obsession.

Mishaps on the road and a healthy rivalry between the men enliven the run to Brighton. There, a mix-up over accommodations puts Alan and Wendy into a nightmare hostelry (run by Joyce Grenfell, in a marvelously eccentric cameo), where domestic differences flare and subside. Alan wages a bet with Ambrose that he can beat his cocky friend on the return trip to London, and the rival drivers resort to an incredible succession of juvenile pranks to upset one another. When Genevieve is ultimately the victor, Alan and Wendy are reconciled.

*Genevieve* burst brightly upon the British film scene, garnering acclaim for William Rose's sly-humored screenplay. Producer-director Henry Cornelius's *(Passport to Pimlico)* well-paced guidance of this delightful battle of the sexes helped win *Genevieve* Britain's Academy Award for 1953's Best British Film.

Of the actors, More and Kendall stand out by dint of their more colorfully written characters. For 27-year-old Kendall, the chic, trumpet-playing Rosalind finally gave her a role that matched her talent and brought her to Hollywood's attention. A final note of praise for Larry Adler's unusual harmonica score, whose merry wit adds a novel touch that helped make this movie so entertaining.

The National Board of Review listed *Genevieve* among 1954's best imports.

# Gervaise

★ ★ ★ ★ ★ ★ ★ ★ ★ ★ ★ ★ ★ ★ ★ ★ ★ ★ ★ ★ ★ ★ ★ ★ ★ ★ ★ ★ ★ ★ ★ ★ ★ ★ ★ ★ ★ ★ ★ ★ ★ ★ ★ ★ ★ ★ ★ ★ ★ ★ ★ ★

Nationality: French                     Year: 1956
Cast: Maria Schell, François Périer, Suzy Delair, Armand Mestral
Director: René Clément          Running Time: 116 minutes
B/W or Color: B/W                 Availability: Public Domain

This excellent, beautifully crafted film was adapted from the Emile Zola novel *L'Assomoir*. Maria Schell stars as Gervaise, a downtrodden Parisian wife and mother who cannot escape the cycle of poverty and degradation of her ghetto environment. Her husband, Coupeau (François Périer), is a brutish alcoholic, engaged in an affair with Virginie (Suzy Delair), her co-worker at the laundry. Gervaise is eventually drawn into the shame she wishes to escape. However, Clément did not direct the film in a somber, cynical fashion; the screen is alive with the teeming life of a slum, where privacy is an unknown quality. The movie has the look of a painting by Renoir or Monet, but without the romanticism. Clément has fashioned his own visual scheme, borrowing only that which furthers the theme of the film. Even the fight scene between Schell and Delair is carefully staged and choreographed.

*Gervaise* is as studied as *Moulin Rouge,* and set in roughly the same 19th-century era in Paris. Schell's acting is magnificent, and this was the film that took her to Hollywood. A highly emotional, introspective actress, Schell was expected to have a big international career. She remained a critics' favorite, but her intensity and lack of glamour, mitigated against widespread popular appeal.

Périer and Delair are memorable as the husband and mistress, fitting neatly into director Clément's pictorial and dramatic scheme as they complement Schell. Clément is responsible for this: he makes the film a tour de force for Schell, complete with poignant close-ups of her suffering, intense face.

*Gervaise* won two awards at 1956's Venice Film Festival, including Best Actress Maria Schell, and the British Film Academy voted it Best Picture of the Year. Oscar-nominated, the movie lost out to *La Strada* as Best Foreign Language Film, but The National Board named it one of 1957's five best foreign-language films.

# Get Out Your Handkerchiefs
## (Préparez Vos Mouchoirs)

★ ★ ★ ★ ★ ★ ★ ★ ★ ★ ★ ★ ★ ★ ★ ★ ★ ★ ★ ★ ★ ★ ★ ★ ★ ★ ★ ★ ★ ★ ★ ★ ★ ★ ★ ★ ★ ★ ★ ★ ★ ★ ★ ★ ★ ★ ★ ★ ★ ★

Nationality: French          Year: 1978

Cast: Gérard Depardieu, Patrick Dewaere, Carole Laure, Riton, Michel Serrault

Director: Bertrand Blier          Running Time: 108 minutes

B/W or Color: Color          Availability: WARNER HOME VIDEO

There seems to be an international impression that Frenchmen have the market cornered when it comes to expertise in l'amour and affairs of the heart. In this Academy Award winner (Best Foreign Film, 1978), as well as in his other films, Bertrand Blier makes it abundantly clear that the French are just as lost when it comes to making love as the rest of us poor folks.

*Get Out Your Handkerchiefs* made a splash when it first opened here and helped to establish Gérard Depardieu as an international star. Like *Going Places* (also starring Depardieu and Patrick Dewaere), this is a "buddy" picture, but this time, instead of amoral roughnecks, we have respectable, middle-class men who have little in common except their lack of understanding of women. Concerned because he cannot make his wife happy, Depardieu offers her to the first man she makes eyes at (in a genteel fashion, of course) in a café. Dewaere is the surprised recipient of this gift. Although confident at first, he is dismayed to discover that he, too, is unable to bring happiness to the lady. Like Depardieu, he is confounded. What does the lovely Carole Laure want? The obsessiveness with which these two men try to solve the mystery is the basis of the movie and the springboard for Blier's zingy humor.

Both heroes decide a baby will make Laure happy, but once again, they fail. It is a 13-year-old boy who becomes the proud papa. Here it must be stressed that the film never becomes smutty—it has a dreamy, almost playful feel. Pauline Kael reports, "Blier's art is an exaggeration; he takes emotions and blows them up so big that we can see things that people don't speak about—and laugh at them." Blier goes behind Mona Lisa's smile in *Get Out Your Handkerchiefs*.

*(The videocassette is dubbed in English.)*

# The Ghost Goes West

**★★★★★★★★★★★★★★★★★★★★★★★★★★★★★★★★★★★★★★★★★★★★★★★★★★★★**

**Nationality**: British          **Year**: 1935 (U.S. release: 1936)
**Cast**: Robert Donat, Jean Parker, Eugene Pallette, Elsa Lanchester
**Director**: René Clair          **Running Time**: 90 minutes
**B/W or Color**: B/W          **Availability**: EMBASSY HOME
                                     ENTERTAINMENT

Producer Alexander Korda had planned this adaptation of Eric Keown's *Punch* magazine story *Sir Tristram Goes West* for Charles Laughton. But Laughton chose to accept Hollywood's offer of *Mutiny on the Bounty*. The project was assigned to the French director René Clair, whose successes included *Le Million* and *Sous les Toits de Paris*. Clair wanted Laurence Olivier as his star, but Korda now insisted on the deftly urbane Robert Donat. It was only the beginning of their many artistic differences over a Robert Sherwood screenplay that was retitled *The Ghost Goes West*, and whose sharp satirical touches included gondolas in a castle moat and an all-black, kilt-clad jazz band.

Donat's role in the film is a dual one, as both Murdoch Glourie, a dour 18th-century ghost, and his 1930s descendant, Donald Glourie, who's reduced by circumstances to sell his ancestral Scottish castle to an American grocery-chain millionaire (Eugene Pallette). Stone by stone, the ancient edifice is shipped across the ocean, to be completely reconstructed—with modern plumbing—among the palm trees of Florida. The Glourie ghost accompanies those family stones, having been condemned to haunt Glourie Castle until a rival clan's insult is avenged. Romance enters the picture in the person of the tycoon's pretty daughter Peggy (Jean Parker), who understandably confuses the young Scotsman with his all-too-visible spectral ancestor.

Due to Clair's unfortunate differences with Korda, *The Ghost Goes West* was his only British film. But its inherent grace, wit, and charm managed to survive Korda's subsequent re-editing and the movie remains a vintage comedy classic (named one of the ten best pictures by The National Board) and paved the way for Clair's equally delightful American fantasy film of 1942, *I Married a Witch*.

# Ginger and Fred
## (Ginger e Fred)

★ ★ ★ ★ ★ ★ ★ ★ ★ ★ ★ ★ ★ ★ ★ ★ ★ ★ ★ ★ ★ ★ ★ ★ ★ ★ ★ ★ ★ ★ ★ ★ ★ ★ ★ ★ ★ ★ ★ ★ ★ ★ ★ ★ ★ ★ ★ ★ ★ ★ ★

*Nationality*: Italian-French-West    *Year*: 1986
German

*Cast*: Giulietta Masina, Marcello Mastroianni, Franco Fabrizi

*Director*: Federico Fellini          *Running Time*: 128 minutes

*B/W or Color*: Color                 *Availability*: MGM/UA HOME
                                      VIDEO

As *Ginger and Fred* opens, Ginger steps pertly off the train and proceeds into the central hall of Rome's main railroad station. In Fellini's vision, the station is ringed with giant billboards and neon lights advertising processed foods. Dangling from the lofty ceiling is a gargantuan package of stuffed pigs' feet, a homemade specialty now available in a cardboard container with a guaranteed shelf life of months. Fellini's images, if not predictable, are often familiar. To complain that we've seen his tarts and dwarfs before is as superficial as to bemoan the sight of yet another Matisse odalisque. *Ginger and Fred* works and when another generation, too distant to be wearied by any hint of déjà vu, judges this film, it might find *Ginger and Fred* a masterpiece.

A television variety show brings together two entertainers from the Thirties to make a guest appearance. Ginger and Fred were never particularly good dancers, even in their prime, but they let us see they were always realistic about that. They knew that creating illusions was their business, and when they were lucky they could share a bit of the illusions themselves.

Those consummate artists, Giulietta Masina and Marcello Mastroianni, play not merely to each other but to Fellini's intent. They sustain perfectly controlled realizations of characters with sharply defined limits, surely a more difficult achievement than gasping through the plagues and afflictions that line the road to the Academy Awards.

The National Board chose *Ginger and Fred* as one of the five best foreign films of the year.

(*The videocassette is in subtitled Italian.*)

# The Go-Between

* * * * * * * * * * * * * * * * * * * * * * * * * * * * * * * * * * * * * * * * * * * * * * * * * *

*Nationality*: British          *Year*: 1971
*Cast*: Julie Christie, Alan Bates, Dominic Guard, Margaret Leighton, Michael Redgrave, Michael Gough, Edward Fox
*Director*: Joseph Losey          *Running Time*: 116 minutes
*B/W or Color*: Color          *Availability*: TV only

T he past is a foreign country," muses the film's narrator. "They do things differently there." Thus, Michael Redgrave sets the tone for Harold Pinter's engrossing adaptation of the L. P. Hartley novel about the effect of a secret love affair on an impressionable boy one summer in England's Norfolk countryside. Redgrave plays the elderly bachelor Leo Colston, who makes a tentative, sentimental journey back to the scene of a 50-year-old trauma. At the age of 12, middle-class Leo (Dominic Guard) was invited to summer at the rambling country estate of his upper-crust school pal Marcus Maudsley. At once smitten with his friend's beautiful older sister Marian (Julie Christie), Leo becomes the unsuspecting go-between for her love letters to their tenant farmer Ted Burgess (Alan Bates), despite her imminent marriage to a dull but socially acceptable gentleman. When Leo discovers that his two favorite grown-ups are secret lovers, the confused boy refuses to carry further missives. Marion's suspicious mother (Margaret Leighton), who had observed Leo furtively tucking an envelope away, forces him to take her to the lovers' trysting place—with results that are predictably devastating.

*The Go-Between* is a marvelous film, as opulent to the eye as it is challenging to the intellect. Hartley's fascinating blend of old-world gentilities and progressive sexual undercurrents make this a compelling exercise in high-styled, romantic melodrama. The casting is perfect, but Margaret Leighton and 15-year-old Dominic Guard steal the acting honors. *The Go-Between* won 1971's Grand Prix at Cannes, and The National Board listed it among the year's best.

# The Gods Must Be Crazy

★★★★★★★★★★★★★★★★★★★★★★★★★★★★★★★★★★★★★★★★★★★★★★★★★★★★★★

*Nationality*: South African          *Year*: 1981 (U.S. release: 1984)
*Cast*: N!xau, Marius Weyers, Sandra Prinsloo, Louw Verwey
*Director*: Jamie Uys          *Running Time*: 109 minutes
*B/W or Color*: Color          *Availability*: PLAYHOUSE VIDEO

I n an old popular song about the benefits of civilization as against the primitiveness of the jungle, the songwriter opts for the wilderness, essentially summing up *The Gods Must Be Crazy*: a zany comedy, but one with substance, beautifully written and directed by Jamie Uys, a veteran African filmmaker.

A Coke bottle drops from a low-flying plane—and changes the lives of an isolated tribe of small Kalahari desert bushmen. The tribe's leader, Xi (N!xau), knows the object is a gift from the gods, useful to carry water, to blow through to make a big sound, to grind corn, to spin as a toy, and the entire community finds a use for it. The trouble is that there is only one bottle. These simple bush people, unacquainted with personal possessions, punishment, or fighting, suddenly become fanatical about their bottle—snatching it away from one another until one day a child deliberately hits another with it. Seeing this final enormity, Xi is now determined that their gift must be returned to the gods and undertakes to make the journey to the edge of the world.

Interspersed with the tribal sequences are glimpses of bustling city life: a sour-looking woman, hair in rollers, drives two blocks to a mailbox to mail her letter; bored children in a prisonlike school; clerks in offices busily filing and unfiling to the musical cacophony of blaring horns, construction noises, and time clocks.

On his mission, Xi encounters white men whom he assumes are gods. Nothing he sees surprises or frightens him, since obviously anything is possible in this land of deities. The people he meets are mostly caring: the lovable, bumbling microbiologist (Marius Weyes) whose earnest efforts to woo the mission teacher (Sandra Prinsloo) result in some marvelous sight gags, even the revolutionaries who hold the school hostage and are so inept that they hark back to early slapstick villains. Xi, taking all this in stride, continues toward his ultimate goal.

One of the many remarkable things about this amusing yet serious and touching film is that N!xau is not an actor. He is playing himself. He is the chief of a South African desert tribe. The movie's unexpected success generated a sequel, untitled at this writing.

# Going Places
## (Les Valseuses)

\* \* \* \* \* \* \* \* \* \* \* \* \* \* \* \* \* \* \* \* \* \* \* \* \* \* \* \* \* \* \* \* \* \* \* \* \* \* \* \* \* \* \* \* \* \* \* \* \* \* \* \* \* \* \*

**Nationality**: French         **Year**: 1974

**Cast**: Gérard Depardieu, Patrick Dewaere, Jeanne Moreau, Miou-Miou, Brigitte Fossey

**Director**: Bertrand Blier       **Running Time**: 117 minutes

**B/W or Color**: Color        **Availability**: RCA/COLUMBIA PIC-
TURES HOME VIDEO

If you care for things down and dirty, then this French crime romp is for you. A popular pair, Patrick Dewaere and Gérard Depardieu, make a mockery of the law and also double Miou-Miou's pleasure—as well as that of a number of other willing females—along the way. It's the best-known work of Bertrand Blier, son of the great French character star Bernard Blier. The young Blier wrote a best-selling novel, *Les Valseuses (The Waltzers)*, in 1972, then adapted it with the aid of Philippe Dumarcay and directed it for the screen. While Miou-Miou does much of her emoting in the nude, and Dewaere and Depardieu are no slouches in that department either, the distaff side is represented rather discreetly. This includes turns by the great Jeanne Moreau, Brigitte Fossey (the little girl from 1952's *Forbidden Games)*, and newcomer Isabelle Huppert in a last-minute appearance.

Petty thieves Depardieu and Dewaere have many adventures, mainly of a sexual nature. They encounter beauty salon proprietor Jacques Rispal and take off with his mistress, Miou-Miou. They force young mother Brigitte Fossey to make love on a train, then pick up ex-convict Jeanne Moreau. The latter stays with them for a while, then commits suicide. Moreau's son (Jacques Chailieux) joins them, but commits murder after arousing the cold Miou-Miou. The trio then seduce young Isabelle Huppert (then 18), after stealing her father's car.

The totally uninhibited nature of this comedy-drama-actioner is probably less shocking today, but may not appeal to all tastes. It's energetic, youthful, and completely Gallic in flavor. Although Depardieu later took on roles of a more serious nature to cement his reputation as an actor, Dewaere was dissatisfied with the way his career—and life—were going. He committed suicide at the age of 35.

*(The videocassette is dubbed in English.)*

# The Gold of Naples
## (L'Oro di Napoli)

★★★★★★★★★★★★★★★★★★★★★★★★★★★★★★★★★★★★★★★★★★★★★★★★★★★★

Nationality: Italian

Year: 1954 (U.S. release: 1957)

Cast: Toto, Sophia Loren, Vittorio De Sica, Silvana Mangano

Director: Vittorio De Sica

Running Time: 107 minutes (135 minutes in Italy)

B/W or Color: B/W

Availability: TV only

Succulent slices of Neapolitan life are served by master craftsman Vittorio De Sica and sprinkled with the seasoned talents of Toto, Sophia Loren, Silvana Mangano, and De Sica himself in *The Gold of Naples*.

Upon its arrival in America, *Gold* consisted of four vignettes. Originally (and only at the 1955 Edinburgh Film Festival), it contained six. The segment dealing with a child's funeral procession was eliminated, and Europe enjoyed a *Gold* of five nuggets. Missing from prints seen in the United States was also an episode concerning a joke played on a snobbish nobleman by a drugstore counsellor. An even shorter version (minus De Sica) was later shown as *Every Day's a Holiday*.

In the delightfully droll episode called "The Racketeer," Toto plays a harassed host to an abusive bully. After years of oppression, he suddenly gains the courage to rebel.

"Pizza on Credit" features Sophia Loren as an unfaithful wife who forgets her wedding ring at her lover's apartment and tells her pizza-vendor husband that it probably fell into the morning's dough. A harried check among recent customers precedes the ring's return by the lover, whom the suspicious husband does not recognize as having sampled *his* wares.

Vittorio De Sica gives a brilliant performance as "The Gambler," an aging count whose wealthy wife won't support his habit. Thus, he's forced to engage in card games with his doorman's 8-year-old son, who easily and wearily wins.

In *Gold*'s most dramatic segment, Silvana Mangano is excellent as "Theresa," a former prostitute whose marriage of convenience to a rich man undergoes a change of heart, as she falls in love with her husband.

Superb photography and music add luster to *The Gold of Naples*. But the ultimate luster is De Sica's. Complimented by an interviewer on his self-direction in this film, De Sica remarked, "That was painful. A line of dialogue can be said a thousand ways; you need someone behind the camera to tell you which is the right one."

# Goldfinger

\* \* \* \* \* \* \* \* \* \* \* \* \* \* \* \* \* \* \* \* \* \* \* \* \* \* \* \* \* \* \* \* \* \* \* \* \* \* \* \* \* \* \* \* \* \* \* \* \* \*

Nationality: British           Year: 1964
Cast: Sean Connery, Gert Frobe, Honor Blackman, Shirley Eaton
Director: Guy Hamilton        Running Time: 108 minutes
B/W or Color: Color          Availability: CBS/FOX VIDEO

The third James Bond film, *Goldfinger,* proved to the world that the most successful series in film history had been well and truly launched. United Artists now planned one a year. The budgets were bigger, the gimmicks and gadgetry more plentiful, the locales more exotic, the opening teasers longer, and the villains more diabolical.

Sean Connery was firmly in control as the cool, commanding, indestructible double agent, and unlike the paltry $30,000 he received for *Dr. No,* this time he took home $10 million. Here the evildoer is Auric Goldfinger (German actor Gert Frobe), a mysterious financier who is illegally tampering with the U.S. and U.K. gold reserves. Honor Blackman plays the provocatively named Pussy Galore, butch as in the novel, but not entirely cold to Bond's advances.

Bond first foils Goldfinger in a crooked card game in Miami Beach, then seduces his accomplice, the beauteous Jill Masterson (Shirley Eaton), who dies after her entire body is painted in gold. 007 meets the villain again during a rigged golf game, along with his lethal sidekick, the oriental Oddjob (Harold Sakata), whose weapon is a razor-brimmed hat skillfully aimed and tossed. In one excruciatingly painful scene, Bond lies spread-eagled as a laser beam bears down on him.

The smashing finale is Goldfinger's assault on Fort Knox. The producers' request to film inside the actual fort was denied by the U.S. Treasury Department, but Uncle Sam permitted them to photograph the surrounding area and provided American soldiers to act as extras.

Added eye- and ear-catching pluses are Shirley Bassey, singing the title song over the credits, and an Aston Martin DBV, equipped with machine guns and an ejector seat.

Only one question remains—the totally unfathomable decision to dub Gert Frobe's voice, since the actor is fluent in English.

# The Good, the Bad and the Ugly

## (Il Buono, Il Brutto, Il Cattivo)

★★★★★★★★★★★★★★★★★★★★★★★★★★★★★★★★★★★★★★★★★★★★★★★★★★★★★★

Nationality: Italian      Year: 1966 (U.S. release: 1967)

Cast: Clint Eastwood, Eli Wallach, Lee Van Cleef

Director: Sergio Leone      Running Time: 161 minutes (180 minutes in Italy)

B/W or Color: Color      Availability: CBS/FOX HOME VIDEO

I l Buono, Il Brutto, Il Cattivo is the third in the Sergio Leone/Clint Eastwood trilogy of spaghetti Westerns, following A Fistful of Dollars and For a Few Dollars More. Still only a television cowboy in the United States, Eastwood, of whom Leone had never heard, got the part of the No Name Stranger in Fistful after James Coburn requested a $25,000 salary. By the third film Eastwood's take was a quarter of a million dollars plus a percentage, and he had won a poll as the world's favorite movie star.

In the American West during the Civil War, Eastwood is the mysterious stranger, Joe, presumably the good; Lee Van Cleef plays Angel Eyes, a sadistic killer, the bad; and Eli Wallach, a Mexican bandit, Tuco, the ugly. Their quest is $200,000 in gold buried in an unmarked grave. Joe and Tuco pull a con game in which Joe turns Tuco over to various sheriffs, collects the bounty, then saves him from the noose. The partners are allied only in their greed, double-crossing each other whenever possible. The finale, a three-way shootout between the gunmen, takes place in the appropriately named Sad Hill Cemetery.

American reviewers, gunning for this third "pop Western," objected en masse to Leone's excessive violence and brutality, The New York Times even dubbing it "The Burn, the Gouge and the Mangle . . . Zane Grey meets the Marquis de Sade." Only a few appreciated its black humor, its honestly unsentimental approach, and its often laughable performances. As for its ethics, Eastwood does kill 10 of the 20 bodies littering the plains, but they all drew first!

After the public turned out in droves to cheer its new cult hero, a few critics relented, Andrew Sarris going so far as to call the film "a kind of cactus Calvary [and] Eastwood a plausible lower-class hero whose physical redemption is the contemporary correlative of Christ's spiritual redemption."

# Goodbye, Mr. Chips

**★ ★ ★ ★ ★ ★ ★ ★ ★ ★ ★ ★ ★ ★ ★ ★ ★ ★ ★ ★ ★ ★ ★ ★ ★ ★ ★ ★ ★ ★ ★ ★ ★ ★ ★ ★ ★ ★ ★ ★ ★ ★ ★ ★ ★ ★ ★ ★ ★ ★ ★ ★ ★ ★ ★**

*Nationality*: British          *Year*: 1939

*Cast*: Robert Donat, Greer Garson, Paul von Hernried (Paul Henried), Lyn Harding, Terry Kilburn, John Mills

*Director*: Sam Wood          *Running Time*: 114 minutes

*B/W or Color*: B/W          *Availability*: MGM/UA HOME VIDEO

K atherine Chipping (Greer Garson, in her screen debut) tells her professor-husband (Robert Donat), whom she calls Chips, "You have all sorts of unexpected gifts and qualities." So does this outstanding film version of the James Hilton novel, which tells the story of 63 years (1870–1933) in the life of a beloved teacher.

Selected as one of The National Board's ten best for 1939, *Goodbye, Mr. Chips* won Donat a well-deserved Academy Award as Best Actor and received six other nominations: Best Picture, Actress (Garson), Director (Sam Wood), Screenplay, Editing, and Sound. The 1969 color remake, starring Peter O'Toole and Petula Clark, had music added, but most of the charm was missing.

Told in flashback, the passage of years is cleverly achieved by the recurring use of a procession of students giving their names and exchanging snippets of timely conversation. Terry Kilburn plays four generations of the Colley family; John Mills appears as one of them in adulthood.

First seen as an elderly man, Chips recalls his arrival at Brookfield School and his initial experiences teaching Latin—gaining his students' respect but not their friendship. On a holiday with another teacher (Paul von Hernreid, who later changed his name to Paul Henreid), Chipping meets the radiant Katherine Ellis, who succeeds in having him overcome his acute shyness. As easily as she wins his heart, so does the new Mrs. Chips win over the faculty and students at Brookfield. Her death in childbirth—along with the baby—devastates everyone (including the viewer).

Many years later, a dying Chips overhears a doctor saying that it's a pity the old fellow never had any children. "But you're wrong," protests Chips, "I had thousands . . . and all boys."

A toast: To Chips of Brookfield! To a classic film!

# The Gospel According to St. Matthew
## (Il Vangelo Secondo Matteo)

\*\*\*\*\*\*\*\*\*\*\*\*\*\*\*\*\*\*\*\*\*\*\*\*\*\*\*\*\*\*\*\*\*\*\*\*\*\*\*\*\*\*\*\*\*\*\*\*\*\*\*\*\*\*\*\*\*\*

**Nationality**: Italian            **Year**: 1964 (U.S. release: 1966)

**Cast**: Enrique Irazoqui, Margherita Caruso, Susanna Pasolini, Marcello Morante

**Director**: Pier Paolo Pasolini      **Running Time**: 136 minutes (142 minutes in Italy)

**B/W or Color**: B/W             **Availability**: Public Domain

The Gospel According to St. Matthew is probably the finest work of the controversial Italian director Pier Paolo Pasolini (1922–75). At different times a poet, novelist, screenwriter, and film theoretician, his work depicted the seamy and less pleasant aspects of life. In 1975, Pasolini was brutally murdered by an alleged homosexual lover. He was an avowed Marxist and atheist as well, so it comes as something of a surprise to learn that his most honored and accomplished film concerns the story of Christ. Released just one year before George Stevens's mammoth *The Greatest Story Ever Told,* Pasolini's film has none of the deadening reverence that ruined that Hollywood epic. The tone is respectful but never stiff or pretentious, while the technique is deceptively simple. Shot on a low budget, the camera is hand held. The images created, however, are vivid, artful, and full of life. The photographer, Tonino Delli Colli, was certainly no amateur, and he would further distinguish himself with such films as Leone's *Once Upon a Time in the West* (1968) and Wertmuller's *Seven Beauties* (1976). Danilo Donati's austere black-and-white costumes create striking contrasts of characters framed against the rough, beautiful landscape of southern Italy.

There is very little dialogue (most of the text comes straight from the Bible), and the cast of nonprofessional actors (including Pasolini's mother as the elderly Mary) is effective because of his direction, which concentrates on static, close-up reaction shots alternating with long shots of Jesus and his followers walking through vast, empty fields. The music consists of Mozart, Bach, Prokofiev, and modern hymns, such as "Sometimes I Feel Like a Motherless Child." This seemingly incongruous use of music, combined with cinema-verité camerawork, instead creates the feeling that we are witnessing something fresh, alive, and real. Jesus walking on the water, the Sermon on the Mount, and the Last Supper are re-created without posturing, while the Crucifixion scene lasts more than 15 minutes and is unforgettable in its harsh realism and emotional power.

Dedicated to the memory of Pope John Paul XXIII, Pasolini's film won the Special Jury Prize at the Venice Film Festival, as well as being named one of the best foreign films of the year by The National Board.

# Grand Illusion
## (La Grande Illusion)

★ ★ ★ ★ ★ ★ ★ ★ ★ ★ ★ ★ ★ ★ ★ ★ ★ ★ ★ ★ ★ ★ ★ ★ ★ ★ ★ ★ ★ ★ ★ ★ ★ ★ ★ ★ ★ ★ ★ ★ ★ ★ ★ ★ ★ ★ ★ ★ ★ ★ ★ ★

**Nationality**: French      **Year**: 1937 (U.S. release: 1938)
**Cast**: Jean Gabin, Erich von Stroheim, Pierre Fresnay, Dita Parlo, Marcel Dalio, Julien Carette
**Director**: Jean Renoir      **Running Time**: 111 minutes
**B/W or Color**: B/W      **Availability**: CBS/FOX VIDEO

This great antiwar film, as Jean Renoir sadly remarked, didn't prevent a second world war. But what a record of men in a prison camp during World War I! Still included in many ten-best lists, this beautiful, moving, philosophic film is one of the great artistic achievements. The script by Charles Spaak and Renoir is memorable and ideal for ensemble acting. The photography by Christian Matras and Claude Renoir is atmospheric and dreamlike. Eugene Lourie did the magnificent set design, one of the few times in which decor seemed to be an outgrowth of the characters' personalities. (In his autobiography, *My Work in Films*, Lourie remarks about Erich von Stroheim's obsession with details: he asked von Stroheim to suggest articles he would need to decorate his commandant's room, and von Stroheim gave him a mammoth list. Lourie gave the actor a large crucifix to hang over his bed.)

The film is set in a German prison camp for officers in 1917. Von Stroheim attempts an egalitarian friendship with French officer Pierre Fresnay, who is uncomfortable with the arrangement. Clearly a snob who cannot understand the changes to come following the war, the commandant is an elitist who believes in egalitarianism only with those of his social class. He is forced to kill Fresnay in an escape attempt involving Jean Gabin and Marcel Dalio, who are officers only because of the war, rather than from tradition. Sadly, the German cannot understand this betrayal of friendship from one of his own.

The most famous sequence in the film is the drag soldier entertainment. The look on the prisoners' faces as they laugh, and then fall silent, recalling the joys of home, is devastating. The pointlessness of war has seldom been realized more tellingly.

*(The CBS/Fox cassette is in French with English subtitles.)*

# Great Expectations

★ ★ ★ ★ ★ ★ ★ ★ ★ ★ ★ ★ ★ ★ ★ ★ ★ ★ ★ ★ ★ ★ ★ ★ ★ ★ ★ ★ ★ ★ ★ ★ ★ ★ ★ ★ ★ ★ ★ ★ ★ ★ ★ ★ ★ ★ ★ ★ ★ ★ ★ ★ ★ ★

*Nationality*: British　　　　　*Year*: 1946 (U.S. release: 1947)
*Cast*: John Mills, Valerie Hobson, Bernard Miles, Francis L. Sullivan, Finlay Currie, Martita Hunt, Jean Simmons, Anthony Wager, Alec Guinness
*Director*: David Lean　　　　　*Running Time*: 118 minutes
*B/W or Color*: B/W　　　　　*Availability*: CBS VIDEO LIBRARY

There's no music—only the sound of bare trees creaking in the wintry wind as a young boy runs across the Kentish salt marshes at dusk on a Christmas Eve to kneel at his mother's grave. As he rises, he suddenly collides with the sinister, hulking figure of an escaped convict. Thus David Lean begins *Great Expectations* with one of the great shock moments recorded on film, a strong reminder that he is among the finest editors working in motion pictures.

Charles Dickens's voluminous novel was filmed at least four times between 1916 and 1975. But none approached the excellence of this version produced by the brilliant triumvirate of Anthony Havelock-Allan, Ronald Neame, and David Lean. After they judiciously pruned the lengthy, sprawling tale, they concentrated on the orphaned young Pip and how he becomes a young man of "great expectations," due to the generosity of an anonymous benefactor.

Visually, *Great Expectations* excels. Oscars were awarded for its striking production design and art direction, and for Guy Green's exquisitely composed and beautifully lit monochromatic photography. A splendidly chosen cast helps enormously: after 15 years in films, John Mills, as the engaging adult Pip, became a familiar name in the United States; the little-known character actress Martita Hunt was unforgettable as the bizarre old Miss Havisham; and young Jean Simmons attracted great praise for her proud, teenaged Estella—before growing into the coolly adult Valerie Hobson. Not to mention the fine character acting of Francis L. Sullivan, Finlay Currie, Bernard Miles, and Anthony Wager's endearing child Pip. As Pip's adult friend Herbert, 32-year-old stage actor Alec Guinness made an auspicious movie debut.

Understandably, The National Board of Review named *Great Expectations* among 1947's ten best motion pictures.

# The Great Train Robbery
## (The First Great Train Robbery)

★★★★★★★★★★★★★★★★★★★★★★★★★★★★★★★★★★★★★★★★★★★★★★★★★★★★★★★

**Nationality**: British        **Year**: 1979
**Cast**: Sean Connery, Donald Sutherland, Lesley-Anne Down, Alan Webb
**Director**: Michael Crichton     **Running Time**: 111 minutes
**B/W or Color**: Color         **Availability**: CBS/FOX HOME
                                           VIDEO

Every 38 years comes a film called *The Great Train Robbery*. First, in 1903, was the granddaddy of all Western films; second, in 1941, was an excellent modern-day B feature about the hijacking of an entire train; finally, in 1979, came this British thriller, tops in action, comedy, and historical significance. It's based on director-scripter Michael Crichton's 1975 best-seller, which was founded on fact, the first robbery of a moving train, in 1855 England. Sean Connery and Donald Sutherland are the agile stars who play it tongue-in-cheek when they aren't seriously risking their necks. Beautiful Lesley-Anne Down is the female lead of this meticulously researched production, which was shot mainly in Ireland.

In 1855, after more than a year of careful planning, Edward Pierce robbed a train leaving England with a payroll for troops fighting the Crimean War. Connery takes the role of Pierce, with Sutherland portraying his burglar-accomplice (who must escape Newgate Prison during a public hanging) and Down as a mistress-accomplice. As to his motives, Connery says simply in court, "I wanted the money."

Distributor United Artists unnecessarily offered $10,000 to anyone who could prove that the players didn't perform their own stunts. Watching Connery making his way across the cars of a speeding train, unaided by safety devices or stunt double, should be proof enough. The film was a departure for Crichton, who had gained a reputation as a science-fiction writer-director (notably *The Andromeda Strain, Coma,* and *Westworld*). For Connery, it was another opportunity to show how well he operated outside of the James Bond mold, while for producer De Laurentiis—whose efforts are often maligned justifiably—it was a major triumph.

# Green for Danger

\*\*\*\*\*\*\*\*\*\*\*\*\*\*\*\*\*\*\*\*\*\*\*\*\*\*\*\*\*\*\*\*\*\*\*\*\*\*\*\*\*\*\*\*\*\*\*\*\*\*\*\*\*\*\*\*\*\*

Nationality: British

Year: 1946 (U.S. release: 1947)

Cast: Sally Gray, Trevor Howard, Rosamund John, Alastair Sim, Leo Genn, Megs Jenkins

Director: Sidney Gilliat

Running Time: 93 minutes

B/W or Color: B/W

Availability: TV only

The production team of Frank Launder and Sidney Gilliat had established a reputation for bringing off serious subject matter with a wry sense of humor (*I See a Dark Stranger/The Adventuress* and *The Rake's Progress/Notorious Gentleman*). With *Green for Danger,* they turned out one of the best whodunits of the Forties. This drily amusing World War II puzzler, based on Christianna Brand's mystery novel, is cleverly developed by way of a report that Scotland Yard Inspector Cockrill (memorably portrayed by the ominously whimsical Alastair Sim) is giving his superior. The subject: murders in a wartime emergency hospital (formerly a handsome English estate).

Rescue worker Joseph Higgins (Moore Marriott) has been brought in as a casualty. The surgeon (Leo Genn) asks Nurse Sanson (Rosamund John) to prepare for a ten o'clock operation. With everything ready, the patient is wheeled in under the great shadowless lamps, and the anesthetist Dr. Barnes (Trevor Howard) turns on his machine. Suddenly, without warning, Higgins lies dead on the operating table. Soon afterward, young Sister Bates (Judy Campbell) finds evidence that the patient met with foul play. Before she can report it, she's stabbed to death. The investigating Inspector Cockrill discovers that each of five suspects had a motive for the crimes, and when his investigation fails to determine the guilty party, he arranges to "re-stage" the fatal operation, hoping to unmask the killer.

A fine cast plays this delicious melodrama to the hilt, but best of all—in a role that finally brought him American recognition—is the 46-year-old Scottish actor Alastair Sim, a former professor of elocution, whose unique, lugubrious demeanor and often wryly defeated characters lend delightful facets to the screenplays he elected to interpret.

# Gregory's Girl

★★★★★★★★★★★★★★★★★★★★★★★★★★★★★★★★★★★★★★★★★★★★★★★★★★★★★★★

**Nationality**: British        **Year**: 1980 (U.S. release: 1982)
**Cast**: Gordon John Sinclair, Dee Hepburn, Chic Murray, Jake D'Arcy
**Director**: Bill Forsyth        **Running Time**: 91 minutes
**B/W or Color**: Color        **Availability**: EMBASSY HOME
                                                ENTERTAINMENT

Writer-director Bill Forsyth's offbeat rite-of-passage comedy, *Gregory's Girl*, consists of several small ingredients put together just right to create a delightful confection. Far different from the *Porky's* school of teenage movies, it has the vitality of first love and the joy of a goodnight kiss.

When adolescence comes upon 16-year-old Gregory (Gordon John Sinclair), who lives just outside Glasgow, his interest in soccer turns from obsessive to indifferent. Atop his list is how to get to the bottom of the opposite sex and the myriad of mysteries they present. Following the team's umpteenth loss, the coach (Jake D'Arcy) relegates Gregory to goalkeeping and replaces him with Dorothy (Dee Hepburn). Does the lad resent this female usurper? On the contrary, he announces to his friends, "I'm in love."

His fellow travelers through the time warp of adolescence are of no help to him in Gregory's inept attempts to woo his lady fair. Steve (William Greenlees) thinks more about food; Eric (Alan Love) dreams about lenses for his cameras; and Andy (Robert Buchanan) is a trivia-phile. When Gregory learns that Dorothy's ambition is to go to Italy, he immediately signs up for a course in Italian.

Gregory is finally taken in hand by his younger sister Madeline (Allison Forster), about whom one tender fellow remarks: "ten years old with the body of a woman of thirteen!" She coaches her big brother, advising him on dress and behavior.

Dorothy accepts a stunned Gregory's request for a date, but a friend arrives in her place. She, in turn, passes him on to another friend, and the new date does the same. Gregory does not get to fully understand women in one evening, but he does get a good-night kiss.

In his *New York Times* review, Vincent Canby found *Gregory's Girl* "irresistible . . . a movie with an original, distinct personality."

# Hamlet

★ ★ ★ ★ ★ ★ ★ ★ ★ ★ ★ ★ ★ ★ ★ ★ ★ ★ ★ ★ ★ ★ ★ ★ ★ ★ ★ ★ ★ ★ ★ ★ ★ ★ ★ ★ ★ ★ ★ ★ ★ ★ ★ ★ ★ ★ ★ ★ ★ ★ ★ ★ ★

*Nationality*: British          *Year*: 1948

*Cast*: Laurence Olivier, Eileen Herlie, Basil Sydney, Jean Simmons, Felix Aylmer, Terence Morgan

*Director*: Laurence Olivier          *Running Time*: 155 minutes

*B/W or Color*: B/W          *Availability*: CBS VIDEO LIBRARY

Shakespeare's poetic revenge drama about that enigmatic prince of Denmark is the best-known stage classic in the English language. Laurence Olivier had first portrayed him onstage in 1937. And, at 41, the actor-director elected to follow his successful *Henry V* with this fascinating Freudian interpretation of the Bard's masterpiece, condensing and tightening the 4½-hour play. Using black-and-white film stock, because he alleged *Hamlet* struck him as an engraving, best seen in terms of light and shadow, Olivier later admitted the real reason: a battle with the Technicolor people.

Designer Roger Furse's massive sets of Elsinore Castle, as photographed by Desmond Dickinson's restlessly exploring cameras, so dominate this *Hamlet* as almost to become its central "character." But Olivier met that challenge by surrounding himself with a well-chosen cast of experienced British stage actors (one exception, the 18-year-old, pre-stardom Jean Simmons, who quite justified his faith in her). Olivier's Danish prince, with his pale, delicate features and cornsilk hair, is as silver tongued as one might expect; yet his interpretation is his own—an intelligent blend of violent emotion and intellectual calm. But this *Hamlet* was generally conceded to be a brilliant one, craftily rethought in terms of the motion picture.

*Hamlet* met with surprising public acceptance in the United States, and the movie copped a "first" for the British film industry by taking 1948's Academy Award for Best Picture, accompanied by a Best Actor Oscar for Olivier and additional statuettes for Art Direction, Set Decoration, and Costume Design. Sir Laurence (for such he became during *Hamlet*'s production) also won the New York Film Critics' citation as the year's best actor.

# The Happiest Days of Your Life

*★ ★ ★ ★ ★ ★ ★ ★ ★ ★ ★ ★ ★ ★ ★ ★ ★ ★ ★ ★ ★ ★ ★ ★ ★ ★ ★ ★ ★ ★ ★ ★ ★ ★ ★ ★ ★ ★ ★ ★ ★ ★ ★ ★ ★ ★ ★ ★ ★ ★ ★ ★ ★ ★*

*Nationality*: British            *Year*: 1950
*Cast*: Alastair Sim, Margaret Rutherford, Joyce Grenfell, Edward Rigby
*Director*: Frank Launder         *Running Time*: 81 minutes
*B/W or Color*: B/W             *Availability*: TV only

In his popular English stage farce, John Dighton dealt cleverly with the amusing notion of a girls' school being forced to share the premises of a boys' school because of an error made by the Ministry of Education's Resettlement Division in the wake of World War II. George Howe and Margaret Rutherford played the understandably agitated headmaster and headmistress. Miss Whitchurch always remained among Rutherford's favorite stage roles, and when the play reached the screen two years later, she was signed to re-create her characterization. The little-known Howe was replaced by Alastair Sim, since producers Frank Launder and Sidney Gilliat needed a box-office "name" to match Rutherford, who was thereby put on her scene-stealing mettle. Set against the wonderfully eccentric character actress's tweedy, aggressively no-nonsense Miss Whitchurch, Sim's Headmaster Pond is all bewildered confusion and doleful, crushed charm. Their long-running battle of wits and words is delightfully offset by the enthusiastic, middle-aged girlishness of Joyce Grenfell, playing a gangling, kittenish sportsmistress.

A lot of visual humor results from the staff's united efforts to keep visitors at bay long enough to hide boy students from parents of the girl students, and vice versa. At a moment's notice, Greek dancing on the lawn is replaced with rugby, and the school's elderly custodian (Edward Rigby) is constantly on call to help coordinate these lightning changes. The screenplay's outrageous lunacy is as wildly absurd as it is delightfully entertaining. The teamwork here makes it a joy to watch. Margaret Rutherford and Alastair Sim are, of course, at the top of their priceless form, and her startled reaction to the boys' school motto, "Guard Thine Honor," is unforgettable.

195

# A Hard Day's Night

★★★★★★★★★★★★★★★★★★★★★★★★★★★★★★★★★★★★★★★★★★★★★★★★★★★★★

Nationality: British          Year: 1964

Cast: John Lennon, Paul McCartney, George Harrison, Ringo Starr, Wilfrid Brambell, Victor Spinetti

Director: Richard Lester          Running Time: 85 minutes

B/W or Color: B/W          Availability: MPI

Before directing this, the Beatles' first motion picture, U.S.-born "Brit" Richard Lester had been responsible for the little-known, teen-pop flick called *It's Trad, Dad* and *Mouse on the Moon,* an inferior sequel to *The Mouse That Roared.* More important, however, was his radio/TV background with the "Goon" shows and an uninhibited, comic theatrical short with the odd title *The Running, Jumping and Standing Still Film,* starring Peter Sellers, Spike Milligan, and the "Goon" gang.

Lester's selection as director of the popular Beatles' first movie proved a clever choice, for he found immediate rapport with those four music-making mopheads from Liverpool. Completed for only $504,000, the result pleasantly surprised both the motion picture industry and its critics. Much of the film's success is due to Alun Owen's fresh and funny screenplay, especially tailored to suggest how the Beatles cope with their fame. In *A Hard Day's Night* (the group's own zany choice of a title), John, Paul, George, and Ringo simply play themselves, with Owen's script augmented by the improvisational ideas of Richard Lester. All of which makes *A Hard Day's Night* an infectious mixture of Beatlesong and wacky comedy of a kind not seen since the heyday of the Marx Brothers. To the accompaniment of a dozen-odd songs by John Lennon and Paul McCartney, the movie tumbles headlong in a whirl of breezy jokes and sight gags, hand-held photography, and near surreal camera tricks, as the boys romp through their paces with carefree charm and casual good humor.

In 1965, Richard Lester reunited with the Beatles for *Help!* With the addition of Technicolor and Bahamian locations, the cost was nearly double that of its modest, black-and-white predecessor.

# Heat and Dust

★★★★★★★★★★★★★★★★★★★★★★★★★★★★★★★★★★★★★★★★★★★★★★★★★★★★★★★

*Nationality*: British          *Year*: 1983

*Cast*: Greta Scacchi, Christopher Cazenove, Julie Christie, Madhur Jaffrey

*Director*: James Ivory          *Running Time*: 130 minutes

*B/W or Color*: Color          *Availability*: MCA HOME VIDEO

Because this was produced, directed, and written by the remarkable team of Merchant, Ivory, and Jhabvala the interest naturally quickens, and more so, in this case, because Ruth Jhabvala wrote the screenplay from her own novel.

The complexities and passions of life in India for the English are examined from points of view some 60 years apart. Olivia (Greta Scacchi, then a talented beauty new to films) and her husband Douglas Rivers (Christopher Cazenove) are Colonial Service representatives stationed in Satipur. Decades later, Olivia's great-niece Ann (Julie Christie) arrives in Satipur with a tape recorder and a packet of Olivia's letters home, to trace her aunt's life story.

The proper Douglas, a good, conscientious, devoted husband was dull, with no imagination, and couldn't begin to understand his lovely wife's need for excitement. Inevitably, the handsome local Nawab (Shashi Kapoor) began to pay her court, taking her on distant picnics with great panoply, and chaperoned after a fashion by Harry (Nickolas Grace), an English sycophant who lived in the Nawab's palace. In the closely knit English community, tongues start wagging—a fine scandal to enliven their days. For a married Englishwoman to dally with a native, no matter how rich and regal, was really beyond the pale, and the gossip was malicious.

When the contemporary Ann arrives in a now bustling Satipur, the Colonial Service is long gone, the British Raj represented only by the monumental buildings left behind. And now the races mix unselfconsciously. Ann not only boards with an Indian family but quite casually has an affair with her landlord.

This is a captivating movie. The acting is excellent, especially that of veteran Madhur Jaffrey as the imperious Begum, looking down her long cigarette holder as she scorns her inferiors. Director James Ivory has produced another gem, as has cinematographer Walter Lassally.

# Henry V

★★★★★★★★★★★★★★★★★★★★★★★★★★★★★★★★★★★★★★★★★★★★★★★★★★★★★★★

*Nationality*: British　　　　　　*Year*: 1944 (U.S. release: 1946)

*Cast*: Laurence Olivier, Robert Newton, Leslie Banks, Renee Asherson, Esmond Knight

*Director*: Laurence Olivier and Re-　*Running Time*: 134 minutes
ginald Beck

*B/W or Color*: Color　　　　　　*Availability*: CBS VIDEO LIBRARY

**B**efore *Henry V*, Laurence Olivier's renown as a classical actor resulted largely from his stage performances. His only previous Shakespearean film (as Elisabeth Bergner's co-star in the less-than-classic 1936 *As You Like It*) convinced him that the Bard's works were best performed live. Responsible for reuniting Olivier, celluloid, and Shakespeare was Two Cities Films' producer Filippo Del Giudice, whom the actor had impressed in a full-length 1942 radio version of *Henry V*. Originally, Olivier hadn't considered *directing* the movie, and he successively sought to engage William Wyler, Carol Reed, and Terence Young, before resigning himself to the task. With complete artistic freedom, Olivier hired film cutter Reginald Beck, not only to edit but to direct when he himself was in front of the cameras. William Walton was signed to compose the score, and Robert Krasker and Jack Hildyard guided the expensive Technicolor cameras.

Most of the huge cast were former colleagues of Olivier's. The one role he could not cast as desired was that of the French princess. Because of the brevity of the role (although it's actually the female lead), producer David O. Selznick, who had the actor's wife, Vivien Leigh, under contract, refused to let her accept it. Renee Asherson, who got the part, played it to such perfection that many assumed her to be French.

The movie opens on a brilliantly detailed miniature set of Shakespeare's London, focusing on the Globe Theatre, where the play begins and ends. Audiences are offered a mixture of painted scenery and realistic outdoor settings (the Agincourt battle sequence) planned deliberately as a means of holding the interest of non-Shakespearean-oriented moviegoers.

Released in England in 1944, the film scored a great hit, becoming an even bigger one, two years later, in the postwar United States—after a few offending "damns" and "bastards" were removed from the soundtrack. In New York, *Henry V* ran for a record 11 months, winning Olivier the New York Film Critics Best Actor Award and a special Oscar for the movie. The National Board of Review called it 1946's Best Picture and Olivier, Best Actor.

# The Hidden Fortress
## (Kakushi Toride No San-Akunin)

\* \* \* \* \* \* \* \* \* \* \* \* \* \* \* \* \* \* \* \* \* \* \* \* \* \* \* \* \* \* \* \* \* \* \* \* \* \* \* \* \* \* \* \* \* \* \* \* \* \* \* \*

*Nationality*: Japanese

*Year*: 1958 (U.S. release: 1962)

*Cast*: Toshiro Mifune, Misa Uehara, Takashi Shimura, Susumu Fujita

*Director*: Akira Kurosawa

*Running Time*: 139 minutes

*B/W or Color*: B/W

*Availability*: MEDIA HOME ENTERTAINMENT (Cinemateque Collection)

One of Kurosawa's most joyously affirmative works, this allegorical fable is remarkable both for its tremendous style and for the director's interesting (initial) use of widescreen. He interweaves specifically Japanese sources (such as the fire festival, *himatsuri*) with the universal truths of Aesop. Its dazzling geometric compositions notwithstanding, *The Hidden Fortress* is almost a genre Western. Originally shown in the United States in a 90-minute version, the film was restored to its full 139 minutes (and re-reviewed) in 1984, probably prompted by the fact that George Lucas claimed to have based elements of his *Star Wars* on the Kurosawa work. Strikingly original is its telling of the story through the viewpoint of two grubby, bickering farmers, the characters on whom Lucas specifically based his robots R2D2 and C3PO.

The film starts with an epic medieval battle, involving hundreds of samurai and foot soldiers. As the fight ensues, the two chicken-hearted farmers desert. They chance upon some gold bars hidden among firewood, but soon discover it's part of a fortune being smuggled out of the country by a mighty warrior (played by Toshiro Mifune).

The mighty Mifune is in the service of a princess (Misa Uehara, who wears an unusual outfit of blouse and short pants), whose father has been killed. The warrior leads the farmers to the hidden fortress where the princess is waiting to journey—with the royal fortune—to another, safer province.

En route, Mifune must use his samurai training in encounters with mounted soldiers and in a decisive duel with another warrior, whose life he spares. The travelers also meet a group of fire worshippers who burn the precious firewood. The two farmers leave the princess and her protector to the mercy of the villains, but they're rescued by the spared warrior. Restored to their former glory, they have the occasion to have the erring farmers brought before them.

Kurosawa's work has made him the most successful Japanese director internationally.

(*The videocassette is subtitled.*)

# Hiroshima, Mon Amour

★ ★ ★ ★ ★ ★ ★ ★ ★ ★ ★ ★ ★ ★ ★ ★ ★ ★ ★ ★ ★ ★ ★ ★ ★ ★ ★ ★ ★ ★ ★ ★ ★ ★ ★ ★ ★ ★ ★ ★ ★ ★ ★ ★ ★ ★ ★ ★ ★ ★ ★ ★

*Nationality*: French

*Year*: 1959 (U.S. release: 1960)

*Cast*: Emmanuelle Riva, Eiji Okada, Stella Dassas, Pierre Barband

*Director*: Alain Resnais

*Running Time*: 88 minutes

*B/W or Color*: B/W

*Availability*: EMBASSY HOME ENTERTAINMENT

They are both happily married to other people. Their brief encounter in Hiroshima takes place in 1950, against the blinking lights of the Americanized city, where Japanese neon competes with the Casablanca, Cinema Ritz, and the Hiroshima Gift Shop. She is a French actress, making an antiwar film. He is a Japanese architect.

The film opens with a dialogue. She has been to museums, seen pictures of deformed children, and watched tourists weep. He remembers Peace Square when it became as hot as the sun. "You saw nothing in Hiroshima," he tells her. In hotel rooms, down long corridors, in vast, empty stations, on a movie set; they talk, make love, and brace themselves against the moment when she must go back to France. He tells her that he cannot let her leave. She tells him that war has touched her life, too. Her lover was a German soldier, and she was shamed and punished at the war's end by outraged neighbors.

Emmanuelle Riva and Eiji Okada are superb as the star-crossed lovers. The flickering backgrounds pay tribute to the power of black-and-white film. Oriental cadences merge with French pop in a beautiful score by Georges Delerue and Giovanni Fusco, enhancing the film's Kafkaesque effect. When the heroine cries out that she cannot conjure up the face of the dead German soldier, we know that her present lover's face will one day grow dim. Sometimes the two seem to struggle under too heavy a burden of allegory. But their tender, sensual love story points up a terrible truth that makes war both bearable and inevitable: war's walking wounded eventually recover to forget the horrors behind their deepest scars.

The National Board of Review named *Hiroshima, Mon Amour* among the year's best foreign films.

(*The videocassette is in subtitled French.*)

# Hobson's Choice

★★★★★★★★★★★★★★★★★★★★★★★★★★★★★★★★★★★★★★★★★★★★★★★★★★★★★★★★★★

**Nationality**: British        **Year**: 1954
**Cast**: Charles Laughton, John Mills, Brenda de Banzie, Daphne Anderson, Prunella Scales
**Director**: David Lean        **Running Time**: 107 minutes
**B/W or Color**: B/W        **Availability**: EMBASSY HOME ENTERTAINMENT

Harold Brighouse's 1915 play about Lancashire life has been filmed three times, the best produced and directed by David Lean. It was his last small-scale black-and-white movie before leaving British studios for Venice and *Summertime*, en route to *The Bridge on the River Kwai* and *Lawrence of Arabia*.

The setting is a Victorian town in Lancashire, where Maggie (Brenda de Banzie), the efficient eldest daughter of prosperous widower Henry Hobson (Charles Laughton), runs both her dictatorial father's household and his bootmaker shop, while he frequents the pub. Hobson hopes to marry off his three spinster daughters, although he balks at the idea of paying out their dowries. Thirty-year-old Maggie decides to act before it's too late, selecting an unlikely husband, her father's shy assistant Willie Mossop (John Mills). It's tough to resist Maggie, and Willie soon finds himself not only married, but in charge of his own bootshop! Maggie has made Willie her father's chief competitor and given him the gift of self-confidence. She also tricks Hobson, during one of his binges, into providing dowries for her sisters, who quickly find husbands. Deserted by his daughters, this provincial King Lear increases his drinking and becomes ill. He wants Maggie back, and she strikes a bargain: she will return only if he'll offer her husband a partnership. Hobson has no choice.

Witnessing a tyrant's defeat is always a pleasure for an audience, and David Lean makes it a delightful experience, as rich in sets and costumes as in Jack Hildyard's eloquent photography and Malcolm Arnold's catchy score. The fine ensemble playing of Lean's excellent cast belies the fact that Laughton disliked Brenda de Banzie and resented the fact that Robert Donat wasn't cast as Willie. Nevertheless, the British Film Academy voted *Hobson's Choice* 1954's Best British Film.

# The Holly and the Ivy

★★★★★★★★★★★★★★★★★★★★★★★★★★★★★★★★★★★★★★★★★★★★★★★★★★★★★★★★★

**Nationality**: British　　　　　　**Year**: 1952 (U.S. release: 1954)
**Cast**: Ralph Richardson, Celia Johnson, Margaret Leighton, Denholm Elliott, John Gregson, Hugh Williams
**Director**: George More O'Ferrall　**Running Time**: 83 minutes
**B/W or Color**: B/W　　　　　　　**Availability**: TV only

A Christmas story for all seasons, this little gem of a comedy-drama offers some incisive observations of familial communication and the human condition. A completely delightful entertainment bundle of humor and seriousness, it blends acerbity with sentiment and illusion with truth to explore the adult meanings of the yuletide season.

In adapting Wynyard Browne's West End success to film, producer Anatole de Grunwald took a straightforward approach, venturing little from the play's Norfolk country vicarage setting, apart from establishing the various characters in their natural habitats at the movie's start.

The widowed Reverend Gregory (Ralph Richardson) and his family spend Christmas Eve and Christmas Day at his vicarage, where they've gathered for the holidays. Representing the senior contingent are his no-nonsense sister Bridget (Maureen Delany), his genteel sister-in-law Lydia (Margaret Halston), and his late wife's cousin Richard (Hugh Williams). The vicar's son Mick (Denholm Elliott) is home on military leave, and his journalist-daughter Margaret (Margaret Leighton) makes a belated appearance during dinner. The vicar's other daughter Jenny (Celia Johnson) has stayed at the vicarage to look after him and now can find no way to leave even to marry her engineer fiancé David (John Gregson).

Christmas Day brings a family catharsis, and—in a beautifully played reconciliation scene—the vicar and Margaret reach an understanding. Her decision to return home solves Jenny's problem, and the vicar is shaken to realize that he, a man of the cloth, never really knew his own family or reacted to their needs.

Fine performances, under George More O'Ferrall's unsentimentalized direction, make this a profoundly moving drama, leavened with humor and cleverly balancing Christmas-sweet with Christmas-sour.

# The Home and the World
## (Ghare Baire)

\* \* \* \* \* \* \* \* \* \* \* \* \* \* \* \* \* \* \* \* \* \* \* \* \* \* \* \* \* \* \* \* \* \* \* \* \* \* \* \* \* \* \* \* \* \* \* \* \* \* \* \* \* \*

**Nationality**: Indian                    **Year**: 1984 (U.S. Release: 1985)

**Cast**: Soumitra Chatterjee, Victor Banerjee, Swatilekha Chatterjee, Gopa Aich

**Director**: Satyajit Ray              **Running Time**: 130 minutes (141 minutes in India)

**B/W or Color**: Color              **Availability**: EMBASSY HOME ENTERTAINMENT

Based on the book by Nobel Prize-winner Rabindranath Tagore, *The Home and the World*, set in the first decade of this century, concerns itself with the hostility between Hindu and Moslem in India.

This conflict is acted out in microcosm at the beautiful and peaceful East Bengal estate of Nikhil Choudury (Victor Banerjee), with all the elements of true drama. Nikhil, a highly civilized, thoughtful, caring man much influenced by Western liberal ideas, frees his beloved wife Bimala (Swatilekha Chatterjee) from religious restrictive practices, encouraging her to leave the women's quarters, mix with and help entertain his friends.

The stage is thus set for the entry of Sandip Mukherjee (Soumitra Chatterjee), an old friend of Nikhil's who has become a small-time demagogue—and a womanizer. The difference between the two men is absolute. Nikhil is quietly but genuinely concerned about the welfare of all on his estate, whereas Sandip is a flamboyant rabble-rouser, and in the end a coward. Sandip makes his headquarters in Nikhil's house, and sets about seducing his friend's wife. In the name of nationalism he succeeds in bringing chaos, savagery, and death to the once tranquil countryside.

*The Home and the World* shows the loving hand of writer-director Satyajit Ray, who also composed the impressive score. With photographer Soumendu Roy, he explores the varied landscape; introduces love scenes that are more effective for being suggestive rather than explicit; takes us through the idealistic efforts of Nikhil to the inexorable rampaging climax.

*(Embassy offers the film in a subtitled version.)*

# The Horror of Dracula
## (Dracula)

★★★★★★★★★★★★★★★★★★★★★★★★★★★★★★★★★★★★★★★★★★★★★★★★★★★★

**Nationality**: British         **Year**: 1958

**Cast**: Peter Cushing, Christopher Lee, Michael Gough, Melissa Stribling, Carol Marsh

**Director**: Terence Fisher         **Running Time**: 82 minutes

**B/W or Color**: Color         **Availability**: WARNER HOME VIDEO

Hammer Films' 1958 *The Horror of Dracula* is widely held to be not only the best version of Bram Stoker's classic Gothic fantasy, but—for many—the finest supernatural tale ever filmed.

Terence Fisher's *Dracula* (as it was called in Britain) reflects the fast-changing moral attitudes of the late Fifties; its explicit approach to sexuality and its presentation of gore is a far cry from the 1931 Tod Browning version, wherein the camera discreetly panned away whenever Bela Lugosi's vampire count bared his teeth at a fair damsel's pale throat.

This adaptation, by Jimmy Sangster, adhered somewhat closer to Stoker's novel than did the slow-paced Lugosi version, and without any effort at "camp" or tongue-in-cheek humor. Natural dialogue helped, and so did the acting. Christopher Lee endowed the master vampire with an imposing strength and athleticism quite new to the part. And so, in his way, did the coolly efficient Peter Cushing, at 43, nine years Lee's senior. Together, this pair soon became the best-known horror-movie team since Karloff and Lugosi.

But the film's great effectiveness isn't due only to blood and sex. Its marvelous special effects include the awesome metamorphosis of sexy vampire Valerie Gaunt, once she has been heart-staked, into an ancient crone. And, finally, there is the movie's horrifying climax, as Dracula is trapped by the sign of the cross, collapsing and disintegrating in deadly shafts of morning sunlight—until he's only a windblown deposit of dust. *The Horror of Dracula* showed what could be done when serious artisans bring craft, flair, and elegance to a much-maligned film genre.

# I Am a Camera

************************************************************

Nationality: British            Year: 1955
Cast: Julie Harris, Laurence Harvey, Shelley Winters, Ron Randell
Director: Henry Cornelius       Running Time: 99 minutes
B/W or Color: B/W               Availability: MONTEREY VIDEO

B oasting a remarkable performance by Julie Harris (re-creating her Tony Award-winning Broadway performance), *I Am a Camera* is an intelligent screen adaptation by John Collier of John Van Druten's stage play, based on Christopher Isherwood's autobiographical *Goodbye to Berlin*. Directed by Henry Cornelius, best known for his British comedies (*Passport to Pimlico, Genevieve*), *I Am a Camera* concerns Christopher Isherwood (Laurence Harvey) and his adventures living as a tutor in the pre-Hitler Berlin of the Thirties. On the horizon, the impending doom of World War II; more immediately, the menace of the Nazi hoodlums lurking on the ill-lit streets. The incidents related in the film virtually all revolve around Sally Bowles (Julie Harris), an English girl of artless but insistent amorality, whom Isherwood befriends.

The film lives up to its title by unraveling as a series of snapshots and candid observations presented to the audience, by Isherwood, in flashback. But it is Julie Harris who holds together the swiftly shifting moods of farce and drama with great expertise. Her performance is little less than inspired.

In contrast, the musical and its subsequent film version, *Cabaret,* shifted the emphasis from Sally to the decadence of pre-World War II Berlin. In fact, while the musical's main focus was the sleazy nightclub where Sally performed, using it as a symbol of decadence, *I Am a Camera* hardly spends any time in the club. This version concentrates more on the personal relationship between Sally and Isherwood.

It is interesting to note that due to dialogue flippancies and plot unconventionalities, *I Am a Camera* was denied a 1955 Production Code seal of approval. While any shock value it may have then had is virtually nil today, the performance of the film's star still fascinates.

*(Tape quality is very good.)*

# I Know Where I'm Going

★★★★★★★★★★★★★★★★★★★★★★★★★★★★★★★★★★★★★★★★★★★★★★★★★★★★★★

**Nationality**: British        **Year**: 1945 (U.S. release: 1947)

**Cast**: Wendy Hiller, Roger Livesey, Pamela Brown, Nancy Price, Finlay Currie, John Laurie

**Director**: Michael Powell and     **Running Time**: 91 minutes
Emeric Pressburger

**B/W or Color**: B/W           **Availability**: TV only

Set against the striking background of Scotland's Western Isles, this unpretentious love story had little to publicize it when first shown in the United States. Wendy Hiller, its sole international "name," had been off the screen since 1941's *Major Barbara*. And Roger Livesey, her leading man, was the second choice after charismatic James Mason, who had misunderstandings with the producers. Livesey's name was hardly a selling factor outside of the United Kingdom, despite the overseas success of his *Colonel Blimp*.

In the screenplay, written by director Michael Powell and his production partner Emeric Pressburger, Hiller plays 26-year-old Joan Webster, a determined young woman from the "outside," who arrives in the Hebrides to marry a wealthy but elderly businessman. When inclement weather prevents her reaching Kiloran, her fiancé's private (but rented) island, she's confined to the mainland, where she meets—and falls in love with—Torquil McNeil (played by Livesey), the impoverished laird from whom her rich fiancé leases his isolated home. In the eight days she's stranded, Joan not only loses her heart to Torquil, but, charmed by the picturesque locale and the fey wisdom of his down-to-earth neighbors, she gains new values and undergoes a permanent change of plans.

Well cast and well produced, from Erwin Hillie's beautiful location photography of Mull and the Inner Hebrides to Allan Gray's atmospheric score (with that haunting, titular folk song), *I Know Where I'm Going* quietly wins over its audience with the story's freshness, its flavorful characters, and its striking Hebridean setting. Ironically, this movie proved more popular in America than in Britain, running nearly a full year in the Manhattan cinema where it opened.

# I See a Dark Stranger

## (The Adventuress)

★★★★★★★★★★★★★★★★★★★★★★★★★★★★★★★★★★★★★★★★★★★★★★★★★★★★★★

**Nationality**: British       **Year**: 1946 (U.S. release: 1947)
**Cast**: Deborah Kerr, Trevor Howard, Raymond Huntley
**Director**: Frank Launder       **Running Time**: 98 minutes (111
                                          minutes in Britain)
**B/W or Color**: B/W       **Availability**: VIDAMERICA

I *See a Dark Stranger* is one of those delightful late-Forties films that have fallen into unwarranted neglect and obscurity. Its clever blend of suspense and wit made it immensely popular. Its success was no accident, nor were comparisons with Hitchcock's films a coincidence, for its creators were the producer-director-writer team of Frank Launder and Sidney Gilliat, screenwriters of *The Lady Vanishes*.

Deborah Kerr offers a most captivating characterization as the peppery colleen, Bridie Quilty, who grows to young womanhood harboring so active a hatred of all things British that she finally asserts her independence and announces intentions of leaving her little village of Ballygarry to join the I.R.A. In 1944, amidst Britain's war against Germany, Bridie elects to pursue her own war.

In Dublin, Bridie's hopes of serving the I.R.A. are dashed, and she naively allows herself to become the pawn of Miller (Raymond Huntley), a Nazi agent. In short order, Bridie is unwittingly involved in a plot to assist the escape of a Nazi spy from an English prison.

How the single-minded dedication of this misguided daughter of Eire is led astray by the low-keyed pursuit of a romantic British officer, how she gets caught up with him in dangerous escapades and in an Irish funeral procession, and eventually avoids arrest by the sudden end of international hostilities—this is part of the narrative that Launder and Gilliat skillfully manage to make us both accept and enjoy. Which is not to minimize the quiet charm and humor of Trevor Howard, as the naval officer who manages to win the heart and hand of this Hibernian wildcat—and convince her that not every Englishman is an Oliver Cromwell.

The New York Film Critics voted their 1947 Best Actress award to Kerr for the combined versatility of her performances in both this film and *Black Narcissus*, her last picture for Rank.

# I Sent a Letter to My Love
## (Chère Inconnue)

**\*\*\*\*\*\*\*\*\*\*\*\*\*\*\*\*\*\*\*\*\*\*\*\*\*\*\*\*\*\*\*\*\*\*\*\*\*\*\*\*\*\*\*\*\*\*\*\*\*\*\*\***

*Nationality*: French                    *Year*: 1980 (U.S. release: 1981)
*Cast*: Simone Signoret, Jean Rochefort, Delphine Seyrig
*Director*: Moshe Mizrahi            *Running Time*: 102 minutes
*B/W or Color*: Color                    *Availability*: THORN/EMI-HBO
                                                        VIDEO

I sraeli-born director Moshe Mizrahi, whose *Madame Rosa* (starring Simone Signoret) won a Best Foreign Film Oscar, made this poignant picture of an invalid, Gilles (Jean Rochefort), and his sister, Louise (Signoret), who has sacrificed her life to care for him. Against the bleak Brittany coast, Mizrahi unfolds an excellent study of three complex people bound together by their isolation.

Louise's attitude toward her brother is ambivalent: regrets for her lost romantic opportunities promote a growing selfishness, which conflicts with her basic loyalty. Embittered by his helplessness, the wheelchair-bound Gilles ponders the days when he could walk and run. Completing the trio is their neighbor Yvette (Delphine Seyrig), a close friend since childhood, who has become a repressed spinster.

When Gilles falls desperately ill, Louise realizes she might have to face the future alone, and advertises anonymously in the local paper for a male friend. While Gilles recovers, Louise receives only one reply to her advertisement—from her brother! She's touched by his expressed desire to experience love, and sympathetically replies, using an assumed name. As the correspondence continues, their lives brighten. Louise pays more attention to her appearance, and she is gentler with Gilles. Gilles becomes skittish with Yvette, who responds by flirting with him. Their dull lives are growing brighter with excitement and expectation.

The performances are marvelous, from Rochefort's astonishing display of versatility in an offbeat role to the always stylish Seyrig. And Signoret is in top form as a woman discovering the resources she never suspected she had. In his review in *The New York Times,* Vincent Canby wrote: "Part of the satisfaction in watching a vehicle that moves as smoothly as *I Sent a Letter to My Love* is watching the actors at work, being aware of performances past in relation to the ones we are presently seeing."

# I Vitelloni

## (The Young and the Passionate)

★★★★★★★★★★★★★★★★★★★★★★★★★★★★★★★★★★★★★★★★★★★★★★★★★★★★

Nationality: Italian-French    Year: 1953 (U.S. release: 1956)
Cast: Franco Interlenghi, Alberto Sordi, Franco Fabrizi, Eleanora Ruffo, Leopoldo Trieste
Director: Federico Fellini        Running Time: 109 minutes
B/W or Color: B/W              Availability: TV only

Beloved, even by Fellini-phobes, I Vitelloni is the unacknowledged inspiration of many popular American movies such as American Graffiti and Diner. It firmly established the director's reputation abroad and is possibly the first (and still the best) film about young men and their transition into adulthood.

Pointedly set in a village on the Adriatic (Fellini grew up in Rimini), the story is autobiographical in its startling, detailed truths; derived from the collected experiences of scenarists Fellini, Ennio Flaiano, and Tullio Pinelli, it was then molded by the young maestro into an object of great beauty and spirited style.

Fausto (Franco Fabrizi), the gang leader, impregnates his girlfriend Sandra (Eleanora Ruffo) long before he's willing to accept responsibility for anything; he continues to work in a stifling antique store. Alberto (Alberto Sordi), the perennial momma's boy, wants only to entertain his peer group, be it with a drag-queen act or an infantile mocking of road workers. Leopoldo (Leopoldo Trieste), straight from La Boheme, writes terrible plays and falls in love with a chambermaid. The Fellini character is Moraldo (Franco Interlenghi), crucially different from the others in that he leaves the boys' hometown for the city.

In addition to its irresistible surface charm, the film is a milestone in scrupulous observation of non-Hollywood, real-life behavior. I Vitelloni won the Silver Prize (no gold prize was given) at the Berlin Film Festival.

The film was termed "a masterpiece" by John Simon, who ranks it as "one of the ten or twelve great films ever made."

Vitelloni are literally fatted calves; used here, the term describes the overgrown youths aimlessly drifting through life.

"I was trying to say there is something more," stated Fellini, "there is always more. Life must have a meaning beyond the animal."

# If . . .

**★★★★★★★★★★★★★★★★★★★★★★★★★★★★★★★★★★★★★★★★★★★★★★★★★★★★★★★★★★★**

*Nationality*: British          *Year*: 1968 (U.S. release: 1969)
*Cast*: Malcolm McDowell, David Wood, Richard Warwick, Robert Swann,
Mary McLeod
*Director*: Lindsay Anderson          *Running Time*: 111 minutes
*B/W or Color*: Color and B/W          *Availability*: PARAMOUNT
                                        HOME VIDEO

Lindsay Anderson's masterpiece wasn't shown in America until some
cuts were made to remove the X rating it had been given. Beware
of the excessively cut versions that find their way to the TV channels.

The film takes place in an English private school—a microcosm for an
overly structured society that subverts natural humanism and cultivates
a genteel sadomasochism in its place. Even the faculty here seems frozen
in immaturity. "Education in Britain," the headmaster intones, "is a nubile Cinderella, sparsely clad and often interfered with."

As the term progresses three nonconformist seniors, led by the brilliant
Malcolm McDowell in his first starring role, move from cynical criticism
of their surroundings to open revolt and then armed rebellion. On Speech
Day they take to the rooftops and stage a violent reception for visiting
parents, faculty, and students. In 1968 it was a surreal echo of what was
going on at campuses all over the world.

McDowell makes his first screen entrance wearing a bizarre slouch hat,
his features swaddled in yards of scarf, almost a preview of his still-more-
unorthodox presence in *A Clockwork Orange*. The film shuttles between
the arrogant bullying of the boys in the upper forms to the playful exuberance of the new boys. An aura of homoerotic fantasy permeates it
all—the vicious sadism of the seniors against the puppylike adoration of
the youngsters. A delicate boy from the lower form watches an older boy
exercising on the crossbar, and it resembles nothing so much as the ri-
tualized courting of certain showy birds. One of the master's wives
(McLeod) is fine as she sleepwalks naked through the deserted dormitory,
caressing the objects that belong to the boys. As a study of anarchic
revolution in which the revolution is a life-style in itself, it recalls the
classic *Zero for Conduct* of Jean Vigo.

# Ikiru
## (To Live)

\*\*\*\*\*\*\*\*\*\*\*\*\*\*\*\*\*\*\*\*\*\*\*\*\*\*\*\*\*\*\*\*\*\*\*\*\*\*\*\*\*\*\*\*\*\*\*\*\*\*\*\*

Nationality: Japanese

Cast: Takashi Shimura, Nobuo Kaneko, Kyoko Seki, Makoto Kobori

Director: Akira Kurosawa

B/W or Color: B/W

Year: 1952 (U.S. release: 1960)

Running Time: 143 minutes

Availability: MEDIA HOME ENTERTAINMENT (Cinemateque Collection)

Ikiru ranks with Ingmar Bergman's *Wild Strawberries* and Vittorio De Sica's *Umberto D* as a classic film study of old age and preparation for death.

Kanji Watanabe (well played by Takashi Shimura), Akira Kurosawa's protagonist in *Ikiru,* recalls several aspects of the lonely and introspective characters of those movies. An aging petty official, Watanabe learns that he has cancer and will die in six months. "Actually," *Ikiru*'s narrator intones, "he has been dead for 25 years," so engrossed is he in his bureaucratic ways and mummylike existence. Realizing the meaninglessness of his life for the first time, Watanabe attempts to make up for it in his final days. First, he tries retreating into his family, but finds that his son has become distant and cold since his wife's death. He next attempts to find pleasure through a wild night on the town, but no longer knows how to enjoy himself. Then he seeks out the company of a young woman, a former employee in his office. Although this temporary friendship does not work out, through it he discovers a way to help others by using the resources of his old job to construct a playground in a wasteland sump.

Kurosawa effectively breaks Watanabe's story in two. The second half, set at a wake following the bureaucrat's death, relates with irony his efforts to build the park. His colleagues fight to claim credit for the project. At the end of a scene all too typical of Japanese funerals, they drunkenly resolve to be more attentive to their responsibilities, but clearly will soon forget their promises.

In a 1979 poll of Japanese critics, *Ikiru* finished second to *Seven Samurai* as the all-time greatest Japanese film. Kurosawa still regards *Ikiru* and *Seven Samurai* as his own personal favorites among his films.

*(Media offers the film in a subtitled Japanese print.)*

# Illicit Interlude
## (Sommarlek/Summer Interlude)

*★★★★★★★★★★★★★★★★★★★★★★★★★★★★★★★★★★★★★★★★★★★★★★★★★*

*Nationality*: Swedish          *Year*: 1951 (U.S. release: 1954)

*Cast*: Maj-Britt Nilsson, Birger Malmsten, Alf Kjellin, Georg Funkquist, Annalisa Ericsson

*Director*: Ingmar Bergman          *Running Time*: 96 minutes

*B/W or Color*: B/W          *Availability*: NELSON ENTER-
                             TAINMENT

R eviewing this film from Stockholm late in 1951, *Variety*'s critic expressed surprise at its optimistic tone and positive attitude, considering that so many other Ingmar Bergman films had maintained "an
influence of hopelessness." Significantly, Bergman himself has said of the
movie, "This was my first film in which I felt I was functioning independently, with a style of my own, which no one could ape."

*Illicit Interlude* (a title chosen by its exploitation-minded independent
distributor for the American release in 1954) suggests a steamy cinema
experience that is never fulfilled. Aside from one discreet, rear-view nude
bathing scene involving its female star, the picture is better suited to its
alternate title-translation of *Summer Interlude*. Told in flashbacks, this is
the story of a prima ballerina named Marie (Maj-Britt Nilsson) employed
by Stockholm's Royal Opera and courted by David (Alf Kjellin), a journalist. Haunted by the memory of a teenage love affair that blossomed
one idyllic summer (in the Stockholm archipelago, of course!) and ended
tragically in the diving death of her lover Henrik (Birger Malmsten), Marie
plays a nostalgic, off-season visit to the locale, in the course of which she
encounters, among other ghosts of the past, her sinister—and somewhat
lecherous—uncle (Georg Funkquist) and Henrik's dying aunt (Mimi Pol-
lak). Ultimately, the rediscovery of a diary Marie kept that long-ago summer helps exorcise the past, paving the way to a likely future with David.

*Illicit Interlude* is not, however, quite as simple in its narrative as the
above description might indicate. Mood and atmosphere abound
throughout, and the people in Marie's orbit, both past and present, are
characterized with depth and subtlety by Bergman. Not unexpectedly,
Gunnar Fischer's photography of the ballet episodes from *Swan Lake* are
as lyrically shot as his summer location scenes. And Erik Nordgren's score
offers intelligent balance to the dramatic sequence *not* employing Tchaikovsky ballet music.

# I'm All Right, Jack

\* \* \* \* \* \* \* \* \* \* \* \* \* \* \* \* \* \* \* \* \* \* \* \* \* \* \* \* \* \* \* \* \* \* \* \* \* \* \* \* \* \* \* \* \* \* \* \* \* \* \* \* \* \*

Nationality: British          Year: 1959 (U.S. release: 1960)

Cast: Ian Carmichael, Peter Sellers, Terry-Thomas, Richard Attenborough, Dennis Price, Margaret Rutherford

Director: John and Roy Boulting     Running Time: 104 minutes

B/W or Color: B/W            Availability: THORN/EMI-HBO VIDEO

World War II is over, and with it ends the supremacy of the Old Boy network in England. Ian Carmichael takes up his battered lance, seeking a job "with an early closing, not too far from London." Working for his uncle, Carmichael becomes the unwitting subject of a time-motion study, before he has fallen in with "the natural rhythm of the workers" (read: the art of goofing-off on the job). The study proves that near-unemployables even working at a leisurely pace could triple the company's present output. Labor unions are aghast, and the ensuing strike brings Britain to her knees in a film that belongs to a great generation of British comedies.

Richard Attenborough, Terry-Thomas and Dennis Price, ostensibly representing competing missile-makers, play parties to a scam involving Mr. Muhammad, the suave but shifty-eyed representative of the Transberberite Embassy. Peter Sellers is superb as a shop steward who rewrites *The Communist Manifesto* to "from each as little as he can get away with." He is the most damning representation of organized labor to be seen to this day on the screen. As Mr. Muhammad, Marne Maitland adroitly delivers Third World variations of old British proverbs about "a bird by the bush in the hand." Margaret Rutherford is fine as the Thatcheresque *doyenne* of the tea cozy.

This sparkling film makes a serious point. Spouting Tory gospel and proclaiming the obvious, Carmichael is the embodiment of the verities (and some of the decencies) that left the club along with Colonel Blimpisms and the bowler hat.

John Boulting cleverly directed the witty screenplay he developed with Frank Harvey and Alan Hackney—from Hackney's novel *Private Life. I'm All Right, Jack* is still widely considered the best of the Boulting Brothers' social comedies. In 1959, the British Film Academy cited it for Best British Screenplay and named Peter Sellers Best British Actor. The National Board of Review listed it among 1960's best films.

# The Importance of Being Earnest

★ ★ ★ ★ ★ ★ ★ ★ ★ ★ ★ ★ ★ ★ ★ ★ ★ ★ ★ ★ ★ ★ ★ ★ ★ ★ ★ ★ ★ ★ ★ ★ ★ ★ ★ ★ ★ ★ ★ ★ ★ ★ ★ ★ ★ ★ ★ ★ ★ ★ ★ ★ ★ ★ ★

*Nationality*: British       *Year*: 1952

*Cast*: Michael Redgrave, Michael Denison, Edith Evans, Joan Greenwood, Dorothy Tutin, Margaret Rutherford

*Director*: Anthony Asquith       *Running Time*: 95 minutes

*B/W or Color*: Color       *Availability*: TV only

That it took Oscar Wilde's wittiest play 57 years to be filmed owes something to the intrinsic problems of transferring its special qualities to the screen. Anthony Asquith wrote and directed an adaptation that made no pretense of being anything but a cleverly photographed play, even framing his movie within the rise and fall of a theater curtain.

Jack (Michael Redgrave) and Algernon (Michael Denison) are wealthy, eligible bachelors. Jack's enamored of Algy's cousin Gwendolen (Joan Greenwood), while Algy is equally smitten with Jack's ward Cecily (Dorothy Tutin). Since Jack likes to pose as his jaunty imaginary brother "Ernest," and as Algy has assumed both Ernest's name and reputation to impress Cecily, both young ladies naturally think themselves engaged to the nonexistent Ernest. When Jack discovers the situation, he announces that his brother has suddenly died in Paris. The girls reject this subterfuge, and both suitors are forced to admit that there *is* no Ernest. Enter the meddlesome Lady Bracknell (Edith Evans), Algernon's formidable aunt and Gwendolen's mother, intent on obstructing matters—until Miss Prism (Margaret Rutherford), Cecily's governess, reveals an old family skeleton and proves that one of the men is *indeed* Ernest.

Asquith's film takes a straightforward approach to this Wilde and witty comedy of Victorian manners. Greenwood, Redgrave, Tutin, and Denison are affectedly right as the two young couples. But, for many, the actress most immediately associated with *The Importance of Being Earnest* (both on stage and screen) is the inimitable Dame Edith Evans, whose splendidly insufferable dragon of a Lady Bracknell makes gospel of Wilde's most ridiculous dialogue. *The Importance of Being Earnest* is a sparkling glass of the best vintage champagne.

# In the Realm of the Senses
## (L'Empire des Sens)

★★★★★★★★★★★★★★★★★★★★★★★★★★★★★★★★★★★★★★★★★★★★★★★★★★★★★★

Nationality: French-Japanese      Year: 1976 (U.S. release: 1977)
Cast: Tatsuya Fuji, Eiko Matsuda, Aoi Nakajima, Meika Seri
Director: Nagisa Oshima      Running Time: 105 minutes (115 minutes overseas)
B/W or Color: Color      Availability: Not yet available

In the United States, pornography has never become a legitimate artistic expression in cinema. When it achieved notoriety, as in *Deep Throat* and *The Devil in Miss Jones,* there was some hope that it would move into the realm of the aesthetic. But no serious artists would touch these films, only nonunion actors would appear, and not enough money was invested to achieve a professional look.

Not that the situation was different elsewhere. Nagisa Oshima (*The Empire of Passion*) is far from a mainstream Japanese filmmaker. His works all represent assaults on tradition, on ritualistic repression, on imperialistic social tendencies. He has openly criticized peers like Kurosawa for their traditionalist styles and themes. Oshima was ripe for a tale such as this: the true account of a prostitute who killed her lover in 1936 and carried his severed sex organ around the countryside for several days before being arrested. Radicals at the time believed her story was one of cultural suicide and saw her as a national hero. When she died, Oshima decided to make the film.

He has used fine actors, fine technicians, and an obsessively rigid style that complements the subject matter. And, while many details of the subculture he depicts are lost to us, the film works nonetheless. It is so well made and performed that one might argue that it skirts pornography; but it is indeed pornography. Perhaps in the West we need sleaze to define our pornography, because it's all we've ever seen.

If this is not Oshima's best film, it is undoubtedly the one he'll be remembered for—and definitely a watershed in film history.

# In Which We Serve

**********************************************************

Nationality: British                    Year: 1942

Cast: Noel Coward, John Mills, Bernard Miles, Celia Johnson, Kay Walsh, Joyce Carey, Michael Wilding

Director: Noel Coward and David    Running Time: 115 minutes
Lean

B/W or Color: B/W                    Availability: EMBASSY HOME
                                     ENTERTAINMENT

I n Which We Serve is the story of a British destroyer, the HMS *Torrin*, and the men who served aboard her at the start of World War II. In semidocumentary fashion, the movie follows the *Torrin* from construction and launching through battle action to her gallant finish when she is torpedoed off the coast of Crete. An obvious propaganda film, it is based on the real-life service record of a British ship.

That the movie succeeds so well can be attributed to David Lean, then the British film industry's highest paid film cutter, who was recommended to producer-director Noel Coward. Coward was seeking a co-director since his energies were already split among the duties of producer, screenwriter, and actor. Eventually, Coward relinquished the picture's direction to Lean, although they divided credit between them. It provided Lean with a valued boot into a distinguished new career.

Coward knew what he was doing when he engaged a fine editor like Lean. For, with its complex scenario of flashbacks, sketching in the background of its seamen as they desperately cling to life rafts in Cretan waters, *In Which We Serve* sustains a narrative structure that could easily confuse its audience. But this movie successfully etches a picture of embattled patriotism and a unification of Britain's then sharply divided class system that still rings true with its antiwar message.

In the United States, *In Which We Serve* was surprisingly popular, obviously striking a responsive chord in its reflection of ordinary people at war and at home. The New York Film Critics awarded it their Best Picture citation for 1942, and Hollywood followed with a special Academy Award to Coward. The National Board named *In Which We Serve* the year's best, singling out John Mills and Bernard Miles among the best actors.

# The Inheritance
## (Uncle Silas)

★★★★★★★★★★★★★★★★★★★★★★★★★★★★★★★★★★★★★★★★★★★★★★★★★★★★★

*Nationality*: British         *Year*: 1947 (U.S. release: 1951)

*Cast*: Jean Simmons, Derrick De Marney, Katina Paxinou, Manning Whiley, Reginald Tate, Derek Bond

*Director*: Charles Frank         *Running Time*: 98 minutes

*B/W or Color*: B/W         *Availability*: Public Domain

The Inheritance, a marvelously melodramatic film, is notable for being director Charles Frank's debut picture and for being British child-actress Jean Simmon's first major starring role. The film is based on Joseph Sheridan Le Fanu's classic Victorian mystery novel *Uncle Silas,* published in 1864. The novel is considered to be one of the first books of the thriller genre. The screenplay and set designs were by Lawrence Irving.

Simmons stars as Caroline Ruthyn, a young heiress left in the dastardly clutches of her appointed guardian, Uncle Silas (Derrick De Marney), after her father's sudden death of a heart attack. Caroline realizes too late that her father erred in his judgment of his brother, that the disarming old man is still the scoundrel he was purported to be in his younger days. With the help of Caroline's crafty and wicked exgoverness Madame de la Rougierre (Katina Paxinou) and his evil son Dudley (Manning Whiley), Silas sets out to steal Caroline's inheritance. Having to contend with curious cousin Monica and Caroline's amorous suitor Lord Ilbury, Silas devises a convoluted plot to permanently rid himself of his niece, and locks her away in his mansion. The clumsy murder plot backfires, and Dudley kills Madame de la Rougierre by mistake. Caroline escapes into the waiting arms of Lord Ilbury. Summoned by the gatekeeper's son, he has come to rescue her. Dudley is trampled to death beneath carriage horses, and Silas, rather than face the gallows, shoots himself.

Despite its gruesomeness, *The Inheritance* is an excellent suspense thriller. Robert Krasker's photography is as gloomy and menacing as it should be. British art direction for period films is always outstanding and perhaps reached a peak in the Gothic mansion Lawrence Irving designed for the film.

# The Innocent
## (L'Innocente)

*★ ★ ★ ★ ★ ★ ★ ★ ★ ★ ★ ★ ★ ★ ★ ★ ★ ★ ★ ★ ★ ★ ★ ★ ★ ★ ★ ★ ★ ★ ★ ★ ★ ★ ★ ★ ★ ★ ★ ★ ★ ★ ★ ★ ★ ★ ★ ★ ★ ★ ★ ★ ★*

**Nationality**: Italian-French       **Year**: 1976 (U.S. release: 1979)

**Cast**: Giancarlo Giannini, Laura Antonelli, Jennifer O'Neill, Rina Morelli, Massimo Girotti

**Director**: Luchino Visconti       **Running Time**: 115 minutes (128 minutes in Europe)

**B/W *or* Color**: Color       **Availability**: VESTRON VIDEO

The denial of sin and the resultant complexities in a newly amoral world haunt *The Innocent,* Luchino Visconti's last film. We are in *fin de siècle* Italy fooling around with the possibilities of a Nietzschean atheism and free love. Giancarlo Giannini plays Tullio, a superman stand-in bent on testing the limits of traditional morality. It is a nod in the direction of the women's movement for Visconti to show this particular male ego shrinking into bas relief against the two women in his life: his wife (Laura Antonelli) and his mistress Teresa (Jennifer O'Neill).

Or maybe it's just that an Italian double standard and sexual experimentation a la Gabrielle D'Annunzio don't mix: the film is based on D'Annunzio's novel. Nowhere is the tension between an old-fashioned Victorian sweetness and "modern" sensuality more successfully embodied than by Laura Antonelli. For as satiated as we may think we are, Antonelli's sexual turn-out is truly titillating.

It's good to see Giannini freed from the directorial ardor of Lina Wertmuller; interestingly, it was at Giannini's prompting that a 20-minute omission from the film was restored. Jennifer O'Neill successfully goes from passionate free spirit to stock mistress. The photography (Pasqualino de Santis), the costumes (Piero Tosi), and the music (Franco Mannino) are all up to the usual Visconti standard of wonderful operating melange.

*The Innocent* is a fascinating conclusion to an estimable career. (*The cassette is English-dubbed.*)

# The Innocents

Nationality: British                    Year: 1961

Cast: Deborah Kerr, Megs Jenkins, Martin Stephens, Pamela Franklin, Michael Redgrave

Director: Jack Clayton            Running Time: 99 minutes

B/W or Color: B/W                  Availability: TV only

Henry James's 1898 novel *The Turn of the Screw* is a tale of such intriguing ambiguity that scholars still question whether its ghosts are real or simply the neurotic imaginings of its repressed heroine. Truman Capote's hand is clearly seen in the screenplay he helped write with William Archibald, who had adapted the novel for the stage. The film was produced and directed by Jack Clayton (*Room at the Top*).

Miss Giddens, a minister's daughter, is engaged as governess to two children who live on a large country estate. She's greeted by Mrs. Grose, the kindly housekeeper, and sweet little Flora, who announces that her brother Miles is coming home—having been expelled from school for his corrupting influence. Miss Giddens, disarmed by the handsome boy, is impressed by his manners. Life takes an ominous turn for her when she sees—or thinks she sees—an evil-looking man and a tall, dark lady staring at her. Mrs. Grose identifies the couple as former employees, now deceased, who had shamelessly engaged in an illicit relationship. After Mrs. Grose leaves with Flora, Miss Giddens, believing that the ghosts have returned to possess the youngsters' souls, concentrates on "saving" Miles. Following a confrontation with one of the specters, Miles falls lifeless, while the distraught governess kisses him tenderly and prays for his soul. The film ends as it began, with a darkened screen and a pair of prayerfully clasped hands, accompanied only by the sound of occasional birdsong.

Photographically, *The Innocents* is a masterpiece. Filmed at Sheffield Park, a magnificent Sussex estate, Freddie Francis's black-and-white cameras artfully captured the lush gardens, marshy ponds, and Gothic architecture. In the movie's most difficult characterization, Deborah Kerr performs with resourceful subtlety. Megs Jenkins is a warmly supportive Mrs. Grose, and Pamela Franklin's Flora is as engaging as Martin Stephens's Miles is uncannily chilling.

As a *real* horror film, *The Innocents* is a cinematic gem. The National Board of Review named Jack Clayton 1961's Best Director and listed *The Innocents* among the year's best movies.

# The Invaders
## (49th Parallel)

\* \* \* \* \* \* \* \* \* \* \* \* \* \* \* \* \* \* \* \* \* \* \* \* \* \* \* \* \* \* \* \* \* \* \* \* \* \* \* \* \* \* \* \* \* \* \* \* \* \* \* \* \* \*

*Nationality*: British  *Year*: 1941 (U.S. release: 1942)

*Cast*: Eric Portman, Laurence Olivier, Anton Walbrook, Leslie Howard, Raymond Massey, Glynis Johns

*Director*: Michael Powell and Emeric Pressburger  *Running Time*: 104 minutes (123 minutes in Britain)

*B/W or Color*: B/W  *Availability*: VIDAMERICA

Titled *49th Parallel* in the United Kingdom, *The Invaders* is the exciting story of six survivors from a Nazi submarine sunk in the Gulf of St. Lawrence, and their experiences as they desperately endeavor to flee across Canada to the United States. The National Board cited Anton Walbrook and Glynis Johns among its list of best performances for 1942. Emeric Pressburger won an Oscar for Best Original Story.

Shortly after the cold-blooded Lieutenant Hirth (Eric Portman) and five men come ashore for food and supplies, their *U-37* is sunk by RCAF bombers. As they travel through Canada, one man is captured and another dies. At a Hudson Bay trading post, they experience a fateful encounter with a French-Canadian trapper (Laurence Olivier) and his companion (Finlay Currie), after which they commandeer a seaplane that crashes. The four surviving members stop at a Hutterite settlement in Manitoba, where they meet the leader (Anton Walbrook) and a young settler woman (Glynis Johns). The lieutenant and his one remaining subordinate are later befriended by an unsuspecting English author (Leslie Howard). Finally, heading for the American border, Hirth must deal with an AWOL Canadian soldier (Raymond Massey), who proves to be his nemesis.

Eric Portman was cast after the director's original choice for Hirth, Esmond Knight, became unavailable. Glynis Johns replaced Elisabeth Bergner, who, after filming location scenes in Montreal, refused to travel to wartime England. "By careful editing," director Michael Powell decided, "we shall use most of Miss Bergner's exterior scenes . . . (but) she will be doubling for Glynis Johns." Future director David Lean edited the film, and, for the opening scene of the U-boat surfacing in Canadian waters, used a shot from captured German film.

# Investigation of a Citizen Above Suspicion
## (Indagine su un Cittadino al di Sopra di Ogni Sospetto)

★ ★ ★ ★ ★ ★ ★ ★ ★ ★ ★ ★ ★ ★ ★ ★ ★ ★ ★ ★ ★ ★ ★ ★ ★ ★ ★ ★ ★ ★ ★ ★ ★ ★ ★ ★ ★ ★ ★ ★ ★ ★ ★ ★ ★ ★ ★ ★

Nationality: Italian       Year: 1970
Cast: Gian Maria Volonte, Florinda Bolkan, Salvo Randone, Gianni Santuccio, Arturo Dominici
Director: Elio Petri       Running Time: 115 minutes
B/W or Color: Color       Availability: TV only

This cunningly constructed suspense melodrama also succeeds as an angry, satirical exploration of the abuse of power. A police inspector (Volonte) has been promoted to the head of his department. He visits his mistress Augusta (Bolkan), and they play elaborate sexual games that reveal his need for sadomasochistic stimulation. When Augusta sneeringly attacks his sexual inadequacy, he turns on her and kills her. It is clear his primary lust is for power and that she is a dispensable object for his amusement. The inspector has a penchant for acting out fantasies based on famous crimes. He carefully arranges a series of clues to implicate himself—fingerprints, footprints, a thread of his tie under her fingernail—smug in the certainty that his position of authority places him above all suspicion.

As the investigation proceeds, the police focus attention on Augusta's homosexual husband, and then on the lover with whom she has been having an affair on the side, a young anarchist stud the police would love to see proven her assassin. The inspector realizes that convicting an innocent man will not prove his own inviolability. He arranges a final test in which the police must face the indisputable evidence of the murderer's identity, which, if denied, will be the ultimate affirmation of his beliefs.

The Italians have consistently produced the most convincing films that equate political repression with kinky sex, and this stands with the best of them. The police department exists as a microcosm of all oppressive forces, a self-sustaining social evil. The film concludes with a quote from Kafka's The Trial: "Whatever impression he may give us, he is a servant of the law. He therefore belongs to the past and is beyond human judgment." The film won an Oscar as Best Foreign Film.

221

# Iphigenia

★★★★★★★★★★★★★★★★★★★★★★★★★★★★★★★★★★★★★★★★★★★★★★★★★★★★★★

*Nationality*: Greek                      *Year*: 1977

*Cast*: Irene Papas, Costa Kazakos, Costa Carras, Tatiana Papamoskou, Panos Michalopoulos

*Director*: Michael Cacoyannis      *Running Time*: 130 minutes

*B/W or Color*: Color                      *Availability*: RCA/COLUMBIA PIC-
TURES HOME VIDEO

T he third in director Michael Cacoyannis's films based on Greek tragedy, this adaptation of Euripides' final play, *Iphigenia in Aulis*, chronologically precedes *Electra* (1962) and *The Trojan Women* (1971).

As the movie begins, we are informed that a thousand Greek ships lie becalmed in Aulis, awaiting the winds that will take them to Troy at the behest of Menelaus, who's intent on retrieving his kidnapped wife, Helen. Menelaus' brother King Agamemnon orders the killing of animals to feed the waiting army and, in so doing, a sacred deer is destroyed. The high priest Calchas prophesies that the Greek ships will sail to victory at Troy only if the king sacrifices his beloved young daughter Iphigenia. Aga-memnon reluctantly sends for her and his wife Clytemnestra on the pre-tense that the child is to marry Achilles. His subsequent efforts to intercept the wedding caravan fail, and Iphigenia's arrival precipitates much tragic soul-searching and breast-beating before the dark tale's inevitable con-clusion.

Each of Cacoyannis's films of Euripidean tragedy is different in its own fashion, and this *Iphigenia* enjoys its own unique strangeness, from the stark beauty of the barren locations to the spare but ominous underscor-ing of Mikis Theodorakis's music.

Irene Papas's sad-eyed face, with its wonderful Greek profile and Hel-lenic intensity, naturally lends itself to the casting of tragic heroines. Her climactic scene of maternal desperation is suitably powerful. Indeed, the entire cast is no less effective, from the anguished, torn Agamemnon of Costa Kazakos to the stalwart, brave Achilles of handsome young Panos Michalopoulos. And, of course, the haunted-looking, would-be child-bride Iphigenia of 12-year-old Tatiana Papamoskou.

*(The film is available on a subtitled videocassette.)*

# It Always Rains on Sunday

\* \* \* \* \* \* \* \* \* \* \* \* \* \* \* \* \* \* \* \* \* \* \* \* \* \* \* \* \* \* \* \* \* \* \* \* \* \* \* \* \* \* \* \* \* \* \* \* \* \* \* \* \* \* \* \*

Nationality: British           Year: 1947 (U.S. release: 1949)

Cast: Googie Withers, John McCallum, Jack Warner, Edward Chapman, Susan Shaw

Director: Robert Hamer        Running Time: 92 minutes

B/W or Color: B/W          Availability: TV only

Against a shabby setting of glistening-wet streets and alleys, *It Always Rains on Sunday* presents a dramatic slice of London life in which various working-class lives are affected by the presence of an escaped convict. Tommy Swann (John McCallum) has broken out of Dartmoor and returned to his old East End haunts. His picture in the papers reminds Rose Sandigate (Googie Withers) of their brief love affair years earlier, before a "job" landed him in prison. Now wed to a stolid, middle-aged husband (Edward Chapman) with three children, Rose reflects on her drab life. When Tommy subsequently turns up at their home for shelter, she hides him in her room.

But once his whereabouts is revealed, Tommy departs and is pursued through perilous railroad yards until he's captured. This eventful Sunday ends with Tommy's fugitive passage having altered quite a few lives, among them the bereft Rose, who attempts suicide; her betrayed husband, who will forgive but not forget; and the district detective sergeant (Jack Warner) with four new arrests to his credit.

That this realistic blend of chase thriller, love story, family drama, and police yarn comes off so well can be credited to its stylish director, Robert Hamer (*Kind Hearts and Coronets*), with his inspired observation of working-class Londoners, his masterful handling of a large acting ensemble, and his maintenance of the film's melancholy, claustrophobic moods. But most unforgettable is the marvelous, tough-but-vulnerable performance he elicits from the underappreciated Googie Withers, who had already done some of her best work under Hamer's guidance in *Pink String and Sealing Wax* and the "Haunted Mirror" sequence from *Dead of Night*.

*It Always Rains on Sunday* is a small work of great artistry whose present-day obscurity is wholly undeserved.

# Ivan the Terrible, Parts I & II
## (Ivan Groznyi)

★★★★★★★★★★★★★★★★★★★★★★★★★★★★★★★★★★★★★★★★★★★★★★★★★★★

*Nationality*: Russian

*Year*: Part I: 1944 (U.S. release: 1947); Part II: 1946/1958 (U.S. release: 1959)

*Cast*: Nikolai Cherkassov, Ludmila Tselikovskaya, Serafima Birman, Mikhail Nazvanov, Piotr Kadochnikov, Vsevelod Pudovkin

*Director*: Sergei Eisenstein

*Running Time*: Part I: 96 minutes/ Part II: 85 minutes

*B/W or Color*: Part II has two color sequences

*Availability*: CORINTH VIDEO

"The grandeur of our theme necessitated a grandiose design . . . we had to show our characters in a stylized way and make them speak in declamations, often with a musical accompaniment." So wrote Sergei Mikhailovich Eisenstein about his final film, the two-part historical epic *Ivan the Terrible* (a planned third part was never completed). Few films by such a great director have received such widely varying reviews. Many called it artificial and antiquated, while others, such as James Agee, responded to its melodramatic quality, calling it "a visual opera, with all of opera's proper disregards of prose-level reality." Orson Welles considered it "the wonderful result of the maturity of Eisenstein's art." And Stalin banned Part II outright, citing political reasons. In truth, there is validity to all these points, and therein lies the endless fascination of this film.

Essentially a simple story of the sometimes brutal rise to power of the 16th-century Tsar Ivan IV, Eisenstein had his actors conform their bodies and faces to fit into his overall "plastic" design, which was to create a larger-than-life world of royal intrigue and an inquiry into the nature of power. As he had done with his previous film, *Alexander Nevsky* (1938), Eisenstein had the great Russian composer Prokofiev write a score that would be an integral component of the film, sometimes building entire sequences to counterpoint the music. The magnificent sets, lavish costumes, and lighting can be fully appreciated only in a high-quality print that preserves all the attention that was put into the painstaking detail of every shot. Unforgettable images abound: the palace set made up entirely in the shape of a giant eye; the immense shadow projected onto a wall as Ivan contemplates a globe; the extreme close-up of Ivan's pointy beard in the foreground and thousands of followers lined up in the distance, and many others. Eisenstein's early films were renowned for their rapid montage, but the hallmark of *Ivan* is its stunning compositions, particularly in the coronation scene, the battle of Kazan, and the 15-minute color sequence near the end of Part II. The film is a must-see for anyone seriously interested in the power of cinema.

*(Corinth offers excellent subtitled videocassettes of both parts.)*

# A Joke of Destiny

### (Scherzo del Destino in Agguato Dietro l'Angolo Come un Brigante di Strada)

\* \* \* \* \* \* \* \* \* \* \* \* \* \* \* \* \* \* \* \* \* \* \* \* \* \* \* \* \* \* \* \* \* \* \* \* \* \* \* \* \* \* \* \* \* \* \* \* \* \* \* \* \* \* \*

**Nationality**: Italian       **Year**: 1983 (U.S. release: 1984)
**Cast**: Ugo Tognazzi, Piera Degli Esposti, Gastone Moschin
**Director**: Lina Wertmuller       **Running Time**: 105 minutes
**B/W or Color**: Color       **Availability**: LORIMAR HOME VIDEO

A *Joke of Destiny* is certainly one of the most ambitious and praise-worthy attempts to handle a serious theme with wit to reach our screens in some time.

The Italian Minister of the Interior is being driven to an important conference in a computer-controlled, terrorist-proof limousine. The power shuts off, and the minister and his chauffeur are trapped in this state-of-the-art, hermetically sealed craft outside the magnificent villa belonging to a toadying politician, De Andreiis, splendidly realized by Ugo Tognazzi.

All attempts to free the minister fail, as they try to enlist the advice of everyone from Agnelli of Fiat to the supertechnicians of Japan. The film ends on a surrealistic note reminiscent of, if not actually derived from, Buñuel's *The Exterminating Angel.*

When Wertmuller is good, she's great, and the cast she has assembled is a joy to watch. The minister, played by Pierluigi Misasi, does a convincing slow burn as he suffers increasingly from heat prostration and frustration. Tognazzi, best known here for his *La Cage aux Folles,* adds another distinguished performance to his already illustrious career. Degli Esposti is funny and touching in what is possibly the most fully developed role Wertmuller has written for a woman. The role of the pot-smoking grandmother would be a bore if it were not for Livia Cerini's incredible face—rather like Harry Langdon startled at being discovered in drag.

It's one of the brightest adult movies we're likely to see for a long time. (*The cassette is subtitled.*)

# Jules and Jim
## (Jules et Jim)

★★★★★★★★★★★★★★★★★★★★★★★★★★★★★★★★★★★★★★★★★★★★★★★★★★★★

Nationality: French        Year: 1961 (U.S. release: 1962)
Cast: Oskar Werner, Jeanne Moreau, Henri Serre, Sabine Haudepin
Director: François Truffaut      Running Time: 110 minutes
B/W or Color: B/W             Availability: KEY VIDEO

Widely considered François Truffaut's greatest achievement, this adaptation of the Henri-Pierre Roche novel is also a celebration of life: an alternately joyous and sorrowful chronicle of two French and German students, Jim (Henri Serre) and Jules (Oskar Werner), in Paris before World War I, whose friendship is intensified and threatened by the love they share for a woman—the mysterious Catherine (radiantly portrayed by Jeanne Moreau). Along with Jacques Demy's *Lola,* this is one of the exhilarating peaks of the French New Wave: the period story also reflects the sense of spontaneity, invention, and love of life that the New Wave directors themselves experienced. Since the film's release, each new generation of filmmakers referred to *Jules and Jim* as an inspiration. (An early Seventies poll ranked it, along with *Citizen Kane* and *2001,* as one of the most influential movies of all time.)

Truffaut exalted in the New Wave's playful attitude toward the screen, using various speeds, different shaped compositions, freeze frames, even voice-over narration to produce an effect of tumultuous activity and on-going invention. It works because the love story is as unsentimentally tough as it is exuberantly romantic. Jules and Jim's awe and bafflement about women, life, and art are met by Catherine's Sphinx-like embodiment of those imponderable things. This film encapsulates the moment when an artistic movement achieves its ultimate expression. This look at the past contains the essence of the Sixties cultural ferment: youth's discovery of the world through the title pair's experience of great love and great pain. A blessed moment: Moreau singing the theme song, "Le Troubillion," summing up the character's hectic, heedless innocence in plangent, unforgettable rhythms. The superlative score is by Georges Delerue, photography by Raoul Coutard.

# Juliet of the Spirits
## (Giulietta degli Spiriti)

* * * * * * * * * * * * * * * * * * * * * * * * * * * * * * * * * * * * * * * * * * * * * * * *

**Nationality**: Italian-French          **Year**: 1965

**Cast**: Giulietta Masina, Mario Pisu, Sandra Milo, Sylva Koscina, Valentina Cortese

**Director**: Federico Fellini          **Running Time**: 145 minutes

**B/W or Color**: Color          **Availability**: TV only

A plush, poetic gift to his real-life wife, Masina, Fellini makes a sincere—and demonstrably feminist—attempt to look into her psyche, to create Giulietta's *8½* for her. At the same time, instead of merely a fact-based recollection of their life together, it's appropriately changed by art and artifice. It's Fellini's first full-length color film, and he (with the great cinematographer Gianni Di Venanzo) plays like a kid in a candy shop, to the point of giving the movie a sweet, kaleidoscopic glow.

As the character Giulietta, Masina adds a new dimension to the role of rich, bourgeois housewife, beset with self-doubt and the suspicion that her husband, Giorgio (Pisu), is having an affair. Through a seance, the stronger women of her support group introduce Giulietta to the spirits, until her inner life gradually begins to dominate her. Iris ("Love for *everyone!*") and Olaf (a profoundly negative male spirit) are most influential. To further confuse Giulietta, elements of her fantasies are bound up with reality (Milo, for instance, plays both Iris and Giulietta's neighbor, Susy). Giulietta's search for self is on. And Fellini helps: the colors and mirrors of Giulietta's boudoir, the sun-drenched splendor of beach and backyard garden—these are elements integral to a complex, ornate, and formal arrangement of space that echoes narrative events and replaces the intellectual's crutch of words. If *8½* asked of Guido "Can you learn to love others?" this film asks of Giulietta "Can you learn to love yourself?" *The New York Times* stated you are ready for the "experience" of *Juliet of the Spirits* if you can answer yes to: "Are your eyes in good condition, able to encompass and abide some of the liveliest, most rococo resplendence ever fashioned in a fairyland on film? And are your wits so instructed and sharpened that you can enjoy a game of armchair psychoanalyzing in a spirit of good, bawdy fun?"

The National Board of Review voted *Juliet of the Spirits* 1965's Best Foreign Film.

# Kameradschaft

## (Comradeship)

★ ★ ★ ★ ★ ★ ★ ★ ★ ★ ★ ★ ★ ★ ★ ★ ★ ★ ★ ★ ★ ★ ★ ★ ★ ★ ★ ★ ★ ★ ★ ★ ★ ★ ★ ★ ★ ★ ★ ★ ★ ★ ★ ★ ★ ★ ★ ★ ★

*Nationality*: German-French          *Year*: 1931 (U.S. release: 1932)

*Cast*: Alexander Granach, Fritz Kampers, Daniel Mendaille, Elisabeth Wendt, Ernst Busch

*Director*: G. W. Pabst          *Running Time*: 78 minutes (93 minutes in France)

*B/W or Color*: B/W          *Availability*: EMBASSY HOME ENTERTAINMENT

Georg Wilhelm Pabst (1885–1967) has become best known in recent years as the director of *Pandora's Box*, that landmark 1928 German silent for which Louise Brooks will always be best remembered—a perfect screen incarnation of the intelligent beauty waging an inner battle with her sexuality. But Pabst also was the man behind 1931's *The Three-penny Opera/Die Dreigroschenoper* and a somewhat less-well-known Brooks vehicle, 1929's *Diary of a Lost Girl/Das Tagebuch einer Verlorenen*. As the Thirties began, he turned out two controversial motion pictures that raised political arguments by their pacifism: the antiwar *Westfront 1918* and *Kameradschaft*, the story of a mining disaster. Both films shared the intent of demonstrating Franco-German détente at times of crisis.

*Kameradschaft* was based on a real-life disaster that took place a decade before World War I in Courcieres, a French town near the German border. Pabst updated the time to shortly *after* the signing of the Versailles Treaty, using the tragedy of the mine disaster to overcome hostilities and bitterness left in the war's aftermath, as German miners crossed over to aid French miners trapped by the explosion.

In a retrospective appreciation, critic Pauline Kael wrote, "Pabst's study of disaster and rescue is a powerful and imaginative re-creation of a high moment in human comradeship. Technically a brilliant achievement, *Kameradschaft* is famous among film craftsmen for the experimental use of sound, and for magnificent creative editing. The subterranean scenes have a nightmarish authenticity."

The National Board named *Kameradschaft* one of the ten best foreign films of 1932.

*(Embassy offers a subtitled cassette of the 78-minute version.)*

# A Kid for Two Farthings

\* \* \* \* \* \* \* \* \* \* \* \* \* \* \* \* \* \* \* \* \* \* \* \* \* \* \* \* \* \* \* \* \* \* \* \* \* \* \* \* \* \* \* \* \* \* \* \* \* \*

*Nationality*: British        *Year*: 1955 (U.S. release: 1956)

*Cast*: Celia Johnson, Diana Dors, David Kossoff, Brenda de Banzie, Joe Robinson, Jonathan Ashmore

*Director*: Carol Reed        *Running Time*: 96 minutes

*B/W or Color*: Color        *Availability*: TV only

With his reputation as a director of such fine topical thrillers as *Odd Man Out, The Third Man,* and *The Man Between,* Carol Reed made a surprising switch to fantasy with *A Kid for Two Farthings,* Wolf Mankowitz's little story about life in London's East End. Reed has explained that he merely wanted to bring to the screen a book that had charmed him, with its rich ethnic setting and fairy-tale story. And he credited Mankowitz's adaptation of his fragile fable, flavored with its folksy Jewish humor: "Any success the picture has had is due in no small measure to his skillful, racy, warm and witty dialogue."

The "kid" of the title is a little white goat that captures the imagination of a six-year-old who lives with his mother in the shop of an elderly tailor. Inspired by the old man's tales of a magic-powered unicorn, the boy mistakes his kid for that legendary creature, because of a hornlike growth on its forehead. He fully believes in his "unicorn" and its powers—which do, indeed, appear to be working. How else to explain the old tailor's finally getting his longed-for steam presser? Or the neighborhood bodybuilder's unexpected victory in a wrestling match? Other "miracles" follow until, suddenly, the goat dies. As the story concludes, the lad gets a new animal—and there is the suggestion that perhaps his long-lost father will return.

As with *The Fallen Idol,* Carol Reed coaxes from child-actor Jonathan Ashmore a performance of such appeal that, at the little kid's death, one cannot help but be profoundly, empathetically moved. The only drawback is that his accents are too refined for the movie's milieu, as are those of his miscast screen mother, the usually superb Celia Johnson.

# Kind Hearts and Coronets

★ ★ ★ ★ ★ ★ ★ ★ ★ ★ ★ ★ ★ ★ ★ ★ ★ ★ ★ ★ ★ ★ ★ ★ ★ ★ ★ ★ ★ ★ ★ ★ ★ ★ ★ ★ ★ ★ ★ ★ ★ ★ ★ ★ ★ ★ ★ ★ ★ ★ ★ ★ ★ ★

*Nationality*: British                    *Year*: 1949 (U.S. release: 1950)

*Cast*: Dennis Price, Alec Guinness, Valerie Hobson, Joan Greenwood, Miles Malleson

*Director*: Robert Hamer          *Running Time*: 104 minutes

*B/W or Color*: B/W                  *Availability*: THORN/EMI-HBO VIDEO

This stylish comedy has aged superbly. Dennis Price, as Louis Mazzini, impoverished member of a noble family, sets out to eliminate the eight members of the D'Ascoyne family who stand in the way of his dukedom. Starting with Ascoyne D'Ascoyne, Louis keeps score on the back of the family tree. Whether he is agonizing over the unexpected birth of twins; deftly substituting petrol for paraffin in a darkroom lamp; or elegantly taking tea with Edith (Valerie Hobson), while sniffing the air for the acrid scent of her husband's burning remains, the result is sheer enchantment. Saucy Sibella (Joan Greenwood) tempts and taunts in a voice that smoothly combines treacle and cyanide, as she gradually becomes party to Louis's plot.

Alex Guinness plays all eight of Louis's victims. A generation that knows him as the grizzled patriarch of *Star Wars* should particularly love him as Lady Agatha, the suffragette who smashes windows and meets a peculiarly ingenious and violent end. Guinness achieves a tour de force as a corporate cast of one. Originally, the actor had been offered only four of these roles, but he successfully negotiated to play double that number. Prior to this, the actor had appeared in only two movies, *Great Expectations* and *Oliver Twist*, neither of which made him an important film star. In *Kind Hearts and Coronets,* although the nominal leading man is Dennis Price, it's Guinness whom moviegoers best remember.

Alec Guinness was named 1950's Best Actor by The National Board of Review, which also cited *Kind Hearts and Coronets* as one of the year's ten best films. Incidentally, this comedy classic, like its Ealing Studios predecessor, *Tight Little Island,* enjoyed more popularity with U.S. audiences than in its native Britain.

# A Kind of Loving

★★★★★★★★★★★★★★★★★★★★★★★★★★★★★★★★★★★★★★★★★★★★★★★★★★★★★★★

*Nationality*: British          *Year*: 1962

*Cast*: Alan Bates, June Ritchie, Thora Hird, James Bolam, Leonard Rossiter

*Director*: John Schlesinger      *Running Time*: 112 minutes

*B/W or Color*: B/W            *Availability*: THORN/EMI-HBO VIDEO

Arriving on the heels of the popular and groundbreaking *Room at the Top* and *Saturday Night and Sunday Morning*, *A Kind of Loving* was initially shunted off as just another in Britain's string of "kitchen sink" dramas of life in the industrial north. The movie made little impact until it won the Best Picture award at 1962's Berlin Film Festival. Word of mouth eventually made this realistic study of young love gone sour a box-office hit and thrust the little-known Alan Bates into full-fledged stardom. With his first feature length motion picture, John Schlesinger found himself suddenly in the top echelon of British filmmakers.

Vic (Alan Bates) is a draftsman in a Lancashire factory, where he's attracted to a typist named Ingrid (June Ritchie). Their dates culminate in Vic's spending a night with her when her widowed mother is away. Ironically, Ingrid falls in love with Vic just as his purely physical desire is waning. When she discovers she is pregnant, he condescends to marry her, and they move in with her snobbish, disapproving mother. Household tensions grow, and when Ingrid suffers a miscarriage, Vic realizes that the wedding was avoidable. After a drunken argument with her mother, he walks out, returning later to persuade Ingrid that they must have a home of their own. Perhaps they can settle for "a kind of loving."

This downbeat twist on the old mother-in-law triangle is notably vitalized by a sly, witty frankness in the Willis Hall-Keith Waterhouse screenplay. Director Schlesinger makes naturalistic use of the dreary Lancashire locations, while treating the film's human element with a controlled sensitivity that avoids excessive sentiment.

Ritchie and Bates are both excellent in demanding roles, and Thora Hird presents a formidably shrewish mother-in-law. Schlesinger surrounds them with wonderful Midlands actors in support.

# King and Country

★★★★★★★★★★★★★★★★★★★★★★★★★★★★★★★★★★★★★★★★★★★★★★★★★★★★★★★

*Nationality*: British                    *Year*: 1964 (U.S. release: 1966)
*Cast*: Dirk Bogarde, Tom Courtenay, Leo McKern, Barry Foster, James Villiers, Jeremy Spenser
*Director*: Joseph Losey                   *Running Time*: 86 minutes
*B/W or Color*: B/W                        *Availability*: TV only

This is a shattering film, stark and depressing, but thought-provoking in its eloquent commentary on 20th-century man and his military honor code.

Originally, *King and Country* was a 1955 story by James Lansdale Hodson called *Return to the Wood,* which John Wilson later adapted for TV and stage under the title *Hamp.*

The setting is 1917 Belgium, where Private Hamp (Tom Courtenay), a simple-minded young Englishman, awaits court-martial for desertion, after serving three years at the front. Captain Hargreaves (Dirk Bogarde), assigned to his defense, learns that Hamp, grimly accepting the deaths of his platoon buddies, as well as news of his wife's infidelity, simply decided to "go for a walk." The lad's sincerity impresses Hargreaves, and he pleads for justice, claiming that the soldier wasn't mentally responsible. But the court-martial finds Hamp guilty, and even the captain's recommendation of mercy is rejected.

The night before the execution, fellow soldiers visit Hamp in his cell with stolen rum. The drink-sodden evening of desperate gaiety has cruelly ironic results; at dawn, the firing squad fails to kill Hamp, and Hargreaves is forced to put a compassionate bullet through the boy's head. Bogarde calls this one-take scene "The most difficult thing I've ever done."

With such a strong script, dedicated cast and crew, and settings of repellent realism, Joseph Losey completed shooting in 18 days. He is brilliantly served by his actors, especially Courtenay's Hamp, who has little dialogue but a face that reflects what he cannot articulate. Bogarde's Hargreaves is an eloquent figure of inner resentment and outer rigidity, of discipline and frustration. Larry Adler's plaintive harmonica score works as economically as Losey's restriction of gunfire to only one scene—Hamp's execution.

Tom Courtenay won a Best Actor award at the 1964 Venice Film Festival.

# King of Hearts
## (Le Roi de Coeur)

★★★★★★★★★★★★★★★★★★★★★★★★★★★★★★★★★★★★★★★★★★★★★★★★★★★★

Nationality: French/Italian        Year: 1967
Cast: Alan Bates, Geneviève Bujold, Michel Serrault, Pierre Brasseur, Micheline Presle, Françoise Christophe
Director: Philippe de Broca        Running Time: 102 minutes
B/W or Color: Color        Availability: CBS/FOX HOME VIDEO

K*ing of Hearts* is a beautifully filmed tragicomedy satirizing the idiocy of war. Meticulously directed by Philippe de Broca from a screenplay by Daniel Boulanger, the film purportedly stems from a World War I story about French mental patients who, after their hospital was bombed, dressed in American army uniforms and were massacred by German soldiers. The film's premise, that in the insanity of war only the lunatics are truly sane, contributed to its being a counterculture hit in the United States during the Vietnam War.

Mild-mannered Private Charles Plumpick (Alan Bates) is sent into a small French town to disarm a bomb set to explode at midnight. Knocked unconscious, he comes to in a town transformed with costumed characters and circus animals roaming freely. He soon realizes that the dandy townsfolk are the harmless asylum inmates: the Duke and Duchess of Clubs, the Bishop, the effeminate hairdresser, the sensuous madame, General Geranium. As his "court," they hail him as the King of Hearts, perform a regal coronation, and prepare for his royal wedding to nubile virgin Columbine (Geneviève Bujold). When his new-found friends refuse to leave their doomed town, a despairing Plumpick decides to stay with them. But with minutes to spare, a chance comment from Columbine leads Plumpick to the bomb, and the bunker is disarmed. When the Scottish and German troops come upon each other, a massacre results. Only Plumpick is left alive. The lunatics return to the safety of their asylum. Plumpick is reassigned, but he slips away from his company. Holding his caged pigeons, he stands naked before two shocked nuns at the asylum gates, waiting to be committed.

*King of Hearts* is an enchanting film. Pierre Lhomme's photography is dazzling, Jacques Fonteray's costumes are brilliant, and Georges Delerue's score is mesmerizing.

(*The videocassette is English-dubbed.*)

# Kiss of the Spider Woman

★★★★★★★★★★★★★★★★★★★★★★★★★★★★★★★★★★★★★★★★★★★★★★★★★★★★★★

*Nationality*: Brazilian                    *Year*: 1985
*Cast*: William Hurt, Raul Julia, Sonia Braga, Jose Lewgoy, Denise Dumont
*Director*: Hector Babenco          *Running Time*: 119 minutes
*B/W or Color*: Color                    *Availability*: CHARTER ENTER-
                                                                TAINMENT

Despite its campy title and plot, *Kiss of the Spider Woman* succeeds
on several levels, as a political thriller and as a character study.
It also earned a Best Actor Oscar for William Hurt, although co-star
Raul Julia—who is superb—equally deserved the award (he wasn't even
nominated). The film-within-a-film sequences are done as a takeoff on
the style of Forties movies, particularly American B pictures. While at
first the viewer might resist these intrusions into the main plot, as does
Julia's character, eventually one is caught up in the narrative to the point
of wanting to know what happens next. The ending of the film is open
to interpretation.

In a South American prison, two opposites share a cell. One is homosexual Hurt, in jail for molesting a youth. The other, the fiery Julia, is a
journalist and radical who is part of an underground movement. To pass
the time, Hurt describes the plot of an old movie in which the heroine is
an agent operating against the Nazis in World War II. To gain favors as
well as freedom, Hurt agrees to spy on Julia, but their relationship blossoms into friendship, and he attempts to help Julia's cause when he's
finally released. Sonia Braga is seen as Julia's woman, as well as the heroine of the movie and also the Spider Woman, lead character in another
film that Hurt briefly describes. Hector Babenco shot the film entirely in
Brazil in English. From the raw emotions expressed in his *Pixote* (1981),
Babenco has journeyed to a more fantastic world in *Spider Woman*, one
in which reality and illusion may be more closely related than evident at
first glance. The ending is one in which the dreamer tries to enter a real
situation, and the realist retreats into fantasy. Both men know that, despite their efforts, they have not changed anything, and they accept the
situation by attempting to reverse their positions.

Hurt also won the Best Actor Award at Cannes; he and Julia shared
The National Board's first dual award for Best Actor, and their movie
was voted one of the year's ten best.

# Knife in the Water
## (Noz w Wodzie)

★★★★★★★★★★★★★★★★★★★★★★★★★★★★★★★★★★★★★★★★★★★★★★★★★★★★★

*Nationality*: Polish                    *Year*: 1962 (U.S. release: 1963)
*Cast*: Leon Niemczyk, Jolanta Umecka, Zygmunt Malanowicz
*Director*: Roman Polanski       *Running Time*: 94 minutes
*B/W or Color*: B/W               *Availability*: CBS/FOX VIDEO

I t is doubtful whether there has ever been a film director whose private life has been more public than that of Roman Polanski. His mother was killed in a concentration camp; his pregnant wife, Sharon Tate, murdered by the Manson family; and then his infamous tangle with the law in 1976 for statutory rape and his subsequent flight from this country—the litany of tragedy is endless. To most people today he represents merely another funny foreign name, a cue for instant laughter from talk-show hosts and nightclub comedians to indulge in cheap double entendres, a synonym for child molesting, much the same way Elizabeth Taylor became a target of fat jokes. It would be a shame, however, if lost amidst all the gossip was the important fact that Polanski was, and is, a startlingly brilliant and disturbing talent who created some of the modern cinema's most memorable films.

To rediscover Polanski the filmmaker in all his unspoiled purity, we should return to his first feature, *Knife in the Water*. Co-written by Polanski, Jakub Goldberg, and Jerzy Skolimowski (himself an original and highly talented director), the story is an uncomplicated three-character drama that takes on added depth when a rich married couple pick up a hitchhiker and take him along for a day of fun on their yacht. Polanski quickly and efficiently establishes an unnerving sense of paranoia and alienation as the two men engage in subtle psychological warfare to impress the woman, who eventually makes love to the young hitchhiker (Polanski claims to have dubbed the voice for the young man). As in many Polanski films, trust in others is not easily attained, and there is a constant sense of dread, of barely repressed violence, dramatized by the constant placement of characters on the very edge of the frame, hovering dangerously close to the camera. Polanski seems fascinated by triangular compositions in depth, exploring dynamic visual manifestations of the mutable nature of complex human relationships. The clinical, seemingly detached, yet strangely comic treatment suggests some of Polanski's admitted influences: Beckett, Pinter, Kafka, and Buñuel, while one can also sense a similarity to Hitchcock, but Polanski seems to have a deeper identification with his unbalanced characters. This identification would reach its pinnacle in the chilling persona of a withdrawn and homicidal Catherine Deneuve in *Repulsion* (1965) and in *The Tenant* (1976) in which Polanski himself plays a man who experiences a gradual emotional and mental collapse.

*(CBS/Fox offers a cassette with English subtitles.)*

# Knight Without Armour

★ ★ ★ ★ ★ ★ ★ ★ ★ ★ ★ ★ ★ ★ ★ ★ ★ ★ ★ ★ ★ ★ ★ ★ ★ ★ ★ ★ ★ ★ ★ ★ ★ ★ ★ ★ ★ ★ ★ ★ ★ ★ ★ ★ ★ ★ ★ ★ ★ ★ ★ ★ ★

*Nationality*: British          *Year*: 1937

*Cast*: Marlene Dietrich, Robert Donat, Irene Vanbrugh, Herbert Lomas, Austin Trevor, Basil Gill

*Director*: Jacques Feyder        *Running Time*: 107 minutes

*B/W or Color*: B/W          *Availability*: EMBASSY HOME
                             ENTERTAINMENT

A love story that takes place during the 1917 Russian Revolution, *Knight Without Armour* concerns A. J. Fotheringill (Robert Donat), an Englishman working as a translator in St. Petersburg, and Countess Alexandra Vladinoff (Marlene Dietrich), daughter of the Minister of the Interior (Herbert Lomas).

After writing an article that offends the powers-that-be, Fotheringill is ordered to leave the country. He appeals to a friend for help, only to discover that he works for the British as an undercover agent. After disguising Fotheringill as a Russian, he has him contact members of the revolutionary movement, but such activities soon find Fotheringill exiled to Siberia.

Meanwhile, Alexandra has married Colonel Adraxine (Austin Trevor), but is shortly widowed. When the revolutionary forces take over, the Englishman is released and becomes assistant to the new commissar of Khalinsk (Basil Gill), with whom he had been exiled. Fotheringill (still disguised as a Russian) finds himself escorting Alexandra, under arrest, to Petrograd. They are separated, but a frantic Fotheringill finds the countess and helps her to escape from her captors. Now in love with each other, they try to reach the border. During the chaotic days of the Revolution, it is little wonder the lovers are again separated. Fotheringill discovers just in time that the countess is still alive and safely on a train leaving for the border. He catches it as it moves out of the station.

Producer Alexander Korda almost had Robert Donat replaced when the actor was felled by a severe asthmatic attack, but Dietrich insisted that they shoot around Donat until he recovered. (This was a wise decision on Dietrich's part, since the chemistry between her and Donat was extraordinary.) Asthma was to plague Donat throughout his career, limiting his screen appearances and finally causing his death in 1958.

# Kwaidan

★ ★ ★ ★ ★ ★ ★ ★ ★ ★ ★ ★ ★ ★ ★ ★ ★ ★ ★ ★ ★ ★ ★ ★ ★ ★ ★ ★ ★ ★ ★ ★ ★ ★ ★ ★ ★ ★ ★ ★ ★ ★ ★ ★ ★ ★ ★ ★ ★

*Nationality*: Japanese          *Year*: 1964 (U.S. release: 1965)

*Cast*: Rentaro Mikuni, Michiyo Aratama, Tatsuya Nakadai, Keiko Kishi, Katsuo Nakamura

*Director*: Masaki Kobayashi       *Running Time*: 164 minutes

*B/W or Color*: Color            *Availability*: Public Domain

Pulitzer Prize-winning New Orleans journalist Lafcadio Hearn moved to Japan and pursued with a passion the chronicling of that country's legends and ghost tales. Using the nom de plume Uagumo Koizumi, his body of work far exceeded that of any other Japanese scholar. He was deeply respected and celebrated in his adopted home. In 1964 Kobayashi brought four of these stories to the wide screen in a film titled *Kwaidan*. Indeed one—"In a Cup of Tea"—is slight, a throwaway, an attempt at comic relief, something at which the great director is not terribly adept. But the other three are profoundly artistic statements, peerless demonstrations of camera movement, composition, lighting, and color.

As the movie was shot almost entirely in an empty airplane hangar, Kobayashi horrified Toho Studios executives by averaging three set-ups a day, pushing the film, according to them, millions over budget. The music, often mistaken for sound effects, was by avant-garde composer Toru Takemitsu—eerie, elemental tones of wood being split, hard stones from the island of Shikoku being struck together, etc.

"The Black Hair" is the first story. Slow and ritualistic, it tells of a samurai who deserts his loving wife for power and money and leads a barren life. He eventually returns to find her and make amends. But the consequences of his betrayal force him to face the finality of what he's done.

In its initial U.S. release, the most popular story, "The Woman of the Snow," was not included. This folk tale again concerns a woman's timeless love and dedication, and the irretrievable penalty of a man's betrayal.

"Hoichi the Earless" finds a blind temple musician reciting the story of the deaths at sea of an entire clan. Unbeknownst to him, he is telling the story to the ghosts of the lost family. Discovering this, temple priests attempt to save him, with tragic results.

If you are a devotee of mesmerizing, eloquent style, you must see Kobayashi's *Kwaidan*.

# La Balance

★ ★ ★ ★ ★ ★ ★ ★ ★ ★ ★ ★ ★ ★ ★ ★ ★ ★ ★ ★ ★ ★ ★ ★ ★ ★ ★ ★ ★ ★ ★ ★ ★ ★ ★ ★ ★ ★ ★ ★ ★ ★ ★ ★ ★ ★ ★ ★ ★

**Nationality**: French          **Year**: 1983

**Cast**: Nathalie Baye, Philippe Léotard, Richard Berry, Christophe Mala-voy, Jean-Paul Connart

**Director**: Bob Swaim          **Running Time**: 102 minutes

**B/W *or* Color**: Color          **Availability**: TV only

This is a spectacularly successful French police thriller, full of atmo-sphere, full-bodied characterizations, honesty, morality, and action. But beyond its success as a film, it's a remarkable achievement for writer-director Bob Swaim.

Swaim, an American who lived in France for 20 years as a student of anthropology, eventually decided to switch careers, and began making short films. *La Balance* is his second feature and, true to his earlier train-ing, he spent several months researching the Brigades Territoriales, an elite police force created to infiltrate the criminal underworld of Paris, in order to write an ethnographically accurate screenplay. He has assembled a world of cynical plainsclothesmen, pimps, prostitutes, and informers—and it is the brigade's delicate relationship with these informers that is the origin of the title.

The actors are marvelous, almost documentary in their delivery. Phi-lippe Léotard is the weak-looking Dede, the pimp-lover of the prostitute Nicole, portrayed by Nathalie Baye. Léotard's looks are counterpointed by his strength as he is manipulated by both the police and underworld toughs. The police are portrayed as unpleasantly as the mobsters, but this is not a tale of heroes. It's a study of cause and effect on the dark fringes of society, a masterful blend of European filmmaking sensibilities—non-linear and absorbed as much with mood as with plot—and Hollywood style, tautly choreographed chases and shootouts.

# La Cage aux Folles

*(Birds of a Feather)/La Cage aux Folles II/La Cage aux Folles 3:*
*The Wedding*

★ ★ ★ ★ ★ ★ ★ ★ ★ ★ ★ ★ ★ ★ ★ ★ ★ ★ ★ ★ ★ ★ ★ ★ ★ ★ ★ ★ ★ ★ ★ ★ ★ ★ ★ ★ ★ ★ ★ ★ ★ ★ ★ ★ ★ ★ ★

*Nationality*: French-Italian      *Year*: 1978/1980/1985
*Cast*: Michel Serrault, Ugo Tognazzi, Michel Galabru, Claire Maurier
*Director*: Edouard Molinaro      *Running Time*: 91 minutes/100
    minutes/91 minutes
*B/W or Color*: Color      *Availability*: CBS/FOX HOME
    VIDEO

This outrageous Franco-Italian farce about a middle-aged show-business gay couple facing an unusual "family" crisis has, to date, become the highest-grossing (in excess of $17 million) foreign-language film ever shown in the United States.

Its source is Jean Poiret's 1973 play, a work that draws its title from the Saint-Tropez nightclub operated by longtime lovers Albin and Renato, in which the more flamboyant Albin stars in drag shows under the name of Zaza. Complications ensue when Renato's son Laurent announces his engagement to a nice young lady whose stuffed-shirt family expresses the desire to meet Laurent's parents—and Zaza pretends to be the boy's mother.

Edouard Molinaro (*Back to the Wall, Seven Capital Sins*) directed this landmark comedy, as well as its almost equally successful sequel, *La Cage aux Folles II,* which retained the same leading players. In France, Michel Serrault's performance as Albin copped him a Cesar (the French Academy Award) for 1978's Best Actor. Hollywood gave no Oscars but saluted *La Cage aux Folles* with three nominations: for Molinaro's direction; the screenplay adaptation of Molinaro, Francis Veber, Marcelle Danon, and Jean Poiret; and the costume designs of Piero Tosi and Ambra Danon.

In 1984, Jerry Herman's musical adaptation of this story became an instant Broadway hit, and late 1985 witnessed the emergence of a second sequel film, *La Cage aux Folles 3.* But by now the theme was wearing somewhat thin, and, unlike its two predecessors, the third movie was a quick failure, both in Europe and the United States.

(*The CBS/FOX videocassettes of all three* La Cage aux Folles *films are offered in English-dubbed editions.*)

# La Chèvre

★ ★ ★ ★ ★ ★ ★ ★ ★ ★ ★ ★ ★ ★ ★ ★ ★ ★ ★ ★ ★ ★ ★ ★ ★ ★ ★ ★ ★ ★ ★ ★ ★ ★ ★ ★ ★ ★ ★ ★ ★ ★ ★ ★ ★ ★ ★ ★ ★ ★ ★ ★ ★

Nationality: French                    Year: 1982 (U.S. release: 1985)
Cast: Pierre Richard, Gérard Depardieu, Pedro Armendariz, Jr., Michel Robin
Director: Francis Veber               Running Time: 91 minutes
B/W or Color: Color                    Availability: TV only

One of The National Board's five best foreign films for 1985, *La Chèvre* (*The Goat*) actually was made (and released in France) in 1982 but was not shown in the United States until after the success of *Les Comperes* (1984), the second collaboration of writer-director Francis Veber and stars Pierre Richard and Gérard Depardieu. Their third comedy, *Les Fugitifs*, opened in France in 1986.

The premise of *La Chèvre* is that the best way to find a missing accident-prone person (a rich man's daughter) is to send an equally accident-prone person (Pierre Richard) in pursuit—on the theory that he'll make all the same blunders. Richard proves himself the man for the job by being asked to sit down in a room of empty chairs and managing to select the only broken one. He's dispatched to Mexico, accompanied by a skeptical private detective (Gérard Depardieu).

Their merry misadventures lead them to the woman's kidnapper, a burned-out village, and an almost destroyed mission—where the two "victims" meet then dreamily walk off hand-in-hand, onto a pier that promptly collapses and floats away with the hapless couple.

Veber, strongly influenced by American comedies of the Thirties, particularly those of Frank Capra and Leo McCarey, has incorporated numerous sight gags—some reminiscent of the Hope-Crosby "Road" pictures and silent-screen comedies (watch that fade out). Richard, who gained fame as *The Tall Blond Man with One Black Shoe* (written by Veber), is a gifted clown—whether sinking in quicksand or being grabbed by a gorilla—and Depardieu quietly scores as his nonplussed straight man. No question about it—*La Chèvre* is inspired slapstick.

Having written 17 screenplays (including *La Cage aux Folles I* and *II*), Veber's directorial debut was *The Toy* (*Le Jouet*), which was later made into an American comedy with Richard Pryor.

# La Dolce Vita

★★★★★★★★★★★★★★★★★★★★★★★★★★★★★★★★★★★★★★★★★★★★★★★★★★★★★★

*Nationality*: Italian-French　　　　*Year*: 1960 (U.S. release: 1961)
*Cast*: Marcello Mastroianni, Anita Ekberg, Anouk Aimée, Yvonne Furneaux, Magali Noel, Alain Cuny, Nadia Gray
*Director*: Federico Fellini　　　　*Running Time*: 175 minutes
*B/W or Color*: B/W　　　　　　　*Availability*: REPUBLIC PICTURES
　　　　　　　　　　　　　　　　　HOME VIDEO

Federico Fellini gained international fame and recognition with this three-hour epic exposing the decadence of European high society. Basically a string of vignettes about moral corruption, *La Dolce Vita* created a scandal with its depiction of the rich and famous cavorting about Rome, indulging in drunken orgies, suicide, and all-around profligacy. Marcello Mastroianni plays a journalist who aspires to serious writing but finds it impossible to break away from his self-indulgent life as a gossip columnist.

There is no unified plot, but, rather, a series of incidents in which Marcello comes to terms with the emptiness of his life. The opening shot of a stone Jesus being flown by helicopter to the Vatican sets the tone of social satire mixed with surreal imagery. Anita Ekberg plays a voluptuous blond starlet who flirts with Marcello and symbolizes his indecision. Her wild dancing in a strapless black dress and taking a pre-dawn bath in the Trevi Fountain are among the cinema's most memorable icons.

The middle of the film concerns a visit to a small town where two children claim to have "seen" the Virgin Mary—which turns out to be a hoax. The Vatican condemned the film outright and found this scene particularly offensive. After Marcello learns that an intellectual writer-friend has killed his two children and himself, he loses control and goes to a decadent, all-night party. The film ends at dawn, when the party breaks up and Marcello walks down to the beach. A little girl waves to Marcello; he stares at her sweet, innocent face for a moment, then shrugs and walks away to join the others—an ambiguous ending to a challenging film.

*La Dolce Vita* is a vast fresco of a film, its wide-screen frames overflowing with brilliant and startling images. It was named Best Film at Cannes, followed by similar accolades from the New York Film Critics and The National Board. Hollywood awarded *La Dolce Vita* an Oscar for Best Costume Design.

*(The videocassette is subtitled.)*

# La Femme Infidèle
## (The Unfaithful Wife)

★★★★★★★★★★★★★★★★★★★★★★★★★★★★★★★★★★★★★★★★★★★★★★★★★★★★★★★★★★★★

**Nationality**: French-Italian      **Year**: 1968 (U.S. release: 1969)
**Cast**: Stéphane Audran, Michel Bouquet, Maurice Ronet, Serge Bento, Michel Duchaussoy
**Director**: Claude Chabrol      **Running Time**: 98 minutes
**B/W or Color**: Color      **Availability**: TV only

Of all the filmmakers of the French New Wave (Godard, Truffaut, Resnais, Rohmer, et al.) Claude Chabrol has had perhaps the most diverse output, both in artistic intent and commercial consideration. His best films, however, must rank as some of the finest that France has ever produced. These include *Que La Bête Meure!* (1969), *Juste Avant la Nuit* (1971), *Le Boucher* (1970), *Une Partie de Plaisir* (1975), and *Les Noces Rouges* (1973). These are all penetrating Hitchcockian studies of suspense, love, and murder among the French bourgeois, however, with Chabrol's uniquely bizarre and personal psychological insight.

*La Femme Infidèle* may just possibly be the best of all. It is the story of a mild-mannered insurance broker (Bouquet) who discovers that his wife (Audran, Chabrol's real-life spouse) is having an affair, and in a fit of passion kills her lover (Ronet). Strangely enough, this brings the married couple closer together, with Audran developing a newfound love and respect for Bouquet.

This is a superbly realized thriller with a long, silent sequence following the murder in which the corpse and all the incriminating evidence are carefully disposed of, obviously inspired by the identical scene in 1960's *Psycho*. Chabrol's direction is, as usual, meticulous and brilliantly controlled, as is his screenplay.

Many scenes are masterly, such as the aforementioned disposal of the corpse, as well as the murder itself and the frequent police inquiries, all creating an almost unbearable tension. We begin secretly to root for the killer, hoping he will get away with his deed, for after all, it is a crime of passion.

Two years later Chabrol would make a film that is almost an inversion of this plot with *Juste Avant la Nuit*. Bouquet and Audran once again star as a well-to-do married couple, only this time it is Bouquet who takes a lover, and he kills *her*, with the similar result of earning new love from his wife.

The National Board listed *La Femme Infidèle* among the best films of the year.

# La Guerre Est Finie

\*\*\*\*\*\*\*\*\*\*\*\*\*\*\*\*\*\*\*\*\*\*\*\*\*\*\*\*\*\*\*\*\*\*\*\*\*\*\*\*\*\*\*\*\*\*\*\*\*\*\*\*\*

Nationality: French-Swedish        Year: 1966
Cast: Yves Montand, Ingrid Thulin, Geneviève Bujold, Dominique Rozan, Françoise Bertin
Director: Alain Resnais        Running Time: 121 minutes
B/W or Color: B/W        Availability: TV only

Alain Resnais has made one of his most accessible films about the confusion of politics in the Sixties. Brilliantly employing the inter-relation of time and place, a technique he had virtually discovered for the cinema, Resnais's hero, the world-weary Diego (Yves Montand), brings a message from the past to bear upon the present—he's a living, breathing memory, impossible to dismiss as historical fallacy.

Diego, whose confused identity presages Antonioni's *Passenger* by nearly a decade, travels between Spain and France on behalf of a 30-year-old cause. He is a courier for the anti-Franco underground, traveling across the border under assumed names to smuggle leaflets into Spain. Diego cut his teeth on the Spanish revolution and remains in the futile service of demogogic older men who have as clearly lost their way as their war. "In the suburbs of Paris," says Diego, criticizing his comrade coffee-house ideologues, "you can make the reality of Spain conform to your dreams." And he seriously questions whether a man living in exile can bring about a change in his own country. Diego's inner turmoil echoes the burden of political idealism: He sees both Marianne, a mistress of 12 years (Ingrid Thulin), and a student, Nadine (Geneviève Bujold). As political myth and reality intertwine, so does his sexual life. His encounter with Nadine functions as both homage to Godard and as a dreamlike stylization that suggests it may be a mere projection of desire. The impotence (and ide-ological potency) of Marxism as a ruling principal of political action is thus contrasted with Diego's personal dilemma and made concrete by Resnais's precise counterpointing of generations. The film stands as one of the Sixties' most clear-minded—yet utterly elegant—works of politi-cal art.

*The New York Times* reported: "It is a powerful study of a man's commitment to a consuming and bewildering belief," and Judith Crist wrote: "[It] is an outstanding film for our time and certainly the out-standing offering at the [N.Y. Film] Festival."

# La Nuit de Varennes

★★★★★★★★★★★★★★★★★★★★★★★★★★★★★★★★★★★★★★★★★★★★★★★★★★★★★★

Nationality: French-Italian          Year: 1982 (U.S. release: 1983)

Cast: Marcello Mastroianni, Jean-Louis Barrault, Hanna Schygulla, Harvey Keitel, Jean-Claude Brialy

Director: Ettore Scola          Running Time: 133 minutes (150 minutes in Europe)

B/W or Color: Color          Availability: RCA/COLUMBIA PICTURES HOME VIDEO

E ttore Scola's film presents a peripheral view of a famous historical incident: the ill-fated flight of Louis XVI and Marie Antoinette from Paris to Varennes, where their bid for loyalist resurgence is foiled. In the literate screenplay by Scola and Sergio Amidei, the drama is shifted away from the doomed king and queen. A cross-section of French society rides symbolically following the king's coach, and it is through them that this drama is played out: Restif de la Bretonne (Jean-Louis Barrault), scandalous writer of the times; Casanova (Marcello Mastroianni), celebrated lover; Thomas Paine (Harvey Keitel), American revolutionary; Sophie de la Borde (Hanna Schygulla), lady in waiting; as well as a sprinkle of lesser members of the nobility. The coach becomes a sort of *Grand Hotel* on wheels, abundant with brief flirtations, memoir, and irony.

Rich in period detail and almost documentary in approach, Scola's film is most effective in depicting a visual sense of chaos. It contains moments of very real charm: Casanova and a fellow passenger sharing a Mozart duet while walking in the woods; the passengers recalling the almost magical impression he has had upon them. History is broken down into intimate details of humanity.

Very much a film that depends upon its actors, *La Nuit de Varennes* is fortunate in its choices; particularly in Mastroianni, who creates a wonderfully complex portrait of a vain man aging gallantly. Full of generous and wise gentleness, he most precisely evokes the film's theme of faded elegance.

The National Board named *La Nuit de Varennes* one of 1983's five best foreign-language films.

(*The videocassette is subtitled.*)

244

# La Ronde

★ ★ ★ ★ ★ ★ ★ ★ ★ ★ ★ ★ ★ ★ ★ ★ ★ ★ ★ ★ ★ ★ ★ ★ ★ ★ ★ ★ ★ ★ ★ ★ ★ ★ ★ ★ ★ ★ ★ ★ ★ ★ ★ ★ ★ ★ ★ ★ ★ ★ ★ ★ ★ ★ ★

*Nationality*: French           *Year*: 1950 (U.S. release: 1954)

*Cast*: Simone Signoret, Gérard Philipe, Danielle Darrieux, Simone Simon, Daniel Gelin, Isa Miranda

*Director*: Max Ophuls         *Running Time*: 97 minutes

*B/W or Color*: B/W          *Availability*: NELSON ENTERTAINMENT

This *Grand Hotel* of French films never dates; it is as joyous today as it was when it created U.S. censorship problems in 1951. Director Max Ophuls picked a distinguished play—*Reigen,* by Arthur Schnitzler—but it is the cast that is a marvel. Most of the great French stars were gathered together for this film (with the addition of the Austrian Anton Walbrook and Italy's Isa Miranda). Ophuls masterfully weaves them into the plotline, and rarely were they showcased so brilliantly, set off by the handsome *fin de siècle* decor.

Schnitzler wrote his play to illustrate how venereal disease is spread, as A goes to bed with B, and B goes to bed with C—until they come full circle. But Ophuls took this mechanical theme to show a disease of a spiritual nature, employing a symbolic merry-go-round and a master of ceremonies (Walbrook) to show a meaningless whirlwind of restless emotion. As background, a beautiful Oscar Straus waltz captures the sadness and restlessness of these love-starved characters. While the emcee cynically and wittily comments on them—even participating as a minor character—they are locked in an emotional trap, unable to break the circle.

*La Ronde* is a classic that doesn't depend on a knowledge of the original to appreciate its greatness. Jean d'Eaubonne's production design, deliberately artificial in some sections, is magnificent and superbly enhanced by the cinematography of Christian Matras. Ophuls, who understood the power of sensuality in a compassionate, artistic way, was the perfect director for this story. Though *La Ronde* explores the insincerity behind sex, the film never panders and never romanticizes.

*La Ronde* won Venice Film Festival awards for its screenplay and decor and was an Oscar nominee for Best Screenplay and Art Direction/Set Decoration. The British Film Academy gave it 1951's Best Film award.

(*The videocassette is subtitled.*)

# La Strada

## (The Road)

★★★★★★★★★★★★★★★★★★★★★★★★★★★★★★★★★★★★★★★★★★★★★★★★★★★★

Nationality: Italian        Year: 1954
Cast: Anthony Quinn, Giulietta Masina, Richard Basehart, Aldo Silvani
Director: Federico Fellini        Running Time: 107 minutes
B/W or Color: B/W        Availability: EMBASSY HOME
                                         ENTERTAINMENT

*L*a Strada was the first non-English language picture to win the Academy Award as Best Foreign Film, which prior to that had been only an honorary award. Co-authored by its director, Federico Fellini, the screenplay also received an Oscar nomination.

La Strada exists on many levels but basically deals with the subject of loneliness. After playing in 62 pictures, Anthony Quinn became a star for his portrayal of the brutal, itinerant circus performer who travels the Italian countryside.

In need of an assistant, Zampano (Quinn) buys a half-witted waif, Gelsomina (Giulietta Masina, Mrs. Fellini offscreen), from her poverty-stricken mother. She becomes his servant and concubine and does her best to learn the clown routines he's concocted. With their pathetic act, the pair go on the road.

Spending the winter with a small circus, Zampano ends up in jail after a harsh confrontation with Matto the Fool (Richard Basehart), an acrobatic clown who has been kind to Gelsomina. Their second encounter is more violent and ends in Matto's death. When Gelsomina becomes the voice of Zampano's conscience, he abandons her but cannot erase her memory. Years later, he learns that she has died and drinks himself into a stupor—ending as a tragic figure.

Although highly successful, Fellini had trouble financing this profoundly moving story. A number of producers agreed to underwrite La Strada on the condition Burt Lancaster and Silvana Mangano were cast. Masina had asked Quinn to read her husband's screenplay while filming Angels of Darkness (Donne Proibite) with him in 1953. He was immediately impressed with the story and signed with Fellini, who now had no trouble finding backing. The actor agreed to accept 25 percent of the profits rather than a salary, but (on his agent's advice) later sold his interest for $12,000. Quinn and Basehart were justly applauded for their fine portrayals, but it's Giulietta Masina's unforgettable performance that shines.

The picture was named one of the five best foreign films of the year by The National Board.

(Embassy offers the film both dubbed and subtitled.)

246

# La Traviata

★ ★ ★ ★ ★ ★ ★ ★ ★ ★ ★ ★ ★ ★ ★ ★ ★ ★ ★ ★ ★ ★ ★ ★ ★ ★ ★ ★ ★ ★ ★ ★ ★ ★ ★ ★ ★ ★ ★ ★ ★ ★ ★ ★ ★ ★ ★ ★ ★ ★ ★ ★ ★ ★

*Nationality*: Italian               *Year*: 1982 (U.S. release: 1983)
*Cast*: Teresa Stratas, Plácido Domingo, Cornell MacNeil, Alan Monk
*Director*: Franco Zeffirelli        *Running Time*: 105 minutes
*B/W or Color*: Color                *Availability*: MCA HOME VIDEO

What more could be done with *La Traviata*? Never ask that question of Franco Zeffirelli, whose mark is instantly recognizable here. Dead silence accompanies the colorful opening credits. Then, suddenly, Verdi's music explodes all around. A sumptuous villa in Paris, peopled by shadows. The camera scans the gray, mysterious, misty blue interior with its shrouded furniture and an oval portrait of an exquisite young woman, now dead. But as the camera zooms into the bedchamber, she rises from her deathbed like a wild-eyed banshee and rushes toward the music. She stops, looking upon her reflection—the beautiful, laughing, sensuous sinner, the Violetta that was, in a gossamer white ball gown. Her setting is brilliantly lit chandeliers, shimmering candles, and a magical blend of rusty, rosy pinks. Verdi's music swells to the rafters, and the familiar story of *La Traviata*—about the star-crossed love of a consumptive Parisian courtesan and a naive country youth—begins.

Teresa Stratas as Violetta epitomizes and personalizes every passion, every pain, every pleasure that is Violetta. Stratas transcends the written words and music with an intensity rarely seen on the motion-picture screen. And who could resist Plácido Domingo's Alfredo—sensitive, handsome, and not ashamed of his love for Violetta. Even without credits, one would know that this is a Zeffirelli film. He brings a special passion and love to his movies. Without words like lush, opulent, lavish, and sumptuous, one would be unable to describe this film. It is extraordinary in every aspect—writing, direction, cinematography, art direction, costumes, acting, and singing.

*La Traviata* won Oscar nominations for its sets and costumes, and The National Board voted it one of 1983's best foreign films.

(*The videocassette is subtitled.*)

# The Lacemaker
## (La Dentellière)

\* \* \* \* \* \* \* \* \* \* \* \* \* \* \* \* \* \* \* \* \* \* \* \* \* \* \* \* \* \* \* \* \* \* \* \* \* \* \* \* \* \* \* \* \* \* \* \* \* \*

**Nationality**: French-Swiss-West German        **Year**: 1977

**Cast**: Isabelle Huppert, Yves Beneyton, Florence Giorgetti, Anne-Marie Düringer

**Director**: Claude Goretta        **Running Time**: 108 minutes

**B/W or Color**: Color        **Availability**: TV only

Swiss filmmaker Claude Goretta created one of the most delicate, subtle films about the fragility of human relationships in *The Lacemaker*. Very much in the humanistic tradition of Jean Renoir, it weaves a seemingly simple story about a romance between opposites: François (Yves Beneyton), a talkative, opinionated student, and a silent, uncommunicative beautician's assistant named "Pomme" (Isabelle Huppert). They meet through friends in a French resort, then decide to continue their affair in Paris. But the fact that each continually misses the other's emotional beats defeats the romance. He tries to bring her into his intellectual world, and she retreats more into herself. He thinks she doesn't contribute to the relationship and leaves her. She has a nervous breakdown and is sent to an asylum. When he visits her, the look of silent, convoluted hatred, frustration, and lack of understanding on her face is shocking and unforgettable.

Huppert is remarkable as the lacemaking girl who lets other people live her life for her then reproaches them silently when they cannot understand her. Beneyton, as the talkative student, is pompous in a likable fashion. He makes his audience see the nervous lack of confidence underlying his seemingly opinionated exterior. Also outstanding is Florence Giorgetti as Marylene, her outgoing friend who unwittingly sets the tragedy in motion by bringing "Pomme" to the resort.

Natural locations add meaning to the story, particularly in the scene of the lovers against the Normandy cliffs. The Pierre Jansen music is lush and sensual in the best manner, never intrusive but making the psychological points of the screenplay and direction more apparent. Pascal Lainé wrote the adaptation of his novel, and he deserves credit for translating his literal, written ideas into visual terms. *The Lacemaker* is one of the most psychologically penetrating films in many years. At Cannes, it won 1977's Ecumenical Prize.

# Lady Chatterley's Lover

★ ★ ★ ★ ★ ★ ★ ★ ★ ★ ★ ★ ★ ★ ★ ★ ★ ★ ★ ★ ★ ★ ★ ★ ★ ★ ★ ★ ★ ★ ★ ★ ★ ★ ★ ★ ★ ★ ★ ★ ★ ★ ★ ★ ★ ★ ★ ★ ★ ★ ★ ★ ★

*Nationality*: French-British        *Year*: 1981
*Cast*: Sylvia Kristel, Shane Briant, Nicholas Clay, Ann Mitchell
*Director*: Just Jaeckin        *Running Time*: 104 minutes
*B/W or Color*: Color        *Availability*: MGM/UA HOME
        VIDEO

D. H. Lawrence's scandalous 1928 novel has, to date, reached the screen twice: initially, in a forgettable 1955 French film, shot in black and white and released in the United States in an era when foreign films carried the promise of taboo sights. That movie's title alone was sufficient to draw sophisticated crowds, as well as prurient thrill-seekers. It wasn't until 1959 that American bookstores were able to sell unexpurgated editions of the notorious book, with all of its then-sensational four-letter words and X-rated plot situations. An X-rated motion picture would have, therefore, seemed a "given" for the much-banned story of a titled young English wife who, faced with the permanent invalidism of her war-injured husband, follows his suggestion that she might care to find sexual fulfillment with another man, which she subsequently does—to the heights of passion—with their gamekeeper. But this 1981 French-British co-production (filmed in English) elects to sidestep the pornographic film that might have been for an art-house production, exquisitely photographed in the BBC "Masterpiece Theatre" tradition.

Just Jaeckin's *Lady Chatterley's Lover* is a highly underrated movie, and a second viewing renews the satisfaction of a handsome visual treat that carries the requisite undercurrent of eroticism while artfully avoiding any tendency toward vulgar exploitation. The temptations must have been present, yet the finished product displays only the most painstaking care, from Anton Furst's production design to the wonderful period costuming of Shirley Russell. Sylvia Kristel makes a beautiful Lady Chatterley, and Nicholas Clay is the handsomely rugged object of her passion, while as the unfortunate husband, Shane Briant skillfully reveals an appropriate array of conflicting class-conscious emotions. But the real star of the film is undoubtedly cinematographer Robert Fraisse, who makes the most of the handsome country estate where the picture was so lovingly shot.

# The Lady Vanishes

★★★★★★★★★★★★★★★★★★★★★★★★★★★★★★★★★★★★★★★★★★★★★★★★★★★★★★

*Nationality*: Great Britain          *Year*: 1938

*Cast*: Michael Redgrave, Margaret Lockwood, Dame May Whitty, Paul Lukas, Basil Radford, Naunton Wayne

*Director*: Alfred Hitchcock          *Running Time*: 97 minutes

*B/W or Color*: B/W          *Availability*: Public Domain

Nothing can be wrong with a film starring (the oh, so young!) Michael Redgrave and Margaret Lockwood; teaming Basil Radford and Naunton Wayne for the first time as those archetypical Englishmen, Charters and Caldicott; with a screenplay by Sidney Gilliat; and with direction by Alfred Hitchcock. And nothing is.

This classic from the hand of the master is a delightful comedy-suspense tale of spies on a seedy Balkan train that is decidedly not the Orient Express. Dame May Whitty is Miss Froy, the middle-aged Englishwoman who suddenly vanishes from a train that hasn't stopped, and Margaret Lockwood is the young heroine who is the only person who cares about what became of her. For their own selfish, personal reasons, various other passengers deny any knowledge of Miss Froy's existence: Michael Redgrave has already had a run-in with Lockwood, whom he sees merely as a spoilt rich nuisance, and wants nothing to do with her pleas for help. Charters and Caldicott want only to get back to England before the cricket test match is over. Having already been held up by an avalanche, they are determined not to become involved in anything that will further delay their return. And Paul Lukas, as a somewhat furtive doctor, obviously has something to hide.

In this, his first film, very unsure of himself in transition from stage to studio, Redgrave seems to think that Hitchcock's most infamous statement might have been directed at him. "I do not know," he writes in his autobiography, "whether Hitchcock's famous 'actors are cattle' remark was coined for my benefit, but I well remember him saying it in my presence." But in spite of this and of Hitchcock's reputation as a tyrant, everyone connected with this picture appears to have had fun in its making.

(*Of available tapes, the superior one is that issued by The Criterion Collection. It's really smashing!*)

# The Ladykillers

\* \* \* \* \* \* \* \* \* \* \* \* \* \* \* \* \* \* \* \* \* \* \* \* \* \* \* \* \* \* \* \* \* \* \* \* \* \* \* \* \* \* \* \* \* \* \* \* \* \* \* \* \* \* \* \* \* \*

*Nationality*: British          *Year*: 1956

*Cast*: Alec Guinness, Cecil Parker, Herbert Lom, Peter Sellers, Danny Green, Katie Johnson

*Director*: Alexander Mackendrick   *Running Time*: 95 minutes

*B/W or Color*: Color          *Availability*: THORN/EMI-HBO VIDEO

Mrs. Louisa Wilberforce (Katie Johnson) is a sweet little old lady who lives in a dilapidated little old house in London with the three parrots that her late sea-captain husband bequeathed to her (putting them safely aboard the last lifeboat, before he went down with his ship). She often visits the local police station and invariably forgets her umbrella, taking time to explain that she must not really care for it because she always leaves it behind.

Into her house and life move Professor Marcus (Alec Guinness) and his group of "musicians:" Major Courteney (Cecil Parker), Louis Harvey (Herbert Lom), Harry Robinson (Peter Sellers), and One-Round Lawson (Danny Green). While they practice, actually using a recording to fool Mrs. Wilberforce, the quintet are really planning the robbery of a security van.

The heist takes place on schedule, and the landlady becomes an unwitting accomplice by collecting a trunk (filled with money) from the depot. They're aghast when she returns to the police station—with the trunk— to get her umbrella. Taking time out to chastise a man for mistreating his horse, she eventually has the police carry the trunk home for her.

Mrs. Wilberforce learns the truth and insists that the money be returned. The professor decides that she must be killed. But in attempting to do so, the five men meet *their* deaths.

Not paying any attention to her, the police tell Mrs. Wilberforce to keep whatever money she's talking about. She agrees to take their advice and instructs the officer who returns her forgotten umbrella to keep it. After all, she now can afford "a dozen new ones."

At 77, larcenous Katie Johnson stole *The Ladykillers* away from her fellow actors and won a British Film Academy Award, as did William Rose's amusing screenplay.

Director Alexander Mackendrick revealed years later that the eccentric facial makeup used by Alec Guinness in the film was an inside joke patterned after critic Kenneth Tynan, who, in 1953, had written that the actor "has no face."

# Last Holiday

★★★★★★★★★★★★★★★★★★★★★★★★★★★★★★★★★★★★★★★★★★★★★★★★★★★★★★

Nationality: British            Year: 1950

Cast: Alec Guinness, Beatrice Campbell, Kay Walsh, Bernard Lee, Wilfrid Hyde-White

Director: Henry Cass            Running Time: 88 minutes

B/W or Color: B/W               Availability: TV only

Author J. B. Priestley often preoccupied himself with the elements of time and fate in people's lives. As the central character of his *Last Holiday* tells newfound friends at the story's climax, "We haven't just *passed* the time, we've *filled* it—with something good. After all, we don't know how much time we've got left."

When George Bird, the reticent young bachelor of *Last Holiday*, learns that he's dying, he quits his salesman job, withdraws his savings, and books into an expensive little seaside hotel, where he plans to go out in style. Some weeks later, when he leaves the resort (having discovered he's *not* dying, after all), he is a changed person. His stay there has brought him friends, monetary opportunities, and local fame, and has made him aware of the needs of others. However, when the other guests learn that Bird isn't dying—that he's just another "ordinary person"—they revert to their petty selves and speak disparagingly of him. Here Priestley adds an ironic twist: Bird's departing car crashes and, dying in a hospital, he dictates a last, loving message to his "friends."

It's an oddly affecting story that Priestley relates here, and Henry Cass, its uncelebrated director, never had better material to work with. Alec Guinness, for a change performing without makeup, offers a subtle, understated delineation of Bird, admirably devoid of self-pity. He is well supported by, among others, Kay Walsh's tough-shelled but understanding hotel housekeeper Mrs. Poole, and Ernest Thesiger's eccentric Sir Trevor Lampington, who proves Bird isn't dying of Lampington's Disease, since *he*, after all, *invented* the disease—and *he's* still alive!

The fact that Priestley refused to accept a happy ending may have contributed to the film's disappointing British box office. But like many other English movies of its era, *Last Holiday* met with far greater approval in the United States, where *any* Alec Guinness film was then an "event."

# The Last Metro

**********************************************************

Nationality: French          Year: 1980

Cast: Catherine Deneuve, Gérard Depardieu, Heinz Bennent, Jean Poiret, Andre Ferreol

Director: François Truffaut       Running Time: 133 minutes

B/W or Color: Color           Availability: KEY VIDEO

On the surface, *The Last Metro* is about a French theater group in Paris struggling to survive during the Nazi occupation between 1942–44. Catherine Deneuve, the most beautiful theatrical entrepreneur east of Hollywood, has become manager of the group because the director, her Jewish husband, brilliantly played by Heinz Bennent, has vanished. The play in rehearsal is suitably titled *The Disappearance*.

The real drama concerns her husband who is hidden precariously in the cellar of the theater to escape deportation to a concentration camp. She visits him nightly and uses his notes to help her with the next day's rehearsals. A Nazi theater critic, evilly characterized by Jean Louis Richard, embodies the German encouragement of French anti-Semitism during the war. He skulks around the theater, sniffing out "Jewishness" in the play like a human bloodhound. The drama *behind* the scenery is what haunts and terrifies us.

The film is beautifully shot by Nestor Almendros, who manages to capture the muted, unnatural quality of the occupied city. His dark photography does far more than the period clothing and automobiles to evoke their sad era.

Truffaut has shown great maturity in this film, picturing people's reactions to profound distress. Grim as the situation may be, there are compensating moments of humor, understanding, and courage. The theater is only a microcosm for the drama taking place all over Paris and in all of Europe at the time. *The Last Metro,* with its overtone of finality, is actually the last train available to theatergoers before the wartime curfew takes effect. It is also a compelling journey into France under the German occupation.

# Last Tango in Paris
## (L'Ultimo Tango a Parigi)

**★★★★★★★★★★★★★★★★★★★★★★★★★★★★★★★★★★★★★★★★★★★★★★★★★★★★★★**

Nationality: Italian-French     Year: 1972

Cast: Marlon Brando, Maria Schneider, Jean-Pierre Léaud, Massimo Girotti, Catherine Allegret

Director: Bernardo Bertolucci     Running Time: 129 minutes (133 minutes in Europe)

B/W or Color: Color     Availability: CBS/FOX HOME VIDEO

A sensation in its day, this once-contested, X-rated film remains a milestone. While sex and nudity are freely exploited in the contemporary cinema, the explicit scenes in this motion picture were nothing short of a breakthrough. Director Bernardo Bertolucci intended *Last Tango in Paris* as a serious study of loneliness in a sexual society where relationships can be all too casual. The partly improvisational dialogue is a result of a close collaborative effort among Bertolucci and his stars Maria Schneider and, especially, Marlon Brando, who patterned his characterization on his own life and relationships.

As an American expatriate living in Paris, Brando portrays a failure whose wife has just committed suicide. At a vacant apartment, he encounters hedonistic young Maria Schneider. She's there to find a flat for herself and her fiancé (Jean-Pierre Léaud), a budding film director. When Brando forces her into a passionate affair, she agrees to an anonymous relationship totally founded upon sex. His later willingness to talk about his unhappy past results in Schneider's seeing him in a different light— no longer the intriguing sexual aggressor, but, rather, an aging and pathetic creature. His outrageous, drunken behavior at a tango contest has tragic results.

*Last Tango* was originally planned as a vehicle for Jean-Louis Trintignant and Dominique Sanda. But circumstances interfered, and they were replaced by Brando and newcomer Schneider, the illegitimate daughter of French actor Daniel Gelin.

Oscar nominations went to director Bertolucci and Brando, who won the 1973 Best Actor awards of both the New York Film Critics and the National Society of Film Critics.

*(With dialogue partly in French, the videocassette is subtitled.)*

# Last Year at Marienbad
## (L'Année Dernière à Marienbad)

**************************************************************

Nationality: French-Italian       Year: 1961 (U.S. release: 1962)
Cast: Delphine Seyrig, Giorgio Albertazzi, Sacha Pitoeff, Françoise Bertin, Luce Garcia-Ville
Director: Alain Resnais       Running Time: 93 minutes
B/W or Color: B/W       Availability: Public Domain

It is not often that a film as experimental as this succeeds in winning over a large audience. Resnais uses his characters as objects within an architectural frame, manipulating them more as puppets than humans, but it somehow seems exactly right within the context of the film. The movie carries its own logic, never subject to the ordinary sequences and relationships of time and space but operating within an infinite continuum. There are no terminal points to fix on as a succession of evocative images are flashed across the screen. As a thesis, it recalls the work of Maya Deren, but happily it escapes being didactic. Although the movie is black and white, the texture and tonality are rich and highly charged.

The story, as such, tells of a romantic encounter between a man and a married woman who meet at a European spa and embark upon an affair which he succeeds (or does he?) in convincing her had begun the previous year. All this occurs in an elegant palace, actually filmed not at Marienbad but in glorious Nymphenburg, just outside Munich, one of the world's baroque treasures. The lover-narrator conveys his dreams or fantasies to us through visualizations of experiences we can never be certain actually happened. The settings are sumptuous; the actors, who move dreamlike from frame to frame, are exquisitely dressed and belong to a world where no one is plagued by so much as a hangnail. Their emotions are frozen, ghosts perhaps, of the same emotions that existed and died in these same surroundings years ago. The music is elegantly conjoined to the images, waxing sadly lyrical for Delphine Seyrig, or sharply contrapuntal for the more startling shifts in action. It is futile to search for a logic outside the film, but it can be a rewarding experience to allow oneself to be moved at the filmmaker's direction, almost as the actors are.

# The Lavender Hill Mob

★★★★★★★★★★★★★★★★★★★★★★★★★★★★★★★★★★★★★★★★★★★★★★★★★★★★★

Nationality: British                    Year: 1951
Cast: Alec Guinness, Stanley Holloway, Sidney James, Alfie Bass
Director: Charles Crichton          Running Time: 78 minutes
B/W or Color: B/W                    Availability: THORN/EMI-HBO
                                                VIDEO

Henry Holland (Alec Guinness) is an innocuous London bank clerk who for 20 years has been in charge of transporting gold from the mint to the Bank of England. He has devised a fool-proof way of stealing a shipment but has yet to figure out how to get the gold out of the country. Enter Pendlebury (Stanley Holloway), who manufactures and transports gilded leaden paperweights shaped like miniature Eiffel towers. With the addition of Lackery (Sidney James) and Shorty (Alfie Bass), an inept duo who will actually stage the robbery, Holland becomes the mastermind of *The Lavender Hill Mob*.

All goes according to plan until six of the solid-gold miniatures are accidentally sold to British schoolgirls on holiday. Holland and Pendlebury are able to retrieve five, but the sixth is to be a present for the student's favorite policeman. At a police exhibition, the pair snatch the paperweight and lead the officers on a merry car chase through London.

Holland escapes to Rio de Janeiro, where he boastfully explains the caper to an interested listener. As the two men rise, their attachment is clear. Manacled, they walk to the door.

The National Board selected T.E.B. Clarke's screenplay as the best of 1951, and the film won the British Film Academy Award. Clarke won a 1952 Oscar for Best Story and Screenplay, and Guinness received an Oscar nomination as Best Actor.

Guinness (whose name is an anagram for Genuine Class) became an international star playing eight roles in *Kind Hearts and Coronets* (1949). Audrey Hepburn (in her fourth film) appears in one scene as Guinness's south-of-the-border girlfriend, Chiquita. Her one line: "Oh, but how sweet of you! Thank you!" delivered in flawless English.

*The Lavender Hill Mob* stands guilty of tickling funny bones and inciting laughter.

# L'Avventura

## (The Adventure)

**★★★★★★★★★★★★★★★★★★★★★★★★★★★★★★★★★★★★★★★★★★★★★★★★★★★★★★**

*Nationality*: Italian-French      *Year*: 1960 (U.S. release: 1961)
*Cast*: Gabriele Ferzetti, Monica Vitti, Lea Massari, Dominique Blanchar
*Director*: Michelangelo Antonioni   *Running Time*: 145 minutes
*B/W or Color*: B/W          *Availability*: Public Domain

Antonioni's enigmatic drama of shifting romantic relationships among well-heeled Italians centers on a Mediterranean yachting party cruising off the Sicilian coast. Central to the story are a middle-aged architect named Sandro (Gabriele Ferzetti), his neurotic mistress Anna (Lea Massari), who has grown increasingly dissatisfied with their occasional, mostly sexual get-togethers, and her friend Claudia (Monica Vitti), the only one present who's not accustomed to wealth. After swimming and sun-bathing, they explore a bleak, volcanic island, where a sudden storm briefly confines them. In its aftermath, the group discover that Anna seems to be missing, and they search the island in vain. Sandro and Claudia refuse to believe their worst fears, continuing their search on the mainland, where reports indicate that Anna may have been there ahead of them. As their quest continues, the pair gradually become less intent on locating the missing Anna as they are increasingly drawn to one another. Passion overcomes feelings of guilt, and they become lovers at a hotel in Taormina.

*L'Avventura* immediately attracted controversy when it was unveiled at the 1960 Cannes Film Festival, where it won a Special Jury prize. The producer devised a cunning advertising campaign to make the movie popular: in essence, it praised *L'Avventura*'s champions for being among the elite, whereas those who found it otherwise were dismissed as ignorant fools—with the result that the film immediately appealed to the European intelligentsia, who flocked to sit in rapt silence. In the United States, *L'Avventura* made Antonioni's name a household one in film-buff circles. And if one were naive enough to ask whatever became of the missing Anna, the director's standard reply was—"It isn't important."

# Lawrence of Arabia

**★ ★ ★ ★ ★ ★ ★ ★ ★ ★ ★ ★ ★ ★ ★ ★ ★ ★ ★ ★ ★ ★ ★ ★ ★ ★ ★ ★ ★ ★ ★ ★ ★ ★ ★ ★ ★ ★ ★ ★ ★ ★ ★ ★ ★ ★ ★ ★ ★ ★ ★ ★ ★ ★ ★**

*Nationality*: British        *Year*: 1962

*Cast*: Peter O'Toole, Alec Guinness, Anthony Quinn, Jack Hawkins, José Ferrer, Claude Rains, Omar Sharif

*Director*: David Lean      *Running Time*: 220 minutes

*B/W or Color*: Color      *Availability*: RCA/COLUMBIA PICTURES HOME VIDEO

A legend in his own time, T. E. Lawrence was a British soldier, adventurer, poet, philosopher, and artist. Exactly what he was and what inspired him has long been an enigma, and this classical epic attempted to find out. If the Robert Bolt screenplay did not fully answer the questions, even with material taken from Lawrence's autobiography, *The Seven Pillars of Wisdom*, then the sweeping beauty and scope of this magnificent film more than compensate. David Lean directed on location in Arabia. While the original grandeur is necessarily lost on a cassette (at least until wide-screen receivers are readily available), one can still appreciate just what has been accomplished here. The film earned seven Oscars: for Best Picture, Director, Freddie Young's Cinematography, the Art Direction, Sound, Anne V. Coates's monumental Editing, and Maurice Jarre's extraordinary Music Score. These qualities can't be diminished by the dimensions of the TV screen.

In 1935, a motorcycle accident in England takes the life of soldier T. E. Lawrence (Peter O'Toole). Flashbacks recall his eventful life as Lawrence of Arabia, a troubled man of vision. Sent to unite dissident Arab tribes, he gains world renown by a daring defeat of the Turks. The Arabs come to look upon him almost as a god, and only a humiliating torture by a Turkish Bey (José Ferrer) prevents him from believing that he might be just that. A thirst for killing and a pleasure in pain also prove to be his undoing, as attempts to finally unite the tribes are defeated. He leaves Arabia as a failure to himself.

The acting is uniformly superb, including O'Toole, Alec Guinness's wily desert prince, Anthony Quinn, Jack Hawkins's General Allenby, Ferrer, Anthony Quayle, Claude Rains (in one of his last films), Arthur Kennedy, and Sharif. The critics were lavish in their praise, one calling this "the first spectacular for adults." The film reflects the care and total dedication to his craft that Lean has always shown—in the quarter century following, he devoted his time to just three more films (*Dr. Zhivago*, *Ryan's Daughter*, and *A Passage to India*).

(*The film has been edited over the years, so check the length.*)

# The League of Gentlemen

\* \* \* \* \* \* \* \* \* \* \* \* \* \* \* \* \* \* \* \* \* \* \* \* \* \* \* \* \* \* \* \* \* \* \* \* \* \* \* \* \* \* \* \* \* \* \* \* \* \* \* \* \* \* \* \* \*

*Nationality*: British        *Year*: 1960

*Cast*: Jack Hawkins, Nigel Patrick, Roger Livesey, Richard Attenborough, Bryan Forbes, Kieron Moore

*Director*: Basil Dearden        *Running Time*: 114 minutes

*B/W or Color*: B/W        *Availability*: TV only

"Think of it as a full-scale military operation," ex-Lieutenant Colonel Hyde (Jack Hawkins) of the British army informs the seven officers who have joined him for lunch. He happens to be speaking about a planned bank robbery and is not above threatening blackmail to have his guests comply. The group, all of whom left the service under questionable circumstances, agree to assist Hyde in making an unscheduled withdrawal of a million pounds.

The not-quite-magnificent seven are driver Nigel Patrick, master of disguise Roger Livesey, radio expert Richard Attenborough, con man Bryan Forbes, combat trainer Kieron Moore, smokescreen wizard Terence Alexander, and explosive genius Norman Bird.

After raiding an army camp for weapons, they steal a large furniture truck to use in their escape from the bank. Unfortunately, a young boy notes the truck's license plate and informs police, who, in turn, foil the best-laid plans.

A very stylish heist film, *The League of Gentlemen* begins in high form. The opening credits are shown against a dark London street, reminiscent of film noir. Suddenly, a manhole cover stirs. Eyes peer out and then disappear, as a street-cleaning truck approaches. After it passes, the eyes reappear. The cover is lifted and Jack Hawkins—dressed in formal attire—emerges. Brushing himself off, he steps into a gleaming Rolls-Royce. Accompanying the action is a rousing military theme.

Bryan Forbes, author of the screenplay, joined director Basil Dearden, producer Michael Relph, Hawkins, and Attenborough to form the production company that made this film. It followed *The Angry Silence*, which Forbes and Attenborough produced together, and preceded *Whistle Down the Wind*, which marked Forbes's directorial debut.

# Le Million

Nationality: French               Year: 1931

Cast: René Lefèvre, Annabella, Louis Allibert, Vanda Gréville, Paul Olivier

Director: René Clair               Running Time: 89 minutes

B/W or Color: B/W               Availability: Public Domain

The films of Clair are with us still, and his reputation is to be envied. Few filmmakers ever approached his comedic skill and his choreographed movements. His movies, especially his early sound comedies, are matchless for entertainment and beauty.

Le Million is particularly infectious. The plotline is simple: a man leaves a winning lottery ticket in a discarded jacket and attempts to retrieve it. But in this case, the play is not the thing. The film is a warm and witty visual poem told in pictures and music. René Lefèvre is especially charming as the hapless hero, and he is matched by the piquant Annabella. There is a deliberate fairy-tale look about the sets, superbly executed by Lazare Meerson, and Georges Perinal's cinematography promotes a childlike acceptance of the events depicted. The ballet at the finale, with all the participants in the merry chase and cavorting in rhythm, is justly famous. But the encounter of Lefèvre and Annabella at the theater, with their romantic moment counterpointed by the tired stagehands, is charming.

Clair was at the height of his powers when he made this film. No one approached him in the execution of beautiful, balletic comedies. Le Million is certainly René Clair's finest film.

The National Board named Le Million one of 1931's five best foreign films, and, in a 1967 Canadian Centennial Commission poll of international film historians and critics, the movie tied with Kind Hearts and Coronets for seventh place among the best comedies of all time.

# The Leopard
## (Il Gattopardo)

**★ ★ ★ ★ ★ ★ ★ ★ ★ ★ ★ ★ ★ ★ ★ ★ ★ ★ ★ ★ ★ ★ ★ ★ ★ ★ ★ ★ ★ ★ ★ ★ ★ ★ ★ ★ ★ ★ ★ ★ ★ ★ ★ ★ ★ ★ ★ ★ ★ ★**

*Nationality*: Italian-French     *Year*: 1963

*Cast*: Burt Lancaster, Alain Delon, Claudia Cardinale, Rina Morelli, Paolo Stoppa, Serge Reggiani

*Director*: Luchino Visconti     *Running Time*: 195 minutes

*B/W or Color*: Color     *Availability*: TV only

One of cinema's most impressive and least romanticized evocations of time (the 1860s) and place (around Palermo) comes not as a wistful peasant recollection, but as a memoir of the deposed Italian upper crust. Stepping off from Giuseppe Tomasi di Lampedusa's well-known novel, Visconti uses CinemaScope to give this story of the twilight of the aristocracy a lush Sicilian grandeur. It also has an epic pace, and a literary, detailed sense of felt life. From the breathtaking historical tableaux of the family at Mass (as the civil war rages near the house), to the large-scale investigations of *Risorgimento* battles, Visconti is not beneath showing vestiges of social decorum among chaos. As Don Fabrizio, Prince of Salina, Burt Lancaster attacks his performance with both a warm pater familias and a cooler reserve of strength and vigor. His idealistic nephew Tancredi (Alain Delon), who has joined Garibaldi, and his rapturously sweet fiancée Angelica (Claudia Cardinale) are the don's glimpse at the future. The famous, final ballroom scene (which lasts over an hour) is Visconti's farewell to the titled world of the landed gentry; it's also his tour de force as a director.

There is top-notch work by cinematographer Giuseppe Rotunno, memorably underscored by Nino Rota's music. And the print, restored to its original length of more than three hours in 1985 (*The Leopard* was cut to 165 minutes for its 1963 U.S. release), has—believe it or not—been respected on TV: the top and bottom of the print are matted so that it can be enjoyed in its proper ratio. *The Leopard* was named one of the five best foreign films of the year by The National Board.

# Les Grandes Manoeuvres

* * * * * * * * * * * * * * * * * * * * * * * * * * * * * * * * * * * * * * * * * * * * * * * * * * *

Nationality: French       Year: 1955

Cast: Michèle Morgan, Gérard Philipe, Brigitte Bardot, Yves Robert, Simone Valere

Director: René Clair       Running Time: 106 minutes

B/W or Color: Color       Availability: TV only

There is always something wonderful about a René Clair film, and artfully aided this time by Jerome Geronimi and Jean Marsan, *Les Grandes Manoeuvres* easily finds its place among Clair's best.

In this seemingly light film, there is an undercurrent of sexual desire and a portent of impending doom. A warning is given, however: "Dragoons . . . ah, look at them from the window—never at close quarters," but this is not heard by the heroine. She is Marie-Louise, played quietly, carefully, and very coolly by an extraordinarily beautiful Michèle Morgan. A suave divorcee, she owns a hat shop in the small town where a French cavalry regiment awaits orders for maneuvers just before World War I. Among the dashing dragoons is Lieutenant Armand de la Verne, played by the handsome Gérard Philipe with a finesse that easily convinces us that any female he encounters will immediately succumb to his charms. He is convinced of this also. So much so that he bets his fellow officers that he can seduce the aloof Marie-Louise. He does—and she falls in love with him and he with her. But the story of the wager is told to Marie-Louise, and she confronts Armand, who admits his guilt but adds that he is hopelessly in love with her. She does not believe him.

A finely tuned film, the leads are fabulous, and the supporting cast is, too. Among them is the young, dark-haired Brigitte Bardot. She is effervescent and charming (hardly a clue to her future sex-kittenship) and a good foil for the very dignified Marie-Louise. The costumes by Rosine Delamare are perfect, and Robert LeFebvre's photography masterful. *Les Grandes Manoeuvres* is an elegant film—full of the legendary Clair wit and charm.

# Les Liaisons Dangereuses

\* \* \* \* \* \* \* \* \* \* \* \* \* \* \* \* \* \* \* \* \* \* \* \* \* \* \* \* \* \* \* \* \* \* \* \* \* \* \* \* \* \* \* \* \* \* \* \* \* \* \* \* \* \*

**Nationality**: French        **Year**: 1959 (U.S. release: 1961)
**Cast**: Gérard Philipe, Jeanne Moreau, Jeanne Valerie, Annette Vadim, Simone Renant, Jean-Louis Trintignant
**Director**: Roger Vadim        **Running Time**: 106 minutes
**B/W or Color**: B/W        **Availability**: TV only

When Roger Vadim announced that he planned to film a modern-day version of *Les Liaisons Dangereuses,* the controversial 1786 novel by Choderlos de Laclos, there were attempts to prevent production; and, after filming was completed, the French government decreed that it could not be exported because it was detrimental to the French.

*Time* magazine declared that *Les Liaisons Dangereuses* was "an offensive against taste . . . At the same time it is a wickedly funny comedy of promiscuities *a la francaise* . . . clearly the best movie Vadim has made."

The de Laclos novel, which depicted diabolical aspects of love and seduction with wit and high style, presented its protagonists as former lovers. In his update, Vadim (who also co-authored the screenplay) made them a married couple who aid and abet each other's extramarital affairs. Valmont de Merteuil (Gérard Philipe) is a compulsive seducer, an eternal Don Juan. His wife, Juliette (Jeanne Moreau), is a cruel, intelligent woman.

When her latest lover, Danceny (Jean-Louis Trintignant), prematurely discards Juliette to marry a young student named Cecile (Jeanne Valerie), the vindictive woman encourages Valmont to seduce the girl, which he does. He also meets Marianne (Annette Vadim, the director's second wife—following Brigitte Bardot and preceding Jane Fonda), a virtuous wife and mother. Marianne resists Valmont's advances, but he follows her to Paris and she succumbs to his charm. He finds himself emotionally involved for the first time in his life; however, Juliette forces him to give up Marianne, who goes insane.

Juliette is later responsible for Danceny killing Valmont and, in attempting to burn her husband's letters, she's horribly disfigured by fire. At the inquest of Valmont's death, a witness scornfully observes that Juliette "carries her soul on her face."

Valmont was the next-to-last role for Gérard Philipe (1922–59), who died of a heart attack six months after this film was completed.

Vadim's movie has no relation to the 1987 Broadway import of the London success, *Les Liaisons Dangereuses,* which is based on the novel.

# L'Etoile du Nord

\* \* \* \* \* \* \* \* \* \* \* \* \* \* \* \* \* \* \* \* \* \* \* \* \* \* \* \* \* \* \* \* \* \* \* \* \* \* \* \* \* \* \* \* \* \* \* \* \* \* \* \* \* \* \* \*

Nationality: French          Year: 1982
Cast: Simone Signoret, Philippe Noiret, Fanny Cottencon, Julie Jezequel, Jean Rougerie, Jean-Pierre Klein
Director: Pierre Granier-Deferre          Running Time: 101 minutes
B/W or Color: Color          Availability: TV only

Philippe Noiret and Simone Signoret are wonderful in this subtle, unusual mystery-romance. *L'Etoile du Nord*, based on a Georges Simenon mystery novel set in the early 1930s, tells the story of Edouard (Noiret), a middle-aged, somewhat dumpy, but good-natured and occasionally charming man, who returns to Europe after losing his job in Egypt, where he's lived and worked for many years. He meets an enterprising and very attractive young blonde, Sylvie (Fanny Cottencon), on the train. She has Edouard introduce her to a wealthy Egyptian businessman, Nemrod, and later doesn't attempt to hide from Edouard that she's sharing Nemrod's bed. Sylvie gets off the train at Brussels, where she visits her mother, Madame Baron (Simone Signoret), who runs a modest boarding house for students. Edouard and Nemrod continue on to France, and, during that trip, Nemrod is murdered. Edouard, who knows no one in France, travels back to Brussels to find Sylvie. She realizes that he's in some sort of trouble and puts him up at her mother's boarding house. Edouard's clothes are bloodstained, but he claims that he doesn't remember how they got that way. The unsuspecting Madame Baron and Edouard become good friends, but as news of the murder spreads, Madame Baron begins to have doubts about her new friend.

This is, on the surface, a deliberately plotted mystery, yet there is a great deal more going on. The film is more concerned with the nature of its protagonists, and how the actions of this "criminal" affect others, as well as the way in which we, as the audience, perceive his deeds. The film focuses on a man who, we suspect, might be guilty of a crime, but we hesitate to judge him harshly because of the happiness he brings to Madame Baron's life. The film provocatively reveals, through the touchingly reserved performance by Simone Signoret, that the truth is often something we'd rather not accept.

# The Lion in Winter

*Nationality*: British             *Year*: 1968
*Cast*: Peter O'Toole, Katharine Hepburn, Jane Merrow, John Castle, Timothy Dalton, Anthony Hopkins
*Director*: Anthony Harvey        *Running Time*: 134 minutes
*B/W or Color*: Color              *Availability*: EMBASSY HOME
                                   ENTERTAINMENT

Selected as one of The National Board's ten best for 1968, *The Lion in Winter* received seven Academy Award nominations: Best Picture, Actor (Peter O'Toole), Actress (Katharine Hepburn), Director (Anthony Harvey), Screenplay (James Goldman), Score, and Costumes. This was Hepburn's third Oscar; Goldman won his for the adaptation of his 1966 Broadway play, and John Barry captured his for his memorable, period-flavored score.

In her *New York* magazine review, Judith Crist found the film "as intellectually delicious as the stage play and surpassing it in depth of characterization, as well as in atmosphere and setting." She noted that "those of us who found Rosemary Harris and Robert Preston so satisfying in the Broadway production can but marvel at the handiwork of Miss Hepburn and Mr. O'Toole."

In 1183, Eleanor of Aquitaine (Hepburn) is summoned to France, where a Christmas court is to be held by her estranged husband, Henry II of England (O'Toole), who plans to choose a successor to his throne. The queen, who has been under house arrest in England by Henry's orders, arrives to champion her son, Richard the Lion-Hearted (Anthony Hopkins), but the King's choice is his youngest son, John (Nigel Terry), to whom he hopes to marry off his mistress, Princess Alais (Jane Merrow). A third son, Geoffrey (John Castle), nurtures ambitions of his own, and Alais's brother King Philip II of France (Timothy Dalton) arrives with still other schemes. The intrigue and in-fighting make the holiday season anything but festive and, at yuletide's end, nothing has been resolved, although king and queen part with mutual respect. "You're still a marvel of a man," Eleanor tells him. "And you're still my lady," Henry responds. Here O'Toole is repeating his portrayal of Henry, whom he had played in *Becket*—and for which he had also been nominated for an Oscar.

# The Living Daylights

\* \* \* \* \* \* \* \* \* \* \* \* \* \* \* \* \* \* \* \* \* \* \* \* \* \* \* \* \* \* \* \* \* \* \* \* \* \* \* \* \* \* \* \* \* \* \* \* \* \* \* \* \* \* \* \* \* \*

**Nationality**: British                    **Year**: 1987
**Cast**: Timothy Dalton, Maryam d'Abo, Jeroen Krabbé, John Rhys-Davies, Joe Don Baker, Art Malik
**Director**: John Glen                 **Running Time**: 130 minutes
**B/W or Color**: Color                 **Availability**: CBS/FOX VIDEO

For James Bond, double agent 007, 1987 is a twenty-fifth anniversary. His screen debut was in 1962's *Dr. No*, and he has subsequently starred fourteen times in the most successful screen series in film history, selling one and a half billion theater tickets.

Loosely based on a short story from Ian Fleming's collection titled *Octopussy*, *The Living Daylights* is a cause for celebration, not only by audiences but some old Bond pros and one vibrant newcomer. This is director John Glen's fourth consecutive Bond film. Richard Maibaum has scripted all but three. John Barry has composed the scores for ten (and makes his screen debut conducting an orchestra). Designer Maurice Binder contributes his fifteenth imaginative opening credits, and this fifteenth mind-boggling array of high-tech gadgetry includes a couch that swallows occupants, a ghetto blaster that blasts, and an Aston Martin Volante equipped with skis and lasers.

New to the game but devastating as James Bond #4 is Timothy Dalton. A veteran of the Royal Shakespeare Company, with Lord Byron, Heathcliff and Mr. Rochester portrayals among past accomplishments, Dalton brings a refreshing new dimension to Double-oh-Seven. Handsome, romantic, *mucho* macho, Dalton plays a warmer, yes, more human hero than predecessors Connery, Lazenby, and Moore.

The nonstop action swirls around Bond's attempt to ferret out a phony KGB defector involved in gun running and cocaine smuggling. In Gibraltar, Austria, Czechoslovakia, and Morocco, he is pitted against Russian villains (Jeroen Krabbé, John Rhys-Davies) and a ruthless arms dealer (Joe Don Baker), aided by an Afghan freedom fighter (Art Malik), and hugged and kissed by a beautiful Czech cellist (Maryam d'Abo)—but hugs and kisses only. The British press refer to this as "the safe sex" Bond.

Queried if he worries about comparisons to his predecessors, Dalton replied: "I have to make the part my own. I intend to approach this project with a sense of responsibility to Ian Fleming."

Rest in peace, Mr. Fleming.

# Lola

✦✦✦✦✦✦✦✦✦✦✦✦✦✦✦✦✦✦✦✦✦✦✦✦✦✦✦✦✦✦✦✦✦✦✦✦✦✦✦✦✦✦✦✦✦✦✦✦✦✦✦✦✦✦✦

*Nationality*: French　　　　　*Year*: 1961 (U.S. release: 1962)
*Cast*: Anouk Aimée, Marc Michel, Jacques Harden, Corinne Marchand
*Director*: Jacques Demy　　　*Running Time*: 91 minutes
*B/W or Color*: B/W　　　　　*Availability*: TV only

Jacques Demy is best known for his 1964 musical, *The Umbrellas of Cherbourg*, but time has proven *Lola*, his feature-film debut, to be his finest film—the most marvelous, peerless confection of the French New Wave. In Nantes, a seaside town (Demy's birthplace), an inter-related group of people—all unhappy, longing for a lost love or distant relatives—live by the painfully sweet promise of songs, comics, and movies. Lola (the young, alluring Anouk Aimée) is a B-girl whose heart is always elsewhere—out to sea with the sailor who hasn't yet made good his promise to return. Demy's masterstroke—his genius—is in accepting and sharing his characters' illusions. *Lola* irradiates an optimistic world view. Demy orchestrates undiluted happiness as everything turns out right for each of his hopeful characters, from the youngest and least experienced to the oldest and most scarred. In her review of the film, Pauline Kael likened *Lola* to "an adolescent's dream of romance, formed from old movies."

The filmmaker isn't pushing irony as in the endings of Buñuel's *Susana* or David Lynch's *Blue Velvet*. This is the genuine thing: bliss. It's like nothing else in the history of movies. Imagine a musical in which the viewer's heart does the only singing. Cinematographer Raoul Coutard rates co-star status with his iridescent, wide-screen camerawork. The score is by Michel Legrand with a song lyric by Demy's then-wife, director Agnès Varda (*Cleo From 5 to 7*). The matchless cast includes the exquisite Elina Labourdette as the lonely, well-bred widow Madame Desnoyers. The title pays homage to Max Ophuls's *Lola Montes*. There's also a shy, connecting reference to Godard's *Breathless*. There have been other *Lola*s (1982 German, 1986 Spanish), but Demy's version is the miraculous one. Incidentally, Demy continued the story of Lola in 1968's *Model Shop*, which also starred Anouk Aimée.

267

# Lola Montes
## (The Sins of Lola Montes)

★★★★★★★★★★★★★★★★★★★★★★★★★★★★★★★★★★★★★★★★★★★★★★★★★★★

*Nationality*: French-German      *Year*: 1955

*Cast*: Martine Carol, Anton Walbrook, Peter Ustinov, Ivan Desny, Oskar Werner

*Director*: Max Ophuls      *Running Time*: 110 minutes

*B/W or Color*: Color      *Availability*: EMBASSY HOME ENTERTAINMENT

How does a pantheon director make a successful spectacle using a characterless star? Build the film around her, and make her the object, rather than the force. Max Ophuls did this with Martine Carol in *Lola Montes*, his last film. Instead of creating a life of the legendary 19th-century temptress with a strong actress, Ophuls was more concerned with analyzing the society that made Lola Montes a byword for forbidden pleasures.

Ophuls was asked by his producers to use the new CinemaScope process, and in this he succeeds magnificently. While bypassing a conventional plotline, he explores the pictorial possibilities inherent in the story. The camera becomes the *raison d'être*, swirling through the gingerbread, baroque palace and the spectacle of the story-framing circus ring. Color is a dominant force in this beautiful, sensuous film: red and gold predominate during Lola's affair with Franz Liszt; midnight blue and gray for scenes of her youth; silver and gold for Bavaria. The circus costumes are garish, while those in Bavaria are warm and wintry. If Ophuls seems concerned with technology over narrative, then it's only to emphasize the subject's romanticism. Lola's appeal lay more in the dreams of a sensation-seeking public than in anything she actually accomplished. She was a media figure before there really *was* a media.

Peter Ustinov, as the ringmaster, is the most memorable character in the film, and Anton Walbrook is regal as the king of Bavaria. Few films document the romantic impulse of the 19th century so well. Ophuls intellectualized the whole theme of this film. He once stated that "It is the people who surround Lola Montes that excite me." So the film should be thought of as a comment on celebrity; indeed, the final scene of Lola selling the touch of her hands, like a religious idol, to a long line of men is one of the most brilliantly conceived scenes in film history.

*(The videocassette is in subtitled French.)*

# The Loneliness of the Long-Distance Runner

## (Rebel with a Cause)

★★★★★★★★★★★★★★★★★★★★★★★★★★★★★★★★★★★★★★★★★★★★★★★★★★★★★★

Nationality: British                     Year: 1962
Cast: Tom Courtenay, Michael Redgrave, Avis Bunnage, Peter Madden, James Bolam, Julia Foster
Director: Tony Richardson          Running Time: 104 minutes
B/W or Color: B/W                      Availability: TV only

As so frequently happened in the Sixties, Britain's Midlands provided the background for this modest contemporary story of an alienated Everyman (Tom Courtenay, in his celebrated film bow) and his resistance to the pressures of society—and success. Alan Sillitoe (*Saturday Night and Sunday Morning*) adapted his short story, and although there's little to induce audience sympathy in *Runner*'s Colin Smith, Courtenay's performance is so engaging that it's hard to picture anyone else in the part. Lean, slight, and wiry of build, Courtenay offers a disarming blend of brooding intensity and shuffling shyness, with his plain, high-cheekboned face, sunken eyes, and disdainful mouth. As the young Borstal reformatory outcast, whose only talent seems to be running, Courtenay exhibits an eccentric but refreshingly unmannered personality, bolstered with nervous energy and a grim, unsmiling naturalism that encases an extraordinary acting talent. In a subsidiary role, Michael Redgrave plays the Borstal governor with a tweedy, pipe-puffing reserve that seems just right for the hearty ineffectuality of his character. In a large cast, Avis Bunnage makes an indelible impression as Colin's termagant, working-class mother.

Producer-director Tony Richardson takes pains to show us what makes Colin Smith tick, and although we may not sympathize with much of his behavior, we can understand and, in a way, even share his ultimate gesture of defiance against authority. With economy of style and brilliant technique, Richardson simultaneously follows Colin's reform-school progress and explores the past events that dispatched him there. Flashbacks build and flesh out Colin's story, whose startling climax suddenly fuses the two parallel narratives with surprising force.

# The Long Good Friday

* * * * * * * * * * * * * * * * * * * * * * * * * * * * * * * * * * * * * * * * * * * * * * * * * * * *

*Nationality*: British       *Year*: 1980 (U.S. release: 1982)
*Cast*: Bob Hoskins, Helen Mirren, Eddie Constantine, Dave King
*Director*: John Mackenzie       *Running Time*: 114 minutes
*B/W or Color*: Color       *Availability*: THORN/EMI-HBO
      VIDEO

The setting is London and the time is the present, but when Bob Hoskins makes his dynamic entrance as a ganglord, you may be reminded of Cagney, Muni, or, most particularly, Edward G. Robinson in the Warners' crime sagas of a half-century ago. Short and square, blunt-featured, with a distinctive gravelly voice and a pronounced cockney accent, Hoskins offers an altogether bravura performance, the one that began his climb to international stardom.

In the opening sequences of the film you meet Harold Shand (Hoskins), the wealthy kingpin of the London underworld, secure in his power and just about to conclude the biggest deal of his life, involving a huge gambling complex in the London dock area. To do this, he must convince his American mafia partners (Eddie Constantine is one) that he can keep order and control. Immediately his confidence is shattered when several of his henchmen are murdered and the restaurant they are about to enter is blown up. It is suddenly war, but against an unknown enemy, since he has no clue as to the identity of his new adversaries. This begins a relentless underworld search, and the film's most graphic scene takes place when Shand has the major crime figures in London rounded up and brought to a warehouse where they are hung upside down on meat hooks while he interrogates them. His frustration mounts as it becomes clear that his opposition is not another crime family, but the Provisional Irish Republican Army. Once his enemy is revealed, Shand sets about to wreak his kind of murderous vengence. But in this case, his enemy proves formidable and unstoppable. The final scene is powerful, ironic, and inevitable.

The strength of *The Long Good Friday* is in the power of the playing. In addition to Hoskins, there is the brilliant Helen Mirren as Shand's shrewd, sexy mistress. The miracle here is that you find yourself drawn to and fascinated by these characters in spite of their insatiable violence and savagery.

# Look Back in Anger

\* \* \* \* \* \* \* \* \* \* \* \* \* \* \* \* \* \* \* \* \* \* \* \* \* \* \* \* \* \* \* \* \* \* \* \* \* \* \* \* \* \* \* \* \* \* \* \* \* \* \* \*

*Nationality*: British  *Year*: 1959

*Cast*: Richard Burton, Mary Ure, Claire Bloom, Edith Evans, Gary Raymond

*Director*: Tony Richardson  *Running Time*: 99 minutes

*B/W or Color*: B/W  *Availability*: EMBASSY HOME ENTERTAINMENT

One of The National Board's five best foreign films for 1959, *Look Back in Anger* had already ushered in a new era of British drama with its 1956 London stage premiere.

The John Osborne play gave birth to the angry young man, antihero character who would represent numerous playwrights and rebels against the Establishment for years to come.

Jimmy Porter (Richard Burton) frequently speaks out against the world, England, class distinction, politics, and religion. He shares a cramped attic flat in London with wife, Alison (Mary Ure), who defied her parents to marry beneath her station, and Cliff (Gary Raymond), a friend with whom he runs a candy shop.

Enter Helena (Claire Bloom), an actress-friend of Alison's, who objects to Jimmy's treatment of his wife. Without revealing her pregnancy, Alison returns to her parents and, ironically, Helena becomes Jimmy's lover. After the wife's miscarriage, the Porters reconcile.

Mary Ure (who, at the time, was married to John Osborne) created her role on stage and won a Tony nomination as Best Actress for the 1958 Broadway production. She was soon to leave Osborne for Robert Shaw and, in 1975, to die of an overdose of alcohol and drugs.

Dame Edith Evans appears as Ma Tanner, who owns the shop operated by Jimmy and Cliff. On stage, her character was only referred to and never seen.

The film was independently made by Woodfall Productions, formed by John Osborne and Tony Richardson. It was the first feature directed by Richardson, who had staged the play. His later films include *The Entertainer, A Taste of Honey, The Loneliness of the Long-Distance Runner,* and *Tom Jones.*

Nigel Kneale wrote the screenplay for *Look Back in Anger*, and Osborne provided additional dialogue. The cinematography by Oswald Morris received considerable praise.

# Lord of the Flies

★ ★ ★ ★ ★ ★ ★ ★ ★ ★ ★ ★ ★ ★ ★ ★ ★ ★ ★ ★ ★ ★ ★ ★ ★ ★ ★ ★ ★ ★ ★ ★ ★ ★ ★ ★ ★ ★ ★ ★ ★ ★ ★ ★ ★ ★ ★ ★ ★ ★ ★ ★ ★ ★

Nationality: British        Year: 1963

Cast: James Aubrey, Tom Chapin, Hugh Edwards, Roger Elwin, Tom Gaman

Director: Peter Brook        Running Time: 91 minutes

B/W or Color: B/W        Availability: KING OF VIDEO

Peter Brook's adaptation of William Golding's horrific 1954 novel about the dark side of human nature is unique in that the major roles are played by everyday schoolboys and that Brook used Golding's dialogue, but no formal script. Brook's Lord of the Flies is as powerfully suspenseful and thought-provoking as the perennially best-selling book.

Students evacuated by air during a fictional nuclear war crash onto an uninhabited island. With prodding from bespectacled, overweight Piggy, the boys choose level-headed Ralph as chief. Ralph tries to maintain order and keep a signal fire going, but irrational fear of a "beastie" and the lack of adult supervision erode the boundaries of this frail civilization. Jack, the aggressive and belligerent would-be chief, turns his followers into hunters. Jack's "tribe" slaughters a pig and offers its head to the beastie. Slowly, the boys revert into chanting primitives whose sole instinct is to survive, with only Ralph, Simon, and Piggy clinging to the safety of logic. When the contemplative Simon climbs down from the mountaintop, after discovering the beastie's true identity, he is brutally murdered. Piggy also meets a violent death at the hands of his schoolmates. Ralph flees for his life until he finally drops in exhaustion—at the feet of a naval commander.

Considering the intensity of Golding's writing, Brook's film brilliantly succeeds in capturing the essence of the novel. The ease with which the children embrace evil is the real horror. Though performed by amateurs, the lead characters are all too believable, under Brook's skilled direction. His one glaring error is the omission of dialogue during the key scene between Simon and the impaled pig's head. For some strange reason, Brook filmed the classic confrontation in silent close-ups.

The National Board listed Lord of the Flies among 1963's best films.

# Los Olvidados
## (The Young and the Damned)

★ ★ ★ ★ ★ ★ ★ ★ ★ ★ ★ ★ ★ ★ ★ ★ ★ ★ ★ ★ ★ ★ ★ ★ ★ ★ ★ ★ ★ ★ ★ ★ ★ ★ ★ ★ ★ ★ ★ ★ ★ ★ ★ ★ ★ ★ ★ ★

Nationality: Mexican        Year: 1950 (U.S. release: 1952)
Cast: Estela Inda, Alfonso Mejia, Roberto Cobo, Miguel Inclan
Director: Luis Buñuel       Running Time: 88 minutes
B/W or Color: B/W       Availability: Public Domain

Los Olvidados (actually, *The Forgotten Ones*) remains a monumental statement about the unredeemable social and human forces at work behind poverty, presented by an unwaveringly truthful Luis Buñuel, in both neorealistic and surrealistic terms.

It was initially received with trepidation by critics unready for the harshness of its stance: Bosley Crowther's review in *The New York Times* complained that "this wild coincidence of evil and violence is not explained, nor is any social solution even hinted, much less clarified. A foreword merely states that the correction of this problem of poverty and delinquency is left to the 'progressive forces' (whatever they are) of our times."

In the early Fifties, we were still in the grips of the Hollywood film community's moral code, which disallowed unredemptive endings. This study of cause and effect found no romantic or optimistic solutions and boldly, shockingly presented its findings. The cast of beggars, blind and legless, of delinquents, of lost souls was culled from the street itself. The performances, though occasionally a bit stiff, are effective in their honesty.

Buñuel's foundation in surrealism permeates this film's bleak vision. The erotic image of a young girl pouring milk on her legs, the foreboding, abstract presence of roosters at scenes of violence, the constant ambience of marauding dogs—all conspire to elevate the experience beyond a simpler, docudramatic context. Pauline Kael said it well: "Buñuel . . . creates scenes that shock one psychologically and remain shocking despite one's best efforts to pigeonhole them or explain them away."

*Los Olvidados* won Buñuel 1951's Best Director award at Cannes.

# Loss of Innocence
## (The Greengage Summer)

★★★★★★★★★★★★★★★★★★★★★★★★★★★★★★★★★★★★★★★★★★★★★★★★★★★★

*Nationality*: British        *Year*: 1961

*Cast*: Kenneth More, Danielle Darrieux, Susannah York, Claude Nollier, Jane Asher

*Director*: Lewis Gilbert       *Running Time*: 99 minutes

*B/W or Color*: Color       *Availability*: TV only

B ased on the novel *The Greengage Summer* (the film's title in England), by Rumer Godden (among her works is *Black Narcissus*), *Loss of Innocence* is the story of the season during which 16-year-old Joss Grey (Susannah York) comes of age.

While on holiday in France, Joss's mother falls ill and has to be hospitalized. The teenager oversees her two younger sisters and brother, but is resented by Madame Zizi (Danielle Darrieux), who runs the Marne River chateau hotel where they're staying. The older woman becomes jealous when her lover Eliot (Kenneth More) takes an interest in the children and especially in Joss.

The charming Englishman, in reality an international jewel thief, escorts Joss and her siblings on trips to the cathedral at Rheims, the Marne battlefields, and the champagne cellars of Pommery.

Eliot also comes to her aid when Joss is attacked by Paul (David Saire), a worker at the hotel. Paul's accidental death forces Eliot to flee, but his concern for Joss betrays him to the police. "In this summer," Eliot tells Joss as they part, "you became a woman." A wiser Joss can now better understand and even feel sympathy for Madame Zizi.

French star Danielle Darrieux, making a rare appearance in an English-language film, brings great style to her character, and the popular Kenneth More increased his box-office appeal with this charming portrayal. It is Susannah York, however, who steals the picture as the captivating and poignant Joss.

This was York's third film, following *Tunes of Glory* (as Alec Guiness's daughter) and the Norman Wisdom comedy *There Was a Crooked Man*. She also appeared in *Tom Jones, A Man for All Seasons,* and, in 1969, received an Oscar nomination (as Best Supporting Actress) for *They Shoot Horses, Don't They?*

# Love
## (Szerelem)

✦✦✦✦✦✦✦✦✦✦✦✦✦✦✦✦✦✦✦✦✦✦✦✦✦✦✦✦✦✦✦✦✦✦✦✦✦✦✦✦✦✦✦✦✦✦✦✦

*Nationality*: Hungarian          *Year*: 1971 (U.S. release: 1973)
*Cast*: Lili Darvas, Mari Toröcsík, Ivan Darvas
*Director*: Károly Makk          *Running Time*: 92 minutes
*B/W or Color*: B/W          *Availability*: TV only

The Hungarian filmmaker Károly Makk made his stateside reputation with *Love,* one of the rare Eastern Bloc movies to manage a skillful and emotionally satisfying blend of politics and drama. Adapting two novellas by Tibor Déry, Makk gets inside the emotional anxieties of an elderly woman (played by Darvas) and her young daughter-in-law (Mari Toröcsík)—both learning to cooperate and understand each other in the absence of the son and husband who was recently jailed as a political prisoner. Toröcsík keeps this news from the ailing Darvas by forging letters that describe the son's success as a filmmaker in the United States. This small-scale story takes place mostly in the cramped apartment the women share—the narrative fluctuates and expands in the gentle flashbacks of the mother's youth and the wife's courtship. Through this strategy Makk describes the circle of adoration and concern surrounding a character who is only briefly glimpsed. *Love* becomes a phantom portrait of family bonds, of the ineffable loyalty and compassion the two women share. Makk's orchestration of two opposing sensibilities is accomplished primarily through the exquisitely nuanced performances of Darvas and Toröcsík. They display insight into the dogged vanities of old age and the complex longing of an abandoned wife who needs to communicate and break out of her isolation. Toröcsík was hailed as the premier Hungarian actress of the Seventies. Both she and Darvas were runners-up for the 1973 Best Actress award from the National Society of Film Critics. Both *Time* magazine and *The New York Times* listed *Love* on their end-of-the-year best films lists.

Writing in the *New Republic,* Stanley Kauffman said, "This is a film of depth and delicacy, small-scale but true. Bedridden, always feeble, Lili Darvas nevertheless creates an entire woman, tender, domineering, cultivated, silly, perceptive, frightened of dying without her son at her side." *Love* was Darvas's last film; she died in 1974, aged 72.

# A Love in Germany
## (Eine Liebe in Deutschland)

\* \* \* \* \* \* \* \* \* \* \* \* \* \* \* \* \* \* \* \* \* \* \* \* \* \* \* \* \* \* \* \* \* \* \* \* \* \* \* \* \* \* \* \* \* \* \* \* \* \* \* \*

*Nationality*: West German-French   *Year*: 1983 (U.S. release: 1984)

*Cast*: Hanna Schygulla, Piotr Lysak, Marie-Christine Barrault, Armin Müller-Stahl, Daniel Olbrychski, Bernhard Wicki

*Director*: Andrzej Wajda          *Running Time*: 107 minutes

*B/W or Color*: Color               *Availability*: RCA/COLUMBIA PIC-
                                    TURES HOME VIDEO

Of *A Love in Germany*, Polish director Andrzej Wajda states, "It is the first time I dared to make a movie in Germany. The film was shot in Brombach, where the actual events once happened." Its reception there, he said, was cool.

The true events to which Wajda alluded first resurfaced in a novel by Rolf Hochhuth, set partly in the present, but mostly in 1941 Germany, detailing the flagrant love affair of a Polish P.O.W. and a grocer's wife, whose absent husband is in service. How this woman's unbridled emotions drove her to fulfill a sexual alliance that scandalized not only her neighbors, but also the whole Nazi regime, is detailed in a screenplay that shifts back and forth between World War II and the present, as the woman's grown son returns with *his* teenaged son to revisit the town where, at seven, he was a confused witness to his mother's compulsive behavior.

Hanna Schygulla quite becomes this drab, pitiable creature who, for her transgressions, was exiled to a work camp until the end of the war. Watching Schygulla's intensely realistic performance here, it's difficult to conjure up the glamorous creatures she portrayed for her late Svengali, Fassbinder, in *Lilli Marleen* and *The Marriage of Maria Braun*. In a simpler characterization, Piotr Lysak is just right as the shy and rather colorless young Pole, whose own passions rise to the surface when, after the breakup of their affair, he refuses to let the Nazis "Germanize" him and is executed.

The National Board of Review named *A Love in Germany* among the five best foreign-language films of 1984.

(*The videocassette is in German with unusually readable English subtitles.*)

# Love on the Dole

\*\*\*\*\*\*\*\*\*\*\*\*\*\*\*\*\*\*\*\*\*\*\*\*\*\*\*\*\*\*\*\*\*\*\*\*\*\*\*\*\*\*\*\*\*\*\*\*\*\*\*\*\*\*\*\*\*\*\*

*Nationality*: British          *Year*: 1941 (U.S. release: 1945)
*Cast*: Deborah Kerr, Clifford Evans, George Carney, Mary Merrall, Geoffrey Hibbert, Joyce Howard, Frank Cellier
*Director*: John Baxter          *Running Time*: 99 minutes
*B/W or Color*: B/W          *Availability*: VIDEO YES-
                              TERYEAR

In only her third motion picture, 20-year-old Deborah Kerr gives a remarkable performance (her first starring role) as a sweet and modest girl, driven by circumstance into early maturity when she realizes that the only salvation for her destitute family lies in compromising herself.

Walter Greenwood's story of life among the economically strapped working classes of Depression-era Lancashire—the obvious forerunner of the "kitchen-sink" dramas of the early 1960s—could hardly have proved diverting to British audiences in those early years of World War II, despite the excellence of its cast and the realism of its narrative.

Sally Hardcastle (Kerr), who shares a bedroom with her younger brother Harry (Geoffrey Hibbert), supplements her family's modest income by working in a mill. Unemployment looms over the house as her father subsequently faces lay-off, and Harry is let go from the engineering firm where he's an apprentice. Sally becomes engaged to an engineer named Larry, a Labour agitator who's unsure of their future together. When he dies in a violent workers' demonstration, the bottom falls out of her world. The unemployed Harry faces family ostracism for impregnating his girl Helen (Joyce Howard), and Sally, to keep her family from utter poverty, turns to the lustful blandishments of wealthy, middle-aged Sam Grundy (Frank Cellier). It's a decision that hardens her and turns her parents against her, but Grundy's influence will mean jobs for her father and brother.

*Love on the Dole* remains a strong and well-made film, despite its limited budget. And, above all, there's the beauty and burgeoning talent of young Deborah Kerr in what remains one of her favorite movies.

(*Video Yesteryear's print is, for the most part, of excellent quality.*)

# The Lovers
## (Les Amants)

★ ★ ★ ★ ★ ★ ★ ★ ★ ★ ★ ★ ★ ★ ★ ★ ★ ★ ★ ★ ★ ★ ★ ★ ★ ★ ★ ★ ★ ★ ★ ★ ★ ★ ★ ★ ★ ★ ★ ★ ★ ★ ★ ★ ★ ★ ★ ★ ★ ★ ★

**Nationality**: French        **Year**: 1959
**Cast**: Jeanne Moreau, Alain Cuny, Jean-Marc Bory, Jose-Luis De Villa-longa
**Director**: Louis Malle        **Running Time**: 90 minutes
**B/W or Color**: B/W        **Availability**: TV only

The *Lovers* of the title are 30-year-old Jeanne (Jeanne Moreau) and a young architect named Bernard (Jean-Marc Bory), who meet when her car breaks down and she accepts his offer of a ride. Invited by her husband (Alain Cuny) to spend the weekend, Bernard finds himself a third guest—the others being Jeanne's friend, Maggy (Judith Magre), and Jeanne's lover, Raoul (Jose-Luis De Villalonga). That night, Jeanne and Bernard make love and the following morning they leave together to make a new life.

*Saturday Review* termed the love scenes "as explicit as anything ever done before on the screen." Writer-director Louis Malle objected to critics labeling the film (his second feature) erotic or immoral, claiming that Americans "rarely understand or appreciate the points we are trying to make."

The picture made an international star of Jeanne Moreau, who had worked with Malle in his debut film, *Ascenseur Pour L'Echafaud (Elevator to the Scaffold)*, not released in the United States until after the success of *The Lovers*. Moreau enjoyed an offscreen relationship with Malle and *The Lovers* was based on her idea. Its intention, she explained, "was to show the poetry and power of love."

Moreau claimed that Malle "was the first director who refused to let me wear makeup—and I was so relieved. Before that . . . I had makeup to hide the black rings under the eyes, to make me have high cheekbones; I was covered with makeup."

*The Lovers'* controversy centered on a crucial scene that depicted a woman's reaction to lovemaking. "I knew that if I acted the love scenes the way Louis wanted," Moreau admitted, "he might like me as an actress but he would hate me as a woman. I took the gamble and lost." The picture ended their personal attachment, but they worked together on two later occasions.

# The Lovers of Teruel
## (Les Amants de Teruel)

\* \* \* \* \* \* \* \* \* \* \* \* \* \* \* \* \* \* \* \* \* \* \* \* \* \* \* \* \* \* \* \* \* \* \* \* \* \* \* \* \* \* \* \* \* \* \* \* \* \* \* \* \* \* \* \*

**Nationality**: French        **Year**: 1962

**Cast**: Ludmila Tcherina, Rene-Louis Lafforque, Milko Sparemblek, Milenko Banovitch

**Director**: Raymond Roleau      **Running Time**: 90 minutes

**B/W or Color**: Color         **Availability**: TV only

The U.S. rights to this ballet-dream film have long since run out. For a while, Continental Distributing continued to play their 35mm print theatrically despite the lapse of rights, but finally that stopped, and *The Lovers of Teruel* is never seen on the big screen anymore.

Recently it appeared on home video, with the extent of its wide-screen format trimmed damagingly and its expressionistic use of blue-green hues improperly transferred to tape. Still, it exists, more or less, with its enjoyably pretentious directoral conception by Raymond Rouleau, its supreme score by Mikis Theodorakis, its stylized cinematography by Claude Renoir (*Black Orpheus, French Connection II*), and its haunting ballet-performance by the immortal Ludmila Tcherina.

Mme. Tcherina has been hailed as the most beautiful woman in the world. In such films as *The Tales of Hoffmann*, a strong case can be made for this claim. Her life in ballet has been haunted by a bad press. Co-star Robert Rounseville (*Tales of Hoffmann*) characterized her as "pure business." Whatever the truth may be, she attends to the legend of Teruel with pure emotion. Her ballet, performance, and dream trauma as the martyred lover doomed to perform her own tragedy as part of a traveling dance company are full of illuminating passion and sorrow.

Apparently once was not enough for Mme. Tcherina. She danced the legend of Teruel again in *Honeymoon* (1961), under the direction of Michael Powell, who had formerly guided her through *Hoffmann* and *The Red Shoes*.

# Loves of a Blonde
## (Lasky Jedne Plavovlasky)

★★★★★★★★★★★★★★★★★★★★★★★★★★★★★★★★★★★★★★★★★★★★★★★★★★★★★

**Nationality**: Czechoslovakian    **Year**: 1965 (U.S. release: 1966)
**Cast**: Hana Brejchova, Vladimir Pucholt, Milada Jezkova, Josef Sebanek
**Director**: Milos Forman    **Running Time**: 88 minutes
**B/W or Color**: B/W    **Availability**: RCA/ COLUMBIA
PICTURES HOME VIDEO

While the world of cinema was startled in the late Fifties and early Sixties by the swift and stunning emergence of the French New Wave, other exciting schools of filmmaking seemed to arise in almost every corner of the world, each tagged a "new wave." In the mid-Sixties, the Czech cinema had its moment of glory with such films as Jan Kadar's *The Shop on Main Street* (1964), Jiri Menzel's *Closely Watched Trains* (1966), and Ivan Passer's *Intimate Lighting* (1965). The Czechs established a small but prestigious niche with these films characterized by their observations of the small, quiet details of human behavior and daily existence. They were fresh, funny, and touching.

None of these characteristics is more evident than in the work of Milos Forman. His second feature, *Loves of a Blonde,* is a delightful romantic comedy about a young girl (Brejchova) who works in a shoe factory. Her boring life is interrupted one night when she attends a local dance and becomes enamored of the pianist (Pucholt). They spend the night together and then go their separate ways. The girl, however, is so much in love that she packs her bags and shows up unannounced at the boy's parents' house, but he is not ready for commitment.

The plot is slight, but the beauty of the film is in the subtle nuances depicting the awkwardness and desire that make up any relationship. Forman is a consummate people-watcher, and one of the great set pieces in the movie is when three forlornly comic soldiers attempt to pick up some girls at the dance. It is a superbly directed sequence, not immediately related to the central story, yet it adds a dimension of truthfulness and hilarity to the overall effect of the film.

Forman has often been compared to directors François Truffaut and Ermanno Olmi for their shared attributes of observing human beings with perception and gentleness. *Loves of a Blonde* certainly lives up to that reputation and paved the way for Forman to eventually come to Hollywood, where he would win a truckload of Oscars with *One Flew Over the Cuckoo's Nest* (1975) and *Amadeus* (1984).

(*The RCA/Columbia cassette has English subtitles.*)

# The Loves of Isadora
## (Isadora)

★ ★ ★ ★ ★ ★ ★ ★ ★ ★ ★ ★ ★ ★ ★ ★ ★ ★ ★ ★ ★ ★ ★ ★ ★ ★ ★ ★ ★ ★ ★ ★ ★ ★ ★ ★ ★ ★ ★ ★ ★ ★ ★ ★ ★ ★ ★ ★ ★

*Nationality*: British          *Year*: 1968 (U.S. release: 1969)

*Cast*: Vanessa Redgrave, James Fox, Jason Robards, Ivan Tchenko, John Fraser, Bessie Love

*Director*: Karel Reisz          *Running Time*: 177 minutes

*B/W or Color*: Color          *Availability*: TV only

Vanessa Redgrave's wonderfully flamboyant performance dominates director Karel Reisz's sprawling film about the controversial dance innovator Isadora Duncan (1878–1927), whose legendary life of devotion to art and free love offered a challenge that few actresses could have resisted.

Redgrave tackled Isadora with uninhibited enthusiasm: "She did what she wanted to do without worrying much what people thought, and I'm fond of that."

Prior to filming, Redgrave spent six months training with a choreographer, and despite the actress's raw-boned physique and six-foot height, her execution of the dance sequences is certainly acceptable as an *interpretation* of Duncan's art. The complex screenplay takes her from a bizarre teenager obsessed with the heritage of Ancient Greece to her music-hall debut to affairs with artist Gordon Craig (James Fox), sewing-machine magnate Paris Singer (Jason Robards), and the lover she marries, Russian poet Sergei Essenin (Ivan Tchenko). Isadora also finds time for dance recitals and a pair of illegitimate children, whose tragic auto death haunts her. By 1927, she's a foolish eccentric dictating her memoirs on the French Riviera. In the movie's final sequence, as Isadora rides off with a handsome young Bugatti driver, her trailing scarf catches in a wheel-spoke, and she meets a swift and terrible death.

The film's nearly three-hour length dismayed Universal, the U.S. distributor, and they cut the movie by 46 minutes, changed its title from *Isadora* to the more promising *The Loves of Isadora*, and promoted it to an Oscar nomination for Redgrave. The National Board listed the film among the year's ten best.

# The L-Shaped Room

* * * * * * * * * * * * * * * * * * * * * * * * * * * * * * * * * * * * * * * * * * * * * * * * * * * * * *

*Nationality*: British                    *Year*: 1962 (U.S. release: 1963)

*Cast*: Leslie Caron, Tom Bell, Brock Peters, Cicely Courtneidge, Avis Bunnage, Emlyn Williams

*Director*: Bryan Forbes                  *Running Time*: 124 minutes

*B/W or Color*: B/W                       *Availability*: TV only

The *L-Shaped Room* in question is a squalid "bed-sitter" on the top floor of a rundown London boarding house that becomes home for a despairing young Frenchwoman (Leslie Caron). Pregnant from a loveless affair with an actor, she's determined to have an abortion. But a visit to an accommodating but repulsive "gynecologist" (Emlyn Williams) changes her mind; she'll stay on at the boarding house and have her child. The young woman then becomes involved with a fellow lodger and aspiring writer (Tom Bell), but he ends their relationship when he learns of her pregnancy, declaring that he could never accept another man's child. After she gives birth, he visits her hospital room with a copy of his first completed story, "The L-Shaped Room." She returns home to France, and the film closes as her sad little room becomes host to yet another single young woman.

Director Bryan Forbes's screenplay excels in its pungent dialogue, mixing cool cynicism with tough compassion. In Lynne Reid Banks's book, the heroine was English, and making her French (to accommodate Caron's casting) raises some unanswered questions. What is her background, and why did she come to London? And would a Frenchwoman of 27 really be so sexually naive? But Caron pulls out all the stops to offer a mature and subtle characterization of such stunning pathos that she won the British Film Academy's Best Actress award. She's given strong support by Tom Bell's unpublished writer, Brock Peters's maladjusted black, and—in a surprising change of pace—comedienne Cicely Courtneidge, as a pathetic old lesbian actress.

In Britain, this realistic study of loneliness ran to 142 minutes, 18 of which were cut for the United States. And, even at approximately two hours, American critics carped at its length. But The National Board of Review listed it among 1963's best films.

# M

Nationality: German         Year: 1931 (U.S. release: 1933)

Cast: Peter Lorre, Otto Wernicke, Ellen Widmann, Inge Landgut, Gustav Grundgens

Director: Fritz Lang         Running Time: 99 minutes (originally 118 minutes)

B/W or Color: B/W         Availability: EMBASSY HOME ENTERTAINMENT

Fritz Lang's talking picture baptism remains a virtual textbook of movie story-telling technique.

Made in spite of attempted Nazi interference (hearing of the film's pre-production title, *Murders Among Us,* they, understandably, assumed it was about them), *M* is a sophisticated, highly experimental piece of cinema dealing with equally radical events. It is two parts straightforward and based on fact, one part Langian pulp. In the director's words: "It seems there is a latent fascination in murder, that the word arouses a tangle of submerged and suppressed emotions . . . I have tried to approach the murderer imaginatively to show him as a human being possessed of some demon that has driven him beyond the ordinary borderlines of human behavior, and not the least part of whose tragedy is that by murder he never solves his conflicts."

Forsaking the expressionistic extremes so pronounced in the majority of his silent and other sound pictures, Lang, his technicians, and artisans strove for a wholly studio-created documentary style. Suffering few of the crudities that mark many early talkies, making innovative use of sound and jump cuts, the results have scarcely dated at all.

As the compulsive child murderer pursued simultaneously by police and underworld factions, Peter Lorre is positively fascinating in his screen debut. Bland, almost childlike himself at times, Lorre's performance shifts from subtle to grandiose, alternately eliciting sympathy and disgust. His tortured confession before a kangaroo court composed of Berlin's most wanted criminals is unforgettably riveting. Whistling his haunting "theme song" (Grieg's "In the Hall of the Mountain King"), so colorless he can be identified and apprehended only after being branded in chalk with a telltale M, the characterization is inspired and influential to this day.

With or without comparison, Joseph Losey's 1951 remake is an extremely minor film. Considering its subject matter, it's actually surprising that no one has attempted to revamp the story for contemporary audiences. One producer did have aborted plans to do an update, starring—of all people—John Belushi!

# Madame Rosa
## (La Vie Devant Soi)

\* \* \* \* \* \* \* \* \* \* \* \* \* \* \* \* \* \* \* \* \* \* \* \* \* \* \* \* \* \* \* \* \* \* \* \* \* \* \* \* \* \* \* \* \* \* \* \* \*

*Nationality*: French          *Year*: 1977

*Cast*: Simone Signoret, Claude Dauphin, Samy Ben Youb, Michal Bat-Adam, Constantin Costa-Gavras

*Director*: Moshe Mizrahi          *Running Time*: 105 minutes

*B/W or Color*: Color          *Availability*: VESTRON VIDEO

Accolades came easily for *Madame Rosa*. The 1975 book by Emile Ajar won the Prix Goncourt, France's most prestigious literary award. Simone Signoret was awarded the Cesar (equivalent of the Academy Award), and the film won Best Picture designation. In the United States, it was voted an Oscar as Best Foreign Film. On a more monetary level, it broke all house records at its premiere in New York. While dealing with controversial topics, it is a quiet tale of dramatic intensity. For Signoret, it was an opportunity to give one of the best performances of her later years. It also provided a reunion with director Constantin Costa-Gavras, here as an actor, and co-star Claude Dauphin, in one of his last roles.

A survivor of Auschwitz and a former prostitute, Jewish Madame Rosa (Signoret) lives in Paris' Belleville section and cares for the children of working prostitutes. Her favorite is Arab boy Samy Ben Youb, who's lived with Signoret for most of his life. She tries to help him resist the hookers' efforts to turn him into a pimp, while doctor Claude Dauphin cares for her declining health. A chance meeting with Michal Bat-Adam and Costa-Gavras, who play two sympathetic parents, shows the boy an alternate way of life, but he remains loyal to Signoret. Samy survives the truth about his mother and father and Signoret's death, attempting to stay with her body in a secret hideaway.

The film was seen by Mizrahi as a natural extension of his previously made *I Love You, Rosa* (1972) and *The House on Chelouche Street* (1973), and employed the services of his favorite actress, Israeli star Michal Bat-Adam. Signoret saw her character as someone who was beautiful in the way of people who were once beautiful—an attitude she must have well understood. The film was given perhaps the greatest praise by Ajar to Mizrahi: "You did not betray me."

# Maedchen in Uniform
## (Girls in Uniform)

★★★★★★★★★★★★★★★★★★★★★★★★★★★★★★★★★★★★★★★★★★★★★★★★★

**Nationality**: German         **Year**: 1931 (U.S. release: 1932)
**Cast**: Dorothea Wieck, Hertha Thiele, Ellen Schwannecke, Emilia Unda
**Director**: Leontine Sagan      **Running Time**: 90 minutes
**B/W or Color**: B/W          **Availability**: EMBASSY HOME
                                       ENTERTAINMENT

Fifty years after its 1931 release, this landmark German motion picture was hailed as "at once a strident warning against the consequences of Hitler's regime and the first truly radical lesbian film."

In its day, this study of a sensitive student who falls in love with one of the teachers at a strict boarding school and attempts suicide caused controversy and was banned by Goebbels. Its source was a stage play, *Gestern und Heute*, by Christa Winsloe, who helped adapt her work to the screen, and it was directed by the Reinhardt-trained Leontine Sagan. Sagan's only other movie was the 1932 *Men of Tomorrow*, made in England for Alexander Korda, after which she confined her activities to the stage in Britain and South Africa. But *Maedchen in Uniform* made enough of an international mark, with the frankness of its theme, to ensure her becoming an international legend.

The title, like the opening shots of the picture, is meant to convey the impression of young girls under subjection to strict militarized discipline like that of the Prussian army. The purpose of the picture—just as obvious as that of Dickens, who portrayed the evils of some of the schools of his day—is to protest the harshness and cruelty of that method of education for girls, during the most sensitive period of their lives. It is a passionate and moving protest, in the form of a dramatic conflict between martinet severity and sympathetic understanding and love.

Its story is simple, its strength the extraordinary care that has gone into its filming, the unpretentious but highly skillful suspense of the drama, and the unerring judgment in casting.

The movie was remade in 1958 with Lilli Palmer and Romy Schneider, but the results were surprisingly unimpressive.

*(Embassy's videocassette, in German with English subtitles, is of fairly good visual quality, but with a noisy soundtrack.)*

# The Magician
## (Ansiktet/The Face)

\* \* \* \* \* \* \* \* \* \* \* \* \* \* \* \* \* \* \* \* \* \* \* \* \* \* \* \* \* \* \* \* \* \* \* \* \* \* \* \* \* \* \* \* \* \* \* \* \* \* \* \* \*

Nationality: Swedish                          Year: 1958 (U.S. release: 1959)
Cast: Max von Sydow, Ingrid Thulin, Gunnar Björnstrand, Naima Wifstrand, Bibi Andersson
Director: Ingmar Bergman          Running Time: 102 minutes
B/W or Color: B/W                        Availability: EMBASSY HOME
                                                       ENTERTAINMENT

Undeniably a complex film, this darkly comic exercise in Gothic mysticism is so loaded with allegorical and mythical allusions that it was once the subject of much controversy and variations of interpretation. As its director, Ingmar Bergman, himself has said, "It caused a certain amount of confusion when it came out. It was regarded as odd, artificial, complicated, and theatrical."

But no matter how dense the intellectual may find *The Magician*, Bergman was obviously amusing himself while filming it, and the result is a fascinating excursion into the bizarre and the uncanny. A troupe of traveling performers, led by a mesmerist, is en route to 19th-century Stockholm when they're detained by provincial police and forced to spend the night in the home of a wealthy merchant, for whom they're asked to give a special command performance the following day. Following a night of sexual tensions and general insomnia, the magician and his aides are challenged during their performance, and their leader is humiliated and partially exposed as a trickster. His bizarre path of revenge centers on the apparent murder of the host's coachman and a subsequent attic autopsy, in which Ingmar Bergman's cinematic trickery far surpasses that of his dramatis personae. This unusual movie's denouement must be seen to be savored.

Bergman was then enjoying the first full wave of American appreciation. *The Magician* stirred filmgoers' imaginations and inspired awe, not only in the astonishing cleverness of Bergman's fertile imagination, but also in the brilliant skills of his acting "stock company," from the exotically disguised magician of Max von Sydow (a visual cross between Conrad Veidt's *Cabinet of Dr. Caligari* somnambulist and Edgar Allan Poe) to the delightful witchery of elderly Naima Wifstrand, who plays his occult-powered grandmother. The entire enterprise would hardly be so effective without the inspired black-and-white cinematography of Gunnar Fischer.

*(Embassy offers the film in both dubbed and subtitled versions.)*

# Mahler

* * * * * * * * * * * * * * * * * * * * * * * * * * * * * * * * * * * * * * * * * * * * * * * * * * * *

*Nationality*: British              *Year*: 1974 (U.S. release: 1975)
*Cast*: Robert Powell, Georgina Hale, Richard Morant, Lee Montague, Rosalie Crutchley
*Director*: Ken Russell              *Running Time*: 126 minutes
*B/W or Color*: Color              *Availability*: THORN EMI VIDEO

K en Russell enjoys disemboweling legends, and his *Mahler* continues that tradition. Visually stunning, *Mahler* contains some of Russell's most manic hyperbole, as well as devastating insights. Originally scheduled as a big-budget German production, the picture had to be shot in drastically revised fashion when German backing dropped out.

The film is mainly flashbacks revolving around Mahler's return to Vienna several months before his death. There's little attempt made at creating an historical document. Russell seeks the *essence* of his subject. There are fine scenes (Mahler's country retreat at Mainernigg, evoking the early 20th century ravishingly), and there are memorable ones (Mahler with his two children, beating out the third Kindertotenlieder song).

The performances range from Robert Powell's complex and fascinating Mahler to Rosalie Crutchley and David Collings, appropriately foreboding as Marie Mahler and Hugo Wolf. Georgina Hale, who plays Mahler's overshadowed wife, Alma, won a British Academy Award as 1974's Most Promising Newcomer. At that year's Cannes Film Festival, Ken Russell's contribution to *Mahler* was recognized with a special prize.

After making note of two sequences in which Russell's artistic imagination evokes "camped-up" references to Wagner and the Nazis, respectively, *Variety* commented: "the picture is not only very easy on the ears, with Mahler's music coming across stirringly as performed by Amsterdam's Concertgebouw Orchestra under Bernard Haitink's direction, but also extremely beautiful to look at, thanks to Dick Bush's stunning Technicolor lensing."

*(The videocassette lists a running time of only 110 minutes.)*

# Major Barbara

★ ★ ★ ★ ★ ★ ★ ★ ★ ★ ★ ★ ★ ★ ★ ★ ★ ★ ★ ★ ★ ★ ★ ★ ★ ★ ★ ★ ★ ★ ★ ★ ★ ★ ★ ★ ★ ★ ★ ★ ★ ★ ★ ★ ★ ★ ★ ★ ★ ★ ★ ★ ★

**Nationality**: British        **Year**: 1941
**Cast**: Wendy Hiller, Rex Harrison, Robert Morley, Emlyn Williams, Robert Newton, Sybil Thorndike, Deborah Kerr
**Director**: Gabriel Pascal        **Running Time**: 121 minutes
**B/W or Color**: B/W        **Availability**: TV only

Hard-to-please playwright George Bernard Shaw was so satisfied with the outcome of his *Pygmalion*, a popular and critical hit of 1938, that he willingly cooperated with its producer, Gabriel Pascal, in bringing a second Shaw stage play, the 1905 social comedy *Major Barbara*, to the screen. This time, Pascal would direct as well as produce. He cast a distinguished collection of stage veterans in the leading roles, topped by *Pygmalion*'s marvelous Eliza Doolittle, Wendy Hiller.

In this typically witty and ironic satire, Shaw spotlights poverty as the basis of all social evils, centering on a determined young Salvation Army major named Barbara Undershaft and her platonic relationship with a rich and romantic professor, who joins up with the army band just to be in her company. Representing Shaw's philosophies in the comedy-drama is her munitions-tycoon father, Andrew, who maintains that money, not prayers, will be the poor's salvation.

This is a straightforward version of Shaw's play, which Shaw was persuaded to make more cinematic with the addition of "connecting" scenes. With such burgeoning talents as David Lean and Harold French as "associate directors" and Ronald Neame as cameraman, Pascal nearly doubled his planned ten-week shooting schedule, under wartime restrictions, before *Major Barbara*'s completion.

Wendy Hiller was praised for the sincere intensity and intelligent humor of her acting, while Rex Harrison was personable and articulate as her romantic *vis-à-vis*. At 32, Robert Morley already possessed the skills to portray a convincing father to 28-year-old Hiller, and Robert Newton is the perfect low-life heel as he brutalizes the army lassie portrayed, in her film bow, by the luminous young Deborah Kerr.

# Make Mine Mink

✶✶✶✶✶✶✶✶✶✶✶✶✶✶✶✶✶✶✶✶✶✶✶✶✶✶✶✶✶✶✶✶✶✶✶✶✶✶✶✶✶✶✶✶✶✶✶✶✶✶✶✶✶✶✶

*Nationality*: British           *Year*: 1960
*Cast*: Terry-Thomas, Athene Seyler, Hattie Jacques, Billie Whitelaw, El-
speth Duxbury
*Director*: Robert Asher        *Running Time*: 100 minutes
*B/W or Color*: B/W          *Availability*: VIDAMERICA

A merry farce, *Make Mine Mink* was based on a play, *Breath of Spring*, by Peter Coke, that was turned into the 1971 Kander-and-Ebb Broadway musical *70, Girls, 70*, starring Mildred Natwick, Hans Conried, Lillian Roth, and Abby Lewis.

Set in Kensington, London, the action centers on Major Rayne (Terry-Thomas), a former military officer who becomes the leader of a band of comical crooks. The group rents rooms from Dame Beatrice (Athene Seyler), a charming elderly woman who, unaware that's she penniless, continues to contribute to pet charities. Her loyal boarders go to elaborate extremes to hide the truth from her.

When a mink coat is accidentally delivered to the house, it inspires the Major to organize the lodgers into an unlikely band of fur thieves. The maid (Billie Whitelaw) has a criminal past and tries to discourage them, but to no avail. Hattie Jacques (familiar to audiences from the *Carry On* series) and Elspeth Duxbury are a distaff version of Laurel and Hardy who embrace with glee the wrong side of the law. The kindly noblewoman stumbles onto their dealings; however, all ends happily.

Bosley Crowther, in his *New York Times* review, thought the film was "as implausibly broad as is the cleavage between Terry-Thomas' two front teeth."

The star, born Thomas Terry Hoare-Stevens in 1911 in North London, made his film debut in a small role in *Helter Skelter* (1949), but it was his second picture, *Private's Progress* (1956), that established the gap-toothed comedian as a prime example of the English "silly ass." His popular movies include *I'm All Right, Jack* (1959), opposite Peter Sellers, and the American comedies, *It's a Mad, Mad, Mad, Mad World* (1963) and *How to Murder Your Wife* (1965)—his favorite among his features. Alas, ill health has forced Terry-Thomas to retire.

# A Man and a Woman
## (Un Homme et une Femme)

★ ★ ★ ★ ★ ★ ★ ★ ★ ★ ★ ★ ★ ★ ★ ★ ★ ★ ★ ★ ★ ★ ★ ★ ★ ★ ★ ★ ★ ★ ★ ★ ★ ★ ★ ★ ★ ★ ★ ★ ★ ★ ★ ★ ★ ★ ★ ★ ★ ★ ★ ★

Nationality: French          Year: 1966
Cast: Anouk Aimée, Jean-Louis Trintignant, Pierre Barouh
Director: Claude Lelouch     Running Time: 102 minutes
B/W or Color: Color         Availability: WARNER HOME VIDEO

Before MTV, before automobile manufacturers started investing millions in soft-focus TV commercials, there was *A Man and a Woman*. It was a landmark film in 1966, phenomenally successful, and rich in awards. Director Claude Lelouch and female star Anouk Aimée received Academy Award nominations. The picture won Oscars for Best Foreign Language Film and Best Original Story and Screenplay, and it was co-winner of the Cannes Festival Grand Prix. It was the great make-out movie—lush, romantic, sentimental, a love story to sing along with, shed a tear over, but ultimately to feel good about. Its two greatest assets: the dazzling color photography (Lelouch was his own cameraman) and the now famous theme music.

Aimée and Jean-Louis Trintignant, both widowed, meet while visiting their respective children at a boarding school in Deauville. When he drives her back to Paris, we learn he is a famous race-car driver; she is a highly paid movie script girl. They begin to fall in love, but he goes off to race at Monte Carlo. She sends a telegram calling him back. He races through the night with a rain-swept windshield and blurred lights and pounding music. When together, the dead husband stands between them. He drives off angrily, but on reflection decides to try one more time. He surprises her on the railroad platform, and they rush into each other's arms. Dissolve with theme reaching ultimate orgiastic climax. Da Da Da da-da-da-da-da da-da-da-da-da.

Throughout, Aimée and Trintignant, both exceedingly attractive, play their parts with becoming restraint and make you believe in all that happens. So successful was this movie that Lelouch made a sequel with the same stars in 1986, *A Man and a Woman: 20 Years Later*. It was a resounding failure, a victim of incessant TV imitation and those 20 years.

*(The videocassette is English-dubbed.)*

290

# The Man Between

***************************************************

Nationality: British          Year: 1953
Cast: James Mason, Claire Bloom, Hildegarde Neff, Geoffrey Toone
Director: Carol Reed          Running Time: 100 minutes
B/W or Color: B/W          Availability: TV only

The National Board selected James Mason as Best Actor of 1953 for his performances as Ivo Kern in *The Man Between*, the captain in *Face to Face*, Rommel in *The Desert Rats*, and Brutus in *Julius Caesar*. The busy British-born actor (1904–84) also appeared in three other releases that year.

Set in postwar Berlin, *The Man Between* casts Mason as Kern, a former lawyer involved in black market activities. He is not above blackmailing his own wife, Bettina (Hildegarde Neff), who thought him dead when she married a British army doctor (Geoffrey Toone). When the doctor's sister, Susanne (Claire Bloom), visits, she is attracted to Kern, but before the relationship develops she is mistaken for her sister-in-law, kidnapped, and taken to East Berlin. Kern helps her to escape and, realizing that he loves her, sacrifices his life to save hers.

This was Mason's second film with his favorite director, Carol Reed. "My two experiences with him," Mason later said, "were impeccable." The first remained the actor's favorite film, *Odd Man Out* (1947). Mason described Reed as "one of my super heroes in the film world; he was the most devoted of directors."

Many critics compared *The Man Between* to Reed's earlier work, *The Third Man* (1949), set in postwar Vienna, in which Orson Wells, as Harry Lime, also dealt in the black market.

"I was never really bitten by the theater bug," Mason once said, "but I was mad about the movies." He received three Academy Award nominations: *A Star Is Born* (1954), *Georgy Girl* (1966), and *The Verdict* (1982), strongly disagreeing with actors "like Brando and George C. Scott turning rather loudly against the Oscars . . . it's like using a mallet to squash a fly!"

# A Man Escaped
## (Un Condamné à Mort S'Est Echappé)

★★★★★★★★★★★★★★★★★★★★★★★★★★★★★★★★★★★★★★★★★★★★★★★★★★★★★

Nationality: French                     Year: 1956 (U.S. release: 1957)
Cast: François Leterrier, Roland Monod, Charles Le Clainche, Maurice
Beerblock, Jacques Ertaud
Director: Robert Bresson            Running Time: 102 minutes
B/W or Color: B/W                     Availability: TV only

A Robert Bresson film that is suspenseful, exciting, and thrilling?
Bresson is noted for his fanatical austerity, slow pace, and lack of
conventionality, yet A Man Escaped is a totally entertaining and engrossing film and a masterpiece. Based on the true story of French Resistance
leader André Devigny's escape from Lyon prison as he was about to be
executed by the Gestapo in 1943, Bresson creates his finest work on the
theme of man's essential isolation in a callous, insensitive environment.
Devigny supervised the production of the film, re-creating his prison cell
to exact specifications in the studio.

As with all his films, Bresson used nonprofessional actors for the cast.
In the lead role, François Leterrier, a 27-year-old student, gives a remarkable performance as a man with an obsessive dedication to escaping from
jail. After trying to flee from a moving car and then being beaten by the
Nazis, he spends almost an hour of the film alone in his cell. What follows is a hypnotic tour de force of composition, editing, and sound-ef-
fects as he uses a spoon, some bedsprings, and his clothing to effect an
escape. Bresson concentrates on the absolute essentials. We hear boots
walking outside the cell, firing squads, and German voices, while the camera
stays inside with Leterrier. We are prisoners just as he is, and the sense
of claustrophobia is palpable. Long, close-up shots of his face and the
spoon digging into the wall are brilliant examples of pure filmmaking
and gripping in their masterful simplicity.

Mozart's Mass in C Minor is beautifully integrated into the soundtrack
and helps to create a sense of spiritual enthrallment. "A miracle of objects" is what Eric Rohmer called this film, and François Truffaut claimed
it to be "the most crucial French film of the past ten years." In its complete rejection of the superfluous and the gimmicky, A Man Escaped is
like no other prison picture ever made and is one of the finest accomplishments of world cinema. The National Board voted it one of 1957's
five best foreign-language films.

# A Man for All Seasons

★★★★★★★★★★★★★★★★★★★★★★★★★★★★★★★★★★★★★★★★★★★★★★★★★★★★★★★

*Nationality*: British                    *Year*: 1966

*Cast*: Paul Scofield, Wendy Hiller, Leo McKern, Robert Shaw, Orson Welles, Susannah York

*Director*: Fred Zinnemann              *Running Time*: 120 minutes

*B/W or Color*: Color                    *Availability*: RCA/COLUMBIA PIC-
TURES HOME VIDEO

Visually entrancing, sensitively directed, and brilliantly acted, *A Man for All Seasons* led The National Board's ten best list for 1966. The board also selected Fred Zinnemann as Best Director, Paul Scofield as Best Actor, and Robert Shaw as Best Supporting Actor. The New York Film Critics also cited the picture, Zinnemann, and Scofield. Of its eight Oscar nominations, there were six wins: Picture, Director, Actor, Screenplay (by Robert Bolt, based on his play), Cinematography, and Costumes. Shaw and Wendy Hiller (nominated as Best Supporting Actress) lost. Scofield had created the role of Thomas More on stage (winning a Tony Award in 1962).

The story unfolds between 1528 and 1535, when More was executed. A devout Catholic, scholar, and philosopher, More was a member of Henry VIII's High Council but angered the king (Shaw) by not sanctioning his divorce from his first wife.

Wendy Hiller is his devoted wife and Susannah York his loving daughter. Leo McKern plays the villainous Cromwell; Orson Welles is seen briefly as Cardinal Wolsey, and John Hurt portrays the ambitious Richard Rich. An unbilled Vanessa Redgrave has no lines as Anne Boleyn.

The moving scene where More bids farewell to his wife and daughter remains the director's favorite moment from among all his films. And a particular location shoot among the strangest. "Something eerie happened," relates Zinnemann, "when we needed a snowy landscape for the Duke of Norfolk's ride to see the dying Cardinal Wolsey. It was almost April and there was no snow on the ground anywhere in England, which forced us to rent two enormous trucks full of Styrofoam. When we arrived on location, snow started to fall and, at dawn, the hills were white. Stranger still, just after we had finished shooting, the sun came out and the snow melted in half an hour, as if on cue."

It stands as a film for all seasons.

# The Man from Snowy River

**★ ★ ★ ★ ★ ★ ★ ★ ★ ★ ★ ★ ★ ★ ★ ★ ★ ★ ★ ★ ★ ★ ★ ★ ★ ★ ★ ★ ★ ★ ★ ★ ★ ★ ★ ★ ★ ★ ★ ★ ★ ★ ★ ★ ★ ★ ★ ★ ★ ★ ★ ★ ★ ★ ★**

*Nationality*: Australian          *Year*: 1982 (U.S. release: 1983)
*Cast*: Kirk Douglas, Tom Burlinson, Sigrid Thornton, Jack Thompson
*Director*: George Miller          *Running Time*: 104 minutes
*B/W or Color*: Color          *Availability*: CBS/FOX VIDEO

Confused readers might be surprised to learn that Australia has *two* film directors named George Miller: one is responsible for the popular *Mad Max* series as well as a segment of *Twilight Zone—The Movie*; the other has worked mostly in TV miniseries, the best of which (*All the Rivers Run*) has been seen on American television. *The Man from Snowy River* marked his big screen bow, and it's a wonderfully entertaining and visually breathtaking, old-fashioned Western from Down Under. Indeed, its wedding of the right ingredients was so felicitous that this movie was Australia's biggest all-time box office champion—until 1986 and the arrival of *"Crocodile" Dundee*.

Filmed in the wild splendors of Victoria, *The Man from Snowy River* has the look of an American super-Western and the sound of Australia. The story takes place in the late 19th century, centering on a young man named Jim Craig (played by Tom Burlinson), who's orphaned at the outset when his father is killed during a hunt for wild mountain horses. Jim goes to work as a ranch hand for a wealthy man named Harrison (Kirk Douglas, enjoying an actor's field day, since he also doubles as Harrison's evil, peg-legged mountaineer brother Spur), whose daughter Jessica (Sigrid Thornton) provides the obligatory love interest. Based on an epic Australian poem, *The Man from Snowy River* has all the best ingredients of popular entertainment as well as refreshingly personable young leading actors who are probably unfamiliar to most American viewers. *Variety* summed it up well as "a rattling good adventure story."

# The Man in the White Suit

\* \* \* \* \* \* \* \* \* \* \* \* \* \* \* \* \* \* \* \* \* \* \* \* \* \* \* \* \* \* \* \* \* \* \* \* \* \* \* \* \* \* \* \* \* \* \* \* \* \* \* \* \* \* \* \* \* \*

*Nationality*: British           *Year*: 1951 (U.S. release: 1952)

*Cast*: Alec Guinness, Joan Greenwood, Cecil Parker, Michael Gough, Ernest Thesiger

*Director*: Alexander Mackendrick    *Running Time*: 85 minutes

*B/W or Color*: B/W            *Availability*: THORN/EMI-HBO VIDEO

The late Forties and early Fifties were a rich era for the British comedy film. Inventive and fertile, their writers and directors proved immensely clever at satirizing various aspects of English life.

In *The Man in the White Suit,* which directly followed *The Lavender Hill Mob,* Alec Guinness plays shyly industrious Sidney Stratton, a textile chemist who, in a forbidden research lab, develops a dirt-resistant cloth that won't wear out. But this amazing white fabric has its drawbacks: it resists color dyes and its consumer acceptance would obviously threaten both labor and management. Stratton wears his miracle suit, while textile executives deny its existence to the press and the worried mill workers strike. The corporation bosses kidnap Stratton, but he escapes and, in the ensuing chase, his suit, which glows in the dark, makes him a vulnerable target. When his pursuers grab him, his suit pulls apart like cotton candy, leaving their quarry in his underwear, shirt, and necktie. In the final scene, Sidney strides triumphantly down a street, accompanied by the amusing sounds that have become the picture's *leitmotif*—the musically syncopated, bubbling gurgles that signal he's on the track of a new chemical triumph.

This clever little classic was written for the screen by Roger MacDougall, John Dighton, and the film's director, Alexander Mackendrick (*Tight Little Island*), who succeed in spoofing a potentially serious theme with tongue-in-cheek slyness. But *The Man in the White Suit* wouldn't be half so much fun without its wonderful cast: Guinness at his blank-faced, antic best; croaky-throated Joan Greenwood, as the mill owner's spirited daughter, who loves him; and such marvelous character actors as stuffy Cecil Parker, dullish Michael Gough, forceful Vida Hope, and that ancient eccentric, Ernest Thesiger.

The National Board named this one of 1952's ten best films.

# Man of Iron
## (Czlowiek z Zelaza)

★★★★★★★★★★★★★★★★★★★★★★★★★★★★★★★★★★★★★★★★★★★★★★★★★★★★★

*Nationality*: Polish           *Year*: 1981
*Cast*: Jerzy Radziwilowicz, Krystyna Janda, Marian Opania
*Director*: Andrzej Wajda       *Running Time*: 140 minutes
*B/W or Color*: Color          *Availability*: TV only

Essentially about the 1980 shipyard strike at Gdansk and the subsequent acceptance of Solidarity, the workers' union, *Man of Iron* mixes documentary footage of that event with staged sequences and fictional characters. The film focuses on Tomczyk (Jerzy Radziwilowicz), a shipyard worker, and follows his evolution from student striker in 1968 to his present role as a supporter of the labor movement. Equally dedicated is his wife Agnieszka (Krystyna Janda), and together they embody a spiritual and political struggle that still exists in Poland. Similarly, a counteractive element is represented by Winkiel (Marian Opania), a radio journalist of uncertain loyalties. He alternately supports Solidarity or the government that has sent him to smear Tomczyk. Andrzej Wajda's film is remarkably outspoken in its enthusiastic support of Solidarity, combined with obvious criticism of the government; it is as much a cause as it is a film.

Unlike most political art, which either reduces important issues to superficial melodrama or propaganda, *Man of Iron* is an inventive, multidimensional collage of flashbacks, television images, documentary footage, and romantic drama. Wajda has taken all of these elements and composed them in an intelligent film that manages the difficult task of humanizing history without making it false. The fictional story of Tomczyk and Agnieszka mirrors the larger tableau of the strike and negotiation process: their struggle is the distillation of the struggle of all the workers, and the objectives of Solidarity leader Lech Walesa (who appears in the movie) are their objectives. It is Wajda's achievement that he has made a film that is so moving while able to project such a strong political statement.

*Man of Iron* won the Golden Palm at Cannes and was a nominee for 1981's Best Foreign Language Film Oscar.

# The Man Who Could Work Miracles

\* \* \* \* \* \* \* \* \* \* \* \* \* \* \* \* \* \* \* \* \* \* \* \* \* \* \* \* \* \* \* \* \* \* \* \* \* \* \* \* \* \* \* \* \* \* \* \* \* \* \* \* \* \*

*Nationality*: British
*Year*: 1936 (U.S. release: 1937)
*Cast*: Roland Young, Joan Gardner, Ralph Richardson, Ernest Thesiger
*Director*: Lothar Mendes
*Running Time*: 82 minutes
*B/W or Color*: B/W
*Availability*: EMBASSY HOME ENTERTAINMENT

When three heavenly observers wish to determine the future of humanity, they endow an average man, George McWhirter Fotheringay (Roland Young), with the ability to work miracles.

H. G. Wells wrote the whimsical screenplay, which *The New York Times* claimed, "dares admit that the cosmic may also be the comic." It concludes, however, that earthbound people are not yet ready for Utopia, and probably would encounter untold difficulties should evolution be speeded up.

A rabbity draper's clerk in the Essex village of Dewhinton, Fotheringay discovers his unexpected gift during an evening at the Long Dragon Inn, when he causes a hanging lamp to turn upside down and continue burning. Downright unimpressed, the innkeeper ejects the miracle worker. His newfound power enables Fotheringay to levitate objects, make animals materialize, fade a little girl's freckles, and even make people vanish (he sends a policeman to blazes, thinks better of the situation, and banishes him to San Francisco instead). But the gift has no influence on the human heart, and our clerical hero is unable to compel a perky shopgirl (Joan Gardner) to fall in love with him.

Attempting to better the lot of mankind, Fotheringay assembles the world's greatest minds—past and present—to devise a plan for a peaceful world. When they request more time, an exasperated Fotheringay commands the Earth to stand still. In the resulting confusion, he relinquishes his powers, and the world returns to normal. "Once an ape, always an ape," notes one of the heavenly observers (played by a barely recognizable and then unknown George Sanders).

Roland Young makes a perfect Everyman, and Ralph Richardson is wonderful as a blustering colonel who goes after the clerk with his elephant gun.

*The Man Who Could Work Miracles* remains to this day a delightfully humorous fantasy.

# The Man Who Fell to Earth

★★★★★★★★★★★★★★★★★★★★★★★★★★★★★★★★★★★★★★★★★★★★★★★★★★★★★★★★

Nationality: British               Year: 1976
Cast: David Bowie, Rip Torn, Candy Clark, Buck Henry
Director: Nicolas Roeg            Running Time: 118 minutes (140
                                  minutes in original British version)
B/W or Color: Color               Availability: RCA/COLUMBIA PIC-
                                  TURES HOME VIDEO

Androgynous rock star David Bowie made his screen debut in this cerebral science-fiction cult classic directed by Nicolas Roeg. The film, adapted from the 1963 Walter Tevis book, was cut by 22 minutes to allow the film an R rating.

Thomas Jerome Newton (Bowie), a frail, exotic alien, comes to earth to save his drought-stricken, dying planet. He brings with him enough fantastically original patents to create the World Enterprises Corporation. Leaving his loyal patent lawyer Oliver Farnsworth (Buck Henry) in charge, the reclusive, homesick alien finds companionship and love with Mary-Lou (Candy Clark). From the bowels of New Mexico, Newton sets up his final project, a private space program building a ship to take him home. He is aided, and eventually sabotaged by, chemist Nathan Bryce (Rip Torn), a man who becomes suspicious of Newton's motives and metabolism. Newton's flight is prevented by a CIA-type organization plotting against World Enterprises, whose power is unsettling the U.S. economy; he is kidnapped and torturously examined by heartless scientists. Finally, his hopes for returning home to his beloved wife and children dashed, the despairing Newton is allowed to escape—a pathetic alcoholic condemned to a life of exile, betrayed and alone, a stranger in a strange land. His fate is all too human.

The Man Who Fell to Earth soars on John Phillips's eerie, haunting soundtrack (to which Bowie did not contribute) and Anthony Richmond's beautiful cinematography. The dangling screenplay actually contributes to the film's overall startling effect. The abstract and intricate elements Roeg brings to his intriguing, technically masterful production, his fractionalized editing, riveting cross-cutting, and discordant images create a disorienting, intense, and erotic film.

# The Man Who Knew Too Much

* * * * * * * * * * * * * * * * * * * * * * * * * * * * * * * * * * * * * * * * * * * * * * * * *

**Nationality**: British           **Year**: 1934
**Cast**: Leslie Banks, Edna Best, Peter Lorre, Nova Pilbeam
**Director**: Alfred Hitchcock       **Running Time**: 84 minutes
**B/W or Color**: B/W          **Availability**: Public Domain

"So sure is Hitchcock's touch in creating an electric atmosphere," stated *The New York Times* review, "that the audience is enthralled."

*The Man Who Knew Too Much* is the only one of Alfred Hitchcock's 54 features that he ever remade. Many critics prefer the original because of its compactness (46 minutes shorter than the 1956 version, which starred James Stewart and Doris Day).

Both versions contain humor and suspense. The plot involves a vacationing couple who witness a murder and try to foil an assassination attempt at London's Albert Hall, even though their child has been kidnapped to prevent their interference. In the first, the main characters are British tourists traveling with their daughter in Switzerland; the second (which is in color) has Americans visiting Marrakesh with their son. In both, the murder victim who sets the action in motion is named Louis Bernard.

Leslie Banks and Edna Best portray the British couple, and Peter Lorre, in his first English-language film (having made an impression in Fritz Lang's German classic *M*), plays the assassin. Cast as the daughter is Nova Pilbeam, whom Hitchcock would later star in *Young and Innocent* (1937).

Because of the final siege in the film, Hitchcock encountered censorship problems. Since British police do not carry firearms, they had to appear unfamiliar with the rifles that are distributed to them. As in the original, it is the wife who carries out most of the final action.

In the Albert Hall sequence in the 1934 version, which was shot in a studio, a painting reflected with a mirror into the camera lens doubled as most of the concert audience.

Hitchcock's greatest British success, the film reestablished his prestige after the mediocre musical *Waltzes from Vienna* and triggered his reputation as master of suspense. He followed this picture with *The 39 Steps* and *The Lady Vanishes,* and then accepted David O. Selznick's offer to work in Hollywood.

*(Of the various tapes available, Hal Roach offers one of good quality.)*

# The Man Who Loved Women

## (L'Homme Qui Aimait les Femmes)

* * * * * * * * * * * * * * * * * * * * * * * * * * * * * * * * * * * * * * * * * * * * * * * * *

*Nationality*: French        *Year*: 1977

*Cast*: Charles Denner, Brigitte Fossey, Nelly Borgeaud, Leslie Caron, Nathalie Baye

*Director*: François Truffaut        *Running Time*: 119 minutes

*B/W or Color*: Color        *Availability*: RCA/COLUMBIA PICTURES HOME VIDEO

The late, great François Truffaut was fascinated with the way the written word and narration could be utilized in films to involve the viewer in a story. He was also obsessed with women, often to the point of idolatry. One can think of his work with such luminaries as Jeanne Moreau, Catherine Deneuve, Françoise Dorléac, Julie Christie, Isabelle Adjani, Jacqueline Bisset, and Fanny Ardant. They all made fine films for others, but somehow Truffaut's films seemed to present them in a new light. Through his camera lens they were more than just gorgeous creatures to be looked at, they were magical, mysterious figures who transported men to a state of confusion and desire.

Truffaut used both women and writing in one of his most unusual features, *The Man Who Loved Women*. The story concerns a man (Charles Denner) who claims that because his mother didn't love him as a child, he had embarked on a relentless campaign of womanizing. However, the relationships did not fulfill or satisfy him, and so, to release himself from feelings of emptiness, he decides to write a book detailing his exploits with the opposite sex. As he narrates the tale, we see in flashback the alternately comic and sad encounters with his many paramours. Truffaut depicts Denner as a driven, somewhat unlikable man who simply can't control himself—yet he never judges him. Among the women, Leslie Caron, Nelly Borgeaud, Geneviève Fontanel, and Brigitte Fossey (25 years after playing the little girl in Clément's *Forbidden Games*), are all delightful and captivating. Appropriately, Denner ends up in the hospital and dies when he falls out of bed, desperately trying to touch the nylon stockings of the nurse. The mixture of romantic escapades and black comedy is successful, and the film leaves one pleased but disturbed.

*The Man Who Loved Women* was named one of the year's five best foreign language films by The National Board, while *The New York Times* included it on their ten best list. An unsuccessful remake by Blake Edwards was released in 1983, starring Burt Reynolds.

*(The videocassette is dubbed in English.)*

# Marius/
## (Fanny/Cesar)

* * * * * * * * * * * * * * * * * * * * * * * * * * * * * * * * * * * * * * * * * * * * * * * * * *

**Nationality**: French

**Year**: 1931 (U.S. release: 1933)/ 1932 (U.S.: 1948)/1936 (U.S.: 1948)

**Cast**: Raimu, Pierre Fresnay, Orane Demazis, Charpin, Alida Rouffe

**Director**: Alexander Korda/Marc Allegret/Marcel Pagnol

**Running Time**: 125 minutes/120 minutes/170 minutes

**B/W or Color**: B/W

**Availability**: TV only

M*arius, Fanny,* and *Cesar* comprise Marcel Pagnol's Marseilles trilogy, which covers 20 years in its characters' lives and combines romance, sentiment, comedy, and the waterfront-setting's local color. All three films were written and produced by Pagnol, who also directed the last.

*Marius* tells the story of the restless title character (Pierre Fresnay) and Fanny (Orane Demazis), whose parents own adjoining shops. His father, Cesar (Raimu), operates the café and her mother, (Alida Rouffe), the fish store. Torn between his love for Fanny and for the sea, Marius is encouraged by the self-sacrificing Fanny, who willingly shares his bed, to answer his true love's call. He goes off to sea, not knowing that she's pregnant.

The film's cast (most of whom were making screen debuts) is the same as the popular Pagnol play, which premiered in 1929. Raimu became France's leading character actor of the Thirties, and Pierre Fresnay would give a memorable performance in Renoir's 1937 classic *Grand Illusion*.

In *Fanny,* directed by Marc Allegret, the young mother-to-be marries Cesar's old friend Panisse (Charpin), the sailmaker, who's many years her senior. Cesar becomes the baby's godfather and sides against Marius when the young man returns from the sea.

*Cesar* reunites Fanny and Marius after the death of Panisse. Fanny reveals to her son (Andre Fouche), now 20, his real father's identity, and eventually the one-time lovers marry and begin life anew.

In 1938, MGM remade Pagnol's trilogy as *Port of Seven Seas,* starring Wallace Beery, Maureen O'Sullivan, Frank Morgan, and John Beal. Directed by James Whale, the screenplay was by Preston Sturges.

Joshua Logan directed *Fanny* (1961), starring Charles Boyer, Leslie Caron, Maurice Chevalier, and Horst Buchholz. Its background music was the Harold Rome score of Logan's 1954 Broadway musical of the same title.

# The Mark

★★★★★★★★★★★★★★★★★★★★★★★★★★★★★★★★★★★★★★★★★★★★★★★★★★★★★★★★★

Nationality: British            Year: 1961
Cast: Stuart Whitman, Maria Schell, Rod Steiger, Donald Wolfit
Director: Guy Green          Running Time: 127 minutes
B/W or Color: B/W          Availability: TV only

"Its writers, director and principals . . . must be credited with courage and imagination," stated The New York Times review of The Mark, "by tackling a theme that is universal but often taboo."

The title refers to the stigma attached to a child molester, in this case Jim Fuller (Stuart Whitman), a Canadian working in England who served three years in prison for the near-rape of a 10-year-old girl. He is on parole and undergoing therapy. We learn about his past (the youngest in his family, he had five sisters, a dominating mother, and a weak father) in flashbacks during sessions with his understanding psychiatrist, Dr. McNally (Rod Steiger).

In the British Midlands, Fuller works for Donald Wolfit. He shies away from friendly co-worker Ruth Leighton (Maria Schell) but finally accepts an invitation to have dinner at her home. There, he meets her 10-year-old daughter (Amanda Black) and is concerned that his former feelings will resurface. After realizing that his emotions are paternal, he makes love to her mother. A newspaperman aware of his past, photographs Fuller with the girl and prints the picture in the newspaper—along with a write-up of his former crime. He is a marked man.

Fuller is fired and evicted from his lodgings. Ruth also rejects him, and he moves to another town. After talking to his psychiatrist, Ruth finds Fuller and they reconcile—with the knowledge that he may once again become the mark.

Stuart Whitman, in the best role of his career, received an Academy Award nomination as Best Actor but lost to Maximilian Schell (Maria's brother) for Judgment at Nuremberg.

As the psychiatrist, Rod Steiger (who would win the 1967 Best Actor Oscar for In the Heat of the Night) received excellent notices.

The Mark and The Angry Silence (1960) are considered director Guy Green's best work.

# Marriage, Italian Style
## (Matrimonio All' Italiana)

**★★★★★★★★★★★★★★★★★★★★★★★★★★★★★★★★★★★★★★★★★★★★★★★★★★★★★★★**

**Nationality**: Italian          **Year**: 1964
**Cast**: Sophia Loren, Marcello Mastroianni, Aldo Puglisi, Tecla Scarano, Marilu Tolo, Pia Lindstrom
**Director**: Vittorio De Sica      **Running Time**: 102 minutes
**B/W or Color**: Color          **Availability**: TV only

For years, it seemed that whenever Vittorio De Sica joined forces with Sophia Loren to make a movie, something wonderful happened. It did when he directed her in *Gold of Naples, Two Women, Yesterday, Today and Tomorrow,* and the winning team continued to display top form in *Marriage, Italian Style.* The comedy received an Academy Award nomination as Best Foreign Film.

Set in Naples, this battle of the sexes involves Loren's efforts to marry her longtime lover, played by Marcello Mastroianni (who had co-starred with her in *Yesterday, Today and Tomorrow*).

Domenico (Mastroianni) receives word that Filumena (Loren) is dying and, on the way to her bedside, recalls their years together. They met during World War II, and after the war she managed his bar and bakery while also running his house and caring for his invalid, senile mother.

Filumena's last wish is to be married and, after the wedding, she confesses that her illness was a pretense. An infuriated Domenico has the marriage annulled. Filumena next reveals the up-to-then secret existence of three sons (whom she supported in foster homes), informing Domenico that one of the boys is his; however, the price of knowing which one is a band of gold.

In the *New York Times* review, Bosley Crowther wrote; "Miss Loren is delightfully eccentric . . . and often poignant." And "Mr. Mastroianni is marvelous . . . They are brilliantly supported. Aldo Puglisi is vastly comical as a valet . . . Tecla Scarano does a fine job as an efficient, hand-clasping maid. . . . Note, too, that Pia Lindstrom plays a nubile and delectable shop girl—one of Domenico's passing fancies." (Lindstrom, the eldest daughter of Ingrid Bergman, later became a critic on TV.)

One of the screenplay's five writers, Eduardo De Filippo, had authored the play *Filumena Marturano,* on which it was based, and had starred in a previous film version, made in 1951.

# The Marriage of Maria Braun
## (Die Ehe der Maria Braun)

\*\*\*\*\*\*\*\*\*\*\*\*\*\*\*\*\*\*\*\*\*\*\*\*\*\*\*\*\*\*\*\*\*\*\*\*\*\*\*\*\*\*\*\*\*\*\*\*\*\*\*\*\*\*\*\*

*Nationality*: German          *Year*: 1978

*Cast*: Hanna Schygulla, Klaus Lowitch, Ivan Desny, Gottfried John, Gisela Uhlen

*Director*: Rainer Werner Fass-          *Running Time*: 120 Minutes
binder

*B/W or Color*: Color          *Availability*: RCA/COLUMBIA
HOME VIDEO

This is one of several brilliant films from the talented young German director Rainer Werner Fassbinder, whose 1982 death was a great loss to the art of cinema. The movie concentrates on a beautiful young woman played by the infinitely intriguing Hanna Schygulla. Her wartime marriage to a soldier occurs during an air raid, when the marriage registry itself trembled under Allied bombing.

After a short time together, the soldier leaves for the front, and Maria must provide for herself in an almost leveled Germany. Enterprising, as well as a beautiful and seductive woman, she trades a family pin for a sexy dress and begins her postwar career in a bar open only to GIs. After believing her husband dead, she takes up with a black GI and becomes pregnant. At this melodramatic point, her husband returns unexpectedly and she accidentally kills the GI. Her husband accepts the blame and is imprisoned. Maria, again on the lookout for a new way of life, becomes involved with a wealthy industrialist, who supplies her with the goodies of an emerging Germany.

As we watch Maria's upward movement from a half-destroyed apartment to a fine suburban home, we hear the hammers restoring a destroyed wartime Germany to a prosperous, modern, postwar economy. Fassbinder cleverly uses the sound of the construction hammers on new buildings to parallel those of the machine guns that battered the German consciousness during the war.

The film, of course, equates its protagonist with her nation. Maria Braun is Germany and Germany is Maria Braun. Her striking face changes as her economic star rises, and Maria Braun has indeed made the same materialistic marriage as her native land. It is a riveting film and a particularly fascinating one from a young man who had been part of the economic miracle himself.

The National Board named *The Marriage of Maria Braun* one of the best foreign films of the year.

# Masculine-Feminine
## (Masculin-Feminin)

★ ★ ★ ★ ★ ★ ★ ★ ★ ★ ★ ★ ★ ★ ★ ★ ★ ★ ★ ★ ★ ★ ★ ★ ★ ★ ★ ★ ★ ★ ★ ★ ★ ★ ★ ★ ★ ★ ★ ★ ★ ★ ★ ★ ★ ★ ★

*Nationality*: French-Swedish        *Year*: 1966

*Cast*: Jean-Pierre Léaud, Chantal Goya, Marlene Jobert, Catherine-Isabelle Duport

*Director*: Jean-Luc Godard        *Running Time*: 103 minutes (110 minutes in France)

*B/W or Color*: B/W        *Availability*: Public Domain

N ot the first teen flick but the greatest. Godard's survey of post-adolescent Left Bank students was an instant classic, a masterful study of the aching differences between boys and girls. Paul (Jean-Pierre Léaud of *The 400 Blows* in his first grown-up and still finest performance) meets Madeleine (Chantal Goya), a would-be rock singer, and is hopelessly smitten, even when her interest in him freezes him into indifference. This story of young love apotheosizes the essence of male-female mutual attraction and the tragedy of their closely related alienation. The phenomenon is unforgettably encapsulated in Paul's first meeting with Madeleine as he watches her casually comb her perfect new hairdo. He's lost in love and at the same time isolated within the depths of his personal romanticism.

Godard lightens what could have been a wearying load of Gallic tristesse by relating Paul and Madeleine's battle of the sexes to the era's most pressing political topics: Vietnam, civil rights, urban violence, militant rock and roll. A tangent episode features an interview with Miss 19 Consumer Product, a pageant winner who forever illustrates the naiveté, self-absorption, and baffling innocence of youth. Love, Godard observes, is the tragic force that ends that idyll. The film is based on two short stories by Guy de Maupassant, "The Sign" and "Paul's Mistress." The originality of Godard's script betrays little outside influence; it springs from an alert contemporary consciousness. This utterly fragmented work may be Godard's best. Brigitte Bardot, who had worked with Godard in *Contempt,* appears briefly as herself in a café-bar, discussing a play with actor-director Antoine Bourseiller (according to a cast member, B.B.'s appearance in *Masculine-Feminine* was improvisational and the result of her having strolled into Le Zoo bar at Vincennes, where Godard was shooting a location sequence).

# Max Havelaar

★ ★ ★ ★ ★ ★ ★ ★ ★ ★ ★ ★ ★ ★ ★ ★ ★ ★ ★ ★ ★ ★ ★ ★ ★ ★ ★ ★ ★ ★ ★ ★ ★ ★ ★ ★ ★ ★ ★ ★ ★ ★ ★ ★ ★ ★ ★ ★ ★ ★ ★ ★

*Nationality*: Dutch-Indonesian     *Year*: 1976 (U.S. release: 1979)

*Cast*: Peter Faber, Sacha Bulthuis, Maroeli Sitompul, Rutger Hauer

*Director*: Fons Rademakers     *Running Time*: 165 minutes (170 minutes in Europe)

*B/W or Color*: Color     *Availability*: TV only

**M**ax Havelaar takes its title and its story from a classic Dutch novel published in 1960 under the pseudonym "Maltatuli" (Latin: "Much have I suffered"), written in sprawling outrage by Eduard Douwes Dekker, a cashiered official from the Dutch colonial administration in Indonesia. The subject is the ruthless, corrupt economic and social exploitation of that former overseas empire to which the author had been firsthand witness (and victim). The movie unrolls, then, as a grand scale historical saga inspired by moral, rather than romantic, fervor. Sickened by the prevailing ethics of inaction, the main character—superbly played by Peter Faber—on his own initiative takes bold steps to ameliorate widespread, self-perpetuating injustice, and in so doing must pay a staggering price in terms of personal security.

The director, Fons Rademakers, is highly regarded in his native country but little known here. In this instance, he clearly demonstrates mastery in making a rather subdued narrative visually engrossing, teeming with exciting detail. The film's leisurely pace is entirely in keeping with its dignity of content. It was photographed mostly in the wilds of Java and in Holland, and the dialogue is spoken in Dutch and Indonesian.

Since the film is an import from the Netherlands, *Max Havelaar* is somewhat obscure for American audiences. But as a product of a mature and inventive mind, it is intelligent and affecting, much more than just a curiosity piece.

In the title role, Peter Faber gives a suitably attractive and flamboyant performance, depicting a strong and compassionate man who is ultimately defeated by the corrupt greed of the entrenched bureaucracy. Fons Rademakers's direction suits the epic scope of his film to the scale of his subject matter, and the cinematography of Jan De Bont displays unusual artistry, evoking pictorial compositions that are often strikingly beautiful.

# Mayerling

\* \* \* \* \* \* \* \* \* \* \* \* \* \* \* \* \* \* \* \* \* \* \* \* \* \* \* \* \* \* \* \* \* \* \* \* \* \* \* \* \* \* \* \* \* \* \* \* \* \* \* \* \* \*

*Nationality*: French        *Year*: 1936 (U.S. release: 1937)

*Cast*: Charles Boyer, Danielle Darrieux, Suzy Prim, Jean Dax, Gabrielle Dorziat

*Director*: Anatole Litvak       *Running Time*: 90 minutes

*B/W or Color*: B/W       *Availability*: EMBASSY HOME ENTERTAINMENT

This is the film that made major stars of Charles Boyer and Danielle Darrieux who respectively played the Archduke Rudolph, heir to the throne of the Austro-Hungarian Empire, and the bewitching Baroness Marie Vetsera. Their love affair created a scandal at the Imperial Court, and the unyielding old Emperor, mindful of the rumblings of revolt, forbade them to see one another. Unable to live without each other, they committed suicide at Mayerling, the royal hunting lodge. In the film, the legendary tragedy is told in purely romantic terms, with Boyer and Darrieux dazzling as the doomed lovers. History, however, treats them more skeptically: Rudolph, a liberal, had many enemies at court. His stifled ambitions, his debauchery, and his humiliation of his wife made him almost universally disliked. The beautiful 17-year-old baroness surely knew she was playing with fire. But it is this 1936 film that we all want to believe.

Apart from a brief Hollywood sojourn for the 1938 comedy *The Rage of Paris,* Danielle Darrieux remained in France to become one of its biggest stars, with some attendant scandal about Nazi collaboration during World War II. Boyer, as we know, went on to join Hollywood's greatest.

In 1956, Anatole Litvak remade the story for TV, starring Mel Ferrer and Audrey Hepburn. In 1951, Jean Delannoy directed *The Secret of Mayerling* with Jean Marais and Dominique Blanchar, while in 1968 Omar Sharif and Catherine Deneuve starred in the latest version of the legendary romance that has fascinated people since the turn of the century.

The National Board of Review listed the original *Mayerling* among 1937's best foreign films and cited Danielle Darrieux's performance.

# Men
## (Männer)

★★★★★★★★★★★★★★★★★★★★★★★★★★★★★★★★★★★★★★★★★★★★★★★★

Nationality: West German    Year: 1985 (U.S. release: 1986)
Cast: Heiner Lauterbach, Uwe Oschenknecht, Ulrike Kriener
Director: Doris Dörrie    Running Time: 99 minutes
B/W or Color: Color    Availability: VISTA HOME VIDEO

Julius Armbrust has it made and knows it. He is the creative director at a Munich ad agency, lives in an elegant house with his beautiful, charming wife, Paula, and two lovely children, drives a Maserati sedan, and is enjoying a fitful sexual liaison with one of his office staff. But there is a bruise on this seemingly perfect apple. His wife, he discovers, is having an affair.

Following his initial trauma, Julius moves out of the house, ends his sexual liaison, takes a leave of absence from the agency, and, reversing the usual film roles (in which the wife struggles to regain her erring husband), embarks on a calculated campaign to win Paula back.

On the surface, Men is delightful and amusing; just under the surface, however, it makes some trenchant comments on contemporary life, especially among affluent "yuppies." It suggests, for example, that the relentless demands of a career can desiccate human emotions, impoverish intimate relationships, and reduce people to things.

In sum, this is a multilayered film by a highly talented director with a substantial and impressive mastery of her craft, a director who knows how to pace a film, how to make serious points without being didactic, and how to get fine performances from her actors.

The stunning box-office success of Men has catapulted Dörrie into the front rank of West Germany's post-Fassbinder generation of young directors. The film has become something of a cult for Germans in their twenties or thirties, and astonishing numbers of people have been to see Men several times. "A lot of people say it is a kind of film we haven't had in a long time in Germany—and that may be," says Dörrie.

The National Board of Review named Men one of the year's five best foreign films.

# Mephisto

\* \* \* \* \* \* \* \* \* \* \* \* \* \* \* \* \* \* \* \* \* \* \* \* \* \* \* \* \* \* \* \* \* \* \* \* \* \* \* \* \* \* \* \* \* \* \* \* \* \* \* \* \* \* \*

Nationality: Hungarian          Year: 1981
Cast: Klaus Maria Brandauer, Krystyna Janda, Ildiko Bansagi, Karin Boyd, Rolf Hoppe
Director: Istvan Szabo          Running Time: 144 minutes
B/W or Color: Color          Availability: T.V.S., INC.

**M**ephisto follows the rise of Hendrik Hofgen, whose acting career begins with an obscure, high-minded theater group and culminates in being recognized as Nazi Germany's greatest and most popular star. A stiff price is paid by Hofgen for this recognition—he must renounce his family (they flee Germany), betray his friends, and transcend honor, morality, and politics. Faust-like, the actor sells his soul to the Nazis in return for their insuring his rise to stardom. And Faust-like, in the end he must pay the devil.

The character of Hendrik Hofgen (played by Austrian actor Klaus Maria Brandauer) is based on the life of Gustav Grundgens (1899–1963) from a novel by Thomas Mann's son Klaus Mann, who was both Grundgens's lover as well as his brother-in-law, since the actor was married to Mann's sister Erika. With Goering as his champion, Grundgens's rise to fame paralleled the rise of the Third Reich. (Although written in 1936, Mann's controversial book was not published until 20 years later.) The disintegration of Germany is limned in the character of Grundgens, a mercurial man, at times frenzied and passionate. But the film sidesteps the issue of his homosexuality, involving him instead in a series of explicit liaisons with a beautiful, sensuous black dancer.

Klaus Maria Brandauer was first introduced to U.S. audiences in 1972's *The Salzburg Connection,* but he didn't attract widespread attention here until 1982, when *Mephisto* had its general American release. If you've been charmed by Brandauer in *Out of Africa* (for which he received a Best Supporting Actor's Award from The National Board), the actor's dazzling tour de force acting in *Mephisto* offers still greater proof that he's probably Germany's best actor on stage and screen today.

Hungarian director Istvan Szabo here produces his best movie to date. *Mephisto* won an Oscar for Best Foreign-Language Film and The National Board's D. W. Griffith Award as well.

# Miss Julie
## (Fröken Julie)

**************************************************

Nationality: Swedish        Year: 1950 (U.S. release: 1952)
Cast: Anita Björk, Ulf Palme, Anders Henrikson
Director: Alf Sjöberg        Running Time: 90 minutes
B/W or Color: B/W        Availability: EMBASSY HOME
                                        ENTERTAINMENT

A film of great visual beauty and stunning theatricality, Alf Sjöberg's *Miss Julie* is one of those rare screen adaptations that manages to retain the spirit of its original source while at the same time exposing hidden depths and meanings in pure cinematic terms. In other words, the film is not just an adaptation of a literary work, but an extension of it, making it a totally separate entity from its source material.

The source material in this case is August Strindberg's 1888 stage play, also adapted for the screen by director Sjöberg, which describes the tragic consequences of a sadomasochistic affair between a valet (Ulf Palme) and a count's daughter (Anita Björk). The original play, limited to the kitchen in a great country estate, has been magnificently and logically opened up to take advantage of the outdoor scenes that are only talked about on stage. Sjöberg's strong sense of imagery is especially evident in the flashbacks used to illustrate Miss Julie's and the valet's past. Sjöberg's screenplay permits him to move from one time level to another with ease, so that the past and present are presented in the same frame, making for an interesting conjunction of immediate and previous events. The mingling of living and dead, past and present, creates strong, impressive dramatic effects.

The passionate, tormented performance of Anita Björk matches the power of the screenplay and the physical production each step of the way. Her sensitivity and talent help to create a fascinating and disturbing portrait of a girl torn between her passion and convention. The rest of the performances in *Miss Julie* are as expertly played, down to the smallest role (note 21-year-old Max von Sydow as the groom).

*Miss Julie* remains the masterpiece of director Sjöberg, who was instrumental in the renaissance of Swedish cinema in the Forties and the country's most important director before the advent of Ingmar Bergman.

*(Quality of videotape is exceptional.)*

# The Mission

★★★★★★★★★★★★★★★★★★★★★★★★★★★★★★★★★★★★★★★★★★★★★★★★★★★★★★

**Nationality**: British                   **Year** 1986

**Cast**: Robert De Niro, Jeremy Irons, Ray McAnally, Liam Neeson, Aidan Quinn

**Director**: Roland Joffe          **Running Time**: 124 minutes

**B/W or Color**: Color             **Availability**: WARNER HOME VIDEO

Selected by The National Board as one of its ten best films of 1986, *The Mission* received the Golden Palm at the Cannes Film Festival and was nominated for seven Academy Awards: Best Picture, Director (Roland Joffe), Cinematography (Chris Menges), Editing, Score, Art Direction, and Costumes.

Robert Bolt's screenplay involves church politics and spiritual strength in 1756 South America, centering on two Jesuit priests and their violent reactions when their order, pressured by the governments of Spain and Portugal, decides to close the mission that has been established among the Guarani Indian tribe. The priests vow to keep the mission open.

Father Gabriel (Jeremy Irons) abhors violence and refuses to fight, while Father Mendoza (Robert De Niro), a former slave trader, reverts to his mercenary ways to lead a vastly outnumbered group of Indians.

In his *New York Times* review, Vincent Canby wondered if audiences would recognize the "parallels between the 18th century and the late 20th century, when many priests in Latin America have also found themselves at odds with Rome."

*The Mission* was the second feature directed by Joffe, who received a 1984 Oscar nomination as Best Director for his initial film, *The Killing Fields*.

Joffe encountered difficulties in selecting the 300 extras needed for the film. "We looked for a tribe who had met missionaries," he explained, "but still had its own tribal history intact." In Colombia, he found the Waunana tribe, most of whom had never seen a car or a photograph. "I told them the story of the film. They understood it immediately. They asked me how people in these stories prepared. I said that they train. They said, 'Then we must train, because we want to do it well.' They got to a point where they would direct themselves."

A standout performance as the papal legate is given by Ray McAnally. When told of the slaughter that has occurred, he objects to the conclusion that "the world is thus." "No . . . ," he answers, "thus have we made the world. Thus have I made it."

# Mr. Hulot's Holiday
## (Les Vacances de Monsieur Hulot)

\* \* \* \* \* \* \* \* \* \* \* \* \* \* \* \* \* \* \* \* \* \* \* \* \* \* \* \* \* \* \* \* \* \* \* \* \* \* \* \* \* \* \* \* \* \* \* \* \* \* \*

Nationality: French        Year: 1953

Cast: Jacques Tati, Nathalie Pascaud, Louis Perrault, André Dubois

Director: Jacques Tati       Running Time: 96 minutes

B/W or Color: B/W        Availability: EMBASSY HOME ENTERTAINMENT

C hug-along, chug-along," says the little shabby car: Mr. Hulot is on his way to a hotel at St. Marc-sur-Mer for his holiday. He not only succeeds in getting there, but manages immediately and unintentionally to liven things up for his fellow guests and the hotel staff. Tall, slightly stooped, with a characteristic bouncing walk, looking rather like a middle-grade civil servant, his every move spells calamity.

Apart from a superb talent for mime, Jacques Tati does nothing overtly humorous; he is just simply funny. He leaves a door open, and a sudden gust of wind blows everything around a room; he plays Ping-Pong and somehow turns the chairs around so that two bridge players end up at different tables; his flat tire becomes covered in leaves and is taken for a funeral wreath. Trying, as always, to be helpful, Hulot manages to shut an acquaintance in the rumble seat of a car. Mr. Hulot well deserved his place on The National Board of Review's 1954 Best Foreign Film list.

Jacques Tati studied art to follow in the footsteps of his father as a picture restorer, but he became more interested in sport, playing rugby for Paris's top team. He then turned to the music hall, making his name in pantomime.

It was after his war service that Tati started making movies: short films on sporty subjects. Then, in 1947, his first feature established his comic genius—the hilarious *Jour de Fête,* in which he played a country postman inspired by the American mailman's slogan "Neither snow, nor rain, nor heat, nor gloom of night stays these couriers from the swift completion of their appointed rounds." The ensuing adventures and misadventures could have been conjured up only by Tati. His talent is truly in the great comic tradition of Charlie Chaplin and Buster Keaton.

# Mona Lisa

\* \* \* \* \* \* \* \* \* \* \* \* \* \* \* \* \* \* \* \* \* \* \* \* \* \* \* \* \* \* \* \* \* \* \* \* \* \* \* \* \* \* \* \* \* \* \* \* \* \* \* \* \*

**Nationality**: British          **Year**: 1986

**Cast**: Bob Hoskins, Cathy Tyson, Michael Caine, Clarke Peters, Kate Hardie

**Director**: Neil Jordan          **Running Time**: 110 Minutes

**B/W *or* Color**: Color          **Availability**: HBO/CANNON VIDEO

The seamy side of London is brilliantly photographed by Roger Platt in this movie chronicling the viciousness of men who control the "working girls." But the film is also arresting on many other levels, particularly in the well-drawn characters and their motivations—above all, the naive George. Writer-director Neil Jordan created this role especially for the remarkable actor Bob Hoskins, who won Best Actor awards from the New York and Los Angeles film critics and the Cannes Film Festival. He is on screen in every sequence, and he is magnificent.

George is a no-account small-time crook who combines the sweet innocence of a William Bendix with the cheeky gangster of a James Cagney. On returning from prison he is lost and bewildered when his wife slams the door in his face, refusing to let him speak to their 15-year-old daughter. Disconsolate, he bunks down with an old cockney friend who takes life as it comes and doesn't bother anyone, unlike the pernicious Mortwell (Michael Caine), who oozes manipulative power as the czar of London's underworld.

As a sop to George for having taken the fall for him, Mortwell throws him the job of driving for and protecting one of his call girls, the breathtakingly beautiful Simone (Cathy Tyson), a tough lady, intense, intelligent, and with no illusions about her life. The relationship between George and Simone is ambivalent, but one thing they do share is a fear and hatred for Mortwell. When Simone asks George to look for her friend who has disappeared from the streets, he agrees to search the places Simone can't or wouldn't dare to enter. George isn't very bright, but he's true to his own standards. Looking for the young girl, his heart aches for his own daughter, and his quest through Soho's sordid sex-for-sale shops disgusts him. Although the climax pits George against Mortwell, he never understands what's really taken place or the extent to which he's been used.

# Monika

## (Sommaren med Monika/Summer with Monika)

\* \* \* \* \* \* \* \* \* \* \* \* \* \* \* \* \* \* \* \* \* \* \* \* \* \* \* \* \* \* \* \* \* \* \* \* \* \* \* \* \* \* \* \* \* \* \* \* \* \* \* \*

**Nationality**: Swedish      **Year**: 1953 (U.S. release: 1959)
**Cast**: Harriet Andersson, Lars Ekborg, John Harryson, Ake Fridell
**Director**: Ingmar Bergman      **Running Time**: 97 minutes
**B/W or Color**: B/W      **Availability**: TV only

A product of Ingmar Bergman's early "middle period," *Monika* faced censorship problems in the early Fifties because of a nude bathing scene that was quite integral to the plot about the birth and death of a young love. A nice boy named Harry (Lars Ekborg) unwisely falls in love with—and makes pregnant—a young tramp during the course of a summer island idyll. Monika (Harriet Andersson) is as restless, defiant of her parents, and disdainful of social conventions at the film's opening as she is at its close. Her lover willingly shoulders the responsibilities of premature marriage and fatherhood, but Monika isn't ready for that herself, and she willfully walks out on domesticity to face an uncertain life of her own choice. At fadeout, she's seated in a sleazy dive, staring brazenly into the camera in a manner that tells us her future will only be more of her past.

At 19, the sensuous and striking Harriet Andersson was already a veteran of some ten movies when an infatuated Bergman selected her for the title role in his bittersweet tale of misguided adolescence. In her director's words, Andersson "was devastating. We were all stuck on her. There's never been a girl in Swedish films who radiated more uninhibited erotic charm than Harriet." And the critics seemed to agree: Britain's *Monthly Film Bulletin* called her Monika, "a portrait as vivid as it is uncompromisingly real"; *Variety* said, "Miss Andersson emerges as a sultry, dynamic find as she firmly outlines the character and instability of Monika, the creature of a summer."

Most of *Monika* was shot with a small cast and crew on the island of Ornö in the Stockholm archipelago during August 1952. Due to a tiny budget, much of the production was improvised, and since cinematographer Gunnar Fischer had only one silent Mitchell camera, dialogue and sound effects had to be post-dubbed. But the results were rewarding, and Bergman later admitted to an interviewer, "It's close to my heart and one of my films I'm always happy to see again."

# Monty Python and the Holy Grail

★★★★★★★★★★★★★★★★★★★★★★★★★★★★★★★★★★★★★★★★★★★★★★★★★★★★★★

**Nationality**: British          **Year**: 1975

**Cast**: Monty Python's Flying Circus (Graham Chapman, John Cleese, Terry Gilliam, Eric Idle, Terry Jones, Michael Palin)

**Director**: Terry Gilliam and          **Running Time**: 90 minutes
Terry Jones

**B/W or Color**: Color          **Availability**: RCA/COLUMBIA PIC-
TURES HOME VIDEO

Having achieved international fame and acclaim in the early Seventies for their perennially popular BBC TV comedy series, it seemed perfectly reasonable for the Pythonites "official" feature debut to be a merciless satirical assault on their homeland's most revered historical legend. The theatrically distributed *And Now for Something Completely Different* (1972) had been merely a warm-up exercise, stringing together a surefire barrage of their most celebrated television sketches (many of which were already considered classics).

This time the talented writer-performers, with careful and irreverent attention paid to myth and history, have forced themselves to contend with a monumental story and theme—and managed to remain true to their unbound, scattershot form in spite of it. The movie is not nearly so much a sendup of fable, literature, history, or movies as it is a rich, well-conceived environment for the team of collaborators to let loose their trademark of free-association humor. Python-type comedy perhaps works best under these conditions, as in their more recent *Life of Brian* (1979) and *The Meaning of Life* (1983).

Ostensibly concerned with King Arthur (Graham Chapman), his equally dense and incompetent cadre of knights, and their quest for the biblical Holy Grail, story and plot are secondary matters. What keeps things humming, providing the real structure, is the never-ending parade of running gags and inspired vignettes, all brilliantly conceived within themselves. The original, longer screenplay suggests that an even more disjointed film was initially planned.

The whimsically outrageous expedition's nonsense logic, sick sight gags, and cartoon animation are effectively bolstered by an unexpectedly grim and realistic re-creation of Dark Ages existence. An especially impressive achievement, in light of the production's reputed cost of less than half a million dollars!

# Moonlighting

* * * * * * * * * * * * * * * * * * * * * * * * * * * * * * * * * * * * * * * * * * * * * * * *

*Nationality*: British          *Year*: 1982

*Cast*: Jeremy Irons, Eugene Lipinski, Jiri Stanislaw, Eugeniusz Hacz-kiewicz

*Director*: Jerzy Skolimowski          *Running Time*: 97 minutes

*B/W or Color*: Color          *Availability*: MCA HOME VIDEO

Moonlighting takes place in London, where three Polish laborers and their English-speaking foreman Nowak (Jeremy Irons) are working illegally on a visa over the Christmas holidays to renovate the London house of a compatriot referred to only as "the Boss." Nowak has chosen his men because he believes them to be stupid—the traditional butt of Polish jokes. He begins to suspect that "the Boss" may think the same of him. He alone learns of the military coup attempting to destroy the Solidarity movement. All ties to home suspended, there is no "boss" to answer to any longer, only himself. He keeps his fellow countrymen in the dark. He systematically begins to abuse his power until the crew is living under virtual house arrest. His actions become increasingly compulsive and alienating, but "the Boss" will have his London refuge if he ever gets out of Poland.

Anyone equating Nowak's actions with the repressive measures of the Polish regime would, of course, be correct, but the film ultimately depicts an authoritarian personality that is not solely the province of Soviet bloc nations. Indeed, much of the film's strength lies in its refusal to make any simple, polemical statement, and a synopsis of the plot must fail to convey how comic, trenchant, and unpredictable *Moonlighting* really is.

At the center of this anxious managerial farce is Jeremy Irons's compelling performance as Nowak. He is by turns naive, desperate, bold, double-dealing, and sympathetic. Irons reveals a wider emotional range and versatility than audiences have seen to date.

The film was awarded a prize at Cannes for Best Screenplay.

# Morgan!
## (Morgan—A Suitable Case for Treatment)

★ ★ ★ ★ ★ ★ ★ ★ ★ ★ ★ ★ ★ ★ ★ ★ ★ ★ ★ ★ ★ ★ ★ ★ ★ ★ ★ ★ ★ ★ ★ ★ ★ ★ ★ ★ ★ ★ ★ ★ ★ ★ ★ ★ ★ ★

**Nationality**: British        **Year**: 1966
**Cast**: David Warner, Vanessa Redgrave, Robert Stephens, Irene Handl
**Director**: Karel Reisz        **Running Time**: 97 minutes
**B/W or Color**: B/W        **Availability**: THORN/EMI-
                                          HBO VIDEO

**M**organ! burst upon the Sixties celluloid world just as America's counterculture was coming of age in the real one. At a time when the antiheroes of John Osborne and Kingsley Amis were popular, this David Mercer script (from his TV play) featured a misfit named Morgan Delt (David Warner), a slightly loony Bohemian artist (he collects simian artifacts and paints gorilla pictures) whose appeal was immediate, especially to collegiate audiences. Critic John Simon called *Morgan!* "the first underground movie made above ground."

A lovable but pathetic rebel, Morgan escapes his own miserable world by fantasizing a happy existence in the jungle. Despite his primitive powers and often charming brashness, his up-to-now pliant, loyal wife, Leonie (Vanessa Redgrave), divorces him for his art dealer, Napier (Robert Stephens). Leonie's taking another mate really sends Morgan round the bend. The "gifted idiot" resorts to fiendish games. Setting a detonator under his ex-wife's bed, in the malicious hope it will explode when she and her lover lie down, he then forces her to go to a Welsh farm where he plays Tarzan and his Mate. Finally, in a gloriously madcap scene that, as late as 1986, was still being "aped" (the German film *Men* and an early episode of TV's *L.A. Law*), Morgan crashes Leonie's wedding to Napier wearing a gorilla suit, a chest-thumping King Kong run totally amok.

Lanky, Royal Shakespearean actor David Warner, whose only prior film was *Tom Jones,* is perfectly cast as the "beatnik with a broken heart" (*New York Times*), and Vanessa Redgrave received an Academy Award nomination. The film is hilariously funny, but it is more than just a fast-paced farce. Beneath its rollicking absurdities is rich satire that probes in an entertainingly fresh and moving manner some of the sadder truths of the times.

# Moulin Rouge

★★★★★★★★★★★★★★★★★★★★★★★★★★★★★★★★★★★★★★★★★★★★★★★★★★★★★★★

**Nationality**: British          **Year**: 1952

**Cast**: José Ferrer, Colette Marchand, Suzanne Flon, Zsa Zsa Gabor, Katherine Kath, Muriel Smith

**Director**: John Huston          **Running Time**: 119 minutes

**B/W or Color**: Color          **Availability**: TV only

One of The National Board's five best foreign films of 1953, *Moulin Rouge* is the colorful, fictionalized biography of the diminutive French artist Henri de Toulouse-Lautrec, who died in 1901 at age 36.

Based on a novel by Pierre LaMure, the screenplay was written by Anthony Veiller and director John Huston. Unaware that José Ferrer had optioned the novel for a stage production, Huston called him to offer him the lead in the proposed film. "It's very hard to nonplus John Huston," claims Ferrer, "but I did, when I told him I owned the movie rights."

To reduce his height, Ferrer walked on specially made shoes attached to his knees. "People ask, 'How did you make yourself short?' " says Ferrer. "Before I can answer, most of them say, 'Trick photography, right?' "

Zsa Zsa Gabor plays Jane Avril, the inspiration for the artist's most famous poster. Her singing of the movie's theme (which became very popular) was dubbed by Muriel Smith, star of Broadway's *Carmen Jones*, who appears as one of the star dancers at the Moulin Rouge.

Huston made the crippling fall that Toulouse-Lautrec suffered as a child more dramatic by having it occur on a staircase instead of the true-life fall from a chair.

Of its seven Academy Award nominations, there were two wins: Costumes and Art Direction. Ferrer, who also appears as the artist's father, lost to Gary Cooper (*High Noon*), Huston to John Ford (*The Quiet Man*), Colette Marchand as Best Supporting Actress to Gloria Grahame (*The Bad and the Beautiful*), and the picture itself to *The Greatest Show on Earth*.

In small roles future notables Jill Bennett, Peter Cushing, and Theodore Bikel can be glimpsed.

Oswald Morris's cinematography cleverly interpreted Huston's idea that the film itself should resemble a Toulouse-Lautrec painting.

# The Mouse That Roared

**✶✶✶✶✶✶✶✶✶✶✶✶✶✶✶✶✶✶✶✶✶✶✶✶✶✶✶✶✶✶✶✶✶✶✶✶✶✶✶✶✶✶✶✶✶✶✶✶✶✶✶✶✶✶**

*Nationality*: British               *Year*: 1959

*Cast*: Peter Sellers, Jean Seberg, David Kossoff, William Hartnell, Timothy Bateson, Leo McKern

*Director*: Jack Arnold               *Running Time*: 83 minutes (90 minutes in Britain)

*B/W or Color*: Color               *Availability*: RCA/COLUMBIA PICTURES

Before *Dr. Strangelove* there was *The Mouse That Roared*. Peter Sellers, who played three roles in each film, dealt with the apocalypse in the later movie and matters of state in the earlier. Both deal with the bomb. In the sunnier and more good humored *Mouse*, it's the Q bomb that causes the excitement. For the first time, Sellers was a star on his own, no longer supporting other comics or vying for attention as a member of the Crazy Gang. His agreeable funning made him an international star and led to many comic triumphs. Here, the ripe talent undertakes three roles in emulation of his former co-star Alec Guinness; naturally, he plays a woman in one. The much-maligned Jean Seberg showed a reasonable flair for comedy, which would be underutilized throughout most of her career. Also new to comedy was director Jack Arnold, who later embraced the genre. At the time, he was best known for the existential science-fiction classic *The Incredible Shrinking Man* (1957).

The tiny duchy of Grand Fenwick faces ruin because its entire economy is based upon the export of a wine to the United States, and a cheap imitation is being marketed. The prime minister convinces Grand Duchess Gloriana that the only solution is to declare war on the United States and then enjoy the benefits this country always bestows upon a defeated nation. However, Field Marshal Bascombe manages to win by capturing the dreaded Q bomb, its inventor, David Kossoff, and daughter Jean Seberg. Grand Fenwick is thus able to dictate to the mighty American nation. Sellers is Bascombe, Gloriana, and the minister. Nothing is sacred. "The Colonel Bogey March" is heard to mock militarism, and Columbia's logo-lady is frightened by a mouse before the main credits. Leonard Wibberley's novel, with a screenplay by Roger MacDougall and Stanley Mann, focuses on the very real problem of the bomb. Small countries have the least to gain from the nuclear race, so why shouldn't they have the balance of power? This well-received import inspired a sequel. None of the same hands got together on *Mouse on the Moon* (1963), which spoofed the space race.

# Murder at the Gallop

\* \* \* \* \* \* \* \* \* \* \* \* \* \* \* \* \* \* \* \* \* \* \* \* \* \* \* \* \* \* \* \* \* \* \* \* \* \* \* \* \* \* \* \* \* \* \* \* \* \* \* \* \* \* \*

*Nationality*: British          *Year*: 1963
*Cast*: Margaret Rutherford, Robert Morley, Flora Robson, Charles Ting-
well, Stringer Davis
*Director*: George Pollock          *Running Time*: 81 minutes
*B/W or Color*: B/W          *Availability*: TV only

N one of Margaret Rutherford's variably amusing Miss Marple mys-
tery-comedies has, to date, appeared on videocassette. Nor have
they been seen on TV with any regularity. Perhaps the time has come for
a new generation to discover the joys of watching this inimitable English
character actress in her late prime. After a lifetime of unforgettable performances on stage and screen, Rutherford first assayed this beloved Agatha Christie heroine in 1961's *Murder, She Said*, a delightful movie whose
popularity quickly spawned *Murder at the Gallop, Murder Most Foul*,
and *Murder Ahoy*, produced when their robust star was in her late sixties
and early seventies. The first film in the series was good, but *Murder at
the Gallop* was by far the best. Not only was its script (based on Christie's novel *After the Funeral*) the cleverest, but, with Robert Morley as
her co-star and Flora Robson in support, Rutherford was on her scene-
stealing mettle. Purists complain that the beloved, blustering Rutherford
was hardly Christie's concept of amateur sleuth Jane Marple, either in
face, form, or personality (with Helen Hayes's several TV impersonations
of that lady perhaps ringing truer to her literary counterpart). But to a
host of moviegoers everywhere, Margaret Rutherford and Miss Marple
will always remain synonymous.

*Murder at the Gallop*'s main setting is a rather sinister country inn,
where murder threatens to eliminate the heirs to the estate of an elderly
recluse, who fell—or was pushed—to his death. In delightful fashion,
Jane Marple quite expectedly busybodies herself into the midst of the
mystery, at one point trading in her signature tweed cape for a riding
habit, and even venturing to dance the Twist. And, as usual, Rutherford's
real-life husband, Stringer Davis, puts in a few fussy appearances as Miss
Marple's neighborhood friend "Mr. Stringer."

In reviewing this film, *Time* magazine called Margaret Rutherford,
"possibly the funniest woman alive" and likened her to "an earnest rhi-
noceros." *Murder at the Gallop* might be difficult to locate, but it's well
worth the hunt.

# Murder on the Orient Express

★★★★★★★★★★★★★★★★★★★★★★★★★★★★★★★★★★★★★★★★★★★★★★★★★★★★★

*Nationality*: British          *Year*: 1974

*Cast*: Albert Finney, Lauren Bacall, Ingrid Bergman, Sean Connery, John Gielgud, Richard Widmark

*Director*: Sidney Lumet          *Running Time*: 127 minutes

*B/W or Color*: Color          *Availability*: PARAMOUNT HOME VIDEO

Placing second on The National Board's ten best list for 1974, *Murder on the Orient Express* received six Oscar nominations: Best Actor (Albert Finney), Best Supporting Actress (Ingrid Bergman), Screenplay, Cinematography, Score, and Costumes. Bergman won the Academy Award (her third), but graciously remarked that it should have gone to Valentina Cortese in *Day for Night*. (Due to a ridiculous ruling, Cortese's splendid performance was nominated the year *after* that picture had won the Oscar as Best Foreign Film.)

Finney played Agatha Christie's Belgian detective Hercule Poirot, who solves a complicated murder aboard a snowbound train. The victim (Richard Widmark) was an American millionaire named Ratchett, despised by all. Poirot must use his "little gray cells" to find the guilty party. It could have been almost any of the passengers: wealthy American Lauren Bacall, Swedish missionary Ingrid Bergman, a count and countess (Michael York and Jacqueline Bisset), a princess (Wendy Hiller) and her maid (Rachel Roberts), a British colonel (Sean Connery, escaping his James Bond image), a teacher (Vanessa Redgrave), the millionaire's secretary (Anthony Perkins), or his valet (John Gielgud). The glamorous train is cluttered with suspects and clues.

Writing in *Films in Review*, Marcia Magill called the picture "a love letter to . . . the detective story." She termed Paul Dehn's screenplay "clever and true to Agatha Christie's ingenious mystery skills," observing that "the sets and way of life in Europe of the Thirties are a nostalgic tribute to a lovely, lost existence none of us, sadly, will ever know again."

Christie had earlier withheld permission for the 1934 novel to be filmed, "Dame Agatha needn't have worried," noted Magill, who concluded, "Sidney Lumet's direction is crisp and knowledgeable."

The British Film Academy named Ingrid Bergman the year's Best Supporting Actress, John Gielgud Best Supporting Actor, and gave Richard Rodney Bennett the Anthony Asquith Award for his mischievous *Murder on the Orient Express* score.

# Murmur of the Heart
## (Le Souffle au Coeur)

\* \* \* \* \* \* \* \* \* \* \* \* \* \* \* \* \* \* \* \* \* \* \* \* \* \* \* \* \* \* \* \* \* \* \* \* \* \* \* \* \* \* \* \* \* \* \* \* \* \* \* \* \* \* \*

*Nationality*: French                    *Year*: 1972

*Cast*: Lea Massari, Benoit Ferreaux, Daniel Gelin, Marc Winocourt, Michel Lonsdale

*Director*: Louis Malle          *Running Time*: 118 minutes

*B/W or Color*: Color          *Availability*: TV only

Set in Dijon, France, in 1954, *Murmur of the Heart* deals with incest—in an intelligent, affectionate, even comic way.

An autobiographical film (*Le Souffle au Coeur*), it was written and directed by Louis Malle, whose original screenplay earned him an Academy Award nomination.

In his *New York Times* review, Vincent Canby described the film as "a beautifully detailed movie about growing up." Critic Judith Crist found the performances "sheer perfection" and commented, "Their work . . . is not for the lover of the lurid or the erotic. It is for the lover of humans."

A sensitive, precocious 14-year-old boy (Benoit Ferreaux) lives with his overprotective Italian mother (Lea Massari), his gynecologist father (Daniel Gelin), and two older, taunting brothers (Marc Winocourt and Fabien Ferreaux—Benoit's real-life brother). A jazz enthusiast who writes essays about Camus and suicide, his growing concern is his burdensome virginity and how to lose it.

An attack of scarlatina sends him to a health resort in his mother's charge. There he flirts with girls and discovers that his mother has a lover, a fact that he promises to keep secret. When a woman regards him as "my poor little thing," he is quick to reply: "Madam, I am neither poor, nor particularly little. And I'm certainly not yours."

The encounter between mother and son is tastefully handled and seemingly frees the boy from Oedipal urges. He then has an experience with a girl his own age, thereby feeling able to take his place alongside his father and brothers when they pay a surprise visit the next morning.

Benoit Ferreaux was chosen from 300 schoolboys auditioned for the part. *Murmur* marked Louis Malle's return to commercial films after making a documentary. His first American film, *Pretty Baby* (1978), would depict yet another adult-child relationship.

# My Beautiful Laundrette

\* \* \* \* \* \* \* \* \* \* \* \* \* \* \* \* \* \* \* \* \* \* \* \* \* \* \* \* \* \* \* \* \* \* \* \* \* \* \* \* \* \* \* \* \* \* \* \* \* \* \* \* \*

**Nationality**: British          **Year**: 1985 (U.S. release: 1986)

**Cast**: Gordon Warnecke, Daniel Day Lewis, Saeed Jaffrey, Roshan Seth, Shirley Anne Field

**Director**: Stephen Frears        **Running Time**: 93 minutes (97 minutes in Britain)

**B/W or Color**: Color          **Availability**: KARL/LORIMAR HOME VIDEO

**M**y *Beautiful Laundrette* is one of the finest films of recent years and surely one of the most unexpectedly successful. Shot in 16mm for British TV on a budget of $900,000 with a largely Pakistani cast, a swift 90-minute running time, and a seriocomic plot revolving around a gay Pakistani and a laundromat, *Laundrette* hardly seems a good bet for hit status. But a hit it is.

Directed by Stephen Frears, who was responsible for Albert Finney's widely acclaimed *Gumshoe* (1971) and *The Hit* (1984) plus two dozen TV films in between, *Laundrette* first attracted attention at the Edinburgh Film Festival. It went on to wow 'em at the Miami Film Festival, was voted most popular film at the Rotterdam Festival, best film of the year by the *London Evening Standard* newspaper, and on and on. At its most basic, *Laundrette* is an outrageously original look at Pakistanis in contemporary London. Yet it's hardly what you'd expect of a film dealing with minorities in an established society. There's no preying on the little guy here. Indeed, it's more the other way round. When we first meet Omar (Gordon Warnecke), he's a decent, devoted young son in need of a job. His alcoholic father (Roshan Seth) sets in motion a sort of Paki "networking." Omar reacquaints himself with an old school friend, Johnny (Daniel Day Lewis). They have little in common except they love each other. Before you know it, they're rehabilitating a slum laundromat into a glitzy discotheque gathering place called Powders.

*My Beautiful Laundrette* is as tough as it is tender. It's as sharply witty as it is warmly wacky. And it's every bit as contemporary as it is classically good, old-fashioned, feel-good filmmaking. The National Board singled out Daniel Day Lewis as the year's Best Supporting Actor and listed the film among its ten best.

# My Brilliant Career

★ ★ ★ ★ ★ ★ ★ ★ ★ ★ ★ ★ ★ ★ ★ ★ ★ ★ ★ ★ ★ ★ ★ ★ ★ ★ ★ ★ ★ ★ ★ ★ ★ ★ ★ ★ ★ ★ ★ ★ ★ ★ ★ ★ ★ ★ ★ ★ ★ ★ ★ ★ ★

*Nationality*: Australian       *Year*: 1979 (U.S. release: 1980)

*Cast*: Judy Davis, Sam Neill, Wendy Hughes, Robert Grubb, Alan Hopgood, Julia Blake

*Director*: Gillian Armstrong       *Running Time*: 101 minutes

*B/W or Color*: Color       *Availability*: VESTRON VIDEO

Directed by Gillian Armstrong from a screenplay by Eleanor Whitcombe, *My Brilliant Career* was in turn based on a semiautobiographical novel published in 1901. The author was 16 years old at the time she wrote the book: it took her just weeks to finish, but five years to find a publisher.

Judy Davis plays the young girl Sybylla as brilliantly as the title demands. She has been raised in poverty on a farm resembling that of a poor sharecropper in the American South, actually the Australian Outback. Her mother married for love far beneath her original status. Sybylla is restless and dreamy, inept and ambitious—and homely. Not knowing what else to do with her, her parents send her to live with her wealthy grandmother. There she acquires beautiful new clothes and a certain amount of polish, but loses not a whit of her tomboyish spontaneity. She flirts with the town's most eligible bachelor (Sam Neill), wins his heart, then refuses his proposal of marriage; she wants to devote herself to her writing career.

This well-constructed, charming evocation of a bygone era is lovely to watch. The thought of a woman's turning down the man she obviously loves in order to pursue her dream of writing—as though the two were incompatible—seems farfetched today, but Sybylla had the example of her own family. So to Sybylla's friends and relations her act of renunciation represents something in the nature of a revolution.

# My Life to Live

## (Vivre Sa Vie)

*************************************************************

Nationality: French       Year: 1962 (U.S. release: 1963)

Cast: Anna Karina, Saddy Rebbot, Brice Parain, André Labarthe

Director: Jean-Luc Godard       Running Time: 82 minutes (85 minutes in France)

B/W or Color: B/W       Availability: TV Only

D ivided into 15 segments, this story of the rise and fall of a Parisian call girl was intended to be a detached, sociological analysis. But writer-director Jean-Luc Godard's emotions and artistry got in the way, creating a rigorous, moody tribute to the actress who plays the lead part, Anna Karina, his wife at the time. With baleful eyes and a Louise Brooks haircut, Karina, the star of eight Godard films, brings a Brechtian aspect of self-portraiture to *My Life to Live*. The theme of prostitution as capitalism's designated social role for women is expanded by Karina's presence into an illustration of the exploitation inherent in the filmmaking collaboration between a director and actress. The film was also a major influence on Jane Fonda's work with Alan Pakula in *Klute*.

Karina's character is named Nana—an anagram of her own name as well as a reference to Zola's heroine and Jean Renoir's 1928 silent film starring his own wife, Catherine Hessling. Godard researches the ideology behind the objectification of women. Nana turns to prostitution after failing to support herself as a shop girl. The pathos of her exploitation by men comes through despite Godard's insistent attempts to put a cold, formal structure between himself and his wife. Godard's own regard for Karina breaks through in two memorable sequences: when Nana goes to the movies and her tears are intercut with the on-screen tears of Falconetti as Carl Dreyer's Joan of Arc; later, as Nana listens to a reading of Poe's "The Oval Portrait" Godard himself breaks in on the soundtrack to interject, "This is our story Anna; the artist painting a picture of his wife." This autobiographical moment is one of the most startling examples of how Godard transcended the typical boundaries of film. Karina herself transcends her other screen appearances with the quiet poignancy of her acting here. Raoul Coutard's sharply contrasting black-and-white photography is a ravishing asset.

# My Name Is Ivan
## *(Ivan's Childhood/Ivanovo Detstvo)*

★★★★★★★★★★★★★★★★★★★★★★★★★★★★★★★★★★★★★★★★★★★★★★★★★

*Nationality*: Russian                     *Year*: 1963
*Cast*: Kolya Burlaiev, Valentin Zubkov, Y. Zharikov, S. Krylov
*Director*: Andrei Tarkovsky          *Running Time*: 84 minutes
*B/W or Color*: B/W                      *Availability*: TV only

In the Soviet Union, the name Ivan is equivalent to John, and, as in the West, it is an extremely popular name. This film is about a 12-year-old Ivan, an orphan who served as a scout for the Red Army during World War II. His job was to slip behind the German lines, spy on the despised enemy, and bring back information to his own people.

Through impressionistic, symbolic images, director Andrei Tarkovsky shows us the boy's bright early life with his mother, then her death and the boy's hopeless involvement in a war that has destroyed his childhood. The film vividly illustrates the profound effect of war on children, and that impact is powerfully seen because it is crystallized through Ivan's eyes. Played with great sensitivity by Kolya Burlaiev, young Ivan upstages the entire cast, although all are convincing and believable. Ivan's private motivation for spying, having little to do with patriotism, is to avenge the death of his adored mother and sister, and we are made to feel all the more keenly the loneliness of the stricken boy.

Two interesting notes about *My Name Is Ivan:* one, the use of Christian symbolism—a rising sun behind an iron cross—and two, the epilogue with its plea for peace. Since any film from the Soviet Union serves as a window on that country's collective conscious or unconscious mind, this Russian motion picture about the effect of the war on its Ivans moves us with its universal concern.

# My Uncle
## (Mon Oncle)

\* \* \* \* \* \* \* \* \* \* \* \* \* \* \* \* \* \* \* \* \* \* \* \* \* \* \* \* \* \* \* \* \* \* \* \* \* \* \* \* \* \* \* \* \* \* \* \* \* \* \* \* \* \*

Nationality: French                    Year: 1958
Cast: Jacques Tati, Jean-Pierre Zola, Adrienne Servantie, Alain Becourt
Director: Jacques Tati               Running Time: 116 minutes
B/W or Color: Color                 Availability: Public Domain

The late, great, incomparable and irreplaceable Jacques Tati made only five feature films in his career as writer-director-actor, but each one is a gem. His sense of humor is unique; his delicate touch unmatched in French comedy; and in 1958 My Uncle (Tati's third movie) was voted Best Foreign Film by the New York Film Critics and The National Board.

Here, Tati is again Mr. Hulot (of Mr. Hulot's Holiday), at home in his small-town attic apartment overlooking the village square where the greengrocer sells produce from his van; the street cleaner leans on his broom, buttonholing every passerby like a Gallic Ancient Mariner to expound his views on the news of the day; and there stands the local bar, where Hulot receives his phone calls.

All this is in stark contrast to his sister's home—and stark is the word for this ultramodern house, with its minimal furniture, hygienic kitchen (where nothing is touched by hand yet nevertheless is sprayed regularly for possible microbes), and where Hulot's young nephew is not allowed to get anything dirty or have a spot on his clothes. Everything here is absolutely symmetrical, and the trees in the garden are not permitted to shed their leaves. The prized, upright fish fountain in the exact middle of the garden is turned on only when guests arrive.

Shabby, easygoing Hulot gets along well with his nephew, his natural awkwardness finding an equal level with the child's gawkiness. They have fun together, while Hulot tolerates the youngster's pranks. But when Hulot works briefly in his brother-in-law's plastics factory, nothing goes quite right—with the hose tubing somehow coming out like link sausages.

This lovable, lanky clown lifts his umbrella, puts on his raincoat, pivots around on his long legs, and marvelous things happen: inanimate objects take on lives of their own, and, oblivious, he walks smilingly away from the chaos he has left behind.

# The Naked Night
## (Sawdust and Tinsel/Gycklarnas Afton)

\* \* \* \* \* \* \* \* \* \* \* \* \* \* \* \* \* \* \* \* \* \* \* \* \* \* \* \* \* \* \* \* \* \* \* \* \* \* \* \* \* \* \* \* \* \* \* \* \*

Nationality: Swedish                 Year: 1953 (U.S. release: 1956)

Cast: Harriet Andersson, Ake Grönberg, Hasse Ekman, Gudrun Brost, Anders Ek, Gunnar Björnstrand

Director: Ingmar Bergman           Running Time: 92 minutes

B/W or Color: B/W                  Availability: EMBASSY HOME
                                   ENTERTAINMENT

I ngmar Bergman's *The Naked Night* represented a turning point for his career. A flop in its own country, the film caught on with international critics, who took notice that a challenging and occasionally brilliant new artist was at work in Sweden. Though he had made a dozen films from 1946 to 1952, *The Naked Night* seemed to indicate a new direction, both in theme and style. Whereas the early works were invariably seminaturalistic studies of young lovers at odds with an insensitive world, portrayed in a realistic yet poetic manner, this new film took a sharply pessimistic and dark tone in its allegorical tale of a traveling circus troupe, complete with twisted sexual dynamics.

The look of the picture is also startling in its extreme degree of almost expressionistic stylization. Bergman once said, "I just want you to look at the human face. The actor's most beautiful means of expression is his look." Indeed, one is struck by the remarkable amount of extreme close-ups of faces, juxtaposed with tilted long shots. The characters often enter a scene deep in the frame and move forward, directly up to the camera, stopping only inches away from the lens. In this respect, and others, the photography of Hilding Bladh, Göran Strindberg, and Sven Nykvist is innovative and peerless throughout. In terms of pure technique, this must undoubtedly rate among the most imaginative and artistically accomplished black-and-white films ever made.

Much of the action takes place outdoors, and another dominant aspect of the story is the way water and rain, and the landscape itself, are used to point up the feelings and relationships of the characters.

Finnish director Jorn Donner's assessment is correct, that "in terms of sheer competence, Bergman has not advanced from *The Naked Night*. It belongs among the rare films that continue to grow, to live with the spectator."

(*The Embassy cassette is subtitled and offered under the title* Sawdust and Tinsel.)

# Never on Sunday
## (Pote tin Kyriaki)

\* \* \* \* \* \* \* \* \* \* \* \* \* \* \* \* \* \* \* \* \* \* \* \* \* \* \* \* \* \* \* \* \* \* \* \* \* \* \* \* \* \* \* \* \* \* \* \* \* \* \* \* \* \*

*Nationality*: Greek                    *Year*: 1960
*Cast*: Melina Mercouri, Jules Dassin, Georges Foundas, Titos Vandis, Mitsos Liguisos, Despo Diamantidou
*Director*: Jules Dassin              *Running Time*: 91 minutes
*B/W or Color*: B/W                   *Availability*: MGM/UA HOME VIDEO

Lines of dancers stamp like elephants. *Ouzo* is gulped neat as the cash register rings up the score. Here, in this Greek café, are gathered the devoted clients of Ilya (Melina Mercouri), daughter of joy, queen of Piraeus harbor, who does no business on the Sabbath. In comes killjoy Homer (Jules Dassin), a Yank, who orders coffee. Homer decides to acquaint Ilya with the glory that was Greece, subjecting her to a crash course in the Great Books. Ilya has her own version of the Greek tragedies: Medea *pretended* to kill her children to get her man back; Oedipus was a good son, who "loves so much his mother." Homer kills her pleasure in these classic tales by carefully explaining how they really turn out.

Outstanding in Ilya's entourage are Despo Diamantidou, a comically seductive hooker, built like a pouter pigeon (she later turned up with Mercouri in the Broadway musical adaptation, *Illya, Darling*), and Georges Foundas is touching as Tonio, who, if he "saves" Ilya, will do it because he takes delight in everything about her.

Ilya creeps guiltily from her Shakespearean sonnets and Mercator projections to play a song on her phonograph. It is the Oscar-winning *Never on Sunday*, by Manos Hadjidakis, who wrote the score. The lyrics sum up Ilya's sweetness: "No one goes by my door for whom I do not feel love." The charm of this joyous film was only partially obscured by an American bubble-gum translation of the title song that fouled the air waves for a time. Mercouri won Best Actress Award at the 1960 Cannes Film Festival.

*(The videocassette is in English.)*

# Night Is My Future
## (Musik i Mörker/Music in Darkness)

\* \* \* \* \* \* \* \* \* \* \* \* \* \* \* \* \* \* \* \* \* \* \* \* \* \* \* \* \* \* \* \* \* \* \* \* \* \* \* \* \* \* \* \* \* \* \* \* \* \* \* \* \* \*

Nationality: Swedish          Year: 1948 (U.S. release: 1963)
Cast: Mai Zetterling, Birger Malmsten, Bengt Eklund, Olof Winner-strand, Naima Wifstrand
Director: Ingmar Bergman          Running Time: 87 minutes
B/W or Color: B/W          Availability: VIDEO YESTERYEAR

This somber 1948 romantic drama wasn't shown in the United States until 1963. By then, the name of its director, Ingmar Bergman, held an art house prestige that this straightforward little story could scarcely live up to, with its sentiment-laden account of a lonely young pianist's accidental loss of sight and his subsequent difficulties in adjusting to blindness and winning the girl he loves.

This film's inclusion in the present volume is chiefly due to its interest for Bergman buffs, coming as it does from an era when postwar European filmmaking so frequently wallowed in the gritty—if not downright tragic—realism reflected by the French and Italian cinema. Apart from one brief sequence in which Bergman interprets the blind youth's post-accident delirium with a surreal montage, there is little that stamps this, his fourth picture as a director, a Bergman work. The film's acting is adequate to the screenplay fashioned from her novel by Dagmar Edqvist, with two of Scandinavia's then most beautiful young actors (Mai Zetterling and Birger Malmsten) as its protagonists, lit and photographed with care by Goran Strindberg. And it's interesting to note the extravagant early work of so familiar a Bergman-stock-company performer as Gunnar Björnstrand, briefly seen as the hero's volatile violinist-colleague in a restaurant sequence.

Bergman holds little sentiment for *Music in Darkness* (as the title directly translates), calling it "a silly little film," though he acknowledges that it was his first popular success in Scandinavia. Hitchcock-like, he even makes a fleeting appearance near the end as a passenger aboard the young couple's honeymoon train.

(*Video Yesteryear's print is subtitled, but its picture quality is murky, sometimes rendering the titles unreadable.*)

# The Night of the Shooting Stars
## (La Notte di San Lorenzo)

**************************************************************

*Nationality*: Italian

*Year*: 1982 (U.S. release: 1983)

*Cast*: Omero Antonutti, Margarita Lozano, Claudio Bigagli, Massimo Bonetti

*Director*: Paolo and Vittorio Taviani

*Running Time*: 106 minutes

*B/W or Color*: Color

*Availability*: MGM/UA HOME VIDEO

Although their 1977 *Padre Padrone* was a critical success, Paolo and Vittorio Taviani didn't hit commercial pay dirt until the 1982 release of *The Night of the Shooting Stars*. In *New York* magazine, David Denby said, "Its abrupt, frequently harsh style with crazy barbaric poetry . . . leaves one rather startled." *The Night of the Shooting Stars* is the Taviani brothers at their best; Marxist commedia dell'arte that is so robust that it dazzles us as it intellectually stimulates us. Told as a bedtime-for-bambino story of a mother's distant past, the movie concerns a summer week in 1944 when occupying Germans leave a small Italian town. A group of townspeople, fearing that the Nazis have mined their village and plan to blow it up in the face of the advancing American army, leaves late one night to "find the Americans," who are but a few valleys away. Led by a powerful peasant patriarch (played astutely by Omero Antonutti), the ensemble of citizenry forms a colorful unit. This is much more than those "charming" views of peasant life that Italy occasionally exports. *The Night of the Shooting Stars* is reality as memory as phantasmagoria.

The Tavianis balance their slices of town life: scenes of coy lovemaking are dovetailed with violent death; battles between runaways and the last gasp of Fascist partisanship in a Tuscan wheatfield are breathtaking in their beauty and seeming verisimilitude. These scenes show the Tavianis to be graphic, stunningly lyrical dialecticians. While involving us with the story, their style comments upon it, our watching of it, and the mother's retelling of it. It is that self-reflexive edge that is the Taviani strength. Their films grab one by the eyes and ears and resonate indelibly in the mind.

*(The videocassette is subtitled.)*

# The Night Porter

## (Il Portiere di Notte)

★★★★★★★★★★★★★★★★★★★★★★★★★★★★★★★★★★★★★★★★★★★★★★★★★★★★

Nationality: Italian          Year: 1974

Cast: Dirk Bogarde, Charlotte Rampling, Philippe Leroy, Gabriele Ferzetti, Isa Miranda, Amadeo Amadio

Director: Liliana Cavani         Running Time: 115 minutes

B/W or Color: Color          Availability: EMBASSY HOME ENTERTAINMENT

Director Liliana Cavani worked with Luchino Visconti on *The Damned*, that towering exposition of sexual decadence among the Nazis. In *The Night Porter* she attempts to go the master one better, and while she doesn't succeed, the film is a classic exploration of sexual politics and has a following among disciples of the bizarre.

The night porter is Max (Dirk Bogarde), the switchboard operator at a sinister Viennese hotel in 1957. Max sees to the special needs of the hotel's guests. He can satisfy the countess' (Isa Miranda) taste for rough young men, or he can be an audience for Bert's (Amadeo Amadio) grotesque dance recital, and reward him with a hypodermic needle in the buttock. Max's life is upturned when Lucia (Charlotte Rampling), the wife of an American symphony conductor giving a recital in Vienna, arrives. It is clear they were once more than friends. They resume their former relationship, which is a graphic investigation of some of the kinkiest sado-masochistic stunts ever filmed. What makes it particularly morbid is that Lucia was a prisoner in the concentration camp where Max was an officer and where their perverted relationship began.

Opinions are divided as to the success Cavani attains in extracting romance from the monstrous relationship her principals engage in. She labors at defining the frightening interdependency between torturer and tortured, and while it is possible that no one has ever done it better, at least on this level, it remains a curiosity, a high-class porn flic.

*The Night Porter* is handsomely filmed in dark, rich tones well suited to the theme. Bogarde's characterization is an appropriate mix of the sensual and the authoritarian, while Rampling's limited repertoire of emotions is not particularly strained by the script's demands.

*(The videocassette is in English.)*

# A Night to Remember

★★★★★★★★★★★★★★★★★★★★★★★★★★★★★★★★★★★★★★★★★★★★★★★★★★★★

**Nationality**: British          **Year**: 1958

**Cast**: Kenneth More, Ronald Allen, Robert Ayres, Honor Blackman, Anthony Bushell

**Director**: Roy Baker          **Running Time**: 123 minutes

**B/W or Color**: B/W          **Availability**: TV only

The maiden-voyage sinking, on April 14, 1912, of Britain's "unsinkable" and luxurious ocean liner *Titanic*, in the iceberg-imperiled North Atlantic, remains a sea tragedy of such awesome proportions as to continue inspiring the documentarians and fiction-makers of the various media. British filmmakers had unimpressively tackled the subject in 1929's *Atlantic*, while 20th Century-Fox's 1953 *Titanic* showed great technical expertise in its studio-tank re-creation of the events but dissipated the story's power with the inclusion of Hollywood-style personal dramas.

Best of all such efforts was this splendid 1958 J. Arthur Rank production, brilliantly adapted by Eric Ambler from Walter Lord's 1955 non-fiction best seller. Ambler's screenplay takes a near-documentary approach to the subject; there are no real starring parts in this account of the tragedy; it is a true ensemble effort for all concerned. *A Night to Remember* remains a triumph for director Roy Baker and his dedicated production crew, especially art director Alex Vetchinsky and special-effects director Bill Wallington, who made such creative use of the facilities at Pinewood Studios. Equal credit is, of course, due cinematographer Geoffrey Unsworth and film editor Sidney Hayers for keeping suspenseful a situation whose unfortunate outcome is only too familiar. But this film also makes us care *how* that awful tragedy happened. As a moving and detailed reconstruction of a great maritime disaster, *A Night to Remember* remains faithful to Walter Lord's carefully documented book, never resorting to cinematic cliché or undue sentimentality.

The National Boad of Review named it one of 1958's best films.

# Night Train
## (Night Train to Munich)

\*\*\*\*\*\*\*\*\*\*\*\*\*\*\*\*\*\*\*\*\*\*\*\*\*\*\*\*\*\*\*\*\*\*\*\*\*\*\*\*\*\*\*\*\*\*\*\*\*\*\*\*\*\*\*\*\*\*\*\*\*\*\*\*\*\*\*\*\*\*

Nationality: British          Year: 1940

Cast: Margaret Lockwood, Rex Harrison, Basil Radford, Naunton Wayne, Paul von Hernreid (Paul Henreid)

Director: Carol Reed          Running Time: 93 minutes

B/W or Color: B/W          Availability: Public Domain

A splendid mixture of comedy and suspense, *Night Train* (called *Night Train to Munich* in England) was inspired by the success of *The Lady Vanishes*, directed by Alfred Hitchcock. It was, stated the *New York Times* review, "written by the same needle-sharp wits that penned *The Lady Vanishes* and directed . . . by a brilliant newcomer named Carol Reed."

Like *The Lady Vanishes*, *Night Train* starred Margaret Lockwood and featured comic relief by Basil Radford and Naunton Wayne, repeating the British tourist roles (Charters and Caldicott) that they had created in the earlier film. The *Times* review described them as "the hilariously monotoned pair . . . who are quite put out by the declaration of war, but even more dismayed at the inevitable loss of a set of golf clubs left in Berlin." Radford and Wayne would star in their next team effort, *Crooks' Tour*, and appear together (as the same tourists) in five films following that.

Based on a novel by Gordon Wellesley, the screenplay was co-authored by Frank Launder and Sidney Gilliat. Anna Bomasch (Margaret Lockwood) leaves Czechoslavakia when the Nazi invasion is imminent. Captured and sent to a concentration camp, she and fellow prisoner Karl Marsen (Paul von Hernreid, later Paul Henreid) escape to England. They meet Gus Bennett (Rex Harrison), a member of a musical troupe who is actually a British secret agent. After leading Marsen to her father (James Harcourt), Anna discovers that Marsen is working undercover for the Gestapo.

When the Bomasches are arrested and taken to Berlin, Bennett follows and sets things right—aboard the night train to Munich.

The climactic cable-car shootout has since been imitated frequently (most memorably in *Where Eagles Dare*).

Again referring to *The Lady Vanishes*, the *Times* review noted that *Night Train* is "the swiftest and most harrowing thriller to come out of England since the Hitchcock work."

# The Nights of Cabiria
## (Le Notti di Cabiria)

\* \* \* \* \* \* \* \* \* \* \* \* \* \* \* \* \* \* \* \* \* \* \* \* \* \* \* \* \* \* \* \* \* \* \* \* \* \* \* \* \* \* \* \* \* \* \* \* \* \*

**Nationality**: Italian-French          **Year**: 1956

**Cast**: Giulietta Masina, François Perier, Amedeo Nazzari, Franca Marzi, Dorian Gray

**Director**: Federico Fellini          **Running Time**: 110 minutes

**B/W or Color**: B/W          **Availability**: TV only

One of Fellini's most haunting, resonant films once more stars his wife, Masina, as the lovable and hopeful prostitute Cabiria. The pictures groundbreaking, progressive imagining of street life is plausible in the neorealist sense yet contains the grandly ordered structures of art and a humane, very Catholic sensibility.

The film begins literally with the childlike Cabiria's baptism into an understanding of her own fragility and self-delusion: rescued from drowning, she sends away her saviors, and it's not until later she admits that her boyfriend, Giorgio, was trying to kill her. "I have everything I need," is her spoken prayer. Yet she's quick to fall in love, first with a man (François Perier) she's met at the theater, sweetly and tragically convinced that her acceptance by him is guaranteed. She sells her drab little home and prepares to marry him; instead, he robs her. Back on the street, Cabiria is whisked away to the fast life of the Via Veneto, whereupon a film star (Amedeo Nazzari) shows her the house of her petit-bourgeois dreams and *la dolce vita*—as illusory, she discovers, as the movies. First appearing as Cabiria in a tiny role within Fellini's *White Sheik*, Masina brings to the part the faux naif elements of Gelsomina in *La Strada*, but with a hard-edge facade and updated awareness.

*Nights of Cabiria* was remade and bowdlerized by Bob Fosse into the play *Sweet Charity* (1968). The picture won the Academy Award for Best Foreign Film and the New York Film Critics' award. Giulietta Masina was named Best Actress at Cannes.

The reviews were uniformly excellent. *Saturday Review* said, "Fellini is one of the few directors who is not afraid to rely on imagery, to let the camera speak for him. But there are things that happen in his pictures that transcend mere technique. . . . They are neither tricks nor effects, but the product of that subtle interplay of technique and emotion which we call art. At 36, Federico Fellini is without question Italy's greatest film artist today." And the *New York Post* summed it up, "This is a picture worthy of Fellini's genius."

# 1900
## (Novecento)

★★★★★★★★★★★★★★★★★★★★★★★★★★★★★★★★★★★★★★★★★★★★★★★★★★★★★

*Nationality*: Italian-French-German *Year*: 1976 (U.S. release: 1977)
*Cast*: Robert De Niro, Gerard Depardieu, Dominique Sanda, Donald Sutherland, Burt Lancaster, Sterling Hayden
*Director*: Bernardo Bertolucci     *Running Time*: 243 minutes
*B/W or Color*: Color     *Availability*: TV only

Not a movie for the faint-hearted, uncommitted, or casual filmgoer, *1900* contains the always engaging, often exhilarating style of a master, Bernardo Bertolucci. It has been hailed as Italian cinema's first great epic film, taking place in the province of Emilia between 1900 and 1945. It is a powerful and rewarding motion picture, equally interested in the fates of the padrone Alfredo (Robert De Niro) and the peasant Olmo (Gerard Depardieu). They are the grandsons of Burt Lancaster and Sterling Hayden, who were born on the same day—one the heir to a moneyed landholding family and the other a bastard offspring of an impoverished peasant family.

Bertolucci's view of the 20th century includes the dissolution of social stability and family loyalty, the rise and fall of Fascism, the vissicitudes of class and capitalism, the myriad combinations of sexuality and psyche. His gifts encompass an unerring eye and ear for detail—for the grand sweep of landscape, but also for the meticulously musical rhythms of the dialogue and editing.

In Olmo's brusque refusal of Alfredo's consolation on the loss of his child, the viewer feels a tightening of their lifelong bond. In the malevolent Attila (Donald Sutherland), we see the facility with which the powerful ingratiate themselves in the families of landowners.

Bertolucci designed the film to follow seasons: summer for childhood, autumn and winter for the rise of Fascism and the second World War, spring for the days that followed.

At the 1976 Cannes Film Festival, a five-and-a-half-hour version of *1900* was shown. Twenty minutes were cut for European distribution, and then the length was reduced to four and a half hours. When it was shown at the 1977 New York Film Festival, *1900* ran four hours and five minutes.

Vittorio Storaro's cinematography, combined with Ennio Morricone's bittersweet score, imparts a sweeping, elegiac quality that in the end seems fulfilling in itself.

*1900* is a monument of international cinema.

# O Lucky Man!

\* \* \* \* \* \* \* \* \* \* \* \* \* \* \* \* \* \* \* \* \* \* \* \* \* \* \* \* \* \* \* \* \* \* \* \* \* \* \* \* \* \* \* \* \* \* \* \* \* \* \* \* \* \*

**Nationality**: British          **Year**: 1973

**Cast**: Malcolm McDowell, Ralph Richardson, Rachel Roberts, Arthur Lowe, Helen Mirren

**Director**: Lindsay Anderson          **Running Time**: 166 minutes (186 minutes in Britain)

**B/W *or* Color**: Color          **Availability**: WARNER HOME VIDEO

Overwhelming in its concept and impact is this monumental version of one young man's odyssey through life to an eventual understanding of what it's all about. It was the third narrative work of documentary-maker and critic Lindsay Anderson, reuniting him with Malcolm McDowell and David Sherwin, the star and writer of his previous effort *If . . .* Touching upon matters of great importance in an ironic, comic, and devastating way, the film cleverly and innovatively uses established screen techniques. Its overall impact wowed the critics and the audiences who saw it as an equally fantastic but less brutal variation on *A Clockwork Orange,* which also starred McDowell.

McDowell begins as an ambitious trainee-salesman for England's Imperial Coffee Company and encounters a series of bizarre, often sexual adventures on his way to salvation and success. Among those he meets are Sir Ralph Richardson, a ruthless tycoon, and his rock groupie daughter Helen Mirren. Among the more disturbing images: the sight of Jeremy Bulloch, whose head has been grafted upon the body of a huge pig; and an attempt by a briefly reformed McDowell to save a suicidal housewife, played by Rachel Roberts (who actually committed suicide in 1980).

Made on a monumental scale for less than $4 million—inexpensive even then—the enterprise almost seems as if it were one big in-joke. With few exceptions, the actors have more than one role; most of the filmmakers appear in the film: co-producer Michael Medwin, director Anderson, composer Alan Price, who appears at intervals to sing the philosophical songs, including the title tune ("If you've found the reason to live on and not to die, you are a lucky man"). Anderson, playing the director of a film-within-a-film called O *Lucky Man!*, hits would-be actor McDowell with the script to make him smile, in the most controversial scene. O great film! The National Board voted it one of the year's ten best.

# Odd Man Out

* * * * * * * * * * * * * * * * * * * * * * * * * * * * * * * * * * * * * * * * * * * * * * * * * * *

**Nationality**: British                    **Year**: 1947
**Cast**: James Mason, Kathleen Ryan, Robert Newton, Robert Beatty, Cyril Cusack, Fay Compton
**Director**: Carol Reed                    **Running Time**: 115 minutes
**B/W or Color**: B/W                    **Availability**: TV Only

In his 1981 memoir, *Before I Forget,* James Mason calls this his best film and Carol Reed his favorite director. Mason's character of Johnny McQueen, the Irish fugitive wanted for murder, is an engaging tragic figure engendering considerable audience sympathy. But this is not merely his story; it is also that of the people, both good and bad, with whom he comes into contact in his flight.

*Odd Man Out* centers on the final, dying hours of Mason's revolutionary leader, wounded in the holdup of a linen mill to get funds for "the cause." What seems on the surface like a simple chase thriller is really far more complex. Its characters embody a spectrum of lower-class Irish life, with all the attendant examples of humor, treachery, private enterprise, and native Gaelic sentiment. Standout performances are offered by Fay Compton, as the ordinary suburbanite who's shocked to find herself aiding the fleeing gunman; hatchet-faced Maureen Delany, as the elderly tart whose honeyed voice masks her conscienceless betrayal of Johnny; beautiful Kathleen Ryan, as the steadfast girl whose love for this underdog moves her to draw the gunfire that ultimately ends their suffering; Robert Newton, as the mad, drunken artist driven to capture the dying Johnny's face on canvas; and F. J. McCormick creates an unforgettable figure out of the whimsical little derelict bird-catcher.

Carol Reed fills his celluloid landscape with many brilliant strokes, even employing weather changes to add mood shadings. Robert Krasker's cameras capture it all superbly, while William Alwyn's affecting music—with its driving, dirgelike main theme—underscores all the dreams, frustrations, and agonies of a beleaguered people. The British Film Academy chose *Odd Man Out* as 1947's Best British Motion Picture, and The National Board of Review listed it among the year's ten best films.

# Odd Obsession
## (Kagi/The Key)

**********************************************************

**Nationality**: Japanese      **Year**: 1959 (U.S. release: 1961)

**Cast**: Machiko Kyo, Ganjiro Nakamura, Junko Kano, Tatsuya Nakadai, Tanie Kitabayashi

**Director**: Kon Ichikawa      **Running Time**: 96 minutes (107 minutes in Japan)

**B/W or Color**: Color      **Availability**: NELSON ENTER-TAINMENT

D irector Kon Ichikawa maintains that his *Odd Obsession* is not a movie about sex. That may be so, but sexual obsession certainly functions as his symbolic gameboard in this darkest of black farces.

Kenmochi, an aging art dealer who senses a loss of his sexual potency, attempts to restore his interest in life through escalating sexual stimulants. When injections and hidden photography of his nude wife in a drugged sleep lose their punch, he tries to arouse himself by maneuvering his daughter's fiancé, a handsome young doctor, into an affair with his wife, Ikiko. The sensuous Ikiko, several years her husband's junior and still quite attractive, joins the perverse games by coyly using to her advantage the obedience and modesty traditional to any Japanese housewife. By demurely repeating her husband's "terrible" requests while expressing her shock at them, Ikiko could easily stimulate any man. In pretending to obey Kenmochi, Ikiko is actually deceiving him from the start. Kimura, the smug doctor, smells money, and unscrupulously yields to his lusts. Toshiko, the college student daughter, jealously tries to fight back in the contest for Kenmochi; ironically, though equally corrupt, the modern Westernized Japanese female is no match for her soft, middle-aged mother.

These cold, dispassionate characters are the basic ingredients for the grotesque games that follow in *Odd Obsession*. Season with malice, throw in a few keyholes and several hidden motives and ambiguities that fool no one, and stir them with heavy irony. The result: a special prize at Cannes with "Special commendation for audacity of its subject and its plastic qualities."

*Odd Obsession* is based on Junichiro Tanizaki's 1958 novel *Kagi* (*The Key*), which uses parallel his-and-hers diaries for its narrative. Ichikawa's film was made the following year, retaining all of Tanizaki's humor and sadomasochistic perversions. While changing to a linear narration, he also added a surprise ending, which adds another layer of irony to Tanizaki's work.

# The Official Story
## (La Historia Oficial)

★★★★★★★★★★★★★★★★★★★★★★★★★★★★★★★★★★★★★★★★★★★★★★★★★★★★

**Nationality**: Argentinian      **Year**: 1985

**Cast**: Norma Aleandro, Hector Alterio, Analia Castro, Chunchuna Villafane

**Director**: Luis Puenzo      **Running Time**: 112 minutes

**B/W or Color**: Color      **Availability**: PACIFIC ARTS VIDEO

In 1985 *The Official Story* took the Best Foreign Film Oscar; Best Picture Award in Toronto; was cited by The National Board; and its star, Norma Aleandro, won Best Actress at Cannes (tying with Cher) and at Cartagena. All this for a first-time director, Argentina's Luis Puenzo, whose movie is all the more effective for its obliqueness—a subtle commentary on the right-wing terror squads that gripped that country in the 1970s.

Alicia (Aleandro), a respected teacher, and her successful husband, Roberto (Hector Alterio), whose business and social contacts extend to the highest government echelons, enjoy their privileged life with their adopted daughter Gabi (Analia Castro). But imperceptibly, their lives change in a post-Falklands War jittery atmosphere.

There are hints and rumors of a mystery concerning Gabi's "adoption"; an old friend of Alicia's returning from exile describes torture she'd undergone before leaving the country (Norma Aleandro, herself an Argentinian exile, returned home after the junta's collapse to play Alicia); Alicia's gradual awareness of the demonstrating Mothers of the Plaza de Mayo, dressed in black, silently holding up pictures of missing children and grandchildren; all force Alicia to heed her conscience and accept as real the stories she has tried not to believe—and also to face the growing nagging conviction that Gabi could indeed be one of these missing children. But when questioned, her husband won't discuss the subject.

By now the ruling junta is falling apart. At the same time Alicia's once happy life is also disintegrating—culminating in one chilling, revealing scene that comes as a total shock.

In making this powerful, award-winning picture, Luis Puenzo has set himself a high standard for his future films.

340

# Oh! What a Lovely War

★ ★ ★ ★ ★ ★ ★ ★ ★ ★ ★ ★ ★ ★ ★ ★ ★ ★ ★ ★ ★ ★ ★ ★ ★ ★ ★ ★ ★ ★ ★ ★ ★ ★ ★ ★ ★ ★ ★ ★ ★ ★ ★ ★ ★ ★ ★ ★ ★ ★ ★ ★ ★

*Nationality*: British               *Year*: 1969
*Cast*: John Mills, Dirk Bogarde, Laurence Olivier, Michael Redgrave, Vanessa Redgrave, Maggie Smith
*Director*: Richard Attenborough     *Running Time*: 132 minutes (originally 144 minutes in Britain)
*B/W or Color*: Color                *Availability*: TV only

World War I depicted as a smart musical revue on the boardwalk at England's Brighton Beach? That's the conceit used as a framework for this lavishly expanded version of Charles Hilton's 1960 BBC-radio show, *The Long Long Trail*. Adapted for the stage by Joan Littlewood under the title *Oh! What a Lovely War*, it had been one of the West End hits of 1963. This screen expansion was by spy novelist Len Deighton (*The Ipcress File*), who was originally director Richard Attenborough's co-producer on the project. But Deighton later withdrew, requesting that his name be removed from the movie's credits, because he felt that Attenborough's handling of the once savagely satiric material "should have been tougher."

What onstage had been a sharply tuned and daringly original work was now, in the opinion of some critics, a star-studded audiovisual marshmallow and the year's "prettiest musical extravaganza." True, the film's producers hoped for a commercial success and employed cameo "name" actors (at deferred salaries) and colorful production values to attain that end. *Oh! What a Lovely War* is none the less powerful, either as trenchant antiwar satire or as an outstanding example of the filmmaking art.

Its structure is immensely complex, cleverly juxtaposing period songs, historical reenactments, and blackout sketches as that Brighton pier, in 1914, flashes an electric sign announcing World War I and selling tickets for the "ever popular War Game—complete with songs, battles and a few jokes." The public is even kept regularly apprised of the body count until, at the end, in 1918, the scoreboard registers a tally of 9 million casualties. The movie's final shot, with a helicopter-borne camera rising to reveal seemingly countless graves marked with identical white crosses, is a shattering panorama that even its detractors surely must admire.

# Oliver!

★★★★★★★★★★★★★★★★★★★★★★★★★★★★★★★★★★★★★★★★★★★★★★★★★★★★★★★

**Nationality**: British       **Year**: 1968

**Cast**: Ron Moody, Oliver Reed, Shani Wallis, Mark Lester, Jack Wild, Harry Secombe, Hugh Griffith

**Director**: Carol Reed       **Running Time**: 153 minutes

**B/W or Color**: Color       **Availability**: RCA/COLUMBIA PICTURES HOME VIDEO

I f ever there was a right choice for director of this film musical it was Carol Reed. He had worked several times with motion pictures told from a child's point of view, *The Fallen Idol,* and *A Kid for Two Farthings* among them. In addition, his style, in its tone and romanticism, was akin to David Lean's when the latter attempted such Dickens classics as *Great Expectations* and *Oliver Twist* in the Forties.

The stage musical *Oliver!* was a resounding success in America and abroad, and money was lavished on the screen version. However, there was an almost unorthodox attention given to the art direction by John Box and the cinematography by Oswald Morris. Lurid blues and greens saturated the sets, and the costumes were basically colorless, while Morris's use of fog filtration on the camera lens de-Technicolored the film's visual feel. According to Morris, "What we wanted to get away from was that awful, hard, garish Technicolor 'Western' look, where they had ultramarine skies, orange-colored cowboys, lush green grass, and deep blue seas. No way could you put Dickens on the screen with those sort of colors." At first, Columbia worried about the experimentation financed with their megabucks, but the virtuosity of the work was appreciated, and the film won several Academy Awards, including Best Picture. It was also named as one of the ten best by The National Board of Review.

Ron Moody is a complex, sympathetic, singing and dancing wonder as Fagin, and it's a tragedy that he has never lived up to the magic of this first starring vehicle. As the villainous Bill Sikes, Reed chose his nephew, Oliver, and proper menace was lent to the role. In the climactic half hour, Reed abandoned the musical genre and went for pure melodrama of the kind that characterized his earlier efforts, such as *The Third Man,* full of oblique angles and sumptuous detail. The deaths of Nancy, then of Sykes, are emotionally gripping sequences that rank with Reed's best work.

# Oliver Twist

★★★★★★★★★★★★★★★★★★★★★★★★★★★★★★★★★★★★★★★★★★★★★★★★★★★★

Nationality: British          Year: 1948 (U.S. release: 1951)
Cast: Robert Newton, Alec Guinness, Kay Walsh, John Howard Davies, Francis L. Sullivan
Director: David Lean        Running Time: 116 minutes
B/W or Color: B/W        Availability: CBS VIDEO LIBRARY

Two years after the triumph of their *Great Expectations,* producer Ronald Neame and director David Lean returned with another, equally impressive Dickens adaptation in *Oliver Twist.*

No brief description can do justice to the grubby period sets and meticulous character performances that give this motion picture such a wonderful feel of Dickensian authenticity, from gloomy workhouse to the undertaking establishment of Mr. Sowerberry to London's dirty slums and back alleys and, finally, that secret attic den of the master thief Fagin.

Once again, David Lean's casting lends credibility to each characterization, from the all-vital naturalness of young Oliver to even the smallest of bit parts. In the title role, John Howard Davies—30 years before turning TV producer with such comic gems as *Monty Python's Flying Circus* and *Fawlty Towers*—makes a striking film debut with the perfect blend of eagerness and gaunt vulnerability, directed to perfection by Lean. As Bill Sikes, Robert Newton is appropriately despicable. It's fascinating to ponder how the part might have been portrayed by Robert Donat, who was rejected as vocally unsuitable. Kay Walsh makes a pathetic Nancy, and Alec Guinness—buried under grotesque makeup for this, his second movie—offers an oily, rasping-voiced Fagin. It was the very success of his characterization that brought the picture censorship problems, because of its alleged "anti-Semitism." Consequently, *Oliver Twist* didn't reach American theaters for three years—and was finally shown in a Fagin-diminished version. The U.S. public never saw this classic in its original edition until 1970, when New York's Museum of Modern Art finally showed it during a David Lean retrospective.

(*The CBS Video Library offers an excellent videocassette of the full-length British original.*)

# On Her Majesty's Secret Service

★ ★ ★ ★ ★ ★ ★ ★ ★ ★ ★ ★ ★ ★ ★ ★ ★ ★ ★ ★ ★ ★ ★ ★ ★ ★ ★ ★ ★ ★ ★ ★ ★ ★ ★ ★ ★ ★ ★ ★ ★ ★ ★ ★ ★ ★ ★ ★ ★ ★ ★ ★ ★

*Nationality*: British                    *Year*: 1969

*Cast*: George Lazenby, Diana Rigg, Telly Savalas, Bernard Lee, Lois Maxwell, Desmond Llewelyn

*Director*: Peter Hunt                    *Running Time*: 140 minutes

*B/W or Color*: Color                    *Availability*: CBS/FOX HOME VIDEO

**B**uried and disregarded by time for its sin against 007—the casting of Australian unknown George Lazenby in the Sean Connery role—*OHMSS* is, for many, a personal favorite in the James Bond lexicon. It's a delightful adventure film, ranking with *Gunga Din, The Vikings,* and *Raiders of the Lost Ark* as sheer spectacle and very good fun.

The film's prologue has Lazenby, as Bond, being outfoxed in a fight scene on a moonlit beach, at which point he turns to the camera and says, befuddled, "This never happened to the other fella!" It was a wonderful way to break the ice for those so entrenched in Connery's image that they would accept none other. Apparently box-office figures indicated that the good-natured attempt had failed, and Connery came bouncing back for the next installment. A pity, for Lazenby was more rugged than Roger Moore and was adept at humor, much of it amusingly self-effacing. In one scene, he lets a minicomputer open a safe, while he sits nearby reading *Playboy.* Later, in the enemy's Alpine nest, he comes to dinner amidst a bevy of rapacious beauties wearing a kilt.

The first half of the film is leisurely paced and beautifully shot. Bond falls in love. His partner in romance is Diana Rigg, tall, stylish, and strong support for the newcomer Lazenby. When the story kicks into gear, it never slackens its pace for a moment. We're in for a super ski chase and avalanche, an inadvertent demolition derby, a cable car escape at night, and a superbly shot bobsled finale you'll never forget.

While Telly Savalas as Blofeld, the arch villain, is less menacing than one might like, small displeasures are forgiven. This is a grand film— even with over half its image sheered away by the video format.

# Once Upon a Time in the West
## (C'era una Volta il West)

**********************************************************

**Nationality**: Italian  **Year**: 1969
**Cast**: Henry Fonda, Claudia Cardinale, Jason Robards, Charles Bronson
**Director**: Sergio Leone  **Running Time**: 165 minutes
**B/W or Color**: Color  **Availability**: PARAMOUNT
HOME VIDEO

This Sergio Leone super-Western ran four astonishing years in France, broke box office records in Germany, South America, and Japan—but bombed in the States. In early scenes, Henry Fonda (that all-American good guy) shoots a helpless child in cold blood, and U.S. audiences were outraged. Uncertain of how to market the nearly three-hour movie, Paramount deemed it overlong and indiscriminately edited it by half an hour. (Beware of this 140-minute version!) Nevertheless, the picture established the "spaghetti Western" as an art form, and the full-length *Once Upon a Time in the West* has now achieved cult status in America among those who appreciate Leone's inspired cinematic excesses.

Along with Fonda's repellent villain, the marvelous cast includes Jason Robards as the robber with a heart of gold, Charles Bronson as the quietly mysterious stranger bent on revenge, and Claudia Cardinale as a fancy widow from New Orleans. The Sergio Leone-Sergio Donati screenplay is riveting, though at times too intricate and confusing.

The overall theme is greed and lawlessness—the wide-open West with no holds barred. Fonda and his vicious gang deliberately slaughter a family for their right-of-way land. The opening sequence, set around a hot, desolate railroad station, is memorable: a gunman, patiently waiting for the train with a fly buzzing around his face, is perfect pantomime. And Ennio Morricone's evocative score is outstanding.

In 1980, Martin Scorsese launched a campaign for color film preservation. Many movies made since 1950 are on inferior stock, which fades and deteriorates in a comparatively short time. To dramatize his cause, Scorsese chose *Once Upon a Time in the West* (most existing prints were in poor condition) to restore to its original state. The resulting restoration was shown, to great acclaim, at that year's New York Film Festival.

# One of Our Aircraft Is Missing

\*\*\*\*\*\*\*\*\*\*\*\*\*\*\*\*\*\*\*\*\*\*\*\*\*\*\*\*\*\*\*\*\*\*\*\*\*\*\*\*\*\*\*\*\*\*\*\*\*\*\*\*\*\*\*\*

*Nationality*: British       *Year*: 1942

*Cast*: Godfrey Tearle, Eric Portman, Hugh Williams, Pamela Brown, Googie Withers, Peter Ustinov

*Director*: Michael Powell, Emeric    *Running Time*: 103 minutes
Pressburger

*B/W or Color*: B/W       *Availability*: REPUBLIC PICTURES HOME VIDEO

The British writing-producing-directing team of Michael Powell and Emeric Pressburger is known primarily for highly stylized, color films such as *A Matter of Life and Death* (1946), *Black Narcissus* (1946), and *The Red Shoes* (1948). However, two of their finest early efforts were *49th Parallel* (1941) and *One of Our Aircraft Is Missing*. Both are highly dramatic, tension-filled black-and-white films that start with the premise of soldiers stranded in alien territory trying to find their way back to safety. *One of Our Aircraft Is Missing* was produced with the full co-operation of the RAF, the Air Ministry, and the Royal Netherland government. It begins with an abandoned bomber flying across the North Sea and then exploding as it hits a pylon. This is all portrayed in a thrilling, documentary-style sequence. We then find out what happened to the crew. The six airmen were forced to bail out over Holland and into occupied territory when the plane was hit following a bombing mission over Stuttgart. The Dutch hide the men and give them disguises in order to escape the Nazis and return to England. There are exciting and suspenseful sequences as they make their way across the country, eluding the Germans at every turn.

The six British fliers are a fairly typical group of characters meant to represent English society, and the tag of "propaganda" could be applied to the film, but that would not be a negative term, since almost all war films from this period were meant to inspire patriotism and courage. The cast is uniformly excellent, and one of the Dutch citizens is played by a young Peter Ustinov in his fourth film role. Ronald Neame's splendid photography and David Lean's tight editing contribute to the overall high quality of the picture. Soon, they would both go on to very successful directing careers of their own.

Oscar-nominated for Best Original Screenplay, *One of Our Aircraft Is Missing* made the annual ten best lists of *The New York Times* and The National Board, which also cited Googie Withers's outstanding performance.

# Open City
## (Roma, Città Aperta)

★★★★★★★★★★★★★★★★★★★★★★★★★★★★★★★★★★★★★★★★★★★★★★★★★★★

**Nationality**: Italian               **Year**: 1945 (U.S. release: 1946)

**Cast**: Aldo Fabrizi, Marcello Pagliero, Anna Magnani, Maria Michi, Harry Feist, Giovanna Galletti

**Director**: Roberto Rossellini        **Running Time**: 105 minutes

**B/W or Color**: B/W                  **Availability**: Public Domain

This influential landmark in the Italian neorealist cinema was the first great European film to reach the United States after World War II. Originally planned as a short documentary about Don Morosini, an Italian priest and member of the Resistance who was shot by the Germans in 1944, director Robert Rossellini's first feature to gain worldwide attention eventually evolved into this full-length, fictional docudrama of occupied Rome, as developed by him and co-scenarists Sergio Amidei and Federico Fellini.

*Open City* is the episodic story of Manfredi (Marcello Pagliero), a Resistance leader hunted by the Gestapo. Pina (Anna Magnani), a friend's pregnant fiancée, offers him temporary shelter, but when she is shot down in the street, he takes refuge with his mistress, Marina (Maria Michi), a cheap actress and dope addict, who betrays him to the Nazis. Tortured mercilessly by the enemy, Manfredi refuses to talk and eventually succumbs. Following his death, the Gestapo executes Don Pietro (Aldo Fabrizi), an activist priest who has supported the Resistance. As the movie ends, Rossellini's cameras follow a group of children, who have witnessed the execution, as they trudge back into the city. Perhaps theirs will be a better world.

This influential film's documentary look (sometimes grainy, at other times well composed and lit) reflected Rossellini's difficulties in creating a motion picture concurrent with the Nazi withdrawal from Rome. But its powerful, gritty realism paved the way for such subsequent Italian neorealist classics as De Sica's *Shoeshine* and *The Bicycle Thief*, and Zampa's *To Live in Peace*.

The National Board of Review voted Anna Magnani Best Actress of 1946 for her role in *Open City* and also named the movie Best Foreign Language Film.

*(Video Yesteryear offers a cassette of mediocre quality with subtitles that are often difficult to read.)*

# The Organizer
## (I Compagni)

* * * * * * * * * * * * * * * * * * * * * * * * * * * * * * * * * * * * * * * * * * * * * * * * * * * * * *

*Nationality*: Italian-French    *Year*: 1963 (U.S. release: 1964)

*Cast*: Marcello Mastroianni, Renato Salvatori, Annie Girardot, Bernard Blier, François Perier

*Director*: Mario Monicelli    *Running Time*: 126 minutes

*B/W or Color*: B/W    *Availability*: TV only

U nionized labor has become so restrictive of economic progress that nowadays it is hard to remember unions were once a progressive social force. *The Organizer* recalls it vividly and with cinematic art.

The scene is a textile factory in Turin in the 1890s, and the story line is an old-fashioned labor classic: illiterate workers, oppressed beyond endurance, are organized by an idealistic schoolteacher and go out on strike for the first time. They return to work without tangible gains, but the strike has given them a new sense of the righteousness of their cause, and their united strength has been felt by the millowners. Marcello Mastroianni plays the bearded, bespectacled "organizer" and fully reveals how accomplished an actor he is. An excellent cast supports him and includes Renato Salvatori, Bernard Blier, Gabriella Giorgelli, and Annie Girardot. The script, by Age-Scarpelli and Mario Monicelli (who also directed), is warmly human and not without humor. The realistic sets are true to the time and place. Giuseppe Rotunno's black-and-white photography has the charm of old photographs. The music of Carlo Rustichelli is often inspiring.

In the *New York Herald-Tribune,* Judith Crist wrote, "*The Organizer* is a stirring and stinging social document—and one of the best movies of this and many a year. Don't miss it." And she went on to advise the reader, "Don't let that 'social document' or the fact that this Italian film is about a strike throw you. Above all it has the leavening of humor, the subtle appreciation of the human comedy that provides the over-all grace for a film concerned with universal problems and social experience."

*The Organizer* was Oscar-nominated for its Original Story and Screenplay by Age-Scarpelli and Mario Monicelli (the winner was Peter Stone's *Father Goose,* starring Cary Grant), and The National Board named it one of 1964's five best foreign-language films.

# Orpheus

## (Orphée)

★ ★ ★ ★ ★ ★ ★ ★ ★ ★ ★ ★ ★ ★ ★ ★ ★ ★ ★ ★ ★ ★ ★ ★ ★ ★ ★ ★ ★ ★ ★ ★ ★ ★ ★ ★ ★ ★ ★ ★ ★ ★ ★ ★ ★ ★ ★ ★ ★

**Nationality**: French          **Year**: 1949 (U.S. release: 1950)

**Cast**: Jean Marais, Maria Casares, François Perier, Maria Dea, Edouard Dermithe

**Director**: Jean Cocteau          **Running Time**: 95 minutes

**B/W or Color**: B/W          **Availability**: EMBASSY HOME ENTERTAINMENT

I n Greek mythology, Orpheus was a celebrated musician who married the nymph Eurydice. When she dies from a poisonous snake's bite, he journeys to the Underworld and is granted the right to return with her on the condition he not look at her during the long trip up to sunlight. A love-sick Orpheus cannot resist—and loses Eurydice forever. Cocteau used this legend as a basis for his 1926 one-act play, which was loosely adapted for this 1949 film.

The story begins simply enough with Orpheus sitting at a modern café in Paris, having a drink. Jazz music wafts through the air. Suddenly a fight erupts, and a young man is knocked to the ground, bloodied. A car silently pulls up, escorted by two motorcycles. The passengers stoop down to pick up the youth and motion to Orpheus to help them put him in the car. Once inside, Orpheus realizes the young man is dead and that the "Princess" who is driving is really Death. When they reach their destination the Princess and the now-resurrected youth walk through a mirror and into a land that is referred to as "the zone." Orpheus is fascinated by this mysterious process and crosses through the mirror himself to the other side. When the Princess falls in love with Orpheus, she is condemned to die. Orpheus returns to the real world unharmed.

A synopsis cannot be made of a film which is, after all, more of a poem than a motion picture. Cocteau viewed the cinema as a means for creating poetical images and used the camera "not like a pen, but like ink."

As Orpheus, Jean Marais has the perfect look of a Greek statue, while Maria Casares as the Princess is hauntingly exotic. With *Orpheus* and his other fantasy masterwork, *Beauty and the Beast* (1946), Cocteau established himself as the lyrical poet of filmmaking.

# Ossessione
## (Obsession)

**********************************************************

Nationality: Italian          Year: 1942 (U.S. release: 1977)

Cast: Clara Calamai, Massimo Girotti, Elia Marcuzzo, Juan de Landa

Director: Luchino Visconti       Running Time: 135 minutes

B/W or Color: B/W             Availability: TV only

Although he did not obtain the rights (which were owned by MGM), Visconti made this film version of a story similar to James M. Cain's *The Postman Always Rings Twice* in 1942, four years before the Hollywood version. Massimo Girotti and Clara Calamai play the illicit lovers who kill the woman's husband (Juan de Landa). In the MGM movie, directed by Tay Garnett, John Garfield and Lana Turner kill Cecil Kellaway. Visconti's version was not officially seen in the United States until October 1976, when it played at the New York Film Festival. (It was officially released in June 1977.) In his *New York Times* review, Vincent Canby noted, "Comparing the Visconti *Ossessione* with the Garnett *Postman* is to stand a production of *Traviata* next to a McDonald's television commercial, which is not meant to underrate the American film, which is as effectively steamy, tough and terse as the Hollywood law allowed in those days." (A much steamier version was made in 1981, starring Jack Nicholson, Jessica Lange, and John Colicos.)

In one of film history's most accomplished directorial debuts, Visconti (who apprenticed Jean Renoir in the Thirties) transcended the generic themes of Cain's potboiler about murder, obsession, and betrayal. The director introduced modern philosophy and a serious, near-documentary observation of World War II Italy into the Cain story. He achieved his own form of psychological epic melodrama that was to provide the structure for later Visconti works: *La Terra Trema, Bellissima, The Leopard, The Job, Senso,* and *White Nights*. The latter 1957 film included a brief, noteworthy appearance by Clara Calamai, whose role in *Ossessione* is regarded as her most memorable. In 1972 Bertolucci paid homage to *Ossessione* by casting Massimo Girotti in *Last Tango in Paris*.

The legacy of *Ossessione* comes from Visconti's giving the ordinary lust-murder-fate trajectory a fatal grandeur. It is generally accepted as having begun cinema's Italian neorealist movement, which featured such filmmakers as De Sica, Rossellini, and Antonioni.

# Otello

\*\*\*\*\*\*\*\*\*\*\*\*\*\*\*\*\*\*\*\*\*\*\*\*\*\*\*\*\*\*\*\*\*\*\*\*\*\*\*\*\*\*\*\*\*\*\*\*\*\*\*\*\*

**Nationality**: Italian        **Year**: 1986

**Cast**: Plácido Domingo, Katia Ricciarelli, Justino Diaz, Petra Malakova, Urbano Barberini

**Director**: Franco Zeffirelli      **Running Time**: 122 minutes

**B/W or Color**: Color         **Availability**: MEDIA HOME ENTERTAINMENT

Zeffirelli's *Turandot, Tosca,* and *La Boheme* have been criticized as "gasp" productions; the curtain goes up in the opera house as the set is unveiled, there is a gasp, and then thunderous applause. Purists believe that the visual overkill takes away from the music. The same controversy surrounds the film version of Verdi's *Otello,* starring Plácido Domingo in the title role, Katia Ricciarelli as Desdemona, and Justino Diaz as Iago.

Some music lovers quarrel with the dropping of two arias, one being Desdemona's "Willow Song." *The New York Times*'s Vincent Canby feels that the "pictorial splendor keeps interfering with the flow of this most intense, most dramatically packed of Verdi's great musical dramas." On the other hand, says the New York *Daily News,* "every movement, set and prop is there for an obvious purpose." The *News* quotes Sir Laurence Olivier: "Domingo not only acts the part as well as I ever did—he can *sing,* too."

"Zeffirelli casts a spell with *Otello,*" said *USA Today.* "Justino Diaz is such a chillingly evil Iago, he nearly walks off with the film." Zeffirelli himself claims that only the American critics realized that *Otello* was never intended to be an aria-for-aria filming of an opera. As the *News* pointed out, "*Otello* is, first and foremost, a movie, and one that takes full advantage of the opportunities inherent in cinematic art." The National Board of Review threw in its lot with the yeas, when it gave *Otello* the 1986 Best Foreign Film Award. Perhaps it is best to forget the debate and revel in the spectacle.

*(The cassette is in Italian with English subtitles.)*

# Othello

★★★★★★★★★★★★★★★★★★★★★★★★★★★★★★★★★★★★★★★★★★★★★★★★★★★★★★★

*Nationality*: British          *Year*: 1965 (U.S. release: 1966)
*Cast*: Laurence Olivier, Frank Finlay, Maggie Smith, Joyce Redman, Derek Jacobi
*Director*: Stuart Burge          *Running Time*: 166 minutes
*B/W or Color*: Color          *Availability*: TV only

For much of his stage career, Laurence Olivier studiously avoided the role of Othello. In 1938, he had portrayed the villainous Iago opposite Ralph Richardson's Moor in an unsuccessful Old Vic production of the Shakespeare classic. But he harbored little desire to assay the Venetian Moor himself, calling the part "a terrible study and a monstrous, monstrous burden for the actor." It was critic Kenneth Tynan who finally persuaded him to tackle the role in celebration of Shakespeare's quatercentenary.

This film version of John Dexter's National Theatre Company production of *Othello* is a straightforward, studio-bound movie record of the stage play, shot in three brief weeks without recourse to exterior sets or location photography. Nor were any textual cuts made; this *Othello* runs just fourteen minutes short of three hours.

In its limited U.S. release, *Othello* won considerable acclaim, as well as Academy Award nominations for Olivier, Frank Finlay's Iago, Maggie Smith's Desdemona, and supporting actress Joyce Redman.

Shakespeare's classic tale of jealousy, deception, and multiple vengeance had reached the screen on at least four previous occasions, and although Olivier's *Othello* may not be the definitive film of Shakespeare's tragedy, it does contain a great deal of theatrical power and, as a record of one of that actor's greatest stage triumphs, it's invaluable. Olivier's brilliantly original characterization and physical makeup stirred critical controversy, focusing on the actor's artful use of blackface, kinky hair, and ethnic mannerisms. The subtleties of Finlay's coldly cerebral, rather muted Iago make the conflict between Othello and his crafty chief lieutenant all the more explosive. And Maggie Smith invests Desdemona with warmth and passion.

As a motion picture, this *Othello* remains somewhat less towering than Olivier's other Shakespearean masterpieces *Hamlet, Henry V,* and *Richard III,* but it nevertheless showcases a great performance, judiciously preserved.

# Outcast of the Islands

★★★★★★★★★★★★★★★★★★★★★★★★★★★★★★★★★★★★★★★★★★★★★★★★★★★★

*Nationality*: British        *Year*: 1951 (U.S. release: 1952)

*Cast*: Ralph Richardson, Trevor Howard, Robert Morley, Wendy Hiller, Kerima, George Coulouris

*Director*: Carol Reed        *Running Time*: 102 minutes

*B/W or Color*: B/W        *Availability*: TV only

Filmed primarily in Ceylon, *Outcast of the Islands* is based on the Joseph Conrad novel. William Fairchild's screenplay strays at times but maintains the overall spirit of the story. Carol Reed's direction was acclaimed by critics, and Bosley Crowther, in his *New York Times* review, pointed out that "Reed, the British film director whose forte heretofore has been the urbane suspense melodrama, has come up with something new for him in *Outcast of the Islands* . . ."

Trevor Howard stars as Peter Willems, who loses his job as a clerk due to his dishonesty but is helped by an old benefactor, Captain Lingard (Ralph Richardson). Taken to a Malaysian settlement, where Lingard is the main trader, Willems is put up at the home of the captain's agent, Almayer (Robert Morley), who is married to Lingard's adopted daughter, played by Wendy Hiller. Willems quickly goes to seed in the tropics and becomes infatuated with the native chieftain's daughter, Aissa (Kerima). "I know only the despair of her presence," Willems admits, "and the agony of her departure."

Aissa is used by villager Babalatchi (George Coulouris) to get Willems to betray Lingard and reveal the secret passage downriver that the captain has shown him. "You're not a human being to be destroyed or forgiven," Lingard tells the traitorous Willems, "you are my shame." Though he still has Aissa, Willems is banished.

Richardson, then 50, was made up to look older. Crowther's review noted that the actor "manages to handle the pomposities of a philosophical role . . . with authority and style." That critic also found Howard's performance "superb" and thought that Kerima (whose role was silent) made "an eloquent show." Of Robert Morley, he observed: "[His] performance is full of bile and selfishness." Morley's daughter, Annabel, played his nasty child in the film.

*Outcast of the Islands* remains an intelligent internal drama of a man's decline.

# Paisan
## (Paisa)

★ ★ ★ ★ ★ ★ ★ ★ ★ ★ ★ ★ ★ ★ ★ ★ ★ ★ ★ ★ ★ ★ ★ ★ ★ ★ ★ ★ ★ ★ ★ ★ ★ ★ ★ ★ ★ ★ ★ ★ ★ ★ ★ ★ ★ ★ ★ ★ ★ ★ ★

Nationality: Italian       Year: 1947 (U.S. release: 1948)
Cast: Maria Michi, Gar Moore, Bill Tubbs
Director: Roberto Rossellini       Running Time: 120 minutes
B/W or Color: B/W       Availability: Public Domain

O*pen City* introduced the non-Italian world to director Roberto Rossellini's talents, and *Paisan* underscores our continued appreciation of them. This film is about the Allied movement northward through Italy in 1943–45, from the original landings in Sicily to a final sequence in the Po Valley. *Paisan* is handled in a semidocumentary manner with a map on screen that shows the terrain the liberating Allied armies had to retake, mile by mile, from the Germans.

In a country that has been raped and starved by constant battle and occupation, there was little money for making movies. Rod Geiger provided the actual raw film, as well as the American actors. Rossellini did the rest. He used the scarred countryside and cities of Italy for his sets and his fellow countrymen (paisans), largely unprofessional, for his actors. The ravished landscape and its grim inhabitants are photographed in just the right tone of gray to capture the mood of the time and the place.

The film consists of six loosely connected sequences taking place at significant, different geographical points. In Sicily, a sympathetic girl is killed in the random, senseless way of war. As the armies move north to Naples, a black GI loses his shoes, and his credulity, to a poverty-stricken Italian family. In Rome, a prostitute tries to make an American soldier less lonely, and in Florence, an American nurse seeks out an old lover. Three American chaplains—Protestant, Catholic, and Jewish—spend the night together in a Franciscan monastery. Their interaction is one of the humorous highlights of the film. Still another sequence involves the partisans of the Po Valley.

Each short episode conveys the anguish of the individual trapped in a war not of his own making. The entire film, beautifully underplayed throughout, is a potent vision for the viewer.

# Panique
## (Panic)

\* \* \* \* \* \* \* \* \* \* \* \* \* \* \* \* \* \* \* \* \* \* \* \* \* \* \* \* \* \* \* \* \* \* \* \* \* \* \* \* \* \* \* \* \* \* \* \* \* \*

Nationality: French          Year: 1946 (U.S. release: 1947)

Cast: Michel Simon, Viviane Romance, Mat Dalban, Paul Bernard, Emil Drain, Guy Faviers

Director: Julien Duvivier        Running Time: 86 minutes

B/W or Color: B/W        Availability: Public Domain

J ulien Duvivier's *Panique* is a cunning and smashingly effective murder thriller in the French film-noir style that manages to keep the audience on the edge of its seat, even though we know who done it all along. The great Michel Simon plays one of his typical oddballs, hopelessly in love with Viviane Romance. However, she loves Paul Bernard, a shady type who treats Simon with disdain. Simon stands in his darkened room night after night, peering out his window into the room of the couple as they make love. One night, he witnesses them involved in a murder, and he tells Bernard he will go to the police unless Romance consents to be his lover. The couple concoct an intricate plan to incriminate Simon for the murder, and the climax of the film involves an angry mob in pursuit of Simon, who's eventually killed after falling from the roof of a building. The guilty pair walk away, but the police discover a photograph in Simon's pocket that incriminates them.

The story is slow to develop but is extremely skillful as an exercise in tension and audience manipulation. Simon, as always, gives a superb performance as the sympathetic misfit, and Bernard matches him every step of the way with his sly characterization of an unrepentant villain. There is a great scene in the middle of the film where all the characters go to an amusement park, and suddenly Simon finds himself at the center of a gang of mad bumper-car drivers, smashing into him from all sides. The final shot is also at the park, where the trapped couple ride a roller coaster up and down, up and down, knowing that they'll be arrested when they get off.

Duvivier's masterwork will always be *Pepe le Moko* (1937), but *Panique* comes close to equaling it as smooth, dark, and proficient screen entertainment. Perhaps Pauline Kael summed it up best when she called the film "so well conceived cinematically that whether you like it or not, you may be forced to agree it's a near-perfect movie."

# A Passage to India

★ ★ ★ ★ ★ ★ ★ ★ ★ ★ ★ ★ ★ ★ ★ ★ ★ ★ ★ ★ ★ ★ ★ ★ ★ ★ ★ ★ ★ ★ ★ ★ ★ ★ ★ ★ ★ ★ ★ ★ ★ ★ ★ ★ ★ ★ ★ ★ ★ ★ ★ ★ ★ ★ ★ ★

Nationality: British           Year: 1984

Cast: Judy Davis, Victor Banerjee, Peggy Ashcroft, James Fox, Alec Guinness, Nigel Havers

Director: David Lean          Running Time: 163 minutes

B/W or Color: Color          Availability: RCA/COLUMBIA PICTURES HOME VIDEO

David Lean's films have shown a remarkable ability for getting inside his characters—from the working-class family of *This Happy Breed* to the middle-class, middle-aged lovers of *Brief Encounter* to the larger than life *Lawrence of Arabia*. And in *A Passage to India*, the sahib wives like Mrs. Turton (Antonia Pemberton), with little facial expressions here and there, tell the whole story of their contempt for the people whose country the British annexed.

Making that titled passage from Britain to Chandrapore, where her straitlaced son is city magistrate, is Mrs. Moore (Peggy Ashcroft). Also along is Adela Quested (Judy Davis), the young man's fiancée, who shares Mrs. Moore's enthusiasm for the "adventure" of India. Uneasy with the British disdain for socializing with the people they rule there, the newcomers are pleased to make the acquaintance of a young local physician named Dr. Aziz (Victor Banerjee), who escorts them on an outing to the distant and forbidding Malabar Caves. But once there, Adela, alone with the doctor, runs from the dark caverns, claiming that he assaulted her. And Aziz is arrested by the British authorities, who are quick to believe an Indian's guilt (or is Adela the guilty one?).

*A Passage to India* has been brought to glorious life in this faithful, location-filmed adaptation of E. M. Forster's 1924 novel, which exposed the racial and political tensions of the British raj. David Lean not only directed, but also wrote the screenplay and edited this, his first film since *Ryan's Daughter*, 14 years earlier.

The National Board of Review voted *A Passage to India* 1984's best film, citing David Lean's direction, and named Peggy Ashcroft and Victor Banerjee best actress and actor. In Hollywood, the movie tied with *Amadeus* for most nominations (each got 11), but scored only two wins: for Best Supporting Actress Ashcroft and Maurice Jarre's Best Original Score.

# Passport to Pimlico

★★★★★★★★★★★★★★★★★★★★★★★★★★★★★★★★★★★★★★★★★★★★★★★★★★★★★★★★

Nationality: British          Year: 1949
Cast: Stanley Holloway, Hermione Baddeley, Margaret Rutherford, Paul Dupuis, Basil Radford, Naunton Wayne
Director: Henry Cornelius      Running Time: 84 minutes
B/W or Color: B/W              Availability: PRISM ENTERTAIN-MENT

**P**assport to Pimlico is the quintessential Ealing comedy: this one pits a small local community against state authority; it also eventually matches the individual against cooperative efforts for the common weal—the World War II spirit of "pulling together" versus the newly emerging "I'm all right, Jack" syndrome.

Pimlico, an inner London borough, has its own distinctive neighborhood atmosphere, but its residents are now split over what to do with the large bombsite dominating the area. Ex-air warden Pemberton (Stanley Holloway) is proposing it be turned into a community recreation area; bank manager Wix (Raymond Huntley) is pushing for a commercial development.

While the Town Council is deliberating these proposals, the issue suddenly becomes irrelevant. A hitherto undiscovered bomb explodes on the site, and the resultant crater reveals not only a treasure trove of antiquities, but documents purporting to prove that Pimlico is actually part of the ancient French Duchy of Burgundy. Margaret Rutherford plays a professor who verifies the documents, testifying before the courts that Pimlico does indeed belong to Burgundy (Alastair Sim was offered this role but turned it down; Rutherford is a superb substitute).

When word gets around, ration books are destroyed; all national regulations ignored; the local policeman promotes himself to chief; Wix defies his head office to run the bank his own way; and passport controls are set up around this little piece of France in England. Everybody, of course, gleefully ignores all austerity restrictions. Trouble begins when low-lifes move in, and the rest of London flocks into Burgundy for unrationed goods. Then the British government gets into the act when those two stalwarts of civil service ineptitude, Basil Radford and Naunton Wayne, muddy the situation even further.

Through the inspired lunacy of its characters, T.E.B. Clarke's screenplay takes to task Britain's interminable and dreary postwar austerity.

357

# Pather Panchali
### (Song of the Road)/Aparajito
### (The Unvanquished)/The World of Apu (Apur Sansar)

★★★★★★★★★★★★★★★★★★★★★★★★★★★★★★★★★★★★★★★★★★★★★★★★★★★★★

Nationality: Indian

Year: 1955 (U.S.: 1958)/ 1957 (U.S.: 1959)/1959 (U.S.: 1960)

Cast: Kanu Bannerjee, Karuna Bannerjee, Pinaki Sen Gupta, Soumitra Chatterjee, Sarmila Tagore

Director: Satyajit Ray

Running Time: 112 minutes/113 minutes/103 minutes

B/W or Color: B/W

Availability: TV only

Pather Panchali is a poetic document of Indian life. Director Satyajit Ray, influenced by the neorealism of Vittorio De Sica and the documentaries of Robert Flaherty, set out to film the moving and realistic story of an Indian boy's evolution. Ray, who both wrote the screenplay and directed the film, proceeded with absolutely no backing. In fact, he sold his wife's and mother's jewelry (a veritable last resort in an Indian family) to do a rough cut. The quality of his work brought rapid government support and gently and tenderly opened a door on Indian life to western audiences.

Photographed in filtered black and white, the film has a special vision and a sense of validity that is almost documentary. It is the story of the boy Apu, from a poor Indian family in a Bengal village. The movie delineates their problems with the slow, listless tempo of a hot afternoon. Ravi Shankar's music is exactly the right accompaniment.

Aparajito, the second film in the Apu trilogy, follows the family to Benares and reveals Apu's incredulity at urban life. It deals with his rejection of his hereditary priesthood and his choice of a western university education.

The World of Apu, the third and final film, follows the destiny of Apu, who's now a thin, awkward young man who marries out of pity and grows to love his sad-eyed but grateful bride. The trilogy's universality provides a classic dimension that transcends nationality and haunts us long after its final scene.

Pather Panchali and The World of Apu were named the Best Foreign Films of, respectively, 1958 and 1960, by The National Board. Aparajito was listed among the five best for 1959.

# Pauline at the Beach
## (Pauline à la Plage)

\* \* \* \* \* \* \* \* \* \* \* \* \* \* \* \* \* \* \* \* \* \* \* \* \* \* \* \* \* \* \* \* \* \* \* \* \* \* \* \* \* \* \* \* \* \* \* \* \* \* \* \* \* \* \*

*Nationality*: French       *Year*: 1983

*Cast*: Arielle Dombasle, Amanda Langlet, Pascal Greggory, Feodor Atkine, Simon de la Brosse, Rosette

*Director*: Eric Rohmer       *Running Time*: 94 minutes

*B/W or Color*: Color       *Availability*: MEDIA HOME ENTERTAINMENT (Cinematique Collection)

**P**auline at the Beach, Eric Rohmer's third and most entertaining entry in his "Plays and Proverbs" series (*The Aviator's Wife* and *Le Beau Marriage* preceded it), is a delightfully witty comedy about love's vagaries. The story involves six people who get caught up in an amusingly complicated series of misunderstandings about who loves whom and why.

It's summer on a Normandy beach, where cousins Pauline (Amanda Langlet)—the 15-year-old title character—and Marion (Arielle Dombasle)—a beautiful, sophisticated Parisian fashion designer in her mid-twenties—are vacationing. Marion is in the process of getting a divorce; it seems her husband is too suffocatingly devoted to her. Marion is at once cynical yet searching for an all-consuming love "that burns." Pauline, who turns out to be the wisest of the bunch, has only brief flirtations to her credit. Marion meets Henry (Feodor Atkine), a balding man in his mid-thirties who's divorced and is at least as cynical about romance as Marion, who takes him to bed before the day is over. It isn't long before Henry becomes uneasy about Marion's growing affection. Then there's Pierre (Pascal Greggory), a handsome and well-toned perpetual student who tries to talk Marion into loving him rather than the slippery Henry. Meanwhile, Pauline finds Sylvain (Simon de la Brosse), a boy her age who seems to share her commonsense approach to relationships. Louisette (Rosette), a looser-than-most "local" girl who sells candy on the beach, rounds out the field.

Rohmer, as he has with the others in this series, opens the film with a quote—this time it's from the 12th-century French romantic poet Chretien de Troyes: "A wagging tongue bites itself." Indeed, there is much talk here, as in most Rohmer films, and the way the various characters deceive themselves—always a key Rohmer ingredient—is never more clearly dramatized than here.

(*Media's videocassette is subtitled.*)

# Pepe Le Moko

**************************************************

*Nationality*: French         *Year*: 1937 (U.S. release: 1941)

*Cast*: Jean Gabin, Mireille Balin, Liné Noro, Gabriel Gabrio, Lucas Gridoux, Charpin, Legris

*Director*: Julien Duvivier         *Running Time*: 86 minutes

*B/W or Color*: B/W         *Availability*: TV only

*Caveat emptor*. Never confuse this wonderful old Julien Duvivier film with the pallid 1938 Boyer-Lamarr remake, *Algiers*. The French original offers brooding seascapes; the sound of foghorns; gendarmes in handsome uniforms; the Casbah; the cynical French colonial cat-and-mouse game (a la Louis and Rick in *Casablanca*), as played by Jean Gabin as Pepe, and Lucas Gridoux as Inspector Slimane. Among the "usual suspects," the chief one here is bank robber Pepe. In the Casbah's honeycomb of winding streets and balconies, Pepe is safe. Yet he chafes at his lady, Ines (Liné Noro), who keeps him on a short leash.

Enter Gaby (Mireille Balin), who, with an appalling lack of street smarts, strolls the Casbah decked in diamonds. She has but to whisper "Champs Elysées," to have homesick Pepe fantasizing about the Paris Metro. While he never, as reported, says, "tu es le Metro," they murmur the names of Paris streets to each other. "What did you do before the diamonds?" he asks. "I wanted them," says Gaby, telegraphing that she has a "past." He, of course, forgives.

The photography is superb, the music haunting. Gabin gives a luminous and sexy performance, reminiscent of his great 1938 *Quai des Brumes*. Surely it is worth enduring a few flickering white-on-white subtitles. The sadness at the end is less for Pepe's fate than for the disappearance of Pepe's world. Even when they betray him, his friends—Gabriel Gabrio, Charpin, Legris—are hoods with a code. Pepe takes us on a nostalgic pilgrimage to a lost pinnacle of Western civilization, before Gabin developed wattles; when there was still honor among thieves. And the film won honors from The National Board for Best Foreign Film of 1941.

# Persona

★ ★ ★ ★ ★ ★ ★ ★ ★ ★ ★ ★ ★ ★ ★ ★ ★ ★ ★ ★ ★ ★ ★ ★ ★ ★ ★ ★ ★ ★ ★ ★ ★ ★ ★ ★ ★ ★ ★ ★ ★ ★ ★ ★ ★ ★ ★ ★ ★ ★ ★ ★

Nationality: Swedish                    Year: 1966 (U.S. release: 1967)
Cast: Bibi Andersson, Liv Ullmann, Gunnar Björnstrand, Margaretha Krook
Director: Ingmar Bergman            Running Time: 81 minutes (84 minutes in Europe)
B/W or Color: B/W                       Availability: Public Domain

I ngmar Bergman says the nucleus of *Persona* derived from a photo he saw of actress Bibi Andersson sunning against a wall with her friend Gunnel Lindblom—and of how their perceived interresemblance moved him to create this "poem of images."

On the surface, this rich, dreamlike fantasy concerns an actress, Elisabeth (Liv Ullmann), who, stricken with silence during a performance of *Electra*, remains voluntarily autistic. When she retreats to an isolated beach house, her silence mocks, then intrigues, the nurse Alma (Bibi Andersson), who cares for her. Despite real (or imagined) betrayals of trust, Alma gradually reveals more and more of herself, until finally confessing her guilt over a teenage sexual encounter that led her to an abortion. The two women's identities (in one of the scholarly cinema's most famous images) gradually fuse, then separate. But as the title suggests, the surface is merely the mask of the true character or, as Jung suggests, of our public roles, which when abandoned, leads to mute unconsciousness.

*Persona* was wildly interpreted when it first appeared as being about everything from lesbianism to vampirism, but it is important to note that the film is irrefutably Christological in both its overt symbolism and intricate relationship to Bergman's oeuvre. It's a meticulous and moving continuation of his "Silence of God" trilogy (*Winter Light, The Silence*, and *Through a Glass Darkly*), with the incarnate deity (or the purely psychological projection) present and listening, yet oddly unconsoling. A tantalizing, abstract introduction—a sacrificial lamb, the nailed palm of a hand, a spider—colors the film's reading; the mise-en-scene is austere enough to suggest Dreyer. Be it sacred or profane, *Persona* is a haunting, important work from one of cinema's great filmmakers. Winner of Best Picture, Director, and Actress (Bibi Andersson) awards from the National Society of Film Critics, *Persona* was voted one of the year's best foreign-language films by The National Board.

# Phar Lap

★★★★★★★★★★★★★★★★★★★★★★★★★★★★★★★★★★★★★★★★★★★★★★★★★★★★★★

Nationality: Australian               Year: 1983 (U.S. release: 1984)
Cast: Tom Burlinson, Martin Vaughan, Judy Morris, Ron Leibman
Director: Simon Wincer               Running Time: 107 minutes (118
                                     minutes overseas)
B/W or Color: Color                  Availability: PLAYHOUSE VIDEO

B ased on fact, this Australian film celebrates one of the greatest horses to ever run a race. Phar Lap was a down-and-out loser that came from behind not only to become a champion but the best damn champion anyone had ever seen.

The beauty of *Phar Lap* is that David Williamson's screenplay combines the standard shots of preparation for the big event with glimpses of corruption, greed, betrayal, and disloyalty—unpleasant traits not only in the people who want Phar Lap to lose but also in the owners themselves. Here, in the obligatory scene where one of the owners is asked to throw the big race for a large amount of money, the owner—the man who found Phar Lap and trained him when everyone else said the big, red horse was hopeless—takes the money and scratches Phar Lap. He doesn't do it for noble reasons, he simply wants the money.

The story ends sadly and touchingly, as an unbeatable champion confronts the fact that good doesn't always win over evil.

A note on Phar Lap's name: he was originally called Far Lap, but Australian racing clubs demanded that each horse's name be at least seven letters long. The *F* was changed to *Ph*, which did not alter the actual *sound* of the first word. And a word about Phar Lap's heart: when an autopsy was performed on the horse after his untimely death, it was discovered that his heart was four times as large as the average animal his size. Some said this was why he was able to race like the wind; others were more sentimental.

# Picnic at Hanging Rock

**✦✦✦✦✦✦✦✦✦✦✦✦✦✦✦✦✦✦✦✦✦✦✦✦✦✦✦✦✦✦✦✦✦✦✦✦✦✦✦✦✦✦✦✦✦✦✦✦✦✦✦✦✦✦✦**

*Nationality*: Australian                *Year*: 1975 (U.S. release: 1979)

*Cast*: Rachel Roberts, Dominic Guard, Helen Morse, Jacki Weaver, Anne Lambert

*Director*: Peter Weir                *Running Time*: 115 minutes

*B/W or Color*: Color                *Availability*: VESTRON VIDEO

If Peter Weir can be regarded as Australia's best contemporary director, then this can be considered his masterpiece. Based on the superb 1967 novel by Lady Joan Lindsay, the film reveals a series of clues as to what may or may not have occurred. Although it was then the biggest grosser in Australian movie history, *Picnic at Hanging Rock* wasn't released stateside until 1979, after the success of Weir's later picture, *The Last Wave*. Filmed principally at the real Hanging Rock in Victoria, South Australia, for a mere $450,000, it has a power beyond Weir's other work, even his excellent American-made *Witness* (1985).

On Valentine's Day, 1900, several girls from fashionable Appleyard College in Victoria go on a picnic to Hanging Rock. The place exerts a mysterious force on four of the students, who walk into a forbidden area and disappear. Mathematics teacher Vivean Gray searches for them, but only one—a hysterical Christine Schuler—returns. Later, Karen Robson is found, but neither girl can explain what happened. The events, including a suicide by orphaned Margaret Nelson, prove to be too much for strict headmistress Rachel Roberts. Driven mad, she is found dead at the foot of the rock. Roberts, who replaced Vivien Merchant in the part, makes a vivid impression in her limited role. All aspects of film technique, including slow motion and varied camera angles, are brought into play, but the mystical musical score by Bruce Smeaton is perhaps the most effective single ingredient. Both wistful and haunting, it creates a mood that most horror films attempt with far less success.

# Place of Weeping

★ ★ ★ ★ ★ ★ ★ ★ ★ ★ ★ ★ ★ ★ ★ ★ ★ ★ ★ ★ ★ ★ ★ ★ ★ ★ ★ ★ ★ ★ ★ ★ ★ ★ ★ ★ ★ ★ ★ ★ ★ ★ ★ ★ ★ ★ ★ ★ ★ ★ ★ ★ ★ ★

*Nationality*: South African  *Year*: 1986
*Cast*: James Whyle, Gcina Mhlophe, Charles Comyn, Norman Coombe
*Director*: Darrell Roodt  *Running Time*: 88 minutes
B/W *or Color*: Color  *Availability*: TV only

With an appealing mixture of naiveté and sophistication, 24-year-old Darrell Roodt has written and directed a remarkable movie reflecting the climate of today's South Africa. He has done this in a docu-drama manner that owes something to John Ford as well as his own highly original style.

Tokkie Van Rensburg (Charles Comyn), a white farmer and therefore complete lord of his domain, fires Joseph, a black worker, for asking for additional food. (Starvation-level rations are part of the pay given farm-hands.) When, desperately hungry, Joseph later tries to steal a chicken, Van Rensburg catches him and beats him to death. A number of people, sparked by a persistent white journalist (James Whyle), endeavor to bring the burly farmer to trial. One by one, the witnesses against him are killed—widening the racial conflict until it involves African rebels encamped in distant hills. The film makes clear that the farmer believes he's done nothing wrong. If a farm animal turned on him, he would kill it. Joseph is just another farm animal. It is this conviction that brings about Van Rensburg's destruction and the destruction of his family.

The movie does not portray graphic violence. Roodt has directed this gem of a film with wise sparseness, sparing the audience the details of the senseless deaths. We know murder is being committed: the menace is visably there. There is no need to bludgeon us with the bloody particulars.

This film about South Africa, produced, directed, written, and acted by South Africans, would rate kudos under any circumstances. In today's world, it is remarkable.

# The Playboy of the Western World

★★★★★★★★★★★★★★★★★★★★★★★★★★★★★★★★★★★★★★★★★★★★★★★★★★★

*Nationality*: Irish                     *Year*: 1962

*Cast*: Siobhan McKenna, Gary Raymond, Elspeth March, Michael O'Briain, Liam Redmond

*Director*: Brian Desmond Hurst      *Running Time*: 99 minutes

*B/W or Color*: Color                 *Availability*: THORN/EMI-HBO
                                       VIDEO

A distant figure stumbles and rises over charcoal gray rocks as night falls on an isolated shore in County Mayo, Ireland. This is our first glimpse of the Playboy of the Western World. As Gary Raymond plays Christy Mahon, we discover the playboy to be a young, handsome, funny, eloquent, bedraggled, and delectably innocent kid—a perfect foil for the older Pegeen Mike, the innkeeper's daughter.

Rather than detract from the original play, which calls for a fine, wild-looking, twentyish heroine, the meticulous Siobhan McKenna adds another dimension and convinces us—perhaps unintentionally—that a sensible and secure, older and wiser woman is exactly what the motherless Christy Mahon needs. After all, he did spend "eleven long days walking the world."

When Christy's murdering of his "Da" turns out to be a fraud, Pegeen's romantic imaginings are shattered, and she rejects him. When he "repeats" his patricide, repulsed, she rejects him again and agrees with the other villagers that he should be hanged.

Christy's dad rises from the dead for a second time and rescues him—from the madding crowd and, alas, also from Pegeen. And woe—Pegeen Mike tears herself asunder, simultaneously realizing her mistake as she murmurs the now-famous and heartbreaking lines, "Oh, my grief, I've lost him surely. I've lost the only Playboy of the Western World." It is our misfortune, too; we feel the grief.

The screenplay by Brian Desmond Hurst is excellent, and not only are we treated to the magnificently poetic and lyrical language of Mr. Synge, but visually Mr. Hurst has given us a banquet. The seacoast scenes are breathtaking, and the glorious mountains simply add to the primitive beauty of the wild west country.

A fine supporting cast, including Elspeth March as the Widow Quin and Niall McGinnis as Old Mahon, comes lustily to life under Mr. Hurst's skilled direction. This beautiful color film is a total joy and treat to the ear and eye, the heart and soul. It is moving, never maudlin, funny, never foolish. Three cheers for the Irish!

# Port of Call
## (Hamnstad)

\*\*\*\*\*\*\*\*\*\*\*\*\*\*\*\*\*\*\*\*\*\*\*\*\*\*\*\*\*\*\*\*\*\*\*\*\*\*\*\*\*\*\*\*\*\*\*\*\*\*\*\*\*\*\*

Nationality: Swedish        Year: 1948 (U.S. release: 1961)
Cast: Nine-Christine Jönsson, Bengt Eklund, Erik Hell, Berta Hall
Director: Ingmar Bergman    Running Time: 99 minutes
B/W or Color: B/W           Availability: EMBASSY HOME
                            ENTERTAINMENT

Ingmar Bergman has admitted of this film's style, "It's in the spirit of Rossellini throughout." Roberto Rossellini's gritty neorealism greatly appealed to the Swedish director who, with only his fifth film, was desperately searching for a style ("I still had nothing of my own to offer").

Shot on location in and around the docks of Gothenburg, *Port of Call* centers on a troubled young woman named Berit (Nine-Christine Jönsson), who's seen at the beginning attempting suicide in the harbor. She is saved from drowning by Gösta (Bengt Eklund), a sailor who befriends her, offering not only pleasant solidity, but perhaps more lasting affection than the various men with whom she previously had been all too frequently involved. Berit's deep sense of inferiority, which manifests itself in her promiscuity, isn't helped by the negative presence of a disapproving mother (Berta Hall) or the death of her friend Gertrud (Mimi Nelson), following a bungled abortion. Victims of their lower-class social background, yet refusing to be defeated by it, Berit and Gösta are ultimate survivors. "We won't give up," maintains the seaman at the movie's fadeout. And the now-optimistic Berit counters, "And soon it will be summer."

*Port of Call* is a very atmospheric work, and Gunnar Fischer's artful camerawork, as in so many of Bergman's early films, is as responsible as apparently were the films of Rossellini ("Rossellini's films were a revelation—all that extreme simplicity and poverty, that grayness"). *Port of Call* has also served to remind some critics of Marcel Carné's *Quai des Brumes,* and so has Erland von Koch's brooding score for the Bergman picture.

*Port of Call* marks an interesting stepping-stone in the early career of a master filmmaker, and, as such, deserves rediscovery.

*(Embassy offers both dubbed and subtitled cassettes.)*

# Port of Shadows
## (Le Quai des Brumes)

★★★★★★★★★★★★★★★★★★★★★★★★★★★★★★★★★★★★★★★★★★★★★★★★★★★★

*Nationality*: French          *Year*: 1938 (U.S. release: 1939)
*Cast*: Jean Gabin, Michèle Morgan, Michel Simon, Pierre Brasseur
*Director*: Marcel Carné          *Running Time*: 89 minutes
*B/W or Color*: B/W          *Availability*: TV only

One of The National Board's best films for 1939, *Port of Shadows (Le Quai des Brumes)* is strongly reminiscent of the Warner Bros. films of the Thirties. Based on the famous Pierre MacOrlan novel (with its action updated from 1914 Paris to present-day Le Havre), it's a celebrated French film noir.

In fog-bound Le Havre, army deserter Jean Gabin saves Michèle Morgan from the clutches of vicious waterfront hoodlum Michel Simon and his gang. Following their chance meeting, the doomed pair share only one night together. Gabin kills Simon, Morgan's "guardian," and is gunned down by one of Simon's henchmen (Pierre Brasseur).

The National Board cited Jean Gabin and Michel Simon on its list of best performances of the year.

Both Marcel Carné, who directed, and Jacques Prévert, the script writer, transcend the usual clichés of this genre and create a unique world of doomed romance. This is the picture (the year's second most popular in France, following only *Snow White*) that resulted in both Gabin and Morgan receiving Hollywood contracts during World War II.

Everything works in this film: the direction, script, cinematography, performances, and music by Maurice Jaubert. From the moment Gabin steps down from a truck, lights his cigarette, and exchanges a few terse words with the driver of the truck, the viewer knows that this is no manufactured movie hero. Gabin was the genuine tough article, the outcast at odds with society.

Just as the film provided the quintessential example of Gabin's prewar screen image, it established Michèle Morgan's appeal. Over 30 years later, David Shipman would write, "for many a middle-aged American or Englishman, Mlle. Morgan remains a warm, fond memory—something tenuous, exquisite, glimpsed, inevitably, through the mist of [*Port of Shadows*]."

The film also reflects the mood of despair in pre–World War II France. "A swimmer for me is already a drowned man," says one of the characters. Considered the first classic of poetic realism, the picture has many imitators; however, *Port of Shadows* remains a singular achievement.

# Prick Up Your Ears

\* \* \* \* \* \* \* \* \* \* \* \* \* \* \* \* \* \* \* \* \* \* \* \* \* \* \* \* \* \* \* \* \* \* \* \* \* \* \* \* \* \* \* \* \* \* \* \* \* \* \* \* \* \* \*

*Nationality*: British                          *Year*: 1987

*Cast*: Gary Oldman, Alfred Molina, Vanessa Redgrave, Julie Walters, Wallace Shawn

*Director*: Stephen Frears                  *Running Time*: 111 minutes

*B/W or Color*: Color                          *Availability*: SAMUEL GOLDWYN
HOME ENTERTAINMENT

P*rick Up Your Ears* is the horrifying, hilarious, true black comedy of Joe Orton's ménage macabre. Gary Oldman (Sid Vicious in *Sid and Nancy*) re-enacts the Pygmalion romance between Orton, the Leicester boy, and the older, better-educated Kenneth Halliwell (Alfred Molina), who is Professor 'Iggins to Orton's Eliza Doolittle. As we know, it ends badly.

Orton goes on to write *Entertaining Mr. Sloane, Loot,* and *What the Butler Saw*. He picks Halliwell's brains and cruises male lavatories in search of pickups. Halliwell, once artistically ambitious, thinks up *titles* for Orton's plays and finally realizes that 'Iggins's role has been reduced to picking up Eliza's laundry.

"You even sleep better than me," says Halliwell. Then he bludgeons his lover to death and kills himself.

Oldman is superb as Orton. The physically repulsive, malevolent Molina is oddly cast but effective. The real-life Halliwell was a *decorative* nonentity. Wallace Shawn plays John Lahr, author of the fine biography *Prick Up Your Ears*, which resurrected Orton's diaries and resuscitated his literary reputation long after his death in 1967. Shawn plays Lahr as a B.B.C.-type "Big Noise From Winnetka" Yank with a low-key view of the playwright's evil, irresistibly funny world.

Shawn's corn-pone cadences set off Vanessa Redgrave's marvelous Nancy Mitford delivery as agent Peggy Ramsay. As the lovers' ashes are mingled by a well-wisher who worries about proportions, she purrs, "It's a gesture, dear, not a recipe." As Orton's mother, Julie Walters does well by the Leicester contingent, which prefers to recall a younger Orton's bedding of a bridesmaid in the days before John changed his name to Joe and acquired his fatal touch of class.

# The Private Life of Henry VIII

★ ★ ★ ★ ★ ★ ★ ★ ★ ★ ★ ★ ★ ★ ★ ★ ★ ★ ★ ★ ★ ★ ★ ★ ★ ★ ★ ★ ★ ★ ★ ★ ★ ★ ★ ★ ★ ★ ★ ★ ★ ★ ★ ★ ★ ★ ★ ★ ★ ★ ★ ★ ★ ★ ★ ★

Nationality: British          Year: 1933

Cast: Charles Laughton, Robert Donat, Binnie Barnes, Elsa Lanchester, Wendy Barrie

Director: Alexander Korda          Running Time: 96 minutes

B/W or Color: B/W          Availability: EMBASSY HOME ENTERTAINMENT

In Academy Award annals, *The Private Life of Henry VIII* broke new ground in 1933 as the first British production to win an American statuette when Charles Laughton was named Best Actor for his portrayal of England's colorful 16th-century Tudor monarch.

This popular serving of lusty British history, with its surprising tongue-in-cheek humor, concerns King Henry's fixation on marriage and the importance of producing a legitimate heir to the throne. Bypassing Katharine of Aragon, the first of his six wives, the screenplay quickly beheads Anne Boleyn (Merle Oberon in an early bit role), offers slightly more footage to Jane Seymour (Wendy Barrie), who dies in childbirth, and considerably more to the entertaining battle of wits between Henry and the well-organized Anne of Cleves (Elsa Lanchester, in a blonde wig and scene-stealing German accent). After divorcing this marital opponent, Henry weds and beheads Catherine Howard (Binnie Barnes), charging adultery with court favorite Thomas Culpepper (Robert Donat). At the movie's close, an elderly Henry has become the surprisingly obedient husband of a bossy Catherine Parr (Everley Gregg).

Producer-director Alexander Korda's celluloid serving of romanticized English history revitalized Laughton's then-flagging screen career. Despite its seeming visual richness, *The Private Life of Henry VIII* owes its "splendor" to the resourcefulness of Vincent Korda, whose flimsy sets were built, lit, and photographed (by Georges Perinal) to give the finished product a deceptively expensive appearance. Amazingly, filming was accomplished in five weeks. In New York, the movie broke all opening-day records at Radio City Music Hall, while in Great Britain it made Korda's name famous and provided a much-needed shot in the arm for a floundering film industry. The National Board of Review named *The Private Life of Henry VIII* one of 1933's ten best films.

# The Promoter
## (The Card)

★★★★★★★★★★★★★★★★★★★★★★★★★★★★★★★★★★★★★★★★★★★★★★★★★★

**Nationality**: British          **Year**: 1952

**Cast**: Alec Guinness, Glynis Johns, Valerie Hobson, Petula Clark, Edward Chapman

**Director**: Ronald Neame          **Running Time**: 91 minutes

**B/W or Color**: B/W          **Availability**: INDEPENDENT UNITED DISTRIBUTORS

The Promoter (titled *The Card* in England) is the history of a social climber in a stuffy community. It's the droll but uncynical study of a washerwoman's son, Henry Machin (Alec Guinness), who rises to prominence by means of forgery and deceit. His victims, however, usually seem the better as a result of his schemes and ironically do not object to paying the price.

In his *New York Times* review, Bosley Crowther defined the Guinness character as "an unabashed rogue," adding that Machin was "not exactly a bona fide crook . . . simply an enterprising young man who . . . invents and resorts to maneuvers a scrupulous person might call sharp."

Seemingly a milquetoast, Guinness uses cunning to alter his grades at school, forge his name on an invitation to a fancy ball, dance with the countess (Valerie Hobson), outwit his employer, and become a rent collector. Managing his own installment-buying service he is eventually chosen mayor of the town. A jealous politician complains that the honor is not deserved. Then the countess informs him of Machin's special contribution: "He has made us laugh."

Bosley Crowther also complimented female lead Glynis Johns for her portrait of "an equally crafty young lady." Of Guinness and Glynis, Crowther observed: "The whole amusement and delight in the picture is watching how neatly they perform."

The two meet when Guinness tries to collect back rent from her dancing school. Though she is more than a worthy opponent, it is Guinness who gets even at the end.

Seen as one of the women in Guinness's life is Petula Clark, who later became a popular singer and co-starred with Peter O'Toole in the 1969 musical version of *Goodbye, Mr. Chips*.

Eric Ambler's screenplay was based on a novel by Arnold Bennett (from his *Five Towns* series) and received expert handling by a superb cast under the inspired direction of Ronald Neame.

# Purple Noon
## (Plein Soleil)

★★★★★★★★★★★★★★★★★★★★★★★★★★★★★★★★★★★★★★★★★★★★★★★★★★★★★★★

Nationality: French-Italian      Year: 1961
Cast: Alain Delon, Maurice Ronet, Marie Laforet
Director: René Clément      Running Time: 115 minutes
B/W or Color: Color      Availability: TV only

The film was released originally in Europe under the title *Plein Soleil* ("bright sunlight"), which was certainly a more accurate title, since there has never been a more vividly color-filled, sun-drenched film noir. Set in the gloriously scenic Italian Riviera and in Rome, the picture-postcard scenery, as photographed by Henri Decae (*The 400 Blows, The Cousins*), is worth the price of rental. While the tangled plot is not always totally credible, the excitement level remains high, right up to the surprise ending that had moviegoers jumping out of their seats.

Based upon *The Amazing Mr. Ripley,* the highly regarded thriller by Patricia Highsmith (who also provided the novel for the Hitchcock classic *Strangers on a Train*), the film introduces a decadent duo: Alain Delon as the poor, jealous, paid companion of the rich, sadistic Maurice Ronet. As they sail down the Italian coastline in Ronet's elegant yacht, Ronet's ambivalent girlfriend (Marie Laforet) is further reason for Delon's discontent. Finally taunted beyond endurance, Delon murders his tormentor in a particularly graphic and grisly scene.

The remainder of the film depicts the ever-more-ingenious schemes that Delon devises as he takes over the identity, the fortune, and the fiancée of the dead man. Directed and co-written by the distinguished René Clément (*Forbidden Games* and *Gervaise*), *Purple Noon* is a stylish shocker, all the more so for its sumptuously beautiful look. Somewhat incongruously, *Purple Noon* is subtitled in English in most versions; the characters, though supposedly American, speak only French or Italian!

# Pygmalion

★ ★ ★ ★ ★ ★ ★ ★ ★ ★ ★ ★ ★ ★ ★ ★ ★ ★ ★ ★ ★ ★ ★ ★ ★ ★ ★ ★ ★ ★ ★ ★ ★ ★ ★ ★ ★ ★ ★ ★ ★ ★ ★ ★ ★ ★ ★ ★ ★ ★ ★ ★ ★

*Nationality*: British                *Year*: 1938

*Cast*: Leslie Howard, Wendy Hiller, Scott Sunderland, Wilfrid Lawson, Marie Lohr

*Director*: Anthony Asquith and        *Running Time*: 95 minutes
Leslie Howard

*B/W or Color*: B/W                    *Availability*: EMBASSY HOME
                                       ENTERTAINMENT

Here is the original George Bernard Shaw story that most Americans know better as the musical *My Fair Lady. Pygmalion* was first produced in London in 1914, and Mrs. Patrick Campbell played Eliza Doolittle to Herbert Tree's Professor Higgins. When Mrs. Campbell blurted out, "Not bloody likely," the reaction was comparable to the kind of sensation caused a quarter of a century later by Clark Gable saying, "Frankly, my dear, I don't give a damn."

*Pygmalion* was nominated for an Academy Award as Best Picture, and its co-stars won Oscar nominations as Best Actor and Actress. Portraying Higgins is Leslie Howard, who shared directing honors with Anthony Asquith (son of Prime Minister Lord Asquith and Nancy Tennant Asquith, the first woman member of Parliament). Wendy Hiller plays Eliza, the cockney flower-seller whom phoneticist Higgins uses to demonstrate his theories that accents determine class labels. Wendy Hiller later starred in the second of Shaw's filmed plays, *Major Barbara*—opposite Rex Harrison, the future Higgins of *My Fair Lady*.

The excellent cast includes Scott Sunderland as Colonel Pickering and Wilfrid Lawson as Eliza's vulgar dustman-father Alfred Doolittle.

Selected as one of the ten best films by The National Board of Review, *Pygmalion* won Oscars for its writing. The often-changing rules in that category allowed W. P. Lipscomb, Cecil Lewis, and Ian Dalrymple to win for Best Adaptation, while Best Screenplay was won by the Grand Old Man himself, George Bernard Shaw. His reaction: "It's an insult for them to offer me any honor, as if they had never heard of me before—and it's very likely they never have."

Shaw had adamantly refused to have his plays filmed until he met producer Gabriel Pascal. They became fast friends, and Shaw agreed to a deal—provided he himself write the screenplay. "Not the least regard will be paid to American ideas," insisted Shaw, "except to avoid them as much as possible."

# Quartet

\* \* \* \* \* \* \* \* \* \* \* \* \* \* \* \* \* \* \* \* \* \* \* \* \* \* \* \* \* \* \* \* \* \* \* \* \* \* \* \* \* \* \* \* \* \* \* \* \* \* \* \* \* \* \*

**Nationality**: British          **Year**: 1948 (U.S. release: 1949)

**Cast**: Jack Watling, Mai Zetterling, Dirk Bogarde, Françoise Rosay, Honor Blackman, George Cole, Susan Shaw, Mervyn Johns, Hermione Baddeley, Cecil Parker, Nora Swinburne

**Directors**: Ralph Smart ("The Facts **Running Time**: 120 minutes of Life"); Harold French ("The Alien Corn"); Arthur Crabtree ("The Kite"); Ken Annakin ("The Colonel's Lady")

**B/W or Color**: B/W          **Availability**: TV only

Unlike *Dead of Night,* in which various stories are linked to a common thread, none of the four Somerset Maugham yarns in *Quartet* has any tie whatsoever, save for the narration supplied—somewhat uneasily—by their 74-year-old author. Characteristic of Maugham, each of these tales has its humor and its ironic twists, ending on notes of surprise. But it is the exploration of character that is of the essence here, and a well-chosen cast brings the package vividly to life. Although the stories were shown in a different order in Britain, this assessment reflects the *American* release print.

"The Facts of Life" recounts what happens when a naive young tennis player in Monte Carlo ignores his father's advice about gambling and women. A glamorous adventuress seduces him and nearly gets his casino winnings—until he steals back his bankroll and, unintentionally, gets hers as well.

In "The Alien Corn," Maugham is at his most serious, detailing the tragic efforts of a young aristocrat to become a great concert pianist—a goal that ultimately proves beyond his reach, after he plays for a celebrated mistress of the keyboard.

"The Kite" dissects, with poignant irony, lower-middle-class life and a family of kite-flying enthusiasts disrupted when the only son leaves the "nest" to marry a disdainful girl of whom his overbearing mother disapproves.

And "The Colonel's Lady" is a gentle, neglected wife who publishes a startling volume of verse detailing an extramarital interlude that her husband of 30 years misinterprets as being autobiographical. But the final joke is on him.

Skillfully adapted for the screen by R. C. Sherriff, *Quartet* proved so successful an entertainment package that it fostered a pair of Maugham sequels, the 1950 *Trio* and *Encore* in 1951.

*Quartet* was named one of 1949's ten best by The National Board.

# The Queen of Spades

*************************************************************

**Nationality**: British                    **Year**: 1949

**Cast**: Anton Walbrook, Edith Evans, Yvonne Mitchell, Ronald Howard

**Director**: Thorold Dickinson and    **Running Time**: 95 minutes
(uncredited) Rodney Ackland

**B/W or Color**: B/W                    **Availability**: HBO/CANNON
VIDEO

Alexander Pushkin's ghost story of *The Queen of Spades* may be best known for the sprawling opera that Tchaikovsky composed in 1890. But the tale is better served by this handsome movie version, produced by Russian-born Anatole de Grunwald.

In 1806 St. Petersburg, Herman (Anton Walbrook), an impoverished army officer, is obsessed with learning how to win at faro. When he learns that an aged countess (Edith Evans) once sold her soul for that secret, he determines to wrest the knowledge from her, and thus he courts the old lady's impressionable young ward (Yvonne Mitchell). But before he can force the countess's secret from her, Herman unintentionally frightens her to death. A subsequent visit from her ghost discloses the winning card combination—three, seven, and ace. Herman stakes everything and loses. Instead of an ace, he turns up the queen of spades, on which he seems to see the dead woman's face—and to hear her tapping cane and rustling petticoats—as he descends into madness.

Rodney Ackland's marvelously detailed screenplay afforded designer Oliver Messel a wonderful opportunity for establishing an elaborate, baroque atmosphere. The artistry with which these sets are lit and photographed by Otto Heller plays a vital role in building the brooding, almost surrealistic terror that Thorold Dickinson's direction sustains. The film began production with scenarist Ackland as director, but those who controlled the purse strings held little faith in his methods, and Dickinson replaced him.

At 60, stage luminary Edith Evans made her belated talking-picture debut, and although her role is relatively brief, she dominates the screen. That she continues to haunt the viewer—even as she does Herman—throughout the film is comment enough. Not to be overshadowed, Walbrook delineates Herman in the grand Teutonic manner.

Thorold Dickinson's *Queen of Spades* remains among the screen's few great ghost stories.

# Ran

★★★★★★★★★★★★★★★★★★★★★★★★★★★★★★★★★★★★★★★★★★★★★★★★★★★★★

*Nationality*: French-Japanese     *Year*: 1985
*Cast*: Tatsuya Nakadai, Mieko Harada, Akira Terao, Jinpachi Nezu, Daisuke Ryu
*Director*: Akira Kurosawa     *Running Time*: 160 minutes
*B/W or Color*: Color     *Availability*: CBS/FOX HOME VIDEO

At 75, Akira Kurosawa could sit back and relax in the knowledge that he is forever assured an honored place in the history of film-making. But happily for his admirers, he is still working, and *Ran* is true to his epic-making form. With dazzling, sweeping vistas, battle scenes rivaling those of *Henry V* and *Alexander Nevsky*, this Asiatic King Lear-like story presents a feast for eyes and ears.

This Lear, Lord Hidetora (Tatsuya Nakadai), has three sons (Akira Terao, Jinpachi Nezu, and Daisuke Ryu) and one Lady Macbeth-clone daughter-in-law (Mieko Harada), a really tough lady who plots murders as easily as planning the daily menu. Lord Hidetora escapes the assassination attempts of his two eldest sons but goes mad in the process and is finally reunited with the son he rejected and now knows to be the only one who truly loved him. One by one, most of the characters meet with violent ends, illustrative of the maxim that he who lives by the sword shall perish by the sword.

*Ran* would be translated in Japanese as "war" or "conflict," but Kurosawa wanted to emphasize an older Chinese interpretation of the word, which meant "chaos." And chaos is certainly what results from the greed, savagery, and intrigue that characterize this martial family. Hidetora himself had been responsible for the sacking of scores of villages and castles, earning implacable enemies, not the least being his vicious daughter-in-law, whose family he has massacred and who, apart from plotting Hidetora's murder, demands her sister-in-law's head, "salted so that it won't decompose."

*Ran* is a spectacle par excellence from a director noted for spectacle. The photography of Takao Saito and Masaharu Ueda, the marvelous costumes of Emi Wada, and majestic music of Toru Takemitsu contribute magnificently. *Ran* was voted 1985's Best Foreign Film by The National Board, which also named Akira Kurosawa Best Director.

(*CBS/Fox offers a subtitled videocassette.*)

# Rashomon
## (In the Woods)

★★★★★★★★★★★★★★★★★★★★★★★★★★★★★★★★★★★★★★★★★★★★★★★★★★★★★

Nationality: Japanese                Year: 1950 (U.S. release: 1951)
Cast: Toshiro Mifune, Machiko Kyo, Masayuki Mori, Takashi Shimura
Director: Akira Kurosawa             Running Time: 88 minutes
B/W or Color: B/W                    Availability: EMBASSY HOME
                                     ENTERTAINMENT

R ashomon was the first Japanese film openly to compete in the Western market. Its director, Akira Kurosawa, became a name to reckon with, and its star, Toshiro Mifune, went on to a brilliant international career as Japan's best-known actor outside of his own country.

Rashomon won the Golden Lion award at Venice in 1951 and was chosen as Best Foreign Film by both The National Board of Review and the Academy of Motion Picture Arts and Sciences. Films in Review called the movie "an almost perfect example of the universality of the film medium" and concluded, "almost every camera shot—long, middle, close and panoramic—was composed as a painter composes. The subtleties of costume, acting, direction and photography are breath-taking."

Rashomon has a timeless theme: human beings tell things the way they would like them to appear. Set in Japan of 1200 years ago, it recounts the story of a merchant traveling with his wife through a forest, of the wife's rape, and of the husband's death at the hands of a bandit. But exactly how did it all happen? Kurosawa's account of this violent crime is told in flashback from four different points of view. What actually transpired is left to the viewer's interpretation—a then-unusual departure from the film of straightforward narrative structure. In the movie's various critical evaluations, some felt that the Japanese were saying to the world: "Who knows who is guilty or who, in terrible truth, is without guilt?"

In 1964, Rashomon was remade, Western-style, in an American version called The Outrage. Martin Ritt directed Michael Kanin's screenplay with an impressive cast headed by Paul Newman, Claire Bloom, Laurence Harvey, and Edward G. Robinson, but the result was an ineffective failure.

(Embassy offers an excellent subtitled print, as well as an English-dubbed version.)

# The Red Shoes

★ ★ ★ ★ ★ ★ ★ ★ ★ ★ ★ ★ ★ ★ ★ ★ ★ ★ ★ ★ ★ ★ ★ ★ ★ ★ ★ ★ ★ ★ ★ ★ ★ ★ ★ ★ ★ ★ ★ ★ ★ ★ ★ ★ ★ ★ ★ ★ ★

*Nationality*: British                    *Year*: 1948

*Cast*: Anton Walbrook, Moira Shearer, Marius Goring, Leonide Massine, Robert Helpmann

*Director*: Michael Powell and          *Running Time*: 136 minutes
Emeric Pressburger

*B/W or Color*: Color                    *Availability*: PARAMOUNT
                                         HOME VIDEO

In the Thirties, producer Alexander Korda had commissioned this ballet story from a staff writer, Emeric Pressburger, but the screenplay was never filmed. In 1947, Pressburger and his partner Michael Powell wanted to reactivate the project and Korda sold the script back to them for £12,000.

*The Red Shoes'* story line loosely derives from a Hans Christian Andersen horror tale about a little girl whose enchanted slippers nearly dance her to death—until a benevolent executioner chops off her feet, allowing them to dance off to hell on their own, while the child carries on with wooden feet.

In the film, a young hopeful (in a remarkable performance by titian-haired ballerina Moira Shearer) rises to principal dancer with a European ballet company. Her career is complicated by a divided allegiance to her young composer-husband (Marius Goring) and a disapproving martinet impresario (Anton Walbrook). Eventually, she dances the dramatic lead in a new ballet called *The Red Shoes*, choreographed to her husband's music, about a young woman whose bewitched toe-shoes literally dance her to death. It makes a star of the ballerina, but the ballet's tragic theme repeats itself when the ballerina dances to her own death in front of a train. At the film's finale, *The Red Shoes* ballet begins without its leading lady, a spotlight eerily following her choreography in tribute.

Cinematographer Jack Cardiff dazzlingly captured the outwardly glamorous, privately gritty world of the ballet. Oscars were awarded for art direction and interior decoration, as well as the two commissioned ballet scores for the "Heart of Fire" and "Red Shoes" dance sequences. The film was immensely popular in the United States, where it ran for over two years in New York City.

The National Board of Review named *The Red Shoes* one of 1948's ten best films.

# Rembrandt

* * * * * * * * * * * * * * * * * * * * * * * * * * * * * * * * * * * * * * * * * * * * * * * * * * * * * * *

*Nationality*: British          *Year*: 1936
*Cast*: Charles Laughton, Gertrude Lawrence, Elsa Lanchester, Edward Chapman, Walter Hudd, Roger Livesey
*Director*: Alexander Korda          *Running Time*: 85 minutes
*B/W or Color*: B/W          *Availability*: EMBASSY HOME ENTERTAINMENT

After the success of his alliance with Charles Laughton on *The Private Life of Henry VIII*, Alexander Korda searched for a suitable follow-up vehicle. *Cyrano de Bergerac* never came to pass; nor did Laughton star in any of the other Korda projects planned for him—*The Scarlet Pimpernel, Things to Come,* or *The Ghost Goes West*. Eventually, Korda and Laughton agreed on a biofilm of Rembrandt van Rijn, the 17th-century Dutch painter.

For art-collector Korda, *Rembrandt* was a labor of love. Unfortunately, it remained one of his few box-office failures. The film's pace is deliberate and its continuity episodic as it moves from 1642 and completion of the great *Night Watch* canvas to the artist's death in 1669. An intelligent screenplay managed to avoid the usual romantic motion-picture falsehoods but still reveal an egotistical, wenching, but religious and dedicated genius undeterred by either poverty or lack of sponsorship. Although Rembrandt's first wife, Saskia, is never shown, the movie covers his relationship with his coarse housekeeper-mistress Geertje (Gertrude Lawrence, with whom Laughton was at odds) and Hendrickje (the actor's wife, Elsa Lanchester), the servant whom he marries after their child is born. When she dies prematurely, Rembrandt retreats into doddering old age, working on a self-portrait with paints made possible by the donation of a former pupil.

Laughton journeyed to the Netherlands to research the artist for this glowing, multifaceted portrayal that the hard-to-please British film critic C. A. Lejeune ventured to call "probably the finest acting performance ever recorded on celluloid."

*Rembrandt* is Korda's finest directorial effort. His production expertise is reflected in his brother Vincent Korda's carefully researched sets, so artfully lit and photographed by Georges Perinal that they actually seem to duplicate the celebrated "north light" that illuminates Rembrandt's paintings.

The National Board of Review listed *Rembrandt* among the ten best films of its year.

# The Return of Martin Guerre
## (Le Retour de Martin Guerre)

★★★★★★★★★★★★★★★★★★★★★★★★★★★★★★★★★★★★★★★★★★★★★★★★★★★★★★

Nationality: French          Year: 1982

Cast: Gérard Depardieu, Nathalie Baye, Roger Planchon, Maurice Barrier

Director: Daniel Vigne       Running Time: 111 minutes (123 minutes in France)

B/W or Color: Color        Availability: EMBASSY HOME ENTERTAINMENT

T he Return of Martin Guerre dramatizes the true story of a man who claimed to be someone he may or may not have actually been. And while the Guerre mystery was eventually solved, its denouement won't be revealed here. It's too integral to the film's enjoyment.

The real Guerre was a young peasant farmer of 16th-century France who obeyed village elders by entering into an arranged, teenage wedding with an agreeable neighbor Bertrande, by whom he had a son before vanishing, suddenly and mysteriously. When Guerre resurfaced eight years later, his appearance had changed: he was now a man of more rugged form and outgoing, humorous disposition. His still-faithful wife willingly welcomed him back to her hearth and bed, and they had two more children. But then a quarrel arose between Martin and his uncle Pierre over money, and the older man took his nephew to court, alleging that he was an imposter. Complications multiply when a pair of passing vagabonds claim that "Martin" was actually a former soldier named Arnaud, and that the real Martin Guerre lives elsewhere, having lost a leg in battle.

How these complications affect the villagers and imperil the movie's central characters are part and parcel of the story, which is played to perfection, especially by Gérard Depardieu, as the alleged Martin Guerre, and the beatific-faced Nathalie Baye as Bertrande. Director Daniel Vigne gives astonishingly accurate attention to the look and feel of postmedieval rural France, owing a great debt to the set and costume designers. The carefully lit cinematography of Andre Neau gives The Return of Martin Guerre the appearance of a Brueghel painting come to life. The National Board named this movie among 1983's best.

(Embassy offers the film in both dubbed and subtitled versions.)

# The Return of the Soldier

**★★★★★★★★★★★★★★★★★★★★★★★★★★★★★★★★★★★★★★★★★★★★★★★★★★★★★★**

*Nationality*: British       *Year*: 1981 (U.S. release: 1985)
*Cast*: Glenda Jackson, Julie Christie, Ann-Margret, Alan Bates
*Director*: Alan Bridges      *Running Time*: 101 minutes
*B/W or Color*: Color       *Availability*: THORN/EMI-HBO
                                          VIDEO

On the eve of World War I, Chris (Alan Bates) has slipped away from his glitteringly elegant guests, and, in the courtyard of his splendid country house, is taking leave of his hounds and horses.

Surely J.M.W. Turner inspired the photography for this view of the English countryside (though Stephen Goldblatt is actually responsible). Sargent, too, could have painted the lovely house authentically furnished down to every detail, and certainly would have wanted to capture on canvas its graceful, languid mistress, Kitty (Julie Christie), a true period beauty. But the serene Edwardian atmosphere belies disturbing undercurrents: the repressed lust for her cousin Chris, of the rather dowdy Jenny (Ann-Margret actually manages to look plain in this part); an empty, unused, lovingly furnished nursery . . .

While Chris is off in the army, the two women spend their days waiting for him, while in turn they're waited upon by their own army of servants.

This self-indulgent existence is shattered when Margaret (Glenda Jackson) appears. She is a shabby, lower-middle-class housewife, but, as an attractive and sensitive girl 20 years earlier, she had loved and been loved by Chris. Margaret informs Kitty and Jenny that Chris is in the hospital, suffering from shell shock and amnesia. Intellectually, he knows this is 1916, but remembers only the people he knew earlier—Margaret and Jenny, but not his own wife, Kitty.

Alan Bridges's direction is gripping and the acting incomparable. It's as though every member of the ideal cast had been born to play these particular roles. With top-notch directing and acting present, background music can be unnecessary. Fittingly, *The Return of the Soldier* has almost no music, other than the little that comes out of an old wind-up gramophone.

# Richard III

★ ★ ★ ★ ★ ★ ★ ★ ★ ★ ★ ★ ★ ★ ★ ★ ★ ★ ★ ★ ★ ★ ★ ★ ★ ★ ★ ★ ★ ★ ★ ★ ★ ★ ★ ★ ★ ★ ★ ★ ★ ★ ★ ★ ★ ★ ★ ★ ★ ★ ★ ★ ★ ★

**Nationality**: British  **Year**: 1955 (U.S. release: 1956)

**Cast**: Laurence Olivier, John Gielgud, Ralph Richardson, Claire Bloom, Cedric Hardwicke

**Director**: Laurence Olivier  **Running Time**: 158 minutes

**B/W or Color**: Color  **Availability**: EMBASSY HOME ENTERTAINMENT

Of Sir Laurence Olivier's first three Shakespeare films, *Richard III* is generally held to be the most straightforward, vivid, and satisfying. Again, he served in the triple capacity of producer, director, and principal actor, with such unflagging vitality and talent for self-criticism that he inspired a superb cast of Shakespeare-seasoned actors to give their all.

Olivier and company give *Richard III* so full-bodied a performance that the play need never be filmed again. The actor's direction is courageously bold and striking, but it is, after all, an actor's *picture,* and Olivier the actor is in top form, dominating the film with his rich, classic portrayal of this deformed monster, a figure of subtle calculation and frightening evil. Olivier plays with such diabolic intensity—full of nuance and unpredictable movement—that it is often difficult to recognize this handsome, classical actor, despite his mellifluous tones and brilliant vocal interpretation. But it is truly a great Shakespearean performance, right through to the climactic Battle of Bosworth Field and Richard's desperate final outcry, "My kingdom for a horse!"

After Olivier's formidable Richard, one must cite Ralph Richardson's scheming Buckingham, John Gielgud's brief but distinguished Clarence (whose forced drowning in a keg of wine provides one of the film's more lurid moments), and Sir Cedric Hardwicke's forceful characterization of old Edward IV, whose throne Richard covets and wins. Claire Bloom makes a beautiful, well-spoken Anne, at once stirred and repulsed by Richard's courting. Mary Kerridge is a colorful Queen Elizabeth, and Pamela Brown, as court mistress Jane Shore, once again proves the eloquence of pantomime and an expressive face.

The British Film Academy called *Richard III* the year's Best Film and justly gave Sir Laurence Olivier its Best Actor prize. The National Board named it one of the best films of 1956.

# Rider on the Rain
## (Le Passager de la Pluie)

\* \* \* \* \* \* \* \* \* \* \* \* \* \* \* \* \* \* \* \* \* \* \* \* \* \* \* \* \* \* \* \* \* \* \* \* \* \* \* \* \* \* \* \* \* \* \* \* \* \* \* \*

Nationality: French-Italian      Year: 1970
Cast: Charles Bronson, Marlene Jobert, Gabriele Tinti, Jill Ireland
Director: René Clément      Running Time: 119 minutes
B/W or Color: Color      Availability: MONTEREY HOME VIDEO

When he appeared in this French-made suspense melodrama, Charles Bronson was a veteran of some 46-odd movies, most of them American made. Nevertheless, Rider on the Rain was undeniably a notch or two above most of his previous efforts, and it offered the rugged action star an opportunity for good grooming and a smart wardrobe in a well wrought script directed by René Clément, whose best work include Gervaise, Forbidden Games, and Purple Noon. Indeed, Rider on the Rain is very much in the Purple Noon tradition. An American army colonel (Bronson) has gone undercover to track down an escaped sex criminal who made off with army funds. In the south of France, he stumbles into a strange murder case that may have some connection with his mission: while her husband is away, a wealthy young Frenchwoman (Marlene Jobert) is attacked and raped in her own home by a mysterious intruder, whom she manages to kill. She then disposes of the corpse. Although it would appear to be that of the American sex offender, nothing is exactly what it seems in this stylish Hitchcockian thriller.

Much of the movie encompasses a battle of wits between Bronson and Jobert, and their charismatic teaming does much to lift the screenplay into an exceptional category. In European cinemas, house records were broken by the movie, and for the 21 weeks of its Paris engagement, it drew capacity crowds. In the United States, Rider on the Rain got some enthusiastic reviews, and even had that rarity for a Bronson picture—arthouse prestige. Bronson considers it his "real beginning" as a star, and gives credit to his wife, Jill Ireland, who talked him into accepting the role.

(Monterey's cassette is of the English-dubbed version.)

# Rififi
## (Du Rififi Chez les Hommes)

**********************************************************

**Nationality**: French                    **Year**: 1955 (U.S. release: 1956)
**Cast**: Jean Servais, Jules Dassin (Perlo Vita), Carl Mohner
**Director**: Jules Dassin                  **Running Time**: 115 minutes
**B/W or Color**: B/W                       **Availability**: Public Domain

Jules Dassin's first American films were characterized by brooding moods punctuated with scenes of soaring, violent visual power—the prison escape that climaxes *Brute Force* and the wrestling match to the death in *Night and the City*. Then blacklisting ended his Hollywood noir period.

Chased off to Europe, Dassin scored an international bull's-eye with *Rififi*, which, ads purported, meant "danger." This story of small-time, expert criminals pulling off a robbery only to be foiled by the unexpected had many Dassin earmarks: the antihero as central characters; a half-hour robbery sequence staged like a ballet and played in total silence; an ending composed of a dreamlike montage of jump cuts as one of the protagonists, while bleeding to death, returns a kidnapped child to its mother. And a further signature—Dassin plays one of the criminals, charmingly.

A later film brought Dassin back to America, his sins washed clean. *Never on Sunday*, featuring Dassin's wife, Greek super-personality Melina Mercouri, earned 40 times its cost at the box office, and that kind of profit instantly canceled out any political indiscretions he may have committed. Once returned, Dassin promptly reworked *Rififi* into *Topkapi*, an enjoyable caper about a museum theft, with the camera keeping an almost fetishist eye on Mercouri and support from Maximilian Schell and Peter Ustinov. It succeeded in more ways than one. An enterprising thief—Murph the Surf—studied the film and duplicated its criminal handiwork when he stole the Star of India sapphire in 1964.

Mercouri has devoted much of her time to politics in her homeland, and, regretfully, Dassin's career appears to be at a standstill.

(*Video Award Motion Pictures offers a subtitled tape.*)

# The Road Warrior
## (Mad Max 2)

**★★★★★★★★★★★★★★★★★★★★★★★★★★★★★★★★★★★★★★★★★★★★★★★★★★★**

*Nationality*: Australian          *Year*: 1981 (U.S. release: 1982)
*Cast*: Mel Gibson, Bruce Spence, Vernon Wells, Emil Minty, Mike Preston
*Director*: George Miller          *Running Time*: 94 minutes
*B/W or Color*: Color          *Availability*: WARNER HOME VIDEO

Like the Trekkies, those devoted fans of the *Star Trek* series, there is also a cult (albeit smaller) equally loyal to the three (so far) Mad Max films. The first was *Mad Max* (1979); *The Road Warrior* was the sequel; and 1985 produced *Mad Max Beyond Thunderdome*. Mel Gibson starred in all three, and George Miller was the director. Most aficionados consider *Mad Max 2* the best of the trilogy.

A futuristic film rather than sci-fi, *The Road Warrior* is set in the grim period following World War III. Civilization has collapsed, and its most precious commodity, gas, is in short supply. Max Rockatansky, a former patrolman whose wife and son were murdered by bikers, locates an oil refinery only to discover that it is being besieged by the Humungus, a muscle-bound horde of leather-bedecked thugs sporting Mohawk hairdos and armed with crossbows. These weirdos are also menacing an outpost of peaceful pioneers. Reluctantly, Max, accompanied by his dog and driving his souped-up hot rod, agrees to bring in a fuel truck so the survivors can escape to a distant land.

Numerous colorful battles and showdowns ensue, most of them resembling sandy demolition derbies, and all of them exceeding any known speed limits as a trailer truck, a supertanker, motor bikes—even a school bus and a homemade helicopter—clash.

Mad Max, the "high-octane Lancelot," is an almost mythical hero and a kind of Shane for the Eighties, strong, silent, unfathomable. The film is unique, almost a first of its kind, unrelentingly exciting and imaginative, and surprisingly witty. The settings, the stunt work, and the visual and special effects are first rate. There has never been a big-screen world quite like Mad Max's inspired junkyard, and therein, perhaps, lies the key to all the fun.

# Rocco and His Brothers
## (Rocco e i Suoi Fratelli)

★★★★★★★★★★★★★★★★★★★★★★★★★★★★★★★★★★★★★★★★★★★★★★★★★★★★★

*Nationality*: Italian        *Year*: 1960 (U.S. release: 1961)

*Cast*: Alain Delon, Renato Salvatori, Annie Girardot, Katina Paxinou, Claudia Cardinale, Roger Hanin

*Director*: Luchino Visconti      *Running Time*: 155 minutes (original Italian version: 180 minutes)

*B/W or Color*: B/W       *Availability*: TV only

Visconti has invested this drama of an Italian peasant family that moves to Milan and is corrupted by urban society with the elemental emotion and power of fine Greek tragedy. The family's devastating fate is firmly tied to an unalterable destiny. The mother (Katina Paxinou) is a simple woman of primal emotions who is incapable of understanding what is happening to her tightly knit family. Simone, played effortlessly and brilliantly by Renato Salvatori, is the role that fills the screen with heart-wrenching scenes. He is lured to the prizefight ring and is ruthlessly exploited by a sleazy manager. We watch the youth, who only a short time earlier was enchanted by his first glimpse of snow, brutalized by his vicious environment. He has a few minor triumphs in the ring, which mask his awareness of what is happening to him. Then he meets Nadia (Annie Girardot), a prostitute down on her luck. When Nadia turns her interest to his brother Rocco (Alain Delon), the jealousy this generates explodes into a devastating rift of all family affection and loyalty. The action moves inexorably to a chilling climax in which Simone rapes Nadia in front of gentle Rocco's eyes, and the brothers fight savagely. The reality of their debasement is movingly conveyed in this high-pitched confrontation. Simone is now hopelessly defiled. He glimpses a truth about himself when he sees a homosexual eyeing him appraisingly in the steam bath and realizes he is simply a commodity for exploitation. Meanwhile, Rocco must surmount his anguish and assume the burden of family responsibility.

Girardot's performance as a woman torn by her emotions often matches the extraordinary level of Salvatori's performance. The action is ably underscored by Nino Rota's compelling music. Many believe this to be Visconti's greatest cinematic achievement.

# The Rocking Horse Winner

* * * * * * * * * * * * * * * * * * * * * * * * * * * * * * * * * * * * * * * * * * * * * * *

*Nationality*: British            *Year*: 1949 (U.S. release: 1950)
*Cast*: Valerie Hobson, John Howard Davies, John Mills, Ronald Squire, Hugh Sinclair
*Director*: Anthony Pelissier      *Running Time*: 91 minutes
*B/W or Color*: B/W                *Availability*: TV only

This strange—and sometimes brilliant—little film hardly deserves its relative obscurity. D. H. Lawrence's uncharacteristic, rather elliptical short fantasy was adapted to the screen with integrity and imagination by writer-director Anthony Pelissier. A gifted 10-year-old (John Howard Davies, a year after portraying Oliver Twist for David Lean) has an unsettling home life due to parents (Valerie Hobson and Hugh Sinclair) being too self-absorbed to pay him much attention. The boy is closer to their handyman (John Mills), who teaches him to ride his Christmas rocking horse like a real jockey. In its toy saddle, the boy makes an exciting discovery: by riding at a frenzied pace, he can predict the outcome of future horse races, pay off the family debts, and satisfy his mother's penchant for extravagance. In short, he can win their love.

The boy raises quite a bundle with his uncanny talent. But his luxury-prone mother's spending drives him to a last, frantic ride on his wooden horse, whipping himself into such a fury that he falls dead. After his funeral, when the handyman gives the boy's mother the banknotes won for her, the repentant woman orders him to burn the "blood money."

Young Davies's acting career was brief; after *The Rocking Horse Winner,* he starred in a third literary adaptation, 1951's *Tom Brown's School Days,* and retired from the screen. But it's his endearingly wistful performance—quite astonishing, in its nuances, for a 10-year-old—that dominates *The Rocking Horse Winner.*

The patrician Valerie Hobson runs an impressive gamut—from selfish greed to humbled contrition—in what is quite likely the best acting of her 18-year film career. As the kindly, afflicted handyman, John Mills balances the tale's more chilling side with a natural cockney warmth.

# The Rocky Horror
# Picture Show

★★★★★★★★★★★★★★★★★★★★★★★★★★★★★★★★★★★★★★★★★★★★★★★★★★★★

**Nationality**: British        **Year**: 1975

**Cast**: Tim Curry, Susan Sarandon, Barry Bostwick, Richard O'Brien, Meat Loaf, Peter Hinwood

**Director**: Jim Sharman        **Running Time**: 95 minutes (100 minutes in Britain)

**B/W or Color**: Color        **Availability**: TV only

Somewhere between *Abbott and Costello Meet Frankenstein* (1948) and Mel Brooks's *Young Frankenstein* (1974) you'd have thought that Mary Shelley's celebrated manmade monster might've run out of voltage as fodder for motion picture parody. Perhaps even as perpetual film reinterpretations of the Frankenstein (or, more deeply, Promethean) myth will always find an audience, so will its apparently endless comic refractions. Richard O'Brien's screen adaptation of his popular stage musical (big stuff in Britain—a dismal flop when imported to New York) is plenty more than the expected riffs on a Boris Karloff cliché.

Springing more from our entire collective sci-fi and B-movie consciousness (as made affectionately clear in the opening "Science-fiction Double-features" number, sensuously crooned by a rouged mouth in a black void), this Frankie warps almost the entire mythos of a genre through a mirror of hedonistically twisted, interchangeable sexuality. The entire focus of the story has been transferred. The creation of life is now reduced to merely a necessary step in the pursuit of "absolute pleasure."

A newly married couple, a stormy night, a stalled car on a deserted road—a castle! (Stop me if you've heard this one before.) A slithering hunchbacked servant (O'Brien), a mad doctor (Curry)—who happens to be a brazen transvestite—and Rocky (Hinwood), his latest creation, a perfect, blond and bronze-muscled male specimen. Add some punk bikers, extraterrestrials (from the transexual planet of Transylvania), even a touch of bedroom farce, and set to over a dozen witty rock-and-roll songs of every variety. This is a fun film—and audiences seemed to realize it before the distributor did.

*Rocky,* as you probably know, emerged as the most prominent cult film of all time.

# Romeo and Juliet

★★★★★★★★★★★★★★★★★★★★★★★★★★★★★★★★★★★★★★★★★★★★★★★★★★★★

*Nationality*: British-Italian  *Year*: 1968

*Cast*: Leonard Whiting, Olivia Hussey, Milo O'Shea, Michael York, John McEnery, Pay Heywood

*Director*: Franco Zeffirelli  *Running Time*: 138 minutes (152 minutes in Europe)

*B/W or Color*: Color  *Availability*: PARAMOUNT HOME VIDEO

Franco Zeffirelli had, in 1967, turned out so surprisingly effective a screen version of *The Taming of the Shrew*, designed as a vehicle for the husband-and-wife team of Elizabeth Taylor and Richard Burton, that he next tackled the very romantic Shakespearean play, the much-filmed *Romeo and Juliet*. Like his previous picture, this was photographed—true to the story's original setting—in Italian locations in and near Verona. Also true to Shakespeare was his choice of appropriately youthful actors for his leads: 16-year-old Olivia Hussey and 17-year-old Leonard Whiting. In so doing, he deliberately sacrificed something in the way of seasoned acting and the reading of the Bard's immortal verse, but the idea was to appeal to a young movie audience—and this Zeffirelli's *Romeo and Juliet* accomplished without dispute. The fresh exuberance of his players and the irreverent zeal with which the director and his two Italian co-adapters approached this timeless theatrical romance resulted in many speeches being cut, transposed, and combined, and some minor characters eliminated. In the words of *Time* magazine, "It is a dangerous game, rewriting Shakespeare, but *Romeo and Juliet* proves that it can be played and won." *Variety*'s advance review from London noted the Sixties "look" that Zeffirelli had given it. *The New York Times* found it to be "The sweetest, the most contemporary romance on film this year," and so did the public, the majority of whom were students being introduced to Shakespeare the easy way.

The National Board named Zeffirelli the year's Best Director and listed *Romeo and Juliet* among 1968's best. Hollywood gave it four Oscar nominations, including Best Picture and Director, but it won only for the lovely cinematography of Pasqualino de Santis and Danilo Donati's Costume Design. Although *not* given an award, one of the film's most memorable aspects was the lovely score by Nino Rota.

# Room at the Top

* * * * * * * * * * * * * * * * * * * * * * * * * * * * * * * * * * * * * * * * * * * * * * * * * * * *

*Nationality*: British        *Year*: 1959

*Cast*: Laurence Harvey, Simone Signoret, Heather Sears, Donald Wolfit

*Director*: Jack Clayton      *Running Time*: 117 minutes

*B/W or Color*: B/W        *Availability*: EVI ELECTRIC VIDEO, INC.

This candid adaptation of John Braine's best-selling novel about a lower-class Brit's aggressive climb upward in a northern industrial town had a seminal and far-reaching influence on the British film industry. The forerunner of frank and realistic movies, *Room at the Top* also established an important director in Jack Clayton, making his feature-film debut at 37.

Neil Patterson's probing, well-crafted screenplay employed down-to-earth dialogue and naturalistic characterization to tell its ironic and engrossingly bitter story. The Oscar awarded Patterson was only one of the various prizes garnered: the British Film Academy called it the year's Best Movie, with Simone Signoret singled out as Best Actress—an accolade triplicated by Hollywood's motion pictures academy, the Cannes Film Festival, and The National Board of Review, which also named *Room at the Top* among the year's ten best films.

Signoret's complex blend of Gallic sophistication and unselfishness—switching to self-destructive despair when her English lover callously leaves her—is the movie's focal performance, despite its brevity. Laurence Harvey, an actor who rarely projected anything on screen but cold, emotionless self-absorption, was apparently inspired by script and direction to give an admirably multitoned portrait of the often likable, opportunistic cad. Heather Sears is sweet as the well-heeled but unworldly girl he must marry, and Hermione Baddeley makes her mark as Signoret's blowsy friend, who never quite trusts Harvey's easy charm.

*Room at the Top* owes its handsome look to Freddie Francis's sharp, gritty, black-and-white photography of Yorkshire and director Clayton's brilliant eye for appropriate settings.

# A Room with a View

★★★★★★★★★★★★★★★★★★★★★★★★★★★★★★★★★★★★★★★★★★★★★★★★★★★★★★

*Nationality*: British                  *Year*: 1986

*Cast*: Helena Bonham Carter, Maggie Smith, Denholm Elliott, Julian Sands, Daniel Day Lewis

*Director*: James Ivory           *Running Time*: 115 minutes

*B/W or Color*: Color             *Availability*: CBS/FOX HOME VIDEO

In 1986, *A Room with a View* won three Oscars as well as a nomination for Best Picture. The National Board of Review named it Best Picture of the year and Daniel Day Lewis Best Supporting Actor; as did the New York Film Critics. These are long-overdue tributes to the 20-year collaboration of producer Ismail Merchant, director James Ivory, and writer Ruth Prawer Jhabvala, whose fine filming of literature is unique among current filmmakers.

Set in Florence and the English countryside, the delectable comedy of manners is structured so deftly that novelist E. M. Forster's characters become living flesh and blood. Lucy Honeychurch (Helena Bonham Carter), an upper-middle-class English girl, is outwardly conventional—but when she sits down at the piano to play Beethoven, hidden romantic fires surface. She is chaperoned in Florence by her spinster cousin Charlotte (Maggie Smith is superb in this role). Staying at the same pensione are a wealth of eccentric and odd British individuals, including Mr. Emerson (Denholm Elliott) with his son George (Julian Sands). Emerson is a journalist who is playfully over-familiar with his fellow guests; George an incorrigible dreamer who "works on the railways" and immediately falls in love with Lucy. Presiding over this establishment is the unflappable owner (Amanda Walker), who speaks both Italian and English with a broad cockney accent. This is an ideal setting for dalliances, mishaps, and misunderstandings.

On her return to England, Lucy perversely becomes engaged to Cecil Vyse (played to perfection by Daniel Day Lewis), a supercilious prig puffed up with his own importance. So when George and his father follow Lucy home, renting a nearby cottage, a delicious comedy of errors ensues.

Everything about this masterpiece is wonderful: the fantastic photography; the acting; the sets; the lovely operatic singing of an unseen Kiri Te Kanawa; the costumes—and above all James Ivory's playfully subtle direction.

# Rosemary
## (Das Maedchen Rosemarie)

★ ★ ★ ★ ★ ★ ★ ★ ★ ★ ★ ★ ★ ★ ★ ★ ★ ★ ★ ★ ★ ★ ★ ★ ★ ★ ★ ★ ★ ★ ★ ★ ★ ★ ★ ★ ★ ★ ★ ★ ★ ★ ★ ★ ★ ★ ★ ★

**Nationality**: West German      **Year**: 1958 (U.S. release: 1959)
**Cast**: Nadja Tiller, Peter Van Eyck, Mario Adorf, Carl Raddatz, Gert Fröbe
**Director**: Rolf Thiele      **Running Time**: 105 minutes
**B/W or Color**: B/W      **Availability**: TV only

The shades of Bertolt Brecht and Kurt Weill hover over this anticapitalist tract based on an actual case. Rosemary's real-life counterpart, Rosemarie Nitribitt, a Frankfurt prostitute, was found strangled, under mysterious circumstances, in her lavish apartment.

Hooker Rosemary (Nadja Tiller) shares an apartment with two pimps, brilliantly played by Mario Adorf and Jo Herbst. We see them carrying a stolen TV set or singing their catchpenny songs to publicize Rosemary's wares. Rosemary graduates into big-league vice when she penetrates a circle of fat-cat industrialists. Under the tutelage of Frenchman Fribert (Peter Van Eyck), she becomes a highly paid cocotte with a sideline of marketable blackmail tapes. Not the brightest of girls, she is unequal to the balancing act she has set in motion. Screenwriters Erich Kuby and Rolf Thiele endow their titans of industry with huge limos and porcine features reminiscent of old George Grosz cartoons. The German foreign ministry took umbrage, as did numerous wealthy parties, who doubtless resented the implication that their class had had Rosemary bumped off. Despite attempts to ban it, *Rosemary* was entered in the 1959 Venice Film Festival. It won the Italian Critics Prize for Best Picture. The score by Norbert Schultz and Rolf Ulrich lacks a show-stopper like "Mack the Knife," yet it wafted through the bland Fifties like a bracing cold blast from the Weimar Republic. *Threepenny Opera*'s Mack the Knife would have endorsed the film's crisp message: when big black Mercedes confronts little black book, bet on the black Mercedes.

# The Rules of the Game
### (La Règle du Jeu)

************************************************************

Nationality: French            Year: 1939 (U.S. release: 1950)
Cast: Marcel Dalio, Nora Grégor, Roland Toutain, Jean Renoir, Paulette Dubost, Mila Parély
Director: Jean Renoir         Running Time: 110 minutes
B/W or Color: B/W          Availability: EMBASSY HOME ENTERTAINMENT

Unquestionably one of the greatest films ever made, *The Rules of the Game* is one of those few classics that seems better with each viewing. So much happens in this film, and it is performed on such a brilliant level by the large cast, that it is like a prism with varied facets. Jean Renoir intended his film to reflect the face of a collapsing French society on the verge of World War II. When the film premiered in Paris, riots were reported, and when the Nazis invaded the French capital in 1940, the film was ordered destroyed.

Octave (Jean Renoir, who played the role himself because Michel Simon was unavailable) invites the aviator hero André Jurieu (Roland Toutain) to a weekend shooting party at the country chateau of a marquis and his wife, whom André loves. The party-loving marquis (superbly played by Marcel Dalio) bought his title, and his guests include aristocrats and celebrities. His wife, Christine (Nora Grégor), is attracted to André but hides behind her social position. Concurrent with this party is the love triangle of the marquis's gamekeeper (Gaston Modot), his coquettish wife (Paulette Dubost), and a poacher (a fine performance by Julien Carette). What begins as dangerously ironic comedy can only culminate in tragedy.

The film's brilliance emanates from this juxtaposition of seriocomic values. Most of the motion picture's characters are concerned with little more than the arcane rules that govern the social and sexual games they play. To violate any, means ruin. The savage bloodletting of a rabbit hunt foreshadows the tragedy of World War II.

*The Rules of the Game* provides a logical follow-up to Renoir's earlier *Grand Illusion,* which concerned the optimism of soldiers in the aftermath of the First World War. This film offers no hope, only artifice.

Originally banned because it indicted the corruption of France, the negative of this movie classic was destroyed in an air raid. Only the diligent efforts of film historians, working with Renoir and piecing together various prints, restored the picture to its previous glory—and present availability.

*(Embassy offers a subtitled videocassette.)*

# The Ruling Class

\* \* \* \* \* \* \* \* \* \* \* \* \* \* \* \* \* \* \* \* \* \* \* \* \* \* \* \* \* \* \* \* \* \* \* \* \* \* \* \* \* \* \* \* \* \* \* \* \* \* \* \* \* \*

**Nationality**: British           **Year**: 1972

**Cast**: Peter O'Toole, Alastair Sim, Arthur Lowe, Harry Andrews, Coral Browne

**Director**: Peter Medak        **Running Time**: 154 minutes

**B/W or Color**: Color         **Availability**: EMBASSY HOME ENTERTAINMENT

Choosing *The Ruling Class* as one of their ten best for 1972, The National Board also selected Peter O'Toole as Best Actor (for this performance and *Man of La Mancha*). Peter Barnes adapted his play for the screen, and Peter Medak directed the irreverent comedy.

*Time* magazine stated that O'Toole's portrayal contained "such intensity that it may trouble sleep as surely as it will haunt memory—funny, disturbing, finally devastating." The actor, whose madcap mayhem earned a fifth Academy Award nomination, described *The Ruling Class* as "a comedy with tragic relief."

As Jack, fourteenth Earl of Gurney, O'Toole leaves an asylum, after eight years, when he becomes heir to the estate of his father (Harry Andrews), who accidentally hanged himself while romping around in long underwear, a tutu, and a three-cornered hat. Jack is convinced he's Jesus Christ and arrives at the estate sporting flowing blond hair, monk's robes, and tennis shoes. His favorite pastimes are stretching out on a huge wooden cross and bursting into song at unusual moments (such as when he leads a group of fox hunters in a rousing rendition of "Dem Bones").

Through a bizarre series of events, Jack assumes a new identity—that of Jack the Ripper. After killing his uncle's wife (Coral Browne) and making it look like the butler (Arthur Lowe) did it, he has his uncle, a psychiatrist, and a bishop committed—following which, he takes a seat at the House of Lords. The modern world, it seems, is ready to accept a Jack the Ripper quicker than a Messiah.

Alastair Sim returned to the screen, after a 12-year absence, to play the befuddled Bishop Lampton.

A controversial film, *The Ruling Class* is a wild mixture of divine madness and savage satire.

(*The videocassette is of the uncut version.*)

# Ryan's Daughter

**★★★★★★★★★★★★★★★★★★★★★★★★★★★★★★★★★★★★★★★★★★★★★★★★★★★★★★★★★**

*Nationality*: British         *Year*: 1970

*Cast*: Sarah Miles, Robert Mitchum, Trevor Howard, Christopher Jones, John Mills

*Director*: David Lean        *Running Time*: 192 minutes

*B/W or Color*: Color        *Availability*: MGM/UA HOME VIDEO

For David Lean, *Ryan's Daughter* "is a love story about a girl becoming a woman. It is also about temptation, about the animal just beneath the skin of us all."

Set against the awesome beauty of Ireland's western coast, it offers natural spectacle combined with a romantic plot underscored by rumblings of the Irish-British troubles of 1916. Lengthy, involving—and leisurely paced—*Ryan's Daughter* takes place against breathtaking Irish vistas, but because of the problematic weather, beach scenes were shot near Capetown, South Africa! Lean's favorite cinematographer, Freddie Young (*Lawrence of Arabia, Doctor Zhivago*), understandably earned his third Lean-oriented Oscar for *Ryan's Daughter*.

Sarah Miles is well cast in a role written for her by her husband, Robert Bolt. A complex young woman of restless energy and romantic idealism, she is torn between a stodgy husband and an exciting lover. Miles's Oscar nomination was well earned. Some critics found Robert Mitchum miscast as her schoolteacher-husband; his is a restrained, gentlemanly portrait of an introverted man, and the actor's nonmacho performance is among his best, with a very credible Irish brogue. As Miles's lover, Christopher Jones offers a compelling portrayal of an embittered British soldier. Trevor Howard obviously relished playing the wise and crusty old village priest, but reports: "We were in that blasted place for over a year. Lean's a perfectionist who must take his time." John Mills's grotesque village idiot won him a Best Supporting Actor Oscar, but Leo McKern is far better as Miles's blustering, treacherous, publican father.

*Ryan's Daughter* is an absorbing motion picture, and The National Board called it one of 1970's ten best.

# Sapphire

✶✶✶✶✶✶✶✶✶✶✶✶✶✶✶✶✶✶✶✶✶✶✶✶✶✶✶✶✶✶✶✶✶✶✶✶✶✶✶✶✶✶✶✶✶✶✶✶✶✶✶✶✶✶✶

*Nationality*: British         *Year*: 1959

*Cast*: Nigel Patrick, Yvonne Mitchell, Michael Craig, Paul Massie, Bernard Miles, Earl Cameron

*Director*: Basil Dearden         *Running Time*: 92 minutes

*B/W or Color*: Color         *Availability*: INDEPENDENT UNITED DISTRIBUTORS

Michael Relph and Basil Dearden spent much of their distinguished producer-director partnership alternating films of pure entertainment with those of social consciousness. Frequently, they chose scripts that combined elements of both. One was Janet Green's highly original *Sapphire,* which offered an intriguing murder mystery wrapped around London's "color problem."

The taut, tasteful economy of Dearden's direction is typified by *Sapphire*'s arresting opening sequence. As the credits roll, a girl's body slams down onto the damp, early morning ground of foggy Hampstead Heath, her dead eyes staring open. Two children and their mother are out for an early walk. The woman stumbles upon the corpse, and her reaction is merely a quick, silent intake of breath as her hand flies to her mouth. The film then cuts to Nigel Patrick's matter-of-fact detective superintendent investigating the crime. In short order, the scene is economically set and the situation firmly and cinematically established.

Sapphire, the murder victim, was a vivacious blonde whose student fiancé becomes a prime target for police questioning. The film centers on two detectives and their investigation, which discloses that the deceased was of racially mixed parentage and was three months pregnant.

Janet Green's script is far more successful as a challenging whodunit than as social commentary, and she evinces more skill at developing red herrings than she does at airing black grievances. We are shown *Sapphire*'s white characters enjoying a close-knit family life, while its "colored" counterparts are depicted carelessly living it up in jazz dives. Despite its drawbacks, however, *Sapphire* works well as a tense and absorbing murder mystery, and if it tends to skirt its sociological responsibilities, this was, after all, only 1959. The British Film Academy named it 1959's Best British Film.

# Saturday Night and Sunday Morning

\* \* \* \* \* \* \* \* \* \* \* \* \* \* \* \* \* \* \* \* \* \* \* \* \* \* \* \* \* \* \* \* \* \* \* \* \* \* \* \* \* \* \* \* \* \* \* \* \* \* \* \* \* \*

*Nationality*: British          *Year*: 1960 (U.S. release: 1961)
*Cast*: Albert Finney, Shirley Anne Field, Rachel Roberts
*Director*: Karel Reisz         *Running Time*: 90 minutes
*B/W or Color*: B/W         *Availability*: TV only

Like *Room at the Top*, this powerful and popular film was based on a novel by one of Britain's "angry young men," Alan Sillitoe. Sillitoe was hired to adapt his book to the screen, and the picture was a startling success that—with its frank new sexual attitudes—helped change the face of British filmmaking.

The self-possessed young antihero Arthur Seaton (naturalistically played by Albert Finney) is a restless factory worker in England's depressing industrial Midlands. Finney had made only one previous movie—a brief role in Laurence Olivier's *The Entertainer*—and although many assumed he was merely playing his regionally accented self in *Saturday Night and Sunday Morning*, the wiry, 23-year-old actor was already a Stratford Shakespeare veteran who had even pinch-hit once for an injured Olivier in *Coriolanus*. Finney's acting dominates *Saturday Night and Sunday Morning*, in which his powerful delineation of a brash and often surly heel was somehow more acceptable in that pre-feminist era.

None of the film's leading characters is entirely sympathetic, although screenwriter Sillitoe and director Karel Reisz engage our attention and manage to sustain our interest as to Arthur's comeuppance, if such it can be termed. Finney's vitally intense portrayal won him a British Academy Award, as did that of Rachel Roberts as Brenda, the hapless, love-starved housewife whose life Arthur scarcely improves. As his girlfriend, Doreen, Shirley Anne Field—with her pert and pretty self-assurance—offers appropriate balance to the miserable Brenda.

American audiences were generally agreed that the thick Midlands accents of the cast deserved subtitles! However, The National Board found *Saturday Night and Sunday Morning* sufficiently comprehensible to award Finney a Best Actor citation and to name the film one of 1961's best.

# The Scarlet Pimpernel

★ ★ ★ ★ ★ ★ ★ ★ ★ ★ ★ ★ ★ ★ ★ ★ ★ ★ ★ ★ ★ ★ ★ ★ ★ ★ ★ ★ ★ ★ ★ ★ ★ ★ ★ ★ ★ ★ ★ ★ ★ ★ ★ ★ ★ ★ ★ ★ ★ ★ ★ ★

*Nationality*: British       *Year*: 1935
*Cast*: Leslie Howard, Merle Oberon, Raymond Massey, Nigel Bruce
*Director*: Harold Young       *Running Time*: 85 minutes
*B/W or Color*: B/W       *Availability*: EMBASSY HOME
                               ENTERTAINMENT

The Baroness Orczy novel *The Scarlet Pimpernel* was ideal for screen adaptation: it contained action, pathos, interesting characters, and an exciting plot. And perfect in the title role (originally scheduled for Charles Laughton) is Leslie Howard, the definitive avenger who blithely intones: "They seek him here, they seek him there, those Frenchies seek him everywhere/Is he in heaven or is he in hell—that damned elusive Pimpernel?"

Set in 1792, as Robespierre engineers the Reign of Terror that sends French citizens to the guillotine daily, this intriguing adventure tale depicts the exploits of one man who symbolizes justice. Sir Percy Blakeney (Howard) organizes a small band to smuggle endangered French people to the safety of England. His signature is the outline of a red flower (from an old family crest) that lies hidden beneath a large stone on his ring. To onlookers, Sir Percy is simply a simpering fop. Even his wife, the beautiful Lady Blakeney (Merle Oberon), is unaware of his secret identity.

Often in disguise (once posing as an old hag), Blakeney consistently eludes his foes. Placed in charge of finding him is Chauvelin (Raymond Massey), who asks Lady Blakeney for help. After she happens to notice the pimpernel symbol on a ring worn by an ancestor in a portrait, Lady Blakeney realizes the truth. Rushing to Sir Percy's side, she is able to join him as he succeeds in defeating the sinister Chauvelin.

Merle Oberon is at the height of her youthful beauty, Raymond Massey makes his character hissable, and Nigel Bruce is a perfect Prince of Wales. As does Leslie Howard, they seem ideal for their roles.

Often reissued, *The Scarlet Pimpernel* was remade in 1950 as *The Elusive Pimpernel,* starring David Niven as Sir Percy. A 1985 TV production starred Anthony Andrews. As enjoyable as the remakes proved, neither compared with the sparkling original.

# Seance on a Wet Afternoon

★★★★★★★★★★★★★★★★★★★★★★★★★★★★★★★★★★★★★★★★★★★★★★★★★★★★★

Nationality: British          Year: 1964
Cast: Richard Attenborough, Kim Stanley, Nanette Newman, Patrick Magee
Director: Bryan Forbes         Running Time: 115 minutes
B/W or Color: B/W         Availability: VIDAMERICA

Despite the fact that kidnapping a child was considered taboo film material in the Sixties, director Bryan Forbes and co-producer Richard Attenborough made a taut, dark, eerie, suspenseful, and engrossing film of Mark McShane's parapsychological novel, with two hauntingly memorable performances by Kim Stanley and Richard Attenborough.

Myra Savage (Stanley) is a demented, middle-aged medium, although her henpecked husband, Billy (Attenborough), is too admiring and loyal to realize the extent of her dementia. Thus he is willing to abet her in her plan, "something so perfect, so pure," to "borrow" a child, demand ransom, then approach the parents and offer to help locate their child through Myra's supernatural powers. The medium's goal is front-page publicity, after which she will hold a seance and reveal clues regarding the child's whereabouts to the police. Billy realizes, however, that their only security lies in his ultimately killing the little girl, which he is loathe to do. It is to the credit of Forbes's sensitive and poignant screenplay that the film's thematic content focuses more on the interaction of the two villains than on their victim's possible fate.

An opening scene, one in which the two bizarre kidnappers prepare their hostage's room, is spellbinding, as is the one in which Billy is to collect the ransom. Gerry Turpin's clever camerawork probes every nuance of this macabre environment, and the sets, the couple's morbid, seedy Victorian house, even an overgrown garden, add further dimension to the somber atmosphere. John Barry's score also serves to play up evocatively the Savages' grisly world.

*Seance on a Wet Afternoon* stands as an example of a film that maintains a firm grip on its subject matter and rarely, if ever, falters.

It was named by The National Board of Review as one of the ten best pictures of the year.

# Secrets of Women
## (Kvinnors Väntan/Waiting Women)

★★★★★★★★★★★★★★★★★★★★★★★★★★★★★★★★★★★★★★★★★★★★★★★★★★

**Nationality**: Swedish  **Year**: 1952 (U.S. release: 1961)

**Cast**: Anita Björk, Maj-Britt Nilsson, Eva Dahlbeck, Gunnar Björnstrand, Birger Malmsten, Jarl Kulle

**Director**: Ingmar Bergman  **Running Time**: 108 minutes

**B/W or Color**: B/W  **Availability**: EMBASSY HOME ENTERTAINMENT

Made at a time when writer-director Ingmar Bergman badly needed a financial success, *Secrets of Women* reflects the then-current vogue for multipart movies, encompassing several stories in one package, usually with a unifying theme. This film, which is set at a lakeside summer cottage in the Stockholm archipelago, focuses on three sisters-in-law awaiting the arrival of their businessmen husbands. They pass the time recounting significant incidents (told in flashbacks) from their marriages. Each recalls something that sheds light on her relationship with her spouse: Rakel (Anita Björk) admits to an infidelity with an ex-lover that nearly resulted in her husband's suicide (until, Bergmanically, he determined that an unfaithful wife is better than no wife at all); Marta (Maj-Britt Nilsson) remembers her youthful Parisian affair with an artist, resulting in a child before their eventual marriage; and Karin (Eva Dahlbeck) tells of returning from a party and getting stuck overnight in an elevator with her husband, an incident that strengthened their relationship. This latter incident is the only part of the movie that's outright comedy, performed in high style by Dahlbeck and Gunnar Björnstrand. Their delightful on-screen chemistry—a sort of Scandinavian Tracy and Hepburn—moved Bergman to cast them in similar roles in *A Lesson in Love*.

In the volume of interviews entitled *Bergman on Bergman*, the director recalls the pleasure of standing in cinema lobbies where this film was playing, listening to howls of laughter from within: "It was the first time in my life people had ever laughed like that at something I'd made."

*(Embassy offers tapes both dubbed and subtitled.)*

# Seduced and Abandoned
## (Sedotta e Abbandonata)

\* \* \* \* \* \* \* \* \* \* \* \* \* \* \* \* \* \* \* \* \* \* \* \* \* \* \* \* \* \* \* \* \* \* \* \* \* \* \* \* \* \* \* \* \* \* \* \*

Nationality: Italian-French      Year: 1964

Cast: Stefania Sandrelli, Aldo Puglisi, Saro Urzi, Lando Buzzanca, Leopoldo Trieste

Director: Pietro Germi

Running Time: 118 minutes (123 minutes in Italy)

B/W or Color: B/W

Availability: VIDEO AWARD MOTION PICTURES, INC.

If the comedy of manners is a film genre not readily identified with Sicily, then writer-director Pietro Germi helped alter that situation, first with 1961's sardonic *Divorce, Italian Style,* then this unrelated follow-up. *Seduced and Abandoned* takes a half hour too long to weave its portrait of a Sicilian town's foibles in establishing family "honor" and justice, but in so doing it offers humorous insights into the old-fashioned codes of manners and mores that apparently still obtained in mid-Sixties' southern Italy.

Agnese, the 15-year-old daughter of a middle-class Sicilian family, is seduced by her sister Mathilde's fiancé, Peppino, who leaves her pregnant. Upon discovering this dishonor, their father, Vincenzo, terminates the engagement and finds Mathilde a new fiancé, the penniless but distinguished Baron Rizieri. When Peppino refuses to wed Agnese (because she is no longer chaste!), Vincenzo attempts to have him murdered but is thwarted by Agnese. Peppino must marry the girl or go to prison for seducing a minor. But his arrogance causes Agnese to reject him as a husband, subjecting her family to ridicule. The embarrassed baron breaks off with Mathilde, who becomes a nun, after Vincenzo suffers a fatal heart attack. Finally, Agnese agrees to wed her seducer.

Basing his film on an Italian statute that absolves a man if he marries the woman he has seduced, Germi mines a good deal of humor from this material with his quite demonstrative, if unfamiliar, cast. As Agnese, Stefania Sandrelli is the perfect target for a lustful young man—as portrayed by the sinister-looking Aldo Puglisi.

The National Board named *Seduced and Abandoned* among 1964's five best foreign-language films.

*(The film is shown with subtitles that are illegible in dinner-table scenes.)*

# The Seduction of Mimi
## (Mimi Metallurgico ferito nell'onore)

\* \* \* \* \* \* \* \* \* \* \* \* \* \* \* \* \* \* \* \* \* \* \* \* \* \* \* \* \* \* \* \* \* \* \* \* \* \* \* \* \* \* \* \* \* \* \* \* \* \* \* \* \* \* \*

**Nationality**: Italian

**Year**: 1972 (U.S. release: 1974)

**Cast**: Giancarlo Giannini, Mariangela Melato, Agostina Belli, Elena Fiore

**Director**: Lina Wertmuller

**Running Time**: 89 minutes (120 minutes in Italy)

**B/W or Color**: Color

**Availability**: CBS/FOX HOME VIDEO

Lina Wertmuller wrote and directed this enticing political and sexual farce with her favorite actor, Giancarlo Giannini, who plays the title role. Mimi is a Sicilian metal worker trying to free himself of some of his island's restrictive traditions. Because he refuses to vote for the local Mafia-backed candidate, he loses his job. He leaves his wife and child and moves on to make the ultimate journey north, to Turin, another world economically and politically from his native Sicily.

In Turin he falls in love with an independent young woman who reflects the freedom of her northern world until she meets Mimi. They set up house together. A short time later, he is unfortunately transferred back to Sicily, where he learns of his wife's unfaithfulness. The rules of the Sicilian game compel him to save his manly honor. He becomes obsessed with the idea of revenge. Since he is a "civilized metallurgist," he resolves not to kill his wife's lover. He will take his revenge another way. He will seduce the seducer's wife! This event turns out to be one of the funniest scenes in the film, although it is essentially brutal in its ugliness. The woman is enormous, and Ms. Wertmuller uses the actress's obese, aging body to great comic advantage. We share Mimi's feeling of horror at his awesome task.

His misadventures bring the Black Hand of the Mafia into his future once again, and we see Mimi, the man who attempted to defy tradition, bewildered by the conflict between his "advanced" attitudes and the overruling old Sicilian world around him.

The film is about the complication of politics in Italy and the use of sex as a political act. It concerns the role of women in both the north and south, and the trap that both politics and sex pose for the average Italian, particularly the Sicilian. It is both funny and sad, a wry yet frequently broad comedy in which Giannini positively excels, registering every possible mood. Elena Fiore and Mariangela Melato are excellent in the accompanying female roles. If Mimi is seduced, so are we, by this delightful but meaningful comedy.

# Senso
## (The Wanton Countess/The Wanton Contessa)

★ ★ ★ ★ ★ ★ ★ ★ ★ ★ ★ ★ ★ ★ ★ ★ ★ ★ ★ ★ ★ ★ ★ ★ ★ ★ ★ ★ ★ ★ ★ ★ ★ ★ ★ ★ ★ ★ ★ ★ ★ ★ ★ ★ ★ ★ ★ ★ ★ ★ ★

Nationality: Italian        Year: 1954 (U.S. release: 1968)
Cast: Alida Valli, Farley Granger, Massimo Girotti, Heinz Moog
Director: Luchino Visconti       Running Time: 115 minutes
B/W or Color: Color          Availability: TV only

"With Senso," one Italian critic wrote, "we see the birth of the first true and authentic Italian historical film." And, as its director, Luchino Visconti, later admitted, "After Senso, everything was easier." Indeed, this handsomely made romantic drama has had a checkered past. In the mid-Fifties, American movie magazines, reflecting the then-current popularity of its stars, Alida Valli and Farley Granger, published advance reviews of an English-language version entitled Summer Hurricane that was never released.

Elegant and costly, Visconti's deliberately paced account of the illicit 1866 love affair of a Venetian aristocrat's wife and a younger Austrian officer was originally shot with an English-language soundtrack adapted by Paul Bowles and Tennessee Williams. However, such was not in evidence when Senso premiered in an Italian-language print at 1954's Venice Film Festival, where Variety praised its "great pictorial beauty and lavish mounting," as well as the acting and direction. This nearly two-hour movie eventually appeared on American TV, cut by half an hour and retitled The Wanton Contessa. It is hoped that a full-length Senso will eventually surface on videocassette.

Visconti originally wanted Ingrid Bergman and Marlon Brando for his ill-starred Senso lovers, but Bergman's then-husband, Roberto Rossellini, refused to allow her to work with another director. Lux Film, which produced the movie, insisted on Granger, who well recalls Visconti's slow, painstaking perfectionism and utter disregard for production costs. Certainly, Senso was not made on the cheap. Sets and costumes are beautifully constructed, and the opera house and palaces of 19th-century Venice and Verona are exquisitely photographed. Alida Valli, then at the height of her beauty, is wonderfully effective in this difficult and tragic emotional role. Granger makes a handsome and credible romantic scoundrel of the faithless young object of her misplaced affections.

# The Servant

* * * * * * * * * * * * * * * * * * * * * * * * * * * * * * * * * * * * * * * * * * * * * * * * * * * * * * * * *

*Nationality*: British          *Year*: 1963 (U.S. release: 1964)
*Cast*: Dirk Bogarde, Sarah Miles, James Fox, Wendy Craig
*Director*: Joseph Losey          *Running Time*: 115 minutes
*B/W or Color*: B/W          *Availability*: THORN/EMI-HBO
                              VIDEO

While *The Servant*'s story line is reasonably simple, the subtextual relationships of its four leading characters are infinitely complex. Wealthy young Tony (James Fox), engaged to marry Susan (Wendy Craig), hires Barrett (Dirk Bogarde) as manservant for the London townhouse he's refurbishing. Soon Barrett is quietly exerting a controlling influence over Tony. Together, they make an elegant showplace of the old Georgian building, as the servant becomes indispensable to his ineffectual master, engendering Susan's immediate dislike. Threatened, Barrett moves in his obviously wanton "sister" Vera (Sarah Miles) as housemaid, and she seduces Tony. After Susan walks out, Tony discovers that Barrett and Vera are lovers and fires them.

Alone, the spineless Tony begins to deteriorate, along with his house, and when he "accidentally" encounters Barrett in a pub, he hires him back. Barrett now takes complete control of both master and household, humiliating the returned Susan, even reinstalling Vera. Drug-oriented parties take place, a symbol of the moral degradation accompanying his new-found domination. The servant has become the master, and vice versa.

A masterfully ambiguous study in corruption, Harold Pinter's adaptation of the Robin Maugham novel offers a variety of possible interpretations. But *The Servant*'s impact is as much attributable to director Joseph Losey. Under Losey's inspired and subtly detailed direction, the actors offer perhaps the best performances of their collective careers. As the Janus-faced gentleman's gentlemen, Dirk Bogarde explores depths previously unrevealed on screen, and Britain's Film Academy rewarded him with its Best Actor award. James Fox won the Academy's "Most Promising Newcomer" vote, and an Oscar went to Douglas Slocombe's exquisite black-and-white photography, while the British Screenwriters Association singled out Pinter's screenplay.

# Seven Beauties

## (Pasqualino: Settebellezze)

\* \* \* \* \* \* \* \* \* \* \* \* \* \* \* \* \* \* \* \* \* \* \* \* \* \* \* \* \* \* \* \* \* \* \* \* \* \* \* \* \* \* \* \* \* \* \* \* \* \* \* \* \*

*Nationality*: Italian          *Year*: 1976

*Cast*: Giancarlo Giannini, Fernando Rey, Shirley Stoler, Elena Fiore, Enzo Vitale

*Director*: Lina Wertmuller          *Running Time*: 115 minutes

*B/W or Color*: Color          *Availability*: RCA/COLUMBIA PICTURES HOME VIDEO

Hailed as the masterpiece of writer-director Lina Wertmuller, this Italian comedy-drama is both harrowing and hilarious. It contains a marvelous performance by her favorite star, Giancarlo Giannini, who became one of the few foreign-language actors to be nominated for an Academy Award. Pasqualino Frafuso is a survivor, not a man of great intellect. At the film's beginning, a narrator translates the dedication to all the survivors of the world.

The action takes place during World War II, as Italian soldier Giannini escapes from a train of wounded in Germany. He relates his history to fellow soldier Piero Di Orio: as a would-be Neapolitan criminal, he killed a pimp for making a prostitute of the eldest of his seven fat sisters. After cutting the body into pieces, he pleaded insanity, but then enlisted in the army to escape prosecution.

As a prisoner in a German camp run by Shirley Stoler, he does anything he can to survive. He tries to make love to Stoler, who is repelled but puts him in charge of his unit. When the war ends, Giannini finds that all the women in his family have become prostitutes.

When Wertmuller and Giannini were in great favor in international film circles, this was hailed as the greatest of their collaborations. It alternates between hilarity and despair, some scenes calling for a strong constitution (or a fast-forward switch). The underlying theme is that survival is worth any price. Shirley Stoler's prison commandant, a role mentioned for Shelley Winters, is presented as a grotesque obstacle to be overcome, or endured. The comedy has a bitter edge, while the tragedy has its poignant side. For once, the majority of the nudity is handled by the male contingent. Tonino Delli Colli's Technicolor photography is outstanding.

# Seven Days to Noon

★ ★ ★ ★ ★ ★ ★ ★ ★ ★ ★ ★ ★ ★ ★ ★ ★ ★ ★ ★ ★ ★ ★ ★ ★ ★ ★ ★ ★ ★ ★ ★ ★ ★ ★ ★ ★ ★ ★ ★ ★ ★ ★ ★ ★ ★ ★ ★ ★ ★ ★ ★ ★

*Nationality*: British               *Year*: 1950
*Cast*: Barry Jones, Olive Sloane, Andre Morell, Sheila Manahan, Hugh Cross
*Director*: John and Roy Boulting     *Running Time*: 94 minutes
*B/W or Color*: B/W                   *Availability*: TV only

This suspenseful doomsday thriller won Oscars for Paul Dehn and James Bernard, who devised its original story for the Boulting Brothers production team. *Seven Days to Noon* begins quietly, with a London postman delivering an envelope to 10 Downing Street. The missive has been sent by an eminent, but disturbed, atomic scientist who warns that he intends to set off a stolen atom bomb in the heart of the city unless the prime minister declares a moratorium on their manufacture. The PM is given a week to do so.

With this gripping situation properly established, John and Roy Boulting proceed to build a minor masterpiece of suspense by hiring little-known actors, shooting on location in the streets of London in the early morning hours and on weekends, and by keeping their topical theme immediate with dramatic understatement. On occasion, they even leaven the tension with wry British humor. Much credit must be given to Roy Boulting's tight editing of director-brother John's complex sequence of London's evacuation, as the film's momentum mounts to the shattering climax, which is staged with documentary-style realism. As the disturbed scientist-fugitive, Barry Jones offers a poignant blend of confused logic and frightened despair. Olive Sloane, a blonde character actress briefly seen to advantage as an aging tart in *The Fallen Idol*, had the best role of her career here, as Goldie, the faded musical-comedy performer whose love for her pampered, little Pekingese, Trixie, signifies the lack of human affection in her middle-aged life. In their support, a large company of equally skilled players helps make *Seven Days to Noon* a totally compelling example of cinematic suspense.

# Seven Samurai
## (Shichinin No Samurai/The Magnificent Seven)

★★★★★★★★★★★★★★★★★★★★★★★★★★★★★★★★★★★★★★★★★★★★★★★★★★★★★★

Nationality: Japanese                    Year: 1954 (U.S. release: 1956)

Cast: Takashi Shimura, Toshiro Mifune, Yoshio Inaba, Seiji Miyaguchi, Daisuke Kato, Kamatari Fujiwara

Director: Akira Kurosawa                 Running Time: 200 minutes

B/W or Color: B/W                        Availability: EMBASSY HOME ENTERTAINMENT

Today, *Seven Samurai* is generally considered the granddaddy of all samurai epics. It is an entertaining, fast-paced classic whose 200-minute length feels like half the time. Numerous imitations, including the American *The Magnificent Seven*, have appeared. A 1979 poll of Japanese critics voted it the best Japanese film ever made. Pauline Kael has praised *Seven Samurai* as "the greatest battle epic since *The Birth of a Nation*." By far the most popular and best-drawing Japanese picture in revival movie houses, it has probably been seen by more Westerners than any other Japanese film.

The vital *Seven Samurai* focuses upon seven hungry, masterless swordsmen who are hired (for rice rations) by a village of impoverished farmers who need protection from roving bandits. The two groups learn to overcome class hostilities and work together to fortify the little hamlet. After the expected battle, the surviving samurai realize that only the farmers are the true victors.

*Seven Samurai* is generally considered an action film, although there is surprisingly little action—only two brief sequences—during the first three hours. The raw, rapid editing of director Akira Kurosawa's innovative telephoto and deep-focus photography thrusts forward the plot, which, for the first time in film, develops the idea of samurai fighting to protect mere peasants and carefully explores the character of each warrior. The climactic battle, Kurosawa's greatest sequence, is an inferno exploding in the mud, which bursts the idealistic illusions set up in previous scenes showing the samurai and the peasants peacefully planning their mutual protection.

*Seven Samurai* was a box-office success upon its release but received mixed critical comments. The uncut version played only in large cities. Other editions of 141 and 160 minutes circulated in second-run houses and abroad for many years. Its Silver Lion at the Venice Film Festival came despite cuts that confused many critics. Fortunately, *Seven Samurai* has survived its mutilations to become the definitive samurai film.

# The Seventh Seal
## (Det Sj&uuml;nde Inseglet)

★ ★ ★ ★ ★ ★ ★ ★ ★ ★ ★ ★ ★ ★ ★ ★ ★ ★ ★ ★ ★ ★ ★ ★ ★ ★ ★ ★ ★ ★ ★ ★ ★ ★ ★ ★ ★ ★ ★ ★ ★ ★ ★ ★ ★ ★ ★ ★ ★ ★ ★ ★ ★ ★ ★ ★

**Nationality**: Swedish        **Year**: 1957 (U.S. release: 1958)

**Cast**: Max von Sydow, Gunnar Björnstrand, Nils Poppe, Bibi Andersson, Bengt Ekerot

**Director**: Ingmar Bergman      **Running Time**: 96 minutes

**B/W or Color**: B/W           **Availability**: EMBASSY HOME ENTERTAINMENT

A weary knight returning from the Crusades encounters a black-en-shrouded figure on a vast expanse of empty beach.

"Who are you?" enquires the warrior.

"Death," replies the stranger nonchalantly.

"Have you come for me?"

"I have long walked at your side" comes the chilling response.

Ingmar Bergman's brooding film poetry achieved a peak in this complex yet ambiguous allegory of Man's external quest for meaning and salvation in a seemingly unknowable universe. The Swedish master's worldwide recognition as an important and innovative original was secured in *The Seventh Seal*'s loosely flowing construct of philosophy, religion, human emotion, and unexpected humor.

Calmly receiving the news of his impending doom, the contemplative knight challenges the Black One to a game of chess—offering his life as the stakes. This framework sets the stage for the wandering knight's various encounters in his travels through a bleak, plague-ridden medieval landscape. Seething with confusion and self-loathing, indifferent to the barbarity and misery that constantly surround him, he seeks redemption or obliteration, but first and foremost—truth. With the figure of Death—amidst the ugliness of life—apparently ever present and inescapable, the knight and his cynically resigned, atheistic companion befriend a troupe of itinerent actors, learning briefly to take delight in their simple pleasures.

The film's settings are sparse and strikingly minimalistic, enhanced by cinematographer Gunnar Fischer's supremely moody black-and-white lensing. Images of the sea, sky, and perpetual horizons remain in the eye.

(*Embassy offers both dubbed and subtitled prints.*)

# Shadows of Our Forgotten Ancestors
## (Teni Zabytykh Predkov/Wild Horses of Fire)

✸✸✸✸✸✸✸✸✸✸✸✸✸✸✸✸✸✸✸✸✸✸✸✸✸✸✸✸✸✸✸✸✸✸✸✸✸✸✸✸✸✸✸✸✸✸✸✸✸✸

**Nationality**: Russian          **Year**: 1964

**Cast**: Ivan Mikolaichuk, Larisa Kadochnikova, Tatiana Bestayeva, Spartak Bagashvili

**Director**: Sergei Paradjanov          **Running Time**: 100 minutes

**B/W or Color**: Color          **Availability**: TV only

More people know Sergei Paradjanov as a cause in the international film community than have actually viewed his films. Paradjanov is an Armenian director, born in Soviet Georgia, who, over the past 20 years, has been permitted to make only three pictures: *Shadows of Our Forgotten Ancestors* (1964), *The Color of Pomegranates* (1969), and *The Legend of Suram Fortress* (1984). These titles are rarely screened in the West, the latter two initially having been banned from export by the Soviet Union.

*Shadows of Our Forgotten Ancestors* won 16 international awards, including Best Production at the Mar del Plata Festival. However, Paradjanov fell into disfavor with Soviet authorities shortly after its release. After nearly a decade of harassment and a trial closed to the public, he was sentenced to a Ukrainian prison camp in 1974. But after five years, he was released, primarily due to worldwide lobbying by critics, filmmakers, and humanitarians.

The haunting *Shadows of Our Forgotten Ancestors* is a story of doomed love against a backdrop of the Carpathian Mountains. Originally advertised in this country as a retelling of the Romeo and Juliet story, it actually depicts one Ivan's futile existence and unhappy, childless marriage after his love, Marichka, accidentally drowns. Far more interesting are its lyrical cinematic elements and depictions of regional rituals. Paradjanov calls this film "a dramaturgy of color," reflecting its visual richness, captured by dazzling, fluid camerawork and backed by the chants, folk songs, rituals, and dances of the region. Paradjanov's two subsequent films represent excursions into the avant-garde, featuring an even more intense use of cinematic language and greatly diminished narrative.

# Shakespeare Wallah

★★★★★★★★★★★★★★★★★★★★★★★★★★★★★★★★★★★★★★★★★★★★★★★★★★★★★

**Nationality**: Indian          **Year**: 1965 (U.S. release: 1966)
**Cast**: Shashi Kapoor, Felicity Kendal, Madhur Jaffrey, Geoffrey Kendal
**Director**: James Ivory          **Running Time**: 115 minutes
**B/W or Color**: B/W          **Availability**: EMBASSY HOME
                                             ENTERTAINMENT

The place is India, the time some 20 years after Indian independence, but for the Buckinghams (Geoffrey Kendal and Laura Liddell, also married offscreen) and their daughter Lizzie (played by real-life daughter, Felicity Kendal) India remains home. They have spent their lives traveling with their Shakespearean acting company and continue to do so, stopping anyplace there is a demand for performances.

One day, when their car breaks down, a young Indian, Sanju (Shashi Kapoor), puts them up at his uncle's estate. All sorts of complications arise when he falls in love with Lizzie.

What is so finely portrayed is the dedication of a rather shabby troupe carrying on in the only manner they know. In spite of any changes in the vast nation, the little troupe still manages to find communities and Maharajahs who want its services, even though engagements grow fewer and farther between. They love their craft and are prepared to play for anyone who appreciates them.

Even when the popular film star Manjula (Madhur Jaffrey), jealous over Sanju's attentions to Lizzie, completely disrupts a performance by arriving late and attracting audience attention, the seasoned Buckingham troupe is not flustered. They're professionals who have encountered far worse during their travels.

As with all of director James Ivory's films, the details are authentic. He and Ruth Prawer Jhabvala co-authored the superb screenplay. The Indian countryside is beautifully photographed by Subrata Mitra, often associated with Satyajit Ray, the famed director who composed the lovely score for this film. It was Ray, incidentally, who began (American-born) Ivory's interest in India. "Seeing his films, the Apu trilogy," says Ivory, "is what really got me started."

The Indian and English actors are only wonderful. *Shakespeare Wallah* is a rewarding experience for discriminating audiences.

# The Sheep Has Five Legs
## (Le Mouton A Cinq Pattes)

★★★★★★★★★★★★★★★★★★★★★★★★★★★★★★★★★★★★★★★★★★★★★★★★★★★

Nationality: French       Year: 1954 (U.S. release: 1955)
Cast: Fernandel, Françoise Arnoul, Delmont, Louis de Funès
Director: Henri Verneuil      Running Time: 95 minutes
B/W or Color: B/W          Availability: Public Domain

From Alec Guinness's masterful delineation of eight roles in *Kind Hearts and Coronets* (1949) to the less-heralded interpretation of seven parts by Jerry Lewis in *The Family Jewels* (1965), comedy talents have been attracted to vehicles that allow them to multiply themselves through the magic of movies.

*The Sheep Has Five Legs* gave Fernandel, France's leading clown, the opportunity to assay six characters: a father and his five sons. In his *New York Times* review, Bosley Crowther considered the film "the best with Fernandel in years" and "the cleverest and most hilarious French comedy we've seen since the war."

To revive the prosperity of the town of Trezignan, its mayor (René Genin) seeks to bring back the now-grown quintuplets, whose birth popularized the place, and stage a grand reunion with their father, crotchety old Edouard Saint-Forget. The godfather, Dr. Bollene (Delmont), is dispatched to round up the quints, who were declared "National Monuments" and removed from their father's home as infants.

The good doctor finds the brothers: Alain, the effeminate proprietor of a lavish beauty salon; Desiré, a poor, easygoing window cleaner with several children; Etienne, a gin-sodden captain of a cargo ship in the South Seas; Bernard, who writes an advice-to-the-lovelorn column under the name of Aunt Nicole; and Charles, a priest whose resemblance to a famous screen comedian who played a cleric (a reference to Fernandel's popular Don Camillo series) has made him a laughing stock in his village. The reunion is a great success, topped by Desiré's wife giving birth again—to six girls!

Critics agreed that the comic highlight was the segment in which Etienne wins a bet with the help of a large (skillfully maneuvered) fly.

*Sheep* received an Academy Award nomination for Best Motion Picture Story.

Born Fernand Contandin in 1903, Fernandel died in 1971.

# Shoeshine
## (Sciuscia)

★★★★★★★★★★★★★★★★★★★★★★★★★★★★★★★★★★★★★★★★★★★★★★★★★★

**Nationality**: Italian        **Year**: 1946
**Cast**: Rinaldi Smordoni, Franco Interlenghi, Aniello Mele
**Director**: Vittorio De Sica       **Running Time**: 105 minutes
**B/W *or* Color**: B/W          **Availability**: TV only

World War II's bequest to the children of almost every country in Europe was despair, corruption, and hopelessness, forever flawing that generation as it grew into adulthood. *Shoeshine* is the shattering film that attacked the demoralizing and dehumanizing existence of those children.

Before the war, a dashing Vittorio De Sica was the Italian matinee idol of bedroom comedies, known locally as "white telephone" movies. Later, he alternated between more routine acting and then directing. *Shoeshine*, his first important postwar film, liberated him from the boudoir and placed him in the forefront of films celebrating life in the streets and the lowly peasant. De Sica became known as "the artist of the poor."

Like other neorealistic films, *Shoeshine* was shot on location, not on sound stages, and most of the actors were nonprofessionals. The combination gave the motion picture an unforgettable level of believability.

The title is taken from the armies of hungry, ragged, sickly Italian urchins who traipsed after GIs with their handmade shoeshine boxes calling out, "Shoosha, Joe!" The story dramatizes the plight of two of these boys, good friends, who are obsessed with the dream of owning a horse. To earn money, they become involved in a black market operation, are unfairly jailed, and deteriorate to such an extent that they are no longer friends.

Although the film had no solution to the problems it mirrors, it was influential in drastically reforming Italian laws dealing with juveniles. Unquestionably a landmark motion picture.

# Shoot the Piano Player
## (Tirez sur la Pianiste)

★★★★★★★★★★★★★★★★★★★★★★★★★★★★★★★★★★★★★★★★★★★★★★★★★★

*Nationality*: French                  *Year*: 1960 (U.S. release: 1962)

*Cast*: Charles Aznavour, Marie Dubois, Nicole Berger, Michele Mercier, Albert Remy

*Director*: François Truffaut          *Running Time*: 92 minutes

*B/W or Color*: B/W                    *Availability*: Public Domain

The connections between the French New Wave and American crime fiction (the pulp novel, the grade-B crime movie) is most evident in Godard's *Breathless* and Truffaut's *Shoot the Piano Player*. The latter's second film (his first was the prize-winning *The 400 Blows*) is based on the American novelist David Goodis's 1956 thriller *Down There*. Truffaut's adaptation gave it an existential gloss, a pop culture amplitude, and a humanist benevolence. Charles Aznavour stars as Charlie Koller, a honky-tonk pianist hiding from the world—until he's brought back into it by an adoring woman who knows his secret, Lena (Marie Dubois).

The tragic end of Charlie's first marriage has made him run from life. But unable to escape entirely, he's compelled to rejoin the fray as vulnerable and helpless as before. Truffaut tells this classical story (it pops up again, slightly altered, in De Palma's *Blow Out*) with a mixture of narrative tones: melodramatic slapstick, musical, film noir, pastorale. The self-consciousness of the New Wave rejected the artifice of a single, sustained mood. Truffaut mirrors the fast-changing attitudes of life, thereby avoiding being stuck in any one genre, in effect, transcending and transforming them all.

Aznavour and Dubois are perfection. Lovely Nicole Berger plays Mrs. Saroyan. The witty story is a double contemplation on love and destiny, showing one man's inability to escape either. This is one of the masterpieces of the pop era.

As Truffaut told interviewer Charles Thomas Samuels: "I made *Shoot the Piano Player* completely without reflection. When people first saw it, they said, 'Why did you make a film about such a disgusting lowlife?' but I never posed this question to myself. You see, I love *Down There* very much. I am always drawn by the fairy tale aura of the American detective novel. . . . When Godard saw *Shoot the Piano Player*, he said, 'This is the first film laid in a country of the imagination.' "

# The Shooting Party

\* \* \* \* \* \* \* \* \* \* \* \* \* \* \* \* \* \* \* \* \* \* \* \* \* \* \* \* \* \* \* \* \* \* \* \* \* \* \* \* \* \* \* \* \* \* \* \* \* \*

**Nationality**: British       **Year**: 1985

**Cast**: James Mason, Dorothy Tutin, Edward Fox, Cheryl Campbell, John Gielgud

**Director**: Alan Bridges       **Running Time**: 97 minutes

**B/W or Color**: Color       **Availability**: THORN EMI-HBO VIDEO

The leisurely, luxuriously elegant life of the English Edwardian country house has been perfectly brought to the screen by Alan Bridges, with help from his cinematographer Fred Tammes, screenwriter Julian Bond, production costume designers Morley Smith and Tom Rand, earning an honored place on The National Board of Review's top ten list. The glittering multistar cast includes Gordon Jackson, Aharon Ipale, Robert Hardy, Judi Bowker, Joris Stuyck, and Sara Badel. And what a marvelous epitaph for that splendid (and sorely missed) actor, James Mason.

The interplay of the characters is refreshingly intriguing: Sir Randolph and Lady Nettleby (Mason and Dorothy Tutin), their family and guests; Lord Gilbert Hartlip (a very stiff-upper-lipped Edward Fox), the acknowledged best shot in England, whose philandering wife (played with engaging impiety by Cheryl Campbell) is nevertheless totally loyal to her husband's interests. Also Lionel Stevens (Rupert Frazer), whose unintended shooting rivalry with Hartlip provides the catalyst for the death that just antedates the all-engulfing tragedy of World War I.

The interaction between these people and Lord and Lady Lilburn (with whom Stevens is in love); Sir Reuben Hergersheimer, Count Rakassyi, and Cicely Nettleby is delicate to bordering on the lewd—the reigning principle still being that anything goes, as long as you don't frighten the horses. However, morality isn't neglected, it strides in in the person of Cornelius Cardew (an enchanting John Gielgud), who advocates animal rights.

But the honors definitely go to Mason for a flawless performance in his last film. When he tells his young granddaughter, "It's not a bad idea to get in the habit of writing down one's thoughts. It saves one having to bother anyone else with them," *our* hearts go out to him. Little Violet, unmoved and uncomprehending, is wandering around his study just touching things. It's a lovely scene. And the movie scores over and over again in this way.

# The Shop on Main Street
## (Obchod na korze)

★★★★★★★★★★★★★★★★★★★★★★★★★★★★★★★★★★★★★★★★★★★★★★★★★★★

*Nationality*: Czech        *Year*: 1965 (U.S. release: 1966)

*Cast*: Josef Kroner, Ida Kaminska, Hana Slivkova, Frantisek Zvarik

*Director*: Jan Kadar, Elmar Klos    *Running Time*: 128 minutes

*B/W or Color*: B/W         *Availability*: RCA/COLUMBIA PICTURES VIDEO

"I'm *nichts . . . null . . .* zero," says Tono Brtko (Josef Kroner), hero of this poignant film about Nazi-occupied Czechoslovakia. Brtko is a henpecked, alcoholic carpenter, whose shrewish wife (Hana Slivkova) keeps nattering at him to "better himself," that is, collaborate with the Nazis. Tono's blustering brother-in-law (Frantisek Zvarik) gets him a sinecure as "Aryan controller" of a small button shop, operated by the Jewish widow Lautmann. Ida Kaminska's Lautmann is something of a grande dame, bawling out her "assistant" Brtko for opening the shop on Sunday. When he tries to warn her about Jewish deportations, she proposes to hide *him*. Then she sees the rabbi being carted off. Street voices come nearer. "A white Jew is worse than a Yid." (For "white Jew," read something like "nigger lover.") "It's you or me," says Brtko. The scales fall from the widow's eyes. Her lips form the word "pogrom." The cinematography turns this grim material into a work of art, as the camera lingers on birds flying over a church or on Mrs. Lautmann's chaste twin beds, a reminder of better days.

Bracketing the horror are Brtko's fantasies. He imagines himself and Lautmann promenading through peaceful streets, where the rabbi once moved, smiling, amid baby carriages and gossiping women. A marvelous Franz Joseph–era band orchestrates a lament for this gentle Mitteleuropa, forever lost to these two magnificent losers. Kroner's Brtko is beautifully drawn—essentially decent—capable of roughing up his wife when she urges him to go after Lautmann's nonexistent fortune. He is capable, too, in a moment of panic, of threatening to bundle Mrs. Lautmann off to the ovens. This film won the 1965 Oscar for Best Foreign Film.

*(The videocassette is in Czech with English subtitles.)*

# Sidewalks of London
## (St. Martin's Lane)

★ ★ ★ ★ ★ ★ ★ ★ ★ ★ ★ ★ ★ ★ ★ ★ ★ ★ ★ ★ ★ ★ ★ ★ ★ ★ ★ ★ ★ ★ ★ ★ ★ ★ ★ ★ ★ ★ ★ ★ ★ ★ ★ ★ ★ ★ ★ ★ ★ ★ ★ ★ ★ ★

*Nationality*: British        *Year*: 1938 (U.S. release: 1940)
*Cast*: Charles Laughton, Vivien Leigh, Rex Harrison, Larry Adler, Tyrone Guthrie
*Director*: Tim Whelan       *Running Time*: 85 minutes
*B/W or Color*: B/W        *Availability*: Public Domain

To gain more autonomy with his films, Charles Laughton joined forces in 1937 with Erich Pommer, the former production head of Germany's UFA organization. Under the name Mayflower Pictures, he and Laughton turned out three interesting failures starring the actor: *Vessel of Wrath/The Beachcomber, Jamaica Inn,* and this study of London's sidewalk "buskers," who perform in the streets of West End theaters for the amusement (and contributions) of theatergoers. Clemence Dane's original screenplay was so heavily rewritten by Laughton, Pommer, and director Tim Whelan that she repudiated the film—although she's the only writer credited.

In her last British movie before Hollywood and *Gone With the Wind,* Vivien Leigh enjoyed her most challenging role as the street-wise cockney pickpocket who uses busker Laughton's personal interest in her to climb the proverbial theatrical ladder. For a time, she's the star of his song-and-dance street act—until socialite-songwriter Rex Harrison makes her the toast of London's musical theaters.

Laughton (who realized little rapport with Leigh during production) is especially fine in the film's climactic scenes, where he briefly reenters her life. She tries to secure him a part in her new show, but he fumbles the audition and, angered by the callous producers, walks out. She runs after him, but he tells her that this isn't his world, as he returns to sidewalk entertaining.

For the fast-rising Leigh, this was a rare "character" role as a guttersnipe with guile and surface charm. And, while she's very effective in this delightful gem of a near-forgotten film, it's Laughton who's really marvelous in a part that could so easily have descended into hammy bathos.

(*Of available videocassettes, Corinth Video offers the best.*)

# A Simple Story
## (Une Histoire Simple)

★★★★★★★★★★★★★★★★★★★★★★★★★★★★★★★★★★★★★★★★★★★★★★★★★★★

*Nationality*: French         *Year*: 1978 (U.S. release: 1980)

*Cast*: Romy Schneider, Bruno Cremer, Claude Brasseur, Arlette Bonnard, Sophie Daumier

*Director*: Claude Sautet        *Running Time*: 110 minutes

*B/W or Color*: Color         *Availability*: RCA/COLUMBIA PICTURES HOME VIDEO

Director Claude Sautet, who explored male friendships incisively in 1974's *Vincent, François, Paul and the Others,* here focuses on the female, in this deceptively named film about the considerable day-to-day problems of a middle-class Frenchwoman named Marie.

Romy Schneider portrays this 39-year-old divorced woman at mid-life crisis. As the film opens, Marie is about to go through with an abortion that will signal the end of a relationship with her lover, Serge (Claude Brasseur). An industrial designer who lives with her teenaged son (a character we barely meet, since this is a simple, *adult* story), Marie is shown coping with her subsequent loneliness, commiserating with women friends, and sharing their marital problems, frustrations, and tragedies (including a husband's suicide). Marie makes an effort to resume a relationship with her ex-husband, Georges (Bruno Cremer), but he opts for the less "demanding" company of a younger woman, and Marie, once again pregnant, decides this time to see it through. As she ruefully admits to her best friend, "It seems that I can't have a man and a child at the same time."

An Oscar-nominated foreign film in 1979 (losing out to Germany's *The Tin Drum*), *A Simple Story* had already garnered acclaim in its native France, where Romy Schneider's expressive performance won her a Best Actress César in a role that had been expressly written for her by Jean-Loup Debadie and director Sautet.

American reviews for the film were generally enthusiastic, especially for the acting and Jean Boffety's cinematography. But *A Simple Story* doesn't linger long in the memory, and perhaps the *New York Times*'s Vincent Canby pegged it accurately as "a pretty movie, extremely well acted but anesthetizing."

*(The videocassette is available only in an adequately English-dubbed version.)*

# A Slave of Love
## (Raba Lubvi)

**********************************************************

Nationality: Russian          Year: 1976 (U.S. release: 1978)

Cast: Elena Solovey, Rodion Nakhapetov, Alexander Kalyagin, Oleg Basilashivili, Konstantin Grigoryev

Director: Nikita Mikhalkov          Running Time: 94 minutes

B/W or Color: Color and B/W          Availability: RCA/COLUMBIA PICTURES HOME VIDEO

One of the finest imports from Russia is this exquisitely beautiful piece about silent moviemaking in the days of the Revolution. That background sets the stage for comedy, drama, romance, action, and historical significance. Director Nikita Mikhalkov came from a family of artists, with father Sergei a poet and brother Andrei Mikhalkov-Konchalovsky a filmmaker. The latter, with Friedrich Gorenstein, contributed the screenplay. While Pavel Lebeshev's color cinematography is a thing of beauty, black and white is used for the film-within-a-film sequences and for actual footage of peasants being executed during the upheaval. The contrasting moods, from comedy to tragedy, are well used, and the opening pretitles set the tone: a takeoff on silent melodramas is followed by a scene of a vicious attack on a revolutionary.

It is 1917, just after the Russian Revolution. In the Crimea, resettled filmmakers are turning out silent melodramas and yearning for the old days in Moscow, while preparing to depart for Paris. The unit is headed by star Elena Solovey, director Alexander Kalyagin, producer Oleg Basilashivili, and photographer Rodion Nakhapetov. The unhappy Solovey, a widow with two young daughters and a lost love (her co-star), finds solace with Nakhapetov. Seemingly carefree, he secretly photographs executions of revolutionaries and proves to be one himself. The footage he shoots leads to a series of events that mark Solovey for death.

The last scene is that of Solovey fleeing on a trolley with a group of soldiers in pursuit. Mikhalkov wisely refrains from showing the inevitable, and the climax is one of the most haunting in screen history. While not an epic in the vein of other memorable Russian efforts, A Slave of Love has its own distinct style as it goes about re-creating a turbulent time, and Elena Solovey creates a vivid impression. Don't be misled by the title or be deprived of the opportunity to see international filmmaking at its finest.

(The videocassette is subtitled.)

# The Sleeping Car Murders
## (Compartiment Tueurs)

\* \* \* \* \* \* \* \* \* \* \* \* \* \* \* \* \* \* \* \* \* \* \* \* \* \* \* \* \* \* \* \* \* \* \* \* \* \* \* \* \* \* \* \* \* \* \* \* \* \* \* \* \* \*

*Nationality*: French　　　　　*Year*: 1965 (U.S. release: 1966)

*Cast*: Yves Montand, Simone Signoret, Pierre Mondy, Catherine Allegret, Jacques Perrin

*Director*: Constantin Costa-Gavras　*Running Time*: 92 minutes

*B/W or Color*: B/W　　　　　*Availability*: TV only

Thanks to the support of several stars, many of whom appear in the movie, Costa-Gavras (raised in France) made his directorial debut with *The Sleeping Car Murders,* selected by The National Board as 1966's Best Foreign-Language Picture. The novice director also co-authored its screenplay (with Sebastien Japrisot, on whose novel the picture is based). Costa-Gavras demonstrates an abundance of cinematic style, and keeps the audience wondering throughout—as the top-notch puzzler is pieced together through flashbacks and guesswork.

The stellar cast in this intriguing tale of murder and blackmail includes Yves Montand, his wife Simone Signoret, and her daughter (by first husband, writer-director Yves Allegret) Catherine Allegret—making her screen debut.

On the overnight train between Marseilles and Paris, ticketless Daniel (Jacques Perrin) meets Bambi (Catherine Allegret), who helps him avoid the conductor and lets him spend the night in an unoccupied berth in her compartment. The next morning, he leaves early; but, having forgotten his suitcase, returns and discovers the body of a perfume saleswoman (Pascale Roberts). It soon becomes apparent that someone is murdering the compartment's occupants, including Cabourg (Michel Piccoli) and fading actress Eliane Darres (Simone Signoret), who was being blackmailed.

Investigating the crimes are Inspector Grazzi (Yves Montand) and his assistant Jean-Lou (Claude Mann), who is new to the force. The inspector prevents Eliane's young lover Eric (Jean-Louis Trintignant) from killing Bambi, but Eric is only an accomplice, and the real murderer is seeking Daniel. Who is the killer?

Calling the film "beautifully plotted," *Films in Review* noted its use of subjective camera ("an enormous revolver fires right into the lens"), its "thrilling, magnificently photographed car and motorcycle chase through the teeming streets of nighttime Paris," and its suspense, "skillfully maintained throughout." Of Catherine Allegret, the reviewer wrote: "[She] combines her mother's style and grace with the appeal of the young Bardot." Unfortunately, the young actress never rivaled her parent's stardom.

# Sleuth

\* \* \* \* \* \* \* \* \* \* \* \* \* \* \* \* \* \* \* \* \* \* \* \* \* \* \* \* \* \* \* \* \* \* \* \* \* \* \* \* \* \* \* \* \* \* \* \* \* \* \*

**Nationality**: British      **Year**: 1972

**Cast**: Laurence Olivier, Michael Caine, Alec Cawthorne, Eve Channing, Karen Minfort-Jones, John Matthews, Teddy Martin

**Director**: Joseph L. Mankiewicz      **Running Time**: 138 minutes

**B/W or Color**: Color      **Availability**: MEDIA HOME ENTERTAINMENT

The most stylish cat-and-mouse game ever filmed, *Sleuth* was directed by Joseph L. Mankiewicz and written by Anthony Shaffer, who based it on his play, which premiered in London. Initially, Cary Grant and Albert Finney were slated for the lead roles.

*Sleuth* received four Oscar nominations: Best Actor (both Laurence Olivier and Michael Caine), Director (Mankiewicz), and Score (John Addison). Fans of Mankiewicz's *All About Eve* will appreciate the name of Eve Channing in the credits (as Olivier's wife), and fans in general will recognize Joanne Woodward in the photographs of Olivier's wife.

In his *New York Times* review, Vincent Canby favorably mentioned Channing and the four other supporting players: Alec Cawthorne as Inspector Doppler, Karen Minfort-Jones as Olivier's mistress, and John Matthews and Teddy Martin as policemen, a nice touch that can only be appreciated by those who have seen the film. Canby also complimented Caine's performance and noted: "To witness Olivier at work . . . is to behold a one-man revue of theatrical excesses—all marvelous."

After finding his way through an elaborate garden maze (a prelude of things to come), Milo Tindle (Caine) arrives at the home of mystery writer Andrew Wyke (Olivier). In love with Wyke's wife, Tindle is there at the invitation of the writer, who plans to slowly humiliate him.

Olivier suggests that the house safe be emptied of his wife's jewelry, thus allowing the insurance money to console him for her loss, while the money from the sale of the gems will allow Tindle to support his wife in the manner to which she's accustomed.

Dressed in a clown's outfit, Tindle stages the robbery and suddenly realizes that Wyke plans to kill the "burglar." This is the first of many surprises that await the audience as well as the characters, who may be more or less than they appear to be.

The role of Wyke (which earned Olivier the New York Film Critics' Best Actor Award) is a tour de force; and, in matching him, Caine is more than able.

# Smash Palace

★★★★★★★★★★★★★★★★★★★★★★★★★★★★★★★★★★★★★★★★★★★★★★★★★★★

*Nationality*: New Zealand          *Year*: 1981 (U.S. release: 1982)
*Cast*: Bruno Lawrence, Anna Jemison, Greer Robson, Keith Aberdein
*Director*: Roger Donaldson          *Running Time*: 100 minutes
*B/W or Color*: Color          *Availability*: VESTRON VIDEO

The New Zealanders are coming! The New Zealanders are coming! Hard on the heels of the Australian filmmakers, the New Zealanders have quite a way to go—both in quantity and quality—to catch up with the prodigious export of their Down Under neighbors. Though their first release, *Sleeping Dogs*, was rather confused and unmemorable, the Kiwis, and writer-director-producer Roger Donaldson in particular, have delivered something both memorable and believable with their second picture.

*Smash Palace* is the honest, crisply intelligent story of Al and Jacqui Shaw (Bruno Lawrence and Anna Jemison), their young daughter Georgie (Greer Robson), and the break-up of their eight-year marriage. Jacqui, bored with the limited life offered around Smash Palace, her husband's wrecking yard, is attracted to her husband's best friend, police officer Ray Foley (Keith Aberdein). After a fight, she leaves Al, taking Georgie with her and begins an affair with Ray. The remainder of *Smash Palace* concerns Al's growing awareness that Jacqui might not come back to him and the way in which a basically decent—but bewildered and angry—husband and father copes with the situation.

Although often reminiscent in theme of *Kramer vs. Kramer* and *Shoot the Moon*, one of *Smash Palace*'s distinctive plusses is its total unpredictability and the resultant elements of suspense and surprise. Roger Donaldson's versatile script can move equally surely from a cozy birthday party scene between father and daughter to one of violent rage. The performances are all first rate, particularly that of Bruno Lawrence, whose portrayal of the frustrated Al could so easily have risked audience empathy. Greer Robson earns special mention as a stand-out in a year of fine performances by child actors.

# Smiles of a Summer Night
## (Sommarnattens Leende)

\* \* \* \* \* \* \* \* \* \* \* \* \* \* \* \* \* \* \* \* \* \* \* \* \* \* \* \* \* \* \* \* \* \* \* \* \* \* \* \* \* \* \* \* \* \* \* \* \* \* \* \*

**Nationality**: Swedish       **Year**: 1955 (U.S. release: 1957)

**Cast**: Ulla Jacobsson, Gunnar Björnstrand, Eva Dahlbeck, Margit Carlquist, Harriet Andersson, Jarl Kulle

**Director**: Ingmar Bergman       **Running Time**: 108 minutes

**B/W or Color**: B/W       **Availability**: EMBASSY HOME ENTERTAINMENT

Ingmar Bergman is not known for light, witty, romantic comedies, but that is exactly what *Smiles of a Summer Night* is, and it's one of the best. In this elegant comedy of manners set in 1901, a group of upper-class characters and their servants romp about a country house for a weekend of love. Some have noted a similarity to Renoir's *Rules of the Game* (1939), but surprisingly, Bergman claims not to admire that classic very much. Woody Allen based his *A Midsummer Night's Sex Comedy* (1982) on *Smiles*, and Stephen Sondheim's famous musical *A Little Night Music* is a direct remake, with songs added.

The story is based around a middle-aged lawyer who has taken a young bride but has yet to consummate the marriage after two years. His son, a theological student with repressed feelings of love for his stepmother, tries to sublimate his passion by having an affair with the family maid. The fun begins when the lawyer takes his wife to see a play and reveals that he once had an affair with its famous leading lady. They all go to the actress's chateau for the weekend, and a game of musical-lovers ensues. The son finally runs off with his stepmother, the lawyer has a liaison with the wife of the man who is to marry the actress, and on and on. But there is an underlying bite to Bergman's treatment. He seems to be saying "look at all these funny, ridiculous people running around for the sake of a little love and sex, but isn't it terrible what we do to one another in the pursuit of selfish pleasure?" Bergman's playful mise-en-scene puts his flawless cast through their paces like an expert ringmaster, building up small details of character through inanimate objects such as parasols, veils, clocks, music-boxes, and an unforgettable trick bed. *Smiles of a Summer Night* re-creates an exquisite past, rich in its complex relationships caught up on a merry-go-round of love and jealousy. The film won a special prize at Cannes for its "poetic humor" and was listed among 1957's ten best foreign films by *The New York Times*.

*(The videocassette is subtitled.)*

# The Soft Skin
## (La Peau Douce)

★★★★★★★★★★★★★★★★★★★★★★★★★★★★★★★★★★★★★★★★★★★★★★★★★★★★

**Nationality**: French               **Year**: 1964

**Cast**: Jean Desailly, Françoise Dorléac, Nelly Benedetti, Daniel Ceccaldi, Sabine Haudepin

**Director**: François Truffaut        **Running Time**: 118 minutes

**B/W *or* Color**: B/W               **Availability**: KEY VIDEO

This surprisingly underrated film by François Truffaut stands tall between the magnificent *Jules and Jim* (1962) and his famed *Fahrenheit 451* (1966). *The Soft Skin* is the first of his full-flung homages to Alfred Hitchcock and probably one of the director's most rigorously "cinematic" films. This is a picture with all stops pulled.

Very simply, we are involved with a love triangle. Pierre (Jean Desailly), a famous editor and lecturer, falls for the beautiful but vapid Nicole (Françoise Dorléac), to the chagrin of his passionate wife Franca (Nelly Benedetti). As Nicole, Dorléac is ample temptation and, along with her sister—Catherine Deneuve—redefined what "beautiful" meant in the swinging Sixties. (Dorléac died three years after *The Soft Skin* in a car accident.)

Truffaut immediately tips his hat to Hitchcock as the audience is keenly caught up in Pierre's "miraculous" catching of his departing flight, as his car zips through the Parisian traffic. Like this nervously cut scene, Pierre's facade of fame and security is about to crumble. The dialogue is sparse, and the action is mostly confined to the interior of the characters, but Truffaut has complete control over these people and the logistics and the ramifications of their affairs.

The difference between the claustrophobia of the triangle here and the expansiveness of the Jules-Jim-Catherine ménage in *Jules and Jim* is astounding, considering their mutual source. Truffaut has called *The Soft Skin* his "violent answer" to *Jules and Jim*, and has explained that love in the city is not as "beautiful" as love in the country so *"The Soft Skin* is truly modern love . . . it has all the harassments of modern life." *The Soft Skin* is a minor gem by a major director.

*(The videocassette is subtitled.)*

# Soldier of Orange

★★★★★★★★★★★★★★★★★★★★★★★★★★★★★★★★★★★★★★★★★★★★★★★★★★★★★★★

**Nationality**: Dutch        **Year**: 1978 (U.S. release: 1979)
**Cast**: Rutger Hauer, Jeroen Krabbé, Edward Fox, Susan Penhaligon
**Director**: Paul Verhoeven       **Running Time**: 150 minutes
**B/W or Color**: Color           **Availability**: MEDIA HOME EN-
TERTAINMENT (Cinemateque
Collection)

**S**oldier of Orange (*Orange* referring to Dutch royalty) is a rip-roar-
ing, solidly entertaining adventure picture relating the true-life escapades of Erik Hazelhoff, a member of the Dutch Resistance during
World War II.

The screenplay, based on Hazelhoff's autobiographical novel (he helped
supervise the filming), balances the human dimensions of war with plenty
of intrigue and derring-do as it follows six college friends through the
war. All become involved with the Resistance movement in one way or
another. The central character, of course, is Erik (Rutger Hauer), a young
Dutch aristocrat who joins the Resistance when the Nazis occupy Holland. From carefree college days prior to the invasion through the first
years of occupation, through Erik's escape to England—where he becomes a bomber pilot and aide to Queen Wilhelmina—the action never
flags.

Rutger Hauer plays Erik with dash, humor, and a strong sense of survival, versus simply "playing the hero." Equally impressive is Jeroen Krabbé
as Guus, the debonair university leader who is Erik's nemesis and later
best friend. Peter Faber, Derek De Lint, Eddy Habbema, and Lex Van
Delden round out the six friends, and Susan Penhaligon is delicious as
Erik's love interest. Edward Fox puts in a strong cameo as a proper British colonel, and Andrea Domburg scores as Wilhelmina, the staunch-
hearted Dutch queen who flees to England during the war.

*Soldier of Orange* holds the attention throughout, thanks to fine ensemble acting, strong narrative, lush photography, and a stirring score.
The movie was shot in English and Dutch, with the Dutch portions subtitled in English.

# The Sound of Trumpets

## (Il Posto)

★★★★★★★★★★★★★★★★★★★★★★★★★★★★★★★★★★★★★★★★★★★★★★★★★★★

*Nationality*: Italian          *Year*: 1961 (U.S. release: 1963)

*Cast*: Sandro Panzeri, Loredana Detto, Tullio Kezich

*Director*: Ermanno Olmi        *Running Time*: 90 minutes (98 minutes in Italy)

*B/W or Color*: B/W         *Availability*: TV only

Profoundly touching without being overweening or precious, *The Sound of Trumpets* is the simple, crowning achievement of Italian neorealism by director Ermanno Olmi, who realized that the movement's manifestations had all but disappeared in the increasingly baroque filmmaking of the late Fifties.

This film is dedicated to those workers on the periphery of urban-industrial Milan in Lombardy who must travel each day to the city for work, despite the palpable Milanese hostility to their presence. However, this movie isn't about the pathos of peasantry, as is Olmi's later *The Tree of Wooden Clogs*.

The angelically innocent Domenico (played by nonprofessional Sandro Panzeri) embodies the sweetest of souls, alienated from his labor and from his natural life-style and filled with gentle yearning for a lovely fellow-worker named Antonietta (Loredana Detto), whom he only occasionally glimpses. By the time of a mournful New Year's Eve party—at which we realize that Domenico had been waiting for months just to see her again—the pain of this promised, failed epiphany is nearly unbearable. As a worker pops a champagne cork, he says, "The gate's open, the trumpets blare, the cannon roars," and we are reduced to examining this grand but empty expression of hope with a scene that follows soon after—the same workers staring hopelessly at the vacated desk and unused coat-hanger of a former worker who had died.

Judith Crist summed it up as "a masterful documentary of the human spirit told in terms of a boy's first job in big business, an introduction to the treadmill to which our society commits so many of us."

At 1961's Venice Film Festival, the picture won the Catholic Film Office award.

# A Special Day
## (Una Giornata Particolare)

★★★★★★★★★★★★★★★★★★★★★★★★★★★★★★★★★★★★★★★★★★★★★★★★★★★

Nationality: Italian-Canadian     Year: 1977
Cast: Sophia Loren, Marcello Mastroianni, John Vernon, Francoise Berd
Director: Ettore Scola     Running Time: 110 minutes
B/W or Color: Color     Availability: RCA/COLUMBIA PIC-
                                                      TURES HOME VIDEO

One of the National Board's best films for 1977, A Special Day received Academy Award nominations as Best Foreign Film and for Marcello Mastroianni as Best Actor. Cinematographer Pasqualino De Santis's use of muted color to simulate black and white adds an unusual effect.

Director (and co-author) Ettore Scola cast Mastroianni and Sophia Loren against type in this story of two lonely people who meet on A Special Day: May 6, 1938, which also marks the historic occasion when Hitler met with Mussolini to proclaim the unity of the two fascist parties. While almost all of Rome turns out for the rally, two who remain home are Antonietta (Loren) and Gabriele (Mastroianni)—neighbors in an apartment complex.

Strangers to each other, they are brought together when Antonietta's mynah bird flies out the window and lands on Gabriele's sill. They spend the afternoon, over coffee, sharing secrets and insecurities.

An uneducated housewife and mother of six, Antonietta's only hope is to have a seventh child, thereby enabling the family to be financially rewarded by the government. Her life has become a series of boring routines, and she's starved for affection. She admits a fantasy involving Il Duce himself, who once galloped by her on horseback while she was shopping in the Villa Borghese.

Gabriele is a homosexual, a radio announcer who has led a double life in order to keep working. He's now without a job or friends; because of his life-style, he's been labeled anti-Fascist and was about to commit suicide when fate (on the wings of the mynah bird) intervened.

The two make love. That evening, Gabriele, now able to deal with difficulties, is arrested; meanwhile, an emotionally replenished Antonietta can better face her family.

Loren and Mastroianni give splendid performances in a story that Films in Review termed "a psychological pas-de-deux."

(The videocassette is dubbed in English.)

# Spetters

★★★★★★★★★★★★★★★★★★★★★★★★★★★★★★★★★★★★★★★★★★★★★★★★★★★★★★

Nationality: Dutch          Year: 1980 (U.S. release: 1981)
Cast: Hans van Tongeren, Renee Soutendijk, Toon Agterberg, Maarten
Spanjer, Rutger Hauer
Director: Paul Verhoeven        Running Time: 115 minutes
B/W or Color: Color          Availability: EMBASSY HOME
                                         ENTERTAINMENT

Paul Verhoeven, the Netherlands' most visible and prolific contemporary filmmaker, is most readily identified with *Soldier of Orange* (1979) and *The 4th Man* (1983). His *Spetters,* a raunchy, free-wheeling 1980 movie about Dutch youth on the loose, bears little relationship to those pictures. Sex, violence, and gutter language abound in this tough, exploitative melodrama, and although the behavior of these motorcycle-obsessed teenagers is often reprehensible, Verhoeven's direction of Gerard Soeteman's episodic screenplay is sufficiently riveting to maintain interest throughout. Add to that a cast more skilled than appealing, and we have in *Spetters* (a colloquial term meaning oil-spray—or perhaps orgasm?) a lusty shocker.

Rutger Hauer portrays the cameo part of a champion motorcycle racer whose celebrity inspires three youths who are fellow racers and off-track buddies. The story takes a tragic turn when the most promising of the trio (Hans van Tongeren) is accidentally crippled and reduced to an embittered, wheelchair future. Another (Toon Agterberg) is a mechanic who resorts to mugging homosexuals to supplement his income—until a curious sort of poetic justice makes him the not-unhappy victim of a gang rape. In the film's most striking performance, sexy Renee Soutendijk plays an ambitious, amoral blonde who, with her burly, gay brother, runs an itinerant lunch wagon catering to the biker crowd—whose sexual favors she samples at random.

If these young Hollanders are rebels without causes, following their nihilistic daily pursuits nevertheless holds the fascination of observing the more dangerous creatures in a zoo from behind the safety of iron bars. They hold a morbid attraction.

*(Embassy offers the movie in Dutch with subtitles, as well as in a surprisingly well-dubbed print.)*

# The Spirit of the Beehive
## (El Espiritu de la Clomena)

* * * * * * * * * * * * * * * * * * * * * * * * * * * * * * * * * * * * * * * * * * * * * * * * * * * *

*Nationality*: Spanish  **Year**: 1973 (U.S. release: 1976)
*Cast*: Ana Torrent, Isabel Telleria, Fernando Fernan Gomez, Teresa Gimpera
*Director*: Victor Erice  **Running Time**: 98 minutes
*B/W or Color*: Color  **Availability**: TV only

The Spirit of the Beehive won its first honors on the Continent at film festivals. London critics extolled the picture anew. It was only when *The New York Times'* Richard Eder (reporting from Colorado's Telluride Festival), admitted it could be "a great film we may never see" that *The Spirit of the Beehive* found a U.S. distributor.

It is not only a major work, but it's one of the best films ever to come out of Spain. Its director, Victor Erice, knows how to work in a clean, Spartan way, employing little camera movement, but inspiring his cameraman, Luis Cuadro, to evoke a mood of loneliness, sorrow, and terror. And Erice understands children—one child in particular, Ana, exquisitely played by a little girl named Ana Torrent. Like *Poil de Carotte* and *Forbidden Games,* this picture is a study of a hungry, imaginative, lonely child lost in the maze of an embittered land. Other fine performances are contributed by Teresa Gimpera, as the mother who maintains correspondence with imaginary friends; and Fernando Fernan Gomez, as the sad, intellectual father, who keeps the beehive of the film's symbolic title.

It is 1940, and one of the few treats the villagers know comes from a film exhibitor traveling with tired, scratchy prints of movies to show in the city hall. He brings James Whale's 1931 *Frankenstein* to the townspeople, and Ana is transported into another world when she sees it and falls in love with the Monster. Convinced by her sister, a tease, that the Monster did not really die, Ana goes out alone day after day, crossing the barren countryside in search of him.

In Richard Eder's opinion: "At its clearest, the movie's formal meaning is always complex, always allusive. But by the time it ends, it has possessed the viewer completely."

# Spring in Park Lane

\*\*\*\*\*\*\*\*\*\*\*\*\*\*\*\*\*\*\*\*\*\*\*\*\*\*\*\*\*\*\*\*\*\*\*\*\*\*\*\*\*\*\*\*\*\*\*\*\*\*\*

*Nationality*: British          *Year*: 1948 (U.S. release: 1949)

*Cast*: Anna Neagle, Michael Wilding, Tom Walls, Marjorie Fielding, Nicholas Phipps

*Director*: Herbert Wilcox          *Running Time*: 100 minutes

*B/W or Color*: B/W          *Availability*: TV only

One of England's most popular stars, Anna Neagle (1904–86) married pioneer filmmaker Herbert Wilcox and formed a team that ranked among the most powerful (and successful) in the British film industry. Among their biggest pleasers were the pictures in which Neagle teamed with Michael Wilding, from *Piccadilly Incident* (1946) to *The Lady with the Lamp*, a 1951 biography of Florence Nightingale. Wilding's marriage to Elizabeth Taylor (he became her second husband in 1952) brought him to Hollywood and an end to his movies opposite Neagle—of which the best remembered is *Spring in Park Lane*, a sparkling musical comedy.

Herbert Wilcox's direction makes the frothy Cinderella-plot play like a happy improvisation. Three cheers for the delightfully lighthearted screenplay by Nicholas Phipps, who appears as the Marquis of Borechester. The sets are lavish, the clothes glamorous, and the champagne corks pop with precision.

Anna Neagle plays Judy, a secretary to her wealthy uncle (a cheerfully droll Tom Walls). Michael Wilding is Richard, a nobleman on the run, who accepted a check for his family's art collection and had the ruddy thing bounce. He takes a job as footman in the same Park Lane mansion where Neagle works, and she quickly surmises that something's afoot with the footman. Their meeting is almost a signal for the opening chords of the Wedding March. The check for the artwork turns out to be good, and everything else turns out simply smashing.

In his *New York Times* review, Bosley Crowther stated that Michael Wilding "comes forward . . . as the easy-going comedian, whose vocal inflections and facial manners are remarkably reminiscent of Danny Kaye's." He found the picture a "sly spoofing of the aristocratic types" and a "lot of lovable fun."

Making his screen debut, tenth-billed as Mr. Bacon, is future star Nigel Patrick.

*Spring in Park Lane* is a frolic for all seasons.

# The Spy in Black
## (U-Boat 29)

**★★★★★★★★★★★★★★★★★★★★★★★★★★★★★★★★★★★★★★★★★★★★★★★★★★★★★**

*Nationality*: British                    *Year*: 1939

*Cast*: Conrad Veidt, Valerie Hobson, Sebastian Shaw, Marius Goring

*Director*: Michael Powell        *Running Time*: 82 minutes

*B/W or Color*: B/W             *Availability*: EMBASSY HOME
                                  ENTERTAINMENT

One of The National Board's ten best for 1939, *The Spy in Black* (also known as *U-Boat 29*) was the first collaboration of director Michael Powell and writer Emeric Pressburger. Among the movies on which they shared the titles of writer-producer-director were *I Know Where I'm Going*, *Stairway to Heaven (A Matter of Life and Death)*, *Black Narcissus*, *The Red Shoes*, and *The Tales of Hoffmann*.

Set in World War I Scotland, this intriguing espionage tale concerns U-boat captain Hardt (Conrad Veidt), who comes ashore at Scapa Flow, the base for the British North Sea Fleet. His contact is a schoolmistress (Valerie Hobson)—in truth, a double agent. Surprise twists and a bittersweet romance are expertly interwoven with elements of duty and deceit.

When Alexander Korda summoned Pressburger, there already existed a screenplay that remained faithful to its source material, a J. Storer Clouston novel. Pressburger completely restructured the plot, changing *The Spy in Black* from a Scottish minister to the German U-boat captain. "When you buy the rights to a famous book which turns out to be useless for a screenwriter's purpose," Michael Powell later explained, "you keep the title and throw away the book."

For three weeks prior to filming, Powell and Pressburger worked with Conrad Veidt and Valerie Hobson. The actors rehearsed the roughed-out scenes, and then everyone would (as Powell later wrote) "tear into them as if we were making home movies." The four were reunited the following year in *Contraband* (released in the United States as *Blackout*).

By the time he played *The Spy in Black*, Conrad Veidt (whose debut was in 1917's *Der Spion/The Spy*) had made over 100 (mostly German) films. His best remembered role was that of Major Strasser in *Casablanca*. The 50-year-old actor died of a heart attack the year it was released.

# The Spy Who Came In from the Cold

**★★★★★★★★★★★★★★★★★★★★★★★★★★★★★★★★★★★★★★★★★★★★★★★★★★★★★★★★★**

*Nationality*: British          *Year*: 1965
*Cast*: Richard Burton, Claire Bloom, Oskar Werner, Peter Van Eyck
*Director*: Martin Ritt          *Running Time*: 112 minutes
*B/W or Color*: B/W          *Availability*: TV only

I n 1965, audiences were hooked on spies and camp. James Bond was at his height of popularity as 007 in *Thunderball*; and *The Man from U.N.C.L.E.* was featured on television, with U.N.C.L.E. theatrical versions in release. While the spy guys were popular, their films were certainly not realistic.

John Le Carré's novels are as far from the world of 007 as Savile Row is from Soho. His books are often grim and not averse to downbeat endings, featuring heroes who are not totally heroic. The lines between us and "them" are often blurred.

Le Carré's first George Smiley novel, the best-selling *The Spy Who Came In from the Cold*, was made into a superior, highly acclaimed film with the late Richard Burton in an Academy Award–nominated performance as the British master spy caught between East and West. Martin Ritt's direction brings a dark, chiaroscuro quality to this cold war story of Alec Leamas (Burton), the British agent who is sent into East Germany to pose as a defector on a last assignment before retirement. His mission is to create a confrontation between Mundt (Peter Van Eyck), the head of the East German operation, and his Jewish second in command, Fiedler (Oskar Werner), who is fanatically jealous of his superior. When the tables are turned, Leamas becomes a pawn in the game. He falls in love with Nan Perry (Claire Bloom), a communist librarian whose eventual death also spells doom for Alec. Rupert Davies plays British spymaster George Smiley, later portrayed by Alec Guinness in the TV miniseries *Tinker, Tailor, Soldier, Spy* and *Smiley's People*.

Subsequent to this film, Richard Burton was offered the part of James Bond in a proposed Kevin McClory production of *Thunderball* (before the rights were picked up for the 1965 film by Broccoli and Saltzman).

A landmark film, *The Spy Who Came In from the Cold* had as a central character a man who was both a professional and a victim. A seasoned veteran with little left in the way of scruples or illusions, Leamas was still unable to believe in the cold-bloodedness of his superiors. The movie never once reduces itself to the expected.

# Stairway to Heaven
## (A Matter of Life and Death)

★★★★★★★★★★★★★★★★★★★★★★★★★★★★★★★★★★★★★★★★★★★★★★★★★★★★★★★★★

*Nationality*: British  *Year*: 1946

*Cast*: David Niven, Roger Livesey, Raymond Massey, Kim Hunter, Marius Goring

*Director*: Michael Powell and  *Running Time*: 104 minutes
Emeric Pressburger

*B/W or Color*: Color *and* B/W  *Availability*: TV only

Written and directed by the team of Michael Powell and Emeric Pressburger, *Stairway to Heaven* is a charming, intelligent fantasy that *Time* magazine found "adult as well as light-hearted" and felt possessed "the admirable quality of taking itself seriously only to kid itself."

Called *A Matter of Life and Death* in England (where it was selected for the first Royal Film Performance), the movie's title underwent a change because distributors were afraid American audiences would reject anything with the word *death* in it.

The fate of RAF squadron leader Peter Carter (David Niven) is determined by a celestial jury while he lies on an operating table. He was scheduled to die when, sans parachute, he bailed out of a burning bomber during the closing days of World War II. However, Conductor 71 (Marius Goring), the heavenly messenger assigned to escort him, got lost in the dense fog over the English Channel. When the Conductor is sent back to collect Carter, the squadron leader doesn't want to accompany him because he has fallen in love with an American WAC radio operator named June (Kim Hunter). The kind doctor (Roger Livesey) who is treating Carter is accidentally killed and is thereby able to defend his friend at the celestial trial, in which the prosecutor is Abraham Farlan (Raymond Massey), an American who hates the British, having been killed in the Battle of Lexington in 1775.

The scenes on Earth are in color and the heavenly sequences in monochrome. Indeed, Goring, who's dressed in 18th-century attire, remarks to the audience, "We are starved for Technicolor, up there."

Kim Hunter was recommended to Powell and Pressburger by Alfred Hitchcock, who had employed her in tests for *Spellbound*. This was David Niven's first postwar picture and helped greatly to reestablish the popularity he had built up before joining the British army at the onset of World War II.

# The Stars Look Down

★★★★★★★★★★★★★★★★★★★★★★★★★★★★★★★★★★★★★★★★★★★★★★★★★★★★★★★★★

*Nationality*: British                    *Year*: 1939 (U.S. release: 1941)
*Cast*: Michael Redgrave, Margaret Lockwood, Emlyn Williams, Nancy Price, Edward Rigby
*Director*: Carol Reed              *Running Time*: 110 minutes
*B/W or Color*: B/W                 *Availability*: Public Domain

Carol Reed's directorial career began inauspiciously in 1935 and enjoyed its first real success with 1938's *Bank Holiday,* a film unfamiliar to most Americans (it was released here as *Three on a Weekend*). But in 1939, he teamed with the young romantic leads of the previous year's Hitchcock thriller *The Lady Vanishes* (Michael Redgrave and Margaret Lockwood) to film A. J. Cronin's 1935 novel about a coal strike in England's North, *The Stars Look Down.* While some English critics considered it Britain's finest motion picture to that date, others carped at the simplification of some of the book's deeper issues.

But Carol Reed knew what he was about, and the forthrightness with which he handled the film's social criticism of Britain's mines and mining conditions helped pave the way for more realism in the British cinema.

As the idealistic central character—a mining-town youth who improves himself with a university education so that he can better support his miner-neighbors' rights—Michael Redgrave offers the first of his many outstanding screen performances. And as the self-absorbed town "bad girl," who coerces Redgrave into marriage and then commits adultery with an old boyfriend (Emlyn Williams), Margaret Lockwood (who had replaced Phyllis Calvert in the role) played so convincingly that one can witness the seeds of such Forties Lockwood heavies as her nonheroines of *The Man in Grey, The Wicked Lady,* and *Bedelia.* Emlyn Williams, of course, does his slimy best as Lockwood's lover and Redgrave's nemesis.

In Britain, *The Stars Look Down*'s popularity raised Carol Reed to one of the most respected of his country's filmmakers. Two years later, when the movie finally had a U.S. release, the New York Film Critics voted Reed a close second as 1941's best director, giving first place to John Ford for *How Green Was My Valley.*

# Stevie

★ ★ ★ ★ ★ ★ ★ ★ ★ ★ ★ ★ ★ ★ ★ ★ ★ ★ ★ ★ ★ ★ ★ ★ ★ ★ ★ ★ ★ ★ ★ ★ ★ ★ ★ ★ ★ ★ ★ ★ ★ ★ ★ ★ ★ ★ ★ ★ ★ ★ ★ ★

Nationality: British          Year: 1978 (U.S. release: 1981)
Cast: Glenda Jackson, Mona Washbourne, Alec McCowen, Trevor Howard
Director: Robert Enders       Running Time: 102 minutes
B/W or Color: Color           Availability: EMBASSY HOME ENTERTAINMENT

Stevie, starring Glenda Jackson, is an affecting portrait of the life of the English poet Stevie Smith. Jackson's engrossing performance contrasts Stevie's daily existence in the London suburb of Palmer's Green with her struggle against the inevitability of death. "Life is like a railway station," says Stevie, and she carries the audience on an engaging journey through her personal world. Intimacy with the audience is further achieved by having her periodically speak directly into the camera.

The action is centered in Stevie's sitting room, convincingly re-created in detail in the studio. Adapted from a stage play, the story focuses primarily on the day-to-day private life and the affectionate relationship that develops between Stevie and her very English aunt, played to perfection by Mona Washbourne. Director Robert Enders, creates a visually stunning film. He breaks up scenes of introspective dialogue and poetry recitations with cross-cutting to the narrator (played by Trevor Howard) and flashbacks to Stevie's childhood. The camera fluidly pans and tracks through the sitting room, kitchen, and bedrooms, underscoring Stevie's orderly external world.

This restrained approach creates the opportunity for establishing Stevie's introspective angst. Confrontation with her aunt's death and her own mortality are sad and poignant moments. As Stevie grows old, the camera lingers on Glenda Jackson's eyes, glowing like dying embers. The scene cuts to a train entering a dark tunnel, never again to emerge into the light.

Glenda Jackson was voted 1981's Best Actress by the New York Film Critics. The National Board not only seconded that honor but also named Mona Washbourne Best Supporting Actress and listed Stevie among the year's ten best.

# The Story of Adele H.
## (L'Histoire d'Adele H.)

\*\*\*\*\*\*\*\*\*\*\*\*\*\*\*\*\*\*\*\*\*\*\*\*\*\*\*\*\*\*\*\*\*\*\*\*\*\*\*\*\*\*\*\*\*\*\*\*\*\*\*\*\*\*

Nationality: French            Year: 1975

Cast: Isabelle Adjani, Bruce Robinson, Sylvia Marriott, Reubin Dorey, Joseph Blatchley

Director: François Truffaut      Running Time: 97 minutes

B/W or Color: Color          Availability: WARNER HOME VIDEO

This story, based on the life of Victor Hugo's daughter Adele, breathes with François Truffaut's simple inspiration and humane engagement with his subject. We join Adele (Isabelle Adjani) in 1862, traveling to Nova Scotia in search of a serviceman named Albert (Bruce Robinson), a feckless French officer who has loved and left her. As they meet, and she desperately tries to claim his devotion, it becomes clear they're talking past each other—she, of his casual marriage proposals; he, of how her famous father has made an issue of their class differences. She resorts to humiliating begging, bribery, and social pressure; she offers him an "open" marriage, and even falsifies a wedding announcement to a French newspaper.

Of Adjani's performance, even high praise is insufficient; her stunning achievement is to display at once the purity of innocent adolescent angst and the lonely desolation of the possessed.

Adele's love is, in fact, spoiled and selfish. What Adele seeks is a triumph of her will, so, when scorned by the object of her desire, she recedes deep within, to find only hubris. One senses she enjoys the honor of the self-imposed exile to Halifax that parallels her father's in Guernsey. Yet the film does not judge her: it is not lost on Truffaut how many characteristics of normal, loving relations bear the mark of sadness. In the end, Adele's "love" reduces her to cinema's most beautiful bag lady—and us to a richer, humbler understanding.

Although Isabelle Adjani was only Oscar-nominated for her performance, the film won her Best Actress awards from the New York Film Critics and The National Board of Review, which also named this the year's Best Foreign Language Picture.

(The videocassette is subtitled but loses the subtlety of Nestor Almendros's great wide-screen photography.)

# Stray Dog
## (Nora Inu)

\*\*\*\*\*\*\*\*\*\*\*\*\*\*\*\*\*\*\*\*\*\*\*\*\*\*\*\*\*\*\*\*\*\*\*\*\*\*\*\*\*\*\*\*\*\*\*\*\*\*\*\*\*\*\*

**Nationality**: Japanese        **Year**: 1949 (U.S. release: 1964)
**Cast**: Toshiro Mifune, Takashi Shimura, Ko Kimura, Keiko Awaji
**Director**: Akira Kurosawa     **Running Time**: 122 minutes
**B/W or Color**: B/W           **Availability**: TV only

In Japan, the detective-crime thriller developed much later than the samurai picture. In fact, when it was released in 1949, Akira Kurosawa's *Stray Dog* was among the first films in its genre. Because of its uncommon depth and seriousness, many still feel that it has been topped only by Kurosawa's 1963 *High and Low*, as Japan's best detective picture.

Amidst the sizzling midsummer heat of postwar Japan, Murakami, a young detective, has his pistol stolen while riding a crowded bus. At that time Tokyo faced severe shortages of everything. Fearful of losing his job, as well as his identity, the rookie cop begins an obsessive search through the "hell" sections of Tokyo. His angst mounts when the pistol is used to kill. Personally taking the blame for all the criminal's acts, Murakami must be reminded, "Stopping his next crime is important. Once does not make a habit, but twice . . . a stray dog becomes a mad dog." By the end, the "stray dog" tag applies to both detective and criminal, as the psychological differences between them virtually disappear, and they struggle indistinguishably in the mud.

Georges Simenon had long been a favorite of Akira Kurosawa, who sought to make the cinematic equivalent of one of Simenon's novels. Although *Stray Dog* has received much praise, plus a Japanese cultural award, Kurosawa does not feel it fulfills his own personal expectations and is cool about discussing it.

Nonetheless, as with *Drunken Angel,* which Kurosawa had made the previous year, he perfectly reflects the problems and tensions of the demoralized Japanese society. Although it is a society in ruins, the humanitarian Kurosawa occasionally offers images of hope and love, little glimmers of optimism in the midst of this despair.

The neglected *Stray Dog* was made in 1949, the same year as *The Third Man* and *The Bicycle Thief,* films that invite many comparisons.

# Sunday, Bloody Sunday

★★★★★★★★★★★★★★★★★★★★★★★★★★★★★★★★★★★★★★★★★★★★★★★★★★★★

Nationality: British                    Year: 1971
Cast: Glenda Jackson, Peter Finch, Murray Head, Peggy Ashcroft, Tony
Britton, Bessie Love
Director: John Schlesinger            Running Time: 110 minutes
B/W or Color: Color                   Availability: KEY VIDEO

John Schlesinger's most intellectual and least sentimental film is a comedy of manners, sexual manners, and very definitely those of the post-
Sixties social revolution. The action centers on what appears, at first, to
be a most unconventional love triangle, but as we learn more about the
protagonists the triangle loses some of its oddness. The film ultimately
establishes some universal truths about love and sex in our part of this
century.

Schlesinger takes two parallel love stories with the same love object.
Daniel Hirsh (Finch) is a successful middle-aged doctor with strong roots
in his upper-middle-class Jewish background. Alex Greville (Jackson) is
a keen, witty career woman in her thirties who has survived a bad marriage. They are both urbane, intelligent, and considerate, and they are
both in love with the same younger man. Bob Elkins (Head) is an artist
still in his twenties who fashions kinetic sculpture of modest merit and
indisputable trendiness. He is narcissistic, unfocused, and selfish, but good
looking and charming enough to make his hold on his two lovers believable. When Bob decides on a career move that will take him to other
shores, his lovers confront the reality of their situation and meet their
desperation and anguish with greater insight than most romantic personalities are ever permitted on screen.

No little credit is due the matchless screenplay by Penelope Gilliatt.
The dialogue is alternately frenzied, rueful, and introspective, but always
hinting at a good deal more beneath the surface of what is actually spoken. The bisexual theme neatly embodies the tone of the new morality
and handily allows us to dismiss the youth's feelings as insignificant compared to the depth of his lovers' emotions. All in all, as mature a love
story as the screen has ever offered.

# A Sunday in the Country
## (Un Dimanche à la Campagne)

★★★★★★★★★★★★★★★★★★★★★★★★★★★★★★★★★★★★★★★★★★★★★★★★★★★★★

*Nationality*: French          *Year*: 1984
*Cast*: Louis Ducreux, Sabine Azema, Michel Aumont
*Director*: Bertrand Tavernier     *Running Time*: 94 minutes
*B/W or Color*: Color          *Availability*: TV only

Monsieur Ladmiral, played nearly flawlessly, in his first major film role, by 73-year-old writer-actor-theater-and-opera impresario Louis Ducreux, is an academic painter who has played it safe and won election to the *Legion d'Honneur,* thus assuring his position and his income. But in refusing to take chances, to risk his talent in original ventures, he has allowed the founding movements of modern art—impressionism and postimpressionism—and life itself to pass him by.

Ladmiral's children represent the two tendencies of his own nature and the opposing responses to life that have warred within him. His stolid son Gonzague, appropriately played by Michel Aumont, has, like his father, opted to play it safe. His father treats him with a formality and a tolerance that verge on contempt, his own self-loathing projected on his son.

It is on his strong-willed, independent daughter Irene, radiantly played by Sabine Azema, that Ladmiral lavishes his love and concern, even as he realizes that he is losing her to the unknown lover in Paris. He confides to her his fears and regrets, his sadness at never having dared, at having lived *une vie manquée.* As they talk, we sense that Ladmiral wants Irene to ask much of life, as he has not. What this sensitive, poignant, and deeply perceptive film shows us is that we can never ask too much of life, but can easily ask too little of ourselves.

*A Sunday in the Country,* like a finely crafted poem, a complex novel, or a great painting, is a work of insight and compassion, deeply felt and brilliantly realized, to be savored and enjoyed again and again.

The National Board named it the year's best foreign film.

# Sundays and Cybele

## (Les Dimanches de Ville d'Avray)

★ ★ ★ ★ ★ ★ ★ ★ ★ ★ ★ ★ ★ ★ ★ ★ ★ ★ ★ ★ ★ ★ ★ ★ ★ ★ ★ ★ ★ ★ ★ ★ ★ ★ ★ ★ ★ ★ ★ ★ ★ ★ ★ ★ ★ ★ ★ ★ ★

Nationality: French          Year: 1962
Cast: Hardy Kruger, Nicole Courcel, Patricia Gozzi, Daniel Ivernel
Director: Serge Bourguignon     Running Time: 110 minutes
B/W or Color: B/W          Availability: Public Domain

The poignant story of the relationship between an amnesia victim and a French schoolgirl, *Sundays and Cybele* won an Oscar as 1962's best foreign-language film—a citation echoed by The National Board of Review.

In an unusual booking, the film premiered in New York before opening in Paris, and Bosley Crowther commented in his *New York Times* review: "Heaven only knows for what rare virtue New York has been rewarded with the first public exhibition of a French masterpiece. But so it has." He continued, ". . . this work of beauty . . . is almost by way of being a cinematic miracle. It is the first feature-length production of a young writer-director, Serge Bourguignon."

Based on a novel by Bernard Eschasseriaux, the screenplay was co-authored by Bourguignon and Antoine Tudal. In the outskirts of Paris, a former pilot (Hardy Kruger), who has lost his memory in a crash, sees a 12-year-old girl (Patricia Gozzi) being left at a boarding school by her father, who later returns with a note. The pilot reads the note, which says that the father cannot visit, as promised, on Sundays. Planning to give the note to the girl, the pilot is mistaken for her father. The child, realizing that she has been abandoned, forms an attachment to the man. Instead of her real name, Françoise, he calls her Cybele, and they spend Sundays together, strolling by an adjacent lake.

A nurse (Nicole Courcel), who lives with the pilot, sees him with the child and fears for the girl's safety, which leads to tragic results.

Bosley Crowther further observed that ". . . it is what *Lolita* might conceivably have been had it been molded by a poet and angled to be a rhapsodic song of innocence and not a smirking joke," and continued his praise: "Patricia Gozzi is sheer magic" and "the performances the director has evoked from his small but brilliant cast establish visions in the memory that one can surely never forget."

Lamentably, Bourguignon never fulfilled his early promise. His fourth (and last, to date) feature, 1969's *The Picasso Summer,* was never released.

# Swann in Love
## (Un Amour de Swann)

★★★★★★★★★★★★★★★★★★★★★★★★★★★★★★★★★★★★★★★★★★★★★★★★★★

Nationality: French-West German   Year: 1984
Cast: Jeremy Irons, Ornella Muti, Alain Delon, Fanny Ardant, Marie-Christine Barrault
Director: Volker Schlöndorff      Running Time: 110 minutes
B/W or Color: Color               Availability: MEDIA HOME EN-
                                  TERTAINMENT (Cinemateque
                                  Collection)

Marcel Proust's monumental, semiautobiographical, seven-volume novel *A la Recherche du Temps Perdu* (*Remembrance of Things Past*) has eluded all efforts to capture its sprawling complexities on the screen. However, the Eighties spawned this lavish film based on its first volume only, published in 1918 as *Du Côté de Chez Swann*. Luchino Visconti once harbored ideas of filming the *Sodome et Gomorrhe* volume, and Harold Pinter published a praiseworthy adaptation, condensing the novel into a screenplay that Joseph Losey once hoped to direct.

*Swann in Love* is a gem of visual style and taste. Its art direction and costume design are impeccable, and Sven Nykvist's cinematography is breathtaking. Reviewing *Swann in Love, Films in Review* stated: "As the opening scenes unfold, the viewer soon realizes he is in the presence of cinematic genius, for each frame forms an indelible image, and reluctantly one is forced to turn from concentration on sets and colors to the actors during this 24 hour period in one man's life."

The day in the life of Charles Swann (played by a French-dubbed Jeremy Irons) centers on this handsome, dandified man-about-19th-century-Paris and his passionate, obsessive pursuit of the fickle but beautiful demimondaine Odette de Crécy (Ornella Muti). Crossing his path during the course of that day are an assortment of persons of style, wit, and class snobbery, among them the homosexual dandy Baron de Charlus (Alain Delon in a surprisingly effective about-face performance) and the cuttingly cruel Duchesse de Guermantes (Fanny Ardant). The hero of *Swann in Love*, however, is cinematographer Sven Nykvist (*Fanny and Alexander*), who provides the overwhelmingly beautiful physical makeup of the film.

(*Media offers the film both in subtitled French and in an excellent English-dubbed videocassette.*)

# Swept Away . . . By an Unusual Destiny in the Blue Sea of August
## (Travolti da un Insolito Destino nell'Azzurro Mare D'Agosto)

\*\*\*\*\*\*\*\*\*\*\*\*\*\*\*\*\*\*\*\*\*\*\*\*\*\*\*\*\*\*\*\*\*\*\*\*\*\*\*\*\*\*\*\*\*\*\*\*\*\*\*\*\*

Nationality: Italian      Year: 1975

Cast: Giancarlo Giannini, Mariangela Melato, Riccardo Salvino

Director: Lina Wertmuller      Running Time: 120 minutes

B/W or Color: Color      Availability: RCA/COLUMBIA PICTURES HOME VIDEO

After viewing Lina Wertmuller's *Swept Away . . . By an Unusual Destiny in the Blue Sea of August,* many will be struck by the Fellini-esque direction of Lina Wertmuller. But after some thought and possibly another look at the film, the performances by Giancarlo Giannini and Mariangela Melato emerge as the film's highlights.

*Swept Away . . .* is the story of Raffaella Lanzetti, a rich woman who is repaid for her extravagance and disregard for injustice by being shipwrecked on a tropical island with her socialist, blindly vengeful, and sadistic cabin boy, Gennarino Carunchio. But in a sudden plot twist, the characters find that switching roles (she becomes the servant, he the master) is easier than one would think, and it is done more than once to make the point. This is another of Wertmuller's social-commentary comedies, like *Seven Beauties,* where she combines politics, sociology, and sex to hold a mirror up to the world's seriousness in the midst of absurdity, and vice-versa.

It is the performances that make this modern fairy tale believable. Giannini's face is a mirror of his character's overactive mind. His eyes light with fire at the slightest hint of political argument, and while his face screws up tensely when trying to restrain himself from his propensity for violence, he becomes seething, romantic, frustrated, and pathologically vengeful all at once.

If it is Giannini's eyes that are his stand-out feature, then it is Melato's mouth that makes her biggest statement. She pouts and sneers her way through her Mediterranean odyssey, as the wealthy and spoiled Raffaella. The actress creates a woman you love to hate, but adds just enough frailty to her characterization that you want to see her only punished, not killed.

The National Board named *Swept Away . . .* among 1975's five best foreign films.

(*The tape is English-dubbed by actors with authentic-sounding Italian accents.*)

# Symphonie Pastorale
## (La Symphonie Pastorale)

*****************************************************

Nationality: French                    Year: 1946 (U.S. release: 1948)
Cast: Michèle Morgan, Pierre Blanchar, Liné Noro, Jean Desailly, Andrée Clement
Director: Jean Delannoy              Running Time: 105 minutes
B/W or Color: B/W                      Availability: TV only

When *Symphonie Pastorale* was originally released in 1946, it took Europe by storm. It was selected with six other entries as a Best Film at the first Cannes Film Festival, where it won Michèle Morgan a Best Actress award, and it won a radio poll in France as the most popular film. Almost every serious film historian knows this film, which critic Pauline Kael calls "emotionally overwhelming," but it is infrequently shown today.

The film is beautifully photographed by Armand Thirard, who expertly utilized the Swiss locations at Chateaux d'Oex and Rossiniere. Interiors were shot in Paris. Pierre Blanchar gives a wonderful performance as the tormented minister who watches the blind girl he adores falling in love with his own son (Jean Desailly), while his long-suffering wife (well played by Liné Noro) tries to suppress her jealousy. But his obsession ultimately destroys his wife and family, and when the girl finally gains her sight and realizes the trouble she has caused, she runs away into the snow. Finding her missing the next day, the pastor searches for the girl, only to find her body being dragged from a stream. He takes her in his arms.

For this role, Michèle Morgan was lured back to her native France from a none-too-successful hiatus in Hollywood, and this movie fully restored her previous stardom. With those beautiful cheekbones and luminous, big eyes, she projects a quiet intensity and a beauty that's as spiritual as it is physical. In addition to her recognition at Cannes she received a Victoire as the year's most popular French actress.

Director Jean Delannoy (*The Eternal Return*) collaborated with Jean Aurenche in adapting André Gide's 1919 novella *La Symphonie Pastorale*. That Gide approved was evident at the Paris premiere, when he inscribed the director's copy of the book: "To Jean Delannoy, for whom this little volume has served as a pretext to create a beautiful film."

# The Tall Blond Man with One Black Shoe

## (Le Grand Blond avec une Chaussure Noire)

************************************************************

*Nationality*: French  
*Cast*: Pierre Richard, Mireille Darc, Bernard Blier, Jean Rochefort  
*Director*: Yves Robert  
*B/W or Color*: Color  

*Year*: 1972 (U.S. release: 1973)  
*Running Time*: 90 minutes  
*Availability*: RCA/COLUMBIA PICTURES HOME VIDEO  

Actor Pierre Richard is a disciple of, as well as an inspiration to, American comedians. Danny Kaye is his particular idol, but there are also traces of Buster Keaton in his work. Richard's films have been remade here, but they always lose in the translation. His *Le Jouet* (1976) became *The Toy* (1982) with Richard Pryor and Jackie Gleason, while the best-known Richard comedy was redone as *The Man with One Red Shoe* (1985), starring Tom Hanks. Actor Yves Robert, who directed *The Tall Blond Man with One Black Shoe* and fashioned its screenplay with Francis Veber, can be seen in this film as the distracted orchestra conductor.

In the title role, Richard is a bumbling concert violinist who becomes a patsy for espionage agents when he's spotted at Orly Airport wearing one black and one tan shoe. Unwittingly, he's drawn into a plot by secret-service agent Jean Rochefort, who's out to obtain evidence against his ambitious deputy, Bernard Blier. Richard blithely falls into every trap that's set for him—to his audience's hilarity. When blond agent Mireille Darc makes love to Richard, he is blissfully unaware she's performing in the line of duty. A real romance blossoms. The movie's amusing ending left the door open for its very funny sequel, *The Return of the Tall Blond Man with One Black Shoe*.

Although the film was given a PG rating for its American release, both Richard and Darc display a bit of back nudity. Tall, blond, and funny, Richard steals his every scene with energetic slapstick. And even his lovemaking is accomplished comically—the lucky amalgam of a facile face, awkward charm, and just a touch of comic genius.

*The Tall Blond Man with One Black Shoe* was a major prizewinner at 1973's Berlin Film Festival, and The National Board named it one of the year's best foreign-language films.

(*The videocassette is dubbed in English.*)

442

# A Taste of Honey

**Nationality**: British        **Year**: 1961 (U.S. release: 1962)
**Cast**: Dora Bryan, Rita Tushingham, Robert Stephens, Murray Melvin
**Director**: Tony Richardson      **Running Time**: 100 minutes
**B/W or Color**: B/W        **Availability**: EVI ELECTRIC VIDEO, INC.

On stage, Shelagh Delaney's play told its funny-sad story of social outcasts with uncompromising honesty and a sketchiness that, despite touching moments, left something to be desired. The tale works better as a film, on which producer-director Tony Richardson collaborated with Delaney. The result is a fluid, almost poetic screenplay, cast without compromise and shot on authentic locations.

In England's industrial north, fatherless, teenaged Jo (Rita Tushingham) lives with her flighty mother Helen (Dora Bryan) in a series of cheap furnished rooms. While Helen enjoys life with her latest lover Peter (Robert Stephens), lonely Jo spends the night with a black sailor named Jimmy (Paul Danquah). After he sails, she returns home to discover that Helen has impulsively married Peter. Jo finds a flat of her own and work in a shoe store, where she meets Geoffrey (Murray Melvin), an equally lonely homosexual, with whom she offers to share her quarters.

Pregnant by Jimmy, Jo's cared for by the resourceful Geoffrey, who even offers to marry her before their happy little world is disrupted by the bossy Helen. Abandoned by Peter, she kicks Geoffrey out, ready to resume motherly duties, in anticipation of her grandchild.

Tony Richardson's hiring of the unknown Rita Tushingham was inspired. As the promiscuous, self-absorbed Helen, comedienne Dora Bryan provides a zestful caricature, as vulgar as she is superficial. Robert Stephens matches her with an oafish flashiness as Peter. Murray Melvin's shy and amusingly resourceful Geoffrey leaves us with a deep sense of loss when Helen ultimately cuts him out of Jo's life.

A Taste of Honey won Cannes Festival awards for Tushingham and Melvin and British Academy Awards for Best Picture, Best Actress (Bryan), Best Screenplay, and Most Promising New Star (Tushingham). The National Board of Review named it one of 1962's ten best films.

# Tess

**★ ★ ★ ★ ★ ★ ★ ★ ★ ★ ★ ★ ★ ★ ★ ★ ★ ★ ★ ★ ★ ★ ★ ★ ★ ★ ★ ★ ★ ★ ★ ★ ★ ★ ★ ★ ★ ★ ★ ★ ★ ★ ★ ★ ★ ★ ★ ★ ★ ★**

*Nationality*: French-British          *Year*: 1979 (U.S. release: 1980)
*Cast*: Nastassia Kinski, Peter Firth, Leigh Lawson, John Collin
*Director*: Roman Polanski          *Running Time*: 170 minutes
*B/W or Color*: Color          *Availability*: RCA/COLUMBIA PIC-
                               TURES HOME VIDEO

Tess was Roman Polanski's first film after he fled the United States when he was accused of statutory rape. Critics and audiences were not sure what to expect, especially since the star of *Tess* was a 17-year-old beauty named Nastassia Kinski, with whom Polanski had been involved. When the opening credits were over and the title "to Sharon" came on the screen, people gasped. Sharon was, of course, Polanski's late wife Sharon Tate, slain by the Manson "family" in 1969.

What followed was the story of a poor, naive girl whose family discovers they have rich relatives and send young Tess off to live at the home of their wealthy cousin Alec. The cousin seduces Tess and she runs away, giving birth to a child who dies in infancy. Shamed and humiliated, Tess goes to work on a farm where she meets Angel, the Parson's kind, young son. They fall in love, and on their wedding night Tess confesses her previous affair only to have her husband suddenly turn cold and distant. She returns to her cousin, who agrees to marry her and provide for her family. Meanwhile, Angel has a change of heart and goes off in search of Tess. He eventually finds her, but she tells him to leave and never return, but later, realizing her cousin's cruel nature, kills him and meets Angel at the train. They run away together, but are caught by the police amid the pillars of Stonehenge.

Some have charged Polanski with softening Thomas Hardy's *Tess of the D'Urbervilles*, of making it a modern feminist tract. But as a film unto itself, its emotional power is undeniable. Physically, the picture is intoxicating in its lushness. Oscars were awarded for Best Cinematography, Costumes, and Art Direction. Though filmed in France, the English countryside is re-created with stunning results. Kinski gives a fine, subdued performance, and Leigh Lawson as her predatory cousin Alec and Peter Firth as Angel are superb. The whole film seems real, alive, and lived-in, re-creating another time and place with absolute fidelity and realism.

The National Board named *Tess* one of 1980's ten best.

# That Man from Rio

## (L'Homme de Rio)

*★★★★★★★★★★★★★★★★★★★★★★★★★★★★★★★★★★★★★★★★★★★★★★★★★★★★★★★*

Nationality: French               Year: 1964
Cast: Jean-Paul Belmondo, Françoise Dorléac, Jean Servais
Director: Philippe de Broca       Running Time: 114 minutes
B/W or Color: Color               Availability: TV only

Philippe de Broca's reputation was based on bittersweet love stories (*Five Day Lover*) and his discovery of film music composer Georges Delerue (*Day of the Dolphin, Anne of the Thousand Days*).

In 1964, De Broca directed a haunting swashbuckler with Jean-Paul Belmondo called *Cartouche*. The director was the first to admit that its initial hour was too farcical, but by the end, it had moved into the realm of true pathos.

His next attempt to combine adventure, comedy, and romance was a monumental success. *That Man from Rio* owed a great deal to Hitchcock's *North by Northwest* in its headlong pace and blending of genres, but where it departed from the master was in its purely European flavor and characterization. Whereas Cary Grant, James Stewart, and Hitch's other romantic protagonists were always treated with grace and "class," Belmondo is a common man, unmannered and doggedly, even rudely, determined to rescue his girlfriend. His attempt is suicidally impetuous, entirely in the hands of fate. The camera is looser than it would have been in Hollywood (De Broca says he comes to the set in the morning and decides where to put it; Hitchcock's storyboarded feel is totally absent).

Françoise Dorléac (whose comedically adroit career ended tragically in an automobile accident shortly after this film was made) is Belmondo's girlfriend, kidnapped by Jean Servais (*Rififi*) for reasons involving a priceless museum artifact. From Paris to Brazil, atop skeletal buildings, on motorcycles, in experimentally edited fight scenes, the pace never slackens. And yet somehow there are those moments of pathos that the director has staked out as part of his cinematic signature.

Belmondo and De Broca attempted to recapture the breakneck energy and mingling of genres a few more times, but, alas, it never quite worked again. However, both had many other successes, and De Broca's *King of Hearts* is a treasure worthy of any video collection.

# That Obscure Object of Desire
## (Cet Obscur Objet du Désir)

★ ★ ★ ★ ★ ★ ★ ★ ★ ★ ★ ★ ★ ★ ★ ★ ★ ★ ★ ★ ★ ★ ★ ★ ★ ★ ★ ★ ★ ★ ★ ★ ★ ★ ★ ★ ★ ★ ★ ★ ★ ★ ★ ★ ★ ★ ★ ★ ★

**Nationality**: French-Spanish    **Year**: 1977
**Cast**: Fernando Rey, Carole Bouquet, Angela Molina, Julien Berthe
**Director**: Luis Buñuel    **Running Time**: 100 minutes
**B/W or Color**: Color    **Availability**: EMBASSY HOME ENTERTAINMENT

This fourth version of Pierre Louÿs's *The Woman and the Puppet* is both the best and the definitive (if not the most faithful) adapation of that saga of a man-destroying woman. Despite the age of the basic material, Luis Buñuel has turned it into a thoroughly contemporary "now" film and by doing so has performed a major service to mankind. When historians, two hundred years hence, look at films that are "mirrors" of the Seventies, here is one done with sophistication, wit, grace, and a total lack of ugliness. Even when it shocks, it does so with impeccable taste. Moreover, though directed by a man who was then approaching 80, it is incredibly young at heart—as sprightly as though made by René Clair in his twenties.

Buñuel's main departure from convention this time is in using two women—Carole Bouquet and Angela Molina—to present different faces and facets of the one woman who drives the hero to despair and distraction.

It's an extraordinarily handsome film, beautifully photographed and excellently acted by Fernando Rey as the harassed male, a role that he has by this time made very much of a specialty without turning it into a stereotype. *That Obscure Object of Desire* is Buñuel's last film. It would be well-nigh impossible to come up with another that could cap a distinguished career in such a graceful, successful, and wholly enjoyable manner.

*(Embassy offers the film both dubbed and subtitled.)*

# Theatre of Blood

\* \* \* \* \* \* \* \* \* \* \* \* \* \* \* \* \* \* \* \* \* \* \* \* \* \* \* \* \* \* \* \* \* \* \* \* \* \* \* \* \* \* \* \* \* \* \* \* \* \* \* \* \* \* \* \*

Nationality: British             Year: 1973

Cast: Vincent Price, Diana Rigg, Jack Hawkins, Robert Morley, Dennis Price, Diana Dors

Director: Douglas Hickox          Running Time: 104 minutes

B/W or Color: Color               Availability: MGM/UA HOME VIDEO

C ritics beware! Vincent Price is having a field day disposing of them in this comedy-horror thriller. It's stylishly directed by Douglas Hickox and contains enough violence to have warranted an R rating originally or to satisfy any bloodlust. Other viewers who prefer to just relish the campy aspects of the plot may push the fast-forward button. Anthony Greville-Bell's screenplay was inspired by the plays of Shakespeare, particularly the manner in which the Bard disposed of certain characters, and by Price's own *Dr. Phibes* movies. A large cast of major British names participates in the doings, causing speculation that they allowed themselves to be disposed of so violently as a means of getting back at all the critics who displeased *them* (or whom *they* had displeased). Certainly many a thespian will silently applaud Price and company as they dispatch the next victim. To set the mood, the opening credits include scenes from Shakespearean works with such actors as Emil Jannings in *Othello* (1922).

Price plays a bad Shakespearean actor named Edward Lionheart who believes he should have won the Critics Circle Best Actor nod. Feigning death, he kills the Circle members in ways inspired by Shakespeare: Michael Hordern as in *Julius Caesar*, Harry Andrews as in *The Merchant of Venice*, Robert Coote a la *Richard III*. Aiding the insane actor are daughter Diana Rigg, sometimes disguised as a boy, and a horde of tramps. Inspector Milo O'Shea and Sergeant Eric Sykes finally run Price to earth, when only critic Ian Hendry is left.

There may be some wish-fulfillment in seeing Jack Hawkins strangle his on-screen wife Diana Dors or in Price electrocuting real-life wife Coral Browne under a hairdryer. Animal lovers, however, may be distressed when Robert Morley chokes to death upon discovering that he's eaten his beloved poodles. Of course, many of the goriest films have a satiric edge to the violence, and this film makes its humor appetizing with intelligent wit. In short, it's a bloody good show!

# The Thief of Bagdad

★ ★ ★ ★ ★ ★ ★ ★ ★ ★ ★ ★ ★ ★ ★ ★ ★ ★ ★ ★ ★ ★ ★ ★ ★ ★ ★ ★ ★ ★ ★ ★ ★ ★ ★ ★ ★ ★ ★ ★ ★ ★ ★ ★ ★ ★ ★ ★ ★ ★ ★ ★ ★ ★

*Nationality*: British        *Year*: 1940

*Cast*: Sabu, Conrad Veidt, John Justin, June Duprez, Miles Malleson, Mary Morris

*Directors*: Michael Powell, Ludwig   *Running Time*: 106 minutes
Berger, Tim Whelan (Uncredited:
Zoltan Korda, Alexander Korda,
William Cameron Menzies)

*B/W or Color*: Color        *Availability*: EMBASSY HOME
                                 ENTERTAINMENT

Was there ever a fantasy more delightful than this? A triumph of special effects, adventure, music, and just plain good humor, this is the work of many hands. Alexander Korda's film empire produced it in sumptuous Technicolor, and there are at least six directors—three uncredited—including the great Michael Powell, American silent-comedy maker Tim Whelan, and Korda himself. The result of all this activity was that the film won four American Oscars, for Art Direction, Cinematography, Photographic Effects, and Sound Effects. It's far better than the opulent but dull Douglas Fairbanks silent (United States, 1924) or the Steve Reeves swashbuckler (Italy, 1961). Its international cast is headed by Conrad Veidt of Germany and the Indian elephant boy himself, Sabu.

In ancient Bagdad, John Justin is the kind but unhappy king who takes bad advice form his wicked vizier, Conrad Veidt. Imprisoned and marked for death, Justin escapes with the aid of a little thief, Sabu. They sail to Basra, and there Justin falls in love with June Duprez, beautiful daughter of silly Sultan Miles Malleson. To further his ends, Veidt uses his magical powers to strike Justin blind and to turn Sabu into a dog. The thief manages to be turned back into his former self, then to steal the All-Seeing Eye with the help of a huge genie, Rex Ingram. All ends happily, of course.

Malleson collaborated with Lajos Biro on the screenplay, and Miklos Rozsa wrote the songs and score. Shooting began at London's Denham Studios, but World War II prevented actual filming, and production moved to Hollywood, with location shooting in the Painted Desert and Grand Canyon. Whether you see this for the first time or the twentieth, it's a film full of delights.

# Things to Come
## (The Shape of Things to Come)

★ ★ ★ ★ ★ ★ ★ ★ ★ ★ ★ ★ ★ ★ ★ ★ ★ ★ ★ ★ ★ ★ ★ ★ ★ ★ ★ ★ ★ ★ ★ ★ ★ ★ ★ ★ ★ ★ ★ ★ ★ ★ ★ ★ ★ ★ ★ ★ ★ ★ ★ ★ ★

Nationality: British

Year: 1936

Cast: Raymond Massey, Edward Chapman, Ralph Richardson, Margaretta Scott, Cedric Hardwicke

Director: William Cameron Menzies

Running Time: 92 minutes (113 minutes in Britain)

B/W or Color: B/W

Availability: NOSTALGIA MERCHANT

Britain's first million-dollar movie, *Things to Come* cost about £300,000 and was in production at three major studios (Elstree, Isleworth, and Denham) for a full year. This visionary tale was based on H. G. Wells's *The Shape of Things to Come*, with Wells himself writing the screenplay. On its release critics were divided about the film's merits, but *Things to Come* has now taken on classic status. The world of tomorrow is bleak and unemotional, and there are elements of fascism, which was a popular concern in the mid-Thirties. And there are premonitions of George Orwell's *1984*, which wasn't written until 1949.

A world conflict begins on Christmas Eve 1939. Everytown (actually, it's London) is destroyed in a 30-year war, which brings plague as well as destruction. Circa 1970, scientists unite as "Wings Over the World" and develop a Utopian society. By 2036, technology is so advanced that only a few people are needed to maintain the state, mainly as button-pushers. Efficiency is paramount, while benevolent emotions are subjugated. However, one man (Cedric Hardwicke) leads a group of radicals who protest progress and makes plans to send a couple into orbit around the moon.

Director William Cameron Menzies, best known as an Oscar-winning American production designer *(Gone With the Wind)*, helped art director Vincent Korda create *Things to Come*'s fantastic sets. Despite the effectiveness of this film, a 1979 Canadian remake, *The Shape of Things to Come*, was undertaken on a low budget. The results were clumsy and uninspired.

A decade earlier, Fritz Lang's German classic *Metropolis* had entertained filmgoers with its futuristic images. *Things to Come* takes its place in cinema history as Britain's Thirties science-fiction counterpart. Fifty years later, its classic reputation rests on the amalgamated artistry of its art direction and imaginative physical production.

# The Third Man

**Nationality**: British          **Year**: 1949 (U.S. release: 1950)

**Cast**: Joseph Cotten, (Alida) Valli, Orson Welles, Trevor Howard, Bernard Lee

**Director**: Carol Reed          **Running Time**: 104 minutes

**B/W or Color**: B/W          **Availability**: THE CRITERION COLLECTION

There is little doubt of the importance theme music has played in the popularity of certain motion pictures, and in the case of *The Third Man*, Anton Karas's seemingly incongruous zither score provided an inspired counterpoint to Graham Greene's intriguing suspense tale of postwar Vienna. But *The Third Man* is much more than a recurring theme on an offbeat musical instrument. Greene's original screenplay offers an entertaining and deceptively simple thriller in an intriguing setting. Of this material, producer-director Carol Reed, in the best Alfred Hitchcock tradition, has wrought a complex masterpiece.

*The Third Man* begins with the arrival in war-ravaged Vienna of an American writer named Holly Martins (Joseph Cotten), who's shocked to learn that Harry Lime, the old friend he had come to visit, has died in an accident that looks like murder. In his search for the truth, the writer discovers that Lime (Orson Welles) is not only alive, but an insidious black marketeer and a murderer. After a chase through the city's ruins and sewers, Martins helps the police trap and kill Lime. In the memorable fadeout, Lime's mistress Anna (Alida Valli), whom Martins had clumsily courted during his investigation, stoically ignores him as she walks from the cemetery down an avenue of bare autumn trees and out of his life. Graham Greene had intended a Hollywood-type happy ending, but Reed staunchly resisted, and *The Third Man*'s impact is all the more powerful for it. Casting Orson Welles as Lime was Reed's idea (one of the producers had wanted Noel Coward!), and this is one of his best (and most restrained) performances.

*The Third Man* won the Grand Prix at the Cannes Film Festival as well as the British Film Academy Award for 1949's Best British Motion Picture. The National Board of Review named it one of 1950's best films.

(*The Criterion Collection offers a sparkling British print of the movie.*)

# The 39 Steps

★ ★ ★ ★ ★ ★ ★ ★ ★ ★ ★ ★ ★ ★ ★ ★ ★ ★ ★ ★ ★ ★ ★ ★ ★ ★ ★ ★ ★ ★ ★ ★ ★ ★ ★ ★ ★ ★ ★ ★ ★ ★ ★ ★ ★

*Nationality*: British          *Year*: 1935

*Cast*: Robert Donat, Madeleine Carroll, Lucie Mannheim, Godfrey Tearle, Peggy Ashcroft, John Laurie

*Director*: Alfred Hitchcock          *Running Time*: 87 minutes

*B/W or Color*: B/W          *Availability*: THE CRITERION COLLECTION

A classic for all time, this was perhaps Alfred Hitchcock's greatest British production. Its style has been copied, but never really surpassed, and the bickering relationship between hero and heroine—who happen to be manacled together—set the tone for many Hitchcocks to come. Acclaimed everywhere, the film was a particular success in the United States, where Hitchcock was the only British director familiar to the public. In his native England, Hitchcock was already being called the Master; some were going even farther and referring to the rotund one as a genius.

Canadian rancher Donat shelters Lucie Mannheim, who proves to be a spy, and finds himself running from police when she's murdered in his flat. Scottish farmer John Laurie wants to turn him in, but wife Peggy Ashcroft helps Donat escape. Respected country squire Godfrey Tearle proves to be the head of the spies, while Madeleine Carroll—a traveler to whom Donat is manacled—turns from antagonist to believer. The key to the 39 steps of a secret formula lies with Mr. Memory (Wylie Watson), a music hall performer.

John Buchan's famed 1915 novel was updated. The original point of the title was forgotten in the fast-paced movie, and half a line had to be added at the conclusion by way of explanation. Hitchcock found that audiences never really cared what the secret plans were, and termed this plot device a "McGuffin." *The 39 Steps* was remade in 1959 and 1978. Both are entertaining without being memorable. Hitch's vision is full of classic scenes, many of which are immediately identifiable with the film: Mannheim's stagger with a knife in her back, Tearle revealing his missing pinky (via trick photography). Above everything else, Hitchcock—whose cameo is as a passerby at a bus stop—is the film's real star.

*(Criterion's sparkling videocassette far surpasses all public domain editions of this movie.)*

# This Happy Breed

\* \* \* \* \* \* \* \* \* \* \* \* \* \* \* \* \* \* \* \* \* \* \* \* \* \* \* \* \* \* \* \* \* \* \* \* \* \* \* \* \* \* \* \* \* \* \* \* \* \* \* \* \* \*

Nationality: British       Year: 1944 (U.S. release: 1947)
Cast: Robert Newton, Celia Johnson, John Mills, Kay Walsh
Director: David Lean       Running Time: 111 minutes
B/W or Color: Color       Availability: TV only

Prior to this, his first solo directorial job, David Lean had officially "teamed" with Noel Coward on *In Which We Serve,* although it's generally conceded to be more of a Lean film than a Coward effort. And apparently the actor-playwright was impressed with Lean, for the budding director's next three films—*This Happy Breed, Blithe Spirit,* and *Brief Encounter*—all derive from Coward plays. *This Happy Breed* hasn't been much seen in recent years, but those who have discovered it (perhaps on public broadcasting stations) have been more than pleasantly surprised, for it's a rewarding and beautifully acted cinematic experience and hardly deserving of its relative obscurity. And, unlike most British films of its period, it's in color, which should make it more accessible to the TV programmers who think their audiences want only color—or colorized—motion pictures!

*This Happy Breed* was the initial film of a newly set-up production company called Cineguild, which was formed by David Lean, producer Anthony Havelock-Allan, and cameraman Ronald Neame. Its subject matter covers 20 years in the working-class lives of the Gibbons family, from 1919 to 1939, encompassing their years as residents of one of a number of matching row-houses in London's Clapham district. As the movie begins, the Gibbonses are just moving in, along with their three teenaged children, the wife's widowed mother, and the husband's unmarried sister. At the fadeout, after two decades of joys and sorrows, life and death, a diminished Gibbons family reluctantly depart the home of their prime years for a smaller flat.

*This Happy Breed*'s screenplay is wonderfully telling and truthful in its small observances. Never oversentimentalized, despite some of its moving plot situations, it's a credit to Lean and his brilliant cast (topped by the flawless Celia Johnson and a remarkably restrained Robert Newton) that nothing ever becomes maudlin. The National Board named Johnson Best Actress of 1947, the year this extraordinary film finally reached the United States.

# This Sporting Life

★★★★★★★★★★★★★★★★★★★★★★★★★★★★★★★★★★★★★★★★★★★★★★★★★★★★★★★

*Nationality*: British        *Year*: 1963
*Cast*: Richard Harris, Rachel Roberts, Alan Badel, William Hartnell, Colin Blakely
*Director*: Lindsay Anderson     *Running Time*: 134 minutes
*B/W or Color*: B/W          *Availability*: TV only

With this movie, Britain's once fashionable cinema of drab realism reached its apotheosis. Admittedly ugly and unpleasant in its setting and its brutalizing human relationships, *This Sporting Life* is nevertheless absorbing drama. And neither of the protagonists elicits much sympathy, although it's difficult to find fault with the brilliantly hard-edged acting of either Richard Harris or Rachel Roberts.

Harris portrays Frank Machin, a brutish coal miner in pursuit of athletic glory with a Midlands rugby team. In short order, he becomes their star player, impressing everyone except Mrs. Hammond (Roberts), the embittered widow with whom he boards. At first, she resists Machin's advances, thinking him a self-centered oaf with an unprepossessing ego. Later they begin an affair—a relationship that he publicly flaunts, as his fame increases. Vicious fights ensue between them, until finally he's forced to leave. When loneliness later drives him back, he finds her close to death from a brain hemorrhage.

With their plain, unglamorous faces, Richard Harris (in his first major role) and Rachel Roberts eloquently illuminate David Storey's adaptation of his novel, articulating the inarticulate in their characters. Harris was named Best Actor at the Cannes Film Festival, and Roberts won the British Film Academy's Best Actress award.

Director Lindsay Anderson refuses to take credit for his leading actor's performance: "The Frank Machin of the film is Richard Harris's creation—and a vital contribution to the whole personality of the picture." But Anderson's modesty cannot dismiss the credit surely due him for *This Sporting Life*'s shattering impact, the vigor of its pace (with its semidocumentary use of natural Yorkshire settings), and the gut-slugging power of its relentless rugby sequences. The National Board of Review cited *This Sporting Life* among the year's best English-language films.

# Three Brothers
## (Tre Fratelli)

★ ★ ★ ★ ★ ★ ★ ★ ★ ★ ★ ★ ★ ★ ★ ★ ★ ★ ★ ★ ★ ★ ★ ★ ★ ★ ★ ★ ★ ★ ★ ★ ★ ★ ★ ★ ★ ★ ★ ★ ★ ★ ★ ★ ★ ★ ★ ★ ★

*Nationality*: Italian-French          *Year*: 1981 (U.S. release: 1982)

*Cast*: Philippe Noiret, Michele Placido, Charles Vanel, Vittorio Mezzogiorno, Andrea Ferreol

*Director*: Francesco Rosi          *Running Time*: 113 minutes

*B/W or Color*: Color          *Availability*: EMBASSY HOME ENTERTAINMENT

Francesco Rosi's *Three Brothers* makes a statement of utmost simplicity: the problems of society are transient, but the love within the family is eternal.

Three brothers who have not seen one another for many years are brought together when they return to the family farm for their mother's funeral. Each brother clearly represents a stratum of current Italian society. The oldest is a judge preparing for the trial of a terrorist. He lives in constant fear for his own life and detests terrorism as a step toward chaos. The middle brother is an idealistic teacher of delinquent children. The third is somewhere between the two—a dissatisfied factory worker who does not condone terrorism but believes that struggle is necessary to bring about change. All three are set in obvious contrast to their father, who has spent his entire life on his farm. While their worlds are filled with anxiety, frustration, and uncertainty, his is one of natural order, a life "guided by the stars and animals."

The accumulation of images in *Three Brothers* creates something that is quite moving. Rosi has approached his subject with great sincerity and is helped by the eloquent presence of Charles Vanel as the father. His face and body, even in the smallest gestures, enlarge the film with moments of quiet grace. Whether he is staring at his now-untended stove, turning from the funeral cortege to receive the gift of an egg, or, most beautifully, in his poetic exchanges with his granddaughter, Vanel nobly proves Rosi's transcendent vision of the cyclical nature of life.

*Three Brothers* was an Academy Award nominee for Best Foreign Film. The National Board voted it one of 1982's five best foreign-language films.

*(The videocassette is subtitled.)*

# Three Men and a Cradle

## (Trois Hommes et Un Couffin)

★★★★★★★★★★★★★★★★★★★★★★★★★★★★★★★★★★★★★★★★★★★★★★★★★★★★★★

Nationality: French                    Year: 1985 (U.S. release: 1986)

Cast: Roland Giraud, Michel Boujenah, André Dussollier, Philippine Leroy Beaulieu

Director: Coline Serreau              Running Time: 100 minutes

B/W or Color: Color                    Availability: VESTRON VIDEO

An adorable French girl moves in with a trio of bachelors—a promising premise, n'est-ce pas?

Mademoiselle, however, is six months old, and the men know as much about diapers as they do about two o'clock feedings. Along with the formula comes a merry mix-up involving drugs, dealers, and police.

*Three Men and a Cradle* won Cesars (the French equivalent of the Oscars) for Best Film, Screenplay, and Supporting Actor. It was also nominated for a 1985 Academy Award as Best Foreign Film.

For filming, they used two babies (one six months old, the other a year) and both are delectable. The tot, of course, becomes the main attraction and changes the lives of and relationships between the three men and their women. The men, at first, make all the droll mistakes that the uninitiated fall heir to, but shortly would qualify for three of Dr. Spock's finest graduate students. Even the women learn a little.

To date, *Three Men and a Cradle* is the most financially successful film to play in France, and its writer-director, Coline Serreau, was signed by Disney to make the American version, *Three Men and a Baby*, starring Tom Selleck, Ted Danson, and Steve Guttenberg.

# The Three Musketeers
## (The Four Musketeers)

\* \* \* \* \* \* \* \* \* \* \* \* \* \* \* \* \* \* \* \* \* \* \* \* \* \* \* \* \* \* \* \* \* \* \* \* \* \* \* \* \* \* \* \* \* \* \* \* \* \* \* \*

**Nationality**: Panamanian      **Year**: 1973 (U.S. release: 1974)/ 1975

**Cast**: Oliver Reed, Raquel Welch, Richard Chamberlain, Michael York, Faye Dunaway

**Director**: Richard Lester      **Running Time**: 105 minutes/108 minutes

**B/W or Color**: Color      **Availability**: USA HOME VIDEO

One of The National Board's best films of 1974, *The Three Muske-eers* was made as one long movie but released as two (with *The Four Musketeers* following in 1975).

Containing a vitality and esprit lacking in most modern adventure films, *The Three Musketeers* is an extremely rich and funny version of the Alexandre Dumas tale, superbly directed by Richard Lester, who keeps the action moving throughout and injects social satire into an irreverent put-on. The contrast between the lives of the poor and the nobility is exploited through excellent editing by John Victor Smith, and the lushness of the decor gives cinematographer David Watkins a chance to create some scenes that contain the quality of a Rembrandt or Vermeer.

Young D'Artagnan (Michael York) provides the thread of continuity in Lester's updated version, which never denigrates the essentials that have made it a timeless best seller. The title characters are played by Oliver Reed (Athos), Richard Chamberlain (Aramis), and Frank Finlay (Porthos).

Involved in the swashbuckling comedy are the lovely Constance (an unusually good comedy performance by Raquel Welch), her elderly spouse (Spike Milligan), the enchanting but empty-headed Queen Anne (Geraldine Chaplin), Louis XIII (Jean-Pierre Cassel), Buckingham (Simon Ward), the villainous Rochefort (Christopher Lee), the evil beauty Milady (Faye Dunaway), and the treacherous Cardinal Richelieu (Charlton Heston, who added a limp as "an acronym of his ills").

Though the acting is pleasurable, this is a director's movie. Born in Philadelphia, Lester achieved his success in England. His work includes the Beatles' first two films, *A Hard Day's Night* and *Help!*, *Petulia*, and *Superman II* and *III*.

# Throne of Blood
## (Kumonosu-Jo)

★★★★★★★★★★★★★★★★★★★★★★★★★★★★★★★★★★★★★★★★★★★★★★★★★★★

*Nationality*: Japanese

*Year*: 1957 (U.S. release: 1961)

*Cast*: Toshiro Mifune, Isuzu Yamada, Minoru Chiaki, Takamaru Sasaki, Takashi Shimura, Chieko Naniwa

*Director*: Akira Kurosawa

*Running Time*: 110 minutes

*B/W or Color*: B/W

*Availability*: MEDIA HOME EN-TERTAINMENT (Cinématique Collection)

B eliefs in superstitions, ghosts, demons, and the supernatural differ considerably between Japan and the West, as both have created their own mythologies. In many regions of Japan, local folklore merges with the Shinto concept of ancestor worship and Buddhist beliefs in rebirth. Ghosts often serve as messengers, sometimes bringing communications from the dead, and should be feared only if one has done evil to someone already departed.

With *Throne of Blood* Akira Kurosawa has made a version of *Macbeth* rooted in Japanese folklore and tradition. While considering the same basic plot as Shakespeare, Kurosawa transposes Scotland to medieval Japan. Many stylistic elements were incorporated from the classical Noh theater, from which Kurosawa also drew the two major female characterizations. The evil Asaji, the Lady Macbeth equivalent, uses Noh-like movements and makeup; her famous hand-washing sequence, staged entirely as mime, is pure Noh. The Japanese witch is also common to Noh, as is her high-pitched voice, her chalk-white makeup, the supernatural reed hut, and spinning wheel.

The Buddhist themes of man's vanity and transience, Kurosawa's message, correspond to Shakespeare's themes. Both the opening and closing sequences of *Throne of Blood* contain awe-inspiring images of a misty mountain, covered with clouds and wooden markers, while a chorus chants about "a proud warrior murdered by ambition."

In between the serenity of the beginning and the end is a frenzied, imaginative film of power struggles, madness, and death. Washizu, one of Toshiro Mifune's most memorable roles, is weaker than most Western Macbeths; his wife, however, is as determined as any Lady Macbeth. Thrilling cinematography capturing the unsettling mist, the magical labyrinthine forest with its moving trees, and the crows' abrupt, metaphorical invasion of the castle combines with commanding performances to give this samurai action melodrama a frenetic pace.

457

# Through a Glass Darkly
## (Såsom i en Spegel)

★★★★★★★★★★★★★★★★★★★★★★★★★★★★★★★★★★★★★★★★★★★★★★★★★★

Nationality: Swedish         Year: 1961 (U.S. release: 1962)

Cast: Harriet Andersson, Gunnar Björnstrand, Max von Sydow, Lars Passgård

Director: Ingmar Bergman      Running Time: 91 minutes

B/W or Color: B/W           Availability: EMBASSY HOME ENTERTAINMENT

In the early years of the Sixties, Ingmar Bergman became involved with what is frequently referred to as his "faith" trilogy. *Through a Glass Darkly* was the first of the trio, and—austere and pessimistic as it is—it's certainly the most accessible of the lot. The focus of the picture is small, being limited to four members of a family spending the summer on a remote island in the Baltic, and it was filmed on Fårö, a locale Bergman was so taken with that he subsequently moved there to live. Karin (Harriet Andersson), recently released from a mental hospital where she has been treated for schizophrenia, is there in the company of her self-involved writer-father David (Gunnar Björnstrand), whose concern for his daughter's health (he's alarmed to realize) is more clinical than personal. Her loving husband Martin (Max von Sydow), though a doctor, finds himself unable to help Karin. Her 17-year-old brother Minus (Lars Passgård), who is just awakening to sex, rounds out the vulnerable quartet, whose initially peaceful sojourn will soon be shattered by the unstable forces of their personal demons.

In *Saturday Review*, Arthur Knight wrote, "Bergman's film unfolds with all the uncompromising, unhurried, slow-gathering momentum of Dreyer's *Ordet*. But where the Dreyer film rose to its climax in the passing of a miracle, Bergman reaches his height in the most horrifying delineation of a mental breakdown ever put on the screen. Ironically, Dreyer moves from his miracle to a finale of despair, while Bergman follows madness with a ray of hope."

*Through a Glass Darkly* was named one of the year's five best foreign-language films by The National Board, and it won an Oscar for Best Foreign Film of 1961.

# Tiger Bay

\* \* \* \* \* \* \* \* \* \* \* \* \* \* \* \* \* \* \* \* \* \* \* \* \* \* \* \* \* \* \* \* \* \* \* \* \* \* \* \* \* \* \* \* \* \* \* \* \* \* \* \*

*Nationality*: British                      *Year*: 1959
*Cast*: Horst Buchholz, Hayley Mills, John Mills, Megs Jenkins, Yvonne Mitchell
*Director*: J. Lee Thompson          *Running Time*: 105 minutes
*B/W or Color*: B/W                      *Availability*: TV only

In her teen years, Hayley Mills was one of the screen's most popular juvenile performers since Shirley Temple, due to a lucky fusion of natural charm, acting talent, and tomboyish appeal. The picture that started it all was *Tiger Bay*, in which the 12-year-old made her professional debut.

In Noel Calef's original novel *Rodolphe et le Revolver*, the young protagonist is a *boy* and, indeed, the role was originally intended for a child actor named Colin Petersen—until director J. Lee Thompson paid a visit to John Mills's home to discuss *his* role in the movie. Meeting young Hayley reportedly inspired him to change the story's central character to a girl and engage the Mills child to play her.

The film's setting is Cardiff, Wales, and its waterfront slum known as Tiger Bay, where a young Polish seaman (Horst Buchholz) kills his faithless mistress in a justifiable rage. A neighborhood waif (Hayley) witnesses the murder, and the sailor tracks her down and abducts the young orphan to save himself from capture. A warm friendship develops between them, and she agrees to stay hidden until he can safely return to his ship, which is about to sail. But when the child falls overboard, he surrenders his freedom by diving to her rescue.

In the leading roles, Mills and Buchholz display an unusual emotional rapport. John Mills's police superintendent is a relatively brief part, but his scenes with Hayley have particular poignance. Director J. Lee Thompson (*Woman in a Dressing Gown*) was at his best drawing forth *Tiger Bay*'s suspense, character development, and its picturesque locations in coastal Wales. It was this film that brought Hayley Mills to the attention of Walt Disney when he was casting his *Pollyanna*, and the contract that followed brought her a popularity her adult roles have not equaled.

# Tight Little Island
## (Whisky Galore)

★ ★ ★ ★ ★ ★ ★ ★ ★ ★ ★ ★ ★ ★ ★ ★ ★ ★ ★ ★ ★ ★ ★ ★ ★ ★ ★ ★ ★ ★ ★ ★ ★ ★ ★ ★ ★ ★ ★ ★ ★ ★ ★ ★ ★ ★ ★ ★ ★ ★ ★

*Nationality*: British          *Year*: 1949

*Cast*: Basil Radford, Joan Greenwood, James Robertson Justice, Gordon Jackson, Wylie Watson

*Director*: Alexander Mackendrick     *Running Time*: 82 minutes

*B/W or Color*: B/W          *Availability*: TV only

Compton Mackenzie's novel *Whisky Galore* developed a delightful fictional plot out of the real-life story of a ship that was wrecked in 1941 off the Isle of Eriskay in the Outer Hebrides of Scotland. In its cargo hold were some 50,000 cases of Scotch, destined for the United States. Since wartime shortages deprived the islanders of this "water of life," as they so quaintly termed it, they quite naturally went to some trouble to rescue the cases of whiskey from the doomed vessel—as much as they could manage under the protective cloak of night.

Screenwriter Alexander Mackendrick moved into feature film directing with this whimsical Ealing comedy, whose success led to his future guidance of two of the best Alec Guinness comedies, *The Man in the White Suit* and *The Ladykillers*.

Filmed largely on the Isle of Barra, at the tip of the Outer Islands, *Tight Little Island* (as it was called in the United States) is set in 1943 and centers on a conflict over that sinking cargo fomented by a Home Guard captain (Basil Radford), who's conscientiously bent on representing the best interests of His Majesty's Customs. The islanders of Todday don't quite see it his way, and with due respect to the sabbath, they nevertheless manage to spirit away the spirits with a skein of masterful and wily Scots strategems, while the lament of bagpipes underscores their covert activities. A wonderful ensemble cast portrays the islanders, limning indelible characters that must be seen to be appreciated; it wouldn't be fair to single them out here.

*Tight Little Island*'s sly ethnic humor and unpretentious comic situations proved a great success in America, and The National Board named it among the year's best films.

# Tim

\* \* \* \* \* \* \* \* \* \* \* \* \* \* \* \* \* \* \* \* \* \* \* \* \* \* \* \* \* \* \* \* \* \* \* \* \* \* \* \* \* \* \* \* \* \* \* \* \* \* \* \* \* \*

*Nationality*: Australian      *Year*: 1979
*Cast*: Piper Laurie, Mel Gibson, Alwyn Kurts, Pat Evison
*Director*: Michael Pate      *Running Time*: 108 minutes
*B/W or Color*: Color      *Availability*: MEDIA HOME EN-
                                    TERTAINMENT

B ased on a first novel by Colleen McCullough (who later wrote *The Thorn Birds*), *Tim* is the unusual love story of a young retarded man and a woman almost twice his age. It marks the directorial debut of Australian actor Michael Pate, who also produced and wrote the screenplay (updating the Fifties time-period of the book).

Tim Melville (Mel Gibson) meets Mary Horton (Piper Laurie) when she hires him to do some chores, because her gardener is ill. His quietness conceals the fact that Tim, as he puts it, doesn't have "a full quid." Learning that he's illiterate, Mary endeavors to teach him to read and write. While his parents approve of the woman's interest in their son, Tim's doting sister Dawn (Deborah Kennedy) becomes jealous of their growing attachment.

During weekends at Mary's beach house, their feelings deepen, Tim explaining that love is not contingent on intelligence. Following the deaths of Tim's parents, his teacher suggests that the pair marry. Despite criticism from neighbors, they do.

*New York Post* reviewer Archer Winsten wrote that Laurie "gives another rendition . . . that places her among the great actresses," and stated that Gibson "demonstrates a communication of simplicity that is astounding." (New York–born Mel Gibson became a star in Australia before making American films.) Winsten considered Alwyn Kurts and Pat Evison, as Tim's parents, "equally perfect."

Piper Laurie made her screen debut as Ronald Reagan's daughter in *Louisa* (1950), but her acting talent was not recognized until she played strong dramatic roles on television in the late Fifties and appeared opposite Paul Newman in *The Hustler* (1961), for which she received an Academy Award nomination as Best Actress. In 1976 she was nominated as Best Supporting Actress for playing Sissy Spacek's mother in *Carrie*.

In one scene, as a tribute to the author (or an inside joke), a copy of *The Thorn Birds* is prominently displayed.

# The Tin Drum
## (Die Blechtrommel)

★★★★★★★★★★★★★★★★★★★★★★★★★★★★★★★★★★★★★★★★★★★★★★★★★★★★★★

**Nationality**: German      **Year**: 1979
**Cast**: David Bennent, Mario Adorf, Angela Winkler
**Director**: Volker Schlöndorff      **Running Time**: 142 minutes
**B/W or Color**: Color      **Availability**: WARNER HOME VIDEO

The Tin Drum is a spectacular view of World War II, seen through the eyes of a child not that thrilled at the prospect of entering a world he considers absurd and grotesque. Oskar Matzerath, played superbly by 12-year-old David Bennent, sets the film's tone at his birth when he says, moments after being pushed into this world, "That more or less settled the question of retreat."

When he is born, Oskar already has a fully developed personality and is looking forward to the tin drum he will receive for his third birthday. When the birthday and the drum arrive, Oskar decides that he is finished with the whole tiresome process of growing and, through sheer willpower, stays at his three-year-old height. His small stature give Oskar (and director Volker Schlöndorff) a unique perspective on the world. His lack of height allows him to crawl under tables and otherwise spy on his family, as the Nazis take over his town. Director Schlöndorff, through Oskar, paints a ridiculous picture of the awkward, looming, and dangerous giants towering over the diminutive boy. Also unique is Oskar's ability to scream at piercing levels. When looking for attention or hoping to create mayhem, Oskar shatters glass with his incredible voice.

Bennent's performance as Oskar is the rhythm to which The Tin Drum marches. Spanning the boy's life from three to 20 years of age, the actor transforms his face and personality perfectly for each stage of life. His slight body and mature visage make him alternatingly menacing and pathetic.

This 142-minute adaptation of Günter Grass's complicated and beautifully written novel is admirable. It neither flattens the characters nor lightens the intent of the book. The film is a tribute to fine cinematic adaptations of acclaimed literature.

# To Forget Venice
## (Dimenticare Venezia)

\*\*\*\*\*\*\*\*\*\*\*\*\*\*\*\*\*\*\*\*\*\*\*\*\*\*\*\*\*\*\*\*\*\*\*\*\*\*\*\*\*\*\*\*\*\*\*\*\*\*\*\*\*\*\*\*

**Nationality**: Italian-French        **Year**: 1979 (U.S. release: 1980)

**Cast**: Erland Josephson, Mariangela Melato, Eleanora Giorgi, David Pontremoli, Hella Petri

**Director**: Franco Brusati          **Running Time**: 110 minutes

**B/W or Color**: Color              **Availability**: RCA/COLUMBIA PIC-TURES HOME VIDEO

I n 1979, the year *The Tin Drum* won a Best Foreign Film Oscar, Franco Brusati's *To Forget Venice* was a strong runner-up, with its multilayered, richly textured story of five adults coming to terms with the past, the present, and mortality. Unlike the director's humorous *Bread and Chocolate*, this complex film has less to say about class structure than about the human condition.

*To Forget Venice* isn't for armchair travelers; we're never shown that city. Instead, the action centers on a retired diva's country house that plays holiday host to two couples. Once a renowned opera star and a great beauty, Marta (Hella Petri) now requires medication to sustain her. Sharing her quarters are her adopted niece Anna (Mariangela Melato) and Claudia (Eleanora Giorgi), a schoolteacher and Anna's childlike lover. Their guests are Marta's brother Nicky (Erland Josephson) and *his* lover (and partner in a vintage-car business), the much younger Picchio (David Pontremoli). Their time together is filled with reminiscences of the past, embittered with hates, fears, and recriminations. Both couples undergo shifting relationships, which are brought to a head by Marta's sudden, unexpected death.

Brusati takes a matter-of-fact approach to homosexuality, and although there is occasional nudity, nothing is sensationalized. Instead, the movie has something to say about adult human feelings and the games supposedly mature people—intentionally or otherwise—play with one another. Brusati often deals in symbols and suggestions, leaving his story line open-ended and his characters much too deeply realized for easy assimilation.

*To Forget Venice* is a motion picture to savor and remember.

*(The videocassette is available in a well-dubbed, English-language version.)*

# Tokyo Story
## (Tokyo Monogatari)

★ ★ ★ ★ ★ ★ ★ ★ ★ ★ ★ ★ ★ ★ ★ ★ ★ ★ ★ ★ ★ ★ ★ ★ ★ ★ ★ ★ ★ ★ ★ ★ ★ ★ ★ ★ ★ ★ ★ ★ ★ ★ ★ ★ ★ ★ ★ ★ ★ ★ ★ ★

*Nationality*: Japanese            *Year*: 1953 (U.S. release: 1972)
*Cast*: Chishu Ryu, Chiyeko Higashiyama, So Yamamura, Haruko Sugimura, Setsuko Hara
*Director*: Yasujiro Ozu          *Running Time*: 139 minutes
*B/W or Color*: B/W             *Availability*: TV only

Though it's characteristic of his simple, utterly humane and profoundly thoughtful style, Yasujiro Ozu's *Tokyo Story* is better than most of his wondrous films and somehow even greater than the sum of its formidable parts. The narrative is unassuming and, in the end, overwhelming: an elderly couple from the village of Onomichi visit their children in Tokyo; they are not cutely old, in the manner of Occidental convention, but somewhat irascible and brutally honest, as in real life. One son, a doctor, has put on airs about his success; and a daughter, who is a beautician, is a bit calculating and vulgar. Only Noriko (Setsuko Hara)—the widowed wife of another son—welcomes them with genuine warmth, and they're soon callously dispatched by the kids to a cheap seaside resort. Both father (Chishu Ryu) and mother (Chiyeko Higashiyama) slowly and very sadly unravel their failings as parents, determining the development of their offspring, finally, to be only "above average."

After the mother dies, further pettiness and cruelty in the children surfaces. In two heartrending scenes (in all of cinema, never were tears more honestly earned), Noriko suggests that she, too, might become similarly hardened (though we suspect she's wrong, if only because of such scrupulous self-analysis); later, the father, tragically depressed, honors Noriko with a keepsake of his wife, while admitting that his own war-dead son was undeserving of an undying loyalty such as hers.

This treasure waited 19 years (nine years after Ozu's death) to get a commercial run in the United States. *The New York Times* named *Tokyo Story* one of its ten best films of 1972.

# Tom Jones

* * * * * * * * * * * * * * * * * * * * * * * * * * * * * * * * * * * * * * * * * * * * * * * * *

*Nationality*: British        *Year*: 1963

*Cast*: Albert Finney, Susannah York, Hugh Griffith, Edith Evans, Joan Greenwood, Diane Cilento

*Director*: Tony Richardson      *Running Time*: 131 minutes

*B/W or Color*: Color         *Availability*: CBS/FOX HOME VIDEO

In 1977, Tony Richardson directed a handsomely appointed version of Henry Fielding's 1742 novel *Joseph Andrews,* about the bawdy misadventures of a young footman. It was hoped that the film would repeat the success formula of 1963's *Tom Jones,* a Fielding adaptation that was nominated for ten Academy Awards and won four: Best Picture, Screenplay, Musical Score, and Director (Tony Richardson). But there was little cause for comparison. Where *Tom Jones* had, by censorship restrictions, been forced to remain merely naughty, sly, and suggestive, *Joseph Andrews* enjoyed the permissiveness of the late Seventies sufficiently to permit license to slip into licentiousness, with nudity abounding and taste abandoned.

Perhaps the tastefulness of *Tom Jones* is part of its wildly entertaining charm. Bawdy Restoration comedy has never been a lucky filmmaking genre, and in 1963 it was an unexpected realm in which to find those English exponents of the angry-young-man drama, writer John Osborne, actor Albert Finney, and director Richardson. But the triumvirate worked in perfect artistic harmony, with their resulting film a 20th-century look at 18th-century manners and morals, given the visual appearance of Hogarth's lusty and uninhibited paintings. Of course, Fielding's original book is more than just a lighthearted farce, but that's the aspect of the story that Osborne and Richardson choose to emphasize, creating a masterpiece of style and originality around Tom Jones (Finney), a cheerful, womanizing youth of dubious parentage whose lust for life threatens to snuff out his future.

Among its many accolades, *Tom Jones* was cited 1963's Best Picture by the New York Film Critics, the British Film Academy, and The National Board, which also named Tony Richardson Best Director.

# tom thumb

★ ★ ★ ★ ★ ★ ★ ★ ★ ★ ★ ★ ★ ★ ★ ★ ★ ★ ★ ★ ★ ★ ★ ★ ★ ★ ★ ★ ★ ★ ★ ★ ★ ★ ★ ★ ★ ★ ★ ★ ★ ★ ★ ★ ★ ★ ★ ★ ★ ★ ★ ★ ★ ★

*Nationality*: British             *Year*: 1958

*Cast*: Russ Tamblyn, June Thorburn, Terry-Thomas, Peter Sellers, Alan Young, Jessie Matthews

*Director*: George Pal             *Running Time*: 98 minutes

*B/W or Color*: Color             *Availability*: MGM/UA HOME VIDEO

I n the mid 1940s, as the Academy Award came deservedly to Hungarian animator George Pal for his work on the Puppetoons, he began preparing three feature projects to expand his Hollywood repertoire. Two of them—*The Great Rupert* and *Destination Moon*—were done in rapid succession, while the third, *tom thumb*, sat dormant through his entire stint at Paramount and became his premiere showcase at MGM in 1958.

*tom thumb* is a lovely musical fantasy, with gobs of double-edged humor aimed at adults as well as children. In addition, it has Peter Sellers and Terry-Thomas as the fairy-tale villains, doing some inspired improvisations under Pal's trusting supervision. The fact that Sellers is mimicking Pal's voice for his entire performance must not have bothered the director—he later developed *The Seven Faces of Dr. Lao* as a vehicle for Sellers, only to learn that MGM wouldn't pay the star's price, and Tony Randall stepped into the seven roles.

Russ Tamblyn plays the part of tom, which had originally been designed for an animated figure. Tamblyn's dancing, surrounded in one exhilarating effects sequence by a host of Puppetoon characters, is a joyous realization of the medium's magic potential. Pal was to direct Tamblyn again in *The Wonderful World of the Brothers Grimm*, the first Cinerama narrative film.

Jessie Matthews, one of the greats of the Thirties British musical stage and screen, plays tom's mother. The Yawning Man Puppetoon who lures tom to sleep is the voice of Stan Freberg. The film won an Academy Award for Special Effects. Pal was as proud of its modest budget ($900,000) as he was of its artistic success.

(*Time has seen to it that all the theater prints have turned pink, but MGM/UA's videocassette retains the original storybook palette of colors.*)

# Tommy

* * * * * * * * * * * * * * * * * * * * * * * * * * * * * * * * * * * * * * * * * * * * * * * * * *

*Nationality*: British          *Year*: 1975
*Cast*: Roger Daltrey, Ann-Margret, Oliver Reed, The Who, Tina Turner, Elton John
*Director*: Ken Russell          *Running Time*: 111 minutes
*B/W or Color*: Color          *Availability*: RCA/COLUMBIA PICTURES HOME VIDEO

Tommy is the greatest work of art the 20th century has produced, in the opinion of its director-adapter-co-producer Ken Russell. You may not agree with the outrageous one, but you will have an exhilarating time. This rock opera, which has no spoken dialogue, originated as a 1969 album by the British group The Who. Although he professed to hate rock music, Russell transferred the work to the screen with lead singer Roger Daltrey in his first acting role. Daltrey's work is outstanding, shining out from a cast of major names that includes burly bad man Oliver Reed, lifting his voice in song as Tommy's stepfather, and Ann-Margret (who doesn't age, despite the story's time span) participating in one of the most uncomfortable sequences ever filmed, as she's doused with soap suds, beans, and chocolate.

With a heavily religious theme, the story tells of Tommy, born on V-E Day in 1945, at the end of World War II. He's the child of Ann-Margret and Captain Robert Powell, who's missing in action. Powell returns years later when she's the wife of sleazy Oliver Reed, who kills him. Tommy is struck deaf, dumb, and blind as a result of witnessing this. Years later, the son (now played by Roger Daltrey) is taken to a succession of healers to cure his afflictions. A cult grows around him as he becomes a pinball champion and when Tommy recovers his senses, he institutes a new religion, which ends disastrously.

Among those who try to heal Daltrey are Jack Nicholson, as a rather sinister specialist; rock star Eric Clapton, as a preacher; and Tina Turner, as the Acid Queen. Pete Townshend composed the score, in concert with fellow Who members John Entwistle and Keith Moon, with Moon appearing as Tommy's dirty Uncle Ernie. If rock opera is too specialized for many tastes, this should provide an excellent introduction to one of the best of the genre.

# Torment
## (Hets/Frenzy)

★ ★ ★ ★ ★ ★ ★ ★ ★ ★ ★ ★ ★ ★ ★ ★ ★ ★ ★ ★ ★ ★ ★ ★ ★ ★ ★ ★ ★ ★ ★ ★ ★ ★ ★ ★ ★ ★ ★ ★ ★ ★ ★ ★ ★ ★

**Nationality**: Swedish    **Year**: 1944 (U.S. release: 1947)

**Cast**: Stig Järrel, Alf Kjellin, Mai Zetterling, Olaf Winnerstrand, Gösta Cederlund

**Director**: Alf Sjöberg    **Running Time**: 90 minutes

**B/W or Color**: B/W    **Availability**: NELSON ENTERTAINMENT

In 1947 Bosley Crowther wrote in *The New York Times*, "This item from the Scandinavian regions is dour and unhealthy in tone. It is curiously reminiscent of some of those grim psychological jobs that were turned out by morbid film-makers in Germany before the Nazis came to power."

The Swedish Östra Real School, where much of the action takes place, has, indeed, much in common with the school in the 1930 German classic *The Blue Angel*. The occupants of these Nordic classrooms share a fascination with loose women and a sadism on both sides of teacher's desk. In *The Blue Angel*, Dietrich, in conjunction with a nasty-minded pack of schoolboys, reduces schoolmaster Emil Jannings to a kind of subhuman geekdom. In *Torment*, a sadistic teacher (Stig Järrel), affectionately known as Caligula, hounds to distraction a promising student named Jan-Erik (Alf Kjellin). Caligula reads a Nazi newspaper and looks a great deal like Heinrich Himmler. When Jan-Erik falls in love with prostitute Bertha (Mai Zetterling), Caligula drives her to her death. Unmasked, Caligula falls apart, revealing the groveling geek inside every sadist's skin.

Says Crowther, "Its merits to the grand prize at the film festival in Cannes last year is hard to see." Yet the film raised Mai Zetterling to international celebrity. The dark lighting and murky insights preview the murky insights and dark mind-cast of Sweden's titan of cinema. Among the credits overlooked by Crowther: a screenplay and an assistant directorship by an unknown named Ingmar Bergman.

# The Trap

★★★★★★★★★★★★★★★★★★★★★★★★★★★★★★★★★★★★★★★★★★★★★★★★★★★★★★★

Nationality: British-Canadian     Year: 1966
Cast: Rita Tushingham, Oliver Reed, Rex Sevenoaks, Barbara Chilcott
Director: Sidney Hayers     Running Time: 106 minutes
B/W or Color: Color     Availability: INDEPENDENT
UNITED DISTRIBUTORS

Adventure, romance, danger, and suspense make *The Trap* an unusual love story, set in British Columbia during late 19th century.

Jean La Bete (Oliver Reed) is a French-Canadian trapper who returns to a pioneer trading post after three freezing winters with a haul of furs and a bag of gold—which he intends to use to buy himself a wife. However, he's too late for the annual auction of female cast-offs sent to the settlement for that purpose.

When the trader's wife (Barbara Chilcott) discovers that her husband (Rex Sevenoaks) has paid a huge sum for La Bete's furs, she agrees to sell the trapper her servant Eve (Rita Tushingham), a mute orphan.

At his log cabin, La Bete tries to teach Eve the ways of the wild: how to trap, fish, shoot; how, in fact, to survive. He also attempts to win her affection through alternate means of cajolery, bullying, threats, and sweet talk. Gradually, the frightened girl's hostility disappears.

When La Bete's leg is crushed in one of his own traps, gangrene sets in and Eve is forced to amputate. Their relationship turns tender and friendly, but she panics upon learning that she's pregnant and goes back to the trading post.

Eventually, Eve accepts a marriage proposal from the trader's clerk, but on the wedding day she disappears—returning to the primitive life and the man she loves.

Rita Tushingham excels in a silent role, her large eyes speaking volumes. This marked his first lead in an A-picture for Oliver Reed, who soon gained international fame in *Oliver!* directed by his uncle Carol Reed. The screenplay was written by David Osborn, who spent several years as a trapper.

There's raw humor and excitement (a crippled Reed being chased by wolves, Tushingham riding a canoe over the rapids), and the spectacular Canadian landscapes never dominate the authentic-looking action of *The Trap*.

# The Tree of Wooden Clogs
## (L'Albero degli Zoccoli)

★ ★ ★ ★ ★ ★ ★ ★ ★ ★ ★ ★ ★ ★ ★ ★ ★ ★ ★ ★ ★ ★ ★ ★ ★ ★ ★ ★ ★ ★ ★ ★ ★ ★ ★ ★ ★ ★ ★ ★ ★ ★ ★ ★ ★ ★ ★ ★ ★ ★

**Nationality**: Italian      **Year**: 1978 (U.S. release: 1979)
**Cast**: Luigi Ornaghi, Omar Brignoli, Lucia Pezzoli, Franco Pilenga
**Director**: Ermanno Olmi      **Running Time**: 185 minutes
**B/W or Color**: Color      **Availability**: TV only

The Tree of Wooden Clogs, winner of the top Cannes festival prize, is a film beautiful in its simplicity. Its overlying theme, the life of hardship and joy of turn-of-the-century Italian peasant families, is subtly charged with political understatement apropos of the time. Basically a one-man film, it was written, directed, photographed, and edited by Ermanno Olmi with a knowing heart.

Two story lines run throughout. One concerns a young boy's introduction to school and, more importantly, his father's reaction. The other follows the romance and marriage of a young farm couple. These studies are filmed with quiet dignity and grace. Olmi adds nothing to the reality of their lives, and takes nothing away. His actors, incredibly, are nonprofessionals and bring to life an authentic flavor in the farm families they represent.

The political undercurrent of the film makes for a potent mix, but Olmi's style is never heavy-handed, always serene. Social injustice is represented by the farmer's eviction from the land he has sharecropped all his life because he cut down a favorite tree of the landlord's to make his son a new pair of clogs to wear to school. Social upheaval is portrayed by violent street confrontations watched silently and unquestioningly by the young couple on their honeymoon.

The Tree of Wooden Clogs is an exquisite film, politically conscious but losing none of its serene, old-world charm. Among its cache of prizes, the picture was voted one of the five best foreign-language films by The National Board, placed on The New York Times annual ten best list, and won a British Academy Award.

# The Trials of Oscar Wilde
## (The Green Carnation)

**★★★★★★★★★★★★★★★★★★★★★★★★★★★★★★★★★★★★★★★★★★★★★★★★★★★★★★★**

*Nationality*: British              *Year*: 1960

*Cast*: Peter Finch, John Fraser, Yvonne Mitchell, Lionel Jeffries, Nigel Patrick, James Mason

*Director*: Ken Hughes              *Running Time*: 123 minutes

*B/W or Color*: Color              *Availability*: TV only

In 1960, two film biographies of Oscar Wilde were released simultaneously in New York. *Oscar Wilde*, in black and white, was directed by Gregory Ratoff and starred Robert Morley, who had played the noted writer on Broadway in 1938. *The Trials of Oscar Wilde* (also known as *The Green Carnation*), a color production written and directed by Ken Hughes and starring Peter Finch in the title role, was preferred by most critics.

Wilde (Finch) files a libel suit against the Marquis of Queensberry (Lionel Jeffries), the father of Lord Alfred Douglas (John Fraser), for calling him a sodomite. Though devoted to his wife (Yvonne Mitchell) and children, Wilde cannot resist young Douglas. At the trial, the marquis's lawyer, Sir Edward Carson (James Mason), provides evidence of Wilde"s relationships with young men and gains an acquittal for Queensberry. Wilde is then tried twice for gross indecency; the first trial ends in a hung jury and the second in Wilde's being sentenced to two years' hard labor. A broken man upon his release, the playwright is advised by his friends to go to Paris.

Both films end with the implication that Wilde and Lord Alfred parted after the trials (and Wilde's imprisonment). In actuality, the younger man joined Wilde in Paris.

In *The New York Times*, Bosley Crowther noted that while Robert Morley had "no doubt a closer resemblance" to Wilde, Peter Finch "makes the distinguished playwright a much more robust, imposing and plausible man. Indeed, he conveys the impression—as do Ken Hughes's direction and script—that Wilde was deeply devoted to his wife and children. . . ." *The New York Herald Tribune* review remarked on "how differently one set of facts can be interpreted" and claimed that "*The Trials* seems more intrinsically cinematic and leaves the impression of having plumbed a little more deeply into the soul of the man."

The British Film Academy gave Peter Finch 1960's Best Actor Award for this performance.

# Tristana

\*\*\*\*\*\*\*\*\*\*\*\*\*\*\*\*\*\*\*\*\*\*\*\*\*\*\*\*\*\*\*\*\*\*\*\*\*\*\*\*\*\*\*\*\*\*\*\*\*\*\*\*\*\*\*\*

*Nationality*: French-Italian-Spanish  *Year*: 1970
*Cast*: Catherine Deneuve, Fernando Rey, Franco Nero, Lola Gaos, Antonio Casas
*Director*: Luis Buñuel          *Running Time*: 95 minutes (105 minutes in Europe)
*B/W or Color*: Color            *Availability*: TV only

One of his last interesting films, *Tristana* is important within Luis Buñuel's *oeuvre* both as a rare example of serious, linear, almost conventional narrative style, and because ideologically, it's attacking a subculture of individuals who went relatively unscathed in his earlier biting satires. As a portrait of Don Lope, R.C.R. (Roman Catholic, Retired), it might be subtitled "The Non-Conformist."

Pointedly set in Toledo, where religion is as prominent as it is permanently entrenched, Don Lope (Fernando Rey) is asked to "keep" a poor, dying woman's daughter, Tristana (Catherine Deneuve). Buñuel details their ordinary life together—walks, chores, café intellectualizing—assuming that viewers will bring to the film an understanding of his surreal inclinations, and that understanding will color their reading of the film's frequent surface tensions. (There's even a Freudian nightmare sequence in which Tristana imagines Don Lope's severed head as the clapper of a bell—Buñuel lurks in the film's shadows.) Don Lope rationalizes his rebellion against the Right (and especially the Church), and his knee-jerk responses suggest he hasn't thought it through—that his vigorous anti-clericalism derives more from fashion than reflection. At one point, Don Lope protects a petty thief on the run by pointing the police, whom he associates with fascism, the wrong way.

When Tristana leaves Don Lope for a painter (Franco Nero), Buñuel's characterizations become more complex: we see Don Lope's true colors, and also Tristana's. She willingly returns to the affluent life-style he provides, in spite of their deteriorating relationship (evidently, the artist—possibly art—provided no peace). In the end, their passionate youthful ideals have been codified into smug, staid behavior. Buñuel suggests that the ultimate bourgeois tendency is refusal to consider oneself bourgeois.

# Tunes of Glory

★ ★ ★ ★ ★ ★ ★ ★ ★ ★ ★ ★ ★ ★ ★ ★ ★ ★ ★ ★ ★ ★ ★ ★ ★ ★ ★ ★ ★ ★ ★ ★ ★ ★ ★ ★ ★ ★ ★ ★ ★ ★ ★ ★ ★ ★ ★ ★ ★ ★

*Nationality*: British          *Year*: 1960

*Cast*: Alec Guinness, John Mills, Dennis Price, Susannah York, John Fraser, Kay Walsh

*Director*: Ronald Neame          *Running Time*: 107 minutes

*B/W or Color*: Color          *Availability*: EMBASSY HOME ENTERTAINMENT

T he sometimes stirring, sometimes mournful bray of bagpipes aptly underscores the dramatic clash of wills that forms the heart of the screenplay James Kennaway developed from his novel *Tunes of Glory*. His well-realized characters and pithy dialogue result in a crisp and polished film, set amid the wintry isolation of a peacetime Highland regiment.

This strong character study is foremost an actors' vehicle, and director Ronald Neame wisely allows his fine cast free reign to flesh out Kennaway's challenging script. *Tunes of Glory*'s power owes much to its brilliant cast. This story of regimental conflict is laced with humor, but it's basically a drama.

Alec Guinness is a crude but popular Scottish colonel who's more at home with drink than discipline; John Mills plays the scholarly martinet who arrives to relieve Guinness of his command. Their subsequent differences with regard to discipline and tradition ignite the drama. In noteworthy support, Gordon Jackson, Dennis Price, and Duncan Macrae convey atmospheric youth struggling to attain both maturity and military discipline. Susannah York and Kay Walsh help balance the predominantly male cast with respective spirit and tartness as Guinness's daughter and mistress.

But the movie belongs to Guinness and Mills, whose brilliant give-and-take acting makes audiences really *care* about these men and their future. Both actors are so good at their characterizations here that it begs the question of how the judges at 1960's Venice Film Festival could justify their selection of Mills as that year's Best Actor.

# The Truth
## (La Vérité)

★★★★★★★★★★★★★★★★★★★★★★★★★★★★★★★★★★★★★★★★★★★★★★★★★★★★★★★★

Nationality: French-Italian          Year: 1960 (U.S. release: 1961)

Cast: Brigitte Bardot, Charles Vanel, Paul Meurisse, Sami Frey, Marie-Jose Nat

Director: Henri-Georges Clouzot          Running Time: 127 minutes (130 minutes in Europe)

B/W or Color: B/W          Availability: TV only

U ntil this film, Brigitte Bardot had seldom been given any credit for her acting talents, despite some very effective performances in movies such as René Clair's Les Grandes Manoeuvres, Claude Autant-Lara's Love Is My Profession, and, of course, Roger Vadim's And God Created Woman. Seemingly, it was a case of B.B.'s naturally photogenic, sensual, and uninhibited persona responding to the guidance of a strong director—one who could cajole, badger, and coax her into digging deeper into her emotional resources than she might otherwise have done. Such is the case with The Truth, in which director Henri-Georges Clouzot reportedly pushed Bardot further, histrionically, than she had ever been pushed before—with results that impressed many of the critics, as well as the star herself ("This is my favorite film. I have had to work harder than I have ever worked before in my life").

Freewheeling, amoral Dominique Marceau (Bardot) is on trial for killing her lover Gilbert (Sami Frey), who was also the fiancé of her virtuous sister Annie (Marie-Jose Nat). Defense attorney Guerin (Charles Vanel) claims it was an understandable crime of passion, while Eparvier (Paul Meurisse), the prosecuting attorney, maintains the act was premeditated and deserving of the death penalty. As the trial proceeds, witnesses reveal Dominique's footloose life-style, and her sordid story unfolds in a web of flashbacks. Ultimately, she realizes that the cards are stacked against her, and while her fate is being decided, Dominique slashes her wrists with a mirror shard.

The Truth won an Oscar nomination for 1960's Best Foreign-Language Film. Clouzot was named Best Director at the Mar del Plata Festival, and Bardot received Italy's David di Donatello award as Best Foreign Actress.

# Two English Girls
## (Les Deux Anglaises et le Continent)

\* \* \* \* \* \* \* \* \* \* \* \* \* \* \* \* \* \* \* \* \* \* \* \* \* \* \* \* \* \* \* \* \* \* \* \* \* \* \* \* \* \* \* \* \* \* \* \* \* \* \* \*

**Nationality**: French            **Year**: 1971 (U.S. release: 1972)

**Cast**: Jean-Pierre Léaud, Kika Markham, Stacey Tendeter, Sylvia Marriott, Philippe Léotard

**Director**: François Truffaut      **Running Time**: 106 minutes (132 minutes in Europe)

**B/W or Color**: Color          **Availability**: KEY VIDEO

Based on the second of the largely autobiographical novels of Henri-Pierre Roché (the first was *Jules and Jim*), *Two English Girls* represents the bleaker side of François Truffaut's cinematic vision. That the film stars his filmic alter-ego, Jean-Pierre Léaud, shows how close he felt to the project. *Two English Girls* remains a monument to many of Truffaut's serious concerns.

The flip side of *Jules and Jim*, *Two English Girls* involves Claude and how his relationship to Anne and Muriel, the duo of the title, helps in his discovery of the connection between the artist and his art. This heady topic is encased in an overly romantic covering that is ethereally shot by cinematographer Nestor Almendros. The romance, as a form, is almost instantaneously dated, yet *Two English Girls* does manage to pull meaning and resonance out of this very literary form.

The movie is filled with the written word. This is one of Truffaut's passions, and along with Claude's art criticism and diaries, the director shows the now-lost power of letter writing. Whereas *Jules and Jim* reflected the *joie de vivre* of the café society of Belle Epoch Paris, *Two English Girls* deals with the dashed passions and sense of loss that took place away from the cafés.

It is doubtful that Truffaut ever shot a more moving sequence than the finale of *Two English Girls*. As Claude looks on at young English girls playing in a Parisian park, searching for one that could possibly be his daughter, the rhythm of regret becomes palpable. In a career filled with emotionally charged images and scenes, Truffaut's editing, camera movement, performances, and narration all come together here in a way they rarely have before. For a little-seen and under-appreciated film, that's saying a lot.

*(The videocassette is subtitled and runs a "restored" 130 minutes.)*

# The Two of Us
## (Le Vieil Homme et L'Enfant)

★★★★★★★★★★★★★★★★★★★★★★★★★★★★★★★★★★★★★★★★★★★★★★★★★★★★★

*Nationality*: French        *Year*: 1968

*Cast*: Michel Simon, Alain Cohen, Luce Fabiole, Charles Denner, Zorica Lozic

*Director*: Claude Berri      *Running Time*: 86 minutes

*B/W or Color*: B/W        *Availability*: RCA/COLUMBIA PICTURES HOME VIDEO

"In my house, France is Pétain," says Grandpa (Michel Simon). He is a wildly prejudiced old blowhard, living in 1944 Vichy France, after the Marshal, ancient hero of Verdun, led the country into ignominious collaboration with the Nazis. Claude (Alain Cohen), a little Parisian boy, is sent to stay with Grandpa's family to escape deportation to a concentration camp. No one must know that he is a Jew. A prodigiously talented dark-eyed imp, Claude carefully memorizes his Gentile name and spells it laboriously on arrival. He remembers to lie low in the bathwater and that he is a Catholic (he never quite makes it through the Lord's Prayer). A deep friendship develops between him and Grandpa. They roam the countryside, with Grandpa spouting the Pétain party line; denouncing the Bolsheviks, the Free Masons, and, above all, the Jews.

Grandpa is *au fond* no worse a fellow than Archie Bunker. His foolishness is often unmasked by Claude's probing little mind. When Grandpa remarks that Jews wear hats at table, Claude's eyes dart to Grandpa's head. Grandpa explains that berets don't count. Claude identifies the mark of a "bayonet thrust to the liver" as an appendicitis scar. Grandpa's World War I wound, he notes, is in the *back*. Their touching relationship ends when G.I.s liberate Paris. Grandpa's verities crumble as his beloved dog dies and Pétain's picture goes into mothballs.

Michel Simon won acting honors at the Berlin, Panama, and Cannes festivals. Claude Berri's first directing assignment has produced a gem with a lovely Georges Delerue score. Its well-drawn characters retain their dignity during the darkest days of the Tricolor.

(*The videocassette is English-dubbed.*)

# Two Women

## (La Ciociara)

★ ★ ★ ★ ★ ★ ★ ★ ★ ★ ★ ★ ★ ★ ★ ★ ★ ★ ★ ★ ★ ★ ★ ★ ★ ★ ★ ★ ★ ★ ★ ★ ★ ★ ★ ★ ★ ★ ★ ★ ★ ★ ★ ★ ★ ★ ★

*Nationality*: Italian                    *Year*: 1961
*Cast*: Sophia Loren, Raf Vallone, Eleanora Brown, Jean-Paul Belmondo
*Director*: Vittorio De Sica          *Running Time*: 99 minutes
*B/W or Color*: B/W                    *Availability*: NELSON ENTER-
                                                              TAINMENT

Selected as one of the National Board's five best foreign films for 1961, *Two Women* firmly established Sophia Loren as an accomplished dramatic actress. She won the Academy Award (the first such citation given the lead in a foreign-language film) and was voted the Best Foreign Actress by the British Film Academy. Among other honors bestowed were the Best Actress awards from the New York Film Critics and the Cannes Film Festival. (She was originally slated to play the daughter in this motion picture, with Anna Magnani as her mother.)

Based on Alberto Moravia's novel, the screenplay was written by Cesare Zavattini. Loren, a widow, runs a small grocery store in Rome. When the store is bombed during the war, she returns with her 13-year-old daughter (Eleanora Brown) to her native village, leaving the store in charge of a neighbor.

Back in her village, a shy schoolteacher (Jean-Paul Belmondo) falls in love with her, and her daughter secretly falls in love with him. While he is forced to guide retreating Nazis over the mountains, Moroccan soldiers rape both mother and daughter in the ruins of a church. The dazed girl becomes alienated from her mother but is reconciled after learning that the schoolteacher has been killed. The two women resolve to struggle on together.

The rape scene is particularly graphic, and Loren's emotional scenes (particularly those when she is trying to explain to her ravaged daughter that love is still possible) received high praise. *Films in Review* said, "Miss Loren makes us believe in this melodrama. Her performance after the rape is one of the most successful displays of deeply felt emotion ever seen on the screen."

# Ugetsu

## (Ugetsu Monogatari/Tales of the Silvery Moonlight in the Rain)

★★★★★★★★★★★★★★★★★★★★★★★★★★★★★★★★★★★★★★★★★★★★★★★★★★★★★★★

Nationality: Japanese               Year: 1953 (U.S. release: 1954)

Cast: Machiko Kyo, Masayuki Mori, Kinuyo Tanaka, Sakae Ozawa, Mitsuko Mito

Director: Kenji Mizoguchi          Running Time: 96 minutes

B/W or Color: B/W                  Availability: EMBASSY HOME
                                   ENTERTAINMENT

Kenji Mizoguchi's lyrical *Ugetsu* is universally regarded as one of the richest, most beautiful films ever made. Each decade the British film journal *Sight and Sound* polls critics on the all-time greatest films, and *Ugetsu* has been ranked in the top ten on each of the last three surveys.

*Ugetsu* traces its origins to Oriental legends. Set near Lake Biwa late in the 16th century, the film presents two parallel stories of love, greed, and strife. A potter and his neighbor leave their village homes to peddle their wares in Kyoto. Although it is a time of war, they are more interested in personal advancement and profits than in protecting their families. Bewitched by a ghost-princess, the potter temporarily finds wealth. Barely escaping her clutches, he returns home to find his family destroyed. His friend, wanting to be a samurai, deceitfully becomes a military hero, but discovers his wife working in a brothel. Both men achieve success, but at heavy prices.

Like Kurosawa's *Throne of Blood,* this timeless legend is set during Japan's medieval civil wars. Both feature the supernatural interacting with the physical world. In *Ugetsu* it strengthens the realism of the narrative. Also, both contain Buddhist themes focusing on the illusion of human ambition.

The major differences between Mizoguchi and Kurosawa can also be readily seen by comparing *Ugetsu* with *Throne of Blood.* Kurosawa is generally concerned with strong, heroic male characters; Mizoguchi focuses on peasants and merchants rather than samurai, and is considered among the world's leading directors at depicting the oppression of women.

The National Board of Review listed the picture among its top ten. The best Hollywood could offer was an Oscar nomination for Costume Design.

*(The videocassette is subtitled.)*

# Umberto D

★★★★★★★★★★★★★★★★★★★★★★★★★★★★★★★★★★★★★★★★★★★★★★★★★★★★★★★★★

**Nationality**: Italian       **Year**: 1952 (U.S.: release 1955)
**Cast**: Carlo Battisti, Maria Pia Casilio, Lina Gennari
**Director**: Vittorio De Sica       **Running Time**: 89 minutes
**B/W or Color**: B/W       **Availability**: EMBASSY HOME
ENTERTAINMENT

U *mberto D* took three years to reach New York. Distributors were understandably reluctant to gamble on a film whose chief character was a lonely, beaten old man, but the instant audience response to this most compassionate drama surprised even the critics.

The central character is played by Carlo Battisti, a college professor who had never acted before. De Sica followed the simplicity of his two earlier neorealist successes, *The Bicycle Thief* and *Shoeshine*, with a story that is stripped down to its austere essentials and recorded with a minimum of camera movement. This is not a social tract. Umberto's environment causes him pain, but it is not held to blame. The film is stark but not bleak. It explores the coldness of a society that can spit men into the streets when their usefulness is eroded, but illuminates all with the radiance of an indomitable human spirit.

Umberto D is a poor pensioner struggling to sustain himself and his mongrel dog. The loneliness of his existence is largely self-imposed. His social contacts are mostly limited to courteous banalities with the rooming house slavey. His landlady is a hard-bitten harridan who is preparing to throw him into the street. Umberto tries to sell off his few pitiful belongings to hang on to the room that has been his only home for the last fifty years. When the old man stretches his hand to beg, in an effort that we can see is crushing him, it is a moment of virtually unbearable candor. Utterly defeated, Umberto tries to kill himself with his dog in his arms, but the animal struggles free and diverts him from the planned suicide.

The film is a memorable portrait of a man whose essential nobility is portrayed in a totally honest and surprisingly unsentimental fashion. Battisti's performance is the eloquent and unmannered triumph of a "natural."

(*The videocassette is subtitled.*)

# The Umbrellas of Cherbourg
## (Les Parapluies de Cherbourg)

★ ★ ★ ★ ★ ★ ★ ★ ★ ★ ★ ★ ★ ★ ★ ★ ★ ★ ★ ★ ★ ★ ★ ★ ★ ★ ★ ★ ★ ★ ★ ★ ★ ★ ★ ★ ★ ★ ★ ★ ★ ★ ★ ★ ★ ★ ★ ★ ★ ★ ★ ★

Nationality: French          Year: 1964
Cast: Catherine Deneuve, Nino Castelnuovo, Anne Vernon, Marc Michel
Director: Jacques Demy       Running Time: 90 minutes
B/W or Color: Color          Availability: U.S.A. HOME VIDEO

Devastatingly beautiful, a many-faceted prism—words easily applicable to both Catherine Deneuve and the ground-breaking *The Umbrellas of Cherbourg*. This is a touching, unpretentious fairy tale of star-crossed lovers we care about, due to the finely drawn characters of writer-director Jacques Demy. The film has been magnificently photographed by Jean Rabier with evanescent rain and brilliant slashes of primary colors. Only less than miraculous in this all-singing, no-talking film is the unaffected singing and from the first moment, we accept it as part and parcel of each character.

Guy (sensitively played by Nino Castelnuovo), an orphan raised by his aunt, is in love with Geneviève (Deneuve), the 17-year-old daughter of an umbrella-shop keeper (Anne Vernon), who disapproves of the 20-year-old auto mechanic. The Algerian War is on, and Guy is called to service. Unknown to him, Geneviève is pregnant. Enter Roland (Marc Michel), a handsome jeweler who's immediately smitten with her. Guy has been wounded and has stopped writing. Her mother urges Geneviève to marry Roland. Two years pass and Guy returns, but Geneviève is gone; he weds his aunt's young companion Madeleine.

Years later, the original lovers meet. She's now married to a wealthy diamond merchant, driving through Cherbourg with her little girl; he's the successful owner of a garage and filling station and the father of a son. Their moment together is brief and heartbreaking.

Michel Legrand's score remains as fresh as a spring morning, with one song ("I Will Wait for You") a longtime standard. Captivatingly directed by Demy and superbly performed, this unusual picture won the 1964 Grand Prize at Cannes and was an Oscar nominee both for Original Story and Screenplay and Best Foreign-Language Film.

(*The videocassette is subtitled.*)

# Under the Roofs of Paris
## (Sous les Toits de Paris)

★ ★ ★ ★ ★ ★ ★ ★ ★ ★ ★ ★ ★ ★ ★ ★ ★ ★ ★ ★ ★ ★ ★ ★ ★ ★ ★ ★ ★ ★ ★ ★ ★ ★ ★ ★ ★ ★ ★ ★ ★ ★ ★ ★ ★ ★ ★ ★ ★ ★ ★

Nationality: French                    Year: 1930
Cast: Albert Préjean, Pola Illéry, Gaston Modot, Edmond Gréville
Director: René Clair          Running Time: 92 minutes
B/W or Color: B/W             Availability: Public Domain

René Clair's first sound film was also France's first all-talking motion picture. But Clair didn't just reproduce sound in this experimental work; he exploded the whole concept, leading the way for all other filmmakers. Exploring the theory of asynchronous sound, he utilized songs, special sound effects, and offscreen dialogue over his visuals to give counterpoint to his scenes. In this way, he created a symphonic movie, rather than simply a dialogue-laden stage imitation. One of the most famous sequences in cinema history, and often copied, is the opening title song, which became an international hit. The street singer (played by the great Albert Préjean) gathers his audience around him, and the camera observes their reactions, then wends its way up and down the street, looking into windows for the neighbors' reactions, then up and over the roofs, as the whole neighborhood joins in the song. Rouben Mamoulian used the same device in *Love Me Tonight* two years later. The fistfight in the railroad yard is orchestrated and scored, rather than simply grunted and panted—as another, more earthbound director might have staged it.

But *Under the Roofs of Paris* is not just an experimental film. It is one of the most charming of Montmartre romances, concerning the street singer and his friend, who both love the same little coquette. As the girl, Pola Illéry is appealing and a flirtatious rival to Clara Bow. The deliberately artificial sets of Lazare Meerson contribute to the idea of a romance existing on an unreal level. The tumbledown little flats are not squalid or sordid, but are the stuff of fairy tales. Georges Périnal's photography has no hard lines, but bathes the screen in a soft glow. The film is the work of a Parisian boulevardier who loved his city and its people.

The National Board named *Under the Roofs of Paris* one of the year's five best foreign films.

# Vacation from Marriage
## (Perfect Strangers)

\* \* \* \* \* \* \* \* \* \* \* \* \* \* \* \* \* \* \* \* \* \* \* \* \* \* \* \* \* \* \* \* \* \* \* \* \* \* \* \* \* \* \* \* \* \* \* \* \* \* \* \* \* \* \* \*

**Nationality**: British         **Year**: 1945 (U.S. release: 1946)

**Cast**: Robert Donat, Deborah Kerr, Glynis Johns, Ann Todd, Roland Culver

**Director**: Alexander Korda      **Running Time**: 102 minutes

**B/W or Color**: B/W           **Availability**: TV only

Vacation from Marriage (or Perfect Strangers, its British title) was filmed under extremely difficult circumstances, the worst of World War II's flying-bomb attacks on England. Amazingly, the result was a charming contemporary story about a stuffy young couple (Deborah Kerr and Robert Donat) whose dull union undergoes its first serious test when he enlists in the Royal Navy and she joins the Wrens. The movie amusingly observes the problems each has in adjusting to wartime service. He learns to relax and is drawn to a widowed nurse (Ann Todd). The wife blossoms under the guidance of an uninhibited service pal (Glynis Johns), gains poise and a serious admirer (Roland Culver).

Three years later, husband and wife reluctantly face their impending reunion, completely ignorant of the changes wrought in the meantime. Indeed, each looks forward to ending a marriage they had never enjoyed. Nothing transpires as anticipated. During one long night, they reminisce, dance, quarrel, part, and then change their minds. As they embrace in their old flat, the camera looks out over London's ruins to the start of a new day.

Vacation from Marriage owes its charm to the brilliance of its ensemble performance, as well as to the witty, knowing screenplay by Clemence Dane and Anthony Pelissier. Deborah Kerr and Robert Donat had previously starred on the stage in Shaw's Heartbreak House, but this was their only film together. Their scenes display a generous give and take that marks the difference between professionalism and greatness.

In his direction, Alexander Korda uses the war only as a device to alter the personalities of his reticent married couple in the process of delivering a gentle and disarming human comedy. The movie enjoyed success on both sides of the Atlantic, and it won Clemence Dane an Oscar for Best Original Story, although—as The New York Times pointed out—"Vacation from Marriage tells an oft-told tale, but tells it easily and well."

# Vagabond
## (Sans Toit ni Loi)

★★★★★★★★★★★★★★★★★★★★★★★★★★★★★★★★★★★★★★★★★★★★★★★★★★★

**Nationality**: French        **Year**: 1985 (U.S. release: 1986)

**Cast**: Sandrine Bonnaire, Macha Meril, Stephane Freiss, Laurence Cortadellas

**Director**: Agnès Varda       **Running Time**: 105 minutes

**B/W or Color**: Color         **Availability**: PACIFIC ARTS VIDEO

Vagabond describes the journey of an 18-year-old woman with a pack on her back, alone, moving south, in the wintry French countryside. This is not a psychological study of a particular individual. It is rather a consideration of what can happen to the entire blue-denim generation who left home, first in the United States and later in Europe, seeking a freedom they related to pleasure.

Actually we know very little of Mona herself. She grudgingly tells us her name and the fact that she worked as a secretary and "hated the bosses." But then Mona also admits to lying easily, so we can't be quite certain of anything she says. Mona's aimless journey, her encounters with hostile outsiders become increasingly difficult. The cold weather prevents her from bathing outdoors. Her small fires in cold, dark corners grow more pathetic as she crouches over them seeking warmth. Near the end, lying on the hard ground, cold and hungry, Mona cries out in profound frustration at an indifferent universe.

Is the film a comment on a system in which the police do a thorough investigation of her death but no social agency has moved to save her life? Does the film question a system that cannot intrigue its young people within the shelter of a lawful society? By the end of the film, although we are still uncertain of a specific message, we sense that we have shared the journey of a generation with serious social problems.

The film certainly merits its Golden Lion award at the 1985 Venice Film Festival and its selection as Best Picture of the Year by the French Critics Association. The heroine, remarkably well played by Sandrine Bonnaire, won the French Cesar award for her efforts.

The photography is superb, a literal gallery of French landscapes from Cezanne to Van Gogh. Agnès Varda, writer and director, was a photographer before she assumed her other roles, and her training is apparent in this thoughtful expression of rare visual pleasure.

# Variety Lights
## (Luci del Varietà)

**************************************************

**Nationality**: Italian                  **Year**: 1950 (U.S. release: 1965)

**Cast**: Peppino De Filippo, Carla Del Poggio, Giulietta Masina, John Kitzmiller, Folco Lulli

**Director**: Federico Fellini and Alberto Lattuada

**Running Time**: 93 minutes

**B/W *or* Color**: B/W                  **Availability**: TV only

Variety Lights is considered to be the first Fellini film, though it was co-directed by the more commercial, less magical Alberto Lattuada. But it has the unmistakable Fellini imprint and encompasses his favorite themes of illusion, the chase after unworthy objects, the return of a fallen one to his original love, and the resignation inherent in dealing with reality. And the movie remains charming, magical, and funny after almost 40 years.

An ambitious but untalented girl (Carla Del Poggio) seduces a small-time vaudeville producer into starring her in his tacky revue. To do this, he must displace his longtime mistress. When he discovers he has been used as a stepping-stone, he returns to his forgiving love. As the producer of the revue, Peppino De Filippo is the archetypical Everyman. Basically decent, he genuinely tries to protect his protégée from men, such as the lecherous industrialist who invites the troupe to his home for an all-night party. Giulietta Masina gives her best early performance (before *La Strada*) as the jilted girlfriend and fellow artiste. She is funny and animated in a wry style not usually associated with her.

Fellini is a master of mise-en-scene, and his depictions of fleabag theaters and hotels is funny and distressingly accurate. The illusions the ragtag performers have about themselves make a fine counterpoint when viewed against the tackiness and sordidness of their surroundings, and they are especially appealing in the scene where they wearily drag themselves back to the village, after being kicked out of the industrialist's home at dawn. Perhaps most telling is the conclusion, where the ruthless actress finds a protector who puts her in a middle-budget revue. The bloated glamour girl in the lead number rides like a queen bee up a stage elevator to make her entrance. When the young actress edges her out, the knowing lead looks wearily at her new competition. She has seen her many times before.

# Vengeance Is Mine
## (Fukushu Suru Wa Ware)

\*\*\*\*\*\*\*\*\*\*\*\*\*\*\*\*\*\*\*\*\*\*\*\*\*\*\*\*\*\*\*\*\*\*\*\*\*\*\*\*\*\*\*\*\*\*\*\*\*\*\*

*Nationality*: Japanese          *Year*: 1979 (U.S. release: 1980)
*Cast*: Ken Ogata, Rentaro Mikuni, Chocho Miyako, Mitsuko Baisho, Mayumi Ogawa, Nijiko Kiyokawa
*Director*: Shohei Imamura          *Running Time*: 128 minutes
*B/W or Color*: Color          *Availability*: TV only

"**I** want to make messy, really human, Japanese, unsettling films," director Shohei Imamura told Audie Bock for her book *Ten Japanese Directors*. In the 1980s, Imamura is the Japanese filmmaker receiving long-overdue recognition in the West, corresponding to Kurosawa, Mizoguchi, and Ozu in the 1950s, 1960s and 1970s, respectively. He loves to film the primitive aspects of Japan—raw, anarchistic societies omitted from the history books, and today's lower strata—capturing these people's crude zest for survival, chronicling a Japan untouched by his colleagues. Imamura still tackles the essence of "Japaneseness." He is best known for his meticulous attention to detail, a documentarylike realism reinforced by detailed characterizations, his vital, gritty topics, and a unique personal vision. Three times his works were selected as Japan's top film of the year: *The Insect Woman* (1963), *The Profound Desire of the Gods* (1968), and *Vengeance Is Mine* (1979). Yet he was a revelation to many of the critics who awarded his *The Ballad of Narayama* the Grand Prix at the 1983 Cannes Film Festival.

*Vengeance Is Mine,* his visceral masterpiece, is arguably the greatest Japanese film of the Seventies. Made after nearly a decade's hiatus from narrative filmmaking, it is Imamura's grisly, unrelenting probe of the criminal mind—here, that of a mass murderer—and is based on a true story.

After his capture, following a nationwide 78-day dragnet in 1964, Iwao Enokizu reflects upon his life: his father's humiliation as a Japanese Catholic during the war; the relationship between the father and the wife, interpreted through his mythomania as incestuous; his own insatiable sexual appetite, closely linked to the violent killings. Imamura describes the crimes in detail, while attempting to understand today's era through this vile person. He concludes by showing us the hollow and forlorn inner soul of modern man.

# Veronika Voss

## (Die Sehnsucht der Veronika Voss)

\*\*\*\*\*\*\*\*\*\*\*\*\*\*\*\*\*\*\*\*\*\*\*\*\*\*\*\*\*\*\*\*\*\*\*\*\*\*\*\*\*\*\*\*\*\*\*\*\*\*\*\*\*\*

*Nationality*: West German      *Year*: 1982

*Cast*: Rosel Zech, Hilmar Thate, Cornelia Froboess, Annemarie Düringer, Doris Schade, Volker Spengler

*Director*: Rainer Werner Fassbinder *Running Time*: 105 minutes

*B/W or Color*: B/W      *Availability*: TV only

When *Veronika Voss* was the opening attraction at the twentieth New York Film Festival, it set such a high standard of excellence with critics and viewers alike that producers involved with movies that followed were in virtual disarray.

This is one of Fassbinder's most visually dazzling films, as well as one of his more brutal. Shot in stunning black and white, *Voss* was the last film Fassbinder saw through postproduction before his death in June 1982.

Set in West Germany in the Fifties (and completing his postwar trilogy, which began with *The Marriage of Maria Braun* and *Lola*), it is the intentionally melodramatic story of a once-famous German movie star, the title character (Rosel Zech), who is now fading fast. Her tragic descent is being helped along by an unscrupulous—not to mention reprehensible—doctor, who gives Voss all the morphine she wants in exchange for furs, jewelry, etc. A young sports reporter meets Voss accidentally, is intrigued by her, and soon discovers what's happening to her. Naive but well-intentioned, he tries to save her before she goes under, but to no avail.

The performances of Rosel Zech, Hilmar Thate as the reporter, Cornelia Froboess as his girlfriend, and Annemarie Düringer as the cold-as-ice doctor are superb.

Vincent Canby of *The New York Times* said of the film, "[It] is a chilly, tough, wicked satire disguised as the sort of schmaltzy, black-and-white, 1950s melodrama that its characters . . . would never bother to see . . . [It] doesn't work in ordinary ways. Unlike *Maria Braun* and *Lola*, it doesn't have any easily apparent social and political targets. It works entirely through the myths of movies. . . . Its melodramatic style is its form of a social-political criticism."

# Victim

★★★★★★★★★★★★★★★★★★★★★★★★★★★★★★★★★★★★★★★★★★★★★★★★★★★★★

*Nationality*: British        *Year*: 1961

*Cast*: Dirk Bogarde, Sylvia Syms, Dennis Price, Norman Bird, Peter McEnery

*Director*: Basil Dearden       *Running Time*: 100 minutes

*B/W or Color*: B/W       *Availability*: EMBASSY HOME ENTERTAINMENT

Styled as a thriller, *Victim* was actually a plea for revision of an ancient British law dealing with homosexuality. *Time* magazine found that "it pursues with eloquence and conviction the case against an antiquated statute."

Melville Farr (Dirk Bogarde) is an eminent Queen's Counsel, who has a wife (Sylvia Syms) but has also had a past relationship with a youth named Jack Barrett (Peter McEnery). After refusing to see his old friend, he discovers that Barrett, who was being blackmailed, has committed suicide, rather than implicate Farr. Full of remorse, Farr risks his reputation and the future of his marriage to find the blackmailer.

The film changed Bogarde's image from romantic idol to mature actor. Although he did appear in one more *Doctor* comedy (the 1963 *Doctor in Distress*), Bogarde stated that he was no longer "the bouncy happy doctor with a little perm in the front lock of my hair." He wore no caps on his teeth and finally allowed himself to be photographed from his right side. Because his head was thought to look too small he had always been filmed from the left. "Every set was built for my left profile . . . in something like 30 pictures," he confessed.

The London *Evening Standard* noted that "his brave, sensitive picture of an unhappy, terribly bewildered man will win him and this film a far wider audience."

Born Derek Van der Bogaerde in London in 1921, Bogarde has credited Basil Dearden (director of *Victim*) with having helped him feel comfortable in front of a camera, when they worked together in the 1950 film *The Blue Lamp*. *Doctor in the House* (his first of four appearances as Simon Sparrow) had made him a box-office star, and his new image, following *Victim*, led to such serious, well-reviewed films as *The Servant*, *King and Country*, *Darling*, *Accident*, and *Death in Venice*.

# Videodrome

★★★★★★★★★★★★★★★★★★★★★★★★★★★★★★★★★★★★★★★★★★★★★★★★★★★★

*Nationality*: Canadian           *Year*: 1983

*Cast*: James Woods, Sonja Smits, Deborah Harry, Peter Dvorsky, Les Carlson, Jack Creley

*Director*: David Cronenberg       *Running Time*: 90 minutes

*B/W or Color*: Color             *Availability*: MCA HOME VIDEO

One of the most unique films of the 1980s, *Videodrome* refuses to create a slot for itself. It seems at times overly intellectualized, yet it works simultaneously on a visceral, emotional level. Its parts are at war with the whole. Interviews with screenwriter-director David Cronenberg and stars James Woods and Deborah Harry reveal that they were well aware when they embarked on this adventure that it might never satisfy mass audiences. How they were able to obtain financing may be more of a mystery than the plot.

Cronenberg has been cooking up fleshy nightmares in Canada for some time. *They Came from Within*—an apartment building full of people infected by giant, vulgar parasites that transmit themselves by creating a sexual urge in their carriers. *The Brood*—Oliver Reed in a grotesque tale of people's minds generating cancerous matter. *Rabid*—porn star Marilyn Chambers as an infected woman who grows an appendage in her armpit that telescopes out to nail victims as she visits movie theaters, luring the raincoat crowd to their deaths.

And *Videodrome*—in which James Woods plays Max Renn, an amoral TV-station owner searching for rich veins of sex and violence in media to seduce viewers away from the competition. One of his technicians picks up a muddled signal from Malaysia, something that could be a snuff documentary series. Renn is hooked by the raw, broken images, unaware of the fact that behind the taboo transmission lurks an insidious organization, reeling him in.

Deborah Harry, her big head framed with red hair, effectively departs from her persona as the lead singer of the rock group Blondie and plays a masochistic turn on Dr. Ruth. Rick Baker's Geigeresque makeup effects are juicily traumatizing.

*The Fly*, a 1986 Canadian remake, appears to be Cronenberg's biggest critical and commercial success to date.

# Village of the Damned

\* \* \* \* \* \* \* \* \* \* \* \* \* \* \* \* \* \* \* \* \* \* \* \* \* \* \* \* \* \* \* \* \* \* \* \* \* \* \* \* \* \* \* \* \* \* \* \* \* \* \* \* \* \* \* \* \* \* \*

*Nationality*: British     *Year*: 1960
*Cast*: George Sanders, Barbara Shelley, Michael Gwynne, Martin Stephens
*Director*: Wolf Rilla     *Running Time*: 78 minutes
*B/W or Color*: B/W     *Availability*: MGM/UA HOME
              VIDEO

A chilling science-fiction thriller, this low-budget production was directed by Wolf Rilla (son of character actor Walter Rilla) and is an outstanding example of its genre.

In the small English village of Midwich, a dozen women have just given birth. There are six boys and six girls, all with flaxen hair and eyes that are luminous and penetrating. The mothers' conception can be traced back to a morning when all life in the village stopped and its inhabitants fell into a coma for several hours.

By the time they're nine years old, the children are intellectual giants; having long since demonstrated powers of mental telepathy, they can easily force their wills upon their elders. One child, David (Martin Stephens), is the son of physicist Gordon Zellaby (George Sanders) and his wife, Anthea (Barbara Shelley). After the deaths of several of the villagers, the physicist realizes that the children plan to use their powers to kill everyone. Since he is the only person they trust, Zellaby realizes it is he who must annihilate the children. Zellaby gathers the alien youngsters in a schoolroom and grimly sets about destroying all twelve.

"Anyone coming upon [the film] cold will exit colder," warned *The New York Times* reviewer, who concluded, "People who send the kids to this one had better head for the hills before they get home." *Time* magazine termed it "one of the neatest little horror pictures produced since Peter Lorre went straight."

Director Rilla, Stirling Silliphant, and George Barclay based their taut, menacing screenplay on *The Midwich Cuckoos*, a novel by John Wyndham. George Sanders gives a skillful portrayal of the torn scientist who is a loving husband and father.

The excellent follow-up was *Children of the Damned* (1964), in which the lethal little league set their luminous sights on destruction of the planet.

# The Virgin and the Gypsy

* * * * * * * * * * * * * * * * * * * * * * * * * * * * * * * * * * * * * * * * * * * * * * * * * * * *

*Nationality*: British                    *Year*: 1970

*Cast*: Joanna Shimkus, Franco Nero, Honor Blackman, Mark Burns, Maurice Denham, Fay Compton, Kay Walsh

*Director*: Christopher Miles         *Running Time*: 95 minutes

*B/W or Color*: Color                    *Availability*: TV only

No movie version of a D. H. Lawrence story has, to date, been more faithful to the spirit of that controversial novelist than this characteristic tale of sexual frustration and emancipation, which was published soon after Lawrence's death in 1930. Modestly budgeted, with a barely known director (Christopher Miles, younger brother of actress Sarah), the film nevertheless conveys the essence of Lawrence, from its milieu of rural desire and hypocrisy to the sexual longings of its characters in early 1920s northern England.

Yvette Saywell (Joanna Shimkus) and her sister Lucille (Harriet Harper) return from a French finishing school to their rector-father's (Maurice Denham) restrictive household. Lucille finds a job, but the unemployed Yvette becomes restive at the rectory. When the girls encounter a handsome gypsy (Franco Nero), Yvette is intrigued by him. When she visits his camp, she meets an unmarried couple (Honor Blackman and Mark Burns) whom her father has barred from the rectory because they are "living in sin." Yvette is plagued by sexual stirrings she does not understand, but an accident at the local dam, and the arrival of the gypsy in time to save her, is the catalyst that sets her free. That night, Yvette and the gypsy make love, but in the morning he is gone. Yvette can no longer stay at the rectory and leaves the village with her unmarried friends.

Christopher Miles's expert guidance of a well-chosen cast unifies the various moral struggles of Lawrence's characters. Joanna Shimkus, wistfully virginal, offers a convincingly subtle transition from innocence to self-confidence, and blue-eyed Franco Nero is appropriately charismatic as the sexual catalyst. *The Virgin and the Gypsy* was listed among 1970's best movies by The National Board of Review.

# The Virgin Spring
## (Jungfrukällan)

* * * * * * * * * * * * * * * * * * * * * * * * * * * * * * * * * * * * * * * * * * * * * * * * * *

*Nationality*: Swedish                    *Year*: 1960

*Cast*: Max von Sydow, Birgitta Valberg, Gunnel Lindblom, Birgitta Pettersson

*Director*: Ingmar Bergman            *Running Time*: 88 minutes

*B/W or Color*: B/W                        *Availability*: EMBASSY HOME ENTERTAINMENT

Set in the Middle Ages, *The Virgin Spring* is based on a 13th-century legend and folk song. If it had been done without Bergman's austere point of view, without the stark pictorial quality, the period details, the montage of symbols, we might have been watching a medieval version of *Death Wish*. It may indeed have been the intelligentsia's answer to the exploitation film.

*The Virgin Spring* has a minimal plot, stark, symbolic overtones, but realistic depictions of the times and the crime. Max von Sydow, Sweden's answer to John Wayne, is on hand as the father who, upon learning that the visitors in his house are the very same villains who earlier that day killed his daughter, unleashes upon them a bloodletting wrath that surpasses even their own savagery.

Von Sydow's feudal knight in *The Seventh Seal* dealt with death and faith far more symbolically than does the vengeful father here. The harrowing scenes of sexual violence and revenge are barely mitigated by the redolent cinematography, and it is easy to understand Bosley Crowther's contemporary review, which stated, "for all its directness and simplicity—its barrenness of plot and perplexities—it is far from an easy picture to watch or entirely commend."

One American director was inspired to strip away the intellectualizations of Bergman's film and attempt a straight exercise in violence. Wes Craven's *The Last House on the Left* opened in 1973. Craven was brought up in a Midwestern Baptist community where movies were frowned upon. The only films he saw as a child were World War II newsreels, such as those showing the liberation of the concentration camps. In his raw, brutal reworking of *The Virgin Spring,* Craven moves to grainier and grainier film stocks during the rape-murder sequence in an attempt to approximate the feelings he experienced watching those newsreels in the 1940s.

*(Embassy offers both dubbed and subtitled videocassettes.)*

# Viridiana

★★★★★★★★★★★★★★★★★★★★★★★★★★★★★★★★★★★★★★★★★★★★★★★★★★★★★★

*Nationality*: Spanish        *Year*: 1961 (U.S. release: 1962)
*Cast*: Sylvia Pinal, Fernando Rey, Francisco Rabal, Victoria Zinny
*Director*: Luis Buñuel        *Running Time*: 90 minutes
*B/W or Color*: B/W        *Availability*: Public Domain

When novelist Enrique Lafourcade visited his friend Luis Buñuel on the set of *Viridiana,* he described the creative mood as highly improvisational. There is a parody of the Last Supper in the film, using the dregs of the lower classes—a blind rake as Christ, et al.—and according to Lafourcade, despite a published screenplay that suggests the contrary, this scene was handled as an on-the-set inspiration. If so, it is indeed remarkable: it is one of the highlights of all cinema. Lafourcade found the film startling and unexpected. Certainly, it is all that—and all the more remarkable for it.

A nun is drugged and raped by her father, who then commits suicide. Emotionally unable to return to the convent, she decides to remain on his estate and minister to God's poor. However, poverty has not enobled the peasants. And they have nasty little plans in store for their angelic mistress.

Although it was made in Franco's Spain, there had never been a possibility of the picture's being released there. In fact, it was smuggled across the border into France. *Viridiana* is decidedly an aggressive statement against both the sociopolitical and Catholic structures in the country.

The Spanish church was a favorite target of Buñuel's, dating back to 1928 when he and Salvador Dali concocted *Un Chien Andalou,* the surrealist short that made them the darlings of European intellectuals. However, Buñuel's abiding preoccupation was established society itself. In one of the longest, most potent bodies of filmed work extant, he remains true to both his surrealism and moral ethical ideals. He left us a string of masterpieces in several languages: *The Exterminating Angel, Los Olvidados, Simon of the Desert,* and *Belle de Jour* among them.

# The Wages of Fear
## (Le Salaire de la Peur)

★★★★★★★★★★★★★★★★★★★★★★★★★★★★★★★★★★★★★★★★★★★★★★★★★★★★★

**Nationality**: French

**Year**: 1953 (U.S. release: 1955)

**Cast**: Yves Montand, Charles Vanel, Vera Clouzot, Peter Van Eyck, Folco Lulli

**Director**: Henri-Georges Clouzot

**Running Time**: 105 minutes (153 minutes in France)

**B/W or Color**: B/W

**Availability**: NELSON ENTERTAINMENT

Four men trapped in an impoverished South American oil town are offered $2,000 apiece if they will drive two trucks across treacherous paths carrying nitroglycerin to put out an oil fire 300 miles away. This is the plot of a film that has been called by filmmaker-historian Basil Wright "possibly the greatest suspense thriller of all time." The film is Henri-Georges Clouzot's *The Wages of Fear*, an unrelenting exercise in high tension and human tragedy that won the Grand Prix at the 1953 Cannes Festival and that the director himself called "an epic whose main theme is courage. And the opposite."

When the trucks begin their deadly trek there's barely a moment to catch one's breath. Once on the road, there are some excruciating scenes in which the men have to drive (carefully) down narrow, rocky roads, across creaky, broken-down wooden bridges, and smash through boulders blocking their way, all the while making sure not to disturb the cargo of nitro. Perhaps the most memorable and harrowing scene is when Montand's partner (Vanel) wades into an enormously deep and wide mud hole to dislodge some tree limbs and gets stuck as the giant truck keeps barreling forward, eventually crushing his legs.

From the opening shot of cockroaches squirming in the sand to the final close-up of a dead man's fire-engulfed hand, this is an uncompromising study of machismo, fatalism, and man's exploitation. The international cast is exceptional, especially a young and rugged Yves Montand as the only driver to survive, at least for a while. Armand Thirard's luminous black-and-white photography and Georges Auric's throbbing music score add immeasurably to create Clouzot's finest film and an unforgettable experience.

William Friedkin's 1977 remake, *Sorcerer*, proved that a prodigious budget can't guarantee real human interest or kinetic excitement.

*The Wages of Fear* won the Best Picture award at Cannes and the British Academy Award of that year.

# Walkabout

★ ★ ★ ★ ★ ★ ★ ★ ★ ★ ★ ★ ★ ★ ★ ★ ★ ★ ★ ★ ★ ★ ★ ★ ★ ★ ★ ★ ★ ★ ★ ★ ★ ★ ★ ★ ★ ★ ★ ★ ★ ★ ★ ★ ★ ★ ★ ★ ★ ★

Nationality: Australian          Year: 1971
Cast: Jenny Agutter, Lucien John, David Gumpilil, John Meillon
Director: Nicolas Roeg          Running Time: 95 minutes
B/W or Color: Color          Availability: TV only

As explained in the opening credits, Walkabout refers to the Aborigine practice of sending a boy at 16 to live by himself off the land.
   The film marked the solo-directing debut of Nicolas Roeg (co-director of Performance), who was also responsible for its cinematography. Previously, he had been the cameraman on such films as Fahrenheit 451, Far from the Madding Crowd, and Petulia; among his later films as a director are Don't Look Now and The Man Who Fell to Earth.
   Considered the first film to successfully display unique atmosphere of the Australian outback landscape, Walkabout begins with a disturbed father (John Meillon), defeated by city life, shooting at his teenaged daughter (Jenny Agutter) and younger son (Lucien John—in real life, the director's son). But they escape, and the man sets fire to his car and kills himself, after which the children are faced with survival in the wilderness.
   The girl insists that they walk across the desert, and they set out—as if on a Sunday stroll. Concerned about appearances she warns her brother to take care of his clothes or else people will mistake them for tramps. The puzzled child asks, "What people?"
   At a dried-up waterhole, they're discovered by an Aborigine boy (David Gumpilil), who helps them adapt to the unfamiliar terrain. Sometime later, the Aborigine, who's attracted to the girl, decorates his body and dances for her; but her reactions are fear and confusion. The next morning, she and her brother find the Aborigine has hanged himself. Fortunately, they also find the road back to civilization.
   Years later, the girl will recall those carefree days spent in the outback, when she swam naked with her brother and their friend.
   An authentic Aborigine, Gumpilil's scenes were explained to him by an interpreter. (In 1986, he appeared in "Crocodile" Dundee.)

# Waltz of the Toreadors

★ ★ ★ ★ ★ ★ ★ ★ ★ ★ ★ ★ ★ ★ ★ ★ ★ ★ ★ ★ ★ ★ ★ ★ ★ ★ ★ ★ ★ ★ ★ ★ ★ ★ ★ ★ ★ ★ ★ ★ ★ ★ ★ ★ ★ ★ ★ ★ ★ ★ ★ ★ ★

**Nationality**: British        **Year**: 1962
**Cast**: Peter Sellers, Dany Robin, Margaret Leighton, John Fraser
**Director**: John Guillermin      **Running Time**: 110 minutes
**B/W or Color**: Color        **Availability**: VIDAMERICA

Seldom has the battle of the sexes been waged with more wit and irony or by such stylish participants as in *Waltz of the Toreadors*. In his *New York Times* review, Bosley Crowther wrote that the film contained "some of the most rollicking comedy . . . that we've ever seen this side of Chaplin or Keaton." Critics also praised Wolf Mankowitz' adaptation of the Jean Anouilh play, which had received five 1957 Tony nominations on Broadway.

Newly retired General Leo Fitzjohn (Peter Sellers, then 36 but made-up to look older) is married to Emily (Margaret Leighton), a nagging woman who claims to be an invalid in order to keep her husband from leaving her. While he enjoys pinching housemaids, the general's real pleasure in life is his 17-year relationship with Ghislaine (Dany Robin), with whom he fell in love while doing the waltz of the toreadors. In an unusual variation on a theme, the love of Fitzjohn and Ghislaine has never been consummated, and she has remained chastely faithful.

One day, Ghislaine unexpectedly arrives at the Fitzjohn home with two letters—passionately written by Emily to her physician. Ghislaine insists that the general is now free; however, a seemingly suicidal Emily has vanished, and the general goes in search of her. Ghislaine retaliates by staging her own suicide, but allows herself to be rescued by Robert (John Fraser), the general's handsome aide (and secretly his illegitimate son).

Following a disastrously unromantic tryst with Ghislaine, the general demands that Emily divorce him. She violently refuses, informing him that, as with her other possessions, he belongs to her. The general then discovers that Ghislaine and Robert have fallen in (and have made) love. Outraged, he orders Robert court-martialed but later halts the proceedings. The general is about to end it all, when the arrival of a new maid gives him a reason to live . . . and perhaps to waltz again.

# War and Peace
## (Voina i Mir)

**\*\*\*\*\*\*\*\*\*\*\*\*\*\*\*\*\*\*\*\*\*\*\*\*\*\*\*\*\*\*\*\*\*\*\*\*\*\*\*\*\*\*\*\*\*\*\*\*\*\*\*\*\***

*Nationality*: Russian        *Year*: 1965–67 (U.S. release: 1968)

*Cast*: Ludmila Savelyeva, Sergei Bondarchuk, Vyacheslav Tihonov, Victor Stanitsin

*Director*: Sergei Bondarchuk      *Running Time*: 373 minutes (433 minutes in the Soviet Union)

*B/W or Color*: Color          *Availability*: TV only

At the time of its release, the Russian *War and Peace* laid legitimate claim to being the longest and costliest motion picture ever made, at a reported excess of $100 million. In its native land, the film was shown in four separate parts, totaling some seven hours and 13 minutes. Shooting began in the autumn of 1962 and took five years to complete. For the famed Battle of Borodino alone, 120,000 men and 800 horses were employed on location near Smolensk. The U.S.S.R. distributor, Sovexportfilm, authorized its editing (by 60 minutes) and its English dubbing. Americans saw it in two lengthy sittings.

Tolstoy's massive classic had been filmed first by the Russians in 1915 and is best known in the West in the spectacular 1956 version King Vidor directed in Italy and Yugoslavia, with Audrey Hepburn, Henry Fonda, and Mel Ferrer in the leading roles. Overlong and simplistic in its exposition, there is really no comparison with the Russian *War and Peace*. *Variety* called it "a film of such staggering scope that it dwarfs previous film spectacles and defies a reviewer's efforts to describe its magnitude. This *War and Peace* is less a cinematic variation than a literal homage to the novel, and as such it is extraordinary." In *New York*, Judith Crist wrote, "The screen has never before been so properly or so beautifully exploited to contain the magnitude of an event or for the depiction of a shattering human experience."

United in voting this epic story of aristocratic interrelationships amid the Napoleonic Wars the Best Foreign Film of 1968 were the New York Film Critics, the Academy of Motion Picture Arts and Sciences, and The National Board of Review.

*(Although previously available in the United States on videocassette, the film is currently out of circulation.)*

# The War Game

\* \* \* \* \* \* \* \* \* \* \* \* \* \* \* \* \* \* \* \* \* \* \* \* \* \* \* \* \* \* \* \* \* \* \* \* \* \* \* \* \* \* \* \* \* \* \* \* \* \* \* \* \* \* \* \*

**Nationality**: British      **Year**: 1966
**Director**: Peter Watkins      **Running Time**: 47 minutes
**B/W or Color**: B/W      **Availability**: Public Domain

The most relentlessly pessimistic film ever made about atomic war, although it is not without its share of gallows wit, is *The War Game*, a docudrama by Peter Watkins.

After the success of his *Battle of Culloden* for BBC-TV, Watkins was regarded as one of the new wunderkind of the docudrama form. *Culloden,* and all of his subsequent work, was characterized by reaching far afield: staging the battle of Bonnie Prince Charlie (or World War III) with documentary realism, using large casts of nonactors, using anachronistic "you-are-there" hand-held-camera interview techniques, punctuating scenes with narration and simple title cards bearing polarizing catch phrases and quotes. In short, a new and dynamic use of the medium.

Unfortunately, Watkins's elevated position in the eyes of the powers-that-be in Britain was painfully short-lived. He was ostracized by the film industry as early as preproduction on *The War Game,* when the Home Office denied him access to information on thermonuclear preparedness and passed the word on to every organization he approached, including the BBC, which eventually refused to air the film. It was finally released theatrically.

What we see in *The War Game* is a painstakingly researched and painfully despairing vision of England in the wake of atomic war, totally unprepared for the fire storms, the radiation sickness, the riots, or the psychological decimation of civilization in the aftermath.

The film was shown in the United States on a double bill with *Dr. Strangelove,* and its sobering vision is as pertinent today as then. Recently, in tribute, the BBC made a sort of emulative feature called *Threads,* chronicling a "nuclear winter." Meanwhile Watkins, whose artistic integrity has cost him dearly in the business world of motion pictures, has somehow managed to produce several important features, including *Punishment Park* (draft dodgers in the United States), *Privilege* (forerunner of *A Clockwork Orange*) and *Edvard Munch.*

# The Way to the Stars
## (Johnny in the Clouds)

★ ★ ★ ★ ★ ★ ★ ★ ★ ★ ★ ★ ★ ★ ★ ★ ★ ★ ★ ★ ★ ★ ★ ★ ★ ★ ★ ★ ★ ★ ★ ★ ★ ★ ★ ★ ★ ★ ★ ★ ★ ★ ★ ★ ★ ★ ★ ★ ★ ★ ★ ★ ★

Nationality: British          Year: 1945

Cast: Michael Redgrave, John Mills, Rosamund John, Douglass Montgomery, Renee Asherson

Director: Anthony Asquith      Running Time: 109 minutes

B/W or Color: B/W          Availability: TV only

The Way to the Stars was Britain's last great World War II film made *during* that long and wearying conflict. Producer Anatole de Grunwald developed the script with playwright Terence Rattigan. Its basic idea stemmed from then-major William Wyler's wartime documentary *The Spirit of St. Louis,* which began as the story of an airfield but evolved into the account of a bomber's crew. Rattigan reworked Wylers unused material into a screenplay about a wartime collaboration of American and British air forces in England. When de Grunwald joined him in a further rewrite, it became *The Way to the Stars.*

With the war obviously nearing its end, Rattigan suggested that the completed movie be updated to include a dramatic "framing" device. Since the story took place in 1942, Asquith shot additional footage that became a *postwar* look at the now-deserted airfield of the film's setting, quietly gone to grass and its barracks empty. Film buffs will note the borrowing of this idea for Henry King's *Twelve O'Clock High* five years later.

In a semidocumentary fashion, the movie affords a glimpse into the lives (often tragically cut short) of various Yanks and Brits as they face and reconcile the natural, small hostilities that begin and end in the common tongue they share—which unites as much as alienates them. The writing and direction are on so intelligent and sincere a level—devoid of battle scenes and clichéd war-movie heroics—that Asquith succeeds in rendering his collection of typical fliers both credible and moving.

In 1946, the London *Daily Mail* instituted its National Film Award, with the first ballot spanning the wartime years 1939–45. *The Way to the Stars* was named the most popular film for those years.

# We All Loved Each Other So Much

## (C'Eravamo Tanto Amati)

**★★★★★★★★★★★★★★★★★★★★★★★★★★★★★★★★★★★★★★★★★★★★★★★★★★★★★★★★**

**Nationality**: Italian          **Year**: 1975 (U.S. release: 1977)

**Cast**: Nino Manfredi, Stefania Sandrelli, Vittorio Gassman, Stefano Satta Flores, Giovanna Ralli

**Director**: Ettore Scola          **Running Time**: 124 minutes (136 minutes in Europe)

**B/W or Color**: Color          **Availability**: RCA/COLUMBIA PICTURES HOME VIDEO

Discovering Ettore Scola is like stumbling upon a diamond mine. He has been around a long time, writing scripts and directing. His work is as creative and experimental as—and even more mainstream than—Fellini's, Antonioni's, De Sica's, and Wertmuller's. He has won the Academy Award for Best Foreign Film (*A Special Day*, with Mastroianni and Loren), and his work, at its best, has an open, lifelike form—allowing its characters to breathe—that surpasses his contemporaries. Yet he is relatively unknown: very few of his films have made it to the United States, and those that are available here are far more accessible on video than in theaters.

*We All Loved Each Other So Much* is generally acknowledged to be Scola's masterwork. Its story spans 30 years and interweaves the lives of three disparate and disappointed friends, centering around the woman that they have all loved at one time or another. There's a serious commentary to be found here about postwar Italy, its aspirations and eventual spiritual and social failures. But the film works on a purely emotional level as well, and its tone is ultimately one of melancholy, with scenes of visual pathos that rank with the works of Chaplin.

Scola himself is modest about such comparisons. He says that his screenplays are 50 percent story and 50 percent memory. And the personal details and feelings resonate very strongly. In this film, the performances of Vittorio Gassman, Nino Manfredi, Stefano Satta Flores, and Stefania Sandrelli are passionately human, laced with humor and tragedy. Armando Trovajoli's lush, haunting score and Claudio Cirillo's cinematography flesh out Scola's directorial vision to perfection. If you are moved by the film, you'll be intrigued to know that Scola varied the theme earlier in 1970's *The Pizza Triangle* and, again later, in 1980's *The Terrace*. (*The videocassette is in Italian with English subtitles.*)

# Weekend
## (Le Weekend)

★ ★ ★ ★ ★ ★ ★ ★ ★ ★ ★ ★ ★ ★ ★ ★ ★ ★ ★ ★ ★ ★ ★ ★ ★ ★ ★ ★ ★ ★ ★ ★ ★ ★ ★ ★ ★ ★ ★ ★ ★ ★ ★ ★ ★ ★ ★ ★ ★ ★ ★ ★ ★

*Nationality*: French-Italian      *Year*: 1968
*Cast*: Jean Yanne, Mireille Darc, Jean-Pierre Kalfon, Valerie Lagrange
*Director*: Jean-Luc Godard      *Running Time*: 103 minutes
*B/W or Color*: Color      *Availability*: TV Only

By 1968, the year *Weekend* premiered at the New York Film Festival, Jean-Luc Godard had established a formidable reputation in world cinema. As critic Pauline Kael noted, "He shook the confidence of other filmmakers." Many mainstream critics didn't understand his jokey, self-referential, and analytic films, but to the new generation of Sixties film enthusiasts he was often referred to as "God" for short, because he opened up a whole new universe of film theory and possibilities. His breezy, ironic films were made with a rare sense of freedom and joyousness, unlike any filmmaker's work since the silent era. Godard's fondness for movie history and experimentation gave him an affinity with the silent pioneers. Paris, during the cultural explosion of the 1960s, was a world waiting to be discovered and documented, just as the world offered itself to the first generation of filmmakers. Godard responded with a set of intelligent, effervescent love stories and political comedies from *Breathless* in 1960 to *Weekend*.

*Weekend* is a cumulative work, representing the end of the joyride. In it a married couple, Roland and Corrine (Yanne and Darc), leave their city apartment to visit—and murder—the wife's parents in the country, hoping to collect on their will. On the way, the couple encounter the breakdown of society through the many different characters they meet (including Lewis Carroll, God, and Saint-Just). It's a surreal road movie, and the highlight is a long traffic jam filmed in one uninterrupted shot (nearly 15 minutes). The automobile—the signal possession of the bourgeoisie—represents the mindset and values of each owner, and Godard's massive traffic bottleneck becomes an amazing, frightening metaphor for a chaotic world, the end of civilization as we know it. This is a savage vision and extremely funny. *Weekend* is Godard at the peak of his artistry.

# The Well-Digger's Daughter
## (La Fille du Puisatier)

**\* \* \* \* \* \* \* \* \* \* \* \* \* \* \* \* \* \* \* \* \* \* \* \* \* \* \* \* \* \* \* \* \* \* \* \* \* \* \* \* \* \* \* \* \* \* \* \* \* \* \* \* \* \***

*Nationality*: French        *Year*: 1946

*Cast*: Raimu, Fernandel, Josette Day, Georges Grey

*Director*: Marcel Pagnol      *Running Time*: 150 minutes

*B/W or Color*: B/W         *Availability*: Public Domain

This film is historic in more than one sense. Released in 1946, it was the first motion picture to be started and completed in France after the end of World War II. In addition, it was written and directed by Marcel Pagnol, a reason for celebration in itself. *Plus,* the movie brought together Raimu and Fernandel, two of France's most talented comedians, to provide the hearty male humor—the red wine and freshly baked bread of this delicious French country repast.

The story is not a new one. During the war, one of Raimu's six motherless and virginal daughters (Josette Day) is seduced by a dashing young aviator, the son of a prosperous family (Georges Grey). He is an old hand with the ladies and is conveniently "missing" soon after the discovery of Day's pregnancy. After a series of summit meetings with his assistant (Fernandel), the well-digger, an honorable man fearful for the good names of his five other daughters, sends the expectant mother away from home. Raimu handles this cliché of a situation with marvelous finesse. His eloquent revelation of his daughter's condition to the young pilot's family is a study in style and dignity.

After finishing the film, Raimu spoke of Pagnol and the legendary director's ability to maneuver the audience's reactions "from laughter to tears and back again in a flash."

*The Well-Digger's Daughter* is to this day one of France's outstanding cinematic contributions. The photography is of an unusually high level, the acting and directing superb. Also, in the postwar year of 1946, it must have been a genuine pleasure to watch a film where the birth of an illegitimate child was an act of profound concern after the worldwide slaughter of the previous five years.

*The New York Times* named this movie one of the year's ten best.

# Wetherby

* * * * * * * * * * * * * * * * * * * * * * * * * * * * * * * * * * * * * * * * * * * * * * * * * * * * * * * *

*Nationality*: British          *Year*: 1985

*Cast*: Vanessa Redgrave, Ian Holm, Judi Dench, Marjorie Yates, Tim McInnerny

*Director*: David Hare          *Running Time*: 102 minutes

*B/W or Color*: Color          *Availability*: MGM/UA HOME VIDEO

The feature-film debut of British playwright and director David Hare *(Plenty)* is a notable effort. Set in the small northeast English town of Wetherby, Yorkshire, and imaginatively photographed by Stuart Harris, *Wetherby* lifts the veneer of civility veiling ordinary lives—to uncover the sexuality and violence seething below.

The day after Jean Travers, a middle-aged schoolteacher, gives a small dinner party, one mysterious guest, John Morgan, returns—and, in front of Travers, deliberately kills himself. It is this inexplicable act of violence that propels the film back and forth in time—reconstructing events leading to young Morgan's suicide.

As Jean Travers, the handsome Vanessa Redgrave sympathetically imbues her character with sass and intelligence, some secretiveness, and charm. Though Morgan, a young doctoral student, manifests low affect (a "central disfiguring blankness"), it is his youthfulness that unleashes Travers's long-repressed passions.

Joely Richardson (daughter of Vanessa Redgrave and director Tony Richardson) plays the schoolteacher 30 years earlier; we witness young Travers's torrid but ill-fated love affair with a stubborn, selfish soldier.

Most noteworthy is Stuart Harris's penetrating camera. Primarily shot in blues, greens, and browns, *Wetherby*'s P.O.V. shots, high contrast lighting, and deep-focus photography provide the film with an extra dimension.

*Variety* called *Wetherby*, "a beautifully directed film in which all the technical elements mesh to form a most satisfying and stimulating whole. It must rank as one of the best British films about personal relationships since the late Joseph Losey's *Accident* in the mid-Sixties."

# When Father Was Away on Business
## (Otac na Službenom Putu)

★★★★★★★★★★★★★★★★★★★★★★★★★★★★★★★★★★★★★★★★★★★★★★★★★★★★★★

**Nationality**: Yugoslavian　　　　**Year**: 1985
**Cast**: Moreno de Bartoli, Miki Manojlović, Mirjana Karanović
**Director**: Emir Kusturica　　　　**Running Time**: 144 minutes
**B/W or Color**: Color　　　　　　**Availability**: TV only

Yugoslavian director Emir Kusturica won Venice's 1981 Golden Lion Award with his first movie, *Do You Remember Dolly Bell?* In 1985, his second picture, *When Father Was Away on Business,* a warm, tender, and funny film about life's complexities, garnered the coveted Palme D'Or at Cannes.

It is narrated by—and seen through the eyes of—Malik (Moreno de Bartoli, a remarkable child who portrays, with both aplomb and naiveté, a youngster growing up in a confused world).

We are in Sarajevo in 1950. The nation is in political turmoil, and Malik's family reflects the uncertainties. His father, Mesha, is a rascally bureaucrat and a womanizer; his mother, an attractive, self-effacing woman—except when she suspects her husband of philandering and lets her temper fly. Then there are Malik's older brother, his grandfather, and his uncles, all of whom contribute both to the family's stability and instability.

Being "away on business" is a Yugoslavian euphemism for being a political prisoner. In the case of Malik's father, the arrest would be ludicrous were it not for the subsequent hardships to his family. His mistress denounces him to his brother-in-law—a petty functionary in the secret police—ostensibly for not following the party line, but actually because Mesha won't divorce his wife to marry her.

Mesha's banishment to a labor camp is followed by postimprisonment rehabilitation. His wife and children join him, with Mesha quickly reverting to form by playing chess during working hours and renewing extramarital affairs. When the family is finally allowed to return to Sarajevo, nothing will have changed. Malik and his brother will grow up in a full family environment: loving, quarreling, but together.

503

# The Whisperers

★★★★★★★★★★★★★★★★★★★★★★★★★★★★★★★★★★★★★★★★★★★★★★★★★★★★★

*Nationality*: British   *Year*: 1967

*Cast*: Edith Evans, Eric Portman, Nanette Newman, Gerald Sim, Avis Bunnage, Ronald Fraser

*Director*: Bryan Forbes   *Running Time*: 106 minutes

*B/W or Color*: B/W   *Availability*: TV only

The elderly have never been popular subjects for motion pictures, and the great films made about them are few: Leo McCarey's *Make Way for Tomorrow* (1937); Vittorio De Sica's *Umberto D* (1952); Akira Kurosawa's *Ikiru* (1952); and *The Whisperers*, written and directed by former actor Bryan Forbes.

Forbes's adaptation of the Robert Nicolson book *Mrs. Ross* was conceived as a vehicle for Dame Edith Evans: "It seemed a tragic waste that nobody had really written a film to make full use of her extraordinary talents." Dame Edith movingly portrays lonely old Mrs. Ross, who lives in a run-down little flat with "voices" that whisper to her from the walls and water pipes. Abandoned by her husband, Archie, she lives on a modest government pension, which she considers merely a loan against the "inheritance" she expects to receive from her late father's estate. Her days consist of visits to the library, a soup kitchen, and the National Assistance Board. But at night there are only the whisperers. Her crooked son Charlie (Ronald Fraser) pays her a visit only to hide stolen pounds in her closet, and when Mrs. Ross later finds the money, she thinks it's her inheritance. Foolishly, she tells an unscrupulous acquaintance (Avis Bunnage), who drugs the old woman and robs her. The next day Mrs. Ross is discovered unconscious in an alley, suffering from pneumonia. While she recovers in a hospital, authorities track down Archie (Eric Portman) and persuade him to return home. They attempt to re-establish a life together, but Archie takes whatever she has left and disappears again, leaving Mrs. Ross alone with her whispering voices.

At 79, Edith Evans dominates the film, creating a rich character who is at once warmly humorous, dottily eccentric, and unsentimentally poignant. Her Mrs. Ross is a brilliant study in understatement, a haunting performance in a heartbreaking movie, which won her Best Actress citations from the 1967 Berlin Film Festival, the New York Film Critics, and The National Board of Review, which also named *The Whisperers* one of the year's ten best.

# Whistle Down the Wind

✮✮✮✮✮✮✮✮✮✮✮✮✮✮✮✮✮✮✮✮✮✮✮✮✮✮✮✮✮✮✮✮✮✮✮✮✮✮✮✮✮✮✮✮✮✮✮✮✮✮✮✮✮✮

**Nationality**: British          **Year**: 1961 (U.S. release: 1962)
**Cast**: Hayley Mills, Alan Bates, Bernard Lee, Norman Bird
**Director**: Bryan Forbes          **Running Time**: 99 minutes
**B/W *or* Color**: B/W          **Availability**: EMBASSY HOME
                                                                    ENTERTAINMENT

This fragile fable, adapted for the screen from Mary Hayley Bell's novella by Keith Waterhouse and Willis Hall, marked the directorial debut of actor-writer Bryan Forbes, in production partnership with Richard Attenborough. In spite of a limited budget, they were able to hire young Hayley Mills for the pivotal role (her mother was the story's author). A prestardom Alan Bates was engaged to portray the mysterious catalyst.

On an isolated Lancashire farm, three children discover a bearded stranger (who is actually a fugitive killer) hiding in their barn. Of strong religious upbringing, the youngsters take the man literally when they seek his identity and he mutters, "Jesus Christ!" Impressionable children soon come from all over to pay him tribute. When one child unintentionally betrays his whereabouts, the authorities close in. After the stranger surrenders, two latecomers arrive at the farm. "You missed Him this time," they're told, "but He'll come again." Alan Bates explains: "I think the picture runs contrary to most people's religious training. It tells us that the church is what you believe, not what other people tell you." With his largely juvenile cast, Bryan Forbes became a virtual Pied Piper, managing to extract totally natural performances and maintaining a fine line between the pitfalls of maudlin sentiment and pretentious symbolism.

Hayley Mills, her Disney vehicles behind her, is touchingly persuasive. Alan Bates, as the mysterious fugitive, imparts a brilliantly subtle blend of seediness and inner light. *Whistle Down the Wind* is a film of unique charm and extraordinary craftsmanship, including Arthur Ibbetson's photography of the stark, wintry Lancashire locations and Malcolm's Arnold's haunting musical score.

# The White Sheik
## (Lo Sciecco Bianco)

\* \* \* \* \* \* \* \* \* \* \* \* \* \* \* \* \* \* \* \* \* \* \* \* \* \* \* \* \* \* \* \* \* \* \* \* \* \* \* \* \* \* \* \* \* \* \* \* \* \* \* \*

Nationality: Italian         Year: 1952 (U.S. release: 1956)
Cast: Brunella Bovo, Leopoldo Trieste, Alberto Sordi, Giulietta Masina
Director: Federico Fellini      Running Time: 88 minutes
B/W or Color: B/W        Availability: TV only

The White Sheik is a perfect example of early Fellini, when he dealt with simple people and their dreams and in terms of fantasy and introspection. This is a neorealistic fairy tale, shot in actual locations, exposing the grittiness of everyday life. Fellini's special genius was in making the most commonplace scenes look magical.

An unsophisticated bride (Brunella Bovo) and her husband (Leopoldo Trieste) travel from their village to Rome, where he has friends who will take them to the courtyard of St. Peter's to have their marriage blessed by the Pope. She darts away to watch the actors in a *fumetti* comic strip starring her idol, "The White Sheik," The amiable crew and actors encourage her fantasies and shelter her, while her frantic husband searches for her. The buffoonish sheik (superbly played by Alberto Sordi) is a fool to everyone but her, and it takes his strong-minded wife to slap the bride into reality and sense. She returns to her marriage blessed with her forgiving husband. Bovo and Trieste are charming as the rural hicks, and Giulietta Masina makes the most of her bit as a prostitute who shelters the saddened husband.

Recalling *The White Sheik* in her 1982 volume *5001 Nights at the Movies*, Pauline Kael wrote, "This affectionate satire on glamour and delusion is probably the most gentle and naturalistic of Federico Fellini's films." And she reminded her readers that it was the inspiration for Gene Wilder's uneven 1977 comedy *The World's Greatest Lover*.

# The Wicked Lady

**✦✦✦✦✦✦✦✦✦✦✦✦✦✦✦✦✦✦✦✦✦✦✦✦✦✦✦✦✦✦✦✦✦✦✦✦✦✦✦✦✦✦✦✦✦✦✦✦✦✦✦✦✦✦**

*Nationality*: British

*Year*: 1945 (U.S. release: 1946)

*Cast*: Margaret Lockwood, James Mason, Patricia Roc, Griffith Jones, Michael Rennie

*Director*: Leslie Arliss

*Running Time*: 104 minutes

*B/W or Color*: B/W

*Availability*: ALMI HOME VIDEO

Following on the popular heels of *The Man in Grey*, the costumed melodramatics of *The Wicked Lady* were roundly condemned by Britain's film critics but nevertheless proved a box-office bonanza, becoming Britain's top-earning movie of 1946. *The Wicked Lady* was also successful in the States, but not until—at the protestations of Production Code officials—the movie had toned down the cleavage of Margaret Lockwood and Patricia Roc. Indeed, the two actresses were recalled to the studio to reshoot, in less décolleté costuming, scenes filmed a year earlier!

With *The Wicked Lady*, the Rank Organisation hoped to duplicate a formula established with *The Man in Grey*, by taking a sensational book (*The Life and Death of the Wicked Lady Skelton*), abbreviating its title, and re-teaming Lockwood with James Mason.

The film's extravagant plot centers on Lockwood, as Barbara Worth, an orphaned vixen who steals Sir Ralph Skelton (Griffith Jones) from his fiancée, her best friend Caroline (Patricia Roc), only to become bored as Lady Skelton. Donning boots, mask, and pistol, she turns highwaywoman. In this diversion, Barbara becomes mistress to the dashing outlaw Captain Jerry Jackson (Mason). After her nocturnal escapades involve murder, she is confronted by Hogarth (Felix Aylmer), a Skelton retainer who promises secrecy if she will reform. Meanwhile, Sir Ralph realizes he still loves Caroline who, in turn, is now courted by Kit Locksby (Michael Rennie), whom Barbara also covets. The ruthless Barbara betrays Jackson and dispatches several gentlemen who stand in her path, including Hogarth, before getting her comeuppance.

A lavish 1983 color remake starred Faye Dunaway and Alan Bates.

# The Wicker Man

**\* \* \* \* \* \* \* \* \* \* \* \* \* \* \* \* \* \* \* \* \* \* \* \* \* \* \* \* \* \* \* \* \* \* \* \* \* \* \* \* \* \* \* \* \* \* \* \* \* \* \* \* \* \* \***

*Nationality*: British                         *Year*: 1973

*Cast*: Edward Woodward, Britt Ekland, Diane Cilento, Ingrid Pitt, Christopher Lee

*Director*: Robin Hardy                    *Running Time*: 102 minutes (86 minutes in Britain)

*B/W or Color*: Color                        *Availability*: MEDIA HOME ENTERTAINMENT

A cult favorite that has never had a general American release—and was even severely cut before being shown in its native Britain—*The Wicker Man* was written for the screen by Anthony Shaffer, who's otherwise best known for the ingeniously puzzling *Sleuth*. *The Wicker Man*, too, has its puzzles, but they're of a different sort. *The Hollywood Reporter* credited Shaffer with "shrouding his characters with the kind of mystery that reaches for artistic significance."

One of *The Wicker Man*'s stars, Christopher Lee, calls this "Quite simply, the most fascinating film of my career—a unique picture and my favorite," additionally observing that it "has created an unparalleled impact wherever it has been shown."

The film's central character is police sergeant Neil Howie (Edward Woodward), who flies to Summerisle, located off the coast of western Scotland, to investigate a 12-year-old girl's disappearance. A man of strong religious beliefs, he's shocked to discover the islanders' obvious disregard for such standard Christian practices as marriage, burial, sexual propriety, and the worship of God. Instead, a rampant air of paganism prevails, with a widespread devotion to the rites of fertility, harvest, and the gods of nature, as sanctioned by the island leader, Lord Sumerisle (Christopher Lee). Howie's island investigations become ever more unsettling, culminating in his introduction to that awesome "wicker man" of the title—a giant, sacrificial image designed for torching.

Reportedly, a major reconstruction job was required to make available a complete print of this cult classic, an achievement celebrated by Media's bargain-priced videocassette. *The Wicker Man* won the Grand Prize at 1973's Festival of Fantastic Films in Paris.

# Wifemistress
## (Mogliamante)

**********************************************************

**Nationality**: Italian              **Year**: 1977 (U.S. release: 1979)

**Cast**: Laura Antonelli, Marcello Mastroianni, Leonard Mann, Gastone Moschin

**Director**: Marco Vicario          **Running Time**: 101 minutes (106 minutes in Europe)

**B/W or Color**: Color              **Availability**: RCA/COLUMBIA PICTURES HOME VIDEO

Marco Vicario has beautifully directed a complex film exploring the male-female relationship on many levels. Set in Italy at the turn of the century, its implications are valid for the Eighties.

When Marcello Mastroianni, who uses his business as a wine merchant to cloak his underground political activities, is sought for a murder of which he is innocent, he goes into hiding in the attic of his neighbor (Gastone Moschin). Mastroianni's lovely wife (Laura Antonelli) is a psychosomatic paralytic who spends her days in bed. But when Mastroianni disappears, she takes the reins of the business and gradually learns of his real life—his pseudonymous political writings, his secret printing press, and his mistresses, one of whom (Annie Belle) is also her best friend.

Antonelli blossoms as an individual and as a woman. Her life now consciously resembles his. Throwing off her frigidity, as she did her paralysis, she joins the political conspiracies and takes as lovers her husband's friends.

Meanwhile, Mastroianni watches the comings and goings in his own house, supplemented with gossip supplied by his host, and is consumed with jealousy. When, finally, he is cleared of murder, he refuses to leave the attic, preferring instead the masochistic anguish of watching his wife, and preparing to shoot himself when he realizes she has guessed his whereabouts and is vengefully tormenting him.

Rodolfo Sonego's screenplay, together with Ennio Guarnieri's photography and the uniformly superior acting, makes the characters live, and we are caught in their conflicts almost as though they were our own.

*(The videocassette is dubbed in English.)*

# The Wild Child
## (L'Enfant Sauvage)

★★★★★★★★★★★★★★★★★★★★★★★★★★★★★★★★★★★★★★★★★★★★★★★★★★★★★

Nationality: French                    Year: 1970
Cast: François Truffaut, Jean-Pierre Cargol, Jean Dasté, Françoise Seigner, Paul Villé
Director: François Truffaut          Running Time: 85 minutes
B/W or Color: B/W                     Availability: TV only

Midway through François Truffaut's brilliant career, he made this quiet little drama founded upon fact. With Jean Gruault, he based his script on the 1806 journal *Mémoire et Rapport sur Victor l'Aveyron*, by Dr. Jean Itard. Then the filmmaker directed himself in his very first acting appearance and what would remain the most important performance of the few he attempted. Set at the end of the 18th century, the film employs silent-film techniques, and iris fades are used. The production is highlighted by Nestor Almendros's black-and-white photography.

In 1798 in the forests of France, a naked young boy (Cargol) is found by peasants. He is more like an animal, running on all fours like an ape. François Truffaut portrays the doctor associated with the Paris Institute for the Deaf and Dumb who becomes interested in the case. He is certain he can be of use. Truffaut determines that the boy is about 12 and probably was left for dead by his parents while still an infant. The wild child becomes a freak attraction for the fashionable folk to see, until Truffaut wins his custody and takes the boy into his home. There, he and housekeeper Françoise Seigner use patience and kindness to civilize and teach the youth all that they can. He is given the name Victor. Although Truffaut despairs, he presses on. One day, Victor escapes to the woods but returns to the doctor, who happily notes that he came back by choice and prepares to continue the lessons.

As the boy, Cargol stays remarkably in character as he evolves into more of a human. Truffaut is so good that one wonders if he could have pursued a career as an actor, had he so chosen.

The National Board named *The Wild Child* the year's Best Foreign Film and cited Truffaut Best Director. The National Society of Film Critics lauded Nestor Almendros's cinematography.

# Wild Strawberries

## (Smultronstället)

\* \* \* \* \* \* \* \* \* \* \* \* \* \* \* \* \* \* \* \* \* \* \* \* \* \* \* \* \* \* \* \* \* \* \* \* \* \* \* \* \* \* \* \* \* \* \* \* \* \* \* \* \*

Nationality: Swedish

Year: 1957 (U.S. release: 1959)

Cast: Victor Sjöström, Ingrid Thulin, Bibi Andersson, Gunnar Björnstrand, Folke Sundquist

Director: Ingmar Bergman

Running Time: 90 minutes

B/W or Color: B/W

Availability: CBS/FOX VIDEO

D r. Isak Borg (Victor Sjöström) is a grand old man about to be honored by his university. He drives to the ceremony with his daughter-in-law Marianne (Ingrid Thulin). On their way, they stop at his childhood summer home, where wild strawberries once grew. In a dream sequence, he sees his dashing brother Sigfrid (Per Sjöstrand) making love to his cousin Sara (Bibi Andersson). A girl who looks like Sara asks for a lift, and she and her two male companions hop in, spreading a joyousness that might have been Isak's had he married Sara rather than his late wife (Gertrud Fridh). Marianne announces that she is going to leave Isak's son Evald (Gunnar Björnstrand), who does not want their unborn child.

Isak's day is punctuated by a car crash and by nightmares. He wakes, dreaming that his corpse pulls him into a coffin; then he imagines himself taking a test in front of a blackboard covered by gibberish, and finally he witnesses his wife's unfaithfulness, half realizing that forgiveness comes easily because he doesn't really care. The father may be egocentric, but ice-water runs in Evald's veins. Brilliant Victor Sjöström projects a basic warmth that is often at odds with his mildly demonic role as Isak. His young passengers adore him.

The film's eerie genius lies in the skill with which the dream scenes blend with Isak's workaday life. In the end, the dream is the reality. The fantasy: the laurel that crowns Isak's four score years and ten. The film won top prizes at the Berlin and Venice Film Festivals, as well as the Danish Academy Award. The National Board named *Wild Strawberries* 1959's Best Foreign Film and Victor Sjöström (or Seastrom) Best Actor.

*(The videocassette is in Swedish with English subtitles.)*

# The Winslow Boy

★★★★★★★★★★★★★★★★★★★★★★★★★★★★★★★★★★★★★★★★★★★★★★★★★★★★★

*Nationality*: British　　　　　　　*Year*: 1948

*Cast*: Robert Donat, Cedric Hardwicke, Margaret Leighton, Frank Lawton, Francis L. Sullivan

*Director*: Anthony Asquith　　　　*Running Time*: 117 minutes

*B/W or Color*: B/W　　　　　　　*Availability*: THORN EMI/HBO VIDEO

Anthony Asquith was born into a life of luxury as the son of an English prime minister. He directed British films that were polished, well-bred, and never less than civilized, specializing in play-to-film adaptations such as *Pygmalion* (1938), *The Browning Version* (1951), and *The Importance of Being Earnest* (1952). One of his finest movies is *The Winslow Boy,* a stellar version of Terence Rattigan's stage hit about a young boy who is expelled from the British naval academy when he is accused of petty theft. His father spends every penny he has plus years of heartbreaking effort in an attempt to clear his son, eventually taking the case to Parliament and a successful suit against the Crown itself. Rattigan based his play on a real-life English case of 1910.

The impeccable British cast is headed by the elegant Robert Donat as the tireless defense counsellor, and Cedric Hardwicke is equally superb as the father who will not be deterred from his quest for justice. The supporting cast is rounded off by the wonderfully porcine Francis L. Sullivan and the eccentric charm of Ernest Thesiger. As the falsely accused boy, Neil North gives a surprisingly skillful performance.

Although the film is somewhat critical of certain British institutions and bureaucracy, the ultimate vindication proves that those in the right can always triumph over adversity. The film is effectively photographed by Frederick Young (*Lawrence of Arabia,* 1962), and there is an abundance of talk, but the talk is very good indeed. And, as the London *Daily Telegraph* so aptly put it, "Only a clod could see this film without excitement, laughter and some slight moisture about the eyes."

# Winter Light
## (Nattvardsgästerna)

★ ★ ★ ★ ★ ★ ★ ★ ★ ★ ★ ★ ★ ★ ★ ★ ★ ★ ★ ★ ★ ★ ★ ★ ★ ★ ★ ★ ★ ★ ★ ★ ★ ★ ★ ★ ★ ★ ★ ★ ★ ★ ★ ★ ★ ★ ★ ★

**Nationality**: Swedish        **Year**: 1963
**Cast**: Ingrid Thulin, Gunnar Björnstrand, Max von Sydow, Gunnel Lindblom
**Director**: Ingmar Bergman      **Running Time**: 80 minutes
**B/W or Color**: B/W      **Availability**: EMBASSY HOME ENTERTAINMENT

This is the second in what has come to be known as Ingmar Bergman's trilogy on faith, the other two being 1961's *Through a Glass Darkly* and 1963's *The Silence*. The threesome are connected in theme but not in characters or plot. Austere in both mood and setting, *Winter Light* takes place in the chilly, snowy setting of a Spartan-looking small-town church whose parishioners are few and whose pastor, Tomas Ericsson (Gunnar Björnstrand), is losing his faith. Widowed for five years, he is tormented by "God's silence" and rejects the creature comforts offered by his schoolteacher-mistress Märta (Ingrid Thulin, made to look dowdy). Visited after communion by a fisherman named Persson, who's depressed with thoughts of atomic annihilation, the pastor offers little solace, instead revealing his own doubts and despairs. Nor can he seem to respond to his mistress's love, and he cruelly rejects her, still harboring grief over his late wife. When Persson shoots himself, Pastor Ericsson goes to comfort the man's pregnant widow. And when he returns to his church for vespers, the pastor finds a congregation of one—the faithful Märta. Perhaps now they will be able to communicate.

Judith Crist, writing in the *New York Herald Tribune*, stated, "It is a taut film, bleak and cold in its abstract ideas, deeply passionate in its concern for the human torment." Much of *Winter Light* is shot in carefully lit close-ups by cinematographer Sven Nykvist. As Bergman has reported of their collaboration, "From early morning until late evening, we stayed in that church registering every gradation of the light. Our common passion is to create light: light and faces surrounded by shadows. This is what fascinates me!"

The National Board of Review named *Winter Light* among 1963's best foreign-language films.

(*Embassy offers the film in both subtitled and well-dubbed prints.*)

# Woman in the Dunes
## (Suna No Onna)

*************************************************************

*Nationality*: Japanese              *Year*: 1964
*Cast*: Eiji Okada, Kyoko Kishida, Koji Mitsui, Sen Yano, Hiroko Ito
*Director*: Hiroshi Teshigahara      *Running Time*: 127 minutes
*B/W or Color*: B/W                  *Availability*: CORINTH VIDEO

An amateur entomologist collecting specimens in a remote area misses his return bus to Tokyo. For self-serving reasons, nearby villagers maneuver him into overnight shelter with a recent widow in a deep sand pit. However, the next morning he discovers that the rope ladder by which he had entered the pit has been removed. Gradually, he learns that he has been trapped, to replace the woman's husband and help shovel the ever shifting sand, which threatens to bury the entire village. He tries to climb out, but the sands hold him back. Eventually, he finds a way to condense fresh water out of the sand, making the villagers' lives easier. By the end, he has left behind his urban existence for a more primitive one. Through returning to nature, he has developed a new sense of identity, a new purpose of life; he even refuses to escape, telling himself he can always run away another day.

This political allegory is the product of two particular talents. Kobo Abe, internationally Japan's best-known author, wrote the screenplay from his novel. His innovative writing style must be considered as avant-garde as the filming of *Woman in the Dunes*.

Director Hiroshi Teshigahara found the means to interpret and provide the proper form for Abe's ideas, and *Woman in the Dunes* is a stylistic tour de force. Several love scenes are charged with an eroticism unparalleled in cinema. Close-ups of porous, landscapelike bodies and the inescapable sweeping sands are textured to unify the allegorical narrative.

*Woman in the Dunes* received the Jury Prize at the Cannes Film Festival. Teshigahara was nominated for an Oscar as Best Director, the only one received by a Japanese director until Kurosawa's for *Ran* in 1986.

(*The videocassette is subtitled.*)

# The Woman Next Door

## (La Femme d'à Côté)

＊＊＊＊＊＊＊＊＊＊＊＊＊＊＊＊＊＊＊＊＊＊＊＊＊＊＊＊＊＊＊＊＊＊＊＊＊＊＊＊＊＊＊＊＊＊＊＊＊

**Nationality:** French    **Year:** 1981

**Cast:** Gérard Depardieu, Fanny Ardant, Henri Garcin, Michèle Baumgartner

**Director:** François Truffaut    **Running Time:** 106 minutes

**B/W or Color:** Color    **Availability:** KEY VIDEO

François Truffaut's twentieth feature since 1959 has an emotional tenor unlike any of his previous films. *The Woman Next Door* concerns ex-lovers who, eight years after the end of a disastrous affair, accidentally become neighbors in a suburb of Grenoble, in which both have settled with their respective spouses. This premise, potentially that of a "sophisticated" French sex comedy, serves instead to introduce a poignant melodrama of adultery that inevitably climaxes in a crime of passion.

*The Woman Next Door* is an assured, highly literate movie. An adept visual storyteller, Truffaut artfully employs the device of a flashback, a variety of rhythmically expressive dissolves, fades, freeze frames, jump cuts, and even iris shots—and a strong sense of mise-en-scene—to enliven what is essentially a character study. This drama of fatal attraction unfolds in a series of finely observed scenes of bourgeois life: at meals, on the tennis court, in a small hotel. These deftly articulate the conflicts that arise between the couple and their marriage partners.

Equally understanding of his actors, Truffaut draws an intense performance from Fanny Ardant, strikingly beautiful in closeup, who makes a haunting film debut in the enigmatic title role. Gérard Depardieu, in his second film with Truffaut, delivers a convincing, well-modulated performance as the errant husband. Véronique Silver, as the film's sympathetic narrator, leads a small but uniformly excellent supporting cast. William Lubtchansky's photography is sensitive to the characters' mercurial shifts of mood and contributes much to the movie's impact, and Georges Delerue's music effectively underscores Truffaut's disturbing tale of lovers who can neither live with nor without each other.

*(The videocassette is subtitled.)*

# Women in Love

\* \* \* \* \* \* \* \* \* \* \* \* \* \* \* \* \* \* \* \* \* \* \* \* \* \* \* \* \* \* \* \* \* \* \* \* \* \* \* \* \* \* \* \* \* \* \* \* \* \* \* \* \*

*Nationality*: British        *Year*: 1969 (U.S. release: 1970)

*Cast*: Alan Bates, Oliver Reed, Glenda Jackson, Jennie Linden, Eleanor Bron, Alan Webb, Christopher Gable

*Director*: Ken Russell        *Running Time*: 129 minutes

*B/W or Color*: Color        *Availability*: CBS/FOX HOME VIDEO

K en Russell is notorious in film circles for the unparalleled irreverence and audacity—both sexual and religious—with which he tackled such big-screen projects as *The Music Lovers* and *The Devils*. One Russell movie both reviewers and audiences agreed possessed quality was *Women in Love*, a faithful adaptation of the 1920 D. H. Lawrence novel by co-producer Larry Kramer. Russell disputes the possibility that this is probably his best film to date, with a slap at the critics: "*Women in Love* was easier for them. It was literal and had just the right amount of violence and erotic things in it. But I don't think it was as good as the others."

The film, deliberately fragmentary and episodic, describes the complex emotional relationships of two young couples in their efforts to express love and friendship. Glenda Jackson and Jennie Linden play sisters of an upper-middle-class family in a Midlands mining town, who are courted, respectively, by a wealthy young mine owner and a school inspector (Oliver Reed and Alan Bates). While one relationship results in a tender love affair—and marriage—the other is stormy and destructive. During a Swiss mountain holiday, the situation reaches a tragic climax.

Larry Kramer's reverent adaptation remains true to Lawrence's original blend of sensuality and subtlety, and Ken Russell employs a bold and stylish visual flair. The most talked about set piece is undoubtedly that firelit, nude wrestling scene between Bates and Reed. The casting of the four lovers is especially fine, with Glenda Jackson taking a slight edge in the acting honors. Her performance won her not only her first Best Actress Oscar but Best Actress awards from both the New York Film Critics and The National Board of Review, which listed *Women in Love* among 1970's ten best.

# The Wrong Box

★★★★★★★★★★★★★★★★★★★★★★★★★★★★★★★★★★★★★★★★★★★★★★★★★★★★★

**Nationality**: British          **Year**: 1966

**Cast**: John Mills, Ralph Richardson, Michael Caine, Nanette Newman, Peter Sellers, Peter Cook, Dudley Moore

**Director**: Bryan Forbes          **Running time**: 105 minutes (110 minutes in Britain)

**B/W or Color**: Color          **Availability**: RCA/COLUMBIA PICTURES HOME VIDEO

Frenetic farce features Britain's best. This delicious black comedy has taken on the trappings of a cult classic. Larry Gelbart and Burt Shevelove, from American TV comedy, took the darkly humorous novel by Robert Louis Stevenson and Lloyd Osbourne, and turned the material into high farce, and Bryan Forbes directed in a style spoofing the silent melodramas, complete with titles. The cast of farceurs, including Peter Sellers as a cat-loving and drink-sodden old doctor, features some of England's best talents. John Mills and Ralph Richardson capitalize on their eccentricities. Michael Caine, young and handsome; Nanette Newman, Forbes's all-time favorite performer and longtime wife; and veteran Wilfrid Lawson are outstanding in their roles. So, too, are the Mutt-and-Jeff team of Peter Cook and Dudley Moore, long before the latter struck out on his own.

In Victorian London, elderly brothers Richardson and Mills are members of a tontine, a trust fund in which the last survivor will inherit a fortune. Since other members have been disposed of, Mills attempts to get rid of Richardson so that young Caine, his grandson, can get the money. However, Richardson's nephews, Moore and Cook, have other ideas. By mistake, they crate up the body of the Bournemouth Strangler, thinking it Richardson's, and a comedy of errors begins.

The humor depends on split-second timing and a pace quickened by Alan Osbiston's fast editing and John Barry's lively score. Funeral and military airs performed by The Temperance Seven have the right amount of mocking humor to them. Of course, the film's title on the side of a cassette box could cause confusion, but that should establish the right mood for the fun ahead.

# The Year of Living Dangerously

★★★★★★★★★★★★★★★★★★★★★★★★★★★★★★★★★★★★★★★★★★★★★★★★★★★★★★

Nationality: Australian       Year: 1982

Cast: Mel Gibson, Sigourney Weaver, Linda Hunt, Michael Murphy, Noel Ferrier, Bill Kerr

Director: Peter Weir       Running Time: 115 minutes

B/W or Color: Color       Availability: MGM/UA HOME VIDEO

Set in 1965 Jakarta, the capital of Indonesia, *The Year of Living Dangerously* tells the story of Guy Hamilton (Mel Gibson), a young, handsome, and ambitious Australian journalist on his first foreign assignment. Although Hamilton's actions form the basis of the film's plot and keep the story moving forward, Billy Kwan (Linda Hunt), one of the more unusual and sympathetic characters of Eighties cinema, defines and shapes the film on a deeper level. Kwan is the film's heart and soul.

Like many Peter Weir films, a clash of culture is central to the theme—this time explored through the friendship between the foreigner Hamilton and Kwan, a deformed, dwarflike native with an undeniably pure spirituality about him. But what exactly are Hamilton's motivations in befriending Kwan: because Kwan has certain connections and can help Hamilton in his work, or because Hamilton recognizes Kwan's unique sensitivity, compassion, and intelligence?

The first half of the film maintains a masterful dramatic balance between the intimate feelings and relationship of the two central characters and the worldly events unfolding around them (the volatile country will soon be plunged into chaos by an attempted Communist coup).

Complications arise when a young, sexy British embassy attaché, Jill Bryant (Sigourney Weaver), arrives on the scene. A romance between Hamilton and Bryant quickly develops, and it's a steamy one. But when Kwan is no longer on screen, the film lapses into conventional—albeit exciting—action adventure, culminating in a riveting, life-at-stake ride to the airport. It is Hunt who most impresses here—she creates a fully dimensional, extraordinarily moving character (of the opposite sex), for which she deservedly won the year's Best Supporting Actress Award from both the Academy and The National Board.

# Yesterday, Today and Tomorrow
## (Ieri, Oggi e Domani)

* * * * * * * * * * * * * * * * * * * * * * * * * * * * * * * * * * * * * * * * * * * * * * * * *

**Nationality**: Italian    **Year**: 1963
**Cast**: Sophia Loren, Marcello Mastroianni, Aldo Giuffré
**Director**: Vittorio De Sica    **Running Time**: 119 minutes
**B/W or Color**: Color    **Availability**: TV only

For a time, the film team of Marcello Mastroianni and Sophia Loren were universally popular—certainly more electric and erotic than their U.S. counterparts, Doris Day and Rock Hudson. While the Americans barely acknowledged sex, the Italians took a more realistic attitude.

*Yesterday, Today and Tomorrow* is the film that gave the ever-popular Italian duo the opportunity to show their ample talent (and for Loren to show her voluptuous figure, too!). It also helped popularize the anthology film in the Sixties. *Yesterday, Today and Tomorrow* is divided into three stories focusing on three women (all played by Loren) living in three separate Italian cities, illustrating how women differ emotionally, economically, and socially.

In "Adelina," Loren is a woman of Naples who has been arrested for selling contraband cigarettes. When it's discovered that Adelina is pregnant, she is protected by an Italian law that states that a woman convicted of a crime cannot be jailed as long as she is breast-feeding her baby.

In order to stay out of jail, Adelina's husband, Carmine (Mastroianni), keeps her constantly pregnant. Dropping from exhaustion, Carmine can't keep up the pace. Caring local citizens solve the crisis.

"Anna" finds Loren as a wealthy, bitchy, upper-class woman of Milan who is having an affair with a poor writer (Mastroianni). He wrecks her expensive car to avoid hitting a child, and an infuriated Anna feels the wrong choice was made.

In "Mara," the sexiest story of the trio, Loren is a Roman prostitute who discovers a young seminary student loves her. When she manages to fend him off, she vows chastity for a week, leaving libidinous boyfriend Rusconi (Mastroianni) sex starved and frustrated.

Watching Loren and Mastroianni strut their stuff under Vittorio De Sica's canny direction is a treat. *Yesterday, Today and Tomorrow* won the Academy Award for Best Foreign Film, as indeed it should have. The National Board also named it among the best foreign films of the year.

# Yojimbo
## (The Bodyguard)

★★★★★★★★★★★★★★★★★★★★★★★★★★★★★★★★★★★★★★★★★★★★★★★★★★

*Nationality*: Japanese     *Year*: 1961 (U.S. release: 1962)
*Cast*: Toshiro Mifune, Eijiro Tono, Kamatari Fujiwara, Takashi Shimura
*Director*: Akira Kurosawa     *Running Time*: 110 minutes
*B/W or Color*: B/W     *Availability*: EMBASSY HOME
                                 ENTERTAINMENT

Yojimbo is set in 1860, a few years before Japan's opening to the West. At that time, Japan had been at peace for two centuries, and the samurai class had already declined greatly (it would be dissolved within two decades), giving rise to the merchant class. No film captures this decline quite like Akira Kurosawa's wily, shaggy, samurai satire.

Toshiro Mifune won the Best Actor Award at the Venice Film Festival for playing a scruffy samurai named Sanjuro (Kurosawa's *Sanjuro* is a sequel), who drifts into a little village beset by its own civil war. Both the sake merchant and the silk merchant have hired bladesmen of various sizes and shapes in their efforts for economic control of this terrorized town. Sensing a chance to clean up, financially and otherwise, the samurai allows himself to be hired as a *yojimbo* (bodyguard), by each side in turn. He craftily pits one side against the other, then observes their mutual decimation from a watchtower.

Samurai pictures are frequently called "Eastern Westerns," and *Yojimbo* is the first film to thoroughly distort conventions of both genres, which often feature a strong loner wandering into an isolated town and discovering a situation with a clear conflict between good and evil. When *Yojimbo* ends, the only survivors are Sanjuro, the merchants, and the sake seller—who did not participate in the final carnage. Kurosawa's explosive humor and pungent irony carry through to the end: Sanjuro mutters as he leaves the devastated village, "Now, there will be quiet in this town." Sergio Leone stole this idea for *A Fistful of Dollars*, giving rise to the "spaghetti Western."

*Yojimbo* is often considered Kurosawa's best picture. It was his first collaboration with Kazuo Miyagawa, Japan's foremost cinematographer, since *Rashomon*. They would not work together again until *Ran*.

*(The videocassette is subtitled.)*

# You Only Live Twice

\* \* \* \* \* \* \* \* \* \* \* \* \* \* \* \* \* \* \* \* \* \* \* \* \* \* \* \* \* \* \* \* \* \* \* \* \* \* \* \* \* \* \* \* \* \* \* \* \* \* \* \* \* \* \* \* \*

Nationality: British          Year: 1967

Cast: Sean Connery, Akiko Wakabayashi, Tetsuro Tamba, Mie Hama, Teru Shimada

Director: Lewis Gilbert          Running Time: 116 minutes

B/W or Color: Color          Availability: CBS/FOX VIDEO

In Ian Fleming's novel *You Only Live Twice,* James Bond travels to Japan to investigate a mysterious man named Shatterhand who lives in a castle by the sea with a poisonous garden where elderly Japanese commit suicide. Bond finds that Shatterhand is really his old enemy Ernst Stavro Blofeld, and in a battle that blows up the castle, he loses his memory. At the end of the novel, Bond, with amnesia, is washed up in the U.S.S.R.

This downbeat story was radically altered by producers Albert (Cubby) Broccoli and Harry Saltzman. Gone were the castle and the deadly garden. Instead, a mysterious spacecraft has been kidnapping Soviet and American space capsules, and civilization is poised on the brink of World War III. Seemingly killed by assassins, "Commander Bond of the Royal Navy" is thought to be dead. In reality, 007 has gone undercover in Japan, where he meets Tiger Tanaka (Tetsuro Tamba), head of the Japanese Secret Service. With the aid of Tiger, Bond discovers that industrialist Osato (Teru Shimada) is working with SPECTRE, and inside a dormant volcano is a huge complex that includes a launch pad for spacecraft. Bond and Tiger's Ninjas (the first time Japanese Ninjas were used in a Western film) invade the complex, and Bond blows it up along with his old enemy Blofeld.

While *You Only Live Twice* is not the most logical Bond film, it is one of the most entertaining, loaded with action from start to finish. Sean Connery holds up well alongside the machinery, and he's ably aided by the beautiful Bond women, the German actress Karin Dor and Japanese actresses Akiko Wakabayashi and Mie Hama.

Lewis Gilbert, a director equally renowned for drama and comedy (*Sink the Bismarck, Alfie, Educating Rita*), proved with this film that he's also more than capable of directing large action pictures. Gilbert also directed the Bond films *The Spy Who Loved Me* (1977) and *Moonraker* (1979).

# Young Scarface
## (Brighton Rock)

★ ★ ★ ★ ★ ★ ★ ★ ★ ★ ★ ★ ★ ★ ★ ★ ★ ★ ★ ★ ★ ★ ★ ★ ★ ★ ★ ★ ★ ★ ★ ★ ★ ★ ★ ★ ★ ★ ★ ★ ★ ★ ★ ★ ★ ★ ★ ★ ★ ★ ★

*Nationality*: British          *Year*: 1947 (U.S. release: 1951)

*Cast*: Richard Attenborough, Hermione Baddeley, William Hartnell, Carol Marsh, Wylie Watson

*Director*: John Boulting          *Running Time*: 86 minutes (92 minutes in Britain)

*B/W or Color*: B/W          *Availability*: TV only

**B**righton Rock, first released in the United States as *Young Scarface*, is writer Graham Greene at his most serious and most characteristic, a work fraught with guilt, in the classic sense, and laden with the ironies that result when man fights his destiny.

Greene collaborated with Terence Rattigan on the screen adaptation of his novel, and director John Boulting had a very precise idea of where he would take it. There is a clear, graphic sense of crime reporting, from the first detailed murder of a reporter right through a series of gangland-style liquidations. It is the quintessential hard-boiled gangster film.

Richard Attenborough, in what may be his most completely realized portrayal, is a young hood, the leader of a second-rate band of punks trying to make it as gamblers in seedy Brighton on England's south coast. He knows his weakness, and the pathetic schemes he pursues to enhance his prestige as a criminal eventually propel him to his doom.

Boulting's staging takes every advantage of the Brighton locations. Roller coasters, shooting galleries, boardwalk loafers, all the carnival props become infernal devices to haunt the disturbed youth.

Greene, as in all his serious works, treats us to a morality play of good versus evil. The hero's personality is split into warring factions of conscience and faith, on the one hand, and the evil he does to survive on the other. He is a lapsed Catholic, never at peace with himself, inevitably taking up with an innocent girl, who is unshakable in her faith. After his death, we are treated to the film's last delicious irony in a scene where a mechanical twist allows the naive girl who married him to maintain the illusion that he really loved her. Hermione Baddeley is notable as the harsh, worn-out, actress who tenaciously pursues him.

# Young Winston

★ ★ ★ ★ ★ ★ ★ ★ ★ ★ ★ ★ ★ ★ ★ ★ ★ ★ ★ ★ ★ ★ ★ ★ ★ ★ ★ ★ ★ ★ ★ ★ ★ ★ ★ ★ ★ ★ ★ ★ ★ ★ ★ ★ ★ ★ ★ ★ ★ ★ ★

Nationality: British      Year: 1972

Cast: Simon Ward, Robert Shaw, Anne Bancroft, Jack Hawkins, John Mills, Anthony Hopkins

Director: Richard Attenborough      Running Time: 145 minutes (157 minutes in Britain)

B/W or Color: Color      Availability: TV only

The great British statesman Sir Winston Churchill (1875–1965) epitomizes Britain in the minds of many people. It was natural that his life and achievements would be the subject of many writings. Surprisingly, this is the only major theatrical film about him. It's based on Churchill's autobiography, *My Early Life: A Roving Commission,* and tells of his youthful army career and entrance into politics. After seeing another Columbia Picture, the World War II epic *The Guns of Navarone* in 1961, Sir Winston decided that its producer and writer, Carl Foreman, would be an ideal choice for bringing his book to the screen. Prior commitments and a great deal of research delayed filming for a decade. The result was, in director Richard Attenborough's words, "the first truly intimate epic." Along with the human story is a grand scale action piece with location work in Morocco and Wales as well as England.

The sweep and the intimacy of Churchill's life are captured in this successful biographical drama. Praise went to Shaw, Bancroft, and especially to Ward, for their performances. Foreman's perceptive script is well served by director Attenborough, who has a way with spectacles. Simon Ward, then 31, was making his starring debut after a few supporting roles, which started with *If . . .* (1968). Ward portrayed a Nazi officer in his next film, *Hitler—The Last Ten Days* (1973), but he never really achieved the fame he should have after this one exceptional portrayal.

# Z

\* \* \* \* \* \* \* \* \* \* \* \* \* \* \* \* \* \* \* \* \* \* \* \* \* \* \* \* \* \* \* \* \* \* \* \* \* \* \* \* \* \* \* \* \* \* \* \* \* \* \* \* \* \*

*Nationality*: French-Algerian      *Year*: 1969

*Cast*: Yves Montand, Irene Papas, Jean-Louis Trintignant, Charles Denner, Georges Geret

*Director*: Constantin Costa-Gavras    *Running Time*: 127 minutes

*B/W or Color*: Color               *Availability*: RCA/COLUMBIA PICTURES HOME VIDEO

The winner of 1969 Oscars for Best Foreign Film and Best Editing, Z is an incomparable cliff-hanging, seat-hugging thriller. The extraordinary camera work of Raoul Coutard and the superb score of Mikis Theodorakis are integral parts of the movie, complementing and adding to the build-up of tensions.

Yves Montand plays a parliamentary deputy (the film is based on the assassination of Greek pacifist Gregarius Lambrakis), who is determined to be the main speaker at a peace rally despite the warnings of his wife (Irene Papas) and friends that an attempt is to be made on his life and that local police will be of no help if there is trouble. Following his speech, the deputy leaves the rally hall to a street crowded with an overflow of supporters, armed police, and political agitators—to be run down by a speeding van; three days later, he dies in a hospital. His irate followers take to the streets in swarms shouting, "Z" (meaning "to be" in Greek, or "alive"). Shot entirely in Algiers, the script was co-authored by Costa-Gavras and Jorge Semprum (*La Guerre Est Finie*). The film unfolds in a dazzling documentary style, concentrating largely on events rather than attempting to develop characterizations.

The magistrate appointed to investigate the case (played by a superb Jean-Louis Trintignant) is supposed merely to go through the motions; unfortunately for the government, he is an honest man and establishes that the deputy was in fact assassinated and the speeding van was a cover-up. Witnesses stream in and out of the courtroom: eyewitnesses, the van driver, police, blustering army officers—and finally the comic-opera colonels and generals. All are members of the assassination plot. Everything about the direction by Costa-Gavras and the editing is flawless. It's impossible to convey the degree of riveting tension that Z possesses.

# Zazie
## (Zazie dans le Métro)

★ ★ ★ ★ ★ ★ ★ ★ ★ ★ ★ ★ ★ ★ ★ ★ ★ ★ ★ ★ ★ ★ ★ ★ ★ ★ ★ ★ ★ ★ ★ ★ ★ ★ ★ ★ ★ ★ ★ ★ ★ ★ ★ ★ ★ ★ ★ ★

Nationality: French                      Year: 1960 (U.S. release: 1961)
Cast: Catherine Demongeot, Philippe Noiret, Vittorio Caprioli, Yvonne Clech, Odette Picquet
Director: Louis Malle                    Running Time: 88 minutes
B/W or Color: Color                      Availability: TV only

Z azie is a whirligig of a film. Seemingly cut with a food processor, it captures the speed, daring, and fun that must have been Paris of the Sixties, at the first flush of the New Wave. Based on Raymond Queneau's novel, Malle's frenzied Zazie is thorny but fun, and the audience must be ready for its pace to take over to have it "work."

Zazie is a disrespectful little girl who's been brought to Paris to stay with her uncle while her mother enjoys three uninhibited days with her lover. Because the Metro is on strike, Zazie's fondest wish (to ride the subway endlessly) is denied her. Instead, the child has a series of wild adventures on the streets and in the seamier nightclubs of Paris. When her returning mother asks Zazie what she has been up to, the little girl replies, "I grew older."

One cannot deny the exhilaration of Malle's depiction of Paris through the eyes of his young but jaded heroine. This is a world in constant flux.

Catherine Demongeot plays the precocious Zazie as a foul-mouthed cynic. She is the surprising precursor of Tatum O'Neal in Paper Moon, Michael Ritchie's Bad News Bears, and the wise-ass pre-teens of TV sitcoms. Most of the actors play several roles, but the real co-star is the city itself. The Eiffel Tower, the cafés, and the traffic are the Tati-like playgrounds upon which the action literally percolates.

The film does to film language what the novel did to French literary language. The cinematic vibrancy and pure speed of Malle's cutting remains fresh. Zazie is New Wave style at high tide—just hold on and ride!

# Zulu

★ ★ ★ ★ ★ ★ ★ ★ ★ ★ ★ ★ ★ ★ ★ ★ ★ ★ ★ ★ ★ ★ ★ ★ ★ ★ ★ ★ ★ ★ ★ ★ ★ ★ ★ ★ ★ ★ ★ ★ ★ ★ ★ ★ ★ ★ ★ ★ ★ ★ ★ ★

*Nationality*: British                     *Year*: 1964

*Cast*: Stanley Baker, Jack Hawkins, Ulla Jacobsson, Michael Caine, Nigel Green

*Director*: Cy Endfield            *Running Time*: 138 minutes

*B/W or Color*: Color              *Availability*: CHARTER ENTER-
                                   TAINMENT

Even though molded in the grand and sweeping tradition of such epic films as *The Four Feathers* and *Gunga Din*, *Zulu* was almost totally ignored upon its American release, but has finally, through telecasts, built up a devoted and highly deserved fan club. Narrated briefly by Richard Burton, *Zulu* is based on a true episode in the British conquest of South Africa's Zululand in 1879. The film's story is of the heroic stand made by 130 British redcoats against 4,000 Zulu warriors in an isolated mission outpost.

Stanley Baker plays the senior officer, a lieutenant in the engineers sent to build a bridge. After refusing to abandon the garrison, he finds himself, with only 8 officers and 97 men—plus the sick and wounded—leading the defense against repeated attacks by hordes of Zulus armed with spears and confiscated British rifles. The bloody, bitter battles last through the night, after which the Zulus withdraw—but not before saluting the bravery of the enemy. Eleven Victoria Crosses, Britain's highest military decoration, were awarded to the men at Rorke's Drift.

Michael Caine, in his first major film, is Baker's second in command, a haughty, rather foppish lieutenant who, nevertheless, shapes up. Originally considered for the role of a cockney enlisted man, the actor was told by American director Endfield he looked more like an officer. "He wasn't acquainted with the British caste system" is Caine's explanation. Jack Hawkins appears as the fanatical missionary who drinks, and Ulla Jacobsson is his stubborn, humorless daughter, both of whom are asked to leave the outpost as Baker considers them demoralizing influences.

Colorful, suspenseful, fast paced, brilliantly acted and photographed, loaded with warm and surprising human touches, and cleverly avoiding all the obvious clichés, *Zulu* ranks as one of the finest war films ever made.